Surburg's Works

Vol III
Worship - Church Year - Music

Edited by
Herman J. Otten

LUTHERAN NEWS, INC., New Haven, Missouri

Surburg's Works

Library of Congress Card
Lutheran News, Inc.
684 Luther Lane
New Haven, MO 63068
Published 2017
Printed in the United States of America
IngramSpark, TN
ISBN #978-0-9864232-1-5

Table of Contents

Worship - Church Year

Music

Worship - Church Year

The Major and Minor Festivals
of the Christian Church Year

From Epiphany to Ash Wednesday

Christian News, January 16, 1984

The Festival of Epiphany (January 6)

Epiphany is one of the Immovable Festivals of the Church Year, which means that it is always observed on the same day namely January 6. This festival has been called by different names. They are: **The Epiphany, Manifestation of Our Lord**, also the **Theophany, the Manifestation of God**. In European countries it was known as **Festum trium regium**, the **Feast of the Three Kings**; in Germany **Drei Koenigetag;** in England, **Twelfth Night**.[1]

Concerning Epiphany, Kleinhans wrote:

Epiphany now seems to be somewhat of an orphan as far as the Western Church Year is concerned, though at one time it was only second to Easter. To us it lies in the shadow of Christmas, though it is nonetheless the second great festival of the Christmas cycle, or in one of its older names "Old Christmas."[2]

While Epiphany has a certain connection with Christmas, it also has a certain independent position from the Christmas cycle. In fact, it begins a new liturgical cycle in the Church Year and advances the latter's teaching about the Person of Christ.

McArthur in his article on "Epiphany" advanced the following relative to the origin of Epiphany and its relationship to Christmas:

> In order to understand Epiphany on 6 January and the complicated problem of its relation to Christmas (q.v.) we must free ourselves from the Western tradition which understands the festival on terms of the coming of the Magi. Its significance as 'Epiphany' or 'Manifestation' conveys, primarily and normatively, not the manifestation of Christ to the Gentiles as such, but rather the manifestation of the revelation of God to the world in Jesus Christ.[3]

Epiphany preceded Christmas as a festival commemorating Christ's birth.[4] The earliest traces of a celebration of Christ's Birth are found in the Eastern Church as early as at the end of the third century when January 6 was observed in a special capacity as the Day of Christ's Birth and of the Epiphany of God as the Lord's Baptism. John Cassian, who visited Egypt between the year A.D. 380 and 400, stated in his Conferences that in Egypt Epiphany was observed as unitive festival, commemorating both the Lord's Incarnation and Baptism. McArthur claims that it was during the fourth century that Christmas reacted as reagent on the original Epiphany in the geographical areas of Constantinople, Asia Minor and Antioch.[5] Gregory of Nazianzus' sermons indicate that by 380 Christmas was being celebrated in Constantinople and was called THEOPHANY or Birthday. The theme was the Incarnation and the Adoration of the Magi.

January 6 was called Holy Day of Lights, or the Day of Holy Lights and the day Jesus' Baptism was commemorated.[6]

McArthur concluded his discussion of the relation of Epiphany to Christmas:

> Thus it seems obvious that, before Christmas was introduced, the Church of Constantinople must have had a festival on 6 January commemorating both the birth and the baptism, and called the Theophany, Manifestation of God is clearly a synonym for Epiphany. When the primary theme the incarnation was transferred to 25 December, the title also was taken. Evidence from Asia Minor is to be found in an Epiphany sermon by Gregory or Nyssa where the situation is obviously the same as Constantinople.[7]

In a sermon preached on Pentecost of 386 John Chrysostom made reference to Epiphany as the first Christian festival, commemorating the appearance of God on earth. But at the end of 386 Christmas was celebrated for the first time. It was only in the preceding decade that the tradition of Christmas, derived from the West, became known in Antioch. At Constantinople the observance of the Incarnation also included the Adoration of the Magi. Unlike Gregory the Great, Chrysostom kept the use of "Theophany" as a name for Epiphany and does not employ it for Christmas. McArthur averred: "There can be no doubt that in Antioch, towards the close of 386 and the beginning of 387, 25 December now was observed as the Christ's Birthday and 6 January the baptism."[8]

In the Eastern Church Epiphany was once a popular time to receive (Baptize) new members — not called **catechumens** ("those who had been instructed") as in the West but **illuminati** ("those who were to be enlightened"), by Christ.[9]

The Method of Determining the Date of January 6

There is no certain reason for the choice of January 6 as a festival day. Strodach claims that the East arrived at January 6 in much the same way as the West determined December 25 as Christ's Natal Day. The East selected a certain starting point for its calculation at arriving at January 6. "In this case," stated Stroduch, "the East began with April 6th as the date of the Crucifixion, and arguing or reckoning, as the Church everywhere always has, on the premise of the 'perfect' Life, **the Annunciation** would be that date also, and therefore the Birthday would be January 6th."[10]

It is also possible that January 6th was chosen because heathen and heretical celebrations were observed at this time and thus the Day was chosen to counteract negative pagan influences.

The Relationship of the Length of Epiphany to Easter

Since Epiphany was an Immovable Festival, this meant that Easter was a Movable Festival. Since Easter may come between March 22nd and April 25th, the number of Sundays after Epiphany depends on the date of Easter. Gwynne informs us: "When Easter falls on one of the earliest days, March 22nd, 23rd, or 24th, there is only one Sunday after the Epiphany; when it falls on one of its latest days, April 22nd, 23rd, 24th, 25th. There are six Sundays."[11] Gwynne, of course, is writing this on the assumption that the Lenten Season is introduced by three Sundays, called Septuagesima, Sexagesima, and Quinquagesima, three Sundays in the ILCW now considered the concluding three Sundays of the long Epiphany Season.[12]

Since the ILCW has eliminated the three pre-Lenten Sundays, there may be as many as nine Sundays after Epiphany.

The Relationship the Ecclesiastical Year to the Civil Year

The Civil year as we have it today in Western Europe and America we owe to Julius Caesar. In Caesar's time the year was measured by the moon instead by the sun, the months later were called **moonths**. But figuring by the moon gave only 355 days to a year, with intercalary days added occasionally by way of correction; summer and winter would in time have changed places, already the seasons were two months in arrears when Caesar decided to change the system of calculation. At the suggestion of Sosigenes, Caesar settled on 365 and a quarter days as the approximately correct solar year; one day was added each fourth year or "leap year." The months were given the names and numbers of days as at present, November and December were skipped, and what would have been November 1, 45 B.C. became January 1, 46 B.C. and the beginning

795

of the new Julian calendar.[13]

After sixteen centuries of the use of this calendar, it was discovered that the Julian calendar was not accurate and that March 11, 1582 was really the day of the vernal equinox, and should have been March 21. Pope Gregory decreed for those churches in communion with Rome that October 5, 1582 should be reckoned as October 15, 1582. This was called the New Style calendar (N.S.), but this change was not accepted in England. However, in 1752 the English Parliament abandoned the Old Style and adopted the New Style. About this action Gwynne wrote:

> By this time the error had increased to nearly twelve days instead of ten, which made Christmas Day of that year (O.S. 1752) to become the feast of Epiphany (N.S. 1753), and caused the ignorant folk to complain that they had been robbed of twelve days of their lives. For this reason also Epiphany came to be called by them "old Christmas."[14]

The Greek and Russian churches still retain the Old Style Calendar.

The Appointed Readings for Epiphany

The Festival of the Epiphany of Our Lord has had certain readings appointed which are the same despite the adoption of new pericopal systems. In the Old Lutheran pericopal system Isaiah 60:1-6 is the appointed Old Testament Scripture.[15] This is also the case in the new ILCW system. Matthew 2:1-12, which sets forth the story of the Coming of the Wise Men, is the standard Gospel. In the LCMS's One-Year System as well as the Three-Year, the Old and New Testament readings are identical.[16] Because the magi who came to worship and present the Christ Child with gifts, Epiphany has been used to emphasize what has generally been called "foreign missions."[17]

The Epiphany Festival and its Season appears to be designed purposely to develop and reveal a definite teaching. Strodach defined its purpose as set forth in the Scriptural readings of the traditional system, followed by Lutherans, Episcopalians, and Roman Catholic to be, in these words:

> He who has come, born a Babe in Bethlehem, conformed to the Law, given a human name, He it is Who has been promised of old, the Christ of God; but this Messiah is Lord indeed, God of God, Light of Light, Very God of Very God and now to be manifested in all the Divine Glory, Son of Man, but Son of God." Shrouded in the flesh but the effulgence of the Divine bursting through to reveal Who He is.[18]

The Gospel Lesson for Epiphany contains one of the most popular stories in the Bible, if one is to judge by mosaic, graffiti and manuscripts hailing from the second and third centuries. In art and in legend the kings from the East (based on the interpretation of Isaiah 60) captured the imagination of Christians, probably sponsored by the contrast between them and the drab shepherds. Matthew's account does not record half of what Christians would like to know about this historic visit to Bethlehem. Many pious legends have grown up about what happened and these legends often have been treated as if they were part of the Biblical account.[19]

Augustine, Chrysostom and other writers mention the number of wise men as twelve. The Greek New Testament used the term "magoi," believed to be a Persian word, rendered "wise men", which really means "keepers of sacred things," "priest-scholars," or "astronomers." Later tradition reduced the number to three. The names given the three were: Melchior, the king of Arabia, a Semite, supposedly 60 years old; Balthasar, king of Ethiopia, a Negro, 40 years old; Caspar, King of Tarsus, and Indo-European, 20 years old. The three are supposed to have begun their journey from Babylon, made their way by camel up the fertile Tigris and Euphrates, the standard route for the traders of ancient times.[20]

The Baptism of Jesus

Kleinhans reports that "many of the Epiphany customs are associated with water or with wine as we might infer if we remember that Epiphany was once the day to celebrate Christ's baptism and the miracle of Cana. In the ancient lectionaries these readings had been once a part of the propers for the day, and Luther favored a return to the account of Christ's baptism, rather than that of the Wise Men. It seems strange that Christ's baptism is completely neglected in the old Church year."[21]

The First Sunday after Epiphany in the Three-Year or One-Year series has the account of Christ's Baptism taken either from Mark 1:9-11 or Matthew 3:13-17. The Collect for this day reads: "Father in heaven, as at the baptism in the Jordan river you once proclaimed Jesus your beloved Son and anointed him with the Holy Spirit, grant that all who are baptized in his name may faithfully keep the covenant into which they have been called, boldly confess their Savior and with him be heirs of life eternal; through Jesus Christ, who lives and reigns with you and the Holy Spirit, one God, now and forever."[22]

Here we have a visualization of the Holy Trinity, the Father speaking, the Son standing in the waters of the Jordan and the Holy Spirit present as a Dove resting on the Son of God. The persons of the Godhead are clearly distinguished.[23]

The Sundays after Epiphany

At one time Epiphany had its own octave, which was associated with the blessing of animals.[24] Although the blessing has remained the octave has now fallen by the way side. Until Gregory the Great's time, the Sundays after Epiphany did not seem to have any liturgical significance.[25] They appear to have been time-fillers between Christmas-Epiphany and the Pre-Lenten Sundays.

According to Kellner at first the Church only observed Easter, Pentecost, Christmas, and Epiphany. This heortologist claimed: "These chief festivals along with others soon added to their number, formed the elements for the organization of a festal system in the Church, as centers round which the lesser festivals grouped themselves."[26] The last step in the development of the Church's Year was to connect the chief festivals with one another, so as to make them parts of a whole.[27]

797

In the oldest service books there were from 4 to 10 Sundays after Epiphany. However, with the growth of Lent and Septuagesima, the number of Sundays varied from 1 to 6, depending on the coming of Easter.[28] In the Old Liturgical system, the propers for the Epiphany Sundays were similar in the Roman, Lutheran, and Anglican liturgical books. This was true about the Gospels and the Epistles. Variations, however, began with the fourth Sunday, where Introits and Graduals are repeated, and with the fifth and sixth, which are called "wandering" days to fill in at the end of the Pentecost season.[29]

The Transfiguration of Our Lord
(Last Sunday of the Epiphany Season)

Christ's Transfiguration was observed in the East as early as the sixth century, but was only accepted in the West very slowly.[30] In the Anglican and Roman Churches it was celebrated on August 6th. It was on the latter day that in 1456 Pope Calixtus III announced the victory of Belgrade, where Hunyady's army overcame the Islamic forces. In 1457 the same Pope extended the observance of the Feast of Transfiguration to the whole church.[31]

Because August 6 frequently fell on a weekday and in August, the Reformers Bugenhagen and Veit Dietrich chose it as a theme for a sermon on the Sixth Sunday after Epiphany. Some of the early Lutheran orders of the sixteenth century followed this custom.[32]

The Gospel for this day was Matthew 17:1-9; in the *Anglican Prayer Book*, it was Luke 9:28-36. The Lutheran, the Episcopalian and Roman *Missal* had the same Epistle, namely, II Peter 1:16-21.[33] In both the LCMS's One-and Three-Year Series, Exodus 24:41-18 was the Old Testament selection, while the Gospel in the Three-Year Series is Matthew 17:1-9; in the One-Year it is Luke's Transfiguration account.

The same collect is suggested in the *LH*, *LW*, and *LBW* and reads: "O God, who in the glorious transfiguration of Thine only-begotten Son has confirmed the mysteries of the faith by the testimony of the fathers, and who, in the voice that came from the bright cloud, didst in a wonderful way make us coheirs with the King of glory and bring us to the enjoyment of the same; through the same Jesus Christ our Lord," etc.[34]

This prayer sets forth the uniqueness and the miraculous character of our Lord's Transfiguration, testifying to His deity and also that the Father called Jesus His Son, whom people were to hear.

An application of this historic event in Christ's life is set forth in another collect only found in the *LBW* and reads: "Almighty God on the mountain you showed your glory in the transfiguration of your Son, give us the vision to see beyond the turmoil of our world and to behold the king in all his glory through your son Jesus Christ our Lord, who lives and reigns with you and the Holy Spirit, one God, now and forever."[35]

The Confession of St. Peter (January 18)

The *Lutheran Worship* has added as a Minor Day of observance, namely, the Confession of Peter.[36] It is also found in *Lutheran Book of*

Worship but not in the *Lutheran Hymnal*. For this day of observance, the Lutheran readings are: the Gospel: Matthew 16:13-19, the Roman *Missal* has the same text as has the Anglican also. However, the Epistle reading is different for the three Communions: I Corinthians 10:1-5 (The Lutheran), 1 Peter 5:1-4 (Roman), and Acts 4:8-13 (Anglican).

Pfatteicher, writing in *The Lesser Festivals I* informs us:

> This festival, restored to the calendar by the Episcopal Church and adopted by the Lutheran Church, marks the beginning of the *w*eek of prayer for Christianity. This week thus begins with a festival in honor of Peter and concludes with a festival in honor of Paul.[37]

There is no question that the confession of Peter to Christ's question, "Whom do you say I am?" The Response by Peter: You are Christ the Son of the Living God, was a great confession. It was the only correct answer to this all-important question. Jesus told Peter that his remarkable statement was not his own, but it was given to him by divine revelation and therefore, it was really God's answer about his own Son. After that great confession Matthew reports that Jesus addressed Peter: "You are Peter and upon this rock I will build my church, and the gates of hell shall not prevail against it" (Matthew 16:11). After making this marvelous confession Jesus to Peter: "I will give you the keys to the kingdom of heaven. Anything you bind on earth will be bound in heaven, and anything you free on earth will be free in heaven."[38]

Peter in his sermons recorded in Acts or in his two Epistles never asserted that he was the head of the church and that Jesus Christ has appointed Him as administrative leader and theological leader of the entire Christian Church. The Collect appointed in the *Lutheran Worship* sets forth the correct meaning of Peter's Confession: "Dear Father in heaven, as you revealed to the apostle Saint Peter the blessed truth that Jesus is the Christ, the Son of the Living God, strengthen us in the same faith in our Savior Jesus Christ, our Lord, who lives and reigns with you and the Holy Spirit one God, now and forever" (pp, 95-96).

In the Roman Catholic *Missal* January 18 is called "The Feast of the Chair of St. Peter,"[39] also the day dedicated to St. Prisca, Virgin martyr. The New *Missal* has this prayer (called a Secret) for St. Peter's Chair Day:

> We beseech thee, O Lord, that the prayer of the blessed apostle Peter may commend the sacrifices and the supplications of Thy Church, so that the celebration we hold for his glory may profit for our pardon, through our Lord.[40]

The Roman Catholic selection or the Epistle is I Peter 5:1-4. In the Roman Catholic lectionary, the Lutheran LCA scholar Pfatteicher said that it can be understood to be directed at the papacy by Peter himself who urges pastoral care of the flock, warns against dictatorial methods, and promises reward at the appearing or the chief shepherd.[41]

On Maundy Thursday evening Christ promised His disciples the gift of the Holy Spirit, Who would guide them into all truth. This applied to all apostles. When Peter wrote his Two Letters to the congregations of Asia Minor, he was not doing this as the representative of Christ on earth, but as one of God's apostles whom Jesus chose and used for the up-building and guidance of the Church. In terms of importance, if comparisons are to be made of the apostles, Paul chosen after the Ascension, accomplished more and played a more important role humanly speaking and contributed thirteen of the twenty-seven inspired books of the New Testament.

The Conversion of St. Paul (January 25)

The Conversion of St. Paul was one of the most important historical happenings in the history of Christianity in the last two thousand years.[42] Luke, doctor and missionary companion of Paul, has given us three different accounts of this significant happening. One account is Luke's version, found in Acts 9:1-22, while Paul in two defense speeches gave two accounts. To the Jerusalem audience (Acts 22:3-21) he related how he became a Christian and later in an appearance before Herod Agrippa he also related how the course of his life had been totally altered by Jesus (Ch. 26). Of these accounts Bruce wrote: "they are subtly adapted to their varying circumstances."[43] In his Letter to the Galatian Paul referred to his former manner of life in Jerusalem in Judaism and how he used to persecute the church of God beyond measure, and tried to destroy it (Gal. 1:13). At the same time he had believed that in pursuing such a course he had been serving God and preserving the purity of the Law. In Philippians 3:6 Paul indicated that his life was "blameless" in regard to the righteousness of the law.

The Conversion of Paul was a sudden one. This is clearly asserted in the narrative account in Acts and also by Paul's statement in his epistles. Dunnett believes that there may have been certain experiences that prepared Paul of Damascus for the Damascene road experience. Thus he wrote:

> The death of Stephen, at which Paul was in hearty agreement (Acts 7:58-3:1l; the heat of his house-to-house campaign against those of the Way (Acts 8:3; 9:1-2; 22:4; 26:10-11) would hardly leave him unaffected; and his furious journey toward Damascus represented the climax of his efforts.[44]

However. when all is said, we agree with Paul Kretzmann, who concluded as follows about Paul's Damascene conversion:

> One fact stands out with a certainty which cannot be denied, namely, that a state of mind less favorable for conversion than that of Saul can hardly be imagined. He was in the very midst of Pharisaic darkness and unbelief, adoring the very name of Christ and full of resentment and hatred toward those that confessed belief, abhorring the very name. But the Lord's manner of dealing with the most hopeless cases and obstinate enemies passes human understanding.[45]

The change in Paul was shown in that Paul responded to the voice of Jesus: "What shall I do Lord?" (Acts 22:10). In Galatians 2:20 Paul shows that he had entered into a new relationship with Christ (Cf. II Cor. 5:16-17).

The second evidence of change in Paul was evidenced in that Paul preached a different message in the synagogue in Damascus, in the very city he had intended to persecute the Christians. Now he proclaims: "He (Jesus) is the Son of God" (Acts 9:20). After the appearance of Christ near Damascus, Paul made this his life's work to prove that Jesus was the Christ (Acts 9:21). Not too long before this Paul "had to do many things hostile to the name of Jesus of Nazareth, even to the extent of declaring "Jesus is accursed." (Cf. 1 Cor. 12:3). He pursued the Christians as if they were wild animals (Acts 26:9-11). The third evidence of Paul's conversion was the conviction that God had convinced him to be "preach God's Son among the Gentiles" (Gal. 1:16).

The Conversion of Paul was humanly speaking a miracle, the results of which are hard to measure. He became the great evangelist who brought the Gospel from Jerusalem to Spain. On three separate missionary journeys he preached in Asia and Europe and founded many churches the Holy Spirit chose Paul to be the writer of 13 inspired Books.

In the Concordia's Three-Year Series, the Epistle is Acts 9:1-22; the Gospel is Luke 21:10-19. In the One-Year Series Acts 9:1-22 and Matthew 19:27-30 with the Old Testament Selection: Jeremiah 1:4-10.[46]

The martyrdoms of Peter and Paul are observed on June 29th.

History of Paul's Conversion as a Festival

In Rome the Conversion of Paul was observed as a feast in the fourth century. In Europe, however, liturgical notice was taken much later.[47] it is Kellner's opinion that the "translation" of the relics of Paul from the catacombs to the basilica of St. Paul during Constantine's reign may have determined the date of January 25.[48] as the festival spread, Paul's Conversion became the dominant theme of the festival. The diocese of Worms adopted it in A.D. 1198, Cologne in 1260.

The dramatic and miraculous element in Paul's conversion Reed claims, had an appeal for the Western Church in the Middle Ages. The Greek Church does not observe Paul's Conversion.[49]

St. Timothy, Pastor and Confessor (January 24)

Lutheran Worship and *Lutheran Book of Worship* list among the Minor Festivals, January 24 as St. Timothy, Pastor and Confessor.[50] *The Concordia Pocket Diary* lists January 24 as the day to remember St. Timothy and two days later, the 26th as St. Titus, Pastor and confessor. Both of these fellow associates of St. Paul are worthy to be remembered, both by the laity and the clergy, because of their service for Christ and as missionaries who helped Paul during his apostolic ministry.

In *The New Roman Missal* the Epistle appointed for St. Timothy Day is I Timothy 6:11-16.[51]

The New Testament tells us considerable about Timothy.[52] His mother and grandmother were Eunice and Lois respectfully (11 Timothy 1:5). His father was a Greek and his mother a Jewess. The women were probably converted to Christianity by Paul on his first missionary journey on his visit to Derbe and Lystra (Acts 16:1-2). When Paul returned to the same region, he was so impressed with young Timothy that the apostle took him with him, possibly to replace John Mark who had left Barnabas and Paul before the conclusion of the First Journey.

Timothy received an excellent religious training from his grandmother and mother. When Paul met Timothy he was an uncircumcised person. Paul chose him to be one of his missionary associates, also because he was "well reported of by his brethren" (Acts 16:1-2; 11 Tim. 1:5; 3:14-15). According to I Timothy 1:18; 4:14, there were certain prophetic indications that Timothy was to serve in the cause of Christ (1 Tim. 1:18; 4:14). Before ordaining him by the laying on of hands, Paul has Timothy circumcised. While the apostle did not consider circumcision necessary for salvation, he felt that Timothy's not being a circumcised individual could present an unnecessary stumbling block when he engaged in evangelism among the Jews.

Timothy accompanied Paul and Silvanus to Troas, where Paul had his famous vision of the Macedonian man who pleaded for Paul to come to Greece (Acts 16:9). The next mention of Timothy is in connection with Paul's stay at Berea, where Paul left Timothy after his departure to Athens (Acts 17:10-14). Later Timothy joined Paul in Athens, from where Paul sent Timothy back to Thessalonica to help the congregations there. Timothy met Paul in Corinth, bringing his mentor a good report about the Thessalonian church (I Thess. 3:6-7). Timothy's name is mentioned by Paul in both his Thessalonian epistles.

Luke reports in Acts that Timothy was with Paul in Ephesus during the latter's Third Missionary Journey (Acts 19:22). After Timothy had returned with Paul to Ephesus, he was sent on a special mission with Erastus across the Aegean world with Paul's First Corinthian Letter (I Cor. 4:17; 16:10-11). It seems Timothy returned to Ephesus (I Cor. 16:11) and with Erastus travelled into Macedonia to make ready for a new stage of Paul's Third Missionary Journey.

According to II Corinthians, Timothy was with Paul when the apostle wrote this letter and also according to Romans 16:21 Timothy was with Paul when the later penned his Romans Epistle. Timothy and certain other person preceded Paul as the latter was on his way through Macedonia to Jerusalem, and waited for Paul at Troas (Acts 20:4-5). Timothy appears to have been with Paul when he wrote the Captivity Epistles (Col. 1:1; Phil. 1:1; Philemon 1), which some scholars believe were written in Rome during the apostle's first Roman imprisonment 60-62 (Others place them during a supposed captivity in Ephesus).

After his release from his first Roman imprisonment Paul left Timothy in Ephesus to attend to necessary church affairs (I Tim. 1:3). The tradition that Timothy was the first bishop of Ephesus is not very sound; because it appears that the apostle John settled there after A.D. 70 and dwelled there till the end of his life. The last reference to Timothy is found in II Timothy 4:6-9, where we learn that Paul during his final imprisonment in Rome yearned to see Timothy and asked him to come before winter. Whether Timothy was able to see Paul before his death we do not know.

Some scholars have inferred from the number of exhortations and injunctions, which Paul uttered to Timothy (cf. I Cor. 16:10-11; I Tim. 4:12; 5:21) that Timothy was a timid soul. Especially in the 60's with the Neronian persecution occurring, Timothy needed to be admonished to fight a good fight and to give a good account of himself. Tradition alleges that Timothy died as a martyr.

St. Titus, Pastor and Confessor (January 28)

The Concordia Pocket Guide and the *Lutheran Hymnal* list January 26 as a day to commemorate Titus,[53] one of the recipients of the Pastoral Epistles. *The Lutheran Book of Worship* differs from the recommended dates for the observance of Titus assigning January 26 to Timothy. Titus and Silas and January 27 as the day to remember Lydda, Dorcas and Phoebe.[54] *The New Roman Missal* assigned February 6 to Titus and also to St. Dorothy, Virgin, Martyr.[55]

It is significant that the New Testament presents its readers with considerable information concerning Timothy and Titus, Paul's fellow missionaries and evangelists. We have more knowledge about these two pastors than about a number of members of the apostolate.

Titus was probably one of Paul's converts I Titus 1:41 and became a valued friend of the Apostle Paul. Titus is not mentioned in Acts but Paul refers to him in II Corinthians, Galatians, II Timothy and Titus.[56] He attended with Paul and Barnabas the Jerusalem Conference reported in Acts 15; Galatians 2:1-4. The great issue at this convention was whether or not the Gentiles who had accepted Christ as Savior still needed to observe the ceremonial law, including circumcision. Titus had come along as a test case. Paul never had Titus circumcised because he was a Gentile, a non-Jew, while Timothy a half-Jew he had had circumcised so that Jews would not be offended. The decision of the Apostolic Conference was that the Gospel did not require circumcision as a part of a person being a Christian and a member of the Christian Church (Acts 15:13-29).

Titus performed an important pastoral work in Corinth. In II Corinthians Titus is spoken of less than eight times and in chapter 8:23 Paul calls him "my partner and fellow worker".

Paul sent Titus into a very difficult situation at Corinth, where the congregation had split up into four parties of cliques. Gross immorality, taking each other into the heathen court, and a number of other religious problems characterized the early history of the Corinthian congregation founded by Paul on his Second Missionary Journey. Titus had success in dealing with the problems of this Grecian church. Titus and this church became attached to each other. Titus seems to have visited this congregation three times, supervising on two occasions the collection for the poor saints in Jerusalem (II Cor. 8:6, 10-11; 22-24). Titus and another person carried Paul's Second Letter to Corinth (II Cor. 8:18).

We know nothing of Titus's life and activity after this until he received from Paul an inspired letter, one of the three Pastorals. From this letter we learn that after Paul's first Roman imprisonment Paul took Titus to Crete, and when Paul left, placed Titus in charge of church work. Instructing him to complete what Paul had begun and to organize the church by the appointment of elders in every city (Titus 1:5). Titus appears to have been a strong personality and steadfast in his ministry among the godless Cretans. II Timothy 4:10 states that Titus has gone to Dalmatia.

The Two Letters to Timothy and the Letter to Titus are important for the directives they give relative to the conduct of the ministry and the importance they ascribe to the preservation of sound doctrine.

In *The New Roman Missal* the prayer assigned for St. Titus Day reads like this: "O God, Who didst adorn blessed Titus, thy Confessor and Bishop, with apostolic virtues grant, through his merits and intercessions, that living righteously and devotedly in this world, we may deserve to reach our heavenly country through our Lord."[57] This prayer assumes that the doctrine of the apostolic succession, namely, that Titus received from Paul apostolic authority to ordain elders in each city of Crete. But in the Pastoral Epistles elders are synonymous with **episcopoi** or **bishops** (Titus 1:7; I Tim. 3:2). The present hierarchy of clergy is a development of the two centuries following the apostolic age.[58] The prayer also assumes that petitions may be made to the saints who have the ability to interceded for those who address their requests to the saints.

The Presentation of Christ (February 2)

Coming within this year's Epiphany Cycle is the Feast of the Presentation of Christ. All liturgical calendars list as the Gospel for this day, Luke 2:22-40. The Presentation of our Lord is observed forty days after Christmas. It is technically a festival of Christ and one not to honor Mary. Luke depicts the Virgin Mary bringing her son to the temple and in accordance with the Mosaic law offering up the appointed sacrifice, which required not only a pair of birds but her Son Himself. In the Eastern Church this day is called "the Meeting," the encounter between the Old Covenant and the New.

According to Reed, Sylvia mentioned the Feast as observed in Jerusalem at the end of the fourth Century.[59] Justinian introduced it in Constantinople in the sixth century.[60] Its earliest name was **Hypapante** (Greek for "Meeting" and the reference was the meeting of our Lord with Simeon. The historic Collect for this day, as well as the Blessing of the Candles, emphasizes the thought of the Presentation and not of Mary's Purification.[61]

However, after the ninth century with the expanding Mary cult, February 2 was called "The Purification of Mary". It would appear, says Reed that the name "is strikingly incongruous with the later dogma of the Immaculate Conception."[62] Both the Lutheran and Anglican Churches have retained the date as a festival of Christ.

February 2nd in the Middle Ages was known as Candlemas (the mass of candles) and refers to the blessing and use of an unusual number of candles in the services of this day.[63] Reed informs us that "this was originally a feature of a pagan festival held in Rome on February 2, which under Christian direction became a penitential procession. The Feast of the Presentation later displaced this but incorporated this particular custom with its own order, possibly because of Luke 2:32 "A light to lighten the Gentiles."[64]

The Collect in the *Lutheran Hymnal* is the same as in the LCA's *Common Service Book* and reads: "Almighty and Ever living God, we humbly beseech Thy Majesty, that as Thine Only-begotten Son was this day presented in the Temple in substance of our flesh, so may we be presented unto thee with pure and clean hearts; through the same Jesus Christ, Thy Son our Lord."[65]

Before the adoption of the new lectionary system by the ILCW, the Old Testament reading was: Malachi 3:1-4; the Gospel Luke 2:22-23. These readings were the same in the *Anglican Prayer Book*, the *Roman Missal* and *The Common Service Book* of the LCA Lutheans.[66]

Lutheran Worship gives different sets of readings, depending whether a pastor uses the One-Year or the Three-Year Series; Old Testament I Samuel 1:21-28; the Epistle; Hebrews 2:14-18 and the Gospel: Luke 2:22-40.[67]

St. Matthias, Apostle (February 24)

Acts 1:15-26 contains the historic account as to the manner Matthias was elected as the 12th apostle to replace Judas Iscariot, who had committed suicide. Luke informs us that Peter led the company of about 120 disciples to make this replacement. It took place in the time between the Ascension and the Outpouring of the Spirit on Pentecost. Matthias was chosen over Barsabbas, surnamed Justus. Both Matthias and Barsabbas were men who knew Jesus from the days of John the Baptist until Christ's Ascension.

The New Testament says nothing of Matthias after his election. This paucity concerning the 12th apostle he also shared with a number of other members of the apostolate. One tradition places Matthias' ministry in Judaea, another has him active in Ethiopia. Horn stated "That there must have been a paucity even of legend is indicated when a ninth-century writer, Autpert, Abbot of Monte Cassio, states that nothing is known of St. Matthias! His day dates from early in the eleventh century, one of the last of the apostles' days, but the reason is not known."[68]

In iconography Matthias is represented as holding a sword by the point, with a stone in his hand, with a book and scimitar.[69]

The Old traditional readings for February 24 are for the Gospel: Matthew 11:25-30; the Epistle Acts 1:15-26. In *Lutheran Worship* the Collect reads: "Lord God heavenly King, whose chosen apostles have witnessed to us regarding your resurrection, grant that your Church, ever preserved from false teachers, may praise your wonderful works and walk in the power of your resurrection, for you live and reign with the Father and the Holy Spirit, one God, now and forever."[70]

The Pre-Lenten Sundays

In primitive times Advent, Christmas and Epiphany made up the Christmas Cycle. The Pre-Easter, Easter-Pentecost and the post-Pentecost seasons made up the Easter or Pascal Cycle. Thus the whole Church

805

Year mirrored what Christ had said and done. At the Reformation this original arrangement was reemphasized.

The season of Pre-Lent were frequently called Pre-Easter. Down throughout the centuries Lent came to assume overtones of fasting and penitence. However, Kleinhans claimed that "the proper mood is one of expectation of waiting, not unlike that of Advent, in which the Christians ought to feel not only sorrow because of his sin and Christ's death, but also joy, because of the triumph of His resurrection."[71]

The first period of the Pre-Lent went from Septuagesima until Ash Wednesday; the second from Ash Wednesday to Laetare Sunday; and the third period from Judica Sunday to Holy Saturday.

The Pre-Lenten Sundays are Septuagesima (70th), Sexagesima (60th) and Quinquagesima (50th). The first Sunday in Lent was known as Quadragesima (40th). The three Sundays cover three and a half weeks. Horn wrote of these Sundays:

> Its origin is quote obscure. The title appears first in the canons of the Fourth Council of Orleans in 541. Before that time, Quadragesima (forty days) was a term applied to the first Sunday in Lent as well as to the entire Lenten fast. Quinquagesima is exactly fifty days before Easter – the only one of the Sundays for which the title is precise. Sexagesima is 57 days and Septuagesima 64 days before Easter. The calendar date of Septuagesima depends, of course, upon the date of Easter. It may occur as early as January 18 and as late as February 22.[72]

Strodach has pointed out that in ancient times there did not appear to be a general rule pertaining as to when Lent was supposed to begin. He wrote relative to the length and manner of the Lenten fast as follows:

> One medieval writer states that the monastic orders began the Fast with Septuagesima, the Greek Church with Sexagesima, and the secular clergy with Quinquagesima. There did appear much emphasis on a forty-day period, a Quadragesima, in imitation of our Lord's Fast in the Wilderness; and as one or another of the classes mentioned might omit, as for example the monastics, Sundays,Thursdays and Saturdays, from the Fast, naturally the fast period would be lengthened. Thus in one case at least the beginning of this period would be thrown back to Septuagesima, in order to include the forty fast days.[73]

The Inter-Lutheran Commission on Worship has eliminated the three Pre-Lenten Sundays, making them instead the three last Sundays of the Epiphany Cycle.[74] In *The Lutheran Hymnal* and the *Lutheran Book of Worship,* Ash Wednesday comes immediately after the Sunday of Christ's Transfiguration.[75]

Footnotes

1. Paul Zeller Strodach, *The Church Year Studies in the Introits, Collects Epistles and Gospels* (Philadelphia: The United Lutheran Publication House, 1924), p. 52.
2. Theodore J. Kleinhans, *The Year of the Lord* (St. Louis (St. Louis: Concordia Publishing House, 1967), p. 55.
3. A. A. McArthur, "Epiphany," J. G. Davies, editor, *The Westminster Dictionary of*

Worship (Philadelphia: The Westminster Press, 1972), p. 170.

4. Edward T. Horne, *The Christian Year* (Philadelphia: Muhlenberg Press, 1957), p. 82.
5. McArthur, **op. cit.**, p. 170.
6. McArthur, **op. cit.**, p. 170.
7. **Ibid.**, p. 170-171.
8. **Ibid.**, p. 171.
9. Kleinhans, **op. cit.**, p. 55.
10. Strodach, *The Church Year*, **op. cit.**, p. 62.
11. Walker Gwynne, *The Christian Year – Its Purpose and Its History* (New York: Longmans, Green, and Co., 1915), p. 61.
12. C. Fitzsimons Allison and Werner H. Kelber, *Proclamation – Epiphany B* (Philadelphia: Fortress Press, 1975), p. v.
13. Gwynne, **op. cit.**, pp. 44-46.
14. **Ibid.**, p. 46.
15. *The Lutheran Hymnal* (St. Louis: Concordia Publishing House, 1941), p. 58
16. *Lutheran Worship* (St. Louis: Concordia Publishing House, 1982), p. 20.
17. C. Thomas Spitz," Sermons Study of Epiphany", *Sermonic Studies – The Standard Epistles, Volume I* (St. Louis: Concordia Publishing House, 1957), pp. 92-93.
18. Strodach, **op. cit.**, pp. 62-63.
19. Kleinhans, **op. cit.**, p. 56.
20. **Ibid.**, p. 56-57.
21. **Ibid.**, p. 58.
22. *Lutheran Book of Worship*, **op. cit.**, p. 20.
23. Adam Fahling, *The Life of Christ* (St. Louis: Concordia Publishing House, 1936), p. 141.
24. Kleinhans, **op. cit.**, p. 58.
25. K. A. Heinrich Kellner, *Heortology – A History of Christ in Festivals from Their Own Origin to the Present Day* (London: Kegan Paulk Trench, Truebner & Co., 1980), p. 170.
26. **Ibid.**, p. 176.
27. **Ibid.**
28. Merrill R. Abbey and O.L. Edwards, *Proclamation – Epiphany – Series A* (Philadelphia: Muhlenberg Press, 1974), p. vii.
29. Horn, **op. cit.**, p. 92.
30. Luther D. Reed, *The Lutheran Liturgy* (Philadelphia: The Muhlenberg Press, 1947), p. 499.
31. **Ibid.**
32. **Ibid.**
33. **Ibid.**
34. *Lutheran Hymnal*, **op. cit.**, p. 60.
35. *Lutheran Book of Worship*, **op. cit.**, p. 17.
36. *Lutheran Worship*, p. 9.
37. Philp Pfatteicher, *Proclamation – The Lesser Festivals I* (Philadelphia: The Fortress Press, 1975).
38. W. Beck, **An American Translation** (New Haven: Leader Publishing Company, 1970), New Testament (Matt. 18:6), p. 22.
39. *The New Roman Catholic Missal*, By F.X. Lusance, F. Walsh, and W. R. Kelbey (New York: Beninger Brothers, 1956), p. 868.
40. **Ibid.**

41. Pfatteicher, **op. cit.,** p. 19.
42. This is the opinion of F. F. Bruce, *The Acts of the Apostle, The Greek Text with Introduction and Commentary* (Grand Rapids: Wm. B. Eerdmans Publishing Company, 1951), p. 196.
43. **Ibid.**
44. Dunnett, "Paul," in H. Von and J. Rea, *Wycliffe Bible Encyclopedia* (Chicago: Moody Press, 1975), II, p. 1293.
45. P. E. Kretzmannn, *Popular Commentary* (St. Louis: Concordia Publishing House, 1921), 1, p. 376.
46. *Lutheran Worship*, p. 96.
47. Reed, **op. cit.,** p. 498.
48. Kellner, **op. cit.,** p. 288.
49. Reed, **op. cit.,** p. 498.
50. *Lutheran Worship*, p. 104.
51. *The New Roman Missal*, **op. cit.,** p. 884.
52. For Timothy's Life and Activities cf. Henry Snyder Gehman, *The New Westminster Dictionary of the Bible* (Philadelphia: Westminster press, 1970), pp. 949-950.
53. *Lutheran Hymnal*, p. 104.
54. *Lutheran Book of Worship*, p. 10.
55. *The New Roman Missal*, **op. cit.,** p. 913.
56. For Titus' Biography cf. Gehman, **op. cit.,** p. 913.
57. *The New Roman Missal*, **op. cit.,** p. 913.
58. On the apostolic succession cf. *The Concordia Cyclopedia* (St. Louis: Concordia Publishing House, 1927), pp. 32-33.
59. Reed, **op. cit.,** p. 499.
60. Reed, **op. cit.,** p. 499; Kilner, p. 18; Gwynne, **op. cit.,** p. 61.
61. Reed, p. 499.
62. **Ibid.**
63. **Kleinhans, op. cit., p. 60.**
64. **Reed, op. cit., p. 499.**
65. **The *Lutheran Hymnal*, p. 85.**
66. **Cf. Reed, p. 498.**
67. *Lutheran Worship, p. 107.*
68. *Horn,* **op. cit.,** *p. 190.*
69. *Ibid.*
70. *Lutheran Worship, p. 96*
71. *Kleinhans,* **op. cit.,** *p. 61.*
72. *Horn,* **op. cit.,** *p. 95.*
73. *Strodach,* **op. cit.,** *pp. 89-90.*
74. *Lutheran Worship, pp. 30-31; Lutheran Book of Worship, p. 17; The Lessons, A,B,C (Minneapolis: Augsburg Publishing Company, no date), pp. 23-24 (A), 23-24 (B), 23-24 (C).*
75. *Ibid.*

Questions

1. Epiphany is one of the ____ Festivals of the Church year.
2. Epiphany preceded ___ as a festival commemorating Christ's birth.
3. When was Christmas first celebrated? ____
4. In the Eastern Church new members were not called ____ but ____.
5. Easter may come between ____.

6. What three Sundays are now considered three Sundays of the long Epiphany Season? ____
7. We owe the civil year as we have it in the Western Europe and America to ____.
8. Epiphany has been used to emphasize what is generally called ____.
9. What was a great confession? ____
10. Peter never said he was ____ of the church.
11. The Conversion of St. Paul is one of the most ____.
12. Paul sent ___ back to Thessalonica.
13. What was the great issue at the Jerusalem Conference? ____
14. Who replaced Judas? ____

Ash Wednesday to Easter Eve

Christian News, February 27, 1984

It was stated in the previous installment on the Christian Year (with its major and minor festivals) that the first period of Lent is actually pre-Lent, which goes from Septugesima Sunday till Ash Wednesday. The next period goes from Ash Wednesday to Sunday Laetare; the next from Laetare until Judica Sunday, also called Passion Sunday. This is followed by Passiontide, from Judica until Holy Saturday. Within Passiontide there is Holy Week itself, culminating in Holy Saturday and its observances.[1]

The Origin of Lent

The word Lent comes from the Anglo-Saxon "lencten," which means "spring". Lent, like other festivals of the Ecclesiastical Year, experienced a development in both the Eastern and Western Churches. A wealth of practices over the centuries developed in different parts of the church.[2] At present, Lent refers to a six-week period of spiritual discipline before Easter as conveyed by the forty-days of the Greek **tessaracoste** or the Latin **quadragesima**. **Careme** is the modern French word for Lent, in old French **Quaresma**, an abbreviation of the Latin Quadragesima.[3]

Horn III has pointed out that the origin of Lent "lies in two directions: the fast which preceded the Pascha (pas-ka), and the period of preparation described for candidates for baptism. Holy Week seems to have developed from the former; the remainder of Lent from the latter."[4]

In the Early Church Pascha commemorated the passion and resurrection of Christ as a unitive festival.[5] In the Early Church, following a Jewish custom, the Lord's Day began at 6 p.m. Saturday evening. The Gospels report that Jesus arose from the dead early on Sunday morning. Christians fasted until 3 a.m. According to the **Apostolic Tradition** of Hippolytus as late as the third century the fast was restricted to Saturday, although sometimes fasting occurred on Friday. This was the case in Rome. According to the **Disdascalia**, the fast was extended to six days. According to Alan McArthur the pre-Pascha fast was gradually extended to forty hours (the time Christ was believed to be in the grave), then to six days before Easter.[6]

It was only in the fourth century, sometime between 350 and 400, that the events of Holy Week were separated from the first five weeks of Lent. Between 350 and the end of the century Holy Week, Good Friday and Easter developed at Jerusalem as separate festivals. One of the early features of Holy Saturday was the Baptism of candidates for church membership. Before Rome became thoroughly Christianized, the weeks before Easter were the time when people were prepared for baptism on Easter Eve. Kleinhans wrote:

> At the beginning of Lent those who wished baptism were publicly exorcised. The bishop admonished them to give up their allegiance to

Satan. During the ceremony they stood barefoot on goatskins.

In this period of instruction the catechumens could not bathe or shave. They could eat only after sundown. If married, they lived in continence. Their chief occupation was meditation and contrition, often within the walls of a monastery or church.[7]

Before 313 A.D. the Christian Church was an underground church, a church not licensed by the government (religio illicita). The church felt that it had to scrutinize carefully every prospective member. The final period before baptism was very rigorous. Catechumens had to fast in preparation of, their baptism, attend catechetical lectures and were periodically examined and scrutinized.[8]

Gradually Lent was expanded into a forty-day period. The idea of a period of forty days was suggested by the fact that Christ fasted for forty days in the wilderness (Mark 4:2; Luke 4:2), Moses' fast on Mt. Sinai (Ex. 24:18; Deut. 9:9) and Elijah's fast on the Mount of God (I Kings 19:8), all of which were of forty-days duration.[9]

Catechumens were allowed to hear the Apostles Creed for the first time on Passion Sunday, and the Lord's Prayer on Palm Sunday. Kleinhans claims that:

"These came in a secret ceremony where they shook hands, promised faithfulness, and stated their desires to become members of the church. The rite was known as **traditio symboli**. On Holy Saturday the confirmands were expected to "return the symbol (the creed, or some explanation, the handshake that came with the creed) in public examination." These "scrutinies"[10] occurred several times during their instruction. The secret character of these instructions goes back to the age of the martyrs.

Originally examinations for the catechumens began on the Wednesday of the third week of Lent, with the last one on Holy Saturday of Holy Week. In the beginning there were seven scrutinies but by the eighth century they were reduced to three, spread over the six-week period of Lent, falling to the first, fourth and last weeks. Some epistle lessons formerly read during Lent recall these ancient practices (E.g. Second Sunday in Lent (I Thess. 4:17); the Third Sunday in Lent (Eph. 5:1-9).

With The Edict of Toleration in 313, when Christianity became a **religio licita**, that is a religion that was licensed by the state; the scrutinies were relaxed and the preparation for the baptism of catechumens became a general period of preparation for the baptism of catechumens. It became a general period of preparation for all people who wanted to become Christians. McArthur noted: "Lent was not instituted as a historical preparation for the Passion, it soon became exactly that."[11]

Observing 36 days of fasting in Lent was thought to represent a tithe of the 365 days of the year — a tithe due to the Lord in fasting and penitence. By adding four days from Ash Wednesday to the First Sunday of Lent and thus at the end of the seventh week or beginning of the eighth week, the number 40 of fast days appeared. The Gelasian Sacramentary has this number for the first time. With Sunday Septugesima the season takes on the character of preparation for Lent.

Horn III has pointed out that the Eastern Church did not adopt the total concept of the Western Church. The Eastern Church exempted Thursdays and Saturdays from fasting, as well as the Sundays and so had an eight-week Lent. Asserted Horn about the longer Lenten season:

Its introduction is gradual. On the Monday after the eighth Sunday before Easter (corresponding to the Western Septugesima), meat is given up: from the seventh Sunday (corresponding to Quinqagesima), Lacticima (eggs and milk) are given up.[12]

The oldest mood for Lent was not that of sorrow or sadness. In the Eastern Church the older liturgies retain the Hallelujahs and looked toward Christ's resurrection, while in the West the concentration of the services was on Christ's suffering and death. In the Western Church, beginning with Septuagesima, the Hallelujah's, the Gloria and the Te Deum, were not used. There was a ceremony observed in the West called "Farewell to Hallelujah." Kleinhans noted "there was a quiet way of saying goodbye to Hallelujah," but "there were also more sensational rites, in which the word was symbolically buried in a coffin or rolled up inside a straw scarecrow and burned."[13]

The Latin Names of Lenten Sundays

The Sundays in Lent bear distinctive names, beginning with Invocavit (or Invocabit), Reminiscere, Oculi, Laetare and Judica (often called Passion Sunday). The Pre-Lenten Sundays are Septuagesima (within a cycle of 70 days before Easter), Sexgesima (within a cycle of 60 days before Easter) and Quinquagesima (the 50th day before Easter).

While the Sundays are not considered a part of the Lenten season, the tendency developed to think morbidly and mediate on Christ's suffering and death. Kellner, an expert on the subject of heortology, complained about this when he wrote:

It is to be observed further that Lent is not devoted to the consideration of Christ's sufferings. This occupies the mind during Holy Week. The aim of Lent is not to move the faithful to dwell upon the passion of Christ, but only to prepare them for keeping Easter worthily... On Palm Sunday for the first time our thoughts are directed to the collect for the day, while in the prayers for the so-called Passion Sunday it is not mentioned.[14]

In the Lutheran Churches the Passion is observed throughout all of Lent, especially in midweek services. The history of Christ's passion was read in pre-Reformation Germany during Holy Week but this has been extended in sermons and meditations of midweek Lenten services. Horn claims that:

"Often the result is that by the time Holy Week arrives both people and clergy are weary of the details of the narrative which are proper to the week before Easter."[15]

In a sermon in the fifth century Leo the Great told his hearers that Lent was observed to help souls to prepare for a beneficial observance of Easter; that during Lent the faithful should be purified and sanctified, to make penance for past sins and break sinful habits. They were also encouraged to give alms, be reconciled and put aside enmity and hatred.[16]

The Middle Ages saw another Lenten custom come into vogue, namely, that of hanging of the Lenten veil, sometimes called the "hunger veil," because of the fast. A veil was hung between the nave and the choir of the churches.[17] In a day when people did not have calendars, it was a way of telling the worshippers that they were in the season of Lent. The Lenten veil was hung from Ash Wednesday to Good Friday. Its use was popular in Westphalia, Hannover and in the Russian Orthodox churches. Since the fourth-century Council of Laodicea (A.D. 360), Lent was declared a closed season (tempora clausa) during which weddings were discouraged; nuptial masses could not be said.

Fasting was found in many sixteenth-century Lutheran church orders, as Brandenberg in 1540 and Calenberg, 1542. Horn claims that "it is a mistake to suppose that Luther wished the custom of fasting to be altogether given up."[18] In the Lutheran and Anglican Churches fasting was placed on an individual basis, just as it had been in the early church. Fasting was considered a good way to practice spiritual discipline.

Shrove Tuesday

The Tuesday before Ash Wednesday is called Shrove Tuesday, taking its name from "shriving" or "the forgiving of sins." In many countries Shrove Tuesday is a time of revealing and celebrating before the great fast. From this day comes the word "carnival", Latin for "goodbye to meat."[19]

Fasting in the time of Charlemagne also included abstainment from dairy products, such as milk, butter, and cheese. For this reason many a good housewife baked up what stocks of butter and milk that she had left into pancakes. In French countries Shrove Tuesday was known as Mardy Gras, or "Fat Tuesday." It was the day the housewife was expected to use up all her fats.[20]

Ash Wednesday and Its Place in Lent

Ash Wednesday marks the beginning of Lent. It was also known as **Caput jejuni** (the head of the beginning of the fast).

Two early Church Fathers, Augustine and Tertullian, inform us that the Lenten fast originated with our Lord's Apostles. Concerning this Strodach wrote:

"While this is not improbable, the statement must be qualified. It is neither the Lent nor the Lenten Fast that we know that is meant, for both of these have undergone a long process of development before they assumed very much of the character, familiar to us."[21]

The name "Ash Wednesday" comes from the medieval custom, continued in the Roman Catholic Church, of sprinkling ashes on the heads of penitents. Horn claims: "Originally these penitents appear to have been persons under church discipline who wished to be reconciled to the church on Maundy Thursday. The ashes were a public acknowledgment of their penance."[22]

The ashes were obtained by the burning of palms of the previous Palm

813

Sunday and pulverizing the ashes. In the present Roman rite the ashes are blessed but only for the penitents. The ceremony of blessing and distribution of the ashes was not retained by the reformers whether Lutheran, Anglican or Reformed, not only because of distaste of the blessing of such things as ashes, but more particularly because the ceremony seemed to be strange contradiction of the Gospel lesson for the day.[23] The Gospel speaks of fasting to God and not to men (Matt. 6:16-21).

Ash Wednesday may occur on any date from February 4 to March 10.

Although the Sundays of Lent are not fast days, it should be noted that the popular name given to the Fourth Sunday in Lent was Mid-Lent Sunday (in French, Mi-Careme); it is commonly called Refreshment Sunday, on account of the Gospel for the day, which contains the story of the miraculous Feeding of the Five Thousand in the wilderness.[24]

The Old Church Year employed the Latin names for the Sundays before Easter as well as the Sundays before Easter and the Ascension. The new Church year adopted by the ILCW has eliminated the Latin names for these Sundays in Lent and the Sundays coming after the Easter celebration and now simply calls the Sundays in Lent as the first the second, the third etc. in Lent. Before the adoption of the New Ecclesiastical Year by Rome and its adoption from them by all Protestant users of the new Roman Church Year, Anglicans, Lutherans and Roman Catholics used the Latin names for these Sundays for hundreds of years.[25]

The Annunciation of Mary (March 25)

Like the Presentation (February 2), the Annunciation was originally a festival of our Lord, rather than that of the Virgin Mary. One of its original names was **Festum conceptionis Domini**. Its date, just like that of the Presentation, is determined by the date of Christmas. When Jesus' birth was determined to be December 25, March 25 became the date for the Annunciation. In England it was known as **Lady Day**.[26]

According to Duchesne, a French Roman Catholic authority on the Church Year, the Annunciation was already established in the Western Church in the seventh century. Gwynne claimed that:

As the commemorating the actual Incarnation of Christ the date was placed just nine months before His Nativity. For this reason also it was reckoned in England and some other countries as the beginning of the civil year. This custom began to prevail in England in the twelfth century, and continued to be generally followed till the reformation of the Calendar by Parliament in 1752.[27]

The event is recorded in Luke 1:26-38. Verse 28: "Hail thou art highly favored, the Lord is with thee," is the basis for the Ave Maria. In the Mozarabic calendar in Spain, the Annunciation, as one of the events preceding the birth of Christ, was observed in Advent on December 18, rather than nine months before His birth.

In the *Lutheran Hymnal*, the Old Testament text for this day was Isaiah 7:10-16 and the Gospel Luke 1:26-30 (p. 86).[28] In *Lutheran Worship*, in the One Year Series, the Old Testament selections are: Psalm 45 and Isaiah 7:10-14, 8:10; the Epistle: I Timothy 3:16 and the Gospel 1:25-38.[29]

Laetare Sunday, Fourth Sunday in Lent or Mid-Lent Sunday within the Lenten season various moods are found. The Fourth Sunday of Lent breaks into the solemnity of Lent in the same way as **Gaudate**, the Third Sunday, breaks into Advent. On Laetare Sunday the Roman Church allows rose as a liturgical color. The traditional Epistle for this Sunday speaks of Jerusalem as "mother of us all," and because of this reading the Sunday has sometimes been called Mothering Sunday. Laetare means "rejoice!" That certainly represents a marked change for the Lenten season. It is also known as "Refreshment Sunday" because of the Gospel, 'The Feeding of the Five Thousand."[30]

Judica, Passion Sunday. The Fifth Sunday in Lent

Judica Sunday, the Fifth Sunday of Lent, marks the beginning of the Passiontide, This season of Passiontide is older than Lent.[31] The chants of these Sunday focuses on the Passion and contain many hymns about Christ's suffering, such as **Vexilla Regis**, **Pange lingua**, and **O Sacred Head Now Wounded**. The appointed Bible readings take up the subject of the crucifixion. This was the Sunday when a veil was placed over the crucifix and pictures and statues were removed only to reappear after Easter.[32]

Holy Week and Its Services and Observances

It is a common mistake to speak of Holy Week as Passion Week. This designation properly belongs to the week that preceded Palm Sunday, the Sixth Sunday of Lent. It is on Judica Sunday that the Gospel lesson begins to tell of Christ's great sacrifice. The correct name for the week before Easter is Holy Week. The German call it "Stille Woche" (Silent Week). The Eastern Church called it "the Great Week." Because of the terrible crimes connected against Christ, it was also named **Nigra** (Black Week) or **Heb. Lamentationis**.[33]

Holy Week has been observed by Christians from the earliest days with great solemnity. Wrote Strodach:

> The object has been to commemorate the last week of our Lord's life and to help the believer relive it all vividly — Holy days, holy hours, indeed that holy companionship. It is no Passion Play, nor is it drama commemoration. It is my heart, my life, my soul, in the light of that suffering. It is the Holy Week — of Fulfillment. Observe how many of the Epistles are Old Testament Messianic prophecies.[34]

Kleinhans claims that "Holy Week largely reflects what the church at Jerusalem once did. In the first two or three centuries Jerusalem was not only the most ancient but also the most influential of the ancient bishoprics, and citing the example of the place where Christ suffered and died was the strongest possible arguments one could raise for imitating it."[35]

In the year A.D. 390 a Spanish pilgrim Silvia Etheria travelled to Jerusalem and she has left a detailed description of the liturgy at Jerusalem. She has written about Easter, Epiphany, and Pentecost, but also gave accounts of the new churches built by Constantine.[36] Her descriptions are the clearest and oldest for Holy Week. When Helena visited the Holy Land, Jerusalem, Constantine's mother had completed churches at the traditional sites which were hallowed by Christ's life-namely, His birth and death places, the room of the Last Supper, and the place where Christ had raised Lazarus. To these places the faithful made pilgrimages. Holy Week was observed in the fourth century by a general release of prisoners and the freeing of slaves, worked ceased that slaves especially could have the opportunity to be instructed in the faith. Action in the law courts ceased and the courts were closed. Constantine and Valentinus's law of 367; Theodosius of 389 closed the courts, and gave rise to the new **Heb. Muta** (Week of Silence).[37] During this week the church gave reconciliation to penitents and emperors could release prisoners. A number of propers, such as the Tuesday and Wednesday Collects and the Monday and Tuesday Graduals contain traces of this ancient practice of releasing prisoners during Holy Week.

The German name for Holy Week was **Charwoche**; the name was probably derived from the Old German **chara**, "Trauer" (sorrow, mourning), or **kar** "Strafe," "Busse" (punishment, penitence).[38]

Palm Sunday, The Sixth Sunday in Lent

The sixth Sunday in Lent has borne various names in the course of time. The earliest are: **Dom. in ramis palmarum** (Lord's Day of Palm Branches), Hosannah Sunday and **Pascha florum** (the Pascal of Flowers).[39] These names are taken from the historic events of this day, given in the Gospel Matthew 21:1-9.

In ancient times the Creed was formally imparted to candidates for Baptism and Confirmation on this Sunday, who in the previous weeks has passed through various stages of preparation. The practice found today in some churches of having confirmation on Palm Sunday is not without ancient precedence. By the seventh century a custom developed, namely that of blessing the Palm and Olive Branches and the procession of jubilation that accompanied the ceremony. The Epistle lesson was taken from the Philippians 2:5-11. This is also the selection in the LCMS's Three-Year Series and in the One-Year Cycle. As far as the Old Testament selection is concerned it is the reading from Zechariah 9:9-12, the prophecy of Christ's entry into Jerusalem; while the Three-Year cycle has Isaiah 50:4-9b, one of the four Servant Passages of Isaiah, which would be in line with the Epistle's central teaching.[39]

Christ's entry into Jerusalem belongs at the beginning of the Lenten season, although liturgically it is fitting for the first Sunday of Advent. The readings for Palm Sunday, or Second Passion Sunday continues the account of Christ's suffering and death. The people, who lined the path taken by Jesus, strewed the path taken by the Lord with palm branches. In the Orient the palm was a sign of honor. The palm was held in high esteem. For some people it symbolized eternal life. In Jerusalem it became a custom that the people would accompany the bishop into the city with palms and marching songs. One of the famous Palm Sunday hymns which developed from the Palm Sunday parade was:

All glory, laud and honor

To thee, Redeemer, King
To whom the lips of children
Made sweet hosannas ring
Thou art the King of Israel
Thou David's royal Son,
Who in the Lord's name comest,
The King and Blessed One.[40]

This hymn was written down by the Bishop of Orleans, Theodulf, who lived at Charlemagne's time. A stanza of this hymn now no longer found in modern hymnals reads:
Be thou, O Lord, the Rider
And we the little ass,
That to God's holy city
Together we may pass.[40]

Monday of Holy Week

On Monday, on His way to Jerusalem, our Lord pronounces judgment on the barren fig-tree as a type of the Jewish Church. Jesus cleanses the Temple for the second time, driving the buyer and the sellers from its courts. The chief priests and the scribes take counsel to put Him to death (Mark 11: 12-20).[41]

Horn claims that till the time of Leo the Great (fifth century) no services were held on Monday and Tuesday of Holy Week. Leo's homily which began on Palm Sunday was continued on Wednesday. The Passion account of Matthew was read on Palm Sunday, Luke's account on Wednesday and that of John on Friday. St. Mark's Passion account was not read in ancient times, because in Medieval times, Mark was considered an abbreviation of Matthew. Later Mark was read on Tuesday; thus leaving Monday without a Passion narrative.[42]

The Lutheran Hymnal has Propers for Monday and Tuesday of Holy Week.[43] *Lutheran Worship* has Propers for each day of Holy Week,[44] as does *The Lutheran Book of Worship*.[45] The Lutheran Church-Missouri Synod's One-Year series lists Psalm 36:5-10; Jer. 17:13-17; Is. 50:5-10 for Old Testament readings and John 12:1-5 as the Gospel. The Three-Year Series assigns Ps. 36:5-10 and Is. 42:19; Hebr. 9:11-15 as the Epistle and John 12:1-11 as the Gospel.[46]

Tuesday of Holy Week

On Tuesday Christ taught His disciples in the Temple, answered many questions put by His enemies, spoke many parables, pronounced a series of woes upon the scribes and Pharisees, sat with His disciples on the Mt. of Olives overlooking the city, and foretold its destruction (Mark 11:20-end).

It was the last day of His public ministry.[47]

Before the adoption of a new three-year lectionary system of readings, the Introit, the Collect, the Gradual, the Epistle and the Gospel were the same in the agendas of the Romans, Anglicans and Lutherans for the

817

Tuesday of Holy Week.

The traditional readings were: Old Testament: Jer. 11:18-20; the Epistle: I Timothy 6:12-14; the Gospel 12:37-50 or March 14:1-15:46.[48]

The LCMS's One Year series has the following: Old Testament Ps. 28; Lam. 1:1,12-17, 20-2la; the Epistle: Heb. 9:16-28; the Gospel John 12:24-43.[49]

Wednesday of Holy Week

On Wednesday Jesus foretold His betrayal. The chief priests agree with Judas for thirty pieces of silver (Luke 22:1-7).

The Wednesday before Easter marks the actual beginning of the events which culminated in the crucifixion of Christ: the Sanhedrin's conspiracy; their covenant made with Judas Iscariot, and because of this, Holy Wednesday was sometimes called **Spy Wednesday**.[50]

In the Ancient Church on Wednesday, Thursday and Friday of Holy Week the office of Tenebrae was used, which, it is believed, developed from the night watchings of prolonged fasts before daybreak.[51]

Strodach has described what was involved in a Tenebrae service. Thus he explained: "The ceremony which gives the office the name, consisted in the extinction of one candle after another, of fifteen placed upon a large triangular stand, following lessons, etc. until the church was left in complete darkness, the significant commemoration was heightened by the use of Psalm 51.[52]

In the *Lutheran Hymnal* the suggested Epistle was: Is. 62:11-63:7 and the Gospel Luke 22:1-23:42 or The Passion History.[53] In *Lutheran Worship*: the One Year Series suggested for Old Testament selections: Psalm 25:14-20; Jer. 15:15-20; Is. 62:10; 63:1-7. The Gospel: Luke 22:1-23: 42. The Three-Year Series has: Psalm 18:21-30; Is. 50:4-9b ; Epistle Rom. 5:6-11; the Gospel: Matthew 26 :14-25.[54]

Thursday of Holy Week or Maundy Thursday

Because this day commemorates the institution of the Lord's Supper, it has always been a day of high significance. Different names have been used when speaking of Holy Thursday. In ancient times it was called **Coena Domini** ("Day of the Supper"), **Natalis Calcis** ("Birthday of the Chalice"), **Dies Mysterium** ("Day of Mysteries"). The name by which the day is commonly known was Maundy Thursday ("Dies Mandati" or "The Day of the Commandment"), and has reference to Christ's injunctions of humility in love given in connection with the foot washing of His disciples (Cf. John 13:34).[55] Besides this there is the command of Christ: "This do in remembrance of Me." So there are the **mandates**, "commands." In Germany, Holy Thursday is called **Gruener Donnerstag** ("Green Thursday"). Kleinhans Claims that "it probably comes from the ancient German '**Gruenen**,' 'To mourn.' By folk etymology, however, it came to mean 'Green Thursday,' since at one period green had been the color of the vestments of the day."[56]

Anciently three masses were appointed to be read on Maundy Thursday for the reconciliation of penitents, for the consecration of holy oil and

818

for the special commemoration of the institution of the Lord's Supper or Holy Eucharist. The consecration oil was used in baptism, exorcism, confirmation, the anointing of sick, and the ordination of priests. This consecration was performed by the bishop.[57]

The first of these two religious observances was dropped in the Lutheran Church; the third commemorated the institution of the Lord's Supper.[58] At Carthage in 397 the Supper was celebrated at Vespers. Christ instituted the Lord's Supper after evening, and it became a synodical rule of North Africa that the rule of fasting for communion was binding except on the day of the anniversary when the Lord celebrated the Supper (Bingham, Antiquities xxi, c. 1. 30, Dowden, p. 41). In the ancient pericopal system, the Epistle was I Cor. 11:23-32 and the Gospel: John 13:1-15. In the ILCW system practically the same readings are appointed; the Old Testament Scriptures is Exodus 12:1-12.[59]

The Collect for Holy Thursday in the *Lutheran Hymnal* and *Lutheran Worship* is the one that had been used before the adoption of the New Church Year pericopic system and reads: "O Lord Jesus, since you have left us a memorial of your Passion in a wonderful sacrament, grant, we beseech, that we may use this sacrament of your body and blood that the fruits of your redeeming work may continually be manifested in us; for you live and reign with the Father and the Holy Spirit, one God now and forever."[60] In this collect both the memorial aspect and the Real Presence are emphasized.

Friday of Holy Week, Good Friday

Good Friday as a separate observance developed in the fourth- century Jerusalem.[61] Hippolytus in the Apostolic Constitutions, written in the third century, does not mention Good Friday. Tertullian in North Africa does not allude to Good Friday. However the pilgrim Etheria, on her visit to Jerusalem after 350, reports a full religious observance of Holy Friday. Horn claims that prior to the fourth century, what is now known as Good Friday was a part of a fast which preceded the Pscha-the single festival which commemorated the redemption and which began at sundown on Saturday. Even in the fourth century the latter fact was the more important.[62]

Good Friday has always been a day of the greatest solemnity and most devoted to religious observance. It was simple in character and shorn of all that might contribute to a festal tone. The day of our Lord's crucifixion has been known by various names. It has been called the Day of the Cross and in early times Pascha Staurosimus (The Pascal Pay of the Crucifixion). Later it was known as Great Friday (Parasceves) and Dies Dom. Passionis (the Day of the Lord's Passion), the German Karfreitag, Trauerfreitag (Friday of mourning).[63] The term Good Friday may refer to the great good that Christ accomplished for mankind in completely paying for the world's sins and reconciled God to the world and the world to God.[64]

A most strict fast was to be followed (sick and aged alone excepted) by church members and applicants for church membership. People were en-

819

couraged to perform works of charity. All notes of joy were suppressed, the glorias were excluded at the beginning of Holy Week, bells were not rung, no kiss of peace given at Communion, all altar ornaments were covered, the vestments were in black, and candles were gradually extinguished (Tenebrae).[65]

On Good Friday the priests wore black vestments. Christ was ritually buried behind the stone altar, the place in ancient churches of Italy, Greece and France where the saints' relics were buried.[66] Formerly it was not permitted for Roman Catholics to commune on Good Friday but the new rite permits the faithful to receive the Eucharist.[67]

In the centuries before the Reformation, Good Friday often began with Black Vespers late on Maundy Thursday. First there would be a reading from the Old Testament and the Gospel followed by the Bidding Prayer- which consisted of a long general prayer, listing all manner of petitions, for all sorts of conditions of men. It is one of the oldest forms of prayer in the Church. The reading of the Passion according to St. John formed the center of the Church's devotion.[68]

The most conspicuous ceremony was the Adoration of the Cross, during which the Reproaches and the hymn, **Pange, lingua glorioa**, "Sing My Tongue the Glorious Battle," and **Vexilla regis**, "The Royal Standard Forward Goes" were sung.[69]

The *Lutheran Hymnal* has three collects for Good Friday;[70] *Lutheran Worship* just one. The only collect in *Lutheran Worship* reads: "Almighty God, graciously behold this your family, for whom our Lord was willingly betrayed, to be given into the hands of sinners, and to suffer death on the cross, who now lives and reigns with you and the Holy Spirit, one God now and forever."[71]

The second collect in *Lutheran Hymnal* reflects the purpose of Christ's suffering and dying: "Merciful and everlasting God, who hast not spared Thine only Son, but delivered Him up for us all that He might bear our sins upon the cross, grant that our hearts may be so fixed with steadfast faith in Him that we may not fear the power of any adversaries, through the same Jesus Christ, Thy Son our Lord."[72]

The third collect, is somewhat similar but at the same time enunciates the outcome and benefits of Christ's death. It reads: "Almighty and everlasting God, who hast willed that thy Son should bear for us the pains of the cross that Thou mightest remove the adversary, help us to remember and give thanks for Our Lord's Passion that we may obtain remission of sins and the redemption from everlasting death; through the same Jesus Christ our Lord, who liveth etc."[73]

The collect in *Lutheran Worship* just states that Christ was betrayed into the hand of sinners and that He suffered death on the cross, but does not state why; nothing is mentioned about the vicarious atonement or the blessings accruing to mankind through Christ's death.[74]

The Epistle Lesson for Good Friday is Isaiah 52:13-53: 12; the Gospel: John 18:1-42 or The Passion History.

Saturday of Holy Week

In ancient times the last day of Holy Week was called "The Great Saturday" or "Holy Saturday." This designation is already found in the liturgical references in the post-Apostolic times. Other names by which this seventh day of Holy Week was known the Vigil of Easter Eve and in Germany called Karsamstag.[75] In other lands it was known as Saturday of Glory. Strodach wrote about Holy Saturday: "While still kept as a strict fast as the day advanced, it gradually turned into joy in the anticipation of the dawn of the Day Resurrection."[76]

The day was to commemorate Christ's rest in the tomb. The Early Church held no services on Holy Saturday. By the fourteenth century the Roman Church developed a series of ceremonies which included the Blessing of the New Fire and the Pascal Candle, chanting the Prophecies (twelve in number), the Blessing of the Font and the Litany of the Saints. The mass which followed has a full set of Propers. The Anglican Prayer Book has an Epistle, Collect and Gospel for this day.

Holy Saturday was the day when the catechumens reached the final stage of instruction and preparation. On Saturday afternoon men and women gathered in the church, the men on one side and the women on the other side- a pattern that perpetuated itself in Lutheran churches in this century when the faithful attended Holy Communion, which sometimes was only celebrated four times a year. Kleinhans reports that the catechumens were once more exorcised against the powers of Satan, and their ears and noses were touched with holy charisma. Facing the West, each of them recited: "I renounce you, Satan, with all your pomp and works and facing the East," "I dedicate myself to you, Jesus Christ, eternal and uncreated light."[77]

During the day light of Saturday the catechumens were left alone to meditate and pray, and they waited with the faithful the Vigil of Easter at which time they were baptized and also received the Lord's Supper.

On Saturday the Alleluia appeared at the Communion Service and white vestments were used by the clergy. Toward the close of the day the services grew in importance and after midnight they eagerly welcomed the early dawn. The traditional ancient Collect for the Easter Vigil read:

> O God, Who didst enlighten the most holy night with the glory of the most holy night with the glory of the Lord's Resurrection: Preserve in all Thy people the spirit of adoption which Thou hast given, so that renewed in body and soul they may perform unto Thee a pure service through Jesus Christ, etc.[78]

In the *Lutheran Hymnal* the Epistle Lesson for Holy Saturday is: I Pet. 3:17-22; and the Gospel: Matthew 26:57-66. *Lutheran Worship* does not list Holy Saturday separately but has at the first service for Easter, the Easter Eve (Evening Prayer of Vespers) and for this, the first service introductory to the Festival of Christ's Resurrection gives the following suggested Scripture Selections for the Old Testament: Dan. 3:1. 3-9. 12-29; the Epistle: I Peter 3:17-22 and the Gospel: Matthew 27:57-60, which is still pre-Easter.[79]

821

Footnotes

1. *Christian News*, February 6, 1984, p. 13.

2. Theodore J. Kleinhans, *The Year of the Lord* (St Louis: Concordia Publishing House, 1967), p. 62. A. A. McArthur, "Lent," in J. G. Davies (ed.) *The Westminster Dictionary of Worship* (Philadelphia: The Westminster Press, 1972), p. 212-214.

3. Walker Gwynn, *The Christian Year* (New York: Longmans, Green and Co., 1515), p. 106.

4. Edward T. Horn III, *The Christian Year* (Philadelphia: Muhlenberg Press, 1957), p. 100.

5. McArthur, **op. cit.**, p. 212.

6. A. A. McArthur, *The Evolution of the Christian Year* (London: SCM Press, 1954), pp. 77ff.; 114f.

7. Kleinhans, **op. cit.**, p. 62.

8. J. D. C. Fischer, "Catechumen, Catechumenate," *The Westminster Dictionary of Worship*, **op. cit.**, p. 122.

9. Luther D. Reed, *The Lutheran Liturgy* (Philadelphia: Muhlenberg Press, 1947), p. 453.

10. Kleinhans, **op. cit.**, pp. 62-63.

11. McArther, *The Evolution of the Christian Year*, **op. cit.**, p. 129.

12. Horn III, **op. cit.**, p. 102.

13. Kleinhans, **op. cit.**, p. 63.

14. Herman Kellner, *Heortology - A History of the Christian Festivals from Their Origin to the Present Day* (London: Kagan Paul, Treanch Tuebner & Co. 1908), pp. 102-103.

15. Horn III, **op. cit.**, p. 103.

16. **Ibid.**

17. **Ibid.**, p. 104.

18. **Ibid.**, p. 105.

19. Gwynne, **op. cit.**, p. 109.

20. Kleinhans, **op. cit.**, p. 64.

21. Paul Zeller Strodach, *The Church Year - Studies in the Introits, Collects, Epistles and Gospels* (Philadelphia; The United Lutheran Publication House, 1924) p. 102.

22. Horne, III, **op. cit.**, pp. 105-106.

23. Massey H. Shepherd, *The Oxford American Prayer Book Commentary* (New York; Oxford University Press, 1950), p. 124.

24. Gwynne, **op. cit.**, p. 105.

25. *The Lessons, ABC* (Minneapolis: Augsburg Publishing House, no date), pp. 25-33.

26. Gwynne, **op. cit.**, p. 109.

27. **Ibid.**

28. *The Lutheran Hymnal*. Authorized by the Synods Constituting The Evangelical Synodical Conference of North America (St. Louis: Concordia Publishing House, 1941), p. 86.

29. *Lutheran Worship*. Prepared by the Commission on Worship of The Lutheran Church-Missouri Synod (St. Louis: Concordia Publishing House, 1982), p. 107.

30. Paul Zeller Strodach, *The Collect for the Day* (Philadelphia: The United Publication House, 1939), p. 93.

31. Strodach, *The Church Year*, **op. cit.**, p. 126.

32. Kleinhans, **op. cit.**, p. 66.

33. Strodach, *The Christian Year*, **op. cit.**, p. 130.

34. **Ibid.**

35. Kleinhans, **op. cit.**, p. 66.

36. "Etheria, Pilgrimage," in Jerald C. Brauer, (ed) *The Westminster Dictionary of Church History* (Philadelphia: The Westminster Press, 1971), p. 309.

37. Strodach, *The Christian Year*, **op. cit.**, p. 130.

38. **Ibid.**

39. Reed, *Lutheran Worship*, **op. cit.**, p. 39.

40. Kleinhans, **op. cit.**, p. 68.

41. Adam Fahling, *The Life of Christ* (St. Louis: Concordia Publishing House, 1936), pp. 527-529.

42. Horn III, **op. cit.**, p. 117.

43. *Lutheran Hymnal*, **op. cit.**, p. 65.

44. *Lutheran Worship*, **op. cit.**, pp. 40-41.

45. *Lutheran Book of Worship* (Minneapolis: Augsburg Publishing House; Philadelphia: Board of Publication, The United Lutheran Church in America, 1978), p. 19.

46. *Lutheran Worship*, **op. cit.**, p. 90.

47. Fahling, **op. cit.**, pp. 530-557.

48. Reed, **op. cit.**, p. 459.

49. *Lutheran Worship*, **op. cit.**, p. 42.

50. Strodach, *The Church Year*, **op. cit.**, p. 139.

51. J. D. Crichton, "Tenebrae," *The Westminster Dictionary of Worship,* **op. cit.**, p. 355.

52. Strodach, *The Church Year*, **op. cit.**, p. 139.

53. *Lutheran Hymnal*, **op. cit.**, p. 66.

54. *Lutheran Worship*, **op. cit.**, p. 42.

55. Reed, **op. cit.**, p. 460.

56. Kleinhans, **op. cit.**, p. 70.

57. Kellner, **op. cit.**, p. 72.

58. Reed, **op. cit.**

59. *Lutheran Worship*, p. 44; *Lutheran Hymnal*, p. 66.

60. **Ibid.**

61. McArthur, "Good Friday," *The Westminster Dictionary of Worship,* **op. cit.** pp. 189-190.

62. Horn III, **op. cit.**, p. 124.

63. Strodach, *The Church Year*, **op. cit.**, pp. 144-145.

64. Gwynne, **op. cit.**, pp. 114-116.

65. Horn, III, **op. cit.**, p. 124.

66. **Ibid,**, p. 126.

67. Reed, **op. cit.**, p. 462.

68. Strodach, **op. cit.**, p. 145.

69. **Ibid.**, p. 145.

70. *Lutheran Hymnal*, **op. cit.**, p. 67.

71. *Lutheran Worship*, p. 44.

72. *Lutheran Hymnal*, p. 67.

73. **Ibid.**

74. *Lutheran Worship*, **op. cit.**, p. 44.

75. Strodach, *The Church Year,* **op. cit.**, p. 147.

76. **Ibid.**
77. Kleinhans, **op. cit.**, p. 73.
78. Strodach, **op. cit.**, p. 147.
79. *Lutheran Worship*, **op. cit.**, p. 47.

Questions

1. The word Lent comes from ____ which means ____.
2. Before A.D., the Christian Church was an ____ church.
3. In French countries Shrove Tuesday was known as ____.
4. The name Ash Wednesday came from ____.
5. The ashes were obtained by ____.
6. Before the adoption of the New Ecclesiastical Year by Rome what had been done for hundreds of years? ____
7. It is a common mistake to speak of Holy Week as ___.
8. Does the practice of confirmation on Palm Sunday have ancient precedence? ____
9. In the Orient the palm was a sign of ____.
10. What was sometimes called Spy Wednesday? ____
11. Maunday Thursday has reference to ____.
12. The term Good Friday may refer to ____.

Easter to Pentecost

Christian News, April 16, 1984

Easter is the climax of the Church year; it commemorates the inner most center of the Christian life and hope. Easter is the Queen of Festivals. It is the Feast of Feasts, the King of Days.[1] Strodach has observed:

> The first day of the week of the Gospel becomes the **Lord's Day**, uniquely His through His victory; and in joyful remembrance the early Church kept this weekly commemoration of His resurrection. This was not displaced, but emphasized, by the annual observance of the "historic" day as the **Lord's Day** of Resurrection are its earliest names.[2]

The word **Easter** is peculiar to the Teutonic and Scandinavian nations. The Anglo-Saxon name for April was Eosturmonath, after the goddess Eostre. Hence the German Ostera. The Latin and Greek Pascha follow the Hebrew Pesach or Passover, and the French Paques has the same origin.[3]

The Easter Vigil

In the early centuries Easter celebration began at dusk on Saturday evening, when lamps and candles blazed throughout the countryside in shops, homes and churches, indicating the beginning of the Easter Vigil - the greatest service of the Christian Year. Even the streets of cities were lit up with lights or torches.[4]

Easter Eve was called "Night of Illumination," "the Service of Lights," or "the Night of Radiance." On this night the Pascal Candle was blessed and lighted, a symbol of the truth that Christ was the Light of the World. On this night those to be baptized, the **illuminandi** - assembled with the faithful to celebrate Christ's resurrection.[5]

It appears that the symbol of light was central to the celebration of Easter, as it was at Christmas. A number of hymns, emphasizing the Light, were sung. One ancient hymn was: "Hail, Gladdening Light." Century after century the image of Christ as the Sun was stressed in Easter hymns, as in the Scandinavian hymn "Like the Golden Sun Ascending."[6] In the modern Greek Church Easter is called **Lampra**, "Bright Day."

According to Tertullian, the Easter Vigil lasted throughout the night, at which there were Scripture readings, antiphons, and prayers. Those who were to be baptized took off their jewelry toward midnight, and after listening to admonitions by the bishop, were baptized; men were first baptized, then the women and then the children. After their baptism the **illuminandi** put on new white tunics, which they wore throughout the whole octave of Easter.[7] This practice caused the Sunday after Easter to be called **White Sunday**.

Easter is one of the Movable Festivals of Christendom. In the Anglican Book of Prayer the Festival of the Resurrection is not called Easter-Sunday but Easter-Day, because Easter always occurs on a Sunday.[8]

The Date of Easter

The Early Church attached great importance to the date of Easter. A discussion arose about A.D. 136 as to when the Easter feast should be celebrated. The controversy was about the issue, whether the feast should be kept on the same day as Jesus kept the **Pascha**, namely the 14th day of Nisan, no matter on what day of the week the Passover chanced to fall, or else on the Sunday following.[9]

One group that insisted that Easter be observed on the 14th were called **Quartodecimans**, from the Latin words of fourteen. This rule was largely followed by Eastern Christians, especially in the region of Ephesus, where it was claimed that Saint John practiced it. By contrast, the Western Churches held that the better day was the Sunday following the full Pascal moon,[10] that being the day of the week when Jesus Himself had sanctified by being raised from the dead.[11] The date of Easter was one of the chief issues for discussion at the Council of Nicea in 325.[12] Kleinhans wrote: "To keep local bishops from establishing their own dates and to bring order out of confusion, the council persuaded Constantine to send out a letter designating Easter as the first Sunday after the first full moon in Spring, or after the spring equinox."[13] However, Nicaea did not want Easter to coincide with the Passover of the Jews. If the full moon fell on a Sunday, Easter would be postponed a week.

In 1984, the date of Easter differs in the various churches of Christendom. Those communions that use as their liturgical language (except the Unitate Churches) Syriac, Greek, Russian, Coptic and Ethiopian celebrate Easter on a date different from that observed in the West. Concerning this Kleinhans has observed: "The Orthodox usually celebrate one to four weeks later than the West, though the difference now is not one of principle but of calendar — the Gregorian versus the Julian."[14]

Gwynne opined about the Easter-date controversy as followed:

The intense feeling which this controversy occasioned about a thing so apparently trifling testifies to the vast practical importance which the early Church attached to the day as a witness to the historic reality of the Resurrection. On this single fact, they knew, rested all else of Christian faith, for if Christ's body never arose from the dead their faith in Him was all in vain (cf. Rom. 1:4; I Cor. 15:14-20).[15]

The feeling about the date of Easter was so strong that for a time a schism occurred between the Eastern and Western Churches. At the end of the second century, Polycrates, Bishop of Ephesus, wrote on behalf of himself and other Eastern bishops defending the tradition of the East, and Victor of Rome, as reported by Eusebius, forthwith endeavored to cut off the Churches of Asia, together with the neighboring churches as heterodox, from the common unity.[16] Many bishops of the West were not in sympathy with Victor's extreme position. Ireneus, famous Bishop of Lyons, wrote Victor as follows:

"When the blessed Polycarp went to Rome in the time of Ancietus (his predecessor) and they had little difference among themselves, likewise respecting other matters, they immediately were reconciled, not disputing much with one another on this head ... and they separated from each other in peace, all the Church being at peace; both those that observed Easter on a Sunday and those that did not observe (it), maintaining peace (Eusebius, Ecclesiastical History, chs. 23-24).

The result was that the Asiatic Churches were left undisturbed in their traditional usage, but it appeared that sometime later before 325, they fell in line with the West.[17]

The history of the Church shows that Easter was considered the greatest holiday of the Church Year. Strodach has observed:

> The contrast with the long fast and the emotions of preceding days adds to this effectively. The Church could hardly wait for its coming. Its celebration began with the ringing of bells and glad acclaim at midnight continuing till dawn. The churches were ablaze with candles and lights. Joyful was the constant greeting, "Christ is risen!" and the answer, "He is risen indeed!"[18]

Easter Day and Week continued for eight days (the Octave of the Feast) and the Easter Week was marked by acts of Christian love; bounteous meals were provided for the poor, in the churches themselves, if no other places were available. The Emperor Theodosius passed a law closing all theaters and circuses during the week. In 533 a law was promulgated ordering Jews to keep out of sight from Maundy Thursday till Easter Monday.[19]

The fifty days between Easter and Pentecost were a time of rejoicing. Of these fifty days, there were forty days of glory. There was no fasting and standing in prayer, no kneeling. The influence of Easter is also seen in the fact that the Apostolic Church chose the first day of the week as the new day of worship in place of the seventh day. The weekly observance of Easter and Christ's annual Resurrection observance were dominant notes in the life of the Early Church and gave a joyful note to early Chrlstianity.[20] However, Reed claims that:

> "The medieval church, with its insistence upon the Friday fast, its development of the lengthy and rigorously penitential season of Lent, and its cultivation of all pervasive atmosphere and uncertainty lost this mood of the early church. It remained for the Reformation to recapture at least some of it."[21]

Initially the entire season of the fifty days from Easter to Pentecost was observed as one continuous festival. In the fourth century the historical sequence of events of the season began to be separated and celebrated individually and successfully, the Resurrection, the Ascension, and Pentecost.[22] The separation into components took place in Jerusalem. Horn claimed:

> "The precedent for the single commemoration of the entire fifty days lay in the Jewish Omer Days — the seven weeks between Passover and Pentecost. But again, while the Christian church took over the festival, it changed the spirit entirely. The Omer days, at least the first part of them were a kind of Lent in spirit, with marriage forbidden as well as haircuts and new clothes. These restrictions were relaxed on the thirty-third day, the Lag b' Omer, which was a kind of folk festival similar to the later European May Day. Contrasted with

this was the early Christian season of continuous celebration."[23]

The Propers for Easter

The *Lutheran Hymnal* lists only one service for Easter Day; the Epistle is I Corinthians 5:6-8 and the Gospel: Mark 16:1-8.[24] The second of the Introits clearly testifies to Jesus' corporeal resurrection. *Lutheran Worship* lists three different times on which the congregation may worship. Easter Eve, the main service on Easter Day and an Easter Day evening service.[25]

For Easter Eve, there are readings according to the One Year Series and also in the Three-Year cycle. In the One Year Series the following are the texts suggested: Old Testament: Dan. 3:1: 3-9, 12-29: Epistle: I Peter 3:17-22 (the text of Christ's descent into Hades on Easter morn); the Gospel: Matthew 27:57-66 (the burial of Jesus).[26]

The Collect used in ancient times also employed in *The Lutheran Hymnal*, begins with the "historic " address: "Almighty God, Who, through Thine Only-begotten Son, Jesus Christ, hast overcome death, and opened unto us the gate of everlasting life: We humbly beseech Thee, that, as Thou didst put into our minds good desires, so by Thy continual help we may bring the same to good effect; through etc."

The second Collect in *The Lutheran Hymnal* speaks of what the outcome should be for those who have celebrated the Paschal Feast, namely "have kindled with heavenly desires a thirst for the Foundation of Life, who is Jesus, God's Son and our Lord."[27]

The Easter Week

The *Lutheran Hymnal* has readings for Easter Monday and Easter Tuesday. *Lutheran Worship* and *Lutheran Book of Worship* have no Easter Monday or Easter Tuesday readings. Horn III claimed that the only weekday in Easter week which was celebrated in his day (1957) was Easter Monday. Formerly there were services each day of Easter week, and after the Reformation many Lutheran Orders had appointments for Monday and Tuesday.[28] The Lutheran and Anglican liturgical books had as Epistle, Acts 10:34-43; the Roman lesson began with verse 37. The Gospel was Luke 24:13-33; the Gospel; Luke 24:13-35, used by all three communions: the Lutheran, the Anglican and the Roman.

For Easter Tuesday in German **Zweiter Ostertag**, the *Lutheran Hymnal* has as the Epistle: Acts 13:26-31; as Gospel the same as Easter Monday.[29]

Missals in France and Spain in the time of Charlemagne indicate that two or three services were held each day of Easter week. The feast of the Resurrection lasted till Pentecost.

For different Easter customs as they developed in many different lands, the reader is directed to the informative book of Kleinhans, The Year of the Lord, pp. 77-81.

The Easter Season

In the old Lutheran, Anglican and Roman Catholic Church Year, the Sundays after Easter bore Latin names.[30] In the new system of readings covering a Three-Year cycle, the Latin names have been eliminated, and the Sundays in the Easter Season are simply known as the Second, Third, Fourth, etc. of Easter.[31] This is the situation in the new LCMS's *Lutheran Worship* and the *Lutheran Book of Worship*.

The Latin names for the Sundays after Easter were derived from the opening of the Collects in Latin.[32]

Quasimodogeniti, The First Sunday after Easter

In *Lutheran Worship* this Sunday is called the second Sunday of Easter. The Latin name was obtained from the verse:

"As newborn babes, desire the sincere milk of the Word." The day is known as St. Thomas Sunday, also White Sunday, and the Octave of the Passover.[33]

Misericordias Domini, The Second Sunday after Easter

In *Lutheran Worship* known as The Third Sunday of Easter. The Latin name is derived from Psalm 33:5: "The earth is full of the goodness of the Lord."[34] This was also known as "Good Shepherd" Sunday because of the Gospel selection which set forth the risen Savior as the Good Shepherd (John 10:1-10).

Jubilate, The Third Sunday after Easter

In *Lutheran Worship* called the Fourth Sunday of Easter. The Latin name was taken from Psalm 66:1: "Make a joyful noise unto God, all ye lands." The Collect used for this Sunday is one of the oldest in Liturgical Use. It comes from the Leonine Sacramentary; it goes back to the time of Leo the Great, who died in 450. That would make this prayer to have been in use for 1500 years. The Collect refers to the newly baptized Christians who had joined the church at Easter.[35]

Cantate, The Fourth Sunday after Easter

In *Lutheran Worship* known as the fifth Sunday of Easter. Again the Latin name is derived from Psalm 98:1: "Oh Sing, unto the Lord a new song."[36] Because of its title, it is often in Lutheran circles the occasion for musicals. It has been noted by Horn that the Gospels for the Third, Fourth and Fifth Sundays got scrambled and how that happened is a mystery. From the Third Sunday after Easter through the Sunday after the Ascension (the Sixth Sunday after Easter), the church reads all of Jesus' farewell discourse, from John 15:26-16:30, but it reads 15:26-16:4 on the Sixth Sunday; 16:5-15 on the Fourth; 16:16-23 on the Third: and 16:23-30 on the Fifth. In addition the festivals of St. Mark and St. Philip and James, which fall within the Easter season, have as Gospels John 15:1-11 and John 14:23-31. All these lessons are appropriate for preparation for Ascension and the coming of the Holy Spirit at Pentecost.[36a]

Rogate, The Fifth Sunday after Easter

Rogate, the Fifth Sunday after Easter (now called the Sixth Sunday of Easter) breaks the pattern in that it took its name from the Rogation

Days during the Week of Ascension.[37] Another name was **Vocem incud-
itates**, and takes its name from the Introit of Isaiah 48:20: "With a voice
of singing declare ye."[38] "Rogate" means "pray ye." The days following Rogate were known as Rogation Days and were observed as a prolonged
Vigil of the Ascension. Reed has pointed out that these Rogation Days
would usually come at the time seed was being sown in the field and was
springing to life. In Gaul, in the fifth century the custom arose after a
siege of devastating earthquake, pestilence and famine, of having church
members go to their churches and thereafter go to the fields changing
litanies and asking God for blessings upon the fruits of the ground.[39]

St. Mark Evangelist (April 25)[40]

In 1984 Easter falls on April 22 and St. Mark's Day is the Wednesday
of the Easter Week. John Mark was the son of Mary (Acts 12:12), a
cousin of Barnabas (Col. 4:10, RSV), companion of Paul (Phil 24) and
Peter (I Pet 5:13). Mark followed the custom of the day of also taking a
surname of Marcus, in addition to his name John. Mark's father is not
mentioned in the New Testament, but his mother appears to have belonged to a well-to-do family in Jerusalem (Acts 12:120). He may have
been the youth that fled when Christ was arrested in the Garden of Gethsemane (Mark 14:51-52).

Luke reports that Mark accompanied Paul and Barnabas (Acts 12:25)
and later was a companion of Paul and Barnabas on the latter's missionary journey (the first) as far as Perga and Pamphylia (Acts 13:5,13). The
cause for Mark's desertion is not stated, but Paul refused to take him
along on his second missionary journey (Acts 14:37-39). Barnabas defended Mark and later Mark and Barabbas went to Cyprus. When Paul
was a prisoner, either in Ephesus or in Rome, Mark appears again as
Paul's coworker (Phil. 24). Later when Peter wrote his first Letter to the
congregations of Asia Minor, Mark was with Peter in Babylon (which
some believe was Rome). At the time of Paul's second imprisonment,
Mark must have proved useful to Paul, because the latter requested
Mark to come to Rome (II Tm. 4:11).

Although the Gospel of Mark is anonymous there are enough ancient
witnesses to ascribe the shortest of the Synoptic Gospels to John Mark.
Markan authorship finds its earliest attestation in the writings of Papias
from the second century and is further confirmed by Ireneus, Clement of
Alexandria, Origen and Jerome.[41]

The *Lutheran Hymnal* suggests as the Epistle for St. Mark's Day, Eph-
esians 4:7-16 and as Gospel. Luke 10:1-9. *The Lutheran Worship* in the
One-Year Series gives Psalm 92:1-4, 12-18; Hosea 11:1-4; and for the
Gospel I John 1-10; John 21:20-24; The Three-Years Series A B C has:
"Psalm 116:12-19; Genesis 1:1-5, 26:31; I John 1:1-2:2; John 21:20-25.

The Collect for St. Mark's Day reads:

"O almighty God, as you have enriched your Church with the precious
Gospel proclaimed by the evangelist Saint Mark, grant us firmly to be-
lieve your good tidings of salvation and daily walk according to your
Word; through Jesus Christ our Lord, etc."[42]

"According to a constant and universal tradition," says Kellner, "he (Mark) was the first Bishop of Alexandria, and his name appears first in all lists of the Bishops of that See."[43] Mark is supposed to have been martyred in A.D. 64 as he attempted to stop the worship of Serapis. In 829 it is alleged that his remains were transferred from Alexandra to Venice, where he now supposedly rests under the high altar of St. Mark's Cathedral. [43a]

Saint Philip and Saint James (May 1)

Philip and James are two of the apostles of we know little but their names. Philip came from the village of Bethsaida in Galilee, and was one of Christ's first disciples. Philip was fellow townsman of Peter and Andrew and brought Nathaniel to Jesus (John 1:43ff.). This Philip should not be confused with the deacon of that name, who with Stephen was one of the first deacons of the Jerusalem church (Acts 6:3). And who, according to Acts 8:55ff., preached in Samaria and later went to the Ethiopian eunuch (Acts 8:26ff.). According to tradition Philip the apostle lived in Hierapolis in Phrygia, where he supposedly died. He is alleged to have had two daughters, who remained unmarried and died in great age, being buried in Hieropolis.[44]

Of James the Less even less is known. The three James mentioned in the New Testament and in Christian tradition, James, the son of Zebedee, the brother of the disciple John, was the only apostle whose death is recorded in Holy Scriptures (Acts 12:2). The day when the church remembers him is July 25. Acts 12:17 and 15:13 mention a James, called the brother of our Lord, said to have been the first Bishop of Jerusalem Church, who was martyred in A.D. 63. He was beaten to death. Horn has suggested that: Perhaps unconsciously, or possibly because of later Roman doctrine which denied the existence of any brothers of Jesus this James, Bishop of Jerusalem, was confused in the church's tradition with James the Less the son of Alpheus and one of the twelve. The result is that we have no certain information about the discipleship, labors or death of James the Less.[45]

Because of the confusion on the different New Testament James's in tradition, there is no information available about the discipleship, labors and death of James the Less. In Christian iconography the confusion has been carried over for James the Less is portrayed with a fuller's club (the instrument with which James of Jerusalem was killed) or he is depicted as a child with palm branch or with a saw in the hand.[46]

The assigning of Saint Philip and Saint James the Less to a date of May 1, is due to the fact of the dedication of the Church of the Apostles at Rome May 1, during the reign of Pope John III (561-579) at which time the bones of these two apostles were transferred to a new basilica. After 561, May 1 appears in Western calendars and in the Gelasian Sacramentary.[47]

In the *Lutheran Hymnal* the assigned Epistle lesson for these saint days is Ephesians 2:19-22; the Gospel: John 14:1-14.[47a] In *Lutheran Worship*, the One-Year Series suggests as readings : Old Testament: Psalm

25:1-10; Malachi 2:16-18; as Epistle: Ephesians 2:19-22. The Three-Year Series has for Old Testament readings: Psalm 36:5-10; Isaiah 35:5-10; Is. 30:16-21; as Epistle 2 Corinthians 4:1-6 and as Gospel John 14:8-16.[48]

The Collect for this day is identical in the *Lutheran Hymnal* and in *Lutheran Worship*. It reads:

> Almighty God, whom to know is life everlasting grant that, even as your Son gave knowledge of everlasting life to the apostles Saint Philip and Saint James by revealing himself to them as the only way to you, so we may by a true and lively faith know him as our only savior now and ever, through our Lord Jesus Christ, who lives and reigns with you and the Holy Spirit One God now and forever.[49]

The Festival of the Ascension
(German: Himmelsfahrt)

The forty days between Easter and Ascension together with the ten days to Pentecost were days of spiritual excitement and the Early Church commemorated them with much joy as they did Easter.[50] Kleinhans claimed that: the church fathers often referred to the whole period as Pentecost, meaning 50 days, without restricting the name to a single day. "Throughout these days, sermons, readings, prayers, and hymns rejected the mood of thanks and praise with no echoes at all of all of the gloom of Good Friday."[51]

By the fourth century Ascension was celebrated as a separate festival.[52] The Greek Church called it "Taking Up." Ephraim, one of the greatest of Greek hymn writers, calls Nativity, Easter and the Ascension "the three feasts of our Lord's Godhead."[53] One of the earliest names was Quadragesima (the fortieth day). Since the Ascension always was celebrated on Thursday, it was also called Holy Thursday. The festival was celebrated in joy and held to complete a symbolic ceremony. After the reading of the Gospel, a Paschal Candle, whose light burned during the forty post-Easter days and represented the presence of Christ in the midst of His disciples, was extinguished.[54]

In Augustine's time (A. D. 354-430) the observance of Ascension was universal, and the feast ranked with Easter and Pentecost. Gwynne has pointed out that a manuscript of a very interesting character was discovered in Arezzo in Italy in 1884.[55] It was "The Pilgrimage of Sylvia," and is dated by scholars at about A. D. 385. This work gives a description of a journey to holy places in Palestine by a devout lady who could read the Fathers in Greek, knew the Bible well, and was a very accurate and quick observer."[56] Sylvia reported that in Jerusalem there was a solemn procession on Ascension day to the Mount of Olives, where Empress Helena, had erected a church as a memorial of the event. Bede, the historian of the English Church, in the eighth century, reported that the celebration of Christ's Ascension was a solemn as that of Easter.[57] In some sections, notably the East, it was a custom to celebrate Ascension in the open fields, if there were no mountain sides or in cemeteries.[58]

In the *Lutheran Hymnal* the Epistle selection for Ascension is: Acts 1:10, the historic account of Christ according to Luke. The Gospel: Mark

16:14-20.[59]

In *Lutheran Worship* the Old Testament Selections are: Psalm 110; Is. 45:18-25 or Daniel 7:13-14; the Epistle Readings: Acts 1:11 or Ephesians 4:7-13. The Gospel Matthew 28; In the Three-Year Series: the Old Testament is Psalm 110; the Epistle: Acts 1:1-11 or Ephesians 4:16-23; the Gospel: Luke 24:44-53.[60] No matter which Hymnal is used. All texts, both Old and New Testaments are appropriate for this great festival of Christ.

The two collects in the *Lutheran Hymnal* emphasize the fact of Christ's visible Ascension into heaven.[61] Although they are brief, they set forth great truths of the Christian faith. In one instance the collect prays that Christians likewise may ascend to be with Christ; while the other prepares for Pentecost by asking the ascended Christ to send His Comforter, the Holy Spirit and thus not to leave His church comfortless.[62] The Collect in *Lutheran Worship* is the same as the second Collect in the *Lutheran Hymnal*.[63]

The Visitation (May 31)

In 1984 the Festival of the Ascension and the Day of Visitation fall on May 31. In the *Lutheran Hymnal* the Visitation of Mary by the Angel Gabriel is observed on July 2, while in *Lutheran Book of Worship* and *Lutheran Worship* May 31 is the day assigned for the commemoration of this historic visit of Gabriel to a virgin in Nazareth.[64]

The Roman Communion lists the Visitation as one of the Marian festivals.[65] The observance of the visitation of Mary can only be traced back to the thirteenth century. Because of its Scriptural basis (Luke 1:39ff.) and the Magnificat which it evoked, it was retained when the Church Year was purified of heretical and anti-Scriptural teachings in Reformation times.

Horn claims that the promotion of the festival of the Visitation was largely due to the Franciscans in the thirteenth and fourteenth centuries, and finally in 1441 the Council of Basel authorized the festival and granted indulgences to those present during the services of that day. Horn also believes that the observance of the Visitation could justifiably be observed in Advent, when Mary visited her cousin Elizabeth.[66]

Sunday Exaudi, The Seventh Sunday of Easter

Exaudi is the Sunday between the Ascension and Pentecost. In *Lutheran Worship* and the *Book of Lutheran Worship* it is known as the Seventh Sunday of Easter.[67] It is interesting that the Propers for this Sunday do not mention the historic fact of Christ's earthly leaving this earth to return to His Father and to enjoy the glory that he left when he assumed humanity in the body of the Virgin Mary. The name Exaudi comes from the Latin Introit from its first word. The thought stressed in the Propers is the expected coming of the Holy Spirit. Exaudi has also been called "Expectation Sunday."[68]

The traditional collect for Exaudi reads: "Almighty God, Everlasting God, make us to have always a devout will towards Thee, and to serve Thy Majesty with a pure heart through Jesus Christ our Lord."[69]

833

The Collect in *Lutheran Worship* is theologically correct and Scriptural and reads: "O King of glory , Lord of hosts, uplifted in triumph far above all heavens, we pray, leave us not without consolation, but send us the Spirit of truth, whom you promised from the Father: for you live and reign with the Father and the Holy Spirit, one God now and forever.[70]

Pentecost, the Festival of the Holy Spirit's Outpouring

Pentecost is the Festival of the Holy Spirit. Heortologists agree that Pentecost is the climax of the whole Pascal season. Pentecost's ancient importance, like that of Epiphany, is demonstrated by the Greek, rather than by its Roman name.[71]

Pentecost has equal rank with the great festivals of the Nativity and the Resurrection. It occurred on the Jewish day of Pentecost (Acts 2:1) and closes the fifty-day period that began with Easter and therefore was called Quinqugesima. The Pentecost Octave was festal in character. All kneeling was forbidden, as were games and play.[72]

The title of Whitsunday, which means "white Sunday" was the more popular title in English-speaking lands, comes from the custom of newly-baptized wearing white garments, just as the Sunday after Easter was once so named.[73] The term Pentecost was preferred to Quinquogesim. In the Septuagint the Jewish festival was called Pentecost. The Early Fathers used the latter term for the Festival of the outpouring of the Holy Spirit. The name Pentecost was also employed in a general sense to designate the 50 days from Easter to Pentecost, but after the Fourth Century to mark the festival itself.[74]

Acts 20:6 tells us that St. Paul kept Pentecost with other Christians at Ephesus and in the year A.D. 58 the apostle Paul spent Easter with the Philippian Christians, not departing till the feast was over, and be then hastened on his journey and even sailed by Ephesus in order to keep Pentecost in Jerusalem (Acts 18:21; 20:6; 16:1). The continuity from Easter to Pentecost is indicated by Luke who wrote in Acts 2:1: "When the day of Pentecost was fully come." The New Testament Pentecost fell originally upon the Jewish festival, the Feast of Weeks (Ex. 34:22; Deut. 16:10), which was also known in pre-Christian times as Pentecost. The Feast of Weeks fell seven weeks after Passover and the Jews celebrated the giving of the law on Mt. Sinai, and, therefore, the institution of the Jewish church. It was observed as a festival of thanksgiving also for the harvest which had been gathered in.[75]

Except for the baptismal service on the Eve of Whitsunday there were few observances associated with Pentecost in the ancient church.[76] The vestments for Pentecost were red, to recall the tongues of fire which rested on the disciples' head. Elaborate hymns to the Holy Spirit developed, largely between the time of Charlemagne and the Crusades. The most famous is probably **Veni, Sancte Spiritus**,[77] which followed the Gradual throughout the week.

In the early centuries Pentecost was the last call for baptism in the Western Church. Horn informs us about the liturgical practices associated with Pentecost as follows:

As at Easter, these ceremonies took place on the vigil and were very similar. The services began on Sunday afternoon and included many lessons, prayers, the blessing of the font, the baptisms, and during the night, the first mass of Pentecost. At first it was understood that Baptism was intended for those whom illness had prevented or some valid reason for being baptized at Easter. Like at Easter eventually these rites were pushed back to Saturday and recently in the Roman Church they were held on Saturday.[78]

Early Christians were quick to see the possible parallels between the Jewish Pentecost and the Christian Pentecost and found occasion not only to thank God for the fruits of the Spirit to replace the Jewish thanksgiving for the fruits of the earth, but also to observe the foundation of the Christian Church, thus to supplant the old dispensation symbolized by the giving of the Law to Moses on Mt. Sinai.[79]

Pentecost Brings Easter to an End

In its earlier development Pentecost brought to an end the high church season which had begun at Easter; there was no octave or prolonged celebration of the Pentecost festival. However, by the time of the development of the Gelasian Sacramentary (Note: a Sacramentary was a book which contained the Liturgy for the Church Year) and in the Gregorian Sacramentary (an early Roman missal) there were services provided for Monday and Tuesday and Saturday after Pentecost.[80]

Like Good Friday and Easter, Pentecost also attracted many customs which were not originally Christian but pagan such as the rites of spring, dancing around the maypole decorating the houses with foliage and playing courtship games.[81] The Church endeavored to counteract these nature rites by introducing drama. The story of Pentecost was acted out, a good way of teaching people in a day of illiteracy. In France churches released a dove from the ceiling of the nave, to symbolize the descent of the dove. In Colonial America the Dutch called Pentecost Pingster, derived from the German **Pfingsten,** the word for Pentecost.[82] In the South, among the Negroes, there took place a week of celebration, for the Negroes Pentecost was a major festival.[83] In Germany it became customary to scatter roses from the roofs of the churches to recall the descent of the Holy Spirit, hence called **Pascha rosatum**. In other places trumpets were blown during Pentecost services to remind the worshippers of the sound of the rushing mighty wind.[84]

In the *Lutheran Hymnal* the Epistle for Whitsunday, the Feast of Pentecost, is Acts 2:1-13, the historic account of the Outpouring of the Holy Spirit, while the Gospel is: John 14:23-31. The *Lutheran Hymnal* has only one set of propers given for one service.[85] The *Lutheran Book of Worship* and *Lutheran Worship* have two and three services listed respectively.[86] The latter two hymnals attempt to return to the practice of ancient times relative to the celebration of Pentecost. Both have Propers for a Pentecost Vigil Service. *Lutheran Worship*'s suggestion of a Pentecost Vigil, a main Pentecost service and a Pentecost day Vespers represents an attempt to restore ancient liturgical practice, this at a time when both the festivals of Ascension and Pentecost make very little impression on the average Lutheran church goer. Few churches today have a service on Ascension Day (always a Thursday) and Pentecost, unfortunately, is considered and treated as just another Sunday. In the larger cities people are already at their summer cottages.

In the LCMS's One Year series the appointed readings are: Old Testament: Joel 3:1-5, the Epistle Romans 8:12-17 and the Gospel John 14:15-21.[87]

The Collect found in the *Lutheran Hymnal*, *Lutheran Worship* and *Lutheran Book of Worship* is the same and emphasizes the truth that God did send his Holy Spirit and the petitioners ask God to send the same spirit on them.[88]

Footnotes

1. Heinrich Kellner, *Heortology – A History of the Christian Festivals from Their Origin to the Present Day* (London; Kegan Paul, Trench, Truebner & Co. 1908), p. 37; L. W. Cowse, and John Selwyn. *The Christian Calendar* (Springfield, Mass: G. C. Merriam Company, 1974), p. 85. Adolf Adam, *The Liturgical Year* (New York: Pueblo Publishing Company, 1981), p. 57.
2. Paul Zeller Strodach, *The Church Year – Studies in the Introits, Collects, Epistles and Gospel* (Philadelphia: The United Lutheran Publication House, 1924), p. 149.
3. Walker Gwynne, *The Christian Year* (New York: Longmans, Green and Co., 1915), p. 65.
4. Theodore J. Kleinhans, *The Year of the Lord – The Church Year – Its Customs, Growth & Ceremonies* (St. Louis: Concordia Publishing House, 1967), p. 75.
5. Edward T. Horn, III, *The Christian Year* (Philadelphia: Muhlenberg Press, 1957), p. 129.
6. Kleinhans, **op. cit.**, p. 75.
7. Horn, **op. cit.**, p. 129.
8. Gwynne. **op. cit.**, p. 65.
9. Kenneth Scott Latourette, *A History of Christianity* (New York: Harper & Brothers, 1953), pp. 137, 156.
10. **Ibid.**, p. 156.
11. Gwynne, **op. cit.**, p. 65.
12. Latourette, **op. cit.**, p. 156.
13. Kleinhans, **op. cit.**, p. 77.
14. **Ibid.**
15. Gwynne, **op. cit.**, p. 68.
16. **Ibid.**, p. 66.
17. **Ibid.**, p. 66.
18. Strodach, *The Church Year*, **op. cit.**, p. 150.
19. **Ibid.**
20. A. A. McArthur, "Easter," in J.G. Davies (ed.) *The Westminster Dictionary of Worship* (Philadelphia: The Westminster Press, 1972). p. 167a.
21. Luther D. Reed, *The Lutheran Liturgy* (Philadelphia: Muhlenberg Press, 1947), p. 464.
22. Horn, **op. cit.**, p. 132.
23. **Ibid.**, cf. also Theodore H. Gaster, *Festival of the Jewish Year*, pp. 51-66.

24. The *Lutheran Hymnal* (St. Louis: Concordia Publishing House, 1942), p. 68.

25. *Lutheran Worship,* Prepared by the Commission on Worship of the Lutheran Church-Missouri Synod (St. Louis: Concordia Publishing House), p. 47.

26. *The Lessons, A B C,* (Prepared by the Inter-Lutheran Commission on Worship, no date), pp. 41-47 (Minneapolis: Augsburg Publishing House, no date), pp. 41-47.

27. *Lutheran Hymnal*, **op. cit.**, pp. 68-69.

28. Horn, **op. cit.**, p. 140.

29. *Lutheran Hymnal*, **op. cit.**, p. 69.

30. Reed, **op. cit.**, pp. 468-469.

31. The selections on the Inter-Lutheran Commission are the same as those of the Roman Catholic Church, cf. *The Lessons, A B C*, **op. cit.**, p. 2.

32. Paul Zeller Strodach, *The Collect for the Day* (Philadelphia Publication House, 1939), pp. 122, 125, 128, 131, 134, 141.

33. Reed, **op. cit.**, p. 465.

34. **Ibid.**, p. 466.

35. **Ibid.**, p. 467.

36. **Ibid.**, p. 467.

36a. Horn, **op. cit.**, p. 145.

37. Strodach, *The Church Year*, **op. cit.**, pp. 166-167.

38. **Ibid.**

39. Reed, **op. cit.**, p. 470.

40. Kellner, **op. cit.**, p. 300.

41. Everett F. Harrison, *Introduction to the New Testament* (Grant Wm. B. Eerdmans Publishing Company, 1964), p. 174.

42. *Lutheran Hymnal*, **op. cit.**, p. 100.

43. Kellner, **op. cit.**, p. 293. Horn, **op. cit.**, p. 193.

43a. Reed, **op. cit.**, p. 501.

44. Horn, **op. cit.**, p. 193.

45. **Ibid.**, p. 194.

46. Horn, **op. cit.**, p. 502.

47a. *Lutheran Hymnal*, **op. cit.**, p. 90.

48. *Lutheran Worship*, **op. cit.**, p. 97.

49. **Ibid.**, p. 97.

50. Kleinhans, **op. cit.**, p 83.

51. **Ibid.**, p. 83.

52. Strodach, *The Church Year*, **op. cit.**, p. 168.

53. A. A. McArthur, "Ascension Day," *The Westminster Dictionary of Worship*, **op. cit.**, p. 41.

54. Horn, **op. cit.**, p. 147.

55. Gwynne, **op. cit.**, p. 69.

56. John Wordsworth, *The Ministry of Grace*, p. 57 as quoted by Gwynne, **op. cit.**, p. 69.

57. Gwynne, **op. cit.**, p. 69.

58. Strodach, *The Church Year*, **op. cit.**, p. 109.

59. *Lutheran Hymnal*, **op. cit.**, p. 71.

60. *Lutheran Book of Worship* (Minneapolis: Augsburg Publishing House; Philadelphia: Board of Publications of the Lutheran Church in America, 1978), p. 22.

61. *Lutheran Hymnal*, **op. cit.**, p. 71.

62. **Ibid., op. cit.**

63. *Lutheran Worship*, **op. cit.**, pp. 55-56; *Lutheran Hymnal*, p. 71.

64. *Lutheran Worship*, **op. cit.**, p. 8; *Lutheran Book of Worship*, **op. cit.**, p. 11.

65. Kellner, **op. cit.**, p. 266.

66. Horn, **op. cit.**, p. 198.

67. *Lutheran Worship*, **op. cit.**, p. 56; *Lutheran Book of Worship*, p. 23.

68. Strodach, Collect for the Day, **op. cit.**, p. 141.

69. **Ibid.**, p. 141.

70. *Lutheran Worship*, **op. cit.**, p. 57.

71. Kellner, **op. cit.**, p. 109.

72. A. Allan McArthur, *The Evolution of the Christian Year* (London: SCM Press, 1953), p. 132; Reed, **op. cit.**, p. 470.

73. Reed, **op. cit.**, p. 470.

74. Kellner, **op. cit.**, p. 110.

75. McArthur, **op. cit.**, pp. 141-144.

76. Kleinhans, **op. cit.**, p. 85.

77. *The Handbook to the Lutheran Hymnal*, compiled by W. G. Polack (St. Louis: Concordia Publishing House, 1942), pp. 167-168.

78. Horn, p. 154. Strodach, *The Church Year*, **op. cit.**, p. 175.

79. **Ibid.**, p. 153.

80. **Ibid.**, p. 174.

81. Kleinhans, **op. cit.**, p. 86-98.

82. Strodach, *The Collect for the Day*, **op. cit.**, p. 143.

83. Herbert I. Priestly, *The Coming of the White Man* (New York: Macmillan, 1929), p. 342.

84. Kleinhans, **op. cit.**, p. 86.

85. *Lutheran Hymnal*, **op. cit.**, p. 72.

86. *Lutheran Book of Worship*, **op. cit.**, p. 23; *Lutheran Worship*, **op. cit.**, pp. 57-60.

87. *Lutheran Hymnal*, **op. cit.**, p 72.

88. **Ibid.**, p. 72; *Lutheran Worship*, p. 58; *Lutheran Book of Worship*, **op. cit.**, p. 23.

Questions

1. What Sunday is the climax of the Church year? ____

2. In the modern Greek Church Easter is called ____.

3. If Christ's body never rose from the dead, then ____.

4. The fifty days between Easter and Pentecost were a time of ____.

5. The Apostolic Church chose the first day of the week a time of ____.

6. The Latin names for the Sundays after Easter were derived from ____.

7. Rogate means ____.

8. Ancient witnesses ascribe the shortest of the Synoptic Gospels to ____.

9. Exaudi has also been called ____.

10. Whitsunday means ____.

11. Do many churches today have a service on Ascension Day? ____

Lutheran Church Year

May 30, 1984

Please find enclosed a continuation of my study on the Lutheran Church year.

This is a follow up of the Ascension and Pentecost portion, which you have not yet published.

Profs and students at Ft. Wayne have told me that they find my study on the Church year interesting and profitable.

May you have an enjoyable summer.

Sincerely,

Surburg

Major and Minor Festivals

October 17, 1984

Dear Pastor Otten:

Enclosed please find the last installment of a series on the Major and Minor Festivals of the Church Year. The previous installment sent to you in July dealt with the church year from "St. Lorenz Day to Luke the Evangelist" (not published).

I believe that this series of articles has contributed to the variety of interesting material published by your informative and very useful *Christian News*. It certainly alerts people to what is going on in the Religious World, in Lutheranism, and in the LCMS. A great defender of orthodoxy.

May God bless you and your literary efforts and may you be able to publish it as it is necessary.

This series, I believe, will constitute a worthwhile contribution to the next edition of *The Lutheran News Encyclopedia* (1983-1993).

Yours in Christ,

Raymond F. Surburg

P.S. Since this is the Centential of Bultmann's birthday, may I call your attention to two articles written by me in *The Springfielder*.

"Bultmann and the Old Testament," vol. 30 (Winter, 1967) pp. 3-26 part I and vol. 33 (Spring, 1967), part II pp. 35-64. In them his philosophy and theology are set forth and criticized. Articles are well-documented.

.

Rudolf Bultmann and The Old Testament: His Approach and Interpretation

(Originally from the Winter 1967 *The Sprinfielder* of Concordia Theological Seminary, Springfield, Illinois)

Following is the first of a two-part essay. The author first discusses Bultmann's philosophical understanding of existence, his hermeneutical principles, his demythologization program and theological understanding of the New Testament. This lays the foundation for a subsequent presentation of Bultmann's approach to and understanding of the Old Testament.

PART ONE

THE OLD TESTAMENT is today a much disputed book, not only among those outside of the church but also among those within it. At various times in the centuries following the ascension of Christ, the Old Testament has been attacked. In the second century Marcion wrote a book to show that the Gospel and the Old Testament contradicted each other. Marcion recommended the separation of Christianity from Judaism because, according to his interpretation, the God of the Old Testament was different from that of the New. The Creator God of the Old Testament was the author of evil works, who was also the author of law, a vengeful and bloodthirsty being; while the God of the New Testament was the author of the Gospel characterized by love, abrogating the law and prophets.

According to Braaten, the rise of the historical method was responsible for placing a great gulf between the Old and New Testaments.[1] For Schleiermacher, the father of modern theology, the Old Testament did not possess the same degree of inspiration as the New, and consequently did not have the normative status of the New. He was in favor of allowing the New Testament to stand by itself because it alone expressed purely the pious self-consciousness of Christians; at best, the Old Testament might be added as an appendix to the New Testament books. Emil Brunner claims that Schleiermacher was guilty of putting the Old Testament on a level with paganism.[2] Thus in *The Christian Faith* Schleiermacher wrote: "Christianity does indeed stand in a special connection with Judaism; but as far as concerns its historical existence and its aim, its relations to Judaism and heathenism are the same."[3]

Adolf von Harnack (1851-1930) took a very hostile attitude toward the Old Testament and in his work Marcion: *Das Evangelium vom fremden Gott* wrote:

> The rejection of the Old Testament in the second century was an error which the great church rightly opposed; holding on to it in the sixteenth century was a destiny which the Reformation was not able to escape; but for Protestantism to preserve it since the nineteenth century as a canonical document is the result of a religious and eccle-

siastical paralysis. To clear the table and to honor the truth in our confession and instruction, that is the great feat required of Protestantism today—almost too late.[4]

In the twentieth century the "German Christians" motivated by anti-Semitism endeavored to persuade the Christians of Germany to get rid of the Old Testament. Alfred Rosenberg in his *Myth of the Twentieth Century* argued that a pure Aryan race should give up a book, written by Jews, which presented a tyrannical God. Although the Nazi threat of eliminating the Old Testament as a part of the Biblical canon was removed by the military defeat of Nazism in 1945, still a low view of the relationship of the Old Testament to the New is currently held by the existentialist school of Biblical interpretation. The Old Testament scholar Hans Wolff asserted in 1962 that for the average theologian in Europe the Old Testament is not normative nor canonical. In most pulpits the Old Testament is not used as the basis for preaching.[5] Concerning this matter Braaten wrote recently: "Modern existentialist theology, as relevant as its insights have been into the nature of human existence, has come to grief in its treatment of the Old Testament."[6] A debate between Gerhard von Rad and Hans Conzelmann had made clear that the Old Testament is regarded with a depreciatory attitude.[7] While it is true that no theologian today is advocating the removal of the Old Testament from the canonical Scriptures, yet as Braaten has said: "Schleiermacher's view that the Old Testament is only historical background, to be studied as a literary aid in understanding the New, lingers on in current existentialist-hermeneutical theology."[8] It is generally conceded that Bultmann has exercised a great influence on theological thought in the last two decades. Those New Testament scholars and theologians who have followed the views of Bultmann as expressed in his various essays, have been led to adopt a low view of the Old Testament, which unlike the New, is not considered to be a vehicle of God's living Word to the church and mankind today.

In this essay an examination will be made of Rudolf Bultmann's attitude toward and his interpretation of the Old Testament, and an evaluation made in the light of the hermeneutical principles of historic Protestantism and of the hermeneutics of the Lutheran Confessions.

Bultmann's academic preparation was mainly designed to fit him for work in the New Testament field. From 1916-1921 he was *professor extraordinarius* at Breslau. In 1920 Bultmann was called as a full professor at Giessen, succeeding the famous Wilhelm Bousset. In 1921 he accepted an invitation as full professor at Marburg where he remained until becoming professor emeritus in 1951. Although primarily a New Testament scholar, Bultmann has expressed himself on the Old Testament and on its relationship to the New. His programmatic essay, "The Significance of the Old Testament for the Christian Faith," became the basis for theological discussion between Bultmann and a number of European and American theologians. It is available in a volume edited by Bernhard W. Anderson as *The Old Testament and the Christian Faith.*[9] Another essay valuable for ascertaining Bultmann's view on the Old Testament is his

"Prophecy and Fulfillment."[10] The first part of his book *Das Urchristentum im Rahmen der antiken Religionen (Primitive Christianity in its Contemporary Setting)* deals with Old Testament heritage.[11] There are also various essays in the three volumes of *Glauben und Verstehen* that deal with different aspects of Old Testament theology and Old Testament interpretation.[12]

In order to assess Bultmann's attitude toward and his interpretation of the Old Testament, it will be necessary to examine his philosophical understanding of existence, his hermeneutical principles, his demythologization program and his theological understanding of the New Testament. Bultmann's approach to and understanding of the Old Testament are determined by his philosophical and hermeneutical principles and procedures as will be shown later in Part II of this essay.

I. Bultmann Influenced by Existentialism

Those who have occupied themselves with the writings of Bultmann are agreed that the eminent New Testament professor has been influenced by existentialist philosophy.[12a] H. P. Owen wrote: "It is well known that Bultmann uses the terms existentialist philosophy in order to expound the nature of self-understanding."[13] Macquarrie has written a volume in which he has compared Heidegger and Bultmann and has shown that Bultmann is an existentialist theologian.[14] David Cairns asserted: "In Bultmann's theology demythologizing and the existential interpretation are connected as indissolubly as are dying and rising again in the Christian faith."[15] The Dutch theologian Herman Ridderbos wrote:

Bultmann's theology can be called an existentialist approach to and exposition of the Biblical message. Existentialist philosophy is very characteristic of the attitude to life of many in our time. The fact that Bultmann's theology is determined completely by philosophical existentialist conceptions of man, life, and the world, explains to a large measure the great number of his adherents and also the sharp opposition to him.[16]

Thus Bultmann's position has been categorized as "existentialist" which means that his theological stance has been affected by his adoption of a philosophical viewpoint, first attributed to Kierkegaard (1813-55), and that came into prominence in the first half of the twentieth century. The school of existentialism claims that existence cannot be conceived, i .e. become an object of thought but that it may be experienced and lived. The fundamental thesis of existentialism contends that existence is prior to essence. Western philosophy since the time of the Greeks had been preoccupied with the idea of ESSENCE, with the general and universal features of anything, rather than with concrete individual, human existence. By emphasizing the priority of existence to essence, a radical new departure in philosophy was initiated. According to Ramm:

This thesis means that my personal existence is prior to existence, my problem of being, my concern with my selfhood, my situation in the world of reality. Man cannot begin with a theory of reality, a metaphysics or ontology; he can begin where he is, human being in the midst of all the contingencies of human existence.[17]

For the existentialist such categories of classical philosophy as "soul," "virtue," "substance," "accidents," "essence," and "existence" are impersonal and inadequate because they do not do justice to the basic character of human life as "change," "consciousness," "process," "movement," "passion" and "decision". The rejection of the emphasis of classical Western philosophy has resulted, according to Harvey, into "two otherwise apparently contradictory tendencies in existentialism: (1) the attack on abstract thought and intellectual detachment ... (2) the highly abstruse development of new categories that aim to do justice to the unique character of human existence."[18] Since it is claimed that existence is prior to essence, one cannot approach life or philosophy rationalistically. It is impossible to view life from the top of the world or to look back upon history as if one stood at the end of it, life cannot be known rationally. It cannot be understood speculatively. Life can only be understood by men and women as existents through participation in existence.

Bultmann has placed himself in opposition to the old theological liberalism in that he has made a sharp distinction between his position and the liberal theology's moral and ethical rationalism as constituting the kernel of the Gospel. For Bultmann the Gospel's content did not consist in timeless truths nor was it to be found in eternal verities, much less in a metaphysical system as held by Wilhelm Herrmann. As Ridderbos has pointed out, for Bultmann the contents of the Gospel consisted of "the actual change and emancipation which the Gospel calls forth in the whole of human existence, as soon as man obeys the call to *Entscheidung.*"[19] In this existentialist interpretation the influence of Kierkegaard is undoubtedly found.

II. Bultmann Influenced by Heidegger

Analyzers of Bultmann's writings and thought, however, believe that it is Martin Heidegger especially, one of Bultmann's former colleagues at Marburg, who influenced Bultmann more than any other modern thinker. James Robinson claimed that Bultmann utilized the categories of Heidegger's *Time and Being* (192 7) "to state the New Testament kerygma in a way accessible to a post-mythological age."[20] Bornkamm stated that Bultmann used Heidegger's philosophical analysis of existence in his Gifford lectures, *Geschichte und Eschatologie*. Bultmann has worked out his understanding of history according to Heideggerrian concepts.[21] The Marburg New Testament professor dedicated the first volume of *Glauben und Verstehen* to Heidegger. Between 1922 to 1928 Bultmann entered into a particularly close relationship with Heidegger and began to draw heavily upon his ideas. It seemed to him that Heidegger's philosophy had a special contribution to make to his study and understanding of the New Testament. Thus Bultmann wrote:

> Above all, Heidegger's existentialist analysis of the ontological structure of being would seem to be more than a secularized, philosophical version of the New Testament view of human life ... Is not

843

that exactly the New Testament understanding of human life? Some critics have objected that I am borrowing Heidegger's categories and forcing them upon the New Testament. I am afraid that this only shows that they are blinding their eyes to the real problem, which is that the philosophers are saying the same thing as the New Testament and saying it quite independently.[22]

Heidegger, Camus and Sartre are twentieth century existentialists who have not worked out their philosophical systems from the viewpoint of Christianity, as Kierkegaard has done. Heidegger has not come to any theistic conclusions. For his point of departure Bultmann has employed the conceptual framework of Heidegger, as reflected in the latter's earlier writings.[22a] At the present time when German theology is emphasizing the use of the later Heidegger for theological thought, Bultmann still continues to defend the superior theological relevance of the earlier Heidegger over the latter Heidegger.[23] Besides obtaining his understanding of man and history from Heidegger, Bultmann has also derived the actualistic idea that a person only exists when he chooses his freedom in responsibility. Although Heidegger does not believe in a personal God, yet Bultmann is convinced that Heidegger's analysis of human nature is in harmony with the New Testament, so that his philosophical concepts are useful in expressing the Christian understanding for modern man.

III. Bultmann's Hermeneutical Principles

Bultmann's interpretation of the Old and New Testaments is radically different from the exegesis as practiced by theological liberalism, neo-orthodoxy or Protestant orthodoxy, whether of the Lutheran or Calvinistic variety. Bultmann has adopted a new system of hermeneutics. Forstman claimed: "If Bultmann is somewhat unusual in that he has written nothing specifically on the subject of authority, he is also somewhat unusual in the amount of attention he has given to the general problem of hermeneutics."[24]

Hermeneutics has been a subject concerning which much study has taken place in Germany since the Reformation, and Bultmann has been particularly influenced by Schleiermacher (1768-1834) and Wilhelm Dilthey (1833-1911). Dilthey in his *Die Entstehung der Hermeneutik* (1900) argued that the self is a peculiar synthesis of thought, will and feeling which is only intelligible in terms of its immediate lived relationships. Traditionally, hermeneutics was considered the science setting forth the principles for interpretation; while the practice of the principles of hermeneutics was known as exegesis. According to the traditional approach to a Scriptural book the "hermeneut" was to set forth what the text said. Making it relevant to the time of the exegete would be the application, not to be confused with what the objective text delineated. This distinction Bultmann has rejected.

The eminent Marburg New Testament scholar has published two essays, in which he has set forth his understanding of hermeneutics, which for him is equivalent to the correct interpretation of a text. They are: "The Problem of Hermeneutics" (1950)[25] and "Is Exegesis without Presuppositions Possible?" (1957)[26] Ideas set forth clearly in these two essays, it should be noted, are to be found scattered through his publications much prior to 1950 and 1957. In the first of these two essays Bultmann in an extended footnote made it clear that he disagrees sharply with traditional hermeneutical rules, taking G. Heinrici, Fr. Torm, and Er. Pascher to task for their inadequate understanding of hermeneutics.[27] On the other hand, Bultmann praised Fritz Buri's critical analysis in which the latter discussed the hermeneutical problems of Protestantism. Thus Bultmann wrote: "However, in its development it is obvious that hermeneutics as the art of scientific understanding is in no way adequately defined by traditional hermeneutic rules."[28] Again in the same programmatic essay he asserted:

> I find myself in agreement with him (i.e. Buri) in the same way, in his struggle for the critical historical comprehension of Scripture, as I am in his refusal to accept a 'pneumatic, suprahistorical comprehension of Scripture' and what is called theological hermeneutics, by virtue of which a 'christological exegesis' of the Old Testament is carried on.[29]

Bultmann contends that exegesis without presuppositions does not exist, although he believes it is possible to approach the interpretation of a text in an unprejudiced manner.[30] He maintains that the "hermeneut" is subject to all conditions which an interpreter of any literary document must observe. It is essential that the interpreter of a text be a master of the language and grammar in which the text was written and have a knowledge of the historical context out of which the document comes and which it reflects.

The historical interpretation presupposes the method of historical-critical research.[31] In this area Bultmann developed the use of form criticism, adopted from Gunkel, and applied it to New Testament studies, as is evident in his *History of the Synoptic Tradition* (4th ed., 1961). For Bultmann the use of the historical-critical methodology meant interpreting history in the sense of a closed continuum, in which individual events are connected by the cause and effect relationship. There may, therefore, be no intrusion of the supernatural into the events of history; consequently, the belief in miracles is excluded.

Hermeneutics, however, must go beyond a mere analysis of form and grammar; it must seek an understanding of the "life moment" of the writer. In his essay "The Problem of Hermeneutics" Bultmann insists that two things specifically are necessary for an interpretation that is more than scholarly routine: *Vorverstandnis* (preunderstanding) and an openness to the meaning of man. The exegete must have a prior understanding of the subject. The *Vorverstandnis* or prior understanding necessary was stated by Bultmann thus:

> A comprehension — an interpretation — is, it follows, *constantly* oriented to a particular formulation of a question, a particular 'objective.' But included in this, therefore, is the fact that it is *governed always by a prior understanding of the subject* in accordance with which it investigates the text. The formulation of the question, and an in-

terpretation, is possible at all only on the basis of such prior under-standing.[32]

A second major point in Bultmann's hermeneutics is his contention that the interpreter must be open to the text's meaning for man, what understanding it has of *"human being in its possibilities as the possibil-ities that belong specifically to the one who understands."*[33] Again he as-serted: "The presupposition for understanding necessary for interpretation is the interpreter's relationship in his life to the subject which is directly expressed in the text."[34] It is necessary to ask the ques-tions of a book which the book itself is answering. According to Bult-mann's understanding of the Bible the latter shows no interest in the facts of past history or in theological data. It rather exposes the life of the reader to the problem of his personal existence. For Bultmann the "hermeneut" is at the same time mediator. "That means that the inter-pretation does not limit itself to making understandable the past as such, but is to show the relation, in its own historical 'vitality,' active in the present."[35]

This implies that the text conveys demand and promise, not only for itself but also for the interpreter. This encounter with the text Bultmann denominates "an existentiell encounter" and requires of the interpreter an "existentiell decision."[36] English translators of Bultmann's writings usually render his term "existentiell" by "existential."

The existential approach to the text means that history must be un-derstood in a different manner than heretofore. In Biblical documents the interpreter is confronted with historical happenings of many cen-turies ago and is faced with words spoken in ages past. To understand history properly the interpreter must not simply view it from the outside as a spectator, but in interpreting historical documents he must stand in history and share responsibility for it. Thus the person trying to under-stand an historical document must participate in history with his own existence. Therefore, in presenting history the scheme of subject and ob-ject, valid in the study of the sciences, cannot be employed when dealing with literary documents.[37]

Another major presupposition of Bultmann's hermeneutics is his the-sis that the understanding of a text is never a definitive one, but one which must remain open, because the meaning of a text is always chang-ing as the Scriptures disclose themselves in a new manner in the future to an interpreter.[38]

IV. Theological Implications of Bultmann's Hermeneutics

This hermeneutical system Bultmann calls "existential hermeneutics." Michalson claimed that all of Bultmann's "theological novelties and ac-cents originate here."[39] The adoption of Bultmann's existentialist hermeneutical principles results in an existentialist theology. There are some important implications for theology which result from the applica-tion of Bultmann's hermeneutics. What are some of the conclusions which, when compared with the teachings of historic Christianity, will be radically different?

From the Bultmannian perspective it is wrong to espouse an objective approach to theology. He rejects such objective certainties as the Word of God, the canon of Holy Scripture, the confessions of the Church, which are simply dismissed as products of the past history of the Church.[40] This means that it is erroneous to entertain an objective approach to the knowledge of God or to formulate *Weltanschauungen,* world views. Belief in God "is not a general truth at my disposal which I perceive and apply."[41] In his essay, published in 1925, entitled "What Meaning Has It, to Speak of God" Bultmann asserted:

If one understands by speaking "of God" speaking objectively "about God" then such speech has no meaning at all, for in the moment in which it appears it has lost its object, God. For where the thought "God" is conceived at all, it means that God is the Almighty, that is, the reality which determines all things. But this thought is not conceived at all when I speak objectively *about* God, that is, when I look upon God as an object of thought, toward which I can orientate myself if I take a standpoint from which I am neutral to the question of God and his being which I can decline or, if they are enlightening, accept . . . For every "speaking *about"* strikes out from a standpoint outside of that about which it is speaking. But there can be no standpoint outside of God, and therefore it is quite impossible to speak of God in general statements and general truths which are true without respect to the concrete existential (existential) situation of the speaker.[42]

He maintains that it is impossible to develop a Christian world view that would be legitimate or valid. In his article "Crisis in Belief" Bultmann asserted:

What we call a theistic or a Christian *Weltanschauung* makes God a principle in understanding the world- an idea. To *belief,* God is the incomprehensible, enigmatic power that surges through my concrete life, and sets limits to it — a power which I can come to know only and for itself.[43]

In a Weltanschauung a person evaluates everything on the basis of a general understanding of the universe, where individual phenomena are seen as instances of the general rule. This is wrong from Bultmann's position, for he stated:

In a *Weltanschauung* I simply escape from the reality of my existence which is actually real only in the 'moment,' in the question involved in the 'moment' and in the decision called for by the 'moment.' We can see in the longing for a Weltanschauung an escape from the enigma and from the decisive question of the 'moment.' It is man's escape from himself; it is the effort to find security in generalizations.[44]

It is sinful for man to attempt to view the world objectively, or to formulate valid general principles which will explain all things, including God. This is sinful for two reasons, according to the Marburg New Testament specialist. Forstman has given them in the following words:

First because it is a man's own construction, his effort which becomes the basis on which he tries to organize his life; and second, because such search for universal, timeless laws is carried on without regard to his own concrete historical life and the claims made upon it.[45]

Bultmann is opposed to those who desire to find *lasting security* which men do when they hold to some world view. He rebuked those who desire some objective security, as the belief in a historical Jesus, in the objective statements of Scripture, in dogmas of faith, or in ethical and moral formulations. According to Bultmann it is impossible to write a biography of Jesus; Jesus did not possess Messianic consciousness. Historical research cannot furnish the Christian with any security.

This analysis of world views and the results of historical research form the pattern according to which Bultmann assesses the historic doctrines of the Christian faith as found in the ecumenical creeds of Christendom. Bultmann employs the logic of Melanchthon's christological statement: "This is to know his benefits, not to contemplate his natures or the mode of his incarnation."[46] For Bultmann faith is found in the *relation* between God and man, and since faith has to do with man's concrete historical existence, doctrines which do not come from the reciprocal character of faith and relate to man's existential existence are beyond human comprehension and thus are meaningless.

In some cases this may mean rejecting traditional doctrines totally, but in other cases it will involve a reinterpretation to show their meaningfulness. Regarding the doctrine of creation, Bultmann wrote:

> The creedal belief in God as creator is not a guarantee given in advance by means of which I am permitted to understand any event as wrought by God. The understanding of God as creator is genuine only when I understand myself here and now as the creature of God.

"Statements of belief," he added, "are not general statements."[47] Bultmann rejects the christological interpretations of the Christian creeds regarding the person of Christ. Knowing the formulation of the doctrine of the person of Christ makes no contribution to the relation between God and man. These christological dogmas make no contribution to a person's concrete existential situation; in fact, they obscure the folcal point of faith, namely "that through Christ our righteousness has been created, that he has been crucified and has risen on our behalf."[48] Any doctrine which does not speak of God's claim upon me is "illegitimate." General statements about God, religious dogmas that do not affect man are, according to Bultmann, sinful, erroneous and illusory.

V. Bultmann's Concept of Revelation

Revelation cannot be identified with past happenings nor can God's revelation be objectified in a written form. The subject and object of revelation are not a series of propositions or body of dogma; it is neither more or less than the living God himself. This emphasis is not unique with Bultmann; other theologians such as Temple, Hebert, Bulgakoff, Barth and Brunner have asserted the same. Bultmann's contributions, however, are to be found in other characteristics ascribed by him to revelation. In his essay "The Hidden and the Revealed God" he claimed that God's act of revelation is concealed in the events that mediate it.[49] No one can ever isolate God's act and present it as an object of observation. "Only the 'natural' happening is generally visible and ascertainable. In it is accomplished the hidden act of God."[50] While Bultmann describes God as speaking through acts, he does not understand them as historical events observable by men. God's acts or deeds cannot be seen by the physical eye, but only by the eye of faith. In his book, *Jesus and Mythology* Bultmann wrote:

> God as acting does not refer to an event which can be perceived by me without myself being drawn into the event as into God's action, without myself taking part in it as being acted upon. In other words, to speak of God as acting involves the events of personal existence... Thus God's love and care *etc.* are not images or symbols; these conceptions mean real experiences of God as acting here and now.[51]

Another aspect of Bultmann's concept of revelation is that it occurs in an "encounter." When a preacher proclaims the kerygma he is not merely pointing to revelation but he is the medium of encounter in which God addresses man and man answers God and this makes preaching itself revelation. This act of revelation is repeated constantly and should never be identified with a system of dogma, but is an act.[52] However, this act of God's self-disclosure in the proclamation of the kerygma would be incomplete unless it results in self-knowledge to the hearer. Revelation does not only reveal the Speaker, but shows also what the hearer can become.[53]

In harmony with his existential approach, revelation is always in the *present*. To place revelation in the past would mean removing it from the sphere of self-understanding. Therefore, to speak of the historical person of Jesus as the Revealer of God is meaningless, for Christ is the means now through whom we have an existentialist encounter.[54] Bultmann in his later writings stresses the difference between the "Jesus of history" and the "Christ of faith."[55] In his response to Schniewind, Bultmann wrote: "I still deny that historical research can ever encounter any traces of the epiphany of God in Christ."[56]

According to Bultmann, Christ is the person through whom God reveals his saving Word. But why does God select the man Christ? Why not Buddha or Socrates? Bultmann's answer is: "Now it also becomes clear that the Revealer is nothing but a definite historical man, Jesus of Nazareth. Why this specific man? That is a question that must not, may not, be answered- for to do so would destroy the offense which belongs ineradicably to the Revelation."[57]

In an essay published in 1941 Bultmann expressed his views on general or natural revelation. According to this article non-Christians can have a knowledge of God as a power transcending their own existence, but they cannot have a positive true knowledge of him. Only Christianity can inform them who this true being is. Thus Bultmann asserted:

> *The Christian belief therefore criticizes* on the basis of its knowledge *not the non-Christian inquiry about God-it can only penetrate into it and illuminate it but first of all the answer which the non-Christian inquiry constructs.* It asserts indeed that man apart from Christianity

could not arrive at an answer at all, even if he carried on to the end in the clarity and seriousness of his inquiry. It asserts that *all answers apart from the Christian answer are illusions.*[58]

It becomes apparent from this statement that Judaism as found in the Old Testament does not know the true God because Christ is not to be found in the Old Testament. This will help to make clear why among other reasons the Old Testament is not, for Bultmann, a true revelation of God and does not possess the authority for Christians ascribed to it by traditional Christianity.

From the application of Bultmann's hermeneutics it becomes dear that it amounts to an anthropological interpretation. His hermeneutics combines anthropology to such a degree that it is impossible to separate the one from the other. The rules of interpretation are to some extent contained in his anthropology[50] which results in his making theology the equivalent to anthropology, and Christology becomes simultaneously soteriology.

VI. Bultmann's Demythologization Program

Bultmann's name has become associated with the term "demythologization." In 1941 Bultmann launched a demand for the demythologizing of the Church's preaching. In his article, "New Testament and Mythology," he linked his famous program of interpretation with demythologization. Forstman claims that this program for demythologization of the New Testament should be discussed as a sub-point of his hermeneutics and should be considered in the total context of Bultmann's thought.[60] Bultmann himself has referred to his "demythologization" on a number of occasions as a hermeneutic method.[61] Already in the last essay of *Glauben und Verstehen,* I (1933) Bultmann defined this program.[62] Wingren claimed that it is strange that "The New Testament and Mythology" occasioned such a furor in theological circles when everything in it was old and familiar.[63]

According to the Marburg: professor the message of the New Testament is drawn from the myths of Jewish apocalyptic literature and from the Gnostic myths of redemption.[64] Since the New Testament writers were affected by their culture and environment, they expressed their cosmology in the framework of a three-level universe, a heaven above, an earth beneath, and a hell under the earth. The New Testament writers believed that nature and human life were influenced by supernatural agents (Satan, demons, angels, God) who can invade and influence the course of human history. Bultmann postulated that the Gospel is also presented under the guise of mythological terms. A pre-existent God sent a heavenly being into the world to effect a salvation, conceived and planned in eternity. This heavenly being performed many miracles which attested to his heavenly origin. Through a substitutionary death He overcame the power of demons. He arose from the dead and ascended into heaven. The New Testament Church expected His early return on the clouds of heaven. History is depicted in the New Testament as proceeding to a literal, cosmic end. According to Bultmann these teachings are

850

mythological. The supernatural is synonymous for him with the mythological.

In dealing with the Bible, both the Old and New Testaments, the interpreter is confronted by a world view that is mythological and impossible. No modern intellectual person can possibly believe or accept the Biblical world view. The supernatural element prominent in both testaments must be reinterpreted, involving the rejection of the miraculous element interwoven into the Biblical narratives. A closed universe does not permit the possibility that the world can be invaded by supernatural beings.

Modern man cannot accept the Biblical world view and could only do so by sacrificing his intellect. The mythology of the New Testament requires not elimination (as in liberal theology) but its reinterpretation, specifically in existential terms. Everything that is incompatible with the temper and outlook of a scientific era must be jettisoned, otherwise a stumbling block is placed into the path of twentieth-century man. The Biblical record must be stripped of every element of myth so that the essence of the Gospel, the kerygma, may be correctly apprehended in Christian preaching.

This type of hermeneutical approach results in the rejection of the following Christian doctrines of historic Christianity and of the Lutheran Confessions: 1. The pre-existence of Christ; 2. The Virgin Birth of Christ; 3. The sinlessness of Christ; 4. The deity of Christ; 5. The substitutionary death of Christ on the cross for mankind's sin; 6. The resurrection of Christ; 7. The ascension of Christ; 8. The future return of Christ in glory; 9. The final judgment of the world; 10. The personality and power of the Holy Spirit; 11. The doctrine of the Trinity; 12. The existence of a spiritual world; 13. Death as a consequence of sin; and, 14. The doctrine of original sin.[65]

This is an imposing list of fundamental Christian doctrines whose repudiation is nothing less than the radical transformation of classical Christianity. As Hughes has asserted: "Indeed the reader's immediate reaction will probably be to ask whether Bultmann has not after all done what he accuses the liberal theologians of the last century of doing, namely, throwing away the kerygma with mythology."[66]

According to Bultmann the mythological elements of the New Testament are in no way an inherent part of the Christian message. In order to overcome the obsoleteness of the New Testament and preserve its truth, one must interpret the *meaning* of the myth. *Entmythologizierung* or demythologizing means the interpretation of the myth, and as Dinkler has observed, it is "therefore a particular application of biblical hermeneutics."[67] The interpreter of Scripture must ask what lies behind the forms of the Bible, that are time bound and historically conditioned? It is especially important to ask: What do these myths say about man's human existence before God? The interpreter must endeavor to discover the concept of man's self-understanding under the concept of myth, and thus an existentialist interpretation must be employed. In setting forth such an interpretation Dinkler claimed that Bultmann uses the "defined categories of Heidegger's philosophy."[68]

Bultmann distinguishes between kerygma and myth as he carries out his program of demythologizing. His existential interpretation aims at giving the abiding truth of the kerygma, contained in the myth. The Greek word *kerygma* means the action of proclamation. In the New Testament *kerygma* refers to the proclamation of Jesus of Nazareth as Christ, Lord, and Savior for us (pro nobis). Bultmann distinguishes between kerygma and myth, kerygma and theology, although he acknowledges that the kerygmatic message of the New Testament is embedded in theological or mythological formulations. Dinkler claimed that the heart of Bultmann's demythologizing program consisted of two things especially:

> The lifting up of the kerygma from the traditional text-pattern as the divine call, and the laying bare of man's response in faith as manifest in his new self-understanding.[60]

What does Bultmann understand under the "kerygma" which needs not to be jettisoned along with the framework in which it is expressed? In one of his essays he defined it as follows:

> The message of the New Testament is not a *weltanschauung* which would teach the *idea* of a forgiving God, or the idea of God's grace; on the contrary, it is the proclamation of an *act* of God, by which he forgives sin . . . The New Testament proclaims that the freedom and arbitrary nature of God's action is authenticated by the fact that he has acted decisively for all the world and for all time in the person of a concrete, historical man, *Jesus of Nazareth.* Through him everyone is addressed and is asked if he is willing to hear God's message of forgiveness and grace here. In Jesus Christ the destiny of every man is decided. He is *the eschatological act of God.* In support Bultmann then quoted 2 Corinthians 5:17-19: Therefore if any man be in Christ, he is a new creature: old things are passed away; behold, all things are become new. And all things are of God, who has reconciled us to himself by Jesus Christ and hath given us the ministry of reconciliation; to wit, that God was in Christ, reconciling the world onto himself, not imputing their trespasses unto them; and hath committed unto us the word of reconciliation.

However, it is significant that Bultmann did not continue the Pauline quotation to the end of verse 21, "For he hath made him to be sin for us, who knew no sin; that we might be made the righteousness of God in him." Concepts such as sinlessness and substitution are out of harmony with Bultmannian cosmological premises.

The center of the kerygma is the fact that God has acted decisively in the event of Christ, a once-for-all event. In his essay "Crisis and Belief" (1931) Bultmann asserted:

> For Christianity belief in God is not belief and trust in God as a general principle, but belief in a definite Word proclaimed to the believer. The event is *Jesus Christ,* in whom, as the New Testament says, God has spoken, and whom the New Testament itself calls the Word.[71]

Since Bultmann insists "that Christian belief has its peculiar character in speaking of an event," and that "on this event a message is based and authenticated which confronts man as *God's Word*" it becomes necessary to determine what does and what does not belong to "the event." Bultmann's interpretation of the "Christ-event" will help to make clear what he means when he claimed the Christian kerygma is a skandalon or stumbling block. The skandalon of the kerygma is the fact that "in the very assertion that belief in God simply cannot and must not arise as a general human attitude, but only as a response to God's Word and that it is this *one* Word—found in the New Testament and based on the Christ-event, which is God's Word."[72]

Bultmann does not regard the Christ-event as unique and supernormal, but as a relative phenomenon which belonged to the normal order of things. The New Testament depicts the Christ event both as miraculous and as historical, but it is impossible to maintain this double viewpoint in a scientific age. The Marburg professor considers Jesus of Nazareth a man[73] whose person and work are to be stripped of the mythological or supernatural and the result, as Hughes remarked, is that Jesus "becomes a relative mortal link in the age-long claim of humanity," and it is on this mere man that the focus of the Christian skandalon is focused.[74] That God chose an ordinary individual through whom to make known the way of redemption is the stumbling block which cannot be avoided. All that Bultmann will allow concerning Jesus is that he was an historical personage and that his crucifixion was an historical event. That Bultmann understood what happened on the cross is clear from the following:

> The Jesus who was crucified was the pre-existent, incarnate Son of God, and as such was without sin. He is the victim whose blood atones for our sins. He bears vicariously the sin of the world, and by enduring the punishment for sin on our behalf he delivers us from death.

But immediately he added: "This mythological interpretation is a mixture of sacrificial and juridical analogies which have ceased to be tenable for us."[75]

The heart of the kerygma, according to Bultmann is Christ crucified and risen. What are the meaning and significance of these two events? He claimed that the cross and resurrection are not separate events. Upon this basis he could say: "Faith in the resurrection is really the same as faith in the saving efficacy of the cross."[76] He stated unequivocably that "the resurrection itself is not an event of past history."[77] To Jaspers he wrote: "He is convinced as I am that a corpse cannot come to life or arise from the grave."[78] Furthermore, to understand Bultmann's interpretation of the death and resurrection of Christ it must be realized that the Marburg professor regards present day preaching as an extension of the Christ-event. In harmony with his existentialist interpretation of history, for Bultmann the event of Jesus Christ is not tied to an event in past time or space but it is represented to the hearer as a present possibility for decision.[79] Thus in his *Theology of the New Testament* Bultmann wrote: "Belief in the resurrection and faith that Christ himself, yes God

853

himself, speaks in the proclaimed word-are identical."[80]

Since Christ meets us nowhere else than in the word of preaching Bultmann reached the conclusion that "the faith of Easter is just this faith-faith in the word of preaching."[81] Not only the Resurrection but also the Incarnation of Christ is an existential and eschatological event which occurs in any person's experience. It is in the proclamation of the message that "the Word of God becomes incarnate. For the incarnation is likewise an eschatological event and not a datable event of the past; it is an event which is continually being reenacted in the event of the proclamation."[82] Through preaching thus men are confronted "with the question whether they are willing to understand themselves as men who were crucified and risen with Christ."[83] By means of the proclamation of the kerygma, the death and the resurrection of Christ offer men the possibility of an existence concerning which a decision must be made.

Bultmann's views on the significance of the death and resurrection of Christ, it hardly needs to be pointed out, differ considerably from the New Testament presentation and the view held by the Lutheran Confessions. In the Bultmannian scheme the crucifixion is recognized as an historical event while the resurrection is a non-historical happening. But in the New Testament both the crucifixion and the resurrection are treated as events occurring on the same level of history. For the New Testament writers both events transpired. [84]

What then is Bultmann's interpretation of St. Paul's phrase "crucified and risen with Christ?" It is tantamount to a formula that affords a "possibility of existence," a sort of formula for existential living concerning which the hearer is challenged through the kerygma to make a decision. This type of existence for which man can make a decision applies only to this life, for there is nothing beyond death toward which the individual can look forward; man may not anticipate a personal resurrection from the dead. Bultmann rejected the idea as abhorrent that death is a punishment for sin as St. Paul teaches in Roman 5:12. Naturalism and idealism regard death as a simple and natural process of nature. [85] Man can look forward to nothing beyond death.

This flight from futurity is in harmony with existential philosophy, which is only concerned with the moment of existence, and is also in agreement with the Bultmannian concept of eschatology. As traditionally understood, eschatology dealt with future and unfulfilled events, with the last things, with the culmination of this age. According to the New Testament the history of this present age will reach its climax in a series of final events, of which the visible second coming of Christ with His holy angels will be the most significant, to be followed by the judgment of all nations and men. Therefore, the element of futurity is an important aspect of New Testament eschatology.

Bultmann's approach to the New Testament results in the surrender of the future which is swallowed up into the present, while simultaneously the past is neglected.[85] "This position has been criticized by Macquarrie as "an excessive devaluation of the objective-historical origins of the Christian faith,"[86] and as a tendency to overemphasize those elements in Christian teaching which are in harmony with existentialism. Bultmann has set forth his position very clearly in the following words:

The Now in which the message is proclaimed is the eschatological Now . .. The paradox of history and eschatology is that the eschatological event has happened within history and happens everywhere in preaching. That means: eschatology in a true Christian understanding of it is not the future end of history, but history must no longer be understood as saving history, but as profane history.[87]

History has been swallowed up in Bultmann's own brand of existentialist eschatology. As Hughes has pointed out, it means the engulfing of salvation history, which according to the Bible has a past, present and future.[88]

Bultmann looks upon the salvation-event as merely "an eschatological occurrence." In his *Theology of the New Testament* he wrote that the salvation happening is not just a fact of the past but that it takes place anew in the present.[89] This is, however, different from the New Testament where the reader is referred back to one decisive event that transpired only once, when Christ lived, died, arose again and ascended into heaven.[90] Bultmann has removed the uniqueness of the events of the historical life of Jesus, the God-man. He has surrendered the objective character of the apostolic message by a substitution of a thorough going subjectivism. What God has done is identified by the "now" of man's eschatological response.

The subjectivism of Bultmann's stance is further apparent in his treatment of the New Testament statements of Christ's deity. To passages which the Christian Church of every age has considered as dearly teaching Christ's deity, he has responded by claiming that "pronouncements" about Jesus divinity or deity are not in fact pronouncements of this nature but are to be understood as statements giving expression to his significance.[91] For Bultmann they do not set forth objective ontological facts, the essential Godhead of Jesus, but are merely value-judgments, made at a given moment in an existential situation. For example, Bultmann suggested that the Petrine confession in John 6:69: "And we believe that thou art the Christ, the Son of the living God" should be understood just as a confession for the "moment" it was pronounced and not as a statement to prove the deity of Christ.[92] In this interpretation Christ no longer is the center of reference but the individual who utters the statement. This results in the subjectivizing of the truth and subjectivity is equated with truth. It is incorrect to say, according to Bultmann, that Christ helps me because He is God's Son, but He is God's Son because He helps me.[93] Such subjectivity reverses the christological teaching of the New Testament and makes it easy to understand the reason why the Chalcedonian definition of Christ's person is dismissed by Bultmann as now impossible for our day. Vital to the theological understanding of the New Testament, as given by Bultmann, is his interpretation of history, which he portrays under the categories of *Historie* and *Geschichte*.[94] *Historie* (history) deals with ordinary events that are open to investigation by the scientific historian. This is general history where the drama of human interaction takes place. Here men plan and accomplish deeds without the aid of supernatural beings. However, such ordinary history is not a source of ultimate value and meaning. On the other hand, true history, or *Geschichte,* must be understood entirely in terms of the living personal encounter, and not in terms of a succession of events or happenings in the past which are outside of the individual. *Geschichte* must be distinguished from the particular event of ordinary history. In *Geschichte* there is a true level of occurrence, there is a time of decision.

Bultmann's existential understanding of history resolves itself into the fact that only that is true history for the individual which is *his* history. According to this conception of history the individual does not place his world and others as objects over against himself as subject. Here Bultmann has followed Heidegger and endeavored to go beyond the distinction of subject and object. Heidegger held that it was incorrect to say that man *has* being, which he then relates to the world; his being is itself being-in-the- world. Man does not exist as an isolated self which is then related to other selves, but man's being is being-for-the-other. According to this Heideggerian concept, adopted by Bultmann, man is unable to detach himself from his own personal setting; he cannot place himself as subject over against other people in history as objects because he is involved in existence, his existence, and so he is the center of history. When Bultmann made the statement that "the true reality for biblical thought is *history,*" he is not referring to the historical events of the Bible. In 1945 in an essay dealing with the Biblical picture of man, Bultmann wrote that "the real life of man . . . develops in the sphere of what is individual-of contingent encounters. In this decision at a given moment ... lies the attainment or the loss of his real being."[95]

In the Old and New Testaments sin separates man from God. Sin needs to be atoned for; in the New Testament Jesus is depicted as the Lamb of God that takes away the sin of the world. Through the death of Christ upon the cross the world has been reconciled to God. Faith in the crucified Jesus, created by the Holy Spirit through the Word of God, is the means by which forgiveness of sins is bestowed upon the sinner. "Therefore being justified by faith, we have peace with God through our Lord Jesus Christ" (Romans 5:1). Bultmann's understanding of sin and justification is conceived of in existentialist terms. Kierkegaard, the father of existentialism, described man as an existent that could either exist the right or wrong way. This distinction was worked out by Heidegger into the categories of authentic and inauthentic existence. Man exists authentically when his original possibilities, belonging to his being as man, are fulfilled. His existence is inauthentic when his possibilities are projected on something alien to himself.[96]

As has already been shown, Bultmann claimed that Heidegger's existentialist analysis is only a secular philosophical exposition of the New Testament view of man. The natural man (the being-of-man-without-Christ) has a concern for himself aroused by anxiety and must again and again choose in a moment of decision (Entscheidung) between the past and future. Man must decide whether he will give himself over to the world of visible objects, the world of the masses, or whether he will obtain his own "actuality" in the relinquishment of all uncertainty by unconditionally surrendering himself to the future over which he has no control. Bultmann's concept of human existence is dominated by the idea of concrete historicality. Man is a sinner not because he is born with original sin or because he has violated a commandment of God. Before faith man's existence is qualified by being a sinner, a creature fallen on the world. By virtue of his natural existence man is already fallen.

Man can lose himself and remain in the past, or he can open himself to the future by throwing away all security and by this means acquire authentic existence. Bultmann identified this with New Testament "faith."[97] When a man makes a decision in the present, he reaches out to the future and it is this reaching out which the New Testament means by eschatology.

Philosophy *knows* what genuine "historic existence" involves but philosophy assumes that all man needs is to be informed what true authentic existence is and he will realize it. However, the New Testament asserts that man's authentic being is not controlled by man. Even though man knows what he ought to be, he cannot realize it. If man is to attain freedom, it must be by "an act of God."[98]

The New Testament does not give a doctrine of man's authentic being but it contains "the proclamation of an act of redemption which was wrought in Christ."

The salvation of man, according to Bultmann, is to be found in "openness to the future: "in his being receptive to the future in which he is making himself accessible in what confronts him in the "now."[99] Freedom, furthermore, is defined as "nothing else than being open for the genuine future, letting one's self be determined by the future."[100] Bultmann asserted that "man falls prey to nothingness and death in cutting himself off from the future in dread," in fact, "the real crux of sin is focused in the dread of the man who is unwilling to surrender to what is mystery to him."[101]

VIII. Reactions and Evaluations of Bultmann's Position

Liberal as well as conservative scholars have reacted critically to Bultmann's conclusions. Thus a liberal theologian like Nels F. S. Ferre made the following evaluation:

All attempts to claim that Bultmann has done away merely with an outworn cosmology, leaving the ontology of the Gospel undisturbed, are stuff and nonsense. Bultmann is no liberal who is bringing Christianity up-to-date by differentiating between outworn and indestructible elements of Christian faith. He is the pioneer of the most radical retranslation and transvaluation of the faith itself into existentialist categories.[102]

The transformation effected by the application of Bultmann's existentialist hermeneutics to the New Testament has been pointedly expressed by David Cairns in these words:

The actual result is to bring before modern man a Gospel without the gospels, so that not without justification we may quote Mary Magdalene and say: 'They have taken away my Lord, and I know not where they have laid him.'[103]

At the 1952 assembly of bishops of the United Lutheran Church of Germany, a pastoral letter was issued denouncing the theology of demythologizing as "false doctrine." In support of this decision an official volume of essays was published by Ernst Kinder in which the charge is made that Bultmann has denied the "objective factualness" of such great redemptive events as the incarnation, atonement, resurrection; ascension and second coming.[104] Theologians belonging to the Roman Catholic Church, as well as Protestant theologians, ranging from liberal to conservative, have rejected Bultmann's restatement of the Christian message.[105] Some of the main objections have been the following: (1) Bultmann's emphasis on the centrality and indispensability of the event Jesus Christ is vitiated by Bultmann's interpretation in such a way that its objective character is denied. (2) Bultmann permits his understanding of the New Testament to be determined by his preunderstanding of the Scriptures and of man according to existentialist categories.

(3) A great deal of what Bultmann classifies as mythological is essential to the Biblical *kerygma,* as for instance, God's participation in history, God's activity through mighty acts, the necessity of Christ being God and man, the need of real atonement.[106]

Footnotes

1. Carl Braaten, *New Directions in Theology Today.* Vol. II History and Hermeneutics (Philadelphia: The Westminster Press, 1966), p. 105.
2. Emil Brunner, "The Significance of the Old Testament for Our Faith," in Bernhard W. Anderson, ed. *The Old Testament and the Christian Faith* (New York and Evanston: Harper & Row, Publishers, 1963), pp. 244-245.
3. Friedrich Schleiermacher, *The Christian Faith.* H. R. Mackin and J. S. Stewart, eds. (Edinburgh: T. & T. Clark, 1928), p. 60.
4. Quoted from Hans Joachim Kraus, *Geschichte der historisch-kritischen Erforschung des Alten Testaments von der Reformation bis zur Gegenwart* (Neukirchen: Verlag der Buchhandlung des Erziehungsverein, 1956), p. 35.
5. Hans Walter Wolff, *Gesammelte Studien zum Alten Testament* (München: Chr. Kaiser Verlag, 1964), p. 325.
6. Braaten, **op. cit.,** pp. 103-104.
7. Exchange found in *Evangelische Theologie,* 24, 3 and 7, 1964.
8. Braaten, **op. cit.,** p. 107.
9. Rudolf Bultmann, "The Significance of the Old Testament for Christian Faith," in Anderson, **op. cit.,** pp. 8-35.
10. Rudolf Bultmann, "Prophecy and Fulfillment," in Claus Westermann, ed., *Essays on Old Testament Hermeneutics.* English translation by James Luther Mays (Richmond, Va.: John Knox Press, 1964), pp. 50-75.
11. Rudolf Bultmann, *Primitive Christianity in Its Contemporary Setting* Translated by R. H. Fuller (New York: Meridian Books, 1956), pp. 15-102.
12. Rudolf Bultmann, *Glauben und Verstehen,* Zweiter Band, (Tübingen: Verlag J.C.B. Mohr [Paul Siebeck], 1952), "Adam, wo hist du?," pp. 105-116; "Das Christentume

als orientalische Religion," pp. 187-210; "Die Bedeutung det alttestamentlichen jüdischen Tradition für das christliche Abendland," pp. 236-245. In *Glauben und Verstehen,* Dritter Band, zweite unveranderte Auflagc (Tübingen: J.C.B. Mohr [Paul Siebeck,] 1962), "Der Mensch und seine Umwelt nach dem Urteil der Bible," pp. 151-165.

l2a. Professor George W. Davis has entitled his sympathetic investigation of Bultmann's contribution to theological thought: *Existentialism and Theology* (New York: Philosophical Library, 1957), 88 pp. Cf. his statement on p. viii.

13. H. P. Owen, "Revelation," in Charles W. Kegley, ed. *The Theology of Bultmann* (New York: Harper and Row, Publishers, 1966), p. 45.

14. John Macquarrie, *An Existentialist Theology. A Comparison of Heidegger and Bultmann* (London: SCM Press, Ltd., 1955).

15. David Cairns, *A Gospel without Myth?* (London: SCM Press, Ltd., 1960), p. 41.

16. Herman Ridderbos, *Bultmann.* Translated by David H. Freeman (Grand Rapids: Baker Book House, 1960), p. 9.

17. Bernard Ramm, *A Handbook of Contemporary Theology* (Grand Rapids: William B. Eerdmans Publishing Company, 1966), p. 46.

18. Van A. Harvey, *A Handbook of Theological Terms* (New York: The Macmillan Company, 1966), pp. 92-93.

19. Ridderbos, **op. cit.,** p. 15.

20. James H. Robinson, "The Historicality of Biblical Language," in Anderson, **op. cit.,** p. 150.

21. Gunther Bornkamm, "The Theology of Rudolf Bultmann," in Kegley, **op. cit.,** p. 8: cf. also Bultmann's own statement in *Jesus Christ and Mythology* (New York : Charles Scribner's Sons, 1958), p. 45.

22. Rudolf Bultmann, "New Testament and Mythology," in Hans Werner Bartsch, *Keryma and Myth.* Revised translation by Reginal Fuller (New York: Harper & Brothers, 1961), pp. 24-25.

22a. Cr. Ian Henderson, *Myth in the New Testament* (Chicago: Henry Regnery Company, 1952), pp. 21-38.

23. James M. Robinson and John A. Cobb, *The Later Heidegger and Theology,* vol. I (New York: Harper & Row, 1963), p. 63.

24. H. Jackson Forstman, "Bultmann's Conception and Use of Scripture," *Interpretation,* 17:459, October, 1963.

25. Rudolf Bultmann, "The Problem of Hermeneutics," in *Essays Philosophical and Theological.* Translated by James C. G. Craig (New York: The Macmillan Company, 1955), pp. 234-261.

26. *Existence and Faith. Shorter Writings of Rudolf Bultmann.* Selected, translated, and introduced by Schubert M. Ogden (New York: Meridian Books, 1960), pp. 289-296.

27. Bultmann, *Essays Philosophical and Theological,* **op. cit.,** p. 235. footnote 2.

28. **Ibid.,** pp. 236-237.

29. **Ibid.,** p. 255.

30. Ogden, *Existence and Faith,* **op. cit.,** p. 289.

31. **Ibid.,** p. 291; Cf. also Rudolf Bultmann and Karl Kundsin, *Form Criticism. Two Essays on New Testament Research.* Translated by Frederich C. Grant (New York: Harper & Row, 1962), pp. 17-31.

32. Bultmann, "The Problem of Hermeneutics," *Essays Philosophical and Theological,*

op. cit., p. 239.

33. Ibid., p. 246.

34. Ibid., p. 239.

35. Rudolf Bultmann, "Reply," in Kegley, op. cit., p. 28. Cf. also Chapter 4 "Modern Biblical Interpretation and Existential Philosophy," in *Jesus Christ and Mythology* (New York: Charles Scribner's Sons, 1958), pp. 45-49.

36. Ogden, op. cit., p. 295.

37. Ibid., p. 294.

38. Ibid., p. 295.

39. Carl Michalson, "Rudolf Bultmann," in George L. Hunt, ed. *Ten Makers of Modern Protestant Thought* (New York: Association Press, 1958), p. 102.

40. Otto Michal, "Event of Salvation and Word in the New Testament," in Kegley, op. cit., p. 170.

41. Bultmann, "The Crisis in Belief," *Essays Philosophical and Theological,* op. cit., p. 7.

42. Rudolf Bultmann, "Welchen Sinn hat es von Gott zu reden," in *Glauben und Verstehen.* Erster Band, Dritte, unveränderte Auflage (Tübingen: Verlag J.C.B. Mohr [Paul Siebeck,] 1958), p. 260.

43. Bultmann, *Essays Philosophical and Theological,* op. cit., p. 8.

44. Ibid.

45. Forstman, op. cit., p. 450.

46. As quoted by Forstman, op. cit., pp. 450-451.

47. Bultmann, *Jesus Christ and Mythology,* op. cit., p. 63.

48. Bultmann, *"Die* Christologie des Neuen Testaments," in *Glauben und Verstehen,* I, p. 260.

49. Bultmann, "Concerning the Hidden and Revealed God (1917)," in Ogden, op. cit., p. 28.

50. Bartsch, *Kerygma and Myth,* op. cit., p. 197.

51. Bultmann, *Jesus Christ and Mythology,* op. cit., pp. 68-69.

52. Bultmann, "Revelation in the New Testament," Ogden, op. cit., p. 78.

53. Ibid., pp. 85-86.

54. Ibid., p. 88.

55. Cf. Owen, "Revelation," in Kegley, op. cit., p. 44.

56. Bartsch, *Kerygma and Myth,* op. cit., p. 117.

57. Rudolf Bultmann, *Theology of the New Testament* (London: SCM Press, 1955), II, p. 69.

58. Bultmann, "The Question of Natural Revelation," *Essays Philosophical and Theological,* op. cit., p. 98.

59. Gustav Wingren, *Theology in Conflict. Nygren-Barth-Bultmann.* Translated by Eric Wahlstrom (Philadelphia: Muhlenberg Press, 1958), pp. 45, 129.

60. Forstman, op. cit., p. 461.

61. Bartsch, *Kerygma and Myth,* op. cit., p. 191.

62. Rudolf Bultmann, "Die Bedeutung des Alten Testaments für den christlichen Glauben," in *Glauben und Verstehen,* Erster Band, op. cit., p. 331, footnote 3.

63. Wingren, op. cit., p. 133.

64. The following is based on Bultmann's essay, "New Testament and Mythology," in Bartsch, op. cit., pp. 1-45.

65. Ernest Rienecker, *Stellungsnahme zu Bultmann's "Entmythologisierung"* (Wup-

pertal: Verlag von R. Brockhaus, 1951), pp. 32-70; P. E. Hughes, *Scripture and Myth* (London: The Tyndale Press, 1956), p. 7. Cf. also Walter Kiinneth, "Bultmann's Philosophy and the Reality of Salvation," in Carl E. Braaten and Roy A. Harrisville, *Kerygma and History* (New York: Abingdon Press, 1962) pp. 94-96.

66. Hughes, **op. cit.,** p. 7.

67. Eric Dinkier, "Myth (Demythologizing) ," in *A Handbook of Christian Theology* (New York: Meridian Books, Inc., 1958), p. 241.

68. **Ibid.**

69. **Ibid.,** p. 242. The same analysis is made by Edwin Good, "The Meaning of Demythologization," in Kegley, **op. cit.,** p. 29.

70. Bultmann, "The Understanding of Man and the World in the New Testament and in the Greek World," in *Essays Philosophical and* **op. cit.,** p. 85.

71. Bultmann, "The Crisis in Belief," in *Essays Philosophical and Theological,* **op. cit.,** p . 11.

72. Ibid., p. 12.

73. Rudolf Bultmann, *Theology of the New Testament.* Translated by Frederick Knobel (SCM Press, Ltd., 1955) , II, pp. 46, 75. Cf. p. 69.

74. Hughes, **op. cit.,** p. 9.

75. Bartsch, *Kerygma and Myth,* **op. cit.,** p. 35.

76. **Ibid.,** p. 41. Cf. also pp. 38-39.

77. **Ibid.,** p. 42.

78. Karl Jaspers and Rudolf Bultmann, *Myth and Christianity* (New York: Noonday Press, 1958), p. 60. Cf. also Bartsch, **op. cit.,** p. 8.

79. Bartsch, *Kerygma and Myth,* **op. cit.,** p. 79.

80. Rudolf Bultmann, *Theology of the New Testament.* Translated by Kendrick Grobel (New York: Charles Scribner's Sons, 1951), I, p. 305.

81. Bartsch, *Kerygma and Myth,* **op. cit.,** p. 41.

82. Bartsch, **op., cit.,** p. 209.

83. **Ibid.,** p. 42.

84. Acts 1:4; 2:23-24; I Cor. 15:4.

85. Bartsch, **op. cit.,** p. 7.

85a. Herbert C. Wolf, *Kierkegaard and Bultmann: The Quest of the Historical Jesus* (Minneapolis: Augsburg Publishing House, 1965), p. 90.

86. John Macquarrie, *An Existentialist Theology,* **op. cit.,** p. 189.

87. Rudolf Bultmann, "History and Eschatology in the New Testament," in *New Testament Studies,* 1:66, September, 1954.

88. Hughes, **op. cit.,** p. 13.

89. Bultmann, *Theology of the New Testament,* **op. cit.,** I, p. 302.

90. Cf. the criticism of Ernst Kinder, "Historical Criticism and Demythologizing," in Carl E. Braaten and Roy A. Harrisville, *Kerygma and History* (New York and Nashville: Abingdon Press, 1962), pp. 69-79.

91. Bultmann, "The Christological Confession of the World Council of Churches," in *Essays Philosophical and Theological,* **op. cit.,** p. 280.

92. **Ibid.**

93. **Ibid.**

94. Bartsch, *Kerygma and Myth,* **op. cit.,** p. 37; Robert T. Knudsen, "Rudolf Bultmann," in Philip Edgcumbe Hughes (ed.), *Creative Minds in Contemporary Theology* (Grand Rapids: Wm. B. Eerdmans Publishing Company, 1966), p. 142; H. P.

Owen, *Revelation and Existence. A Study in the Theology of Rudolf Bultmann* (Cardiff: University of Wales Press, 1957), p. 25.

95. Bultmann, "Adam, Where Art Thou?," in *Essays Philosophical and Theological,* **op. cit.,** pp. 124-125.

96. Macquarrie, *An Existentialist Theology.* **op. cit.,** p. 137.

97. Bartsch, *Kerygma and Myth,* **op. cit.,** pp. 19-20.

98. **Ibid.,** p. 27.

99. Bultmann, "The Understanding of Man," in *Essays Philosophical and Theological,* **op. cit.,** p. 80.

100. Bultmann, *Theology of the New Testament,* Vol. I. p. 335.

101. Bultmann, "The Understanding of Man," in *Essays Philosophical and Theological,* **op. cit.,** p. 81.

102. Nels Frederick Ferre, *Searchlights on Contemporary Theology* (New York: Harper & Row, 1961), p. 109.

103. Cairns, **op. cit.,** p. 88.

104. Ernst Kinder, *Bin Wort Lutherischer Theologie zur Entymythologisierung* (Munich, 1952), The essays by Ellwein, Kinder and Künneth have been translated and published in English translation by Braaten and Harrisville, **op. cit.,** pp. 25-119.

105. Reginald Fuller, *The New Testament in Current Study* (New York: Charles Scribner's Sons, 1962), pp. 12-24.; K. Runia, "Dangerous Trends in Modern Theology," *Concordia Theological Monthly,* 35:355-339, June, 1964.

106. Runia, **op. cit.,** pp. 337-338.

Questions

1. Marcion wrote a book that showed ____.
2. According to Braaten, the rise of the ____ was responsible for placing a great gulf between the Old and New Testament.
3. The "German Christians" endeavored to ___.
4. What has had a great influence on theological thought in the last two decades of the twentieth century? ____
5. Bultmann was influenced by ____ philosophy?
6. The fundamental principle of existentialism is that ____.
7. What did Martin Heidegger do ____.
8. According to Bultmann the meaning of a text is never ____.
9. Bultmann maintained that it is impossible to develop a world view which ____.
10. Bultmann rebuked those who desire some ____ as belief in ____.
11. Bultmann stresses the difference between the "____ of history" and the "____ of faith."
12. According to Bultmann, Christ is not to be found in ____.
13. Bultmann's hermeneutical approach results in the rejection of ____.
14. Bultmann regards the Christ even as ____.
15. According to Bultmann, the resurrection is not an event of past ____.
16. How does Bultmann distinguish between Geschichte and Historie? ____
17. What did the 1952 assembly of bishops of United Lutheran Church of Germany say about Bultmann's theology? ____

Rudolph Bultmann and The Old Testament: His Approach and Interpretation

From the Spring 1967 *The Springfielder*

This is the final installment of a two-part essay. Part One presented Bultmann's philosophical understanding of existence, his. hermeneutical principles, his demythologization program and theological understanding of the New Testament. Part Two discusses Bultmann's approach to and understanding of the Old Testament.

PART TWO

BULTMANN claimed that the Old and New Testaments might be approached from two different perspectives and that the two Testaments might be dealt with as sources for the reconstruction of the religions of Israel and that of primitive Christianity.[1] From this viewpoint a religious and historical continuity between the two Testaments can be found when the latter are simply regarded as historical phenomena in the history of religion.[2] With the religions geschichtliche Schule Bultmann was willing to permit the consideration of the Old Testament as an historical source for one of the many religions of the ancient Near East and to regard the religion of Israel as a sector of the religions of mankind. Treated in this manner the Old Testament can properly be classified with and related to all other religions which espouse ethical monotheism.[3] According to Bultmann this approach deals with Judaism from the outside and is proper for Judaism. To the descendants of Abraham, God manifested Himself through great leaders and prophets; men who from time to time were called by God to serve Him.[4] For the Jews, the Old Testament constituted God's revelation to them. Judaism is within its rights in considering itself as having a history that contains manifestations of God's grace.[5]

For the Christians, the Old Testament has a different significance. When a Christian deals with the Old Testament in terms of Heilsgeschichte and when he considers the New Testament as a continuation of the history of the Old Testament, he is interpreting the Old Testament in a wrong manner, according to Bultmann. The New Testament believer who establishes continuity between the two Testaments becomes guilty of treating the Old Testament as a "bygone age in the history of religion" and thereby proceeds to make his own religion into an objectified phenomenon which can be incorporated into an historical development that unfortunately will result in a relativism.[6]

In discussing Bultmann's understanding of the relationship of the Old Testament to the New, Kraeling has thus characterized the Marburg professor's position:

He first of all rejects certain ways of approaching the problem of the relation of the Old Testament to Christianity as outside of the pale of specifically theological interest. These other ways are legitimate in themselves on neutral or more or less anti-Christian standpoints, but must be ruled out where the discussion is truly theological. He even discards an approach that would ask in a detached manner whether the Old Testament has significance for a faith that sees in Christ the revelation, of God; this mode of questioning he asserts, is still an asking from the *outside-in* which one surveys everything from the historical perspective. Theological questioning can only be from within — from the vantage point' of faith. Can the Old Testament Word of God be heard by me as intended for myself? That he says, is how the question must be formulated?[7]

Those who claim to be Christians and who accept the New Testament must approach the Old Testament from *within* the faith and ask : "What does the Old Testament mean for me, what does it mean for the Church?" Only the second approach has theological relevance for the Christian Church today.[8]

In the writings of Bultmann both methods of dealing with the Old Testament are found. While the trend of Bultmann's views would seem ostensibly to lead to a depreciation and disuse of the Old Testament by Christian people, he still insisted that the Old Testament is important for Christians by virtue of the fact that Occidental Christianity is the product of a mixture of ideas absorbed from the Old Testament and from Greek thought.[9] He attributes importance to the Old Testament for Protestant religious education as may be seen from a reply by Bultmann to an evaluation of his position by Hannelis Schulte, a German religious educator, when the former asserted: "I can see that instruction in the Old Testament should begin with the history of Israel, and therefore should be carried out in such a way that the Old Testament is understood as an historical document."[10]

In his book, *Primitive Christianity in its Contemporary Setting* Bultmann has dealt in outline form with the history, religion, and theology of the Old Testament as background for primitive Christianity. Thus in the introduction of this book he wrote: "The Cradle of Primitive Christianity as an historical phenomenon was furnished by late Judaism, which in turn was a development from Hebrew religion as is evidenced in the Old Testament and its writings."[11] In setting forth his views on the Old Testament Bultmann has followed the conclusions obtained by the use of the historical-critical method as found in the writings of such scholars as Gunkel, Pedersen, Cook, Snaith, Rowley, Eichrodt, Simpson, Koehler, Hempel, Baudissin, Causee, Pfeiffer, Welch, Bousset and Holscher.

I. Bultmann's Interpretation of the
Old Testament from the Outside: The Historical Perspective

1. The Hebrew Philosophy of History

In his Gifford Lectures for 1955, *The Presence of Eternity,* Bultmann has set forth his understanding of the Hebrew philosophy of history. He claimed that the Hebrews entertained a different concept of history than did the Greeks. In pointing out the great difference between Hebrew and Greek historiography Bultmann asserted:

The main point, however, is that the experiences of men are understood as divine ordinances, as blessings or punishments of God, and their deeds as obedience or disobedience to the commandments of God. Israelite historiography is, therefore, not science in the Greek sense.[12]

For the Hebrew historian God was the creator and ruler of history who led history towards its goal. Because of this principle, history was articulated in periods or epochs, each of which has an importance for the whole structure of Old Testament history. Bultmann claimed that Israelite historiography had as its purpose to remind the people of the Old Testament of God's past deeds and of the people's conduct. "Therefore historiography is not a means of education for politicians but a sermon to the people. Looking back into the past means critically examining the past in order to warn the present."[13]

Bultmann accepted the Documentary Hypothesis with its four major documents, namely, the Jahwist, Elohistic, Deuteronomistic and Priestly sources.[14] He saw similarities between Herodotus and the Jahwistic document, especially in the manner in which the latter related events, which Bultmann considered "still largely a series of tales." He claimed that the Jahwist source has as its main central thought the national unity under the aegis of Judah. The beginning and end of historical events are connected by the Jahwist through divine promise. With the fall of the Davidic dynasty the Jahwist account is terminated, although the reader is left with the idea that in the future the Davidic throne will be established.

Like the Jahwist, the Elohistic source portrays the history of Israel as a unity. The Elohistic historian was motivated in his portrayal and evaluation of events by the principle obtained from the great prophets of the eighth and seventh centuries. In the Elohistic tradition of the history of Israel there is a similarity with Herodotus in showing that the law of sequence of human wrong doing and divine punishment controls the course of historical happenings. However, in distinction from the Greek historian, sin is portrayed as apostasy against Jahweh, as a violation of the command only to worship Jahweh. The destruction of Jerusalem and the fall of the Judean state mark the end of the Elohistic narrative, but it does not end on a note of despair as hope is held out that the Davidic dynasty will not be exterminated.

In the Deuteronomistic redaction of Hebrew history, God is depicted as having chosen Israel and as ruling its history. The prophets have influenced the Deuteronomistic interpretation which shows a "permanent cycle of apostasy to idolatry and the divine punishment of defeat and subjugation to foreign rulers, of conversion to God and deliverance."[15] This history also ends with a promise of a future salvation contingent upon repentance by the people and obedience to God's will.

The Priestly narrative divides the past according to periods, the first of which began with Adam, Noah and Abraham, followed by the Mosaic period. The origin of the priestly legislation is depicted as dating back to the Mosaic period. According to Bultmann, the goal of the Priestly narrative, the latest of the four documents, is to show the return of the Jews from exile and the reconstruction of their community under law.

2. Old Testament History from Abraham to the Time of Christ.

Genesis, chapters 1-11 seem to be considered as Urgeschichte in harmony with current Old Testament critical scholarship. Accordingly Bultmann began his history of the Old Testament with Abraham. For the Israelites the Old Testament, God's revelation in history, was bound to their particular history. In writing about God's action in Old Testament times, Bultmann asserted:

> What God has done unto the patriarchs, what he has done unto the people when he summoned Moses, led the people out of Egypt, guided them into the Holy Land, he has done even now to each person, since this history is not past history but present, ever reactualized in the present generation of the people.[16]

From this quotation it would appear that the historical events in the Old Testament times are depicted as actually transpiring. The same inference may be made from the following statement by Bultmann: "Jesus cannot be remembered like Abraham or Moses, nor can his cross be remembered like the crossing of the Red Sea or the giving of the Law at Sinai."[17] It was Jahweh, the God of Moses who made Israel what it was, Bultmann contends. The part played by Jahweh in the history of the Israelite nation was stated by Bultmann as follows:

> It was he who brought the nation out of Egypt and made his covenant with it at Mount Sinai. It was he who led it through the wilderness and gave it the land- the land which is now their heritage, the land of their fathers. These fathers are not the dim figures of a distant past, but abiding witnesses of the nation's history.[18]

The worship of Jahweh was a mighty factor in the history of the nation. "The bond of unity was the worship of Jahweh. He was the God of the nation. Israel's wars were his wars, Israel's glory his glory. The land belonged to him, the land which Israel had conquered, though he gave it to the nation for a heritage."[19] God dealt with Israel as a corporate entity, and not as with individuals. The covenant was inaugurated by sacrifice and perpetuated through the cultus.

When Israel entered Canaan there was danger of influence by the Caananite religion with its belief that God was tied to the land. In the Caananite religion the gods were worshipped as the powers of fertiliity, the forces operating in nature. The prophets fought this idea and contended that God was not tied to the land but to the nation. Because the nation was the product of history, Israel was always concerned with loyalty to that history. Jahweh reminded the Israelites that the past was not to be understood as the story of man's exploits and achievements but was the gift of God! (Deut. 8:17f.). The emergence of the nation from Egypt was a result of Jahweh's actions and thus the nation was constituted by the mighty acts of God.

The passover festival, the feast of weeks, the feast of tabernacles, originally feasts of a pastoral and agricultural people, were transformed by Israel into historical commemorations. Bultmann claimed that these festivals represent the people's sense of history and became monuments in redemptive history. However, eventually the cultus lost much of its former magical association.

Israel's election did not rest on its own merits (Deut. 9: 4-5) but was due to God who ruled its history. Since the divine election of Israel was unmotivated and free, it was necessary that the nation continually be faithful to the cultus of Jahweh. Besides faithfulness in the performance of the cultic acts, the prophets emphasized the need for obedience to the Law of Jahweh. When Israel came to Canaan, it settled down as a nation of agriculturalists. There it came into contact with urban cultures which eventually turned Israel into a national state, surrounded by small and great nations of the Fertile Crescent. Israel's religion was influenced by foreign cults whose religious practices were adopted by the Jews. A decline in moral standards and social sins then began to abound.

The prophets of the Old Testament raised their voices against the foreign cults and also deplored the attendant decline in moral standards. Bultmann is critical of the efforts of the prophets when he wrote:

Unfortunately, however, the prophets combined their preaching of social righteousness with a protest against all political and economic progress as such. They called for a return to a golden age of the past, to the simple life before the State began. They depicted that age as a time when the holy people were faithful to the covenant and lived at peace with God — a Utopian requirement in view of the actual course of history; Israel was so small that she was unable to pursue an independent policy of her own, especially after the schism between the northern and southern kingdoms.[20]

With the establishment of the monarchy, the old tribal structure was replaced by a new organization in the provinces. The army became composed of professional warriors. A new aristocracy of bureaucratic men and officers came into existence. Jahweh was made the head of the state and a temple was built for him according to Canaanite custom. Jerusalem, Bethel and Samaria saw the erection of national shrines. The old communal village life declined as a result of the distribution of wealth. Corruption affected society so that injustice and violence often prevailed. In order to advance the welfare of their respective kingdoms, the kings of Judah and Israel made treaties with other nations.

The prophets voiced their disapproval of the new institutions and their moral consequences. Unfortunately, the prophets failed to perceive the problem of the state, whose kings were not in a position to follow the ideals of the prophets. To insure the strength of the state, the kings had to enter into foreign alliances.[21] Bultmann claimed that the prophets undermined the state:

When they sought to uphold the sovereignty of God by denying the right of the State to administer justice, and insisting that judicial functions should be placed into the hands of the priestly caste, they

867

were undermining the very foundations of the State.[22]

When Israel lost its independence at the time of the exile, the utopian ideals of the prophets nevertheless lived on. The old aristocratic order of patriarchs was supplanted by the rule of the priestly caste. Israel was organized on an hierarchical basis with the high priest as its head. With the decree of liberation by Cyrus, the returned exiles set up a Jewish state. Ezra (444 B.C.) established the Church State which derived its cohesion from the tradition of the past. Postexilic Israel looked back to the old days when it had been independent under David. The rite of circumcision and the observance of the Sabbath were stressed. The people hoped for the restoration of the Davidic kingdom which, however, was never realized. The full realization of the Davidic ideal was projected into the mythical future. "The genuine idea of God as a God who has to come was abandoned, and with it the conception of God as the Lord of history. In the eschatological hope, history was expected to come to an end. By its anticipation of the eschatological future Israel lost its historical moorings."[23]

After the time of the Exile, Israel lost her independence as a state. From 587 B.C. onward, Israel lived under foreign rule, first under the Persians until 350 B.C. During the Persian rule the Jews organized themselves as a theocratic state. During the Greek period, i.e., under the Ptolemaic rule, the Jews continued to enjoy freedom. However, during the time of the Seleucids, the situation changed for the Jews in Judea. Antiochus IV (175-164 B.C.) forcibly tried to Hellenize the Jews, which resulted in the Maccabean revolt. Under the Hasmonean kings Judah was able to achieve independence until Pompey entered Jerusalem in 63 B.C. and set up Roman rule. Herod the Great reigned as a puppet king under the Romans from 37 B.C. to 4 B.C. After his death his kingdom was divided among his grandsons. Judea proper was under the hegemony of Archelaus (4 B.C.-A.D. 6) until the rule of the Roman procurators. Two Jewish revolts, one in 66-70 A.D. and the other in 132 A.D., resulted in the final destruction of the Jewish nation.

3. The Theology and Religious Ideas of the Old Testament

Bultmann held that the Jewish doctrine of creation was not a speculative cosmogony but a confession of faith. God is the Creator, the source of all life from of old and for all time.[24] Like other Semitic deities, Jahweh the God of Israel, began as a tribal god. Israelite thought was not monotheistic from the beginning; before monotheism, henotheism and monolatry had preceded it. When Israel became a state circa 1500 B.C., Jahweh then became the God of the Israelite nation. Polytheism posed a problem for the Israelites when they came into contact with other Near Eastern nations. The prophets emphasized the fact that Jahweh was a "jealous God," who would not permit the worship of other gods. To this Jahweh, the writer of Deutero-Isaiah attributed the creation of the world. Creation myths lie behind the creation accounts in Genesis 1 and 2.[25]

Jahweh was conceived of as a Being transcending the world, whose transcendence received classic expression in the *creatio ex nihilo*, "a notion utterly inconceivable to the Greek mind, though a logical development from the premises of Biblical thought (Jub. 12:4; 2 Macc. 7:28.)."[26] The world is the sphere of God's sovereignty and the stage where man works out his destiny. The Israelites did not think of Jahweh as God of the world in their earliest writings but this was a concept first conceived by the prophets. Jahweh was thought of essentially as righteous will demanding of men righteousness. Through observation of their own history, men in the Old Testament came to recognize that God's sovereignty extended over other nations.

For the Hebrews, knowledge of God was differently conceived of than it was by the Greeks. The latter believed that God could be apprehended by reason and that proofs for His existence could be formulated. "Knowledge of God has nothing to do with God's metaphysical nature. It means to know his will."[27] In the Old Testament, truth is not primarily propositional knowledge "but that which is valid and demands recognition, that which can be trusted."[28] Wisdom is not an abstract science but consists of practical morality. The basic principle of Israelite wisdom is enshrined in the statement: "The fear of the Lord is the beginning of wisdom." God cares for the world which he has made (Psalm 147:8f). The people of the Old Testament realized that nature is beyond man's control. "To this extent suffering and death present no problem, and sickness or natural disasters never evoke questions which might lead to the working out of a theodicy or throw doubt on the existence of God."[29] Suffering can be explained as punishment from God. But why do the wicked prosper? The wisdom literature answers that in the end the wicked will suffer and the righteous prosper (Prov. 24: 19f.; Ps. 37:9-11). Ecclesiastes recommends resignation as the answer to the problem of suffering and concludes that the best thing to do is to submit uncomplainingly to the will of God. The wisdom of God surpasses all human understanding. Often the problem of suffering is bound up with the nation. The suffering of the nation must be borne in the same way as that of the individual, namely, of meekly bowing before the will of God.

4. The Anthropology of the Old Testament

In the Old Testament man is composed of flesh and soul which are not opposed to each other in a dualistic sense. "The soul does not belong intrinsically to a higher world, here imprisoned in a material body. Instead, the soul is the energy which gives life to the flesh. Its seat is generally in the blood, though it is sometimes equated with the divine breath."[30] Life like flesh is mortal and ceases to exist after death. The concept of the immortality of the soul is foreign to the Old Testament; it is an idea taken over from the Greek world into Hellenistic Judaism.[31] The doctrine of the resurrection found in a few late passages in the Old Testament was adopted from the Iranian religion. As a rule the Old Testament confines life to this earth, although it taught that the departed lived in a shadowy existence in Sheol. The idea of a resurrection is to be found only toward the end of the Old Testament in Isaiah 24-27 and in Daniel.[32]

A man's greatest gift is to have a long and happy life. The Old Testa-

869

ment devotees did not distinguish between natural and spiritual life. "Life is never described as good or bad in a moral sense. To live does not mean to live in any particular way."[33]

From a study of the ethical vocabulary of the Old Testament it would seem that Hebrew thought does not depict an ideal conception of man. Men are to meet their obligations to society by upright and responsible conduct. Evil is portrayed as opposition to the will of God. Sin must be either punished or forgiven. The Old Testament does not distinguish between social justice and personal morality. The ethical concepts are addressed to the corporate nation rather than to the individual. Sound principles must be followed if society is to flourish. Most of the ordinances are negative, as for instance, in the Decalogue.

Jahweh as King was the patron of justice, who demanded righteousness and justice. But this was protested by the prophets who claimed that God demands only righteousness and justice, not the performance of the cultus (Amos 5:21-24; Hos. 6:6; Is. 1:11-15). The prophets, however, did not succeed in removing the cultus. "The outcome of their work was its centralization at Jerusalem, which brought to an end the Canaanite vegetation rites and the corruption of the worship of Jahweh. And in addition to this there was an attempt to discover a unity between the cultus and the judicial and moral law."[34] The latter prophets changed the cultus into a demonstration of obedience to God and used it as an effective symbol of Israel's separation from the surrounding nations. Sin is disobedience against God; it is rebellion against lawfully constituted authority. Jahweh is a jealous God who will not permit anyone to have the honor that belongs to Him. In the Old Testament sin is not only ostentation but self-will; it is ingratitude to God. Since sin involves guilt, it necessitates atonement. God punishes men by sending misfortune, sickness or premature death. A way of atonement, however, has been provided by Jahweh through the sacrifical system. At first the ceremonial rites were associated with magic but later they were reinterpreted "as symbols of man's obedience, and the more sin is interpreted in terms of moral guilt, the more do the ceremonies of atonement come to be regarded as an institution of the forgiving grace of God. Man knows he is thrown back upon God's forgiveness."[35]

5. Theological Development since the Exile

One of the significant developments of the Exile was the adoption of synagogues by Judaism which sponsored a non-sacrificial worship. The synagogue services began and ended with prayer and with the reading of Scripture. This resulted in binding Judaism to its past history. As a nation the Jews developed a strong sense of history and election. Bultmann believes there was an unfortunate development in postexilic Judaism. Due to Israel's loyalty to a book it became tied to its past history. "God was no longer really the God of history, and therefore always the God who was about to come. He was no longer a vital factor in the present: his revelation lay in the past. History was likewise brought to a standstill."[36] The leaders of the nation were teachers that expounded the

Scriptures but not men of social action. Israel cut herself off from the out-side world and thus removed herself from the stream of history. She looked for redemption in the future, but it was not to be a real historical event but a fantastic expectation that all history would end for good.

Not only did the Jews cut themselves adrift from history but their God was also removed by them from participation in history. Jahweh no longer seemed to reveal Himself in history. A new concept of God's tran-scendence originated in the two centuries before the birth of Christ. A doctrine of His omnipotence and universal judgment was then developed. From then on the idea of God's transcendence was conceived in meta-physical terms. "He was a superior cosmic power, spatially distant and ontologically distinct from all wordly phenomena."[37] Apocalyptic writings presented fantastic pictures of God's cosmic rule, attended by hosts of angels and the blinding glory of heaven.

God's purpose now embraced not only Israel but all mankind. All peo-ple would one day be required to appear before Jahweh, the Judge of all the earth. The true worship of God was confined to Judaism, which was interested in making converts for Judaism. Proselytes were required to join the Jewish community. In doing this, Bultmann claimed, Israel again cut herself off from a common history with other nations.

Another adverse development, according to Bultmann, in postexilic Judaism was its attitude toward the Book, which no longer was regarded primarily as an historical record of God's dealings with mankind but as a book of divine Law. The focal point of worship became the preaching and hearing of sermons which were supposed to regulate life. This change had two different consequences, according to Bultmann. "First, it meant that the whole life was dominated by religion. Religion was not confined to a special sphere of its own, as distinct from daily life. On the other hand, however, life was alienated from history, which is the natural sphere to which it belongs."[38] The Jews lost sight of their social respon-sibilities and although the Law inculcated morality, there developed a special emphasis on ritualism.

The Law, which went back to the time of Moses, was not capable of undergoing any further development. Since it was God's Law, it was binding for all time. Many new circumstances arose in Judaism that were not covered in the Mosaic Law so that the scribes had to provide new laws to meet new conditions. This lead to discussions among the rabbis and to the formation of various schools of thought, the outstanding ones being — those of the Sadducees and Pharasees, each of which took cer-tain distinctive positions on theological matters.

II. Bultmann's Interpretation and Understanding of the Old Testament from Within-from the Vantage Point of Faith[39]

Bultmann maintained that there is a basic difference between Chris-tianity and Judaism. The New Testament and the Early Church, as well as the Church in subsequent centuries, had a wrong conception of what was truly involved in New Testament religion. Stripped of all false notions, the New Testament does not primarily repeat the teachings of Jesus but above all, it proclaims the person of Christ and ties the relationship between God and man to Christ's person.[40] If Christ's message is stressed then the New Testament would only contain Law, which belongs to the Old Testament. According to Bultmann, that which is specifically Christian is the fact that in Jesus Christ the revelation of God has taken place. Without this emphasis, the religion of the New Testament would be nothing but "a refined Judaism or humanism."

For the person who stands within the New Testament, the Old Testament to have theological relevance must be interpreted existentially. The questions with which the New Testament believer approaches the Older Covenant are: What meaning do its happenings and events have for my personal existence? What message does it have for the Church now? To treat the Old Testament in terms of trying to establish how its events relate to world history is not to deal with it in a genuinely historical manner. To be meaningful the Old Testament must be interpreted in terms of the question of *what* basic possibility it presents for an understanding of human existence (Daseinsversfandnis). It is essential to enter into dialogue with the Old Testament to see how the experiences of Old Testament men may reveal what is truly involved in human existence.[41]

In the opinion of Bultmann, a Christian does not take the Old Testament seriously if he investigates it in order to see what men said twenty centuries ago. He only correctly deals with the Old Covenant when he asks: What message does its books have for my existence? While many Christians in the course of the centuries have misunderstood the Old Testament, Bultmann believed that Paul and Luther grasped the understanding of existence in the Old Testament which they set forth in terms of the antithesis between "Law and Gospel."[42]

When the Old Testament is properly evaluated from the existentialist viewpoint, it will be apparent, as it was to Luther, that the Old Testament is Law. When the New Testament believer asks the question as to what the relationship of the Old Testament is to the New, he perceives that the Old Testament sets forth the Law as an expression of God's demands upon him, while as a sinner he is under grace in the New Testament. The constant demands made by the Old Testament aid the Christian to understand the true meaning of the Gospel. This therefore means that the Old Testament is a presupposition for the New. According to Bultmann, it is essential for the New Testament man to *stand under* the Old Testament. *Under* the new order, represented by the New Testament, the Christian believer stands under the grace of God which is willing to accept him even though he is a sinner. Furthermore, Bultmann affirms that while it is true that the Christian is free from the Law and is under the Spirit, he still needs the Law of the Old Testament. Why is this necessary? "But faith, as the possibility of Christian existence ever to be grasped anew, is a reality only by constantly overcoming the old existence under the Law."[43]

If the Old Testament is necessary as a constant presupposition for the New, does the former maintain its specifically Old Testament character?

This Bultmann negates. That portion of the Old Testament legislation that was cultic or ritualistic in character, only had value for a particular epoch of Hebrew history. The ethical demands of the Old Testament are valid and are still in force, not because they are found in the Old Testament as an authoritative inspired book, but because they emanate from basic relationships of human beings with each other. The Law is found outside of the Jewish Scriptures as Paul asserts in Romans 1:32 that without the benefit of Old Testament instruction the Gentiles know what God demands of them. According to Romans 2:14f., Bultmann avers, the Word of God is written in their hearts.[44]

Although Bultmann affirms that the Gospel presupposes the Law, the Old Testament is not the only source for becoming acquainted with the Law, and thus not identified only with the Decalogue and other legislative formulations in the Old Testament. Without the use of the Old Testament men everywhere are capable of becoming aware of their nothingness and to come to a sense of humility or despair. Everywhere men believe that by self-discipline and by keeping the moral demands they can attain authentic selfhood.[45]

Bultmann believed that in the Old Testament the Decalogue as well as the ethical demands as expressed by the prophets were some of the best statements of ethical requirements in the world and therefore the Old Testament was a useful instrument with which to bring home to man that he is subject to God's demands. But strictly speaking, it must be realized that the Law of the Old Testament was not meant for Christians but was addressed to a particular people, the Jews.[46] The Law is a part of their living history. The reason why in our day we regard the Law of the Old Testament as coming from God is due to the fact that out of the history of which we have come the Old Testament has played an important part.

Bultmann contends that men are subject to many different influences and that in the present situation a number of possibilities for the understanding of the self are to be found. In endeavoring to understand his existence properly, the Christian needs also to consider the Old Testament's view of existence. The Old Testament portrayal of human existence is different than that which comes from the Greeks. Every idealistic or utilitarian demand is rejected. The Old Testament does not depict some ideal of excellence to be striven after, but it sets forth the demand that in obedience to God the neighbor be served in the constant awareness of a sense of inadequacy and guilt.[47] To understand the Old Testament's concept of man one must realize that man is believed to have been created by a higher power and as a creature is delivered to the Lord of the world. History is not to be understood as the result of human activity but of God's power and direction. Thus Bultmann wrote: "But rather he (i.e. man) finds himself put by the divine will in a particular place in the stream of temporal occurrence which for him holds the possibility of either judgment or grace depending on whether he acts in obedience to what God requires of him."[48]

The Old Testament understanding of existence is the same as that found in the New Testament but is radically different from that in Greek literature which presents an idealistic view. Between these two views a choice must be made. Only as the Christian has a critical dialogue with the Old Testament will he be able effectively to grasp what the true significance of the Old Testament is for Christianity.[49]

Bultmann's insistence on the existentialist interpretation of Old Testament materials might lead to some erroneous conclusions as to the value of the Old Testament for Christianity. The old belief that the Old Testament is a revelation of God or His Word for the Christian Church is a faulty conception. Bultmann does not think that in Christian preaching it is proper to refer to the Old Testament as the revelation of God, as has been done heretofore.[50] The statement that the concept of existence is the same in both Testaments might lead to the conclusion that both are a part of the revelation of God to the world and as such to be followed by Christian people.

Since Bultmann holds that faith, righteousness and grace, sin and forgiveness, are basically the same, wherein then does the difference between the Old and New Testaments lie? What new contribution does the New Testament make in comparison with the Old?

As already shown, Bultmann described this difference as being that between Law and Gospel. But just as living under grace presupposes the Law, so in the Old Testament which is Law, there is also to be found simultaneously an existence under grace.[51] It was by an act of grace that God established the possibility of a relationship between Himself and man; it was an act of grace that prompted God to give Israel His law and committed to them a specific assignment, which was to be realized in the course of its historical existence. God is portrayed by an act of grace as forgiving the sins of His people, despite the fact that Israel proved unfaithful time after time, God was willing to show mercy and to forgive their sins.[52] It is possible for Christians to use passages in the Psalter and in the prophetic writings that ask for forgiveness and that offer God's grace. Bultmann holds that inasmuch as the grace of God for the sinner is spoken of in the Old Testament, it must be recognized that the Gospel is evident in the Old Testament, although there are many places where the Gospel is not found in its purity.[53] Often the radicality between sin and grace is not brought out as it should have been. Not all Old Testament passages show that their authors have grasped the radicality of God's grace. This grace has been truly apprehended when the individual waits on God and finds help and boasting only of Him. Many of the Old Testament saints received God's grace and forgiveness in their vicissitudes, and when they did not experience them, they however looked forward to them. From this hopeful outlook, Bultmann claimed the beginnings of eschatology are to be found.[54]

Bultmann averred that insofar as Old Testament writers had the proper understanding of God and of sin and grace, their faith may be considered as hope. Over against this faith, the New Testament then appears as the faith which has fulfillment. The great difference between the Old Testament and the New is to be found in the truth "that in Jesus

874

Christ God has performed the eschatological deed hoped for, that in Christ he has forgiven sin, has called the New Israel, has bestowed his Spirit."[55] Through Christ God reconciled the world to himself. That is God's eschatological deed. Bultmann in this connection rejects the deity of Christ and states that faith is not found in believing in Christ. Thus he asserted: "There is not alongside of God another divine person . . . nor does the Christian faith give assent to metaphysical speculations about the deity of Christ and his natures. Rather, faith is nothing else but faith in God's deed in Christ."[56]

In the light of God's eschatological deed in Ghrist, what then is the difference between the Old and New Testaments? In the New Testament God's grace must be understood radically, and when this is done it follows that forgiveness is not merely tied to the changing fortunes of life of an individual or of a collective group. God's grace, which is pure forgiveness, produces men, strong and new. This means that judgment has taken place; the new era has been inaugurated, all concepts about future events are eliminated. God's grace and forgiveness are made available through the proclaimed Word. Jesus is the Word that has come to lighten the world (John 1:1f.).[57]

If his interpretation about the uniqueness of the Christ event is correct and is granted, Bultmann claimed it follows that the grace of the New Testament is different from the grace of God in the Old Testament. In the latter the grace of God is tied to the destinies of the Hebrew nation. According to the Old Testament conception, because the Jew was a member of the nation he shared in the grace shown in the past history which continues on into the present. Likewise, the Hebrew of the future, as a member of the nation, will share in the grace once given. But this does not pertain to the situation in the New Testament where the grace of God is not tied to an historical event.[58] The act of God in Christ is not an historical event as was the passage through the Red Sea or the making of the covenant at Mt. Sinai. Christ is not to be thought of as Moses or Abraham. The forgiving grace of God is not to be associated with an historical event but is to be found in the proclaimed Word in which Jesus is present.[59] God's grace is not to be found in statements in the New Testament on the basis of which the conclusion is reached that God is gracious, but God's grace comes directly through the proclaimed Word.[60] This furthermore means that the church cannot be conceived of as a sociological entity with a history like other associations of men. The Church is created through the Word of God's forgiveness in Christ and is the community of those who accept the message in faith. Because Christ is the end of the old aeon, the final word that God has spoken and still speaks, Bultmann called, the association of believers, an eschatological congregation, one that stands at the end of history.[61]

In the light of the uniqueness of the New Testament faith, the Old Testament cannot be considered as God's revelation as it was for the Jews. Historical events that had meaning for Israel and were the Word of God to them, do not have that significance for the Christian.[62] To reflect on such historical events as, for example, the Exodus, the giving of the Law at Sinai, or the building of the Solomonic temple, has value inasmuch as they have had influence on the Christian civilization of Europe. However, Bultmann contended that the events of Greek history, such as the death of the Spartans at Thermopylae or of Socrates' drinking the hemlock cup are just as valuable for Christians as are the historical: events of the Old Testament.[63] Any person or group of persons that grapples with history shows the modern Christian what the possibilities are for human existence.

After rejecting the history of the Old Testament as a means of revelation for the Christian faith, Bultmann asks whether the Old Testament completely disassociated from its history can be a revelation for Christian faith. Some Christians would like to consider the Old Testament as being preliminary and as having a restricted value, claiming that in the New Testament God has spoken in a clearer and fuller fashion. But when this position is taken, it merely means that the Church would find in the Old Testament that which it knows from the revelation in the New.[64]

This was the method followed by the New Testament and primitive Christianity which considered everything that had gone before in the Old Testament as preliminary and taught that in the events of Christ's life and in the establishment of the Christian Church, the Old Testament has found its fulfillment as well as a deeper meaning. Early Christianity employed the Scripture-proof text method, according to which many passages in the Old Testament were interpreted as prophecies that found their fulfillment in Christ.[65] In his essay "Prophecy and Fulfillment" Bultmann has set forth how this was done in the New Testament and asserts that this was only possible by the employment of an allegorical exegesis. Passages that were looked upon as prophecies were often no prophecies at all, or at best, only reflect expressions of hope for the future. Bultmann cited numerous examples from the New Testament where Old Testament passages are quoted and said to be fulfilled in Christ.[66] He accuses the New Testament writers of reading from or into these texts what they already knew. Thus he wrote: "If one follows their intention one is obliged to say that the Old Testament becomes clear as prophecy as a result of fulfillment. But what would be the point of such proceeding on the part of God?"[67] The incorrectness of this procedure has been shown by modern critical scholarship. The reasons Christians did this was for polemical reasons against the Jews and for apologetical purposes in dealing with the Gentiles.[68] Emphasis upon the antiquity of many Old Testament prophecies, interpreted messianically, was motivated by the desire to strengthen the salvation event in Christ. However, this was a grave mistake in Bultmann's opinion, because it was an attempt to attain security for faith and so tried to lessen the real stumbling block, the offense of the cross of Christ, which cannot be overcome by objective proofs.

The traditional formula of prophecy and fulfillment of the New Testament writers and of the Early Church Fathers is completely wrong as is also Von Hofmann's view as expressed in his book *Weissagung und Erfullung* (Prophecy and Fulfillment). According to Von Hofmann, the *words* of the Old Testament were not prophetic, but the history of Israel was, to which the Old Testament testifies. Thus for Von Hofmann prophecy is not prediction of coming events for whose realization the world had to wait. No, prophecy is history itself insofar as history was a movement leading to a goal and bore within itself a goal as prophecy or promise. Fulfilled history is to be understood as prophecy; through fulfillment the significance of history has become clear. Since Christ is the goal of history, history is prophecy of Christ and not just the history of the Old Testament, of the covenant people of God, but of the history of the world. Thus Von Hofmann, as quoted by Bultmann, asserted:

> If it is true that all things, great and small, serve to bring about the unification of the world under its head, Christ, then there is absolutely nothing in the history of the world in which something divine does not dwell, and so nothing which must necessarily remain foreign to prophecy.[69]

Bultmann claimed that Von Hofmann's understanding of prophecy actually amounts to sponsoring a philosophy of history that has been influenced by Hegel. Because it has been determined by the Hegelian concept, so Bultmann averred, Von Hofmann's interpretation has its limitations, and Israel's history, of which Christ is the goal, is theologically irrelevant. According to the New Testament, Bultmann claims that Christ is the end of salvation history, "not in the sense that he signifies the goal of historical development, but because he is the eschatological end. Can Old Testament history perhaps be legitimately understood as prophecy on this basis?"[70]

In both of his major essays dealing with the interpretation of the Old Testament, Bultmann emphasized the discontinuity of the Old and New Testaments. In "Prophecy and Fulfillment" he examined the concepts of "the covenant," "the kingdom of God," and "the people of God." After analyzing all three ideas, he reached the conclusion that they cannot be realized in history; all three prove to be an impossible basis for an historical development and so cannot be transformed into reality within history.[71] The people of God in the Old Testament conceived of themselves as a covenant people living under Jahweh's rule, as a real entity in the Near Eastern world. This, according to Bultmann, no longer holds, for in the New Testament there is no sociological historical entity but an eschatologized community. Between the Old Testament community and the New Testament church there is no direct connection. In writing about the New Testament community, Bultmann said: "The community is not a people as a historical entity within the world ... The new covenant is a radically eschatological dimension, that is, a dimension outside of the world, and to belong to it takes its members out of the world . . . The rule of God and so of Christ . . . is eschatological and supramundane in its entirety; and the man who has part in it is, as it were, already taken out of the world . . . The people of God is no longer an empirical historical entity-it does not exist as a people requiring institutional ordinance for its organization."[72] In his book, *The Presence of Eternity* Bultmann again sets forth the eschatological difference between the Old and New Testament conceptions: *"The New Covenant* is not grounded on an event of the history of the people as was the Old Covenant ... *The new people of God* has no real history, for it is the community of the end-time, an eschatological phenomenon."[73] It is clear from these assertions that Bultmann breaks all revelational continuity between the Old Testament and the New.

In Part I of his essay, "Prophecy and Fulfillment" Bultmann does not regard the Old Testament too highly. Its history is said to be filled with contradictions which pervade the self-consciousness and the hope of Israel. The meaning of the Old Testament is negative. The great mistake of the Old Testament is that it failed to eschatologize its great major theological concepts. The rule of God described in the Old Testament cannot be realized in history. "But we find the contradition in the fact that God and the activity are not conceived of in the radically transcendent and eschatological sense."[74] But strangely, the miscarriage of history actually amounts to a promise. Old Testament history is said to be a "miscarriage of history." The history of the Old Testament is a failure because of its character as law, which reveals man's contradictions and thus forces a Christian to Christ. Even though the Old Testament is a failure, it thereby may be considered a preparation for the Gospel.[75]

Bultmann insisted that if the Christian Church feels it needs to use the Old Testament in preaching, the latter must not be interpreted against its original sense, as critical-historical research claims the church of the past has done by the employment of the allegorical method.[76]

While the Marburg sage strictly speaking denies the true revelatory character of the Old Testament, he was willing to permit the latter, to serve as God's Word in an intermediate fashion. Although the Old Testament has words not spoken for Christians nor addressed to them, it is possible for New Testament believers to find reflected a picture of their own existential problems and thus see the Old Testament as a Word of Christ addressed to their needs. In this sense it is possible to denominate the Old Testament "prophecy," and the New Testament as "fulfillment."[77] However, it is not absolutely necessary to use the Old Testament in the manner just described, for the New Testament has a number of books which utilize the Old Testament very sparingly and some not at all. This means the Old Testament can be ignored in Christian preaching and teaching. Bultmann concluded his essay, "The Significance of the Old Testament for the Christian Faith" by asserting that if the Old Testament is to be used in Christian preaching, then two precautions will have to be observed; first, the allegorical method, which robs the Old Testament of its original meaning with its exclusive pertinence to Hebrew history, must be avoided. Second, the materials of the Old Testament should only be used to the extent that they help a Christian to grasp the meaning of human existence."[78]

III. An Evaluation of Bultmann's Approach to and Understanding of the Old Testament

In assessing Bultmann's views of the Old Testament, it will be necessary to examine the historic background from which he has come and see what influences have affected his philosophical and religious beliefs. In the introduction to his book, *Primitive Christianity in Its Contemporary Setting,* Bultmann stated that despite its predominance of Old Testament and Jewish background, primitive Christianity was an amalgam of ideas from many sources, including Gnosticism, Hellenism and paganism.[79] An analagous comparison might also be made about Bultmann's understanding and interpretation of the Old Testament which likewise are the result of philosophical and theological views derived from liberalism, dialectial theology and existentialism. Many different streams of thought have contributed to Bultmann's Old Testament positions which often appear to be contradictory. Gunther Bornkamm claims that Bultmann's theological work has its roots in historical critical research and in the so-called dialectical theology, especially as reflected in the writings of Karl Barth and Gogarten.[80] Bultmann agreed with Bornkamm's evaluation of his theological position and added : "In fact, I have seen and still see it as my task to bind into a unity the intentions at work in that tradition and this movement."[81]

Bultmann rejected the traditional conception of historical Protestantism that God has made available to mankind in the Scriptures of the Old and New Testaments by inspiration of the Holy Spirit, oracles of truth. With the advent of scientific historical criticism, the traditional Christian conception of divine revelation (as found in the various confessional statements of historic Protestantism) was rejected. Since divine truths could not be found in propositional assertions, revealed in a Book, liberal Protestantism of the nineteenth century endeavored to ground theological truth in the religious consciousness, an idea especially proposed by Schleiermacher.[82] The importance of Jesus consisted in this that He had made known to mankind a new concept of religion, viz., that in his feelings man possessed a new kind of God-consciousness. In Christ the new God-awareness reached its perfection.

For Schleiermacher and those who accepted this interpretation of religion, the Old Testament was unimportant as mediating God's revelation. At best the Old Testament could only serve as a propaedeutic to the Christian faith.[83] The Old Testament merely shows how man through an evolutionary method developed the God consciousness concept. Other religions, besides that found in the Old Testament, have records of spiritual experience that exhibited God-consciousness that reached its climax in Christianity. The Religions geschichtliche school proposed that all non-Christian religions, Gentile or Jewish, be investigated by scientifically comparing them and asking to what degree they contributed to the new God awareness, the outstanding characteristic of the Christian faith.[84]

From this vantage point, the religion of the Old Testament only had value for the liberals in helping man become aware of his God-consciousness. Other religions contained just as valid teachings about human existence as does the Old Testament. The history of the New Testament is as much connected with the Greeks as with the Hebrews. Athens and Rome are just as holy as Jerusalem is for Christians. According to liberal Protestantism of the nineteenth century the Old Testament is not a real revelation for the Christian faith. Jesus, in whom the God-consciousness reached its culmination, was a Jew and so He naturally expressed Himself in Jewish forms. The New Testament also contains expressions derived from Hellenism and paganism. To arrive at the real religion of Jesus, liberals contended that the message had to be stripped of its first-century accoutrements. The chaff had to be separated from the wheat, or to use twentieth century jargon, the eschatological kerygma required demythologization.[85]

According to Richardson, the roots of this type of thinking are to be found in the positivistic understanding of history as developed in the eighteenth century.[86] Lessing based the truths of religion on reason and could not find the locus of revelation in history. In the following century the foundation for religious truth was based upon religious experience. During that century the Jesus of history was pursued with great diligence, but as time went on He became more elusive until in the twentieth complete historical skepticism came to be the controlling thought of the day and the real message of Christianity was to be located in the existential encounter.

Richardson asserted that "no new discovery is claimed for the observation that Bultmann's theology is a logical development from nineteenth century Liberal Protestant ways of thinking. The point has often been made hitherto."[87] Karl Barth in his *Kirchliche Dogmatik* spoke of the fact that Bultmann was influenced by W. Hermann and ultimately by Ritschl and Schleiermacher.[88] Paul Althaus was convinced that Ritschl's value judgments had returned in new dress in Bultmann's use of the phrase "the significance for man."[89]

A number of scholars have stated that Bultmann's position leads to a disparagement of the Old Testament.[90] Thus Kraeling wrote : "In spite of the statements already noted pointing in the conservative direction, his main line of argument is negative in its consequence. The value of the Old Testament lies in the sphere of the intellect-in the insight it gives into existence, but what insight we really need we can have without it."[91] Richardson opined that Bultmann's low view of the Old Testament can be traced to the latter's inheritance from Hermann and Ritschl. For Ritschl the Old Testament at best was a propaedeutic for the understanding of the religious ideas of the New Testament. In the later editions of his writings Ritschl went so far as to deny all revelation of the Old Testament and limited revelation to ideas found in Christ.[92]

Hermann, the disciple of Ritschl, was even stronger in his denial that the Old Testament was to be placed on the same plane of revelation as the New. It was Hermann's contention that the Church had erred in placing the Old Testament side by side with Christ instead of keeping Christ apart and above all. In Christ alone all that which is true meets and has its most perfect expression. Thus Hermann wrote: "We cannot even transplant ourselves into the religious life of a pious Israelite with a complete understanding. For the facts which acted on him as the revelation of God have for us this power no longer."[93] Hermann went so far as to represent Christ as standing apart from the Old Testament, of occupying a position of isolation. For Ritschl and his school, according to Lichtenberger, "the only proper religious authority is the person, the word, and the work of Christ, as the testimony of the first Christian community has made us to know them."[94] Not the entire New Testament contains God's revelation but only that part that helps Christians to see their awareness of salvation in Christ. It would, however, be erroneous, according to Ritschl, to look for the revelation in Christ in his "substance" or "nature," to seek for Him through the communication of metaphysical truths that emphasize His deity or describe His relationship to the First and Third Persons of the Trinity.

Many of the distinctive views of Bultmann on the Old and New Testaments have parallels in the thought of the school of Ritschlianism. Richardson claimed that "Bultmann's view on the significance of the Old Testament is entirely in character with his neo-Ritschlian interpretation of the New."[95] There are many statements as reflected in Bultmann's interpretation of the Old Testament that could be traced to Ritschl's and Hermann's influence.[96]

Since Bultmann's publication of the *Romer brief* (1919) Bultmann became involved in the dialectical theology, whose traditions he claimed to have carried out up to the present.[97] Bornkamm averred that the fundamental principles of the dialectical theology have been utilized by Bultmann and have never lost their validity for the Marburg sage and have in fact been further developed in his work.[98] The dialectical theology is characterized by the use of the paradox.[99] Bultmann utilized the paradoxical principle in his writings. There are a number of contradictory positions taken by him in his portrayal of the relationship of the two Testaments to each other, which can best be understood in the light of this principle. It appears to the essayist that Bultmann is resorting to paradox when he conceived of the Old Testament as pure Law when compared with the New, but when the former is considered apart from the New he admitted that the Old Testament contains both Law and Gospel. Another contradictory position is evident when the events of the Old Testament are looked upon as sources for the history of the religion of Israel, but when a Christian uses the same Testament the historical events lose their historical meaning and have value only as they show man how to live existentially. A paradox is also apparent when Bultmann speaks of the giving of the Law on Mount Sinai, the exodus from Egypt, the entry of Israel into Canaan, the building of the Solomonic temple as true happenings, but in the New Testament which purports to be a continuation of the history of the forefathers, the historical events of the life of Christ and the biographical materials relating to the apostles are removed from the realm of history. The same observation holds true relative to the concepts of "the covenant," "the people of God," and "the kingdom of God," all acknowledged by Bultmann as historical realities.

However, when these entities are referred to in the New Testament their historicity is denied and they are placed in a suprahistorical realm and are eschatologized. The patadoxical principle seems to be employed when the Old Testament is considered to be a revelation from God when used by Jewish people, but when the same body of sacred literature is utilized by Christians it ceases to be divine revelation. Bultmann classified the teachings of Christ with Law and allied them with the teachings of the prophets, but when the name of Christ is used in proclaiming the so-called eschatological deed in Christ, then the Gospel of grace is made available. By means of these paradoxes Bultmann has established a discontinuity between the Old and New Testaments.

The teachings of the two Testaments are viewed by Bultmann through the spectacles of existential philosophy.[100] In dealing with the Old Testament from *within- the* only proper method for understanding the literature of the Old Covenant — this is done by Bultmann according to existentialist categories. In his theological exegesis, one of the current systems of philosophy has been employed to determine the meaning of Scripture. Bultmann has attempted a new rapprochement between theology and philosophy.

Some theologians in the Christian Church are suspicious of the place assigned by the Marburg professor to existentialist philosophy. It was Barth who claimed that Bultmann had been responsible for bringing theology back to an Egyptian bondage, in which philosophy determines what the Holy Spirit is allowed to say.[101] From the viewpoint of historical Protestant hermeneutics and the hermeneutics of the Lutheran Confessions, Barth is correct when he charged that the truth of Christianity (which also includes the Old Testament) is perverted and distorted when it is welded to a system of philosophy, in this case existentialism. Heidegger's scheme helps to determine the meaning Bultmann elicits from a Biblical text. Bultmann claimed that the Old Testament only has theological relevance as it is dealt with existentially.

Philosophers themselves have been critical of the school of philosophy chosen by Bultmann. Jaspers, sometimes classified as an existentialist, has faulted Bultmann for his dependence on one singular philosopher — Heidegger — and for basing his views on one book only, *Sein und Zeit*. Jaspers asked the significant question whether a demythologized version of Christianity must not result in another form of human philosophy.[102] According to Richardson, Bultmann's adoption of an existentialist theology was "a genuinely evangelical attempt to escape from the negative and, skeptical consequences of his fundamentally positivistic Gospel-criticism, even though it is achieved at the expense of divorcing the kerygma of the Church from any possible sources of it in the life and teaching of Jesus."[103] If existentialism is found to be a faulty philosophy, Bultmann's interpretation of both the Old and New Testaments is consequently inadequate.[103a]

One of the problems for many theologians and historians in Bultmann's system is his understanding of the relation of theology to history. Historic Christianity, whether of the Roman Catholic, Greek Orthodox or Protestant variety has always considered the Judaeo-Christian faith as an historical religion. The religion of the Old and New Testaments has always found its center not in a code of laws nor in a world view but in a series of historical events that achieved their fulfillment in the life of Christ.[104] As has already been shown in Part I of this essay, Bultmann does not ascribe factuality to the narratives of the Gospels. One of his admirers, Macquarrie, recognized this when he wrote: "Now Bultmann, as we have seen, leaves very little in the way of factual objective history to the Gospel narrative. What history there was, he tells us, has been transformed into myth, so that we can no longer get at the history. He himself transforms the myth into its existential significance and brings the 'salvation history' into the present, that is to say, into the historical existence of the believer who here and now dies and rises with Christ."[105]

Bultmann will not admit the fact that the theology of the New Testament as a whole is based primarily upon Jesus' own interpretation of His mission and person in the light of His understanding of the Old Testament. [106] Because of Bultmann's unique interpretation of historiography, it seems that historical events themselves are not significant. He falls far short of doing justice to the historical dimensions of the Biblical revelation.[107] In the light of his existentialism, historical events only have meaning as they help the individual solve the problems of human existence. Bultmann's concept of "prophecy and fulfillment" becomes an impossibility because in his scheme,[108] the fulfillment of that self-revelation of God that occurred in history is transferred into "the timeless category of personal self-understanding."[109]

The Old Testament cannot be a true revelation of God for the Marburg sage because he does not accept the fact that God directly revealed Himself to men like Abraham, Moses, David, Isaiah, Jeremiah, Ezekiel, Daniel and many others in the course of Biblical history and communicated to them His will and teachings. The New Testament statement of Peter: "Holy men of God spake as they were moved by the Holy Ghost" is completely rejected. Bultmann has stated that the Old Testament was unnecessary for the Christian. The continuing value of the Old Testament is clearly set forth by Paul: "For whatever was written in former days was written for our instruction, that by steadfastness and encouragement we might have hope" (R.S.V. Rom. 15:4).

Just as Bultmann has demythologized John and Paul and turned the Pauline theology upside down,[110] so he has likewise proceeded in a cavalier manner to belittle Old Testament truths. His view of the Ceremonial Law of the Old Testament is extremely low. While it is true that the Ceremonial Law was no longer binding upon Christians after the death of Christ on Calvary, Bultmann failed to appreciate the Biblical truth that the Ceremonial Law was a part of God's economy during the days of the Old Covenant to prepare men for the revelation of the significance of Jesus' work for man's salvation. The Israelite did not distinguish between Moral and Ceremonial Law because the Law of God was of one fabric. All laws were binding upon the chosen people because they had been given by God. Influenced by a wrong understanding of the nature of the Old Testament, Bultmann wrote disparagingly of various aspects of Old Testament teachings. Vischer pointed out in his evaluation of Bultmann's position that the cultic demands were "an essential part of" the understanding of human existence" in the Old Testament.[111] The Epistle of the Hebrews which stresses the superiority of Christ in relation to the institutions and teachings of the Old Testament shows how the tabernacle, the Levitical priesthood and the sacrificial system were preparatory and that in Jesus of Nazareth their typical significance was fulfilled. The cultic demands are described in the Pentateuch as originating with Jahweh and are not ascribed to human origin.

While Bultmann held the moral requirements of the Old Testament in higher esteem than the cultic, he failed to recognize the true character of the Moral Law as given by God. The normative character of the moral requirements as set forth in the Old Testament Scriptures was not acknowledged by Bultmann. The origin of the Moral Law did not spring out of human realtionships. Regarding the Moral Law, Bultmann held that man can know "by nature what the Law demands" and that he can comprehend the moral demands "arising out of the relation to his fellowman which he must acknowledge in his conscience."[112] This would assume that conscience dictates right actions to people. However, conscience is not an infallible guide; conscience can only function in terms of a norm. If the norm is wrong, then conscience will direct the individual to do wrong. It is a well-established fact that conscience does not give the same advice to people faced with identical moral problems. The Old Testament does not portray the Moral Law as arising from some form of human relationship or coming out of its concrete historical form, but ascribes the origin of the Moral Law to God. Jahweh originally placed the Moral Law into man's heart at creation but it became dulled as a result of the fall into sin. The Moral Law written by Jahweh on two tablets of stone on Mt. Sinai and delivered to Moses was incorporated by him in the Pentateuch. Vischer correctly faulted Bultmann for claiming that "thou shalt" simply sprang out of human relationships and not out of the I AM (Ex. 3:14).[113]

Paul and Luther have been cited by Bultmann in support of his Law/Gospel dialetic, according to which the Old Testament is Law and the New Testament, Gospel. However, this interpretation of Paul and Luther is not warranted by the facts. Both Law and Gospel are found by them in the Old and New Testaments. Paul certainly believed that the Gospel was in the Old Testament. He taught that Abraham received the Messianic promise in the statement: "In thee shall all nations be blessed" (Galatians 3:8). In Romans 4 Paul argued that the doctrine of justification by faith was not a new doctrine that he was advocating but that it was found in the Old Testament, dating back to Abraham. Both Abraham and David were justified by faith apart from the works of the Law. The writings of Luther are replete with statements to the effect that Christ alone gives salvation to all men, that all passages of Scripture must be understood in harmony with this basic teaching[114] Bornkamm claimed that Luther found both Law and Gospel in the Old Testament just as the Reformer found Law and Gospel in the New Testament. For Luther, the promises of coming redemption which are found in the Old Testament are not Law but Gospel.[115] On the other hand, the commands and directions for right living found in the New Testament are not Gospel but Law. The true position regarding the relationship of Law to Gospel in the two Testaments might be said to be: in the Old Testament the Law pre-dominates and in the New Testament the Gospel is more prominent. "For the law was given by Moses, but grace and truth came by Jesus Christ" (John 1: 17). If the Old Testament were entirely Law, then Bultmann would be correct in his assertion: "Hence, it can be only for *pedagogical reasons* that the Christian Church uses the Old Testament to make man conscious of standing under God's demand."[116] Braaten seriously questioned Bultmann's Law/Gospel dialectic as an exclusive valid hermeneutical principle for interpreting the Old Testament.[117] The Formula of Concord claimed that from the very beginning of God's church in the Old Testament, Law and Gospel were distinguished. "Since the beginning of the world these two proclamations have continually been set forth side by side in the church of God with the proper distinction."[118]

From the viewpoint of Luther and the Lutheran Confessions it must be said that Bultmann fails to appreciate the Christocentricity of the canonical Scriptures. For Bultmann the historical Jesus is of no particular concern. It is in the kerygma that Christ is known, that is, not historically but existentially. Christ as the Word is important and through the proclamation of the Word, forgiveness is bestowed. In the preaching activity of the Church the Word has revelatory authority. Like Kaehler, Bultmann delivered "the historical" Jesus to the form critics and instead emphasized the "Jesus of faith." Künneth has well described the meaning of Christ in the Bultmannian system: "For Bultmann the name of Jesus Christ represents not a personal living reality of God's saving Revelation in the sphere of history but merely a concept, an ideogram, a symbol or a principle for the event of contemporary preaching."[119]

Jesus, before as well as after His resurrection, taught that He was foretold in the Old Testament Scriptures. To the Jews of His day, Jesus said: "You search the scriptures, because you think that in them you have eternal life; and it is they that bear witness of me," (RSV, John 5:39) "If you believed Moses, you would believe me, for he wrote of me" (RSV, John 5: 46). On Easter afternoon Jesus said to Cleophas and his friend: "O foolish men, and slow of heart to believe all that the prophets have spoken! Was it not necessary that Christ should suffer these things and enter into his glory? And beginning with Moses and all the prophets, he interpreted to them in all the scriptures the things concerning himself" (RSV, Luke 24:25-27).

The sermons of Peter, Stephen and Paul in Acts all assume the continuity of the Old Testament into the New.[120] The apostolic testimony in Acts is unanimous in asserting that there were prophecies in the Old Testament Scriptures that predicted Christ's suffering, death and subsequent glory. Both Peter and Paul held that apart from Christ there is no salvation. The great events of the New Testament were foreseen and foretold by the inspired writers of the Old Testament.[121]

From the viewpoint of historical Protestantism and that of the Lutheran Confessions, Bultmann has broken the unity of the Bible by making unnecessary the canon of the Old Testament. Concerning the importance of the Old Testament canon for Christian theology, Ernst G. Wright wrote:

To understand the meaning of Christ requires attention to the Christian *canon* of Scripture, for the Church' doctrines of both canon and Trinity place the person of Christ within a context of divine activity in history. The meaning and mode of this divine action is the central content of the canon of Scripture through which God is revealed as *our* God and in the form by which he would be known as our God.[122]

Braaten concluded his discussion of Bultmann's views on the Old Testament by asserting: "And thus the overarching unity of the Bible as medium of divine revelation is broken."[123] The Epitome of the Formula of Concord begins with the assertion: We believe, teach, and confess that the prophetic and apostolic writings of the Old and New Testaments are the only rule and norm according to which all doctrines and teachers alike must be appraised and judged, as it is written in Ps. 119:15, "Thy word is a lamp unto my feet and a light to my path."[124]

The evaluation in the preceding pages has concerned itself primarily with Bultmann's understanding of the Old Testament from what he calls *within*. It is here especially that the radicality of Bultmann's position has been evident. Due to the limitations of space, the essayist has not evaluated Bultmann's understanding from what the latter termed the *outside the* viewpoint of the school of comparative religions. Sandmel[125] and Albright[126] are two critical scholars who have challenged aspects of Bultmann's understanding of Old Testament history and religion. The essayist believes that the influence of Gunkel and Wellhausen are evident in Bultmann's interpretation of the Old Testament, and therefore the latter's views share the weaknesses that modern scholarship has detected in Wellhausianism.[127]

Summary

Henderson, in his sympathetic study of Rudolf Bultmann, has noted that in the latter's thought there is a "fundamental paradox and tension." Bultmann wants to be both evangelist and historian. "As an evangelist, he is constrained to proclaim the action of God. As an historian he cannot accept it as a causal factor in the scheme of things."[128] The Marburg sage's Old Testament understanding is likewise characterized by paradoxes and tensions. His existentialism, allied with his views on revelation, history and demythologization do not allow a Christian to find the God of our Lord Jesus Christ in the Old Testament. St. Paul asserted to his associate, Timothy, about the Old Testament Scripture that they were able to "make him wise unto salvation through faith which was in Christ Jesus" (2 Timothy 3:15). The necessity for belief in Christ's redemptive work, effected by His death on the cross and certified by His bodily resurrection, are unessential for Bultmann. This rejection strikes a deadly blow at the heart of the Gospel.

In the opinion of the Scandinavian scholar Lönning, Bultmann by his existentialism has initiated a third major assault on traditional Christianity and thus perpetuated the attacks begun earlier by rationalism and liberalism.[129] Bultmann's approach to and interpretation of the Old Testament, evaluated in terms of the criteria of historical Protestant hermeneutics and of those of the Lutheran Confessions, are deficient and erroneous. While Bultmann's position may not be quite as radical as that of Marcion in the second century, it cannot but have a negative effect on the attitude toward the Old Testament by those who follow the Marburg sage.

Footnotes

1. Rudolf Bultmann, "The Significance of the Old Testament for the Christian Faith," Bernard W. Anderson, ed. *The Old Testament and The Christian Faith* (New York: Harper & Row, Publishers, 1963), p. 8.
2. **Ibid.,** p. 12.
3. **Ibid.**
4. **Ibid.,** p. 31.
5. **Ibid.,**
6. **Ibid.,** p. 13.
7. Emil Kraeling, *The Old Testament Since the Reformation* (New York: Harper & Brothers, Publishers, 1955), pp. 229-230.
8. Bultmann, "The Significance of the Old Testament for the Christian Faith," Anderson, **op. cit.,** p. 12.
9. **Ibid.,** p. 20.; Rudolf Bultmann, "The Significance of Jewish Old Testament Tradition for the Christian West," *Essays Philosophical and Theological.* Translated by James C. G. Greig (New York: The Macmillan Company, 1955), p. 262.
10. Rudolf Bultmann, "Reply," Charles W. Kegley, ed. *The Theology of Rudolf Bultmann* (New York: Harper & Row, Publishers, 1966), p. 285.
11. Rudolf Bultmann, *Primitive Christianity in Its Contemporary Setting.* Translated by R. H. Fuller (New York: Meridian Books, 1956), p. 11.
12. Rudolf Bultmann, *The Presence of Eternity. History and Eschatology* (New York: Harper & Brothers, 1957), p. 18.
13. **Ibid.,** pp. 18-19.
14. **Ibid.,** pp. 19-23.
15. **Ibid.,** p. 20.
16. Bultmann, "The Significance of the Old Testament for the Christian Faith," Anderson, **op. cit.,** p. 30.
17. **Ibid.**
18. Bultmann, *Primitive Christianity in Its Contemporary Setting, op. cit.,* pp. 36-37.
19. **Ibid.,** *p.* 34.
20. **Ibid.,** p. 42.
21. **Ibid.,** p. 44.; Rudolf Bultmann, "Prophecy and Fulfillment," Claus Westermann, ed. *Essays on Old Testament Hermeneutics.* English Translation by James Luther Mays. (Richmond: John Knox Press), p. 69.
22. Bultmann, *Primitive Christianity and Its Contemporary Setting,* **op. cit.,** p. 44.
23. **Ibid.,** p. 45.
24. **Ibid.,** p. 15.
25. **Ibid.,** p. 16.
26. **Ibid.,** p. 17.
27. **Ibid.,** p. 23.
28. **Ibid.,** p. 24.
29. **Ibid.,** p. 26.
30. **Ibid.,** p. 46.
31. Rudolf Bultmann, "Der Mensch und seine Welt nach dem Urteil der Bibel," *Glauben und Verstehen.* Dritter Band. Zweite unveranderte Auflage (Tiibingen: J. C. B. Mohr [Paul Siebeck], 1960), p. 163.
32. **Ibid.,** p. 163.
33. Bultmann, *Primitive Christianity and Its Contemporary Setting,* **op. cit.,** p. 47.
34. **Ibid.,** pp. 50-51.
35. **Ibid.,** pp. 54-55.

36. **Ibid.,** p. 60.
37. **Ibid.,** p. 61.
38. **Ibid.,** p. 62
39. Part 2 will be based mainly on Bultmann's programmatic essay, "The Significance of the Old Testament for the Christian Faith," Anderson, **op. cit.,** pp. 8-35.
40. Bultmann, "The Significance of the Old Testament for the Christian Faith," *Anderson,* **op. cit.,** p. 11.
41. **Ibid.,** pp. 12-13.
42. **Ibid.,** p. 14.
43. **Ibid.,** p. 15.
44. **Ibid.,** p. 16.
45. **Ibid.,** p. 17
46. **Ibid.,** p. 17.
47. **Ibid.,** p. 18.
48. **Ibid.,** p. 20
49. **Ibid.,** pp. 20-21.
50. **Ibid.,** p. 21.
51. **Ibid.,** p. 22.
52. **Ibid.,** p. 23.
53. **Ibid.,** p. 24.
54. **Ibid.,** p. 27.
55. **Ibid.,** p. 28.
56. **Ibid.,** pp. 28-29.
57. **Ibid.,** p. 29.
58. **Ibid.,** p. 30.
59. **Ibid.,** p. 30.
60. **Ibid.,** p. 30.
61. **Ibid.,** p. 31.
62. **Ibid.,** p. 31.
63. **Ibid.,** p. 31.
64. **Ibid.,** p. 32.
65. **Ibid.,** p. 33.
66. Bultmann, "Prophecy and Fulfillment," Westermann, **op. cit.,** pp. 51-54.
67. **Ibid.,** p. 54.
68. **Ibid.,** p. 54.
69. **Ibid.,** p. 56.
70. **Ibid.,** p. 58
71. **Ibid.,** pp. 59-72.
72. **Ibid.,** pp. 62, 63, 67, 71.
73. Bultmann, *The Presence of Eternity,* **op. cit.,** p. 36.
74. Bultmann, "Prophecy and Fulfillment," Westermann, *op. cit.,* p. 73.
75. **Ibid.,** p. 74.
76. Bultmann, "The Significance of the Old Testament for the Christian Faith," Anderson, **op. cit.,** p. 33.
77. **Ibid.,** p. 34.
78. **Ibid.,** pp. 34-35.
79. Bultmann, *Primitive Christianity in Its Contemporary Setting,* **op. cit.,** p. 11.
80. Günther Bornkamm, "The Theology of Rudolf Bultmann," Kegley, **op. cit.,** p. 4.
81. Bultmann, "Reply," Kegley, **op. cit.,** p. 257.
82. Karl Barth, *Protestant Thought from Rousseau to Ritschl* (New York: Harper & Brothers, 1959), p. 330; Hugh Ross Mackintosh, *Types of Modern Theology* (London: Nisbet and Co. Ltd., 1949), p. 60.
83. Hans Joachim Kraus, *Geschichte der historisch-kritischen Forschung des Alten Testaments von der Reformation bis zur Gegenwart* (Neukirchen Kreis Moers: Verlag der Buchhandlung des Erziehungsvereins, 1956), pp. 176-177.
84. Alan Richardson, "Is the Old Testament the Propaedeutic to Christian Faith?,"

Anderson, *op cit.,* p. 36.

85. **Ibid.,** p. 37. Cf. also Alan Richardson, *The Bible in the Age of Science* (London: SCM Press, 1961), p. 113.

86. Richardson, "Is the Old Testament the Propaedeutic to Christian Faith?," Anderson, **op. cit.,** p. 38; Cf. also Alan Richardson, *History Sacred and Profane* (Philadelphia: The Westminster Press, 1964), pp. 118-121.

87. Richardson, "Is the Old Testament the Propaedeutic to Christian Faith?," Anderson, **op. cit.,** p. 38.

88. Karl Barth, *Church Dogmatics.* Volume III. *The Doctrine of Creation,* Part 2 (Edinburgh: T . & T. Clark, 1960), p. 446.

89. Paul Althaus, *Fact and Faith in the Kerygma of Today.* Translated by David Cairns (Philadelphia: Muhlenberg Press, 1959), p. 83.

90. Ernst Voegelin, "History and Gnosis," Anderson, **op. cit.,** pp. 64-65; Carl Braaten, *New Directions in Theology Today.* Volume II. *History and Hermeneutics* (Philadelphia: The Westminster Press, 1966), pp. 103-104.

91. Kraeling, **op. cit.,** p. 238.

92. Richardson, "Is the Old Testament the Propaedeutic to Christian Faith?," Anderson, **op. cit.,** pp. 39-40.

93. The quotation is from Hermann's *Verkehr des Christen mit Gott* (1886), p. 49. as quoted by A. E. Garvie, *The Ritchlian Theology* (Edinburgh: T . & T. Clark, 1899), p. 211.

94. F. Lichtenberger, *History of German Theology in the Nineteenth Century.* Translated and edited by Hastie (Edinburgh: T. & T. Clark, 1889), p. 580.

95. Richardson, *The Bible in the Age of Science,* **op. cit.,** p. 113.

96. Cf. the parallels adduced by Richardson in "Is the Old Testament the Propaedeutic to Christian Faith?," Anderson, **op. cit.,** pp. 42-43.; Richardson, *The Bible in the Age of Science,* **op. cit.,** pp. 113-114.

97. "Autobiographical Reflections of Rudolf Bultmann," Kegley, **op. cit.,** p. xxiv.

98. Bornkamm, "The Theology of Rudolf Bultmann," Kegley, *op. cit.,* pp. 4-5.

99. Cf. Edgar Primrose Dickie, "Dialectical Theology," in Lefferts A. Loetscher ed., *Twentieth Century Encyclopedia of Religious Knowledge* (Grand Rapids: Baker Book House, 1955), I, 335-336.

100. William Hordern, *New Directions in Theology Today. Volume I Introduction* (Philadelphia: The Westminster Press, 1966), p. 51.

101. Karl Barth, *Rudolf Bultmann-Bin Versuch ihn zu verstehen* (Zurich: Zollikon Evangelischer Verlag, 1952), p. 52.

102. Karl Jaspers and Rudolf Bultmann, *Myth and Christianity. An Inquiry into the Possibility of Religion without Myth* (New York: The Noonday Press, 1958), pp. 81-84.; John Macquarrie, *The Scope of Demythologization. Bultmann and His Critics* (New York: Harper & Row, Publishers, 1966), pp. 163-168.

103. Richardson, *History Sacred and Profane,* **op. cit.,** p. 139.

103a. James Barr, *Old and New in Interpretation* (New York: Harper & Row, Publishers, 1966), p. 175.

104. Oscar Cullmann, "The Connection of Primeval Events and End Events with the New Testament Redemptive History," Anderson, **op. cit.,** p. 122; Eric Voegelin, "History and Gnosis," Anderson, **op. cit.,** p. 72.

105. John Macquarrie, "Rudolf Bultmann," Dean G. Peerman and Martin E. Marty, eds. *A Handbook of Christian Theologians* (Cleveland and New York: Harper & Brothers, 1965), pp. 459-460.

106. Alan Richardson, *An Introduction to Theology of the New Testament* (New York: Harper & Brothers, 1958), p. 12.

107. Cf. Gordon H. Clark, "Bultmann's Historiography," Carl F. Henry, ed. *Jesus of Nazareth; Saviour and Lord* (Grand Rapids: William B. Eerdmans Publishing Company, 1966), pp. 213-224.

108. Friedebert Hohmeier, *Das Schrifeverständnis in der Theologie Rudolf Bultmanns* (Berlin und Hamburg: Lutherischer Verlagshaus, 1964), p. 132.

109. Ronald Hals, "The Problem of Old Testament Hermeneutics," *The Lutheran*

Quarterly, 13:99, May, 1961.

110. William Foxwell Albright, *History, Archaeology and Christian Humanism* (New York, Toronto and London: McGraw-Hill Book Company, 1964), pp. 277-278.

111. Wilhelm Vischer, "Everywhere the Scripture is About Christ," Anderson, **op. cit.,** p. 92.

112. Bultmann, "The Significance of the Old Testament for the Christian Faith," Anderson, **op. cit.,** p. 17.

113. Vischer, **op. cit.,** p. 93.

114. Ewald M. Plass, *What Luther Says. An Anthology* (St. Louis: Concordia Publishing House, 1959), II, p. 708.

115. Heinrich Bornkamm, *Luther und das Alte Testament* (Tubingen: J.C.B. Mohr [Paul Siebeck] 1948), p. 70.; Cf. also Kurt Fror, *Biblische Hermeneutik* (Miinchen: Chr. Kaiser Vef lag, 1964), p. 112.

116. Bultmann, "The Significance of the Old Testament for the Christian Faith," Anderson, **op. cit.,** p. 17.

117. Braaten, **op. cit.,** p. 123.

118. Theodore G. Tappert, *The Book of Concord* (Philadelphia: Muhlenberg Press, 1959), p. 562.

119. Walter Künneth, "Dare We Follow Bultmann?," *Christianity Today,* 6:28, October, 13, 1961.

120. Acts 2:14-36; 3:ll-26; 10:34-43; 13:16-41; 26:22-23; 28:23-24.

121. Luke 1:68-79; Romans 1:2-4; I Peter 1:10-12. G. Ernst Wright, "History and Reality: The Importance of Israel's

122. "Historical" Symbols for the Christian Faith," Anderson, **op. cit.,** p. 189.

123. Braaten, **op. cit.,** p. 125.

124. Tappert, **op. cit.,** p. 464.

125. Samuel Sandmel, "Bultmann on Judaism," Kegley, **op. cit.,** p. 219.

126. Albright, **op. cit.,** pp. 2 72-286. Herbert F. Hahn, "Wellhausen's Interpretation of Israel's Religious History: A Reappraisal of His Ruling Ideas," Joseph L. Blau, Arthur Hertzberg, Philip Friedman and Isaac Mendelsohn, eds. *Essays on Jewish Life and Thought* (New York: Columbia University Press, 1959), pp. 299-300.

127. Ian Henderson, *Rudolf Bultmann* (Richmond, Virginia: John Knox Press, 1966), p. 39.

128. Per Lonning, *The Dilemma of Contemporary Theology* (New York: Humanities Press, 1962), p. 126.

Editor's note: Bultmann had many supporters. See "German Theologian Rejected Christianity – Liberal Lutherans Still Praising Bultmann" on pp. 893-896 from the February 27, 1978 *Christian News*, *Christian News Encyclopedia*, p. 292.

Dietrich Bonhoeffer has been lauded by both of the seminaries of the "conservative" Lutheran Church-Missouri Synod and the president of the LCMS, Matthew Harrison, as the greatest Lutheran since Martin Luther. Bonhoeffer said he demythologized the Bible more than Bultmann (*Bonhoeffer and King*, edited by Herman Otten, p. 5). After he attended the Fourth Assembly of the Lutheran World Federation in Helsinki, Finland, in 1963, Kurt Marquart, in an editorial in the August 26, 1963 *Christian News*, reprinted in Volume IX, *Marquart's Works – Lutherans*, noted that the LWF was broad enough for Bultmann "who regards the substance of the Athanasian Creed as so much mythology."

The American Lutheran Publicity Bureau, held in high regard by the leaders of the LCMS, published and praised *Lively Stone – The Autobiography of Berthold von Schenk*. Von Schenk wrote that he held Bultmann in high regard and that he considered it an honor that Bultmann was present when he received his doctorate at the University of Marburg.

The LCMS clergyman says Bultmann was "greatly misunderstood" by conservative Lutherans. He wrote: "There are two ways to consider de-mythologizers like Rudolf Bultmann: one is to condemn him as one who dared to knock down our orthodox prejudices, the other is to rediscover the value of the myth. To speak of myths in the Bible is not to be critical of the Holy Book" (114).

"Bultmann Promoted Kloha's Position – LCMS Theologians May Teach Elizabeth Not Mary Said Magnificat" the lead story in the March 14, 2016 *Christian News,* noted that Bultmann said according to former LCMS Greek scholar William Arndt in 1956, that the text of Luke 1:46 teaches that Elizabeth and not Mary spoke the Magnificat. Jeffrey Kloha of Concordia Seminary in his "Elizabeth's Magnificat (Luke 1:46)," pages 200-219 of *Texts and Traditions: Essay in Honour of J. Keith Elliott* con-cludes: "Therefore, in the context of 1:39-56, Elizabeth is the character who sings the Magnificat" (p. 218). LCMS President Matthew Harrison, the Concordia Seminary, St. Louis faculty and Board of Regents insist Kloha is not guilty of any false doctrine.

"Conservative Fortnightly Pays Tribute To Bultmann's 'Positive Con-tribution'" a Religious News Service story in the August 8, 1975 *Christian News* noted that at Bultmann's 90th birthday Christianity Today com-mended Bultmann for his "positive contributions."

Christian News commented at the time:

Ed. While Bultmann claims to be a "Lutheran," it should be noted that his Christ is not the Christ of historic Christianity. Bultmann's Christ is not God and his Christ never rose from the dead. While Bultmann's the-ology leads to Hell, he has been highly praised by Lutheran moderates. "But even if we or an angel from heaven would bring you any other good news that what we brought you, a curse be on him!" Galatians 2:8. Pray that this great scholar will repent, repudiate all the blasphemy he has written and confess faith in the Risen Christ of the Bible before he dies.

Questions

1. Bultmann accepted the ____ hypothesis.
2. Bultmann began his history of the Old Testament with ____.
3. According to Bultmann creation ___ lie behind the creation accounts of Genesis 1 and 2.
4. What did Bultmann maintain about the immortality of the soul? ____
5. Bultmann rejected the ___ of Christ.
6. Bultmann accused New Testament writers of reading from or into ____ they already knew.
7. Bultmann breaks all revelational continuity between ____.
8. The Marburg sage denies the true revelatory character of ____.
9. Bultmann does not ascribe factuality to ____.
10. According to Bultmann, the Old Testament was ____ for the Chris-tian.
11. Is conscience an infallible guide? ____
12. Did Paul and Luther find the Gospel in the Old Testament? ____

German Theologian Rejected Christianity Liberal Lutherans Still Praising Bultmann

by Herman Otten
Christian News, February 27, 1978

Ed. This article shows that Dr. Raymond Surburg had valid cause to spend so much time exposing the anti-Christian theology of Rudolph Bultmann. Dr. Gerhard Forde, a leading Lutheran defender of Bultmann is highly regarded at Concordia Seminary, St. Louis and Concordia Seminary, Ft. Wayne, where Surburg taught ("Fordeites in Lutheranism" Christian News, May 26, 2014).

Dietrich Bonhoeffer wrote in his Letters and Papers from Prison: *"Bultmann did not go far enough in demythologizing the Bible. I go further."Concordia Seminary, Ft. Wayne, Indiana Professor William Weinrich frequently mentions the "Lutheran" scholar Bultmann in his* Concordia Commentary, John 1:1-7:1 *published by CPH and reviewed in the December 21, 2015 Christian News.*

Some of our critics contend that there is no real theological difference between Lutherans. They tell us that all Lutherans are in basic agreement on the doctrines that really count. We've been told that we never furnish any documentation to show that there is any serious theological disagreement among Lutherans.

For more than 15 years we have been photographing articles, essays, and reports by liberals to show just where they stand. Many of these articles have been reproduced in their entirety to show that we were not quoting out of context. We have quoted liberal Lutherans at considerable length. We have given them many pages of our paper to express themselves. A good number of our readers complain that we give liberals too much space.

Anyone who still wants evidence to show just how far Lutheran "moderates" have departed from historic Christianity should subscribe to such liberal Lutheran publications as *Dialog*, published quarterly by *Dialog* Inc., 2375 Como Ave., St. Paul, Minnesota 55108, $8.50. We have previously urged readers, who want evidence of theological liberalism in Lutheranism, to subscribe to Seminex's *Currents In Theology and Mission*.

Dr. Rudolph Bultmann is featured on the front cover of the Winter, 1978 *Dialog*. The five major articles in this issue praise Bultmann, a liberal Lutheran who denied the entire, historic Christian faith. Dr. Roy Harrisville of the ALC's Luther Seminary, St. Paul, writes that "Bultmann was attractive because he furnished me a good conscience respecting the uses of the historical-critical method, and in the wake of the tradition of Bengel and Schlatter (Heilsgeschlichtler!). Orthodoxy had taught me to fear the inconsistencies in the biblical record" (12).

Dr. Richard Jeske, a professor at the LCA's Lutheran Theological Seminary, Philadelphia, listed in the LCMS's *1978 Lutheran Annual* as a member of the LCMS clergy, agrees in his *Dialog* article on Bultmann with David L. Edwards that "no greater New Testament scholar ever lived" than

Bultmann. The LCMS theologian writes in *Dialog*: "More than any other exegetical theologian of his time and before him, he has insured the place of biblical scholarship in contemporary discussion, moving it from an auxiliary science to center stage.. . That the present situation in the theology is called 'post-Bultmannian' is no insignificant tribute.

"It is also true that Bultmann's intention in every aspect of his life's work was to serve the Church of Jesus Christ. It is tragically ironic that many non-Christians could see this more clearly than many Christians" (26).

Dr. Gerhard O. Forde of the ALC's Luther Theological Seminary, St. Paul, writes in his tribute to Bultmann: "In my student days there was a story making the rounds about the theological bells of Germany. The first bell, it was said, rang in deep and heavy tones: BULT-MANN! BULT-MANN! BULT-MANN! The second was a more cheery and clear tenor: Karl-Barth! Karl-Barth! Karl-Barth! And the third was a tiny treble tinkle: schlink! schlink! schlink! The story turned out to be more prophetic than was intended. For when all is said and done, it is perhaps 'the Bultmann bell' with its ponderous and menacing tones that has echoed through the halls and rattled the windows of theological academia most persistently. It was the Bultmann bell that tolled for many of us the death-knell of the old ways and still threatens to drown us out when we try to say something that is supposed to be 'relevant' to the 'modern world.'

"Who can forget those imperious words spoken with such Olympian finality in the Essay 'New Testament and Mythology?'

"It is impossible to use electric lights and the wireless and avail ourselves of modern medical and surgical discoveries and at the same time to believe in the New Testament world of demons and spirits.

"... All our thinking today is shaped for good or ill by modern science. A blind acceptance of the New Testament mythology would be irrational, and to press for its acceptance as an article of faith would be to reduce Christian faith to the level of human achievement...

"... The only honest way of reciting the creeds is to strip the mythological framework from the truth they enshrine—that is, assuming that they contain any truth at all, which is just the question theology has to ask.

"... There is no longer any heaven in the traditional sense of the word... The mythological eschatology is untenable for the simple reason that the parousia of Christ never took place as the New Testament expected."

The ALC professor indicates that he is in basic accord with what Bultmann says in these radical anti-Christian statements. Professor Forde writes in *Dialog*: "In the first instance, he took us away. He took us away from our cherished ways of thinking in things theological. He woke us from our 'dogmatic slumbers.' He made us aware of what we have learned to call, rather glibly, 'the problem of communications.' Many of us had already gone through the trauma of being weaned from the world views about verbal inerrancy and were only beginning to stammer the new language of Heilsgeschichte, ' revelation in history,' 'truth as encounter,' and all that. It was bad enough to be told the 'facts' we had learned in Sunday School could no longer be supported by an inerrant scripture and needed new warrant by finding their place in the scheme of Heilsgeschichte. But suddenly to be told that the 'facts' themselves were suspect or maybe even irrelevant because they were couched in an outmoded language was the straw that almost broke the camel's back and indeed did for many, as contemporary theology bears eloquent witness.

"Bultmann was a shock treatment for a theology already showing signs of rigor mortis. For many of us Heilsgeschichte was at best a half-way house — good, but not a place one could stay entirely or for long. Bultmann made that clear- though many have yet to learn that lesson. And for those who could take the shock and stay to listen, Bultmann taught many valuable things. He did tell us something about what communicating the Gospel means."

The ALC professor, who is highly praised and defended by the officials of the ALC, says that "Bultmann took us away from the old ways of thinking and speaking. He shattered the chains that had bound us to those old ways. His influence was and still is vast" (28).

The ALC professor concludes: "For my own part, one things seems certain. The basic difficulty with Bultmann's theological program, aside from the critical excesses, is that he did not go far enough. Like just about everybody before him, he thought we still had something going for us. In his case, it was the possibility of 'authentic existence.' He thought he could translate the message into these terms, into that 'something' we still have going for us. In that he did nothing more or less than virtually every theology before – and since. But the truth lies, I think, in realizing at last that we haven't anything going for us: I expect that is what the New Testament is trying to tell us. It is our myth that needs finally to be excised so that Word can save us. Somehow we have to learn how to say that" (30).

Dr. Robert Scharlemann of The Lutheran Church-Missouri Synod is the author of "The Systematic Structure of Bultmann's Theology" in the Winter, 1978 *Dialog*. Robert Scharlemann already in the Spring, 1962 *Dialog* defended Bultmann's view of the resurrection of Christ. Bultmann rejects any real physical resurrection. Robert Scharleman wrote in the Spring, 1962 *Dialog* that "it is possible to conceive that the corpse of Jesus decayed in the grave and that the bones are still there, but that Jesus Christ is at the same time truly resurrected." The LCMS theologian, who was defended by officials of the LCMS when he wrote his *Dialog* article in 1962, said that "The fear of Bultmann's critics that he is dissolving the historically factual exactly parallels the fear of Luther's critics that he was eliminating all morally responsible action."

LCA, ALC, and LCMS liberals continue to praise Bultmann and refer to him as a great Lutheran theologian even though Bultmann rejected the Christian faith. The LCA's Fortress Press published and highly commended Bultmann's *The Johannine Epistles*. The ALC's *Luther Theological Seminary Review* (Fall, 1973) praised this Bultmann book. The December, 1965 *Seminarian* of Concordia Seminary, St. Louis (before the "Exodus") lauded Bultmann's entire demythologizing approach and said that Bultmann "has set the direction which theology must follow if it is to be faithful to its calling. His demand for demythologizing is not only legitimate, it is necessary if the Gospel is to have a place in our time."

Did Rudolph Bultmann accept historic Christianity?

Bultmann claimed that "It is an error to think that the Apostles' Creed is a dogma that the Christian must hold to be true. Faith is not the mere acceptance of certain facts of salvation." "One can say that Jesus is risen in the same manner as Goethe, if one views Jesus' person and work as a phenomenon of cultural history. For the persons and works of great men remain effective in cultural history, and that goes for Jesus, too." "That the reports of a bodily resurrection of Jesus are legends, in my view is correct." "I personally think that the recitation of the creed in the church service should be renounced altogether" (*Christianity and Crisis*, November 14, 1966).

Bultmann says in his *Jesus And The Word* that "I do indeed think that we can know almost nothing concerning the life and personality of Jesus" (Charles Scribner's & Sons, p. 8).

Dr. Walter Maier, Jr. is correct when he observes in his *Form Criticism Reexamined* that "If, for example, the physical resurrection of Jesus from the dead did not actually take place, as Bultmann avers, all belief in Jesus Christ as Savior is useless; ..." (CPH, 1973, 33).

While some liberal Roman Catholic scholars support Bultmann, Father John Steinmueller writes in his *A Companion To Scripture Studies*, Vol. III: "Bultmann's thinking, it should be made clear, demolishes Christianity completely ... He rejects the fall of man, celestial beings, the doctrine of the atonement, the resurrection and ascension, heaven and hell" (Lumen Christi Press, 1969, 24).

Dr. Roy Harrisville of the ALC tells in *Dialog* how highly impressed and thrilled he was when he had a personal visit with Bultmann.

But even such a liberal theologian as Nels Ferre, who rejects the virgin birth of Christ and other basic doctrines of Christianity, writes in a report of a conversation he had with Bultmann: "One question was that of life eternal or life after death. I know that Dr. Bultmann refused to accept this as an aspect of his faith. I kept urging him, 'Is it not possible for us, at least in a classical Christian sense, to accept life after death in some genuine way as part and parcel of the Christian faith?'

"He puffed harder and harder on his pipe. Friends had told me that I had better not try his patience too much or he would show me the door, and that the pipe was a warning signal. But I persisted, 'Dr. Bultmann, don't you really think that — putting aside your understanding of science, the modern mood, existentialism and all the rest — eternal life really is part of the Christian faith?' He said, 'No.' Then he added, 'But of course you can always hope. A person can hope anything'" (*The Extreme Center*, Waco, Texas: Word Books, 1973, 178-180). It appears as if Harrisville almost worships Bultmann when he tells about his visit with him.

The LCA, ALC, and AELC all permit their theologians to express basic agreement with Bultmann and his radical anti-Christian theology. We suggest that when LCMS theologians enter into fellowship discussion with theologians from the LCA, ALC and AELC they get into the real issues by asking questions about the kind of radical theology found in *Dialog*, *Currents In Theology and Mission, Lutheran Quarterly*, etc. They should, for example, ask whether the LCA-ALC-AELC will officially allow theologians to defend the anti-scriptural theology of Bultmann. The LCA-ALC-AELC should be asked if there will be any repudiation of the rank liberalism by LCA-ALC theologians found in *Dialog* and elsewhere. It appears to us that many discussions will be simply a waste of time and money unless the matter of just what kind of theology is going to be tolerated in the LCA-ALC-AELC is taken up.

If the representatives of the LCA-ALC-AELC mention in their defense that such liberals and Bultmann defenders on the staff of *Dialog* as Richard Jeske and Robert Scharlemann are still LCMS theologians, LCMS representatives will have to admit that this is true. Hopefully officials of the LCMS will read *Dialog* and take some firm action against all those liberals in the LCMS who still praise the radical theology of Rudolph Bultmann and other skeptics. There is room for the anti-Christian theology of Bultmann in the territorial and state churches of Europe, the Lutheran World Federation, the LCA, ALC, and AELC. Honest liberals still in the LCMS should leave and join one of these liberal churches.

From St. Luke The Evangelist (Oct. 18) to St. Andrew's Day (Nov. 30)

Christian News, October 29, 1984

Concerning St. Luke there is little information. Luke, "the beloved physician," is supposed to have been one of the seventy and possibly the unnamed companion of Cleophas on Easter afternoon's walk to Emmaus.[1] Luke is mentioned three times in the New Testament: Colossians 4:14; Philemon 24; II Timothy 4:11. In Colossians 4:10,14 Luke is distinguished from the men of the circumcision. Nevertheless, W.F. Albright has argued from the Aramaic form of his name in Greek and the Hebrew idioms in three poems of Luke in chapters 1-2 of the Third Gospel that Luke was a converted Jew.[2] Tradition has it that he was originally a pagan, who was born in Antioch in Syria. He was an early convert to Christianity. Paul referred to him as "the beloved physician (Col. 4:14)" and he became a friend and companion of Paul, and Luke's Gospel is spoken of as the Pauline Gospel, just as the Gospel of Mark is referred to as the petrine Gospel. It has been suggested that Luke may have been left in charge of the church at Philippi between Paul's second and third missionary journeys, and it is believed that Luke may have been with Paul during his two imprisonments, the one at Caesarea and the first Roman incarceration. Luke has been credited by conservative Biblical scholars with the authorship of the Third Gospel and the Book of Acts. This would mean that Luke and Acts are the only books, if the view of Albright is not accepted, of the twenty-seven books of the New Testament, not to have been written under the guidance of the Holy Spirit by men of Hebrew descent.

Luke obviously was a talented man, and a man of education and culture. Tradition claims that Luke was a painter. Reed remarked about this aspect of Luke's life: "His Gospel with its large number of parables and its poetic imagery certainly reveals an unusual appreciation of beauty."[3]

After the New Testament era Luke is said to have proclaimed the Good News in Bithynia in Asia Minor and lived to the age of 84. There is no information about his death and burial, although one tradition places his death and burial at Thebes.[4]

Luke's life was commemorated for the first time in the East. Luke's relics were supposedly found and translated along with those of St. Andrew to Constantinople and deposited in the Church of the apostles on March 3, A.D. 357.[5] It was only in the eighth century that Luke's Commemoration Day appears. Luke was the last of the evangelists to be honored with a feast at Rome and this was the case until the tenth century. October 18, the date for Luke in all the calendars, may also be his death day.[6]

In iconography St. Luke is represented by an ox with an ox lying near, with paints and palette; also as a physician.

In *The Lutheran Hymnal* the appointed Scriptures are: the Epistle: 2 Timothy 4:5-15; the Gospel: Luke 10:1-9.[7] In *Lutheran Worship*, in the One-Year Series (ABC): Old Testament: Psalm 138; Isaiah 43:8-13; or Isaiah 34:5-8; the Epistle: 2 Timothy 4:5-11; the Gospel; Luke 1:1-4; 24:44-53.[8]

The Collect in *Lutheran Worship* reads: "Almighty God, whose blessed Son called Saint Luke the physician to be an evangelist and physician of the soul, grant that the healing medicine of your Word and the sacraments may put to flight the diseases of our souls that with willing hearts we may ever love and serve you; through Jesus Christ, your Son, our Lord, who lives and reigns with joy and the Holy Spirit, one God, now and forever."[9]

The Collect in *The Lutheran Hymnal* is much shorter and speaks only of spiritual healing effected by the wholesome medicine of Thy Word.[10]

Horatio Bolton Nelson in his hymn: "By All Your Saints in Warfare," wrote about St. Luke, the Evangelist:

For that beloved physician
All praise to God show,
The healer of the nations,
The one who shares our woes.
Your wine and oil, O Savior
 Upon our spirits pour.
And with true balm of Gilead
Anoint us evermore.[11]

St. Simon and St. Jude, Apostles (October 28)

The association of these two Apostles may be due to the fact that they are paired together in Luke 4:14-16 and in Acts 1:12,13. There is a tradition which depicts Simon preaching in Egypt, Cyrene and Mauritania, while Jude is said to have raised a family after being married, but to have accompanied Simon. Another tradition portrays the two Apostles as going to Persia, where they labored thirteen years in missionary work and are alleged to have been martyred in the city of Suanir at the same time. According to tradition their martyrdom occurred on July 1. A third tradition identifies Jude with Thaddeus and places his work for Christ and the activity of Simon as taking place in Armenia.[13]

In the West their day of remembrance dates back to the ninth century although why October 28 was selected is not known.[14]

The Scripture selection for Saints Simon and Jude in *The Lutheran Hymnal* are: The Epistle: 1 Peter 1:3-9 and the Gospel: John 15:17-21.[15] In *Lutheran Worship*, in the One-Year Series the texts are: Old Testament: Psalm 119:89-96; Deuteronomy 32:1-4; the Epistle: 1 Peter 1:3-9; the Gospel: John 15:17-21; in the Three-Year Series; Old Testament: Psalm 119:3-80; Jeremiah 26 (1-6) 7-10, the epistle I John 4:1-6 and the Gospel John 14:21-27.[16]

The Collect in *Lutheran Worship* reads: "O Almighty God, whose Church is built on the foundation of the apostles and prophets, Jesus Christ Himself the chief Corner Stone, grant us to be joined together in unity of spirit by their doctrine that we may be made a holy temple acceptable in your sight, through Jesus Christ, your Son, our Lord, who lives and reigns with you and the Holy Spirit one God, now and forever."[17] The Collect in *The Lutheran Hymnal* is like the Introit and other Propers for St. Simon and Jude, those appointed for Evangelists, Apostles' and Martyrs' Days.[18]

Horatio Bolton Nelson in his hymn: "By All Your Saints in Warfare," wrote about St. Simon and St. Jude, Apostles:

Praise, Lord, for your apostles
Who sealed their faith today;
One love, one hope impelled them
To tread the sacred way.
May we with zeal as earnest
The faith of Christ maintain.[19]

Reformation Day (October 31)

This is the only festival of the Second Semester of the Year of our Lord, which is peculiar to the Lutheran Church. On this day, the nailing of 95 Theses to the Church door of Wittenberg by Luther is observed. Reed has stated about this day of remembrance: "The Lutheran Liturgy is unique among the churches of the world in appointing a Festival of the Reformation."[20] This festival, which the *Common Service Book* (LCA) regards as of major rank, may be traced back to the annual commemoration in domestic circles of the translation of the Bible into the German language.[21]

All Saints Day (Nov. 1) was a holy day of obligation and so Luther knew that all the faithful would be attending the service and would be bound to hear his theses. The professor of Biblical Theology of the University of Wittenberg did not dream that these theses would set into motion events, which would eventually result in the formation of a new Church and be the creator of a large division of Christendom. Splitting the Church was the farthest thing from Luther's mind. He was optimistic that reforms could be introduced into the Church of Rome, since before his time a number of Reform Councils had actually met, which aimed at doing for the Church what Luther had in mind, namely, to remove the corruptions that had crept into the Church. Even after 1521, Luther wished merely to maintain evangelical Christianity in the Catholic Church. Horn believed that Luther would have objected to the introduction into the Church Calendar of a Festival of the Reformation, both because it would have given the Lutheran Church the appearance of newness, and because it would not have contributed to the reconciliation of Christendom.[22]

The Festival of the Reformation was observed in the sixteenth century, but only six of the hundreds of church orders had a provision for such a celebration, and not all agreed what the nature of the commemoration should be, or when Reformation Day should be held.[23]

Bugenhagen placed a Reformation celebration in the orders for Brunswick (1528), Hamburg (1529), and Luebeck (1531).[24] The next reference to a Reformation observance occurred in 1563 by Elector Joachim and in Pomerania in 1568. The Pomeranian Church Order designated a festival for St. Martin's Day to commemorate Luther's birth, November 10, 1483.[25] Some Lutheran Orders chose Trinity Sunday, thus following the bright day of the Christian Church on Pentecost. Still others set the Reformation Festival after the Nativity of John the Baptist (June 24), since the Augsburg Confession was promulgated June 24, 1530. Both these early observances died out or were obliterated by the Thirty Years War, a war in which the Roman Church made a final attempt to wipe out in the north, European Protestantism. Gustavus Adolphus, "Lion of the North," at the Battle of Leutzen (1632) saved the cause of the Reformation or of Protestantism,[26] although it was in that same battle that Gustavus Adolphus lost his life.

In 1667 John George II, Elector of Saxony, ordered a Festival of Reformation to be observed on October 31st.[27] During the 17th and 18th centuries the observance of a Reformation Festival on October 31 spread and was customarily observed on the Sunday closest to October 31st.[28] When the Evangelical Synod of Missouri, Ohio, and other states was organized in 1847 in Chicago, and in its first hymnal, October 31 was designated as Reformation Day. In 1957 Horn claimed that in the 1950's Reformation Day was also sponsored by The National Council of Churches of Christ in the United States.[29]

In *The Lutheran Hymnal* the suggested selections are: The Epistle: Revelation 14:6-7; the Gospel: Matthew 1:12-15.[30] In *Lutheran Worship*: suggested Readings in the One Year Series are: Old Testament: Psalm 46; Isaiah 53:1-11; Revelation 14:6-7; the Gospel: Matthew 11:12-15. For the Three-Year series (ABC): Old Testament: Psalm 46; Jeremiah 31:31-34; The Epistle: Romans 3:19-28; John 8:31-36.[31]

The Collect is essentially the same in *The Lutheran Hymnal* and *Lutheran Book of Worship*, and reads: "Almighty God, gracious Lord, pour out your Holy Spirit on your faithful people. Keep them steadfast in your grace and truth, protect and comfort them in all temptations, defend them against all enemies of your Word, and bestow on the Church your saving peace, through Jesus Christ, you Son, our Lord, who lives and reigns with you and the Holy Spirit one God, now and forever.[32]

All Saints Day (November 1)
The primitive Church provided a day for the remembrance of all martyrs. In the fourth century May 13 was chosen for the Festival of All Saints.[33] This date was adopted in the West when the Roman Pantheon was rebuilt and dedicated to St. Mary and All Martyrs, May 13, 610.[34] Originally the Pantheon had been built by Agrippa in 27 B.C., but by the seventh century A.D., the cost of keeping this building in shape and repair was considered by the government to be burdensome, and in view of that fact the Emperor gave the Pantheon to Pope Boniface IV.[35]

In the eighth century Pope Gregory III (731-741) dedicated a chapel to St. Peter and to "all apostles, martyrs, confessors and all just and perfect who are at rest." In A.D. 835 Pope Gregory IV 9287-844) shifted the date of "All Saint's Day" from May 13 to November 1. The festival attracted a large numbers to Rome and because of the food supply in the eternal city was inadequate in May, it is believed that that was the reason for the change from May 13 to November 1.[36]

The early English name for All Saints was "All Hallows," that is, "All Holies."[37] It is from this name for the proceeding day, Halloween, or Even of All Hallows, October 31, is derived. Gwynne, wrote about All Hallows as follows: "It is evident that the adaption of a festival was a national instinct of the human heart and its needs, a day which would not be confined to the remembrance of the great Saints and Martyrs of the whole Catholic Church or of national or local Churches but of all those devout and unnamed or unknown servants of God who "have departed this life in His faith and fear."[38] the purpose of All Saints was plainly to give to every individual Christian opportunity to remember his own holy dead as still "living unto God" in Paradise, still members of the One Holy Catholic and Apostolic Church, the Communion of Saints, "No longer trammeled and fettered, compelled to fight for every life in an enemy's country, but free to work as they never were in the days of their earthly existence."[39]

All Saints Day through the centuries became exceedingly popular with pilgrims. After the Reformation the Lutherans (in many parts of Germany and in Scandinavia), like the Anglicans continued to observe All Saints, but rejected All Souls Day because it was concerned with the souls of purgatory.[40]

In *The Lutheran Hymnal*, the suggested Readings are: The Epistle: Revelation 7:2-17; the Gospel: Matthew 5:1-12.[41] *Lutheran Worship* has no appointed reading for All Saints Day.[42]

The Collect in *The Lutheran Hymnal* reads: "O almighty God, who has knit together Thine elect in one communion, and fellowship in the mystical body of Thy Son Jesus Christ, our Lord. Grant us grace so to follow Thy blessed saints in all virtues and godly living that we may come to those unspeakable joys which Thou hast prepared for those who unfeignedly love thee, through Jesus Christ, Thy Son our Lord, who liveth etc."[43] The Collect in *Lutheran Worship* is essentially the same.[44]

Lutheran Worship contains a number of hymns to be sung in commemoration of the saved dead Christians. Hymn 195 "For All Your Saints, O Lord" and others are suitable for use on All Saints' Day.

Commemoration of the Faithful Departed (November 2)

The Lutheran Hymnal does not list November 2 as a minor day for observation by the devout Lutheran Christian. However, *Lutheran Worship*[45] has included November 2 as a new day of observation. Neither Horn nor Reed list this day as one for Lutherans to commemorate. *Lutheran Book of Worship* does not have November 2 as a minor festival.[46]

In the Roman Catholic Church, November 2, is known as All Souls Day, a commemoration which does not appear before the ninth century A.D.[47] An English liturgical authority claims that "under the special impetus supplied by the reported vision of a pilgrim from Jerusalem, who declared that he had seen the tortures of souls suffering purgatorial fire, that this observance made headway."[48]

November 2, as observed in the Roman Catholic Church, perpetuates the unscriptural teachings concerning purgatory,[49] according to the *Catechismus Romanus* purgatory is defended as: "Besides (hell) there is a fire of purification, when the souls of the pious, after having been tortured for a set time, are purified, so that the entry into the eternal fatherland, into which nothing impure, can be opened unto them."[50] The Council of Trent has decreed: "That there is a purgatory and that the souls there detained are helped by the suffrages of the faithful, but principally by the acceptable sacrifice of the altar."[51]

Concerning the doctrine of purgatory Stump asserted: "Through this fire they are to be finally purified from those sins for which they have not done adequate penance on earth. Connected with this doctrine is the practice of saying mass and offering prayers for the dead, so that their stay in purgatory may be shortened. The attempt is made to prove the existence of purgatory from such passages as 1 Cor. 3:11-15; Matt. 5:26; 12:32; Luke 12:10; 16:9; 1 John 5:16-17; Mal. 3:2 and the Apocryphal passage, I Macc. 12:39-46. Not only does the doctrine of a purgatory have no basis in Scripture, but it is in conflict with the doctrine of salvation by faith alone and with that of the sufficiency of Christ's atoning merit. It implies that God has forgiven some sins, but not others, while in reality forgiveness is the forgiveness of the person, and is either complete or non-existent.[52]

In views of the false doctrine promulgated on November 2, one wonders why November 2 should at all be remembered even though in *Lutheran Worship* the name of the 2nd of November has been changed Commemoration of the faithful. Is that not precisely what the purpose of November 1st is? The New Lectionary System adopted by Lutherans, Methodists, Reformed and Roman Catholics to emphasize the unity of these churches is belied by false doctrines that permeate the Roman Church and is reflected in its church festivals and days of remembrance. Among Protestants, those whose theology has become, liberal, who deny the Trinity, the deity of Christ, the vicarious atonement, the Virgin Birth, the corporeal resurrection of Christ, a literal ascension of Christ into heaven as well as a real-to-be-seen second coming of Christ, how can the mere observance of the same Church year, establish a true Church of Christ, who said that only "When we continue in His Word are we His disciples indeed." All depends how the Scriptural readings of the Church Year are interpreted.

Lutheran Worship has no suggested Reading for November 1, but strangely for November 2 has the following appointed Readings: For the One-Year Series: Old Testament; Psalm 34:1-9; Isaiah 35;3-30; The Epistle: 2 Peter 3:8-14; John 5:24-29 and for the Three Year Series: None.[53]

The Collect for November 2 is: "Almighty God, in whose glorious presence live all who depart in the Lord and before Whom all souls of the faithful who are delivered of the burden of the flesh are in joy and felicity, we give you hearty thanks for your loving kindnesses to all your servants who have finished their course in faith and now rest from their labors, and we humbly beseech your mercy that we, together with all who have departed in the saving faith, may have our perfect consummation and bliss, in both body and soul, in your eternal and everlasting glory; through Jesus Christ our Lord, who lives and reigns with you and the Holy Spirit, one God, now and forever."[54] This is one of the longest Collects in *Lutheran Worship*.

Festival of Harvest (Date Selected by Congregation)

Reed claims that The Festival of Harvest is another unique day in the Lutheran Church Calendar.[55] The Roman Catholic Church observed three Rogation Days-Monday, Tuesday and Wednesday before Ascension Day-with penitential processional litanies followed by a mass for which special propers are provided to implore God's forgiveness and invoke His blessings upon the fruits of the earth.[56] The American Episcopal Prayer Book (not the English) also recognized the Rogation Days, eliminating the Penitential features, and appointed for the harvest festival proper Lessons and a special collect.[57]

According to Reed, the Lutheran Harvest Festival is of a different character. It definitely is a thanksgiving of the fruits of the earth and is observed according to local appointment usually on a Sunday after the harvests have been gathered.[58] A number of Lutheran Church Orders of the sixteenth century, such as Calenberg, 1542; Osnabrueck, 1543; Hildesheim, 1544; Prussia 1558, combined the Festival of Harvest with the Feast of St. Michael. Still other Lutheran Church Orders specified the Sunday either before or after St. Michael's Feast. Again others do not specify a Sunday but simply direct that this festival should be held annually.[59]

In England August 1 (St. Peter's Chains) was Lamma (Loaf Mass) and a thanksgiving for the wheat harvest.[60] Die Evangelische Kirche in Deutschland, reflecting present German custom, has provided for a Harvest Festival (German: Erntedankfest) the first Sunday after Michelmas, except when the Sunday falls on the last Sunday in September, it is celebrated the first Sunday of October.[61] In rural America even in non-liturgical churches a harvest home festival is often observed.[62]

The practice of holding a festival of harvest home has Old Testament Biblical precedent. Among ancient Hebrews, Pentecost was celebrated as a harvest festival. The Feast of Booths (or Tabernacles) which was held in September (Hebrew: Tishri) was a thanksgiving for the harvest of grapes and olives, as Pentecost had been for grain. Later in Europe, the fall Ember days (after September 14) most likely took the place of the Roman harvest festival.

The Lutheran Hymnal gives as Scriptural Lections: Old Testament: Deuteronomy 26:1-11, and The Gospel Luke 12: 13-21.[63] *Lutheran Worship* suggests for the One-Year Series: Old Testament: Psalm 67; Malachi 3:10-12; the Epistle 2 Corinthians 9:6-15; Luke 12:13-21 as the Gospel. For the Three-Year Series: ABC: Deuteronomy 26:1-11; 2 Corinthians

9:6-15; Matthew 13:24-30 (36-45).[64] The *Lutheran Hymnal* and *Lutheran Worship*, each has a different Collect for Harvest Home Festival. The Collect for the observance of Harvest Festival according to The *Lutheran Hymnal* is: "Almighty God most merciful Father, who openest Thy hand and satisfieth the desire of every living thing, we give Thee most humble and hearty thanks that Thou has crowned the fields with Thy blessing and hast permitted us once more to gather in the fruits of the earth: as we beseech Thee to bless and protect the living seed of Thy Word sown in our hearts that in the plenteous fruits of righteousness we may always present in Thee an acceptable thank-offering through Jesus Christ our Lord, who liveth, etc."[65]

A Day of General or Special Thanksgiving or National Thanksgiving

Thanksgiving is uniquely an American Day established by the proclamation of governors of States and the President of the United States. Thanksgiving Day is observed the fourth Thursday in November. In 1621 after the first harvest, a Day of Thanksgiving was proclaimed by the Pilgrims.[66] By 1680 Thanksgiving had been observed as a festival in Massachusetts Bay Colony.[67] George Washington in 1789 proclaimed Thursday November 26 a Day of Thanksgiving. In 1795 George Washington appointed a Day of Thanksgiving and Prayer as a day for the benefit and welfare of the Nation. At the end of the War of 1812, James Madison proclaimed a national day of prayer and thanksgiving. In 1863 President Lincoln appointed an annual day of prayer and thanksgiving, a practice followed by each succeeding occupant of the White House. The date is usually the last Thursday of November.[68]

In Canada Thanksgiving day this year will be observed on Monday October 8th.

The *Lutheran Hymnal* has as Readings for Thanksgiving: The Epistle: 1 Timothy 2:1-8 and as the Gospel: Luke 17:11-19.[69] In *Lutheran Worship*, in the One-Year Series the following are appointed Scriptural Selection: Old Testament: Psalm 68; Isaiah 61:10-11; The Epistle: 1 Timothy 2:1-4; The Gospel: Luke 17:11-19 or Matthew 6:24-34. In the Three-Year Series, ABC: Psalm 65; Deuteronomy 8:1-10; Philippians 4:6-20 or 1 Timothy 2:1-4; The Gospel: Luke 17:11-19.[70]

The Collects in The *Lutheran Hymnal* and in *Lutheran Worship* are nearly word for word the same. In The *Lutheran Hymnal* the Collect reads: "Almighty God, our heavenly Father, whose mercies are new unto us every morning and who, though we have in no wise deserved Thy goodness, dost abundantly provide for all our wants of body and soul, we pray Thee, Thy Holy Spirit that we may heartily acknowledge Thy merciful goodness toward us, give thanks for all Thy benefits, and serve Thee in willing obedience, through Jesus Christ, Thy Son, our Lord who liveth etc.[71]

Mission Festival

Both the *Lutheran Hymnal*[72] and *Lutheran Worship*[73] have Propers for a special day or service: MISSION FESTIVAL. Mission festivals are held at different times during the Church Year. In many communities in the Lutheran Church-Missouri Synod, mission festivals have been and are held during the summer months and during the fall season. Missionaries on furlough, or pastors especially involved in missionary programs of the Synod or District, often are the speakers.

The word "evangelism" and what it stands for has become very popular in Lutheran circles and a great amount of effort has been and is being expanded in fostering evangelism in congregations,[74] thus making the winning of people for Christ a year-long activity. The missionary message of the Bible lends itself for emphasis in connection with a number of different Sundays in the various seasons of the Church Year. Epiphany, Christmas, Easter, Pentecost are naturals for the missionary obligation placed by Christ upon His followers.

Both the Old Testament and the New Testaments are replete with exhortations and admonitions and encouragements to proclaim the religion of the true God. The Gradual for Mission Sunday: "I will praise you, O Lord, among the nations, I will sing of you among the peoples, For great is your love, higher than the heavens, your faithfulness reaches to the skies (Psalm 108:3-4)" sets forth the obligation to make known the religion of the true God to the nations. Again the words of the Introit: "Declare his glory among the nations, his marvelous deeds among the people" (Psalm 96:4,9,10), do the same thing.

The New Testament contains many passages which encourage and command the spreading of the Gospel. The Great Commission has always been recognized as a duty revolving on Christ's followers (Matthew 28:20; Acts 1:8). Unfortunately in our day what is involved in doing missionary work and being an evangelist has been watered down or reinterpreted by modern theological liberalism. This is especially true when it comes to winning Jews, Mohammedans, Buddhists and Hindus for Christ's kingdom. The whole church needs to realize that only Christ is "the way, the truth and the life" and that no person can be saved apart from faith in the atoning work of Christ. What Peter declared to the Jewish leaders in the thirties of the First Christian century is true today, namely, "that there is no salvation in any other name given under heaven by which people can be saved (Acts 4:12)."

The *Lutheran Hymnal* gives as suggested Scriptural Lections: The Epistle: Romans 10:8-10 or Isaiah 12:2-4; 42:1-12; 49:1-6 and as the Gospel: Matthew 9:35-38; Mark 4:26-32.[75]

Lutheran Worship has as its recommended Readings for the one year series: The Old Testament Psalm 96; Isaiah 2:1-3 The Epistle: Romans 10:8b-17; The Gospel: Luke 14:16-24: The Three-Year Series: (ABC): Psalm 96, Isaiah 62:1-7; Romans 10:11-17; Luke 22:44-53.[76]

The Collect for Mission School in *Lutheran Worship* reads: "Almighty God, since you have called your Church to witness that in Christ you reconciled us to yourself, grant that by your Holy Spirit we may proclaim the good news of your salvation that all who hear it may receive the gift of salvation through Jesus Christ, our Lord, who lives and reigns with you and the Holy Spirit, one God, now and forever."[77]

A Day of Humiliation and Prayer (*Lutheran Hymnal*)
A Day of Supplication and Prayer (*Lutheran Worship*)

Both the *The Lutheran Hymnal*[78] and *Lutheran Book of Worship*[79] suggest a Sunday, when a church or for that matter the entire Synod, could observe a day of Humiliation by confessing personal as well as national sins and ask God for forgiveness. Any Sunday would be suitable for such a service. However, it must be noted that such an observance has fallen into desuetude in American Lutheranism. This would be obvious by consulting the many Concordia Pulpits, which always have sermons for the special services of the Church Year, but usually have none for a day of humiliation and prayer.

That "A Day of Supplication and Prayer" is listed in the hymnal of Lutheran Churches is due to the fact that there was a time during four hundred some years of the Lutheran Church that such an observance was held yearly. An examination of Lutheran sixteenth century church Orders reveals that days of humiliation and prayer were observed in Hesse (1526) Luenenberg (1527), Mecklenburg (1552), Cassel (1539) and Wuerttemberg (1568).[80] Some of the Lutheran Orders retained the historic Rogation Days (Rogation Days in the Roman Church were on Mondays, Tuesday, and Wednesday before Ascension Day and following Rogate, the Fifth Sunday after Easter). They were characterized by processions and recitations of litanies.[81] Other Lutheran Churches substituted days of penance for Rogation Days.[82] Also some Lutheran Churches kept the Ember Days (Ember Days were Wednesday, Friday, and Saturday following Pentecost the Exaltation of the Cross (Sept. 14), and St. Lucy (Dec. 13). Later there were added Wednesday, Friday and Saturday after the first Sunday in Lent. In the Lutheran Church Ember days became church days for the quarterly lectures and examinations in the catechism).[83]

After 1983, most Lutheran areas in central and northern Germany observed Wednesday before the last Sunday as such a day.[84] Days of Humiliation were not popular in Germany and in America the Propers are seldom used.

The *Lutheran Hymnal* suggests as Scriptural Lection: Old Testament: Joel 2:12-19 and New Testament Gospel: Matthew 6: 16-21[85], *Lutheran Worship* has suggested the following Scriptural Lections: The Old Testament: Joel 2: 12-19; Psalm 130, Isaiah 1:2-18; The Gospel: Matthew 6:16-21. For the Three Year Series: Psalm 6; Nehemiah 1:4-11a; I John 1:5-2:2; Luke 15:11-32.[86]

The Collect in *Lutheran Worship* reads: "Almighty God, Our Heavenly Father, because you desire not the death of a sinner but rather that he should turn from his evil ways and live, graciously turn away from us the punishment which we by our sins have deserved and which have been borne for us by our Lord Jesus Christ and grant us grace ever to serve you in holiness and pureness of living, through Jesus Christ our Lord who lives and reigns with you and the Holy Spirit, one God now and forever."[87]

Footnotes

1. Jack P. Lewis, "Luke," *Wycliffe Bible Encyclopedia* (Chicago: Moody Press, 1975), II, p. 1056.
2. F. W. Albright, *New Horizons in Biblical Research* (London: Oxford University Press, 1966 l, pp. 49ff.
3. Luther D. Reed, *The Lutheran Liturgy* (Philadelphia: Muhlenberg Press, 1947), p. 507.
4. Edward T. Horn III, *The Church Year* (Philadelphia: Muhlenberg Press, 1957), p. 205.
5. **Ibid.**
6. **Ibid.**
7. *The Lutheran Hymnal*, **op. cit.**, p. 93.
8. *Lutheran Worship*, **op. cit.**, p. 101.
9. **Ibid.**, p. 101.
10. *The Lutheran Hymnal*, **op. cit.**, p. 93.
11. *Lutheran Worship*, **op. cit.**, Hymn 194, Stanza 19.
12. Horn, **op. cit.**, p. 205.
13. **Ibid.**, p. 206.
14. Reed, **op. cit.**, p. 508.
15. *The Lutheran Hymnal*, **op. cit.**, p. 93.
16. *Lutheran Worship*, **op. cit.**, p. 99.
17. **Ibid.**
18. *The Lutheran Hymnal*, **op. cit.**, p. 87.
19. *Lutheran Worship*, **op. cit.**, Hymn no. 194, Stanza 20.
20. Reed, **op. cit.**, p. 509.
21. Strange that two Lutheran Books, Paul Zeller Stodach *The Church Year - Studies in the Introits, Collects, Epistles and Gospels* (Philadelphia: The United Lutheran Publication House, 1924), has no propers for Reformation, nor does he have in his book, *The Collect for the Day* (Philadelphia: The United Lutheran Publication House, 1939).
22. Horn, **op. cit.**, p. 207.
23. Horn, **op. cit.**, 207; Reed, **op. cit.**, p. 509.
24. Reed, **op. cit.**, p. 509.
25. Horn, **op. cit.**, p. 207.
26. Lars P. Qualben, *A History of the Christian Church* (New York: Thomas Nelson and Sons, 1940), p. 350.
27. Horn, **op. cit.**, p. 207.
28. Reed, **op. cit.**, p. 509.
29. Horn, **op. cit.**, p. 208.
30. *The Lutheran Hymnal*, **op. cit.**, p. 84.
31. *Lutheran Worship*, **op. cit.**, p. 115.
32. *The Lutheran Hymnal*, **op. cit.**, p. 84; *Lutheran Worship*, **op. cit.**, p. 115.
33. J. Connelly, "All Saints," J.G. Davies, *The Westminster Dictionary of Worship* (Philadelphia: The Westminster Press, 1972), p. 2.
34. Reed, **op. cit.**, p. 510.
35. **Ibid.**, **op. cit.**, p. 510.
36. Horn, p. 209.
37. Gwynne, **op. cit.**, p. 87.

38. **Ibid.**

39. **Ibid.**, pp. 87-88.

40. Reed, **op. cit.**, p. 510.

41. *The Lutheran Hymnal*, **op. cit.**, p. 93.

42. *Lutheran Worship*, **op. cit.**, p. 116.

43. **Ibid.**, p. 116.

44. *The Lutheran Hymnal*, **op. cit.**, p. 93.

45. *Lutheran Worship*, **op. cit.**, p. 9 (Calendar of the Church Year).

46. *Lutheran Book of Worship*, **op. cit.**, p. 12.

47. J. Connelly, "All Soul's Day," *The Westminster Dictionary of Worship*, **op. cit.**, p. 3.

48. John Dowden, *The Church Year and Calendar* (Cambridge: At the University Press, 1910), p. xiv.

49. Erwin Lueker, *The Lutheran Cyclopedia* (St. Louis: Concordia Publishing House, 1954), p. 874.

50. As cited in *Lutheran Cyclopedia*, **op. cit.**, p. 874.

51. **Ibid.**, p. 874.

52. Joseph Stump, *The Christian Faith - A System of Christian Doctrine* (New York; The Macmillan Company, 1932), p. 394.

53. *Lutheran Worship*, **op. cit.**, p. 105.

54. **Ibid.**

55. Reed, **op. cit.**, p. 511.

56. Horn, **op. cit.**, p. 215.

57. **Ibid.**, p. 211.

58. Reed, **op. cit.**, p. 511.

59. **Ibid.**, p. 512.

60. Horn, **op. cit.**, p. 212.

61. **Ibid.**

62. **Ibid.**, p. 211.

63. *The Lutheran Hymnal*, **op. cit.**, p. 84.

64. *Lutheran Worship*, **op. cit.**, p. 120.

65. *The Lutheran Hymnal*, **op. cit.**, p. 84.

66. Reed, **op. cit.**, p. 513.

67. Horn, **op. cit.**, p. 2100

68. Reed, **op. cit.**, p. 513.

69. *The Lutheran Hymnal*, **op. cit.**, p. 85.

70. *Lutheran Worship*, **op. cit.**, p. 122.

71. *The Lutheran Hymnal*, **op. cit.**, p. 85.

72. **Ibid.**, p. 94.

73. *Lutheran Worship*, **op. cit.**, p. 119.

74. Cf. the article on "Evangelism" by Herman Goeckel, *The Lutheran Cyclopedia*, **op. cit.**, p. 355.

75. *The Lutheran Hymnal*, **op. cit.**, p. 94.

76. *Lutheran Worship*, **op. cit.**, p. 119.

77. **Ibid.**, p. 119.

78. *The Lutheran Hymnal*, **op. cit.**, p.p. 84-85.

79. *Lutheran Worship*, **op. cit.**, pp. 121-122.

80. Horn, **op. cit.**, p. 213; Reed, **op. cit.**, p. 512.

81. **Ibid.**, p. 212, 217 218.

82. **Ibid.**, p. 212.
83. **Ibid.**, p. 212.
84. Reed, **op. cit.**, pp. 512-513.
85. *The Lutheran Hymnal*, **op. cit.**, p. 85.
86. *Lutheran Worship*, **op. cit.**, p. 121.
87. **Ibid.**

Questions

1. Luke's Gospel is referred to as the ____.
2. Luke was a man of ____.
3. What was the farthest thing from Luther's mind? ____
4. Luther wished merely to ____.
5. The Augsburg Confession was promulgated ____.
6. What did Gustavus Adolphus do? ____
7. The English name for All Saints was ____.
8. Halloween came from ____.
9. Lutherans rejected All Souls day because ____.
10. The doctrine of purgatory has no basis in ____.
11. The New Lectionary System adopted by Lutherans, Methodists, Reformed and Roman Catholics is belied by ____.
12. Thanksgiving Day is observed on the ____.
13. The New Testament contains many passages which ____.

Advent and Christmas Teachings Based Upon Matthew's Genealogy of Christ (Matthew 1:1-17)

Christian News, **December 9, 1985**

The Bible contains different types of historical materials, such as straight forward narrative biography and genealogy.[1] In the Old Testament, there are numerous passages that contain genealogical data and genealogical lists. Some of which are lengthy and some rather brief. The principal genealogical materials of the Old Testament are found in Genesis Chapters 5,10,11,22,25,29,30,35,36,46; Exodus 6, Numbers 1,2,7,10,13,26,34; scattered notices in Joshua. Ruth, I Samuel, 2 Samuel 3,5,23; Kings 4:1 Chronicles Chapters 1-9,11,13,15,23-27; 2 Chronicles 23,29; Ezra 2,7,10; Nehemiah 3,7,10,11,12.[2] The longest genealogies are found in Genesis 5 and 11 and in I Chronicles, where no less than nine chapters give names beginning with Adam and leading up to King Saul. Ezra 2 and Nehemiah 7 also contain lengthy genealogies.

What is the purpose of the Old Testament genealogies? Hoehner has enumerated the following as distinct purposes: "1. They show the history of Israel. The earlier genealogies show Israel's kingship with and distinction from her neighbors: 2. They are given to show the ancestry and preservation and the purity of the different tribes in Israel; 3. The genealogies are for the preservation and purity of Israel's Aaronic priesthood and the Davidic line which ultimately led to Christ, the long-awaited Messiah in the Gospels. These genealogies not only were for the preservation of the line but also they were used to demonstrate the legitimacy of the individual in his office: 4. the post-exilic genealogies were to demonstrate the homogeneity of Israel as a nation after their captivities."[3] Thus it would appear that the Old Testament genealogies were essentially the skeleton on which the history of Israel was fleshed out upon.[4]

I. The New Testament Genealogies

The New Testament has only two genealogies: Matt. 1:1-17 and Luke 3:23-28, both giving the ancestry of Jesus Christ by two different lines.[5] The first was written by an apostle of the Lord; the second by a follower who based his Gospel upon historical research, a doctor or physician by profession. Matthew begins his Gospel with a genealogy, which traced the ancestry of Christ back to Abraham; while Luke places his genealogy at the end of the first 30 years of Jesus, just prior to His entry upon His public ministry. Luke traced the ancestry of Christ through Abraham back to Adam. Each of the two evangelists fits his genealogy into the purpose that he had in mind, when by the Holy Spirit he was moved to write his perspective account of Jesus life, activities, preaching and work of redemption. Matthew had the Jewish people in mind and in various ways endeavored to show that Jesus of Nazareth was the promised Messiah, predicted about in many Old Testament Scriptures. Luke, on the other hand, writing to the Gentile world, wished to show that Jesus was a universal Savior, who died and arose again not only for the benefit of the Jews but for all men. So the latter traced his genealogy of Christ back to Adam; while Matthew, aiming his good news to the Jews, emphasized Jesus' Hebrew ancestry beginning with Abraham.[6]

Each of the New Testament genealogies has features and peculiarities which are not found in the other. Since it is not the purpose of this study to deal with both genealogies, but solely with the Matthean, the reader might consult the article by Louis Matthews Sweet in *The International Standard Bible Encyclopedia*, Volume II,[7] or *The Gospels - A Synoptic Presentation of the Text in Matthew, Mark, Luke, and John* by John Ylvisaker.[8]

The statement which Paul made first of all about the Old Testament: "All scripture is given by inspiration of God (theopneustos God-breathed, or God-spiraled) and is profitable doctrine etc." is also applicable to the New Testament genealogies. What specific lessons and teachings can profitably be deduced from Matthews genealogy of Jesus Christ? There are a number of them.

II. It Reminds Us of the Fact that Christianity Is A Historical Faith

The Christian religion centers in a person, an historical personage, namely, Jesus of Nazareth, Son of the Virgin Mary.[9] Joseph was not his real father according to the flesh, but was his legal father. The fact that Christianity has a real person who still lives because He arose from the dead and ascended into heaven, from where He sent the Holy Spirit upon the Christian Church at Pentecost, and the fact that Jesus now is active in exercising his prophetic, priestly and kingly offices, distinguishes Christianity from any past and current religions.[10] There are certain historic happenings which constitute the very core of the Christian faith. Christ's life, death and resurrection are the basis of His redemptive efforts for mankind. Take them away and Christianity ceases to be a saving and helping religion. Christ and his salvatory deeds are the heart and core of Christ's religion. He is the sum and substance of Christianity and everything revolves around Him. This is not the case with Buddhism, Brahminism, Confucianism, Zoroastrianism, Jainism, Taoism, Unitarianism, animism and many other isms that could be enumerated. These all could live and exist today without a knowledge as to their founders or authors. Of these it must be said that they are philosophies or moral codes which people must follow in order to merit whatever the blessings or advantages these religions are said to bestow. One can be a Buddhist without believing in Buddha or be a Parsi without knowing much about the founder Zoroaster. Systems conceived and worked out by Plato, Aristotle, Bacon, Hegel, Marx, Whitehead, Wittgenstein and other great minds can stand apart from whether one believes that their originators and propagators lived. John Dewey's educational and ethical views would be possible or acceptance, even if one knew nothing of the activities of the Columbia professor. The same may be asserted about all systems of philosophy, ethics, and morals the future may produce.

However, such is not the case with Christianity. Christianity stands or falls with Christ, its Leader and Founder. To be a Christian means first of all accepting the living Christ as personal Savior. Furthermore, it involves the existence of a personal relationship between Christ and the believer. Thus being a Christian means having a direct relationship between Christ and His devotee. Buchheimer phrased it like this: "He is the Alpha and Omega, the First and the Last of its being and character. He is the Beginning of its high purposes and its splended hope, and He is the end of all of its teachings and promises. He is the First, Last, Midst all and in all."[11]

The Four Gospels contain numerous statements in which Christ and those who accepted his claims to deity, proclaimed that Jesus of Nazareth was the world's only and sole Redeemer. Jesus asserted His Superiority over all religious teachers.[12] Only he was sent by God, the Father. It was His contention that he did not only show people the way to heaven, but he unequivocally said: "I and the Way, the Truth, and the Life, no man comes unto the Father except by me" (John 14:6). The seven I am's of John's Gospel testify to the same claim.[13] Peter after Christ's ascension enunciated the same stance, when he publicly asserted before high Jewish officials: "Neither is there salvation in any other, or any other name given under heaven by which men can be saved." Therefore Buchheimer has well said: "Hence, it is easy to understand that everything peculiar to Christianity necessarily goes overboard and the whole Gospel scheme of salvation falls dead if the Person of Christ is eliminated, and hence is quite plain to us why in setting forth Christian truth and the Gospel the first book of the Bible should contain the record of the birth of this Person and a table of His generation and genealogy."[14]

III. From the Matthean Genealogy it is Clear that Jesus Was A Man

The living center of Christianity was a real man and not a phantom as early Gnosticism taught. John stressed this truth in his Epistles. Christ was a man, descended from human beings.[15] While the Apostle John is his prologue emphasized the deity, divinity of Christ, Matthew clearly taught that Mary's Son was also a human being. Both Matthew and Luke in their genealogies stressed the humanity of Christ. John agrees with Matthew and Luke about Christ's humanity for in John 1:14 he wrote: "And the Word (in verses 1:1-3 identified with God) became flesh and dwelt among us, and we beheld his Glory, the glory of the only-begotten." Writing before the destruction of Jerusalem in A.D. 70, the author of Hebrews asserted: "Now since all these children have flesh and blood, He in the same way took on flesh in order to die and so take away all the powers of him who had the power of death, that is, the devil, and to free those who, terrified by death, had to be slaves all their lives. It is clear He didn't come to help angels but Abraham's descendants" (Hebrews 2:14-16).[16]

It is true that God could have revealed Himself in angelic form, when as He once stood before Joshua with drawn sword, announcing that He was captain of the host. Christ could have opened the heavens and manifested His glory sitting upon a throne in heaven in a human form. But opined Buchheimer: "But in that event, men, corrupted by sin and disabled for such bright visions, would have fled affrighted before Him calling the rocks and hills to cover them." In the early days of the apostolic period there were false teachers who claimed that Christ's human appearances were a mere phantom or spectre.[17] The New Testament teaches that the INCARNATION of Jesus Christ consisted in God assuming human form. In Mary's womb deity, Godhead, and humanity were united in one Person. Theologians have termed this the theanthropic union. Christ, who was God from all eternity, the Creator of the universe, became a real human being, following the normal course that men and women are made to follow by being conceived by the Holy Spirit in the body of the Virgin Mary, then after the normal time of development in the body of His mother, He was born as a baby in Bethlehem, he progressed through babyhood, childhood, adolescence until He matured and became a man. Then at thirty years of age He entered upon His public ministry. According to Matthew 1, Christ had human ancestors; He was descended from commoners and kings alike.

Jesus needed to be a man for in accord with the eternal plans of the Trinity Jesus was scheduled to die for the sins of all men, to pay mankind's sin debt. The reconciliation of God to man was only possible because Jesus was a man, and at the same time because of His deity the Man Jesus was able to accomplish what no other human being, or religious leader and founder could have achieved. To deny either the humanity of Christ or reject His deity or divinity would have meant the failure of Christ's mission to "save that which was lost." He could not have given His life a ransom for the world had He not assumed human form. Christ's victory over the devil, sin and death were only achievable because "God was in Christ reconciling the world unto himself" (2 Cor. 5:20).

IV. Again, It is Apparent from Matthew's Genealogy that Christ was God's Promised Messiah

It was the purpose of Matthew in his Gospel to show that in different ways that in Jesus the Messianic promises were fulfilled.[18] In many Old Testament prophecies the Messiah as well as the Messianic age were foretold. Throughout the pre-Christian centuries believing Jews were looking for the "redemption of Israel," to be effected by the Messiah.[19] Luther expressed it this way "Behold, the book of the generations of Christ is before thee, therein is written for thy instruction and consolation that the promises made of the Messiah, Jesus Christ were fulfilled with his birth, life, death and resurrection."[20]

How does Matthew's Genealogy Link up with Christ, the Messiah?

Matthew begins his list of Christ's ancestors like this: "The book of the generations of Jesus Christ, the son of David, the son Abraham." Obviously here the word "son" does not mean a father's direct offspring, but rather "descendant of." Matthew in verse 1:2 begins with Abraham, because Yahweh made a covenant with Abraham, usually referred to as "the Abrahamic covenant."[21] There were three components to this **berith**, or agreement and promise to Abraham, the son of Terah. God promised Sarah, who was barren, a son. Abraham was told that his progeny would be as numerous as the "star of the heavens and as numerous as the sand on the sea shore." The climax of the Abrahamic covenant was the promise that through one of Abraham's descendants the nations of the world would be blessed. In addition, Yahweh gave the land of Canaan to Abraham's offspring as the land where they were to dwell. Paul, the apostle, asserted in Galatians that the Seed through whom the nations were to be blessed was Jesus Christ (Galatians 3:16).

Furthermore, Matthew teaches that Jesus was to be descended from David, probably Israel's greatest king, the inaugurator of the golden era of Israel's history. Yahweh made a covenant with David, usually termed "the David covenant," revealed by the prophet Nathan as recorded in 2 Samuel 7: 12-17.[22] The center of this covenant is not Solomon but Jesus Christ, of whom Yahweh revealed that he was going to establish an eternal kingdom. Thus Jesus, the Messiah was of kingly origin, and would establish a spiritual kingdom. Christ was to become the King of the kingdom of power; but especially was He to establish the kingdom of grace, whose saved citizens would enter the kingdom of glory.

Prior to Abraham's time God had made an earlier promise, namely, that the Seed of the woman would crush the serpent's head and would undo the damage to humanity, when the Tempter caused our first parents, Eve and Adam, to eat of the tree of the knowledge of good and evil. To Adam and Eve Yahweh said: "And I will put enmity between you and the woman and between your descendants and your Descendant. He will crush your head, and you will bruise His heel."[23] The Zerah (Hebrew for "seed" or "Descendant) of Genesis 3:15 was the basis for the Abrahamic covenant, where as in Genesis 3 "seed" is not a plural concept but a singular one.

The Messiah was to be born of a woman. In Matthew's genealogical list there are mentioned a number of women, who were ancestresses of Jesus Christ. It is clear from the list of ancestors in Matthew 1:1-17 that the Messiah was linked up with humanity, that in the form of a servant he embarked upon the carrying out of the eternal decree of redemption. Christ was the Lamb slain from before the foundation of the world (Rev. 13:8). There are four persons listed as females in the line of descendants from whom Christ emerged. They are: Ruth, a Moabitess, originally a stranger outside the community of Israel, and a member of the people who were forbidden to enter God's house till the tenth generation. There is Rahab, the harlot of the abominable seed of the Canaanites. The other two women were Tamar and Bathsheba, the wife Uriah, an adulteress.

V. Gross Sinners were Part of Christ's Genealogy.

Thus it is plain that gross sinners were a part of Christ's family tree stretching across at least four thousand years of world history. Speaking of gross sinners there was Ahaz, who required his children to pass through the fire. Then, there is Manasseh, son of Hezekiah, who was so wicked that God caused the Assyrian king Esarhaddon to take Manasseh to Babylon and place him into captivity until Manesseh repented and then God again caused the Assyrian king to allow him to return the rule over the Judean kingdom (2 Chronicles 33:33). Amon, one of the more evil kings of Judah was murdered by his servants.

Why does the Matthean genealogy have such strange and unsavory links in it? Why were these humiliating personalities included between Abraham and Mary? Why were these iniquitous people not passed over? On the basis of Scriptural teaching one might reply that Jesus was born for sinners, to pay for their sins and wash the latter away. Holy Writ states that Jesus took upon Himself sinful human flesh and did not disdain to enter into close relationship with the vilest and grossest of sinners. No sinner is so vile that he cannot repent and receive Christ's forgiveness. Jesus promised: "Him that Cometh to Me, I will in no wise cast out." Averred Buchheimer: "There is no zero in any man (person's) moral condition and character beneath which His gracious offers do not pertain."[24] That was the purpose of Christ's mission "to seek and save that which was lost." The fact that vile sinners are mentioned as forbears of God's Son show the first Gospel's readers that Jesus is the Savior of sinners.

VI. Matthew's Genealogy Shows That Christ Came at the Right Time in World History

Matthew's genealogy shows its readers that in what is now known as the first century before Christ, around 6 or 5 B.C., the time had come for God to send his son into the world. To state Paul's Christmas text: "But when the right time came, God sent forth His Son, born of a woman born under the Law, to free them under the Law and make us free sons,"[25] (Beck). Most translations give the Greek word **pleroma** as "fulness." **The New International Version** translates: "When the time had fully come."[26] "An analysis of Matthew's list of Christ's ancestors and ancestresses shows that Matthew divided his fifty-two names according to a scheme of 3 times 14."[27] Three specific time periods are followed in Matthew's arrangements of men and women who constituted the family tree of Jesus Christ. The first time period begins with Abraham, 2166 B.C. (year of birth) and concluded with David 1010-970 B.C. The second time period begins with David (1010-970 B.C.) and concluded with the Babylonian Captivity (587 B.C., according Wisemann's *Chronicles of the Chaldean Kings*). The third time period begins with the Babylonian Captivity and concludes with Mary, betrothed to Joseph, the legal father of Christ. Since Jesus was born in the reign of Herod the Great, who ruled from 37 B.C. to 4 B.C., this would mean that Christ was probably born in 6 or 5 B.C.[28] Thus Matthew's genealogy covers roughly about 2100 years of Near Eastern history. By comparison the Lucan genealogy begins with 6 or 5 B.C. and goes beyond Abraham and ends with the first man, Adam, who because he was made in the image of God is called "a son of God" Luke 3:38), thus covering at least a period of our thousand years of world history.

What does Paul's expression "when the time had fully come" exactly mean? According to God's timetable a number of preparatory matters had to be taken care of before the world's Redeemer could assume flesh and blood.[29] The Old Testament congregation of believers had to be given a complete picture of the person, lifework and achievements of the Messiah. The members of the Old Covenant were given this information piecemeal over many centuries. The names of Matthew's genealogy list the names of people who waited and yearned for the coming of the Messiah. During Old Testament times the Old Testament Saints were agonizing for the Messiah's coming. Men and women were groping after the truth. It would appear that God had a timetable. Certain religious preparation had to be made before God could send His Son.

Moved by His grace, God had chosen the descendants of Abraham, "the Hebrew" to be the people, eventually the nation, from whom the Messiah, God's Redeemer, should come. To the Hebrews, later called Jews, were given, as Paul stated in Romans 9:4: "They were made God's family. They have the glory (Hebrew: the Shekinah) the covenants, the Law, the worship and the promises. They have the ancestors, and from them according to His body came Christ, who is God over everything, blessed forever."[30] It was the fleshly and spiritual Israel in Old Testament times to whom was given the task to promote Yahweh's true religion in the Near Eastern world.

Linguistically, the world had to be made ready for Christ's coming. God used the contribution of the Greek race in getting the world prepared for Christ's coming and ministry. The Greeks developed a language, which was well suited for the expression of spiritual truth. Alexander the Great, who loved Aristotle, was responsible for spreading the Greek language throughout Greece, Asia Minor, Palestine, Egypt and Mesopotamia.[31] Although Rome conquered Greece, it was Greek culture and civilization that ultimately conquered Rome. Latin was the official court language, while Greek became the language of culture and education and was commonly understood by many different peoples throughout the Roman Empire. The Greek that was commonly used was not Attic Greek but the Koine Greek.[32] The Septuagint (LXX) was the Greek translation of the Hebrew Old Testament and in the two centuries before Christ the LXX was the Bible of the Jews outside of Palestine. Greek, an Indo-European language, was the instrument through which the Gospel was to be spread throughout the Roman world. The Holy Spirit caused the writers of the New Testament to write the books of the New Testament in the Greek language.

Religiously speaking, the Roman world (called by Luke in the Greek New Testament "**oikoumene**", Luke 2:1), was in a state of religious confusion with many different gods and goddesses being worshipped. Many different religious systems were promoted besides the religions of Greece and Rome. There was a general yearning among millions in the Roman empire for the coming of a Savior.

Politically speaking, the time was ready for the coming of God's Son into the flesh. With the rule of Caesar Augustus (27 B.C.-A.D. 14) there developed a period of peace which was favorable for the missionary activity of Christian mission.[32] The Romans had built an excellent systems of roads on which the Roman legions could quickly march to any trouble spot, but the same roads also helped the travels of Christian missionaries. Thus in many different ways the time was ripe for the coming of Christ. As the Biblical reader reads these fifty two names in Matthew's list of Christ forebears, there would come before the mind's eye the history of mankind beginning with the fall and promise in Eden, including the flood, the confusion of language, the call and promise to Abraham, the 215-year stay of the three patriarchs in Palestine, the Egyptian bondage, the exodus, the wilderness stay of forty years, the conquest under Joshua, Israel's history from Joshua to Zedekiah, the histories of Egypt, Assyria, Babylonian, Medo- Persia, and Rome — yes, all these would pass by and be associated with Matthews genealogy.

The Amazon River is supposed to be the most extensive river on earth, it takes its rise in the Andes, and flows in a channel of about 4,000 miles; then enters a valley and empties into the seas. Its current is perceptible two hundred miles in the Atlantic Ocean. In the area traversed by the Amazon there is not a river, not a brook, not a fountain gushing forth from the hills, which does not empty into the sea, and its tides are felt through an upward course of 4,000 miles. So analogously, it might be said that the history of the early ages, its wars and peace, its vicissitudes of men and the nations lead up to the coming of the Christ, and since Jesus' birth for nearly 2,000 years the world has been affected by Christ's birth, life, death, resurrection, ascension and the outpouring of the Spirit sent by the ascended Christ. Christians write of world events as occurring before Christ's birth, as B.C., and of events that transpired after His birth taking place in **Anno Domini**, as A.D. Jews of course, will not recognize this fact, but write C.E., Common Era, or B.C.E., before the common era.

VII. Matthew's Genealogy Shows that God Keeps His Promises

Another educational truth that one can deduce from Matthew's genealogy is the truth that God always keeps His word and promises. God has promised Adam and Eve, a Person who would undo the tragedy of man's fall and loss of eternal life. The Devil would be defeated by the Seed of the woman. He had further promised that the nations of the world were to be blessed through the Seed of the woman. The genealogical list of Matthew shows how God kept His promises by means of the preservation of the Hebrew nation. Matthew's list shows how God went about fulfilling his promises. J.C. Ryle commenting upon this fact wrote: "Thoughtless and ungodly people should remember this lesson and be afraid. Whatever they may think, God will keep His word. If they repent not, they will surely perish — True Christians should remember this lesson, and take comfort. Their Father in heaven will be true to all His engagements. He has said it. He will do it. "He is not a man that He should lie." "He abideth faithful: He cannot deny Himself" (2 Tim. 11:13)."[33]

VIII. Application and Conclusion

It certainly is a privilege to have been one of the forbears of Jesus according to the flesh. It was truly an honor for certain men and women to

917

have belonged to the family tree of Jesus. And yet there is a family in which we may all be the near kinsmen and kinswomen of Christ. There is a relationship with Christ which is in reach of all people. On one occasion Jesus of Nazareth stretched out His hands to His disciples, saying: "Behold, my mother and my brothers; for whosoever shall do the will of my Father, which is in heaven, the same is My brother, and sister and mother." By that statement Jesus meant to teach and show that there is yet another and higher, supernatural and heavenly family, in which all true believers who are justified by faith are adopted. God wants all men to be brothers and sisters in this spiritual sense. All saved people are the sons and daughters of God; Jesus is their Brother.

Footnotes

1. Richard G. Moulton, *The Modern Reader's Bible, Presented In Modern Literary Form* (New York: The Macmillan Company, 1945), pp. 1543-1548: 455ff.
2. Philip Wendell Channell, "Genealogy," *The International Standard Bible Encyclopedia* (Grand Rapids: Wm. B. Eerdman's Publishing Company ,1939), II, pp. 1185-1186.
3. H. W. Hoehner, "Genealogy," *The Wycliffe Bible Encyclopedia* (Chicago: Moody Press, 1975), I, p. 663.
4. **Ibid.**
5. Adam Fahling, *A Harmony of the Gospels* (Grand Rapids: Zondervan Publishing House, no date), p. 18, footnote 2.
6. Charles P. Roney, *Commentary on the Harmony of the Gospels* (Grand Rapids: Wm. B. Eerdmans Publishing Company, 1948), p. 29-30; 2. Graham Scroggie, *A Guide to the Gospels* (London: Pickering & Inglis, LTD, 1948), pp. 254 (relative to Matthew), 364 (Luke).
7. Louis Matthews Sweet, "The Genealogy of Jesus Christ," *The International Standard Bible Encyclopdia*, edited by James Orr (Grand Rapids: Wm. B. Eerdmans Publishing Company, 1939), pp. 1196-1199.
8. John Ylvisaker. *The Gospels – A Synoptic Presentation of the Text in Matthew, Mark, Luke, and John* (Minneapolis: Augsburg Publishing House, 1932), pp. 52-60.
9. Sweet, **op. cit.**, p. 1196a.
10. Cf. P. E. Kretzmann, *The God of the Bible and Others* (St. Louis: Publisher not given, 1913), p. 27.
12. John's Gospel has a number of such declarations. 3:16; 3:39.
13. John 8:12; 10:9; 14:6; 10:11-16; 6:32-35; 15:5; 11:25.
14. Bucheimer, **op. cit.**, p. 27.
15. John Rutherford, "Gnosticism," *The Standard Bible Encyclopedia*, **op. cit.**, III, p. 1243.
16. Hebrews 2; 14-16 in William F. Beck*, The Holy Bible, An American Translation*, (New Haven: Leader Publishing Company, 1976), p. 275 (New Testament).
17. Rutherford, **op. cit.**, p. 1243.
18. Charles R Erdman, *The Gospel of Matthew, An Exposition* (Philadelphia: The Westminster Press, 1946), pp. 14-15.
19. Alfred Edersheim, *The Life and Times of Jesus the Messiah* (Grand Rapids: Wm. B. Eerdmans Publishing Company, 1974), II, pp. 710-741.
20. As cited by Buchheimer, op., cit. p. 28.
21. J.F. Walvoord, "Abrahamic Edward Promise," *Wycliffe Bible Encyclopedia*, **op. cit.**, pp. 12-13; Edward Mack, *The Christ of the Old Testament* (Richmond, Virginia:

The Presbyterian Board of Publication, 1926), pp. 49-50,

22. **Ibid.**, pp. 67-74.
23. Beck, **op. cit.**, p. 4 (Old Testament)
24. Buchheimer, op, cit., pp. 29-30.
25. Beck, **op. cit.**, p. 238 (New Testament).
26. *The Holy Bible, New International Version* (Grand Rapids: Zondervan Bible Publishers, 1978), p. 1250.
27. Charles R. Eerdman, *The Gospel of Matthew, An Exposition* (Philadelphia: The Westminster Press, 1946), pp. 26-27.
28. H. Wayne House, *Chronological and Background Charts of the New Testament* (Grand Rapids: Zondervan Publishing House 1981), p. 72.
29. Cf. Adam Fahling, *The Life of Christ* (St. Louis: Concordia Publishing House, 1936), Chapters 1 and II, pp. 13-58.
30. Beck, **op. cit.**, p. 199 (New Testament).
31. Everett F. Harrison, *Introduction to the New Testament* (Grand Rapids: Wm. B. Eerdmanns Publishing Company, 1964), pp. 49-56.
32. E. A. Judge, "Augustus," *The New Bible Dictionary, Second Edition* (Wheaton, Illinois; Tyndale House Publishers, 1982), p. 107.
33. Rt. Rev. J.C. Ryle, *Expository Thoughts on the Gospels* (New York and Chicago: Fleming H. Revell Company, 1959), Matthew, p. 3.

Questions

1. What is the purpose of Old Testament genealogies? ____
2. Where are the New Testament genealogies found? ____
3. Matthew traces the ancestry of Christ back to ____.
4. Luke traces the ancestry of Christ through Abraham back to ____.
5. Matthew had the ____ in mind.
6. Luke is writing for ____.
7. Paul's statement about the Old Testament is also applicable to ____.
8. Christianity is a ____ faith.
9. What distinguishes Christianity from any past and current religions? ____
10. Christianity stands or falls with ____.
11. Jesus asserted his authority over all ____.
12. The living center of Christianity was a ____.
13. The New Testament teaches that the incarnation of Jesus Christ consisted in ____.
14. What is the anthropic union? ____
15. It is apparent from Matthew's Genealogy that Christ was ____.
16. Jesus, the Messiah, would establish a ____ kingdom.
17. The Messiah was to be born of a ____.
18. ____ were a part of Christ's genealogy.
19. Mathew's genealogy covers roughly ____.
20. Greek became the language of ____.
21. The Septuagint was ____.
22. The Roman roads helped the travel of ____.
23. Who prefers using C.E. and B.C.E. rather than A.D. and B.C. ____.
24. All saved people are the sons and daughters of ____; Jesus is their ____.

The Ascension of Christ
From the Perspective of the Historical-Critical Method Compared with the Biblical and Historical Christian Teaching

Christian News, May 25, 1987

There was a time when Protestantism, Roman Catholicism and Lutheranism believed that on the fortieth day after Easter Jesus slowly ascended from the Mount of Olives, near Bethany, and was received by a cloud into heaven. Two angels were present who spoke with the disciples, who watched Christ's heavenward ascent, saying that this same Jesus would again return visibly in the same manner as He had left the earth and thereby withdrew His physical presence from them. This climactic event was of a miraculous nature as a number of other significant happenings in Christ's life had been from the moment of His conception in the womb of His mother Mary until His ascent to His Father.

However, with the coming of the historical-critical method as a technique for the interpretation of Holy Writ, the historicity and facticity of Christ's true bodily ascension has been questioned and explained away. The traditional separate steps of Christ's state of exaltation have been rejected. These steps are set forth in books of dogmatics of Roman Catholic, Protestant and Lutheran scholars and writers. The literature of the second half of the twentieth century reveals that proponents of the use of the historical-critical method among Roman Catholics, Protestant and Lutheran scholars have rejected the factualness and historicity of the longer account by Luke in Acts 1:1-11 and the shorter versions in the Gospels of Mark and Luke. In doing this they have followed in the footsteps of Freidrich Schleiermacher, the father of modern liberal theology, who in his *Der Christliche Glaube* asserted Christ's ascension: "The facts of the resurrection and the ascension of Christ cannot be taken as an authentic part of the doctrine of the person of Christ."[1] The modern rejecters or re-interpreters of the meaning of Christ's ascension are following in the footsteps of theological liberalism and certain advocates of the theology of neo-orthodoxy who terminate the life of Jesus with His death on Calvary and His deposition in the tomb. Liberal writers of the life of Christ, like those of Emil Ludwig, Edgar Goodspeed and others, have Christ's life ending with His death on Calvary's central cross and His burial.[2]

In this essay, the first part will present the views of Protestant, Roman Catholic and Lutheran scholars who have employed the higher criticism of a negative type to reject or substitute a different interpretation for that which the normal explanation of the Scriptural text would indicate.

Part I
Historical-Critical Interpretations of the Account of Christ's Ascension into Heaven

A. Protestant Interpretations
1. The Ascension in *The Interpreter's Dictionary of the Bible*

James M. Robinson sets forth a liberal and anti-Scriptural view of Christ's ascension into heaven in his article on the ascension in *The Interpreter's Dictionary of the Bible*.[3] The Lord's ascension is discussed by Robinson together with Old Testament ascensions those referred to in the Pseudepigrapha and in such pagan religion as Zoroastrianism, Mithraism, Mandaeism and Gnosticism. The Claremont scholar claimed: "When the earliest Christology identified Jesus with the Son of Man, expected shortly from heaven, the theological necessity of the ascension was apparent" (see e.g. Luke 22:69; Acts 7:56; Euseb. II, xxiii,13).[4] He further averred that: "This orientation can still be sensed when the ascension is for purpose of the installation in an office (Acts 2:36; 5:31, Phil 2:9; etc.), or is associated with the title 'Son of man,' (John 3:13-14, etc; cf. Mark 8:31, etc.), or with the Parousia 3:20 (Luke 19:11ff; Acts 1:11; 3:21; see also Phil. 3:20; Col. 3:1-4; I Thess. 1:10.[5] Thus the Son of man's functions of dominion, glory, a kingdom, the subservience of all (Dan. 7:14), amplified by Ps. 8 of the Son of man (Eph. 1:22; Heb. 2:6-9; etc.) Psalm 110 of the enthronement Lord (Mark 14:62; Acts 2:34-35; Eph. 1:20, Col. 3:11, Heb. 1:3,13, etc.) and Ps. 2 of the adopted Son (Acts 13:33; Heb. 1:55:5; 2:26-27; 12:5, etc.), pointed in the direction in which the Ascension's significance (and terminology grew)."[6] The fact of the ascension was projected as the result of developments within the Christian communities.

What Robinson failed to do was to realize that the ascension and the Parousia or Second Coming of Christ are two events that are separated at least by over 1900 years. The two events are clearly distinguished in Scripture. Denying the true historicity of the ascension, critical scholars work out a system of New Testament theology, which is not true to the revealed New Testament revelation, but is a fabrication of their theological theorization. Robinson claims that Christ's ascension has been misunderstood. Those scholars, who hold what he believes are erroneous views, are said, by him, to do the following: "They took Christ's enthronement at his ascension for the finality of God's victory, and hence were naively ignorant of, or presumptuously ignored the persistent ambiguities of human existence and the all-embracing extent of God's ultimate claim upon creation, insights they kept live by a futuristic eschatology they rejected in favor of the finality of Christ's work of the ascension."[7]

Robinson places the historical episode of Christ's literal and bodily ascension heavenward in opposition to Paul's futuristic eschatology. The Claremont professor further claims that the ascension of Christ is for the New Testament of secondary importance. He asserts that the ascension is only found in Acts 1:9-11 in the New Testament. Asserts Robinson: "The particular crystallization of the ascension motif in Luke-Acts is primarily a reflection of theological considerations. The life of Christ needed to have an ending and thus the ascent is primarily a reflection of theological consideration.[8] Here, Robinson exhibits the technique of a redaction critic, for redaction criticism holds that the evangelists were not so much historians, as was traditionally believed, but creative theologians, who did not hesitate to create events that did not occur and place words into the mouth of Jesus which He never uttered.[9] We ask: "What does that do to the reliability and credibility of the Gospels and to our knowledge concerning the life of Christ?" Of course, Robinson has been involved in the third quest for the historical Jesus! So New Testament students are informed by modern critical scholars that a terminal date was needed for the earthly life of Christ, so Luke developed the view that Christ left this earth by this unique act of levitation, which humanly speaking is not possible. Luke depicted Christ like a human elevator ascending upward.

2. Macgregor on the Ascension in *The Interpreter's Bible*

G. H. C. Macgregor in his exposition of "the Book of Acts" in *The Interpreter's Bible,* claims that there is nothing in Luke's Gospel to indicate that the ascension did not take place on the same day as the Resurrection — a view supposedly shared by Paul, who seems to have ignored the ascension and considered the two events as synonymous.[10] The acceptance of the longer period of time by church tradition was probably due to the desire to make room for the imparting of secret instruction to the inner circle of his disciples by the Risen Jesus, in particular concerning the kingdom of God.[11]

In commenting about Christ's ascension, Macgregor reasoned as other critically-oriented tradition critics have, that because Matthew and Mark do not mention the ascension of Christ, or Paul does not specifically refer to it, (obviously MacGregor does not accept Ephesians as Pauline), that the ascension had no place in the early Christian tradition.[12] In response to this we argue that since Luke concluded his Gospel with an account of Christ's ascension, all statements before these verses deal with the events of the Resurrection Day and since no time is mentioned and the same writer records the fact in Acts 1 that it was on the fortieth day after Easter that Christ left his earth, this should be accepted as the complete and accurate account of the ascension.[13] Assuming that a writer knows what is involved in contradictions and that he purports to research the data for the life of Christ (Luke 1:3) and that he consulted other lives of Christ and interviewed living witnesses, people who knew and had contacts with Christ, fairness demands, unless one is bent on discrediting a writer in an unreasonable manner or has an axe to grind, that Luke should be perceived as a responsible author and that the ending of his Gospel does not contradict the ascension account in Acts 1:1-11, and that the latter is the complete version of what happened on the fortieth day after Easter.

3. Emil Brunner's Views about Christ's Ascension

Emil Brunner, renowned Reformed theologian of Europe, has rejected the stance of the Reformation period's confessional creeds and of the catechisms of various Reformed theology. Brunner in his *Dogmatics* thus wrote about the ascension of Christ: "Within the New Testament writings, however, Luke is the only one to give this account, which is entirely isolated. No other apostle mentions such an event; further, this conception is irreconcilable with that of Paul. For Paul there are no 'forty days,' within which appearances of the Risen Savior took place. Paul indeed sets the appearance of the Risen Christ, which was granted him as the last of the Apostles exactly on the same level as that granted to Peter, the Twelve and the Five Hundred brethren."[14] However, we contend that this event, which happened on the Damascus road, took place long after the "forty days" were over; indeed, after the persecutions. Brunner also asserted that "once more we stand at a point where theology must have the courage to abandon the ecclesiastical tradition. For Paul the Exaltation of Jesus is identical with His Resurrection and the same is true of John: only in John it is more plainly than in Paul, and therefore crucifixion and exaltation are regarded as a unity."[15] Brunner further claimed that this rejection of the literal ascension of Christ into the cloud of heaven must be repudiated, not because it goes against current cosmology, but because the Bible itself demands it.[16]

During the Second World War Brunner preached a series of sermons on the **Apostles' Creed**, later published in book form. Among the twelve sermons published, the reader will not find a sermon on the ascension or His sitting on the right hand of God. Considering that he did not believe that the account of the ascension in Luke was true and that it was a late addition, it is not surprising that he did not preach on these two doctrines found in all three Ecumenical Creeds.[17]

4. Helmut Thielicke's Views on the Ascension

One of the recent recognized theologians in Germany was Thielecke, who was the author of a two-volume *Christian Dogmatics*, called in German, *Der Evangelische Glaube*, translated into English by Bromiley as *The Evangelical Faith*.[18] The English translator calls the attention of the reader to the fact that in Volume 2, Thielicke takes up the two articles of the Creed. Relative to Thielicke's treatment of the locus of Christology, he asserted: "The approach to Christology is not through the two natures but through the three offices, so that atonement and the resurrection can be treated as well as the traditional, if less important Christological themes of the virgin birth, the descent, and the ascension."[19] The reader of Thielicke's second volume will find little on Christ's ascension. The index lists on page 339 "Ascension of Christ," but on reading that page, one will find no reference to the ascension. Thielicke has devoted a considerable number of pages to Christ's resurrection, but has no discussion of the ascension, and session of Christ at the right hand of the Father.[20]

B. Protestant and Roman Catholic Views on the Ascension

In 1975 the Seabury Press of New York City issued *The Common Catechism - A Book of Christian Faith*. This volume has 681 pages plus an index, totaling 690 pages. This catechism was written by Protestant, Roman Catholic and Lutheran theologians and is said to supplement the *Dutch Catechism*.[21] *The Common Catechism* is said to offer both a more explicit theological presentation of the Christian faith and delineate doctrine more explicitly.[22] Where the *Dutch Catechism* begins with fundamental questions of human existence, the publishers claim *The Common Catechism* then goes on to relate them to man's religious experience and beliefs. The two works thus are said to supplement each other and also together constitute a complete library of contemporary religious thought.

The Common Catechism index lists the ascension of Christ as found on pages 173-175, 203, 221, 225, 331, and 410. The manner in which the writers worked out their interpretations on the resurrection and ascension of Christ shows the use of form and redaction criticisms. In describing the resurrection appearances of Christ to the Emmaus disciples, here is the catechism's explanation: "The language describing the meal scene is such that the reader is forced to think of the primitive Christian Lord's Supper. Luke is saying that the community meets the risen Christ in the new interpretation of Scripture and the celebration of the Lord's Supper. In 24:34 Luke then adds the first appearance to Peter."[23]

On page 175 very little is said about the ascension, except to state that "the Gospel (i.e. of Luke) ends with the short account of the ascension (24:50-53)." That is all on the ascension! Nothing on page 203. Page 211 has no specific reference to the ascension. There is no reference to the ascension on page 225. On page 331 the ascension is mentioned incidentally in connection with the fact that Peter was the leader in the Church immediately following the ascension. On page 410 the reader will find these revealing words: "By contrast the ascension of Christ into heaven symbolizes (italics the author's) the power of the Lord in the new creation (Mk 16:19; Luke 24:51; Eph. 4:9f.)."[24]

Thus there are not even three complete lines in 660 pages that treat of the ascension of Christ! The session and second coming are not mentioned or rejected in the light of the alleged new insights in current theology.[25]

C. Roman Catholic Authors on the Ascension
1. The *Dutch Catechism* on the Ascension of Christ

In 1967 Herder and Herder of New York City issued a translation of *De Nieuwe Katechismus* which was commissioned by the Hierarchy of the Netherlands produced by the Higher Catechetical Institute at Nijmegen, in collaboration with numerous others. The English translation has 508 pages. The index lists the discussion of "Ascension" on pages 189-193. *The Dutch Catechism*, compared to *The Common Catechism*, does discuss the Ascension of Christ, but not under a separate caption but in connection with the resurrection of Christ and His session at the right hand of God.[26] *The Dutch Catechism* asks the question: "Where was Jesus during the forty days after Easter, when He appeared to the disciples?" Again: "Was He alone in a certain place in Palestine from which He sometimes came to his disciples?" The answer given these two questions: "No, He was with the Father. It was 'from there' that He made Himself visible and tangible to his own."[27]

The Dutch Catechism takes the position that immediately with the res-

924

urrection Christ was with the Father, thus the ascension of Christ and the session did not occur after the ascension but immediately after the resurrection. This, of course, does not agree with traditional Roman Catholic theology, but the *Dutch Catechism* has become famous for departing from the traditional Roman Catholic position on also other Biblical doctrines.

The Dutch Catechism, like other re-interpreters of Christ's ascension, cites Jesus' words to Mary Magdalene: "I am ascending to my Father and your Father, to my God and your God (John 20:17)."[28] However, the text of John 20:17 does not assert that Jesus was ascending on Easter Sunday, but that this going to the Father was an event to happen in the future. From Acts 1:1-11 we know it was on the fortieth day after the ascension.

The Dutch Catechism sums up its discussion on the meaning of the ascension: "To sum up: Jesus, by virtue of his resurrection is with the Father. This is demonstrated vividly in the last of the apparitions by a symbolical gesture, the ascension, as regards Jesus' present existence as man, we know that He is in the love of the Father."[29]

2. The Ascension of Christ In The Jerome Biblical Commentary

In the Roman Catholic *Jerome Biblical Commentary*, in the article dealing with the resurrection of Christ, Raymond Brown a critical scholar, stated: "Ascension normally evokes the image of Jesus' being lifted into heaven on a cloud after 40 days (Acts 1:3,4). Such an understanding presents several difficulties: 40 is a symbolical number in the Bible and not always to be taken literally; other passages imply an ascension on Easter (Luke 24:51; Jn. 20:17; Mk. 16:16), the notion of ascending to heaven implies figurative language, for heaven is not really to be thought of as above the earth."[30] The Roman Catholic scholar Benoit of the Ecole Biblique in Jerusalem, who died recently, has proposed the following distinction when endeavoring to set forth what the New Testament teaches about Christ's ascension, an explanation Brown is willing to accept. Thus Benoit averred: that if a person is speaking about the terminus of Christ' earthly life and also the last appearance after the resurrection, perhaps Luke symbolizes it by an act of levitation of Christ, usually thought of as the ascension. If, however, one is thinking theologically of the ascension, i.e. as return to the Father or a glorification in heaven at God's right hand, this exaltation was an integral part of the resurrection. Thus Jesus' road from the dead to glory is depicted as appearing to men after the resurrection as one already glorified with supreme power (Mt. 28:18; Luke 24:26).[31] Benoit here reflects the views of critical scholarship and claims that the session really occurred on the day of resurrection and not on the day of the ascension. He goes against the traditional doctrinal stance of the Roman Catholic Church as will be shown in part II of this essay.

3. The Views of Voegtle on the Ascension

The Roman Catholic scholar Voegtle wrote the explanation on "He ascended into heaven," in *A New Look at the Apostles' Creed*, edited by Gerhard Rein.[32] Voegtle, Rector of the University of Freiburg, began his presentation on "He ascended into heaven" like this: "Few phrases of the Apostles' Creed are more perfect examples of the attachment of the Christian message to a long obsolete image of the world than the phrase 'ascended into heaven.' How can we take this statement seriously today?"[33]

In view of the developments of this scientific age when we know that the earth is a sphere, not a disk above which there stretches the massive shell of the firmament with God's throne room, so how can Christians today use this statement of the Apostles' Creed in an intelligent and meaningful manner.[34] Voegtle grants that in the ascension account there are two miracles involved: the levitation of Christ heavenward and the presence of two angels who spoke to the viewers of Christ ascension. The rector of Freiburg University admitted that the Scriptural text of Acts describes an event involving seeing and hearing, both by those present on the Mount of Olives.[35] He stated: "There is unusual emphasis on the vision of the disciples 'before their eyes' — 'from their sight'— 'gazing up' - 'looking up.' And the phrase: 'And while they were gazing after into the sky' obviously calls to mind the image of a prolonged flight upwards."[36] However, despite the clear assertions of the text, that it was an actual ascent which took place in time and space, Voegtle asserted: "But this could not be a literal report of the occurrence you say. In reality, it is merely a figurative expression for an event that defies description."[37] Voegtle admitted that such phrases as "he was caught up" and "before their eyes" means what they actually do, then the writer must have been reporting about an empirically observed event. While Christians believe that it happened, Voegtle does not believe it actually occurred. To negate the Biblical miracle he asks: "Is it deceit, a flight of their imagination, a legend or myth?"[38]

Voegtle claimed that the stranger to theology (i.e. to higher criticism) does not realize how the story was used in ancient times and also in the Bible. In the ancient world and in the Bible not everything which is presented as visible occurrences refer to things which actually happened.[39a] After trying to show that Luke contradicted other New Testament accounts of the resurrection and the ascension, Voegtle comes up with this conclusion: "In conclusion, one more question, should not we reformulate that 'ascended into heaven' does not really refer to an external event in earthly space, but with the help of the then current image of a three-storied universe, to a purely other worldly happening? I cannot think of an adequate substitute, nor do I feel that it is really needed."[39] Voegtle's problem is that he does not believe that the ascension of Christ was a miracle, a concept with which higher-critical scholarship has a problem.

D. Lutheran Critical Scholars' Views on the Ascension
1. Bultmann and the Ascension

Rudolf Bultmann was a Lutheran scholar who did not believe in the ascension of Christ, because he did not hold that Jesus rose from the dead.[40] If Jesus was not raised from the dead, obviously He could not ascend into heaven. Bultmann did not believe in miracles, for according to him God could not intervene in the cause and effect arrangement which we find controlling human events. Furthermore ascending into heaven would assume the validity of a three-story universe, found in both the Old and New Testaments, and modern science has shown the fallaciousness of such a cosmology. The Biblical accounts need to be demythologized in order to get at the truth behind the myth. Bultmann's 1942 essay on demythologization has had a devastating and deliterious effect on many New Testament scholars who were persuaded of the validity of Bultmann's hermeneutics.[41] Today we have the sad spectacle where this Christ-denying interpretation is hailed as the correct understanding for the two great events which occurred in Christ's life.

2. An American Lutheran New Testament Scholar on the Ascension

John Reumann's Jesus in the Church Gospels, a book claiming to present "modern scholarship and the earliest sources," takes the stance that the Gospel writers created their theology and that the Gospel documents present not only different but contradictory views about the life of Christ.[42] The post-resurrection appearances of Christ are said to be "separate tales which never can be put into an ordered framework."[43] Reumann does not indicate whether or not the ascension was a real historical event but claims its value is that it put an end to the appearances of Jesus, which he seems to say, are less and so the ascension "as an acted declaration of finality" to the resurrection appearances of Jesus. How Reumann thinks about the resurrection is stated by him as follows: "Here is the difference which the resurrection makes, it renders dubious any mere quest for the Jesus of history, for one discovers through historical studies that the records are constantly illuminated by the resurrection light. It demands commitment to Jesus who is Lord, and not just a human figure, for the resurrection has stamped Jesus in the New Testament records as not just a figure of the past but one of continuing significance."[44]

Whether or not Jesus stayed upon the earth after His resurrection for forty days is questioned by Reumann, who claims that the Gospels disagree on the order and number of the resurrection appearances. He follows critical scholarship and questions the physical ascension of Christ as given by Luke in Acts 1:11.[45]

3. Aulen on the Ascension of Christ

The Swedish theologian Aulen in his *Faith of the Christian Church* has little to say about the ascension of Christ. In his index to the book, the ascension is not listed, obviously not very important. He devoted two lines to this important event in Christ's State of Exaltation when he commented on Acts 2:23: "God hath made him both Lord and Christ, this Jesus whom ye crucified." He wrote: "The conceptions which set forth this act of exaltation are summarized in the threefold affirmation of the Apostolic Creed about the resurrection, the ascent into heaven, and the sitting on the right hand of God. The continuous work is carried on by this exalted Christ. If we look closer at these three expressions, we note that none of them can be isolated from the others, but that all three together furnish the background against which the continuous work and the dominion of Christ appear to the eye of faith."[46]

4. The Dogmatician Althaus on the Ascension of Christ

Paul Althaus has advanced erroneous views about the ascension of Christ. In his two volumes *Die Christliche Wahrheit* (a Lutheran Dogmatics) Althaus discussed the ascension as a part of the Exaltation (Die Erhoehung) and wrote the following: "Die Gestalt von Ostern und Himmelfahrt is der eine und derselbe. Gott hat Jesus erhoeht." (In English) "The form of Easter and the ascension is one and the same. God hath elevated Jesus."[47] Althaus claimed that in early apostolic preaching there is no distinction between the resurrection and the ascension. He questions the reliability of the most complete ascension account, namely, Luke's in Acts 1:1-11.[48] He has asserted, just like other critically-oriented scholars that Luke's account of Christ's ascension occurring on the fortieth day is a late addition. Such an anti-Scriptural approach must naturally also question the various resurrection accounts found in the four Gospels, when the claim is made that the resurrection and the ascension took place on the same day. Althaus and the scholars associated with his viewpoint are thereby telling us that the New Testament is a confused book whose history may be challenged and if necessary rejected.

5. Werner Elert on the Ascension of Christ

Disappointingly, Werner Elert in *Der Christliche Glaube* devoted less than one page to Christ's ascension and to Christ's resurrection. Elert believes that inasmuch as neither Matthew or John refer to the ascension, that therefore Christ's removal from space and His no longer being held by space was effected by the resurrection and not by the ascension.[49] This German dogmatician appears to ascribe to the resurrection effects and results which Scripture assigned to the ascension.[50] He seems to deny or ignore the fact that Jesus was received by a cloud, which for the disciples, who were watching Christ's ascent heavenward would have been the sky in which the clouds were found. By contrast we cite Heinrich Schmid, who, in *Doctrinal Theology of the Evangelical Lutheran Church,* wrote about the ascension as follows: "After Christ had shown himself to His disciples as one raised from the dead. He ascended to heaven, i.e. His human nature also betook itself into heaven, where it had not been before."[51] Schmid quoted Hollaz as follows on the ascension of Christ: "The ascension is the glorious act of Christ by which, after having been resuscitated He betook himself, according to His human nature, by a true real, and local motion, according to His voluntary determination (Per liberam aconomican) and in a visible manner into the common heaven of the blessed, and to the very throne of God; so that, having triumphed over His enemies, He might occupy the kingdom of God (Acts 3: 21), reopen the closed Paradise (Rev. 3:7), and prepare a permanent inheritance for us in heaven (John 14 :2).[52]

6. The Treatment of the Ascension in
Lutheranism's Most Recent Dogmatics

A two-volume, *Christian Dogmatics*, authored by professors of the Lutheran Church in America and The American Lutheran Church, is also disappointing in its presentation of Christ's ascension into heaven .[53]

928

Braaten, of The Lutheran School of Theology in Chicago, devoted a page and a half to Christ's ascension. In discussing the ascension of Christ, Braaten wrote: "The exaltation of Christ moves from his resurrection on the third day through forty days to his ascension."[54] He further asserted: "The mythical features of his trajectory of exaltation are obvious the moment we ask where Jesus went when He ascended heaven . . . The need to demythologize the story should not, however, weaken our sense for the message it contains."[55] The number "forty" is not to be taken literally as exactly forty days. Relative to the fact that Christ literally ascended heavenward, Braaten asserted: "Not only Rudolf Bultmann, but before him, Luther ridiculed the literalistic images of the ascension common in popular piety as childish ideas."[56] Further he claimed that in one respect the content of Easter and the ascension are one and the same. They both mean that God exalted Christ. While Braaten believed that there are good reasons for the church in its ecclesiastical calendar to celebrate the two festivals forty days apart, dogmatics would be hard pressed to justify the distinction between Easter and the Ascension. The ascension of Christ "is a mystery clothed in the language of myth and symbol. History does not give us the key to unlock it."[57]

7. Kuemmel's Views on the Ascension

Werner George Kuemmel, Professor of New Testament at the University of Marburg, a student of the form critic Dibelius, is well known for his espousal of the historical-critical method in Biblical interpretation.[58] In his article, "Himmelfahrt Christi," in *Religion in Geschichte und Gegenwart*, he expressed the view which is currently held by other New Testament servants that the New Testament data dealing with the resurrection and ascension are contradictory. He argues that the resurrection of Christ and Christ's ascension set forth the same- theological truth. After Christ ascended to His Father on Easter Sunday, He again returned to the earth. The beginning of Luke's version of the ascension in Luke 1:ff. begins with material of a later origin and therefore, is secondary material and legendary.[59] Since Luke's account is in contradiction to the primitive tradition, it is necessary for Biblical scholars and general readers to demythologize the ascension accounts. It is quite obvious that Kuemmel was influenced by Bultmann relative to his claim that the ascension narratives are in need of demythologization.

E. Churches and Theologians Who Accept the Historic Orthodox Scriptural Doctrine of Christ's Ascension
1. Ascension in the New Testament

The ascension of Christ followed the resurrection as the third great face of the state of exaltation. It is alluded to in John 6:62 and predicted in John 20:17. Matthew 28:18-20 presupposes it, the ascension is mentioned in the appendix of Mark's Gospel and recorded in Acts 1:4-14.[60] There is a debate among textual critics and New Testament scholars whether it is mentioned in Luke 24:51. **The New International Version** reads: "While he was blessing them and was taken up into heaven."[61] By contrast **The New English Bible** translates the same verse as follows: "Then he led them out as far Bethany, and blessed them with uplifted hands; and in the act of blessing he parted from them."[62] Beck has a similar translation, not rendering "was taken up into heaven," but simply "was departed from them."[63] The ascension is referred to in Ephesians 2: 6; 4:10; I Timothy 3:16; Hebrews 9:24 and I Peter 3:22. In his Lutheran *Dogmatics* Reu asserted: "The fact that in other places the sitting at the right hand of God appears to be the immediate consequence of the resurrection and that the ascension is not explicitly mentioned, does not justify the conclusion that the ascension is no separate element in the exaltation. The first generations of Christians was definitely convinced that the Lord after the resurrection spent a number of days in physically perceptive communion with his own."[64] Throughout the Apostolic Age the ascension is assumed as a fact among other historical events of Christ's life, as consistent with them as real.

2. Critical Objections Answered by Arndt

William Arndt in his commentary on St. Luke has answered all the objections advanced by critical scholars, many of whose views were presented in part I of this essay. At the very end of his commentary he has "Special Note: The Ascension," covering nearly two pages.[65] Concerning the claim that Jesus ascended into heaven on the day of resurrection, he wrote: "If we had nothing but his account (i.e. Luke 24:50-53), we might conclude, as mentioned before, that the ascension occurred on the same day as the resurrection, because there is no statement anywhere of a longer interval between the episodes in this section and what preceded. Such a view would of course, be connected with great difficulties, because it would assume that Jesus led the group out of the city and made them climb with Him the slopes of the Mount of Olives when the darkness had set in, which appears very strange and unlikely. The first chapter of Acts makes us see this narrative in its proper light. Luke here merely outlines Even Easton, who cannot be accused of too great a penchant for conservative positions, says "The obvious intention is to prepare for the narrative in Acts."[66]

3. The Church Father on the Ascension

The Roman Catholic scholar Ott claimed that "The Fathers give unanimous testimony of Christ's Ascension. All the ancient rules of Faith mention it together with the Death and Resurrection. Cf. St. Ireneus, Adv. haer. I 10, I, III, 4, 2; Terullian, De praescr. 13; De virg vel 1; Adv. Prax. 2; Origin, De princ. I praef 4."[67]

4. The Doctrine of the Ascension; An Historical
Event in Christ's Life the Stand of All Christian Churches

Historically, all Christian denominations and churches, whether they be Roman Catholic, Eastern Orthodox, Lutheran, Episcopalian, Presbyterian, Baptist, Congregational. Reformed, Pentecostal and others who claim they are Christian, unless their theologians have succumbed to the historical-critical method, have held and taught the bodily or corporal ascension of Jesus into heaven. The various confessions or symbols of all Christian Churches accept the three Ecumenical Creeds, the Apostles' Creed, The Nicene Creed and the Athanasian Creed, all three of which have a statement declaring the fact that Jesus ascended into heaven.[68]

5. The Lutheran Confessions on the Ascension of Christ

In the Augsburg Confession of 1530 Melanchthon stated: "The same Christ also descended in to hell, truly arose from the dead on the third day, ascended into heaven and sits at the right hand of God."[69] Luther in his *Small Catechism* and in *The Large Catechism* repeats the historic statements on the ascension as found in the three Ecumenical Creeds.[70] In the *Formula of Concord*, the authors of this Lutheran symbol, in article VIII, "The Person of Christ," asserted: "Therefore we also believe, teach and confess that it was not a plain, ordinary, mere man who for us suffered, died, was buried, descended into hell, and the third day rose from the dead, ascended into heaven, and was exalted to the majesty and omnipotent power of God, but a man whose human nature has such a profound and ineffable union and communion with the Son of God that it has become one person for us."[71] Luther in The Smalcald Articles, Part I, under no. 4 quoted from the Second Article of the Apostles' Creed: "And he arose from the dead."[72]

6. The Historic Position of
The Lutheran Church-Missouri Synod

Of the many statements appearing in the publicana doctrina (public doctrine) here are a few: *The Concordia Cyclopedia* of 1927 defined the ascension of Christ like this: "It was that event in which the risen Christ removed from the society of men and passed in the heavens."[73] *The Popular Symbolics* stated: "Christ's ascension to heaven and His Session at the right band of God (Mark 16:16; Eph.1:20; Heb.1:3) means that He answers, according to his human nature, the full exercise, power and universal divine dominion belonging to it by virtue of the personal union."[74]

7. The Historic Stance of Churches
Following the Reformed Tradition

Calvin in his Institutes of the Christian Religion wrote the following about the ascension of Christ: "His resurrection is properly followed in the Creed by his ascension to heaven . . . received up into heaven therefore he removed his corporeal presence from our view; not that he might no longer be present with the faithful who were still in a state of pilgrimage on earth, but that he might govern both heaven and earth by a more efficacious energy.[75] The Heidelberg Catechism in question and answer No. 46 asserts the ascension as a fact; The Scottish Confession of Faith of A.D. 1560.[76] The Belgie Confession of A.D. 1561 also teaches the ascension as ah historical fact.[77]

The Thirty-Nine Articles of the Church of England also testify to their belief in the historicity of Christ's ascension. The English confession has this statement: "Christ took again His body, with flesh, bones and all things pertaining to the perfection of man's nature, wherewith He ascended into Heaven and there sitteth."[78]

8. The Historic Roman Catholic Stance on the Ascension

Heinrich Ott, in *Fundamentals of Catholic Dogma,* gives the following as the official dogma of the Church of Rome on the ascension: "Christ ascended into Heaven and sits at the right hand of the Father (De Fide)."

Correctly Ott declared: "All the Creeds are in agreement with that of the Apostles' which confess **ascendit ad coelos, sedet ad dextram Dei Patris omnipotentia**." The Caput Firmiter says more exactly "Ascendit pariter in utoque (sc. in anima et in carnal D. 429)."[79] He also cited the standard *Catechismus Romanus* to the effect: "Christ ascended into Heaven of His own power of His transfigured soul which moved His Transfigured body, as it wills. In regard to the human nature of Christ, one can also, following the Scripture assert that He was taken up into heaven (by God) (Mark 16-19; Luke 24:51; Acts 1:9,11). I,7,2.[80]

The Vatican's *Katholischer Kan-Katechismus* (1982), in the German 13th edition, has as assertion 30 the following: "Jesus Christ is King of Heaven and earth. After His resurrection Jesus instructed His disciples for 40 days concerning the Kingdom of God. Thereafter he departed from them as He blessed them and ascended into Heaven. He went with body and soul into the glory of the Father. Through His ascension Jesus has opened for us the way into Heaven and there sitteth."[81]

9. Lutheran Scholars Who Accept the Ascension Account As Held by the Historic Christian Church

In contrast to the Lutheran scholars discussed in Part I, denying the historicity of the ascension on the fortieth day after Easter, various scholars will be referred to who accepted the literal Biblical accounts. Hove, at one time professor at Luther Theological Seminary, St. Paul described the ascension of Christ as follows: "The ascension was an actual, visible rising towards heaven by which Christ, according to his human nature withdrew His visible presence from the earth and entered into His heavenly mode of existence, by which He can invisibly be present everywhere, also according to His human nature."[82] In contrast to professors teaching currently at Lutheran theological seminaries, Hove contended: "It was no illusion, when the disciples be held Jesus taken up toward heaven. Jesus, actually, visibly arose until a cloud received Him out of their sight. This visible rising was to the disciples a proof that He was now withdrawing from them, and the world and His passing into the heavenly mode of existence."[83]

10. President Stump on the Ascension

Joseph Stump, one time president of Northwestern Theological Seminary, Minneapolis in 1932 stated: "The ascension of Christ is the act of the risen Savior by which forty days after His resurrection He visibly ascended into heaven from the Mount of Olives, a cloud covering Him out of their sight (Acts 1:9)."[84]

The Swedish Lutheran dogmatician Lindberg, whose dogmatics was used in the former Augustana Lutheran Synod as text, quoted the definition of Hollaz, previously given earlier in this essay. He further also wrote: "The ascension of Christ was not an **aphanismos** or a disappearance in the sky, but a real ascension; neither after He had disappeared in the sky were there, humanly speaking, successive step in a journey' through all planetary heavens till He had reached the coelum empyreum."[86]

Over against those scholars who claim Jesus ascended on His resur-

932

rection day and not on the fortieth day after Easter Reu asserted: "The fact that at other places the sitting at the right hand of God appears to be the immediate consequences of the resurrection and that the ascension is not explicitly mentioned, does not justify the conclusion that the ascension is no separate element in the exaltation. The first generation of Christians was definitely convinced that the Lord after the resurrection spent a number of days in physically perceptive communion with his own. If such fellowship has been terminated and superseded by a different sort of communion and if observers now address their Lord — who is at the right hand of God — as King and high priest, then they thereby affirm that the risen Lord has ascended to heaven sometime after his resurrection."[87]

John Theodore Mueller has pointed out in his Christian Dogmatics that the heaven into which Christ ascended is not only the heaven of the blessed (John 14:2) (domicum beatorum ascensionis terminem ad quem proprius), but also the right hand of God.[88]

11. The Ascension of Christ Marks His Highest Exaltation

The ascension of Christ marks for the Savior the highest degree of exaltation, it implies His session at the right hand of God, His entering upon the full use according to His human nature, of the divine attributes, of which he relinquished the use and enjoyment during the state of humiliation.

12. What Occurred after Jesus Was Received by a Cloud!

Precisely what took place after the cloud received the risen Lord out the sight of the disciples on the Mount of Olives, believers do not know. Hove wrote about this matter as follows: "We cannot conceive the motion to have continued indefinitely. We do not know what Heaven really is but we do know that it is a mode of existence quite different from our earthly, temporal mode of existence. And of the mode of existence into which Christ passed, Scripture says: "He that descended is the same that ascended far above all heavens (Eph. 4:10)."[89] Therefore, we see that the withdrawal of his visible presence does not mean that He ceased to be present in this world for Christ promised to be with His Church unto the end of the age (Matt. 28:20).[90] Hence, both in his human and divine natures Christ is still with us; and present everywhere. Having finished His work on earth, He triumphed as the Victor over sin and hell. On Christ's ascension rests our peace, rest and hope for the future.[91]

The ascension of Christ was the complete laying aside of the form of a servant, and the full entrance upon a state of transcendence on the part of the human nature and it is now completely glorified, exalted above all human limitations and exercising fully all attributes received from the divine nature through the personal union. Although removed from His Disciples as regards His former made of presence, Jesus is with them in a special sacramental manner in the Holy Supper.[92] Yes, the ascension was a triumph for Christ after His completed redemption and a going to prepare a place for them who believe in Him (John 14:1-2).

13. Christ's Session at the Right Hand of God

Immediately after "he was received in heaven and sat on the right hand of God" is not a circumscribed locality in a spatial heaven, but refers to Christ in infinite power and majesty filling all in all and ruling all things (Ex. 15:1; Ps. 118:16; Ps. 139:7-10; Ps. 48:13; Matt. 26:64).[93] To sit on the right hand of God means to occupy a position of supreme power, might and majesty, not only in this world, but also in the world to come, "and hath put all things under His feet, and gave him to be the Head over all things to the Church; which is His body, the fullness of Him that filleth all in all" (Eph. 1:26-23; I Peter 3:22).

Before Jesus assumed life in the body of the Virgin Mary, Christ's divine nature always was at the right hand of God, i.e. He always exercised sovereignty over all things. With the ascension also His human nature, to which majesty and power were communicated in the state of humiliation and from which he abstained until the resurrection morning, now fully also in the human nature exercises this sovereign rule and dominion."

14. Christ Exercises His Threefold Office in Heaven

Jesus continues in heaven His threefold office, which was begun while on earth according to the divine and human natures. As Prophet He gives His church pastors, teachers, and evangelists for the perfecting of the saints (Eph. 4:8-12); as High Priest He intercedes for His followers (Rom. 8:34); and as King He governs the kingdom of power in the interest of His kingdom of grace (Eph. 1:20-21).[95]

Footnotes

1. Friedrich Schleiermacher, *Der Christliche Glaube*, III, Par. 99, p. 96; English Translation, *The Christian Faith* H. R. Mackin and J. Stewart (T. & T. Clark, 1928).

2. Edgar J. Goodspeed, *A Life of Jesus* (New York: Harper & Brothers, 1950), 200 pages. He concludes his life of Jesus with the burial of Christ.

3. J. M. Robinson, "Ascension," George Arthur Buttrick, *The Interpreter's Dictionary of the Bible* (New York and Nashville: Abingdon Press, 1962), I, p. 245.

4. **Ibid.**

5. **Ibid.**, p. 246.

6. **Ibid.**

7. **Ibid.**, 246a.

8. **Ibid.**, p. 246b.

9. **Ibid.**, cf. Norman Perrin, *What Is Redaction Criticism* (Philadelphia Fortress Press, 1969), 86pp.

10. G. H. C. Macgregor, "The Acts of the Apostles," *The Interpreters Bible* edited by George Arthur Buttrick (New York: and Nashville: Abingdon Press, 1954), Vol. 9, pp. 26-27.

11. **Ibid.**, p. 26-27.

12. **Ibid.**, p. 28.

13. William F. Arndt, *Bible Commentary - The Gospel According to St. Luke* (St Louis: Concordia Publishing House, 1956), p. 500.

14. Emil Brunner, *The Creation Doctrine of Creation and Redemption*. Translated by Oliver Wyon (Philadelphia: Westminster Press, 1952), II, p. 373.

15. **Ibid.**

16. **Ibid.**

17. Emil Brunner, *I Believe in the Living God - Sermons on the Apostles' Creed*. Translated and edited by John Holden (Philadelphia: The Westminster Press, 1956), 16 pp.

18. Helmut Thielicke, *The Evangelical Faith*. Translated and edited by Geoffrey Bromiley (Grand Rapids: William B. Eerdmans Publishing Company 1977), Two volumes.

19. **Ibid.**, Vol. II, p.v. Editor's preface.

20. **Ibid.**, pp. 423-452.

21. *A New Catechism - Catholic Faith for Adults* (New York: Herder and Herder, 1967), 510 pp.

22. *The Common Catechism - A Book of Christian Faith* (New York: The Seabury Press; 1975), cf. the introduction, pp. ix-xv.

23. *The Common Catechism*, **op. cit.**, p. 174.

24. **Ibid.**, p. 331.

25. **Ibid.**, pp. 529-530.

26. *A New Catechism for Adults. Catholic Faith for Adults* (New Herder and Herder, 1967), cf. pp. 185-190.

27. **Ibid.**, p. 190.

28. **Ibid.**

29. **Ibid.**, p. 191.

30. Raymond E. Brown, "Aspects of New Testament Thought," in *The Jerome Biblical Commentary*, edited by Raymond E. Brown, Joseph A. Fitzmeyer and Roland E. Murphy (Englewood Cliffs, New Jersey: Prentice-Hall, Inc., 1968), p. 795.

31. P. Benoit, *Revue Biblique*. Vol. 56 (1949), 161-203; *Theology Digest*, 8 (196), 105-110.

32. Anton Voegtle, "He Ascended into Heaven," *A New Look at the Apostles' Creed* (Minneapolis: Augsburg Publishing House, 1969), pp. 51-56.

33. **Ibid.**, p. 51.

34. **Ibid.**

35. **Ibid.**

36. **Ibid.**

37. **Ibid.**, p. 52.

38. **Ibid.**

39a. **Ibid.**

39. **Ibid.**, p. 55.

40. Rudolf Bultmann, *Theology of the New Testament*, translated by Kendrick Grobel (New York) Scribner Son's, 1955), II, p. 299.

41. Rudolf Bultmann, "On the Problem of Mythologizing" in *New Testament and Other Bible Writings*, edited by S. Ogden (Philadelphia Fortress Press, 1914), pp. 95-144.

42. John Reumann, *Jesus in the Church's Gospels* (Philadelphia: Fortress Press, 1961), p. 134.

43. **Ibid.**, p. 132.

44. **Ibid.**, p. 133.

45. **Ibid.**, pp. 131-132.

46. Gutav Aulen, *The Faith of the Christian Church*: Translated by Eric H. Wahlstrom and G. Everett Arden (Philadelphia: The Muhlenberg Press, 1948), p. 246.

47. Paul Althaus, *Die Christliche Wahrheit Lehrbuch der Dogmatik* (Guetersloh: C. Bertelsmann, 1949), II, p. 272.

48. **Ibid.**, p. 274.

49. Werner Elert, *Der Christliche Glaube* (Hamburg: Furche Verlag Dritte and eneuerte. Auflage, 1956), p. 121.

50. **Ibid.**, pp. 121-122.

51. As cited by Heinrich Schmid, *Doctrinal Theology of the Evangelical Lutheran Church*. Translated by Charles A. Hayes and Henry E. Jacobs (Minneapolis: Augsburg Publishing House, 1961), Reprint of 1875 edition, p. 380.

52. **Ibid.**, p. 380.

53. Carl E. Braaten and Robert W. Jensen, assisted by Gerhard O. Forde, Hans Schwarz, Philip Hefner and Paul E. Sponheim, *Christian Dogmatics* (Philadelphia: Fortress Press, 1984), Two volumes.

54. **Ibid.**

55. **Ibid.**

56. **Ibid.**

57. **Ibid.**, p. 553.

58. Cf. Werner George Kuemmel, *The New Testament: The History of the Investigation of Its Problems*, Translated by S. Maclean Gilmour and Howard Clark Kee (New York: New York and Nashville: Abingdon Press, 1970), 510 pp.

59. W. G. Kuemmel, "Himmelfahrt Christ," in Die Religion in Geschichte und Gegenwart, herausgegeben von Kurt Galling, Band III, 1958), 336.

60. M. Reu, *Lutheran Dogmatics* (Decorah, Iowa: Wartburg Theological Seminary, 1951), p. 233.

61. Alfred Marshall, *The New International Version. Interlinear Greek-English* (Grand Rapids: Zondervan Publishing House, 1976), p. 354.

62. *The New English Bible with Apocrypha* (Oxford and Cambridge: At the University Presses, 1970), New Testament, p. 110.

63. William Beck, *The Holy Bible - An American Translation* (New Haven, Missouri, 1976), New Testament, p. 115.

64. Reu, **op. cit.**, p. 234.

65. William Arndt, *Bible Commentary, The Gospel According to St. Luke* (St. Louis: Concordia Publishing House, 1956), pp. 502-504.

66. **Ibid.**, p. 500.

67. Ludwig Ott, *Fundamentalist of Catholic Dogma*. Edited in English by James Canon Bastible. Translated from the German by Patrick Lynch (New York: Herder and Herder Book Company, 1957), p. 194.

68. *Die Bekenntnisschriften der Evangelisch Lutherishen Kirche*. 2. Verbessete Auflage, (Goettingen: Vandenhoeck & Ruprecht, 1952), p. 21,26,30.

69. Theodore Tappert, *The Book of Concord* (Philadelphia: Fortress Press, 1959), p. 30.

70. **Ibid.**, pp. 345, 413.

71. **Ibid.**, p. 488.

72. **Ibid.**, p. 292.

73. L. Fuerbringer, Th. Engelder and P.E. Kretzmann, *The Concordia Cyclopedia* (St. Louis: Concordia Publishing House, 1927), pp. 41-42.

74. The Engelder, W. Arndt, Th. Graebner and F. E. Mayer, *Popular Symbolics* (St. Louis: Concordia Publishing House, 1934), pp. 51.

75. John Calvin, *Institutes of the Christian Religion*. Translated from the Latin and Collated with the author's last edition in French (Philadelphia: Presbyterian Board

of Christian Education, no date), II, p. 139.

76. Philip Schaff, *The Creeds of Christendom with a History and Critical Notes*. In Three Volumes (New York: Harper & Brothers, 1877), III, p. 448.

77. **Ibid.**, p. 414.

78. E. J. Bickell, *A Theological Introduction to the Thirty-Nine Articles* (New York: Longmans and Green and Co., 1919), p. 139.

79. **op. cit.**, p. 194.

80. **Ibid.**, p. 194.

81. E. Hove, *Christian Dogmatics* (Minneapolis: Augsburg Publishing House, 1950), p. 203.

83. **Ibid.**

84. Joseph Stump, *The Christian Faith - A System of Christian Dogmatics* (New York: The Macmillan Company, 1932), p. 178.

85. Schmid, **op. cit.**, p. 380.

86. Conrad Emil Lindberg, *Christian Dogmatics and Notes on the History of Dogma*. Second Revised Edition. Translated from the Swedish by Rev. C. E. Hoffsten (Rock Island, Illinois, 1928), p. 244.

87. Reu, **op. cit.**, pp. 233-234.

88. John Theodore Mueller, *Christian Dogmatics* (St. Louis: Concordia Publishing House, 1955), pp. 299-300.

89. Hove, **op. cit.**, p. 203.

90. **Ibid.**, pp. 203-204.

91. A. L. Graebner, *Outlines of Doctrinal Theology* (St. Louis: Concordia Publishing House, 1910), pp. 130-131.

92. Stump, **op. cit.**, p. 179.

93. F. Peiper, *Christian Dogmatics* (St. Louis: Concordia Publishing House, 1951), II, p. 329; John Schaller, *Biblical Christology* (Milwaukee Northwestern Publishing House, 1981), p. 109.

94. Henry Eyster Jacobs, *Summary of the Christian Faith* (Philadelphia: General Council Publication House, 1905), p. 158.

95. Edward W. A. Koehler, *A Summary of Christian Doctrine* (Detroit and Oakland: The Reverends L. H. Koehler and Alfred Koehler, 1952). Second Revised Edition, p. 106.

Questions

1. How did the coming of the historical-critical method of Bible interpretation effect the attitude toward the Ascension of Christ? ____

2. Schleiermacher was the father of ____.

3. Edgar Goodspeed has Christ's life ending with ____.

4. What does the *Interpreter's Dictionary of the Bible* teach about the Ascension? ____

5. Redaction criticism holds that ____.

6. What did Macgregor maintain in *The Interpreter's Bible* about the Ascension? ____

7. What did Emil Brunner preach about the Ascension? ____

8. What did Helmut Theilicke write about the Ascension? ____

9. What does Raymond Brown say in the Jerome Biblical Commentary about the Ascension? ____

10. Rudolph Bultmann did not believe that Jesus ascended into heaven because he did not believe Jesus ____ from the dead.
11. The American Lutheran John Reumann questioned ____.
12. The Swedish theologian Aulen has little to say about the ____.
13. What did Paul Althous say about Luke's account of the Ascension? ____
14. Carl Braaten in the two volume *Christian Dogmatics* by professors of the Lutheran Church in American and American Lutheran Church says the number "forty" is not to be taken ____.
15. Hove commented that the Ascension was no ____.
16. What did Joseph Stump say about the Ascension? ____
17. The Ascension of Christ marks for the Savior the highest ____.
18. Heaven is a mode of existence quite different than ____.
19. To sit at the right hand of God means ____.

Advent and Christmas Prophecies in Isaiah/and Micah, Two Eighth-Century B.C. Prophets

The Old Testament Believers Look Forward to the Days of the New Testament

Christian News, December 3, 1990

The Old Testament believers looked forward to the days of the New Testament. The prophet Jeremiah announced the truth that *God* would make a new covenant with the house of Israel.[1] Jesus claimed that the Old Testament spoke specifically of Him. To his contemporaries He averred: "Search the Scriptures for in them you think that you have eternal life and they are they which testify of me (John 5:39)." The Apostle Paul informed Timothy: "And that from babyhood you have known the Holy Scriptures, which are able to make you wise unto salvation through Christ Jesus" (2 Timothy 3:15). "The evangelist St. Matthew made it a special point of emphasis that many events and happenings in the life of Jesus had been foretold in various Old Testament Scriptures. There are a number of times when he wrote: "All things happened that it might be fulfilled that which was spoken by the prophet. . . ."[2] Beginning with the Virgin Conception and Birth till the coming of John the Baptist as waypreparer for the Messiah, the Old Testament announced many facts about the life and ministry of Jesus of Nazareth.

Christ is the center and heart of the 39 books of the Old Testament or the 24 books of the Hebrew arrangement of the Scriptures of the Old Covenant. It is this truth which since the time of Jesus' coming and ministry differentiates Judaism from Christianity.[3] Modern theological liberalism is characterized by its denial of predictive Messianic prophecy.[4] By the repudiation of the clear statements of the New Testament writers as well as the assertions of Christ Himself, theological liberals have denied the deity of Christ and with it also the doctrine of the Trinity, which is the basis of the Three Ecumenical Creeds of Christendom: the Apostles, the Nicene and the Anthanasian Creeds.

Because of the many clear declarations about Christ as Redeemer and Savior in the Old Testament, the Christian Church in its liturgies, catechetics and sermonizing has utilized passages and pericopes that are Messianic in character and content. In fact all major Christian Churches that use a church year have chosen many texts from the Old Testament that speak about Christ and the New Testament Age. A number of pericopal systems have Old Testament Messianic texts for various Sundays of the first half of the church year beginning with Advent and ending with Pentecost.

This is the case relative to the Eisenach,[5] Thomasius pericopal systems,[6] as well as twentieth century systems as given in the Synodical four series of new pericopes.[7] Series A, B, C adopted Old Testament texts that were deemed appropriate by the Inter-Lutheran Commission on

Worship.[8] In all these lectionary systems, Old Testament texts for the Sundays in Advent, Christmas and Epiphany that were deemed to speak about the great events in the life of Christ were selected.

Five of the eighth century B.C. prophets have within them Messianic prophecies. Jonah, Hosea, Amos, Isaiah and Micah contain prophecies about the Messiah, whom the New Testament has identified with David's greater Son, Jesus of Nazareth.[9] Jonah, a prophet of the Northern Kingdom, who preached repentance to Assyria and its capital Nineveh, furnished a type of Christ's entombment and resurrection by his being swallowed by a great fish and spewed out after three days.[10] This is the clear teaching of the New Testament, yes, by Christ Himself. Hosea at the end of each of the first three chapters of his prophetic book has Messianic prophecies that speak of Israel truly being God's people and a new coming David, Jesus Christ, as their spiritual ruler.[10a] Amos prophesies about the restoration of the new Israel, the Israel of God which would embrace Jew and Gentile.[11]

Isaiah and Micah, both contemporaries of each other, are rich in Messianic predictions that announce at least 700 years in advance the conception, birth, childhood of God's Messiah. In preparation for the new year of our Lord, beginning December 2nd the following prophecies from Isaiah and Micah will be discussed, namely, Isaiah 2:2-4; 40:1-3; Isaiah 7:14; and Micah 4:1-4; 5:1-7; Isaiah 9:5-6.

Because of the plenitude of Messianic prophecies Isaiah has been called "The Fifth Evangelist," or his prophetic book has been denominated "The Fifth Gospel." Verses which have been considered Messianic, which includes also passages that predict the New Testament Messianic age, are 2:1-4; 4:1-6; 7:14; 9:5-6; 11:1-11; 40:1-3; 42:1-9; 49:1-6; 50:4-11; 52:13-53:12; 60:1-9; 63:1-6.[12] Concerning the Messianic emphasis in Isaiah, Halley wrote as follows: "Isaiah has been entitled the Messianic prophet because he was so thoroughly imbued with the idea that his nation was to be a Messianic nation to the world, that is a nation through whom one day a great and wonderful blessing would come from God to all nations, and he was continuously dreaming of the day when that great and wonderful work could be done."[13]

The New Testament's Interpretation of Isaiah as Messianic

The New Testament clearly teaches that Isaiah "saw the glory of Christ, and spoke of him (John 12:41)." Various New Testament writers have not only assigned all of the sixty-six chapters to Isaiah, thus negating the theories of Isaiah 1, Isaiah 2, (Deutero Isaiah) or Isaiah 3 (Trito-Isaiah), but apply many Isaianic passages as predictive of Christ's person and ministry.[14]

The Eight Century Prophets of Isaiah and Micah and Advent and Christmas

In preparation for the new church year beginning on December 2, 1990 this presentation will discuss those prophecies in Isaiah and Micah that deal with the coming of John the Baptist, the prediction of the Virgin

940

Conception and Virgin Birth, the deity of the Messiah, His divine names, and the purpose of his ministry. The prophecies that will specifically be discussed are Isaiah 2:24; Isaiah 40:1-3; Isaiah 7:14; 9:5-6 and Micah 4:1-4 and Micah 5:2-4.

The New Testament Era Predicted by Micah and Isaiah

The coming of the Messianic Age was foretold by both Isaiah and Micah, two contemporary prophets of Judah. Thus in Isaiah 2:2-4 it reads: "In the last times the mountain of the Lord's temple will be established at the top of the mountain and be raised above the hills and all the mountains and be raised above the hills and all nations shall flow to it. Then many people will go and say, Come let us go up to the Lord's mountain and to the temple of the God of Jacob, and He will lead us in his ways and we will live in them. The Lord's Instruction comes from Zion and His Word from Jerusalem, And he will judge between the nations and make decisions for many people. Then they shall hammer their swords into plowshares and their spears into pruning hooks. No nation will raise a sword against another or train for war anymore."[15]

The Prophet Micah has the same prophecy in 4:1-4 but adds the verse: "But everyone will sit under his vine and his fig tree with nobody to frighten them, because the LORD armies has promised that (v. 4)." That this is a Messianic passage is recognized by Rabbi Slotki who asserted about Isaiah 2:2-4 as follows: "the introduction (i.e. to chapter (II to IV) describing the glories of the Messianic Age,"[16] and "Rabbi Goldman claims that it is a vision of the end of days, i.e. of the Messianic Age."[17]

What is the Meaning of Isaiah 4:2-4 and Micah 4:1-4? The "last days" (Hebrew: aharim hayammim) refers to the time period before the Second (coming of Christ. During this period "the mountain of the LORD'S house, that is Zion, the Christian Church will be established, in the top of the highest mountains," that is the Christian Zion will tower above every human organization, especially over every idolatrous organization.[18] All nations shall flow to the Christian Church. P. E. Kretzmann opines that "this is said of the Church in the time of the New Testament, when it is established in all the world, high above all religions and churches drawing men from all nations to seek the true God."[19] According to the Book of Acts, the Christian Church was organized in Jerusalem with a membership of 3,000 members which shortly thereafter grew to 5,000 devotees. In obedience to Christ's command the disciple began at Jerusalem, did missionary work in Judea, Samaria, Syria, Asia Minor, in various provinces of Roman Europe and by the year A.D. 1,000 Christianity had spread over most of Europe and had also been taken into Africa and India and China.[20] The spiritual Zion, organized by the Holy Spirit through the preaching of the apostles, carried out Christ's commission to take the Gospel to the ends of the earth.[21]

"The Law of God in the wider sense, including Law and Gospel went out from Jerusalem, the message foretold in the Old Testament by type and direct prophecies, was proclaimed among all nations, and repentance and forgiveness of sin was proclaimed to the nations by Paul and the 12

Apostles. Jesus as Judge and King will judge among all nations (v. 4), He will rebuke many people setting forth His decisions under the influence of Christ's Spirit, who lives in Christians, of whom it is said that they will beat their swords into ploughshares and their spears into pruning hooks, nation shall not rise up against nation, neither will they make war anymore, because in the Church of God as it really exists under the government of the Messiah, the Prince of Peace, there is nothing but peace, unity and love. Here, as Kretzmann has awarded one finds a wonderful description of the Messianic kingdom."[22]

Isaiah 2:2-4 and Micah 4:1-4 have been misinterpreted by those who believe that this oracle represents a wish on the part of these prophets, which expresses the hope that when once nations use their common sense and realize the futility of war, that they will realize this and agree to live together peacefully.[23] Such an existence among nations would truly represent a Messianic age. Every Christmas one will find preachers that express this sentiment, which disagrees with Jesus' statement in the Olivet discourse "that there will always be wars and rumors of wars" (Matthew 24).

Another wrong understanding of this oracle is the idea that when Christ comes a second time to this earth that after his appearance there will be a thousand years of peace on earth, during which time Christ will rule visibly in Jerusalem as King, recognized as such by all people.[24] This interpretation conflicts with Christ's teaching that His Kingdom is not of this world, or the assertion of Christ that "the kingdom of God does not come by observation, nor that men shall say lo or here, for the Kingdom of God in within you."[25]

The interpretation that Isaiah is not to be understood literally but figuratively also agrees with the prediction of the establishment of a new covenant as announced in Jeremiah 31:31-34. The days of the new covenant are said by the Epistle to the Hebrews to be fulfilled in the coming of Christ and the New Testament age.[26]

John the Baptist's Coming Announced by Isaiah

The ministry of Christ was preceded by the appearance of the preaching of repentance to the Jews of Judea and Jerusalem. The appearance of John, son of Zecharias and Elizabeth, marked the opening of the Messianic Age. In the Magnificat, Zechariah clearly stated: "Blessed be the Lord, God of Israel, for He hath visited and redeemed his people, and has raised up a mighty Deliverer for us in the house of David, as he spake by the mouths of his holy prophets which have been since the world began, to deliver us from our enemies, and from the power of all who hate us (Luke 1:68-71)."[27] In this opening prophecy of the New Testament John's father further declared: "He showed mercy to our forefathers. He remembered his holy covenant, the oath which he swore to Abraham, our forefather, that we should be delivered out of the hands of our enemies. And should serve him without fear, in holiness and righteousness all of our days (1:72-75)."[28]

Thus the Messianic era began with the preaching of John the Baptizer, who, his father claimed, was called "a Prophet of the Most High, for thou shall go before the Lord to prepare his way (1:76)." In the opening great chapter of the second half of Isaiah, the prophet in 40:3-5 predicted the coming and work of John the Baptist.[29]

When John the Baptist appeared A.D. 26 in the Judean desert, Matthew, Mark, Luke and John, all four Evangelists, stated that John's preaching was a fulfillment of the prophet Isaiah in chapter 40:3-5. Thus Matthew wrote: "For this is he of whom Isaiah said 'The voice of one crying in the wilderness,'" "Prepare the way of the Lord." Luther,[30] Stoeckhardt,[31] Francis Pieper,[32] P. Kretzmann,[33] Fahling,[34] Fuerbringer,[35] and many others. Considered Isaiah 40:3-5 as foretelling the coming of John. Ylvisaker wrote concerning the matter whether Isaiah 40 predicts John's coming and preaching and baptizing for the remission of sins as follows: "All the Synoptists find in the account of the appearance of John a fulfillment of Is. 40:3. Mark also of Mal. 3:1. As Elijah was called by an angel so was also the Baptist; and as the mission of Elijah was to return to the people to the Lord, even so it was with John. Luke quotes the passage from Isaiah more fully than Matthew and Mark, but each takes it from the Septuagint. Several recent expositors of a recent period assert the quotation from Isaiah refer to the return of the people from exile, and to Jehovah's repossession of the Holy Land. This is not correct. According to verse 9, the people are in the Holy Land, and God is considered as coming to it. And for His return the people shall prepare the way, in order that the glory of the Lord may appear and all flesh may behold it."[36]

Arndt in his commentary on Luke wrote: "The quotation from the prophet Isaiah which is introduced here is found in Is. 40:3-5. The same quotation is given in Mt. 3:3, although in shorter form; in Mk. 1:3 it is used, and in John 1:23, where the words are still more brief. Evidently these words of the prophet were treasured by the early Christians and often repeated in Christian teaching. The prophecy was fulfilled in the coming and work of John the Baptist and is one of the grandest in the Old Testament. It definitely points to the Messianic Age and to the forerunner of the messiah."[37]

Liberal critical scholarship completely rejects the Biblical assertions that Isaiah 40:3-5 announced seven hundred years before the coming of the Messiah's waypreparer.[38] It appears that a number of conservative commentaries have accepted the critical interpretation that Isaiah 40:3-5 speaks of the return of Israel from the Babylonian Captivity.[39]

The Virginal Conception and Virgin Birth Foretold

The prophet Isaiah announced not only the coming of the new age, the Messianic period of world history, but Isaiah by divine inspiration also proclaimed to King Ahaz that the Messiah was to be virgin-conceived and that the Messiah's mother would become pregnant by the Holy Spirit. In other words, the Messiah would have an earthly mother, but not an earthly father.

Kligermann, a Hebrew Christian scholar, wrote about Isaiah's remarkable prophecies about the Messiah: "As we read this book we cannot but

943

feel that here is a prophet who was admitted to closer, a more inward and spiritual, fellowship with God than any of the brethren. His spirit rose to a larger prevision of 'the grace and truth' which 'came to Jesus Christ.' That is what we mean when we call him 'the Evangel' of the Old Testament. He had seen God face to face. His was the vision of 'the Lord sitting upon a throne, high and lifted up,' which made him a PROPHET (Is. 6:1-8). What he had seen, others might see, and it was his ruling task and the endeavor of his life to make them see."[40]

Isaiah 7:14 is said by the Apostle St. Matthew to have foretold the Virginal Conception and the Virgin Birth of Jesus Christ, son of Mary, thus Matthew asserted: "All this happened so that what the Lord had said would be fulfilled. Behold, the virgin will conceive and have a son and they will call His name Immanuel (Matthew 1:22-23)."

The Historical Background of Isaiah 7:14

Isaiah 7:14 was an oracle that was uttered to Ahaz in connection with the Syro-Ephraimitic War of 735-734 B.C.[41] In 735 B.C. Syria and Israel were threatened by the Assyrians under Tiglath-Pileser II. The Syrian King Rezin and the King of Israel, Pekah, wanted to force Judah into a military alliance against Assyria. However, Ahaz, the king of Judah was not interested in warring against the Assyrians. The two kings to the north of Judah wanted to replace Ahaz with Tabeel. While Ahaz was examining his water supply in preparation for an attack by Syria and Israel, Isaiah appeared "at the canal from the upper pool, on the road to the Laundryman's Field." Isaiah encouraged Ahaz to place his trust in Yahweh and simultaneously informed him that within a short time both Syria and Israel would cease to exist. Isaiah was sent a second time by God to Ahaz and encouraged him not to worry about Judah's enemies, so long as the king would completely trust Yahweh. God through Isaiah offered to perform some spectacular sign as proof that Yahweh could do what he has promised. But Ahaz disbelieved and said he did not want to tempt God by asking for a spectacular sign. Upon this refusal to accept Yahweh's offer, the latter through Isaiah then announced that in the future a remarkable event would occur, namely a virgin would conceive and bear a son, and she will call His name "Immanuel."[42]

The Isaiah prophecy was not merely a sign for those times, but it was "the Sign of the Ages."[43] There are seven different points that must be noted about the oracle the Holy Spirit revealed unto Israel.[44] 1. The sign was divinely given ("the Lord Himself") shall give it; 2. It was given to the House of David ("to you" plural) and not merely to Ahab. 3. The sign involved a miracle and did not refer to any baby of the eighth century. It had to match what Yahweh promised to do for Ahaz, making the sign "deep as Sheol" or making it as "high as the heavens." This implied a unique and stupendous miracle. 4. The sign concerned the perpetuation of the House of David till the present sign of the ages would be fulfilled. 5. The sign involved a "virgin" ('almah'). This concept of a virgin is implied by the context and is shown by the fulfillment in Matthew 1:22-23, where parthenos is employed. The Septuagint (c. 250 B.C.) translated 'almah as parthenos.' That this is the ways the Jews understood it shown by the fact that the new LXX translations of Aquila, Symmachus and Theodotion render "almah" as neanis, i.e. "young woman." The claim that "almah" means young woman of marriageable age who may be unmarried or married goes against the possible meaning of the word for almah in Gen. 24:43; Ex. 2:8; Ps. 68:25; Song 1:3; Prov. 30:19. 6. The very name "Immanuel" meaning with us (humanity) is God (deity), requires the incarnation of Christ and argues for the theanthropic person of Christ. 7. Although "Immanuel" would be divine. He would eat what other children ate and thus be truly human. Cf. Luke 2:52.

Isaiah 7:14 is not to be considered as an isolated prophecy dealing with just one specific incidence in the life of Christ, but it is an important link in a whole chain of Messianic prophecies beginning with Genesis 3:15 and ending with Malachi 4:2.[45] The sum total of these great predictions is that a Savior-Redeemer would ultimately come who would deliver Israel from its real peril of its cancerous affliction, affecting it was the head (the wicked Ahaz) on down to the feet (the lowest citizen (Is. 1:26).

Interpretations Rejecting the Direct Prophecy and Fulfillment Conception

A review and analysis of Isaiah 7:14 has shown that many divergent interpretations have been advanced denying the direct prophecy-fulfillment understanding of the Virgin Conception and Virgin Birth interpretation.[46] Radical critical scholarship opposed the understanding of Luther,[47] Eckhards,[48] Stoeckhardt,[49] F. Pieper,[50] Kretzmann,[51] Laestch,[52] Engelder,[53] Mennicke[54] and of non-Lutheran scholars like E. Young,[55] Unger,[56] Hindson and many others as impossible because the Virgin Birth explanation requires the belief in the miraculous and the supernatural, which hostile Old Testament scholarship finds intellectually unacceptable.

Another reason advocated against the direct prophecy fulfillment interpretation is the claim that for Isaiah's second oracle to make meaning to Ahaz that it would have to refer to an event of the eighth century and that a prediction about a birth which would occur seven hundred years later would be meaningless to Ahaz and those who may have heard it. Stoeckhardt has however, pointed out that Isaiah 7:14 and following was an announcement to Arab of a judgment to come on Judah, beginning in 735 B.C. and ending with the punishment of Judah under Roman rule.[58] The prophecy of 7:14 would only be helpful and comforting to those, who in subsequent ages would be waiting for the hope of Israel. The Virgin Conception and Virgin Birth prediction had meaning for the true believers of Isaiah's and Ahab's time. Leupold, citing Junker, claims Isaiah 7:14 "is fundamental to the development of the Messianic concept in Old Testament prophecy."[58a]

An interpretation that does not do justice to Isaiah 7:14 is the one which claims that the prediction to Ahaz has two meanings: a primary and a secondary. The primary one who consists in Isaiah announcing that in the near future that a woman in Judah would become pregnant and bear a son and call the child Immanuel, i.e. God is with us.[59] The secondary meaning would be the way Matthew explained the verse, namely, that a virgin was to bear a son and call Him Immanuel. This interpretation has two serious problems. The Judean woman of Ahaz's time would become pregnant by a man, while in the Matthean account the Holy Spirit brings about the pregnancy. Furthermore, in view of historic developments following the oracle by Isaiah to Ahaz, the two kings from the north, Syria and Israel invaded Judah according to 2 Chronicles 28 and killed 120,000 Judeans and took 200,000 captives. How can such a military disaster be understood as God-with-us? It would appear that those conservative scholars who claim that the "almah" of Isaiah 7:14 is a type of Christ or find two alleged meanings in the text are accommodating themselves to the higher critics, who were responsible for rejecting the second oracle of Isaiah to Ahaz as a true rectilinear prophecy of Jesus' Virginal Conception and Virgin Birth.[60]

Finding two meanings in a text was rejected by Luther,[61] Walther,[62] Fuerbringer,[63] Mennike[64] and the hermeneutics taught in The Lutheran Church-Missouri Synod for over a hundred years. Ascribing two different meanings to a given text is rejected by legal hermeneutics and its practice would lead to allegorization, a system of hermeneutics that bedeviled the Christian Church for over a thousand years.

The Immanuel Section of Isaiah and Immanuel
Chapters 7-12 have been called "the Immanuel Book" by a number of scholars. Besides chapter 7:14 the name Immanuel is found in 8:14, and 8:10. In chapter 8 where Isaiah announced the coming of the Assyrian who would overrun Judah, the prophet addresses Immanuel as Lord of Judah. Calling the land of Judah as belonging to Christ makes sense, because He made the whole world, including Palestine of which Judah was a part.[65] Even though the Assyrians will overflow the land or their wings spread like a bird of prey over the land, God warned that the evil plans of the Assyrians will come to naught, because Immanuel is with the Judeans, God's people.

The Wonder Child with the Four Divine Names
The conception and predicted birth of the Messiah is realized in Isaiah 9:5-6, where the prophet announces the birth of the Messiah. This prophecy is preceded with the description of the Galilean ministry of Christ. "Zebulon and Naphthali were among the tribes of Israel located in the northern territory later called Galilee. The Judeans always disdained the Galileans. But the prophet Isaiah saw, eight centuries in advance, that the 'Stranger of Galilee' would bring the light of life first to that land."[66]

"Unto us a son is given" reminds the readers of John 3:16, where Jesus of Nazareth is called God's Son. The Messiah will be a Ruler, He will exercise the government, not as a burden, but as an epaulet, an insignia of high rank. Five names or possibly six, are listed in behalf of this King. He is described as the miracle, the counselor, mighty God, everlasting

Father, Prince of Peace. Walter A. Maier, Sr. in a Christmas sermon, took the position that the Hebrew "people" should be rendered "the Miracle," because His birth was miraculous as was His whole life.[67] Jesus performed many miracles. His resurrection was a miracle, as was His ascension into heaven. Stolee wrote concerning this matter: "Our Revised Standard Version reads 'wonderful counselor' as one name. But inasmuch as the word wonderful also may be rendered wonder and describes an attribute which is distinct from 'counsellor,' we prefer to omit the comma in this instance (Judges 13:18; Psalm 71:7)."[68]

Isaiah 9:5-6 emphasized both the humanity and the deity of the Messiah. The deity of the Messiah has been rejected by critical Old Testament scholars, who have rendered the second half of verse 6: "and he shall be called in purpose wonderful, in battle God-like, Father of all time, Prince of peace."[69]

The New Berkeley Version renders the text correctly: "For unto us a Child is born to us a Son is given; the government shall be upon His shoulder, and His name shall be called Wonderful, Counselor, Mighty God, Everlasting Father, Prince of Peace."[70] This oracle which in no way speaks about Hezekiah sets forth the theanthropic person of the Messiah, who was to be Immanuel, that is God in human form.[71] "Unto us a Child is born, unto us a Son is given," in these two expressions both the humanity and the deity of Christ was expressed. The child refers to his human nature. As was seen from Chapter 7:14 the Messiah was to come into the world as the virgin's son. Joseph was not his human father, his conception was caused by the Holy Spirit. Jesus was also the eternal Son of the Father who did come from the glory He enjoyed with the Father from all past eternity. In order to effect our salvation he had to be a human being, substituting for mankind, and yet only as God could he atone for the sins of the world.[72]

"The government was to be upon His shoulder." Thus he was destined to exercise supreme rule over all the universe. Old Testament prophecies predicted that the Messiah would be a King.[73] The Messiah would not be able to exercise universal rule and be King of Kings and Lord of Lords, if he were not "the mighty God." There are those who would tone down this truth, which also later would be enunciated by Jeremiah in 23:5-6, where the Messiah's name is called "Yahweh is our righteousness."

The Messiah is further called "The everlasting Father." A better translation would be "the Father of Eternity." The Son is not to be confused with the Father, though He and the Father are one (John 10:30). Christ is eternal, like the Father and the Holy Spirit.

The last of the unique names predicted of the Messiah is that He is "the Prince of Peace". "That was fulfilled when the newborn Son of the Virgin Mary was presented as bringing peace on earth. By the blood shed before His crucifixion and during it. The Messiah, Jesus Christ, made peace between God and mankind. All those who trust in Him are at peace with God and may also be at peace with their neighbor in this world of warfare and hatred."[74]

In Isaiah 9:7 the world is told: "Of the increase of his government and peace there shall be no end, upon the throne of David, and upon His kingdom, to order it, and to establish it with judgment and with justice from henceforth even forever. The zeal of the Lord of hosts will perform this." Millennialist's believe that this prophecy will be fulfilled in the seventh dispensation, when Christ will visibly reign in Jerusalem for nearly a thousand years, in which the Jews, who generally today reject His kingship, will experience a complete change of heart.[75] The truth, however, is that Christ when He ascended on high occupies the seat at the right hand of God, from where he directs human affairs in the interest of His Church. When the Messiah returned for the judgment of the nations, then all nations and kings will recognize Jesus as King of Kings. To the believers He has promised: "To him that overcometh will I grant to sit with Me in my throne, even as I also overcame, and am set down with My Father in His throne" (Rev. 3:21).

Micah's Christmas Prophecy 5:2-5

Micah 5:2-5 is the second Messianic prophecy found in . Lenski asserted about Micah 5:2-4 as follows: "There are two prominent Christmas texts in the Old Testament, Is. 9-6-7 and our text, much like two of the New Testament, Matthew 1,18 etc. and Luke 2,1 etc. Both of these Old Testament texts are so satisfactory because they foretell the wondrous birth in the plainest terms, and then declare the divine greatness of the Child thus born. Our text is even plainer on the first point than the Isaiah text, for in a significant way it refers to the Savior's mother 'she which travaileth,' omitting any reference to a father. Furthermore, the very birthplace is clearly named at this early date, for Micah's activity lies between 697 and 756."[76]

In Micah 4:1-4 having described the glory, peace and victory which during the Messianic period would be the characteristics of the Kingdom of Messiah would bring about, the prophet Micah under the Holy Spirit's revelation in chapter 5 turns to direct predictions of the person and work of the coming Redeemer. The chapter opens this way: "Now gather thyself in troops, daughters of troops. He has laid siege against us. They will strike the judge of Israel with a rod on the cheek" (v. 1).[77] Jerusalem has designated herself as the Church Militant. Judah before the incarnation of the Messiah was characterized by very deep humiliation, when all the former glory had faded away from the Jewish nation. But at the time of greatest degradation, when all the former glory had faded away from the Jewish nation, there then would occur the greatest event of human history, the birth of God's Son, the promised Messiah. A number of Old Testament pericopal systems have listed Micah 5:2-4 as an Old Testament text predicting the Incarnation of Jesus of Nazareth. That Micah 5:2 announced before and the birth of the world's Redeemer is clear from Matthew 2:6, where when Herod the Great consulted the scholars of the Sanhedrin as to where the Messiah was to be born, he was told: "But you, Bethlehem, in the land of Judah, are among the least among the rulers of Judah, for out of you shall come out a Ruler who will shepherd My people Israel." Correctly understood this verse is speaking of a Deliverer who

948

will come from Bethlehem. Micah sees this Deliverer of village birth, one Who in himself was the pre-existence God, standing in the midst of His little flock to feed and strengthen them, as true man and God.

The deity of the Messiah as seen from verse 2 is denied in liberal critical translations, which render "whose going forth are of old from ancient days."[78] *The New English Bible* renders this Hebrew text into English as follows: "But you, Bethlehem in Ephrata, as you are among Judah's clans, out of you shall come forth a governor for Israel, one whose roots are far back in the past, in days gone by."[79] Micah tells that the Ruler who was to come would not be born in Jerusalem, but in Bethlehem, the town where David was born. "Going forth" or "come forth" does not per se denote birth (cf. Micah 4:10), but here it is the context which clearly shows that "going forth" means, because she which travaileth is the mother of the child. No father is referred to here, just as in Isaiah 7:14, where only the mother, the Virgin is said to give birth to the Messiah. Thus two eighth-century prophets refer to this unique fact of Christ's life, that He only had a human mother but not a human father. Not only did the priests at the time of Herod the Great understand Micah 5:2 as referring to the Messiah, but that was also the belief of the people, for in John 7:42 the people said: "Has not the Scripture said that the Church comes from the seed of David and from the town of Bethlehem, where David was?"

The Kingship Predicted by Other Old Testament Passages

The Messiah was to be a ruler in Israel, rather than over Israel. Such a ruler had been foretold long ago and time and time again this fact of His Kingship predicted, such as Gen. 49:10f.; I Sam. 7:12ff.; Psalms 2,22,23; 45,47,72; 110; Is. 9:6f). But now for the first time the Old Testament believer was told it would be Bethlehem.

The Eternal Origins of Israel's Messiah

Laetsch said that "going forth," "from of old," "from everlasting," said of the Messiah that: "The Jewish rabbis in the Christian era refer these words either to the Messiah's name in eternity or to the idea of the Messiah existing in God's mind before the creation of the world." Rationalistic interpreters of the early nineteenth century generally adopted these interpretations. Modern Jewish and Protestant interpreters generally refer "from of old," "from everlasting," "to the rise of the Davidic dynasty." To this view Laetsch objects by asserting: "Yet a lineage dating back to ancient times could not possibly have served as a special characteristic of the future ruler. Every descendant of David and even of Abraham and Adam could trace his lineage back to creation (cp. I Chron. 1-28; 3:1-13)."[80] Laetsch rejects Orelli's interpretation that the words "denote the many preparations made by God from the earliest times in prophecy and history for the foundations of the Messianic kingdom."[81] The reason Laetsch gives for this rejection is: "For the words speak not of the founding of a kingdom, nor, of the preparations for such a kingdom, nor of the prophecies of the going forth of the Ruler. The prophet here speaks of the goings forth and of the birth of a future Ruler. Keil, on the other hand

949

regards the plural 'going forth' as referring both to the origin of the Messiah before all worlds and to His appearances in the olden times."[82]

In Micah 5:3 the prophet predicts that Israel will come subject to foreign nations until the time "that she which travaileth hath brought forth," namely, the Messiah. With Christ's birth, "then the remnant of His brethren shall return unto the children of Israel," with the birth of Christ He would bring together from various nations of the world those whom he would add to the spiritual Israel. Averred Kretzmann, "the humiliation of the house of David and of Israel has been included in the plan of God, but the final result would be, that the Messiah, like his ancestor David would go forth from the humble city of Bethlehem."[83]

The next verse 4, speaks of the truth that the Messiah would stand and feed His people, that the Christ would both rule and nourish His people. The Messiah would perform these things in the strength of God (Is. 9:6). With verse 4 the prophetic description is rounded out. Not only will the Messiah rule over Israel but the greatness of His rule is stated in these words: "He shall stand and feed in the strength of the Lord, in the majesty of the name of the Lord his God; and they shall abide: for now shall he be great unto the ends of the earth." According to Jesus' statements in the Johannine Gospel, there was an intimate relationship between Jesus and the Father. His ruling as a man is unique, because he shares in His Father's divine strength.

The result of his shepherding and other activity shall be the blessedness of peace. This agrees with Isaiah 9:6, where the Messiah is called "Prince of Peace." It also was fulfilled as is apparent from Luke 2:14. As a result of the Christ's work of atonement Paul could write: "But now in Christ Jesus you who were once far away have been brought near in the blood of Christ. For he is our peace, who hath the two of us (Jew and Gentile) one, and hath broken down the part-wall of partition between us."[84] Micah predicted that the Messiah's name would be great unto the ends of the earth. This prophecy has also been fulfilled as the missionary history of the last nineteen hundred years has shown.

Footnotes

1. Jeremiah 31:31-34. Cf. R. C. H. Lenski, *The Eisenach Old Testament Selections* (Columbus, *Lutheran Book Concern*, 1925), p. 17.
2. Matthew 1:22; 2:15,17; 3:2; 4:14; 3:17; 12:17; 13:14,35; 21:4; 26:56; 27:9.
3. Cf. the Statements about Jesus in the Talmud. Cf. *Christian News Encyclopedia* (Washington, Missouri, 1988), p. 3109.
4. S. Mohwinkel, *He That Cometh* (Nashville, Abingdon Cokesbury, 1956), pp. 3-95.
5. Lenski, **op. cit.**, Jeremiah 31:31-34; Malachi 4; 1-6; Isaiah 40:1-8: Deuteronomy 18:15-18; Isaiah 40:1-3; Micah 5:2-4.
6. Martin Reu, *Thomasius Old Testament Selections* (Columbus, The Warburg Press, 1959), Malachi 4:1-6; Isaiah 40:1-10; Isaiah 2:2-5; Isaiah 9:6-7.
7. The selections are listed by Soll, *Pericopes and Selections* (Yakima, Washington, 1929), published by the author, pp. 12-22.
8. Series A,B,C are published by Augsburg Publishing House, Minneapolis. In Series A of The Lessons the following texts are found: Isaiah 2:1-4; Is. 11:1-11; Is.7:10-

14; Is. 9:2-7; in Series B, Is. 40:1-11; Is. 9:2-7; in Series C, Jeremiah 33:14-16; Malachi 3:1-4; Micah 5:2-7.

9. Paul Heinisch, *Christ in Prophecy*, Translated by William G. Heidt (Collegeville, Minn., Liturgical Press, 1956), p. viii-ix.

10. Edward Mack, *The Christ of the Old Testament* (Richmond, Presbyterian Committee of Publications, 1926), p. 95.

10a. Heinisch, **op. cit.**, pp. 77-79.

11. Theo. Laetsch, *Bible Commentary - The Minor Prophets* (St. Louis, Concordia Publishing House, 1956), pp. 190-192.

12. Cf. Listing of Isaianic Messianic prophecies in Thompson, *The New Chain Reference Bible* (Indianapolis, Kirkbride Bible Co., 1928), 246-49. *New American Standard Bible, The Open Bible* (New York, Thomas Nelson, 1935), 1236-1243.

13. Henry H. Halley, *Halley's Bible Handbook* (Grand Rapids, Zondervan Publishing House, 1965), 24th Edition, p. 285.

14. Edward J. Young, *An Introduction to the Old Testament* (Grand Rapids, Wm. B. Eerdmans Publishing House, 1964), p. 206.

15. Translation in Beck's *The Holy Bible - An American Translation* (Leader Publication Company of New Haven, Missouri, 1976), Old Testament, p. 786-737.

16. Rev. Rabbi Slotki, Isaiah, *Hebrew Text and Translation* (London, The Soncino Press. 1949), p. 9.

17. The Rev. Doctor A. Cohen, *The Twelve Minor Prophets* (London, The Soncino Press, 1957), p. 169.

18. G. Stoeckhardt, *Der Prophet Jesaja. Die Ersten Zwoelf Kapitel* (St. Louis, Concordia Publishing House, 1902), p. 22. H. Oswald, *Luther's Works* (St. Louis, Concordia Publishing House, 1977, pp.40-60.

19. P. E. Kretzmann, *Popular Commentary - Old Testament* (St. Louis, Concordia Publishing House, 1924), 11, 291.

20. Lars P. Qualben, *A History of the Christian Church* (New York, Thomas Nelson and Sons, 1940), pp. 134-136.

21. H. C. Leupold, *Exposition of Isaiah* (Grand Rapids, Baker Book House, 1963), Volume 1, pp. 77-73.

22. Kretzmann, **op. cit.**, 11, p. 291.

23. G. Ernst Wright, *The Book of Isaiah - The Layman's Bible Commentary*(Richmond, John Knox Press, 1964), pp. 26-27. President Carter expressed this view at the signing of the Camp David Agreement, with President Sadat present.

24. B. Keller, *Der Prophet Jesaja fuer bibelforschende Christen erklaert* (Neumuenster, Vereinbuchhandlung G. Ihloff & Co., 1928), p. 38; R. Ludwigson, *A Survey of Bible Prophecy* (Grand Rapids, Zondervan Publishing House. 1951). p. 176.

25. John Theodore Mueller, *Christian Dogmatics* (St. Louis, Concordia Publishing House, 1955), pp. 620-621. Cf. refutation of millennialism in F.E. Mayer, Religious Bodies in America (St. Louis Concordia Publishing House, 1956, pp. 424-425.

26. Cf. the interpretation of Lenski, **op. cit.**, pp. 11-33. Also C.F. Zorn, Die Epistel an die Hebraer (Milwaukee, Northwestern Publishing House, 1917), pp. 44-45.

27. Translation of Helen Barrett Montgomery, *The New Testament in Modern English* (Philadelphia, The Judson Press, 1924), p. 152.

28. **Ibid.**

29. William F. Arndt, *Bible Commentary - The Gospel of St. Luke* (St. Louis, Concordia Publishing House, 1956). pp. 65-69.

30. *Luther's Work - The American Edition*. J. Pelikan and H. Oswald, Isaiah, 40-66 (St. Louis, Concordia Publishing House, 1969), pp. 1-14.

31. George Stoeckhardt, "Weissagung und Erfuellung," *Lehre und Wehre*, 30.

32. Francis Pieper, *Christian Dogmatics* (St. Louis, Concordia Publishing House. 1950). I, p. 248.

33. Kretzmann, **op. cit.**, II. New Testament I, p. 13.

34. Adam Fahling, *The Life of Christ* (St. Louis, Concordia Publishing House, 1936), p. 135.

35. Louis Fuerbringer, *Theological Hermeneutics* (St. Louis, Concordia Publishing House, 1924), p. 19, note for paragraph 35.

36. Jon Ylvisaker, *The Four Gospels* (Minneapolis, Augsburg Publishing House, 1932), p. 110.

37. Arndt, **op. cit.**, p. 109.

38. W. K. Lowther Clark, *Concise Bible Commentary* (New York, The Macmillan Company, 1953), p. 537; Sherman E. Johnson, "The Gospel According to Matthew," *The Interpreter's Bible* (New York, The Abingdon Press, 1951), VII, p. 263.

39. Werner Franzmann, *Bible History Commentary* (Milwaukee, Northwestern Publishing House, 1930), omits Is. 40:2-3 as Messianic in his discussion of Messianic Prophecies, pp. 498-506.

40. Aaron Judah Kligerman, *Messianic Prophecy in the Old Testament* (Grand Rapids, Zondervan Publishing House, 1957), pp. 69-70.

41. Cf. Charles F. Pfeiffer, *Old Testament History* (Grand Rapids, Baker Book House, 1873), pp. 334, 358.

42. H. C. Leupold, *Exposition of Isaiah*, **op. cit.**, I, pp. 14-153.

43. Edward E. Hindson, *Isaiah's Immanuel A Sign of His Times or The Sign of the Ages* Phillipsburg, New Jersey, Presbyterian and Reformed Publishing Co., 1978), title pages.

44. Merrill F. Unger, *Unger's Bible Handbook*, **op. cit.**, p. 313.

45. Leupold, **op. cit.**, I, p. 165.

46. Gleason Archer, "Isaiah," Carl F. Henry, *The Biblical Expositor* (Philadelphia, A.J. Holman Company, 1960), II, pp. 133-134; Herbert Wolf and John H. Stek, Isaiah 7:14 in *Concordia Self-Study Bible* (St. Louis, Concordia Publishing House, 1986), p. 1029a.

47. J. Pelikan and H. Oswald, *Luther's Works* (St. Louis, Concordia Publishing House, 1969), 16, p. 34.

48. E. Eckhardt, Homiletisches Reallexikon nebst Index Rerun (Blair, Neb. 1908), Volume beginning with Chiliasmus), p. 560.

49. Stoeckhardt, **op. cit.**, pp. 83ff.

50. Piper, **op. cit.**, I, 242, 248.

51. Kretzmann, *Popular Commentary,* New Testament, I, p. 6.

52. Theodore Laetsch, *Bible Commentary - The Minor Prophets* (St. Louis, Concordia Publishing House, 19—), 272.

53. Fuerbringer, Th. Engelder and P. E. Kretzmann, *The Concordia Cyclopedia* (St. Louis, Concordia Publishing House, 1927), p. 351.

54. Victor E. Mennicke, "Bible Interpretation," Th. Laetsch (Editor), *The Abiding Word* (St. Louis, Concordia Publishing House, 1947), p. 46.

55. Edward J. Young, *The Book of Isaiah* (Grand Rapids, Wm. B. Eerdmans Publishing Company, 1965), Vol. I, Chapter I-XVIII, pp. 236-291.

56. Merrill F. Unger, *Unger's Commentary on the Old Testament* (Chicago, Moody Press, 1931), II, pp. 1161-1162.

57. Hindson, *Isaiah's Immanuel*, **op. cit.**, pp. 1-87, a comprehensive discussion of chapter 7:14ff with excellent bibliography.

58. Stoeckhardt, **op. cit.**, pp. 37-97.

58a. Leupold, **op. cit.**, Vol. I, p. 165.

59. David F. Payne, "Isaiah," Howley, Bruce and Ellison, *The Layman's Commentary* (Grand Rapids, Zondervan Publishing House, 1979), p. 776.

60. Cf. R. Prenter, *Creation and Redemption*. Translated by Theodore L. Jensen (Philadelphia, Fortress Press, 167), pp. 430-431.

61. *The St. Louis Edition of the Works of Martin Luther,* 18:1307; 4:13041.

62. C.F.W. Walther, *Walther and the Church* (St. Louis; Concordia Publishing House, 1938), p. 124.

63. Fuerbringer, *Theological Hermeneutics*, **op. cit.**, p. 12.

64. Mennicke, "Bible Interpretation," **op. cit.**, p. 54.

65. Leupold, *Exposition of Isaiah*, **op. cit.**, I, p. 170.

66. Saint Matthew 3:12-16.

67. Walter A. Maier, Sr., *The Radio for Christ* (St. Louis, Concordia Publishing House, 1939), p. 50.

68. H. J. Stolee, *Isaiah Saw the Lord* (Minneapolis, Bible Banner Press, 1955), p. 25.

69. *The New English Bible With the Apocrypha* (Oxford University Press, Cambridge University Press, 1970), p. 320.

70. *The Holy Bible, The New Berkeley Version in Modern English* (Grand Rapids, Zondervan Publishing House, 1959), p. 693a.

71. J. Bright, "Isaiah I," Matthew Black and H. H. Rowley, *Peake's Commentary of the Bible* (New York, Thomas Nelson and Sons, 1962), p. 497.

72. H. A. Ironside, *Expository Notes on the Prophet Isaiah* (New York, Loizeaux, 1952), p. 60.

73. Franz Delitzsch, *Messianic Prophecies in Historical Succession* (New York, Charles Scribner's Sons, 1891), p. 148.

74. Young, *The Book of Isaiah*, **op. cit.**, I, pp. 339-340.

75. Ironside, **op. cit.**, p. 63.

76. Lenski, *The Eisenach Old Testament Selections*, op, cit., p. 97.

77. *Holy Bible, The New King James Version*, **op. cit.**, 901.

78. Laetsch, *The Minor Prophets*, **op. cit.**, p. 272.

79. *The New English Bible*, **op. cit.**., p. 1150.

80. Laetsch, **op. cit.**, p. 272.

81. **Ibid.**

82. **Ibid.**

83. Kretzmann, *Old Testament*, **op. cit.**, p. 630.

84. Montgomery, **op. cit.**, p. 515.

Questions

1. Jesus claimed that the Old Testament spoke about ____.
2. What does modern theological liberalism say about predictive prophecy? ____
3. Isaiah has been called the ____.
4. Jesus said in his Olivet discourse that there will always be ____.

5. What conflicts with Christ's teaching that His kingdom is not of this world? ____
6. The Septuagint translates "almah" as ____.
7. The claim that "almah" means a young woman of marriageable age who may be married or unmarried goes against ____.
8. Immanuel means ____.
9. The Virgin Birth had meaning for the true ____.
10. Finding two meanings in Isaiah 7:14 was rejected by ____.
11. Isaiah 9:5-6 emphasized both the ____ and the ____ of the Messiah.
12. A better translation of "The everlasting Father" would be ____.
13. Millennialists believe that Isaiah 9:7 will be fulfilled when ____.
14. The deity of the Messiah is denied in liberal critical translation which render Micah 5:2 as ____.
(Ed. This is how the ESV renders Micah 5:2).
15. Micah predicted that the Messiah's name would be ____.

Christ —The God-Man

An Analysis of the Uniqueness of the Biblical Incarnation Texts

(A Study for Advent and Christmas)

**Ed. This study will help pastors preparing
Advent and Christmas sermons.**
Christian News, December 13, 1993

Christ was born between 8 B.C.[1] and 5 B.C.[2] By the year 1995 two thousand years will have elapsed since Christ's incarnation. Within these two thousand years the pendulum relative the humanity and deity of Christ will have swung in opposite directions. In the second and third centuries the Gnostics denied the humanity of Christ, while today there is a tendency to deny His deity. With the Word of God denying Jesus Seminar many facts about the life and ministry are reinterpreted, denied or rejected. With the paganization of Christmas in today's world, it is necessary again and again to set forth the great Biblical teachings about Christ's miraculous birth.

Christ is the center of human history. All the centuries which preceded His coming looked forward to Him, and all times that followed look back to Him. He is the meeting point of God and man, and the foundation and center of the Christian religion. The names which He bore are significant of His mission and work. Jesus was His personal name and signifies that "He shall save His people from their sins." Christ was His official title, the Greek equivalent of the Hebrew and Aramaic "Messiah," and signifies the "Anointed One." One who was anointed by the Holy Spirit without measure.[3]

In this study for the Christmastide Old and New Testament passages, which either explicitly or implicitly show that God became man in the Person of Jesus Christ will he listed and discussed.

These Scriptural declarations will be organized according to two time periods, namely, 1. Christ as Second Person of the Godhead, existing from all eternity prior to the assumption of a human nature, and, 2. The Logos (WORD) becoming man in the course of human history as stated in John 1:14.

I. The Logos in Eternity Prior to Assumption of Man's Nature
1. The Father Begets the Son or the Filiation of the Son

Psalm 2 is a Messianic psalm. In it there is described a dialogue between the Father and the Son.

In verse 7 the Messiah declares: "I will tell of the decree: The Lord said to me. Thou art My Son:

This day I have begotten you."[4] The author of Hebrews cited Psalm 2:7 and shows that these words were never spoken to angels, but only to the Son (Hebrews 1:5).

2. Jesus Claimed to have the Same Glory as the Father

In his high priestly prayer Jesus asserted: "And now, O Father, glorify thou me with thine own self, with the glory I had with you before the world began (John 17:5)."[5]

3. Jesus, like the Father and the Holy Spirit, was God

In the Prologue of his Gospel, John writes: "In the beginning was the Word (Greek: Logos) and the Word was with God, and the Word was God."

4. The Relationship of the Logos to the Father

The Apostle Paul describes the relationship of the Word to the Father: "He is the image of the invisible God, the Firstborn of all creation."[6] (Colossians 1:15). The word "image" (Greek: eikon) means a likeness, but also representation, and further a manifestation. It includes the three ideas of "resemblance, representation, revelation.[7] Said Eerdmans: "It expresses such a likeness as that of a head stamped upon a coin, or such a representation as that of a face reflected in a mirror; yet its fuller meaning, as here, is that of an exact representation. The likeness of the Son to the Father was so perfect as to fit him to be complete and finalization of God to men."[8]

The author of Hebrews informed his readers about Christ: "He who is the radiance of God's glory and the exact likeness of his nature."[9] (13). Weymouth translated this verse like this: "He brightly reflects God's glory and is the exact representation of His being."[10] In Hebrew 1:3 Christ is said to be "the very image of his person" or "the exact representation of his very being." There are two expressions in 1:3 that emphasize in the Greek text the same idea, namely, the perfect revelation of God embodied in Christ.

5. Like the Father and the Holy Spirit, the Word is the Creator of the Universe

John in his Prologue states: "all things come into being through him and apart from him nothing that exists came into being."[12] With this teaching Paul agreed when he wrote the Colossians: "For in him was the universe created, things in heaven, and on earth, the seen and the unseen, thrones, or dominions or principalities, for him all things have been created, and He is before all and in him all things subsist (1:16-17)."[13]

The author of Hebrews teaches that God gave the world a final revelation by His Son, who is predestined Lord of the universe, and through whom He made the world. Here the Logos is portrayed as the medium of creation.[14]

6. God Appointed Jesus Heir of All Things

This assertion points forward to the sovereignty yet to be exercised by Christ. This is the goal of human history. "The Son is to be the universal ruler, and this by virtue of his Sonship. Because He is the Son, therefore, He is the Heir (Gal. 4:7). When Christ became heir he claimed the inheritance. This sovereignty will only be enjoyed until" the kingdom of this world is become the kingdom of our Lord and of His Christ (Rev. 11:15).[15]

7. Christ Upholds and Sustains All Things

The author of Hebrews in his Christological creation passage, declares:

"He being an emanation of God's glory and stamp of his substance and upholding the universe by the utterance of his power,"[16] sets forth the work of Christ's providence which follows the work of creation. The author of Hebrews ascribes various divine works to the preexistent Son.[17]

8. The Word and Source of All Life

In his great Prologue St. John writes: "In him was life, and the life was the light of men" (1:14).

During the course of his public ministry Jesus declared: "I am the Way, the Truth and the Life, no man comes unto the Father except by Me" (John 14:6).

9. The Incarnation of the Word Was Determined in Eternity

In the book of Revelation John writes: "That Christ was the Lamb slain from the foundation of the world" (13:8). The death of Christ was determined in eternity and thus presupposes the Word's human nature. Assuming mankind's human nature was necessary if Christ was to fulfill the law for mankind, be crucified, die and be buried and rise again for mankind's justification. If Christ had not been born. He could not have given His life a ransom for many.

10. The Eternity of the Son was foretold by Solomon in Proverbs 8:22-31

This Christological passage begins like this: "The LORD possessed me at the beginning before his works of old I have been established from everlasting, from the beginning, before there ever was an earth (8:22,23)." "When he marked out the foundations of the earth, then I was beside him as a master craftsman" (8:29b-30).[18]

II. God's Preparation in Time for the Realization of Christ's Incarnation

1. The Messianic Prophecies of the Old Testament

There are over three hundred Messianic prophecies in the Old Testament. The very first Messianic prophecy, given to Adam and Eve, teaches that from Eve there would One be born who would destroy the Devil (Gen. 3:15).[19] Further the Seed of the woman would be born of the family of Shem (Gen. 9:25).[20] Abraham was told that from his descendants would come the Seed through whom the nations of the earth would be blessed (Gen. 12:3).[21] Moses was given the information that the Messiah would be a great Prophet, whom the people would obey (Deut. 18:15).[23] All Messianic prophecies in the Old Testament presuppose Christ's humanity. One of the most remarkable prophecies is that of Isaiah: 'Therefore, the Lord himself will give you a sign; Behold, a virgin will be with child and bear a son, and she will call his name Immanuel" (7:14).[24] Two chapters later Isaiah makes this remarkable announcement: "For unto us a child will be born and a son will be given us and the government will rest on his shoulders; and His name will be Miracle, the Counsellor, Mighty God, Eternal Father, the Prince of Peace."[25] In Isaiah 11:1 the prophet foretold that Christ would be a descendant of David: "There shall come forth a Rod from the stem of Jesse, and a Branch shall grow out of his root.[26] The birthplace of the Messiah was announced in the early eighth century by

Micah, who declared:

"You, Bethlehem (Ephrathah) too small to be one of Judah's clans, from you there will come out for me. One Who is to rule Israel whose real comings are from the eternal past. So He will give up Israel up till the time when a mother will have a Child" (5:2).[27]

The latter verse had been interpreted as being a reference to the Virgin Birth by the prophet Micah.

The prophecy of Jeremiah in chapter 23:5-6 is a remarkable one. Jeremiah predicted: "The days will come, says the Lord, when I will raise for David a righteous Branch who will rule as king and be wise. He will create fairness and righteousness in the earth. When He comes, Judah will be saved and Israel will dwell safely. This is the name by which he will be called, Jahweh—our righteousness."[28] Here the Messiah is identified with Jahweh Himself it reminds us of Christ's statement in John: "I and the Father are one." No matter by what name or title the Messiah is called in the various Old Testament prophecies, they all assume His humanity. As has been shown, there are passages in which both deity and humanity are predicted of the Second Person of the Godhead. In Isaiah 7:14 the Messiah is called Immanuel, i.e. God-with-us, in Isaiah 9:5 "the mighty God."

2. On the Way to Bethlehem

The entire first chapter of Luke describes the events which occurred within a year of Christ's incarnation. Matthew 1:18-25 adds to the information given in Luke One. Both Luke and Matthew record the uniqueness of Christ's birth, beginning with the Virginal Conception. Six months after the announcement of the coming of the way preparer, the angel Gabriel visited Mary in Nazareth, who was betrothed to a man named Joseph. Gabriel said to Mary: "You will conceive and give birth to a Son and you will name Him Jesus. He will be great and will be called the Son of the Most High and the Lord God will give Him the throne of his ancestor David. He will be king over the people of Jacob forever, and His Kingdom will never end (1:32-32)."[29] Since Mary was not living with a man and had not had intercourse. Mary replied: "How can this be?" Gabriel replied: "The Holy Spirit will come over you, and the power of the Most High will overshadow you. And for that reason the Holy Being to be born of you, will be called the Son of God."[30] (1:35)

The Apostle St. Matthew also records the Virgin Conception and Virgin Birth of Christ. "The birth of Jesus Christ took place in this way. His mother Mary had been promised to Joseph to be his wife. But before they came together, she was found to be with Child by the Holy Spirit."[31]

When Joseph saw that his betrothed was with child, and he was not the father, he decided to leave her. But the Lord intervened, informing Joseph that he was wrong in his conclusion about Mary's fidelity. "Do not be afraid to take Mary your wife home, for what in begotten is her is by the Holy Spirit; and she shall bear a son and you are to call him Jesus, for he shall save his people from their sins (1:21)."[32]

3. The Importance of the Virgin Birth

The dogmatician Stump has correctly asserted: 'The immaculate conception of Christ by the Virgin Mary is fundamental to the true conception of the Person of Christ."[33] Again he declared: "Dogmatically the Virgin Birth of our Lord is not a matter of indifference, as is asserted by some. Without it Christ would necessarily sink to the level of a mere human being, with perhaps an infusion of divinity in Him. He could not be the Son of God incarnate, nor could His perfect freedom from original sin be accounted for. Those who reject the Virgin Birth are confronted with a greater difficulty than that which belief in the Virgin birth involves, for they are left without any way which to account for the appearance of human being and only one who is without sin, and towers high above the rest of the race like a mountain peak above the surrounding plain."[34]

4. The Two Genealogies of Christ

Matthew 1:1-17 and Luke 3:23-38 clearly show that Jesus was a human being.[35] In the case of Matthew the genealogy of Christ is traced back to Abraham, the progenitor of the Hebrew nation, and in the case of Luke it goes back to the first human being, Adam. The two genealogies have challenged scholars to account for the different names in each not found in the other.[36] Scroggie suggested that the difficulty in harmonizing the respective genealogical lists is to be accounted for: 1. That both genealogies give the descent of Joseph; Matthew's the real and Luke the legal decent; 2. That Matthew gives Joseph's legal descent as successor to the throne of David, and that Luke gives his real parentage; 3. That Matthew gives the real descent of Joseph, and Luke the real descent of Mary.[37]

5. The "Fullness of the Times" (Galatians 4:4)

The truth that Christ was born, which establishes the historicity of the Incarnation of Christ, is shown by the fact that He was born during the reign of Caesar Augustus, when Cyrenius was governor of Syria.[38] The Incarnation occurred at a time when world conditions in the Roman Empire were ideally suited for the Messiah's coming. Paul alluded to this fact when he wrote in his Galatian epistle: "But when the time had fully come, God sent forth His Son, born of a woman, born subject to Law, in order to ransom those who were subject to Law, that we might receive recognition as sons." (4:4) Weymouth. It was a time peculiarly suited for the introduction Christ's Gospel. The whole civilized world was at length governed by one master. There was nothing to prevent preachers of a new faith going from city to city and country to country because of the excellent road system which traversed the length and breadth of the Roman Empire in Europe and the Near East. The religions of the different nations had been absorbed and had been found wanting. There was a general yearning for a Savior to come. There was general peace in the Roman Empire. Notwithstanding their mighty conquests effected by great conquerors, poets, historians, architects and philosophers, the kingdoms of the world were full of dark idolatries. It was a "due time for God to send His son."[39]

959

III. The Miracle of the Ages: God Assumed Human Nature
1. Luke's Version of the Incarnation

The story of the birth of Christ as related by Matthew is in striking contrast with that of Luke.

Matthew depicts Jesus as king for whom at his birth the reigning Herod trembles in his throne and the Magi adore him, offering royal gifts. Luke represents Jesus as the ideal man and the story is full of human interest. In the most beautiful book written, to quote Renan, Luke's Christmas account of the incarnation must be classified as the most beautiful account of the manner in which God became a man. Luke the physician portrays two lovely peasants traveling from Nazareth in northern Galilee to Bethlehem, and in David's royal city Mary and Joseph are excluded from the inn, placing their newborn child into a manger attended by animals. The first visit to the child was made by shepherds who were directed by an angel. When Christ assumed man's nature, an angel chorus sang: "Glory to God in the highest heavens, and on earth peace to those who have His good will."[40]

2. Saint Matthew's Version of the Incarnation

The genealogy of Jesus declared him to be the Son of David. The story of His birth reveals Him as the Son of God. It includes an explanation of the name which was given and of prophecy which was fulfilled. The story is brief but it bears the features characteristic of Matthew, the "Gospel of the King," of the predicted and rejected Messiah; for it shows that the mother of Jesus is about to be repudiated and that Joseph was to be the legal father, addressed as "the son of David," that Jesus is to save his people from their sins and that an Old Testament prediction is divinely fulfilled in his birth.[41]

3. John's Account of the Incarnation

The Prologue of John's Gospel culminated in these Words: "and the Word became flesh, and dwelt among us, and we beheld His glory, glory as of the only begotten from the Father, full of grace and truth."[42] With 1:14 the earthly life of Christ begins with John the Baptist as the way preparer, which was a fulfillment of prophecies in Isaiah 40:3 and Malachi 4:5.

4. The Incarnation Was God's Gift to Mankind

The Bible clearly presents the Incarnation of Christ as being a gift of God to mankind. The Gospel in a nutshell states: "God so loved the world that He gave his only begotten Son, that whosoever believes in him should not perish, but have eternal life." Paul calls upon the Corinthians to be grateful: "Thanks be to God for His UNSPEAKABLE GIFT."[43]

5. Paul's Testimony to the Incarnation of Christ

Paul has a number of passages that testify to the humanity of Jesus Christ. In the opening words of his Romans letter, he wrote: "It is about His Son, who according to the flesh was born a descendant of David, but according to spirit—a spirit of holiness—was declared by His resurrection from the dead to be the powerful Son of God" (1:3-4).[44] In a great passage setting forth the humiliation and exaltation of Christ, Paul informed the Philippians about Christ, "although He existed in the form of God, He did not consider His being equal with God as a prize to be displayed. Instead, when He became like other human beings. He emptied Himself, taking on the form of a servant. He appeared as man. He became obedient and humbled Himself even to the point or death, yes, death on a cross (2:5-9)."[45] In speaking about the mediatorship of Christ, Paul told Timothy: "There is one God. There is also one Mediator between God and mankind, the Man Christ Jesus" (1 Tim. 2:5)."[46] Paul assured his coworker Timothy, pastor in Ephesus: "Keep in mind Jesus Christ, who is risen from the dead, a descendant of David—this is the Gospel I preach" (2 Tim. 2:8).[47] In his first letter to Timothy Paul closes chapter 3 with what appears to be an ancient hymn or even a part of a confession:

"He in flesh was manifested
In the Spirit was attested;
By the angels was beholden,
Among the Gentiles heralded:
In the world believed on.
And in glory taken up."[48]

6. Hebrews and the Incarnation of Christ

The author of Hebrew begins his great Christological epistle with these significant words:

"God, who in ancient days spoke to our ancestors in the prophets, at many different times and by various methods, has at the end of days spoken to us in a Son Whom he appointed the heir of all things."[49] The assumption of the Epistle to the Hebrew is that Christ became a man, which was necessary for Him to become the Pioneer of their salvation. Thus in chapter 2:14, it is stated: "Therefore, since the children are sharers in flesh and blood, he also similarly partook of the same."[50]

7. The Reality of the Incarnation of Christ

In the second half of the first century A.D. incipient Gnosticism had invaded the Christian Churches.[51] John the Apostle, in combatting this heresy of Gnosticism which denied that Christ had really assumed human nature wrote: "That which was from the beginning, which we have heard, which we have seen with our eyes, which we have looked at and our hands have touched, this is what we are speaking about, namely, The Word who is Life. This Life was revealed; we have seen it and we testify to it, and we proclaim to you the eternal Life, which was with the Father and which was revealed unto us."[52] Thus clearly corroborating what John wrote in the Prologue (1 John 1:1-3).

8. The Miracle of Miracles: God Became Man. Christ is the God-Man

The miracle of Christmas is the truth that the Second Person of the Godhead became man. Isaiah predicted that the Son of Mary would be Immanuel—"God—with us" in one person. Paul is defending the deity of Christ against Gnosticism assured the church at Colosse: "In Him dwelleth all the fullness of Godhead bodily (Greek somatikos)." [53]

9. The Uniqueness of Christ

Stump wrote about Christ's uniqueness as follows: "The Jesus Christ whom the New Testament sets before us is an absolutely unique personality, who is God and man in one person. He is exhibited as a true human being with all the essential marks of humanity, and at the same time as the eternal Son of God who stands in a unique relation of absolute and perfect communion with the Father. There exist in Him a divine and a human side which are clearly distinguishable, yet which are intimately and indissolubly united in oneness of person. The Synoptic, beginning with the human side, follow the historical steps of His career on to the final revelation of His divine majesty and glory; and John, beginning with the divine side, exhibits the fullness of the Godhead dwelling in the humanity of Christ. In the former we have a historical progression which more and more reveals the divine in Him; in the latter we have the simultaneous presentation of the divine and the human, in Him, in the latter we have the simultaneous presentation of the divine and the human."[54]

10. The Personal Union of the Two Natures of Christ

According to Romans 9:5 Jesus has a complete human nature, inherited from the fathers, and is therefore. Himself, a true human being; but at the same time He is "God blessed forever." Thus it appears that the two natures are united so as to constitute one person, one individuality. Hence, there is one Christ, who is both true God and true man (Cf. Athanasian Creed, 28-35).[55]

The *Formula of Concord* has expressed the facts about the personal union in this way: "We believe, teach and confess that the Son of God, although from eternity He has been a particular, distinct, entire divine person, and thus, with the Father and the Holy Ghost, true essential perfect God, nevertheless, in the fullness of the time assumed also human nature into the unity of His Person, not in such a way that there are now two persons or two Christs, but that Jesus Christ is now in one person at the same time, true eternal God, born of the Father from eternity, and true man, born of the most blessed Virgin Mary."[56]

11. The Profundity of the Two Natures of Christ in One Person

The Apostle Paul declared: 'There is no doubt about it: Deep is the mystery of our religion. He appeared in the flesh, was justified in spirit, was seen by angels; was preached among nations; was believed in the world; was taken up in glory."[57]

Here Paul covers the life of Christ from birth to the ascension and the session at the right and of God. What Paul here declared to be "great," is not in its obscurity, but in its importance; it is weighty, significant and sublime, could only be asserted of One who was both God and man in one person. Paul stated the same truth to the Church at Colosse when defending Christ against the Gnostics: "In Him dwells the fullness of the Godhead bodily (2:9)."

12. The Relationship of the Two Natures to Each Other

The two natures are not so mixed and mingled as to make a new composition; neither has one changed into the other, losing its own identity; but, like body and soul, they remain distinct. Nor do they exist beside each other, like two boards glued together, without having and communion with, and interrelation to each other; but again, like body and soul, the divine nature so permeates and penetrates the human nature, and the human nature is so permeated and penetrated by the divine nature that both natures are one. The Athanasian Creed put it this way: "As the reasonable soul and flesh is one man, so God and man is one in Christ."[58]

Schmid, in his *Doctrinal Theology* put it in essence this way: The union of the two natures is so close and inseparable that the one can no longer be conceived of as without or away from the other, but both are to be regarded in all respects united, yet in such a way that each of the two natures retains its own essential character and peculiarities as before, and remains unmingled with the other.[59] One exegete put it this way: "This particular human nature belongs to, and is possessed of the Son of God, where, therefore, the Son of God, the divine nature, is, there is likewise the Son of Man, the human nature. Ever since the Word, was made flesh and the Word is not without the flesh. The two natures are inseparable, though distinct."[60]

13. How Was the Personal Union Effected?

The flesh was not made God. Jesus was not a man for a number of years and was then elevated to the Deity, but the Word (LOGOS) was made flesh (John 1:14); "God sent forth His external Son" (Galatians 4:4). The personal union was then brought about in this manner, that the eternal Son of God received and incorporated into His divine Person another human, nature. This took place at the conception of Jesus (Luke 1:35); the unborn Child of Mary is called "Lord" (1:43).

The unity of the person is the key to such understanding as is possible to us of Christ who is set forth in Scriptures. He is true God and true man; but He is only one person, not two persons. Stump has claimed: "There is not the least indication in Scripture that Jesus was conscious of a double personality. His consciousness embraced His temporal existence as a man and at the same time reached back into the farthest eternity. But it is the consciousness of single person, and through it all runs the sense of the self-identity and unity of the ego. Because of this inner oneness Jesus, speaking to the hostile Jews, was able to say. "Before Abraham was, I am (John 8:58)."[61]

14. The Divine Nature of Christ, the God-Man

Christ has a true divine nature. He is in substantial sense the Son of God. The Scriptural evidence is found in numerous Bible passages. He is "God of God, Light of Light, Very God of Very God, Begotten not made, being of one Substance with the Father." In His divine nature He is the Son of God, Second Person of the Trinity, who is consubstantial and co-equal with the Father and the Holy Ghost. He is the Son of God, not by adoption, nor as one who worked His way into divine sonship by His perfection, but He is divine in the full and substantial sense of the term.

15. The Human Nature of the God-Man

Christ had a body and soul. He is bone of our bone and flesh of our flesh and was in all points tempted as we were, yet without sin (Heb. 4:15). The Gospels give many examples of His humanity.

Christ was born (Luke 2:7), grew from babyhood to full adolescence (Luke 2:42), grew to manhood, associated with other men, entered upon

His public ministry, gathered disciples around Him. He had human wants and feelings. He hungered (Matt. 4:1), thirsted (John 4:7) was weary (John 4:6), slept (Matt. 8:24), prayed (Matt. 26:39), was tempted (Matt. 4:1), rejoiced (Luke 10:21), was sorrowful (Matt. 26:38), suffered, died and was buried.

16. Possible Ways of Speaking About Christ Because of the Personal Union

Because of the personal union of the divine and the human natures in Christ, it is perfectly proper to say not only "Christ is God" (cf. 1 John 5:20), Christ is man (cf. 1 Tim. 2:5), but also to say of Him "This man is God" or "The Son of Man is the Son of God" (cf. Matt. 16:13-17) and "God is man" (John 1:14). The *Formula of Concord*, Epitome, stated it this way: "Hence, we believe, teach, and confess that God is man and man is God, which could not be if the divine and human natures had in deed and truth absolutely no communion with one another."[62]

IV. The Purpose of the Incarnation
1. Christ took to Undo the Work of the Devil
In his first epistle John informed his readers: "He who committing sin is of the devil, because from the beginning the devil is sinning. It was for this cause that the Son of God was manifested, that he might destroy the works of the devil" (I John 3:8).[63]

2. God Became Man that Man Might Be Freed from the Bondage of the law
Paul in his Galatian Christmas text gave the purpose of the incarnation in this way: "But when the fullness of time was come God sent forth his Son, born of a woman, born under the law, to redeem from captivity those under the law, in order that we might receive our sonship" (4:5).[64]

3. Christ Became Incarnate to Deliver Men from the Fear of Death
One of the great Christological teachings of Hebrews is found in 2:14: "Now since all these children share flesh and blood. He also took on flesh and blood to be like them, so that by His death He might take away all the power of him who had the power of death (that is, the devil). And thus He might free those who were subject to slavery all their lives by the fear of death."[65]

4. Christ Assumes Humanity that He Might Be Our High Priest
Christ was a descendant of Abraham "and so in every way He had the obligation to become like His brothers, so that He might be a merciful and faithful high Priest in representing them before God and thus pay for the sins of the people (Hebrews 2:17)."[66]

5. Christ Assumed Human Nature to Help His Believers in Temptations
Hebrews concluded chapter 2 with the words: "Furthermore, because He Himself experienced testing when He suffered. He is able to help others when they are tested."[67]

V. The Implications of the Incarnation for Christ's Followers

Titus 2:11-14 is a selection read in Christian Churches at Christmas, and it contains instructions for daily Christian living. Prior to this pericope, Paul had given moral instructions for various groups, this was climaxed with a hymn of hope, stating how the grace of God should motivate Christian conduct. Here is the hymn in the TEV's rendering of this Greek passage: "For the grace of God has appeared which brings salvation to all people. It trains us to say 'No' to ungodliness and worldly lusts, that we might live sensibly and uprightly in the present world, as we look for our blessed hope, namely, the glorious appearance of our great God and Savior Jesus Christ, He gave Himself as a payment for us to free us from all wickedness and cleanse us to be His own people, eager to do good works."[68]

VI. The Reception of the Incarnate Christ

The prologue of John's Gospel sets forth the major themes of the Fourth Gospel. A great antithesis in this book is belief versus unbelief, rejection of the Messiah versus His reception. The Logos is called "the Light," which lighteth every person coming into the world. The Apostle John, says that John the Baptist came to testify of this Light. Of Christ, the Light of people, John stated: "He was in the world, and through him the world came into being, yet the world knew Him not. He came into His own creation, and his own folk received him not" (1:10).[69] Yet despite the fact the many were rejecting Him, "the Light is shining in the darkness, and the darkness has not overwhelmed it."[70]

Footnotes

1. Stephen L. Caiger, *Archaeology and the New Testament* (London: Casswel and Company, 1931), p. 146.
2. Charles W. Hoehner, *Chronological Aspects of the Life of Christ* (Grand Rapids; Zondervan Publishing Company, 1977), p. 25. Cf. chapter 25.
3. Joseph Stump, *The Christian Faith* (New York: The MacMillan Company, 1932), p. 141.
4. *Thompson Chain Reference Bible,* Third Impression (Indianapolis: J. B. Kirkbride Bible Company, No. 421 "the Messianic Star," Supplement, p. 182.
5. H.B. Montgomery, *The New Testament in Modern English*, Centenary Translation (Philadelphia: The Judson Press, 1924), p. 234.
6. *Holy Bible, New Evangelical Translation* (Cleveland: NET Publishing, 1992), p. 374.
7. Charles R. Eerdmans, *The Epistle to the Colossians and Philemon* (Philadelphia: The Westminster Press, 1938), p. 51.
8. **Ibid.**
9. *New Evangelical Translation*, **op. cit.**, p. 409.
10. Richard Francis Weymouth, *The New Testament in Modern Speech,* Fifth Edition (Boston: The Pilgrim Press, 1943), p. 527.
11. Charles R. Eerdmans, *The Epistle to the Hebrews* (Philadelphia: The Westminster Press, 1934), p. 30.
12. Montgomery, *The Centenary Translation*, op cit., p. 241.
13. **Ibid.**, p. 538.

14. Montgomery, **op. cit.**, Hebrew 1:2b.

15. Eerdmans *The Epistle to the Hebrews*, **op. cit.**, p. 29.

16. Montgomery, **op. cit.**, p. 593.

17. Creation, divine providence, purification of man's sins, session at God's right hand are divine works mentioned.

18. *Holy Bible. The New King James* (Nashville: Thomas Nelson Publishers, 1982), p. 625.

19. Francis Pieper, *Christian Dogmatics* (St. Louis; Concordia Publishing House, 1950), Vol. I, pp. 21,70, 193; 347; 508. 534. 535; Vol. II, pp. 66,70,72,218,249,251,517; Vol. III, pp. 212ff., 411,435.

26. Edward Mack, *The Christ of the Old Testament* (Richmond, VA.: Presbyterian Committee of Publication, 1926), pp. 48-49.

21. **Ibid.**, p. 52.

22. Franz Delitzsh, *Messianic Prophecies in Historical Succession* (New York; Charles Scribner's Sons, 1891), p. 56.

23. Werner Franzman, *Bible History Commentary* (Milwaukee: Northwestern Publishing House, 1986), pp. 292-294.

24. H.C. Leupold, Exposition of Isaiah (Grand Rapids; Baker Book House, 1968), Vol. I, Chapters 1-39, pp. 155-158.

25. Franzman, **op. cit.**. pp. 498-500.

26. Leupoid, **op. cit.**, I, pp. 215-216.

27. George H. Robinson, *The Twelve Minor Prophets* (New York: George H. Doran Company, 1926), pp. 162-103.

28. Theodore Laetch, *Jeremiah* (St. Louis: Concordia Publishing House, 1952), pp. 193-195.

29. *New Evangelical Translation*, **op. cit.**, 1:32-33, pp. 168-169.

36. **Ibid.**, Luke 1:35 p. 109.

31. *New Evangelical Translation*, **op. cit.**, p. 2.

32. Montgomery, **op. cit.**, *Centenary Translation*, p. 4.

33. Stump, **op. cit.**, p. 142.

34. **Ibid.**

35. H. Wayne House, *Chronological and Background Charts of the New Testament* (Grand Rapids: Zondervan Publishing House, 1981), pp. 96-97.

36. William Arndt, *Bible Difficulties and Seeming Contradictions* (St. Louis: Concordia Publishing House, 1987), pp. 176-72.

37. W. Graham Scroggie, *A Guide to the Gospels* (London: Pickering and Inglis: 1948), p. 507.

38. Relative to the census under Caesar Augustus and Quirinius, cf. Arndt, **op. cit.**, pp. 68-71.

39. Lars P. Qualben, *A History of the Christian Church* (New York: Thomas N. Nelson and Sons, 1940), pp. 10-14.

40. *New Evangelical Translation*, **op. cit.**, Luke 2:14, p. 113.

41. Adolph Schlatter, Der Evangelist Mattheus (Stuttgart: Calwer Vereins Buchhandlung, 1929), pp. 7-24.

42. *New American Standard Bible,* (Philadelphia: A. J. Holmon Company, 1973), p. 760.

43. 2 Corinthians 9:15 in *The Holy Bible, The Berkeley Version in Modern English* (Grand Rapids: Zondervan Publishing Company, 1969), p. 200.

44. Romans 1:3-4, *New Evangelical Translation*, **op. cit.**. p. 277.

45. **Ibid.**, p. 367.

46. **Ibid.**, p. 300.
47. **Ibid.**, p. 398.
48. Montgomery, *The Centenary Translation*, **op. cit.**, p. 567.
49. **Ibid.**, p. 593.
56. **Ibid.**, p. 597.
51. John Rutherford, "Gnosticism," in James Orr. General Editor, *The International Standard Bible Encyclopedia* (Grand Rapids: Wm. B. Eerdmans Publishing Company, 1939), II, pp. 1242-1243.
52. *New Evangelical Translation*, **op. cit.**, p. 453.
53. *The King James Version of 1611*, Colossians, 2:9.
54. Stump, *The Christian Faith*, **op. cit.**, pp. 143-144.
55. Theodore Tappert, *The Book of Concord* (Philadelphia: Muhlenberg Press, 1959), p. 20.
56. *Formula of Concord*, Th. D., Article VIII, 6 *Concordia Triglotta* (St. Louis: Concordia Publishing House, 1921), p. 1615.
57. Timothy 3:16 in *New Evangelical Translation*, **op. cit.**, p. 392.
58. Tappert, *Book of Concord*, **op. cit.**, line 35, p. 20.
59. Heinrich Schmid, *Doctrinal Theology of the Evangelical Lutheran Church* (Minneapolis: Augsburg Publishing House, 1889), pp. 294-366.
60. Edward A. Koehler, *A Summary of Christian Doctrine* (Second Revised Edition; Detroit and Oakland: L. H. Koehler and Alfred Koehler, Distributors, 1939), p. 89.
61. Stump, **op. cit.**, p. 144.
62. *Formula of Concord*, Epitome, Article VIII, 10; *Concordia Triglotta*, **op. cit.**, p. 819.
63. Montgomery, *Centenary Translation*, **op. cit.**, p. 658.
64. **Ibid.**, p. 505.
65. *New Evangelical Translation*, **op. cit.**, p. 412.
66. **Ibid.**, p. 412.
67. **Ibid.**, p. 412.
68. *New Evangelical Translation*, **op. cit.**, pp. 404-405.
69. Montgomery, *The Centenary Translation*, **op. cit.**, p. 241.
70. **Ibid.**, p. 241.

Questions

1. Christ was born between _____ and _____.
2. Christ is the center of _____.
3. Did Jesus claim to have the same glory as the Father? _____
4. Is Jesus also the Creator of the Universe? _____
5. What was foretold in Proverbs 8:22-31? _____
6. There are over _____ Messianic prophecies in the Old Testament.
7. Who announced the virgin birth of the Messiah?
8. Who announced the place of His birth? _____
9. What did Jeremiah predict? _____
10. Matthew's genealogy of Christ is traced back to _____.
11. Luke genealogy goes back to _____.
12. Matthew gives the real decent of _____ and Luke the real decent of _____.
13. What is "The Fullness of the Times?" _____

Thanks to God
A Common Theme Characterizes the Observance of the Festival of the Harvest Day of Thanksgiving

Christian News, November 15, 1993

The liturgical calendar of the Lutheran Church lists readings, collects and introits for The Festival of the Harvest and for A Day of Special Thanksgiving.

Reed in his book, *The Lutheran Liturgy*, wrote: "The Festival of Harvest is another unique day of the Lutheran calendar. The Roman Church observes three rogation days—Monday, Tuesday and Wednesday before Ascension—with penitential litanies followed by a Mass for which special propers are appointed which implore God's forgiveness and invoke His blessings upon the fruits of the earth. The American Book of Prayer (not the English) also recognizes these Rogation Days, features and appoints proper lessons and a special Collect."[1]

Reed claimed that the Lutheran Festival of Harvest is of a different nature than the Roman Catholic and Protestant Episcopal, in that the Lutheran stresses a Thanksgiving for the fruits of the earth and is observed differently in each locality, and held after the harvest has been gathered in. According to Reed's research "many sixteenth-century Lutheran Orders (Calenberg, 1542, Osnabruck, 1543, Hildesheim, 1544, Prussia, 1558) combine The Festival of Harvest with The Feast of St. Michael's Day. Others again, simply specify that such a harvest festival be held annually, without specifying the date.[2] Agricultural congregations are the most likely to observe a Festival of Harvest, especially when a plentiful harvest means so much for the economic health of those communities.

The collect in *The Lutheran Hymnal* adequately sets forth the purpose of The Harvest Home Festival and reads: "Almighty, most merciful father, Who openest Thine hand and satisfies the desire of every living thing, we give thee most humble and hearty thanks that Thou has crowned the fields with thy blessing and has permitted us once more to gather in the fruits of the earth; and we beseech thee to bless and protect the living seed of Thy Word sown in our hearts that in plenteous fruits of righteousness we may always present to thee an acceptable thank-offering through Jesus Christ, Thy Son our Lord, who with thee etc."[3]

The Evangelical Lutheran

Church (ELCA) *Lutheran Book of Worship* has this collect: "O Lord, maker of all things, open your hand and satisfy the desire of every living creature. We praise you for crowning the fields with your blessing and enabling us once more to gather in the fruits of the earth. Teach us to use your gifts carefully, that our land may continue to yield her increase, through Your Son, Jesus Christ our Lord."[4] *Lutheran Worship* of The Lutheran Church-Missouri Synod has this collect: "Lord God, heavenly

Father, through whose kindness we have received the fruits of the earth in their season, grant us ever to rejoice in your mercy that neither prosperity nor adversity may drive us from your presence, through Jesus Christ our Lord, Who liveth etc."[5]

The Scripture readings according to the *Lutheran Hymnal* are Deut. 26:1-11; the Gospel: Luke 12:13-21;[6] *Lutheran Worship* has for the one year cycle: Psalm. 67; Mal. 3:10-12; 2 Cor. 9:6-15.[7] *The Lutheran Book of Worship*: Three-year cycle: Deut. 26:1-11; 2 Cor. 9:5-15; Matt. 13:24-30.[8]

The underlying thread through all prayers and Scripture readings is thanks to God for the fruits of the ground, not also forgetting the food that feeds the spiritual life. The theme of thanksgiving predominates the day of Thanksgiving, observed in Canada October 11 and in the United States on November 25.

A Day of Thanksgiving

Thanksgiving is a uniquely Canadian and American Day. In America Thanksgiving Day was established by the proclamation of the President and governors of the various states. The Pilgrims who came from Holland proclaimed a Day of Thanksgiving in 1621 after their first harvest.

By 1680 this observance had become an annual festival in the Massachusetts Bay Colony. In 1789 George Washington proclaimed Thursday, November 26 a Day of Thanksgiving. Again the first American President in 1795 designated a Day of Thanksgiving for the benefit of the welfare of the nation. At the end of the war of 1812 President Madison also did the same. In 1858, twenty-five governors annually appointed a Day of Thanksgiving. Five years later (1863) President Lincoln declared a National Day of Thanksgiving. Every year thereafter, whoever happened to be president, proclaimed the fourth Thursday in November as a Day of Thanksgiving.

The Lutheran Hymnal has its epistle for Thanksgiving Day: 1 Timothy 2:2-8 and the Gospel: Luke 17:11-19.[9] *Lutheran Worship* gives these Scripture selections: Psalm 65; Isaiah 61:10-11; 1 Timothy 2:1-8; Luke 11:11-18.[10] *The Lutheran Book of Worship* gives: Psalm 65; Deut. 8:1-10; Philippians 4:6-20; I Tim. 2:18; Luke 17:11-18.[11]

The Old and New Testaments have at least a hundred passages, in which believers of both covenants are called upon to thank God or are depicted as thanking God for specific blessings, earthly as well as spiritual.

Examples of Thanksgiving In the Old Testament

The first record of thanksgiving is given in the Book of Genesis 9; it occurred at a time when only eight people were still living. Eight people of all mankind had not drowned as a result of a great worldwide flood. Because Noah and his three sons, Ham, Shem, and Japheth and their wives had trusted God; they were still alive and they needed to continue to trust in God, in the days ahead, if the world was their own to rebuild and be better than the one which was destroyed. At this juncture of human history, Noah set the world a living example by erecting an altar of thanksgiving unto the Lord. On the altar he sacrificed of every clean beast and of every clean bird as a token of gratitude for undeserved mercies. Like Noah, we too, can look back upon many undeserved mercies and kindnesses of God in 1993 and we shall do well to erect a similar altar of thanksgiving onto the Lord.

Thanksgiving in the Mosaic Period

In the Mosaic period God gave Israel detailed instructions about five different kinds of sacrifice.

In Leviticus 7:11-13 the text read: "This is the law of the sacrifice of peace offerings which ye shall offer to the Lord: If he offers it for a thanks-offering, then he shall offer with the sacrifice of thanksgiving unleavened cakes mixed with oil, or cakes of finely blended flour mixed with oil. Besides the cakes, as his offering he shall offer leavened bread with the sacrifice of thanksgiving of his peace offering" (New King James).

Killen in *The Wycliffe Bible Encyclopedia* pertinently asserted: "The Bible is full of thanksgiving, the most pronounced examples of which are found in a special OT offering of thanksgiving (Lev. 7:12-15; 22:29; II Chron. 29:31; Amos 4:5), in the many feasts instituted for Israel (Ex. 23:14ff; 34:22-23; Lev. 23; Num. 29; Deut. le)."[12]

Our national celebration of thanksgiving is an echo of two OT feasts of Harvest (Ex. 23:16), called also the Feast of Pentecost and the Feast of Weeks (Ex. 34:22), since it was seven weeks or 50 days after the Passover; and of the Feast of Tabernacles (Lev., 23:34-43). Also called the Feast of Ingathering (Ex. 23:16; 34:22) at the end of the agricultural year. Pentecost marked the end of the wheat harvest in Israel and came in June, while our thanksgiving marks the end of the entire harvest season and comes in the fall, as did the Feast of Tabernacles after the olives, grapes, and other fruits were picked.[13]

Thanksgiving in the Post-Mosaic Periods

In the days of Joshua, after Israel had come into Canaan, the Israelites were told to take of the first fruits of the land and present them to the priest in appreciation of the fact that God (Yahweh) had kept His promise to give Canaan to Abraham's descendants. When David said to the people: "Give thanks unto the Lord and call upon his name, and make his deeds known among the peoples (1 Chron. 16:3-4, 6-7,34). The function of Jeduthun and his sons was to give thanks and to praise God (1 Chron. 25:3). There are at least 23 references in the Psalms commanding Israel to praise God.

Psalms of thanksgiving are Ps. 34:3; 50:14; 92:1-5; 100; 107,136). At Solomon's installation as king, David blessed the Lord and said: "Now therefore, our God we thank thee and praise thy glorious name (1 Chron. 29:13)."

In the prophetic period Hezekiah appointed the divisions of the priests and Levites, each man according to his service, the priests and Levites for burnt offerings and peace offerings, to serve, to give thanks and to praise in the gates of the Lord" (II Chron. 31:2). One of the strangest thanksgivings came from Jonah, while in the stomach of the great fish, for he concluded his prayer with the words: "But I will sacrifice to you with the words of thanksgiving (Jonah 2:9)."

The eighth-century prophet Amos called upon the northern kingdom to offer a sacrifice of thanksgiving with leaven, proclaim and announce the "free will offerings" (Amos 4:5). The prophet Jeremiah announced that in the restored Jerusalem: "then out of them shall proceed thanksgiving and the voice of those who make merry (30:19)." In the days of Nebuchadnezzar Daniel thanked God for giving him wisdom and might and the revelation of the dream and its meaning for the Babylonian king (Dan. 2:22). In the course of the building of the Second Temple the priests and Levites sang together in praising and giving thanks unto the Lord, "because He is good and his mercy endureth forever (Ezra 3:11)." At the dedication of the wall in 444 B.C. Nehemiah reports that two companies gave thanks in the house of the Lord (Neh. 12:24,40).

Examples of Thanksgiving In the New Testament
There are over sixty references to the giving of thanks in the New Testament. Christ, Paul, John, Luke and the author of Hebrews are portrayed as giving thanks.

Jesus and the Giving of Thanks
Christ thanked his heavenly Father for answering his prayers. In the performance of the two miracles of multiplication of bread and fishes, the feeding of the 5,000 and the 4,000 respectively, Jesus is depicted as thanking God for the food before giving orders for its distribution (John 6:11; Matthew 16:36). When Jesus stood before the tomb of Lazarus, He said: "Father, I thank thee that thou art ever hastening to me etc (John 11:42)." One of the healing miracles of Christ involved healing ten lepers and Jesus was disappointed that only one man returned to give thanks to our Lord for His gift of new life (Luke 17:18).

In connection with the institution of the Lord's Supper, Jesus took bread and wine and thanked His Heavenly Father for them before giving them to His disciples (Luke 22:14-20).

Paul on Thanksgiving
A study of the variegated passages in most of the epistles of Paul will be very instructive in showing twentieth-century Christians to Whom through Whom, for whom and for what conditions and gifts, thanks should be rendered. In the apostles kaleidoscopic presentation, present day followers of Christ will learn what things are especially to be subjects of thanksgiving and which should lead to thanksgiving. The noun eucharistia is employed twelve times by the apostle, the verb eucharistet twenty-four times and the adjective eucharestos once, meaning "thanksliving," "giving of thanks," and "thanked."[14]

Who Is to Be Thanked
The true God is the object of all of Paul's thanksgivings. The God to

whom Paul addresses his thanksgivings is the Father and is associated with Jesus Christ. In writing to the Roman congregation, the Apostle to the Gentiles declared: "First, I thank my God through Jesus Christ for all of you etc., (NET)" (1:8) In communicating with Timothy, his spiritual son, Paul said: "I thank Christ Jesus our Lord who made me strong. He considered me to do His work, although I used to be a blasphemer, a persecutor, and a violent person. However, I received mercy because I acted ignorantly in unbelief. Our Lord poured His grace on me abundantly, along with faith and love in Christ Jesus (I Timothy 1:12-14)" TEV. Only those who acknowledge Christ as Savior and Redeemer, can pray to the Father of our Lord Jesus.

For Whom Should Thanksgiving Be Made?

Prominent in Paul's letters are statements thanking God for seven of the churches he had founded or had been organized by others. In expressing gratitude to God through Jesus Christ, the apostle especially was grateful to God for the spiritual blessings bestowed upon them. In some cases he thanked the Giver of all good things for their election, in others he expressed gratitude for their faith in Christ, in yet others for his convert's missionary zeal. The following passages in the Pauline epistles will demonstrate these points: Roman 1:8; 1 Corinthians 1:4; Philippians 1:1,3-4; Ephesians 1:16; Colossians 1:3; 1 Thessalonians 1:2; 2 Thess. 1:3.

Not only entire congregations are the subject of Paul's thanksgivings but individuals such as Philemon (w. 3-4) or Timothy (2 Tim. 1:3). Paul was grateful to God for the help and support that Aquila and Priscilla had given to him and other Christians (Romans 16:4). Paul of Tarsus likewise thanked God for Titus for the care he had given to the Corinthians (2 Cor. 8:16). Paul thanked God for himself. The things for which gratitude are expressed are grace bestowed upon him that through a persecutor of Christ's followers he forgave him and called him to proclaim the good news to both Jews and Gentiles: (1 Timothy 1:12-4).

For What Paul Thanked God Through Jesus

Christ's thirteenth apostle was thankful for spiritual and earthly blessings, the greatest of all spiritual gifts was that God had sent His only begotten Son into the world. Just as Paul wanted to proclaim no one other than Christ crucified, so Paul held the gift of God's Son as unfathomable, so that he cried out: "Thanks be to God for His indescribable Gift (1 Cor. 9:15)." (NET).

Prominent in the list of blessings God has bestowed on Paul were those that spoke of a spiritual nature. Thus he was grateful for freeing him from the bondage of the law (Romans 8:25). He thanked God for the victory over the fear of the law and the sting of death (Co. 15:55). The apostle of the Gentiles thanked God who, as he averred, "always leads us in triumph in Christ and through us diffuses the fragrance of His knowledge in every place" (2 Cor. 2:14). Timothy was told by Paul "that foods needed not to be abstained from, but were to be received with thanksgiving (1 Tim. 4:3-4)." Another cause for thanksgiving was the liberality of the

972

Corinthians for the suffering brethren in Judea, (2 Cor. 9:11-12). On his trip to Rome by ship which was shipwrecked in the Mediterranean, Luke reports in his church history book: Acts, that Paul encouraged the people to eat who had not partaken of food for fourteen days: He took bread and gave thanks to God in the presence of them all, and when he had broken it he began to eat (Acts 27:35).

In his instructions to Timothy Paul told him to teach people to pray for all men and for those in authority, "that we may live peaceful and tranquil lives with all godliness and in good repute (1 Tim. 2:1-3)" In the concluding verses of 1 Thessalonians Paul gives a member of final counsels and says: "Always be joyful, pray without ceasing, give thanks to God in everything (5:17)."

Thanksgiving Resulting In Thanksliving

The author of Hebrews in the application portion of his epistle gives this exhortation: "Wherefore since we are receiving a kingdom which is unshakeable, let us give thanks and offer up an acceptable worship to God with holy awe and fear (Hebrew 12:28)." The same writer among his closing admonitions charges his readers: "In his name, let us continually offer up a sacrifice of praise to God, that is the fruit of lips that confess his name. And forget not to be kind and liberal; for with that sort of sacrifice God is well pleased (13:15-16)." Thanksgiving in Heaven in the Book of Revelation John reveals to us that heaven is filled with the voices of angelic creatures and of the redeemed giving thanks to God (Rev. 4:9; 7:12; 11:17).

Thanksgiving Should Occur Every Day

Golloday in a thanksgiving sermon appropriately encouraged his listeners: "There is one thing about the phrase thanksgiving day which needs to be guarded against. One might get the impression for it that thanksgiving is only an occasional thing—once a year or at least on special occasions."[15]

Footnotes

1. Luther D. Reed, *The Lutheran Liturgy* (Philadelphia: Muhlenberg Press, 1947), p. 511.
2. **Ibid.**, p. 512.
3. *The Lutheran Hymnal* (St. Louis: Concordia Publishing House, 1946), p. 84.
4. *Lutheran Book of Worship* (Minneapolis: Augsburg Publishing House; Philadelphia: Board of Publications, Lutheran Church in America, 1968), p. 39.
5. *Lutheran Worship* (St. Louis; Concordia Publishing House, 1982), p. 126.
6. *Lutheran Hymnal*, **op. cit.**, p. 84.
7. *Lutheran Worship*, **op. cit.**, p. 126.
8. *Lutheran Book of Worship*, **op. cit.**, p. 39.
9. *Lutheran Hymnal*, **op. cit.**, p. 85.
10. *Lutheran Worship*, **op. cit.**, p. 122.
11. *Lutheran Book of Worship*, **op. cit.**, p. 46.
12. R. A. Killen, "Thanksgiving," Pfeiffer, Vos, and Rea, Editors, *Wycliffe Bible Ency-*

clopedia (Chicago: Moody Press, 1975), n, p. 1687.

13. **Ibid.**

14. G. Abbott-Smith, *A Manual of Greek Lexicon of the New Testament* (New York: Charles Scribner's Sons, 1929), p. 190.

15. R. E. Golladay, *The Son of God Rides On* (Columbus: The Book Concern, 1938), p. 384.

Questions

1. Agricultural congregations are most likely to observe ____.
2. The pilgrims proclaimed a day of Thanksgiving in ____.
3. The first record of Thanksgiving is given in the Book of ____.
4. There are over ____ references in the New Testament of giving thanks.
5. Eucharistic means ____.
6. Thanksgiving results in ____.
7. Golloday in a thanksgiving sermon encouraged his listeners to ____.

Objective and Subjective Justification

Christian News, December 12, 1994

In this article, entitled "The Place and Purpose of Advent in the Church Year," I inadvertently ascribed the attempt to wipe out the Jews, as recorded in the Book of Esther, as being done by Mordecai, but it should have read "Haman." Mordecai had raised as his own daughter Esther and refused to bow before Haman, causing the latter to hate and plan to destroy the Jewish people and thus his mortal enemy Mordecai. Some scholars believe that Mordecai may have been the author of the Book of Esther.

In speaking about the Church Year, I wrote that the Sundays after Trinity are in *Lutheran Worship* called Sundays in Pentecost, it should have read "Sundays After Pentecost."

One kind and astute reader questioned my statement on page 7, column 3 where under 2: "The Cruciality for the Acceptance of the Incarnate Christ and the death and Crucifixion of the God-man," I wrote: "Romans 5:12-17 makes clear that all people have sinned and through Christ all have been reconciled." My respondent wrote me: "Do you mean to say that all men have been reconciled toward God, or that God has been reconciled toward mankind?" What I had in mind when I wrote what I did was that through the propitiatory sacrifice of Christ: God through His Son has forgiven all mankind the guilt and the punishment of their sins. No human beings guilty in God's sight can pay the penalty of their sins. In Romans 4:25, Paul stated about the Lord Jesus Christ: "Who was betrayed to death for our transgressions and raised again to life for our justification." LCMS theologians and exegetes have referred to this Justification as "objective Justification." The Brief Statement paragraph 17, "Of Justification" reads: "Holy Scripture sums up all its teachings regarding the love of God to the world of sinners, regarding salvation wrought by Christ, and faith in Christ as the only way to obtain salvation in the article of justification. Scripture teaches that God has already declared the whole world to be righteous in Christ, Rom. 5,19, 2 Cor. 5, 18.21, Rom. 4:25."

However, the fact that all mankind's sins are forgiven still requires that people accept Christ and are justified by faith apart from the deeds of the law. Subjective justification 2 Corinthians 5:20 surely teaches that God has been reconciled toward mankind.

Questions

1. What did Mordecai do? ____
2. No human being can pay ____.
3. What is "objective justification?" ____
4. The fact that all mankind's sins are forgiven still requires that people ____.
5. Subjective justification teaches that God has been ____.

Christmas Texts

A Comparison of the Matthean, Lukan and Johannean Nativity Accounts with Special Reference to John's Prologue

Christian News, December 19, 1994

Christmas or Mass of the Christ is the only festival that has three distinct services appointed for The Festival of the Incarnation or The Nativity of the Church's Lord.[1] Christmas is a festival which is distinctively western in origin. Its earliest name was **Natalis** or **Nativitas Domini**.[2] Weinacht-Holy Night is derived from the solemn vigil which preceded the Feast.

The word Yule comes from the Anglo Saxon geoil, giul, geol and entered into English from the Scandinavian languages and designated the Christmas season. Originally Yule was a heathen festival of the winter solstice, akin to Old Norse "Jol."[3] Christmas is a distinctly English name. It is analogous to such names as Candlemas, Michelmas, meaning the Mass of Christmas Day. The designation of Festival of the Incarnation specifically suggests the purpose of Christmas, namely, of God assuming human nature, for as John 3:16 that God sent His Only begotten Son, or as some readings have, God's One-And-Only Son, into the world to seek and save that which was lost.[4]

Christmas in the course of time became the greatest of the festivals of the church year. According to *Lutheran Worship* there are three distinct services that can be held within a 24-hour period. The great Christmas celebration begins with December 24 at 6 p.m., being ushered in with a Holy Night watch, terminated at midnight. Early at dawn a second service may take place and the holy festivities are concluded by a final service, the main Nativity service.[5] Each of the three services has its own Propers: namely: the Introit (usually composed of psalm verses), a collect for the day, the gradual, the Scriptural readings, and the verse. For all three services, both the Old and New Testaments furnished selections for readings and as texts for homilies or sermons. The following Old Testament texts are suggested in *Lutheran Worship*: Isaiah 92 (3-5), 6-7; Micah 5:2-4 and the following joyous psalms of praise: 2,96,98; additional Old Testament texts are: Isaiah 52:7-10; 37:24-28. From the New Testament there are these: Luke 2:1-20; John 1:1-18; Titus 2:11-14; 3:4-8a; Hebrew 1:1-9.[6]

The doctrine of Christ's assuming flesh and blood is taught throughout the Bible, being clearly stated in John 1:14: 'The Word became flesh."

Paul wrote the Galatians: "When the time finally came, God sent His Son to be born of a woman and to be born under the law."[7] In 1 Timothy 3:16 Paul appears to be quoting from an ancient hymn: "He appeared in the flesh, was justified in spirit, was seen by angels, was preached among nations, was believed in the world, was taken up in glory."[8] In an earlier epistle Paul declared: "For what the Law could not do, because it is weakened by the flesh, God has done by sending His Son to be like sinful flesh, God sent Him to be a sacrifice for sin and condemned sin in His flesh" (Romans 8:3).[9] The Word incarnation is from the Latin meaning "becoming flesh," that is "becoming human." The doctrine of the incarnation teaches that the eternal God became human, and He did so without in any member or degree diminishing His divine nature. A somewhat detailed statement is found in Philippians 2:5-11: "Having this attitude in yourselves which was also in Christ Jesus, who although He existed in the form of God, did not regard equality with God a thing to be grasped, but emptied Himself, taking the form of a bond-servant and being made in the likeness of men, and being found in appearance a man. He humbled Himself by becoming obedient to the point of death on a cross. Therefore also God highly exalted Him, and bestowed upon Him the name which is above every name, that at the name of Jesus ever knee should bow, of those who are in heaven, and on earth, and under the earth, and that every tongue should confess that Jesus Christ is Lord, to the glory of the Father." All the essential attributes of God are ascribed in the Bible to the human Christ.

There are other significant texts which teach the humanity or incarnation of God's Son. Thus Matthew, Mark, Luke, John (in his Gospel), the three epistles and the Apocalypse), Paul in his writings, the author of Hebrews, Peter have recorded texts that declare and assume the humanity of the Second Person of the Godhead. Other Scriptures which should be mentioned are: Galatians 4:1-7; Colossians 1:13-17; 2:9; Hebrews 2:14-18; 2 Peter 1:2.

The Variety of Truths Revealed by the Incarnational Texts

The most beloved Christmas text is that of St. Luke, found in 2:1-20. In that chapter the reader is informed of the time of the birth, the reason why Joseph and Mary travelled from Nazareth to Bethlehem, the necessity of Christ being born in a stable surrounded by animals, the song of the angelic hosts, the appearance of an angel to announce Christ's birth to shepherds and the visitation of the shepherds to the place where the Godman lay. More sermons throughout the centuries have been preached on this Scripture than other texts asserting the fact that God had become a man.

The Matthean account of Christ's birth gives us data not contained in Luke's classical account. Matthew relates the fact that Joseph, of the house of David, was engaged to a Mary, also of the Davidic line. Before these two Davidic descendants lived permanently as husband and wife, Mary was seen by Joseph to be pregnant. Since he had not had intercourse with his betrothed, he assumed that Mary had been guilty of infidelity. He was prevented from not consummating the marriage, when in a dream he received the command by revelation not to leave her, because Mary was with child by the Holy Spirit. Both Luke (Chapter 1:35) and Matthew (1:18) record the miracle of the immaculate conception. The angel told Joseph: "Do not be afraid to take your wife Mary home with you; for her Child is from the Holy Spirit. She will have a son, and you will name Him, Jesus, because He will save His people from their sins."[11] Matthew further declared that the manner of Mary's conception was by the Holy Spirit and was in fulfillment of a prophecy of Isaiah: "Look" the virgin will conceive and have a son, and they will name Him Immanuel, which means "God Is with Us" (7:14).[12]

The most remarkable account of Christ's incarnation was given Bible readers in John's Prologue. A portion of John's introduction to the Fourth Gospel deals with Mary's Son before His conception and miraculous birth. From the Prologue the uniqueness of Mary's Son as God before becoming God-man is described. Here the Biblical reader will learn outstanding truths about the person and work of Jesus Christ before his human birth as John wrote: "And the Word became flesh and lived among us, and we saw His glory, the glory of the Father's one-and-only Son."[12a] While Matthew and Luke tell of the life of Christ from the conception by a virgin to the lowly birth in an inn, John in 1:1-14 informs us about the eternal Christ. Mark begins his account of Christ's life when he was thirty years old, completely by passing the birth of David's greater offspring. What a loss it would be had the world not in their totality the four gospels.

Thus it is apparent that the Apostle John's Gospel contains facts and data not contained in the other three. Why this difference? Good reasons might be given for this situation. Bishop Ryle gave this answer: "But it is enough to remember that Matthew, Mark, Luke and John wrote under the inspiration of God. In the general plan of their respective Gospels, and in the particular details— in everything that they record, and in everything that they do not record—they were all four equally guided by the Holy Ghost."[13]

John's Prologue (1:1-18) is the primordial nucleus of the whole Book. It is difficult to see how certain scholars have claimed that the Prologue plays no part in the rest of the twenty-one chapters constituting the Fourth Gospel. Henry averred: "In majestic prose, this initial portion presents Jesus of Nazareth as the Eternal Logos become flesh (14), creation (v. 5), history (w. 5-16), and conscience (vv. 4,9) finding their meaning and unity in the Divine Redeemer (v. 17). Linking the destiny of the whole of creation to the resurrection of the incarnate and crucified Logos, the Gospel thus sweeps from eternity to eternity."[14]

In the Prologue there are four designations of our Lord which at once capture attention: (1) the WORD, (2) the LIFE, (3) the LIGHT, (4) the SON. Two of these declare His relationship to God, the Father. The other two indicate functions toward the human creation.

The first five verses of John 1 contain a statement of matchless sublimity concerning the divine nature of our Lord Jesus Christ. He it is, when John speaks of the Logos, or word. No doubt there are heights and depths in that statement which are far beyond man's understanding. And yet there are plain lessons in it, which every Christian would do well to treasure up in the mind.

The Prologue of eighteen verses contains the word in Greek of "Logos," which means more than the English vocable "Word." Tenney in his commentary on the Greek Logos wrote: "A word is an idea expressed through combination of sounds and letters. Without the idea or concept behind it, the medium would be meaningless, KXBZ might represent a radio station, but as a combination of letters or sounds, if it could be pronounced, it has no meaning whatsoever, because no concept is attached to it. Just so the term Logos implies intelligence, and the transmissible expression of it. The term was used technically in the Greek philosophy of this period by the Stoics, to denote the controlling reasons of the universe, the all-pervading mind that ruled and gave meaning to all things. Logos was one of the purest and general concepts of that ultimate Intelligence. Reason or will that is called God."[16]

In the interpretation of the Logos of the Prologue it is necessary to distinguish between the philosophical employment and the meaning assigned to the Logos by John. To quote Tenney again: "How could he do otherwise than to adopt to his purpose the vocabulary of his time? If he refused to use it because it had connotations contrary to this meaning he would have to be forced to remain silent for lack of media expression. His usage should be understood in terms of its own definition."[17]

The Greek word Logos should be understood in the light of Christ's person, not by that found in philosophy. With the rise of Jesus of Nazareth a new philosophy had begun, so that John's use of Logos represents a new concept, far removed from that of paganism.

The question which concerned John was this: how shall human beings regard Jesus of Nazareth? Is he to be admired as the best of men, or may He also be worshipped and trusted as God; was he the greatest of the prophets, or is He the Savior of the world? Is our attitude toward Him a test of character? Does belief in Jesus determine life and our eternal destiny?

All these questions are answered in John's Gospel as a whole. These great questions are already set forth in the Prologue, verses 1-18. Scholars have suggested different divisions and different organizations. One suggestion is to divide the Prologue into seven sections, each of which deals with some aspects of the Logos.[18]

The Prologue is an integral part of Johannine Gospel. As each Evangelist begins his book in a manner suited to his narrative, so John goes back to eternity. Matthew and Luke describe the coming of Christ from the human side; John describes it from the Divine side. He traces the course of the pre-existence of the Son from the glory which He had with the Father "before the world was" (17:5). Coming down into the time and the field of human history. With a stately simplicity, John introduces the Lord Jesus Christ out from the eternal past.

A. The Word and Deity (v. 1)

The first predicate of the Logos is that He is eternal. John's Gospel reminds one of Genesis 1:1: "In the beginning God created the heavens and the earth." The Triune God is the Creator of the universe, including the world. When time began the Logos always was. Christ is eternal, Jesus as the Logos was with the Father and the Holy Spirit when the Gospel

979

was proclaimed in the Old Testament. As Paul stated to the Colossians in a great Christological passage in chapter 1, "He was before all things."

The author of Hebrews agrees with John about the deity of the Logos, when he wrote: "He who is the radiance of God's glory and the exact likeness of His nature."[19]

Christ was a Personality; He was not an impersonal principle, but is to be regarded as living, an intelligent and active personality.[20] Further, the Logos, who later tabernacles among men, was deity. The Greek word **theos**, translated God, is employed here without the article. In the second clause the article is used, the emphasis of the word is on individuality, God as a separate person. God as a Person without the article the emphasis is on quality, God as a kind of being. The Word was deity, clearly asserts that the Logos possessed and eternally manifested the very nature of God. Clearly John claims that the Logos was in the beginning with God.

Baxter, commenting on the opening verses of the Prologue, asserted: "Our Lord is the Word, i.e. the expression of God, not only towards man, not only from pre-mundane antiquity, but before all the creation (verses 2,3), fundamentally, eternally, indivisible. He was not merely from the beginning; He already was, 'in the beginning' (verse 1)." "He was not only with God; 'He was God' (verse 1).[21] No exegetical jugglery can really hide the force of the Greek here, especially when it is read honestly with its context." The Jehovah Witnesses New World Translation of the Holy Scriptures translates verse 1 wrongly, when it rendered the opening verse of John's Gospel: "In the beginning was the Word, and the Word was a god."[22] It makes the Word of a different nature and quality than God by its rendering of God with a small "god."

B. The Word and Creation

John unequivocally asserts: "Everything was made by Him, and not one thing that was made was made without him" (verse 3).[23] So far as being a creature of God, as some heretics have averred. He is the Being who made the worlds, the universe, including our earth. Paul in speaking about his commission to the Gentiles, that He Paul should proclaim the unsearchable riches of Christ and also proclaim the new dispensation of that secret purpose, hidden from eternity in the God who founded the universe, in order that now the manifold wisdom of God should through the church, be made known to principalities and powers in the heavenly sphere. The author of the Hebrews was caused to write about Christ: "His Son, whom he hath appointed heir of all things (1:2)." Christ did what Psalm 40:8 declares: "He commanded and they were created." "All things" relates to the universe, its elements, and system of law. The Greek text reads: "Panta di' autou egeneto, kai choris autou egeneto oude en ho gegonen." Literally this says: "All things through Him became, and without him became not one thing." The **Centenary Translation** renders verse 3: "all things came into being through him, and apart from him nothing that exists came into being."[24]

"All things came into being," presupposes a crisis, a transition from

980

what was not to what is. The tense of the verb "egeneto" is aorist, and implies occurrence without relation to elapsed time, an event, not a process. By the use of this tense the interest is not centered in the method of creation so much as the fact of creation. By contrast the word "was" in the first part of the Prologue (1:1), presupposes duration. The Logos exists eternally, the material universe temporarily,

The Word, or Son of God, the Agent of Creation

The work of creation is the work of the Holy Trinity. The opening verses of Hebrews informs its readers: "In the past God spoke to our fathers at many times and in various ways through the prophets. In these last days He has spoken to us through His Son, by whom He also made the world. He who is the radiance of God's glory and the exact likeness of His nature."[25]

Not only did the Word create the universe, He is said to uphold it. Paul, in his great Christological passage stated: "For in Him was the universe created, things in heaven and on earth, the seen and the unseen, thrones, or dominions, or principalities, or powers; by him and for him all have been created; and He is before all, and in him all things subsist" (Col. 1:16).[26] With Paul, Hebrews also agrees: "He who is radiance of God's glory and the exact likeness of His nature maintains everything by His powerful Word" (1:3).[27]

Many scholars, going back to ancient times believe that Solomon in chapter 8 of Proverbs, where Chochmah, or wisdom is personified, describes Christ as being with God at creation. In Proverbs 8:22-31 there is a description of a Person who was with God in the beginning and participating with God, the Father in creation. Luther and others believe that this Person was Christ.[28]

C. The Word and Life

In verse 4 John wrote: "In him was life, and the life was the light of men." The light is shining in the darkness, and the darkness has not overwhelmed it." In verse 9 John further describes Christ, the Life: "The true Light which enlightens every man coming into the world." The beloved disciple claims that Jesus Christ is the source of all spiritual life and light. Christ is the eternal fountain, from which life, physical and spiritual, is obtained. That completely repudiates atheistic and theistic evolution. So far from being a creature of God (as the Jehovah witnesses contend) He is the source of all life and therefore of all creatures.[29] Whatever spiritual life and light Adam and Eve possesses before the fall was from Christ. Whatever deliverance from sin and spiritual death any child of Adam and Eve does enjoy since the fall, whatever light of conscience or understanding anyone has, all flowed from Christ.

The term "darkness" in verse 5 is the first hint of the awesome conflict between light and darkness. Henry noted: "It is a stark reminder that the created universe is now a fallen world, that mankind now is ensnared in sin. Despite creation in God's image, man is spiritually disqualified from fellowship and needs supernatural restoring to sonship (v. 12). In

Genesis 1:1-3 cosmic darkness supplies the setting for the Creator's "Let there be light!" The background of the Logos' Incarnation is the gloom of a fallen spiritual world against which God's Son lights the heart of fallen mankind. The Prologue of John's Gospel shows the world's need for darkness to be removed. The world is unable to save itself, but God so loved the world to send His Son to remove the darkness. The life of the Logos in its manifestation brings illumination.

The word true (Greek: alethinos) refers to true in contrast to the false. The same word **alethinos** is employed of God in 17:3, where the emphasis is on the ultimate character of God's being. **Alethinos** means true in contrast to false, original rather than correct. From the Logos proceeds true spiritual illumination.[30]

D. The Word and the World

In verse 6:13 John describes Christ in history. In these verses the reader is brought to the historic appearance of the Son of God in the Incarnation. They relate the mission of John the Baptist, who was sent to bear witness of the Light that was coming into the world, to prepare men to believe in Christ as the perfect light for every man. The word "world" (Greek: Kosmos) is employed seventy-seven times in the Gospel of John[31] and is one of the distinctive Johannine terms. Here it applies to the material and spiritual environment, in which people live. The immanence of the Logos is asserted in that He has entered into the framework of life, and has taken an active part in it.

Christ who came into the world during the reign of Caesar Augustus toward the end of the first century B.C. and first century A.D. and the world knew Him not. The world as a system had no place for the Logos. The Synoptic Gospels reveal that the Jewish-Gentile world of Christ's time had only a superficial understanding of Him, yes, even His disciples did not really understand him completely before His ascension (Acts 1:7).

E. The Word and Men

Verses 11-13 expatiate yet more on the assertion of verse 10. "World" is a term which is broad and collective and describes humanity and its environment as one system. In verses 11-13 there is an individualization, and they personalize the world's reception of the Christ. "He came into His own folk did not receive Him."[32] The individuals comprising the world did not welcome Him. Since Jesus was the Creator of the world, when He was born. He simply was coming to that which belonged to Him (cf. John 16:32 and 19:27 for the use of "came into own home)."[33] Those who were His own people did not receive Him as the promised Messiah. The idea of "coming into his own" is the expression Christ uttered in the Synoptic parable of the wicked husbandman (Matthew 21:33-46: Mark 12:1-12; Luke 20:9-16). Christ was accepted by the Samaritans (John 4), was sought by the Greek Gentiles (John 12:20), but was rejected by the official representatives of His own people.

Rejection, however, has its counterpart reception. Those who believed in the Logos and thus received Him are given the privilege to be the Sons of God. It was moreover, by an act of God that those who believed and trusted the Logos were begotten as "the sons of God." Believing Christ's name is the key to the reception of the Word that has come into the world.

F. The Word Became Flesh (v. 14)

In verses 14-18 John tells of the appearance of the Logos, "the shining of the true light," the "coming into the world," was by way of incarnation. Verse 14 announces that the Word stooped from the eternal world into the sphere of time and space as a human being to redeem sinners. Verse 14 is very short, if measured by the number of verses, but it is very long, if we measure it by its contents. This single verse contains more than enough matter to fill a volume. The main truth of verse 14 is that reality characterized Christ's incarnation. The plain meaning of this verse is that the Savior took on human nature that, in order to save sinners, "adding to human nature to what He was" eternally, that is Deity.[34]

Verse 14 is the pivotal assertion of the Prologue. The word Logos occurs in verse 14 and connects it with verses 1 and 2. Asserts Tenney: "Verse one speaks of the eternal nature and relation of the Logos to God, verse 14 of a change of relationship to the world of men. Jesus revealed Himself in a human personality, that was visible, audible and tangible. As the author of Hebrews puts it: "Since, therefore the children are the sharers in the flesh and blood, he also similarly partook of the same, in order that through death he might render powerless him that had the power of death, that is, the devil (2:14-15)."[35] Jesus became a man like ourselves in all things, sin only excepted. Like ourselves He was born of a woman, though born in a miraculous manner. Luke tells us that, like ourselves. He grew from infancy to boyhood and in stature (2:52). Like ourselves, he hungered, thirsted, ate, drank, slept—and was weary, felt pain, wept, rejoiced, marveled and had compassion. He played, read Scripture, suffered, being tempted, shed His blood, died and was buried, rose again and really ascended into heaven.

John said that Christ "tabernacled" among men. The Greek **ekenoosen** means to pitch a tent. The verb **skenoo** is used only five times in the New Testament; in John 1:14 and four times in the Apocalypse (Rev. 2:15; 12:12; 13:6; 21:3).[36] Two of these instances refer to God. In the Greek Old Testament the word is largely confined to use with reference to the Tabernacle, where the presence of God dwelt. Possibly John assumed that the reader's knowledge of the Septuagint assumed that the reader would connect this statement of John 1:14 with the Old Testament doctrine of the person of God which guided the children of Israel in the wilderness.

The Logos became man sets forth the union of the two natures in Christ's one Person.[37] This is one of the great mysteries of the Christian religion. The relationship of the two natures involves a number of interesting conclusions. The relationship of the two natures is not meant to be curiously pried into, but to be reverently believed.

The effect of Christ's dwelling on earth among men had a revelatory effect and is stated by John this way: "And we beheld His glory, the glory as of the only begotten of the Father, full of grace and truth."[38] "Beheld" in the original text is **etheasametha**, "Observed." The verb contains the word "theater" and indicates more than a casual glance. In fact, the life of Jesus was studied under every possible condition, favorable and unfavorable. All the information that human investigation would produce was made available by Christ to His contemporaries.[39]

The experience of the disciples evoked the following statement: "Of his fullness have we all received, grace in exchange for grace." In this assertion the reader possesses the element of personal confession by Christ's loyal disciples. The disciples saw in Christ the glory of the Father and the essential features of the character of God (v. 14). From His inexhaustible being they all received an increasing supply of grace (v. 16). The testimony of John is introduced. The witness of prophecy is introduced by John the Baptist, who stated "This was He of whom I said, 'He who comes after me has been but before me, for he was before me.'"[40] Then the Law was mentioned as a symbolical system that foreshadowed the grace and truth which was completely embodied in Jesus Christ.

G. The Word Revealing

The climax of the Prologue is found in verse 18: "No man hath seen deity at any time; the only begotten son of God, who is in the heaven of the Father he hath explained (him)."[41] Tenney observed: "'The intent of the author is to make clear that while the unveiled essence of the deity has never been given to mortal sight, the real character of God can be seen in the Son who is the fullest expression of the Father's life and love.[42] The expression "bosom of the Father" means perfect understanding and love. The nature of the invisible and mysterious God is thus interpreted by One who is qualified to do so through kinship and understanding.

Two climactic affirmations of the Prologue reveal the incomparable superiority of the Hebrew-Christian religion over the pagan religions: (1) the spirituality of God and (2) the divine incarnation once-for-all in Christ (The oldest manuscripts read not only "the only-begotten Son," but "God only begotten)."[43]

H. The Word and John the Baptist

The Prologue speaks of three different times relative to the Word: 1. of eternity, 2. of the birth of the Logos in about 5 B.C. and 3. then leaps from 5 B.C. to A.D. 26, thus bypassing the first thirty years in the life of the Logos. John the Baptist receives no less than six verses in the Prologue, describing the relationship of John the Baptist to the Word.

The appearance of Jesus of Nazareth in Palestine was not an unanticipated event. During the Old Testament period God had given numerous prophecies about the coming of the Messiah. Henry observed: "Prior to the coming of the Light of the world, the lamp of prophetic witness had shone steadily in the night of sin. Four centuries of silence followed the last inspired Old Testament prophecies until John the Baptist announced the Messiah's imminent presence" (1:6-8).[44] John the Baptist refused to be identified with Christ the Light of the World. Thus verse 15 informs

984

us; "This is he of whom I said, 'He who is coming after me has been before me, for he was before me,'"[45] thereby testifying to the eternity and deity of the Logos, Jesus Christ.

John the Baptist had some disciples (John and Andrew were among John's disciples) whom he directed to follow Jesus, who as "the Lamb of God takes away the sins of the world." In connection with his testimony to the Word, John by inspiration said: "This I have seen and I am become a witness to the fact that he is the Son of God,"[46] one of many different witnesses to Christ's deity in John's twenty-one chapters.

Among the Christological statements found throughout the New Testament, the Prologue certainly must be proclaimed as unique, especially when John portrayed the activity of the Second Person of the Trinity before His incarnation. John's Prologue makes a valuable contribution to the events which preceded as well as those which followed Christ's Incarnation.[47]

Footnotes

1. *Lutheran Worship.* Prepared by The Commission on Worship of The Lutheran Church-Missouri Synod (St. Louis: Concordia Publishing House, 1982), pp. 14-17.
2. Paul Zelier, Strodach, *The Church Year* (Philadelphia: The United Publication House, 1924), pp. 40-41.
3. *Webster's New World Dictionary of the American Language* (Cleveland and New York; The World Publishing Company, 1966), p. 1697. College Edition.
4. *Holy Bible, New Evangelical Translation. New Translation* (Cleveland: NET Publishing Company, 1992), p. 178. Hereafter referred to as **TEV**.
5. Cf. footnote 1.
6. *Lutheran Worship*, **op. cit.**, pp. 15-17.
7. **TEV**, p. 350.
8. *The Centenary Translation. The New Testament in Modern English.* Translated by Helen Barrett Montgomery (Philadelphia: The Judson Press, 1924), p. 567.
9. **TEV**, p. 298.
10. The New American Standard Bible. Student's Edition (Philadelphia: A.J. Holman Company, 1973), p. 842.
11. **TEV**, p. 3.
12. **TEV**, p. 3.
12a. **TEV**, p. 173.
13 Rt. Rev. J.C. Ryle, *Expository Thoughts on the Gospels* (New York: Fleming H. Revell Company, 1858), St. John, vol. 1, p. 1.
14. F. H. Henry, "John," in *Biblical Expositor*, edited by Carl F. Henry (Philadelphia: A. J. Holman Company, 1966), HI. New Testament, p. 158.
15. J. Sidlow Baxter, *Explore the Book* (Grand Rapids; Zondervan Publishing House, 1960), Lesson 123, ealin with John, p. 302.
16. M. C. Tenney, *John, The Gospel of Belief* (Grand Rapids: Wm. B. Eerdmans Publishing Company, 1948), p. 62.
17. **Ibid.**
18. **Ibid.**, pp. 63-64.
19. **TEV**, p. 409.
20. Charles R. Erdmans, *The Gospel of John* (Philadelphia; Westminster Press, 1946), p. 18.

21. Baxter, **op. cit.**, p. 302.

22. *New World Translation of the Holy Scriptures* (Brooklyn; Watchtower Bible and Tract Society, 1961), p. 1151.

23. **TEV**, John 1:3; p. 173.

24. *The Centenary Translation*, **op. cit.**, p. 241.

25. **TEV**, p. 409.

26. *The Centenary Translation*, **op. cit.**, p. 538.

27. **TEV**, p. 469.

28. P.E. Kretzmann, *Popular Commentary of the Bible* (St. Louis; Concordia Publishing House, 1922), *Old Testament*, II, p. 225; Carl Manthey Zorn, *Weissagungen und Warnungen aus den Spruechen Salomonis* (Zwickau, Saxen: Johannes Herman, no date), p. 3; Ludwig Fuerbringer, "Persoenliche Weisheit Gottes," *Concordia Theological Monthly*, 4;241-248; 321-329; 461-467; April to June 193.

29. Irvine Robertson, *What the Cults Believe* (Chicago: Moody Press, 1969), p. 47.

30. Marvin R. Vincent. *World Studies in the New Testament* (Grand Rapids; Wm. B. Eerdmans Publishing Company, 1946), II, p. 44.

31. Thus Tenney, **op. cit.**, p. 67.

32. W. Robertson Nicoll, *The Expositor's Greek New Testament* (Grand Rapids: Wm. B. Eerdmans Publishing Company, 1974 reprint), I, The Gospels, p. 687.

33. A. T. Robertson, *Word Studies in the New Testament* (Nashville: Broadman Press, 1932), V. *The Fourth Gospel and The Epistles*, p. 10.

34. Henry, **op. cit.**. p. 158.

35. *The Centenary Translation*, **op. cit.**, p. 596.

36. Abbott-Smith, *A Manual Greek Lexicon of the New Testament* (New York; Charles Scribner's Sons, 1929), p. 409.

37. John Schaller, *Biblical Christology* (Milwaukee; Northwestern Publishing House, 19811, pp. 56-58.

38. *Holy Bible, New King James* (Nashville and New York; Thomas Nelson Publishers, 1982), p. 1032.

39. Vincent, **op. cit.**, p. 52.

40. *The Centenary Translation*, **op. cit.**. John 1:15, p. 242.

41. Tenney's *Translation*, **op. cit.**, p. 72.

42. Henry, **op. cit.**, p. 158.

43. Henry, **op. cit.**. p. 158.

44. **Ibid**., pp. 158-159.

45. *The Centenary Translation*, **op. cit.**, p. 242.

46. John 1:14, *The Centenary Translation*, **op. cit.**, p. 243.

47. Cf. Kenneth Wuest, *Great Truths to Live By*, printed in Wuest's *Word Studies from the New Testament* (Grand Rapids: Wm. B. Eerdmans Publishing Company, 1952), pages 13-39. The article is entitled: "Jesus of Nazareth—Who Is He?"

Questions

1. The earliest name of Christmas was ____.
2. The word Yule comes from ____.
3. The feast of the Incarnation suggests ____.
4. The word Incarnation is from the Latin meaning ____.
5. The most beloved Christmas text is ____.
6. John's use of the term Logos represents ____.

7. When time began the Logos always ____.
8. How does the Jehovah's Witnesses New World translation wrongly translate John 1:1? ____
9. John asserts everything was made ____ Him.
10. The work of creation is the work of ____.
11. The plain meaning in John 1:14 is ____.

Waking up Pastors
Ascension Day

Dear Brother Otten:

Enclosed please find a scholarly essay which was in the preparation a number of months. I believe that its publication by the installment plan might make a small contribution to waking up some pastors and lay people to some of the theological issues and problems still troubling the LCMS as reflected by the Elim literature and *Missouri in Perspective*.

Again, God's blessings on all your endeavors and the stand you have taken for the truth of God's Word and sound Lutheran doctrine and practice.

Blessed ascension tide to you, your family, and congregation.

Yours in Christ,

Raymond F. Surburg

The Significance of the Ascension for Christ and for His Followers
Christian News, May 22, 1995

There are four major events in Christ's life that have been observed by those Churches that use an Ecclesiastical Year: namely, Christmas, Good Friday, Easter and Ascension .[1] In many congregations Christmas receives a great deal of attention, especially in the Advent season, making the Day of the activity's celebration somewhat anti-climactic in character. Even the pagan world observes Christmas, spelled for them Xmas (the x representing an unknown quantity). The pagan world completely misunderstands what Christmas is really about. Good Friday is remembered in Roman Catholicism, Protestantism, Episcopalianism and Eastern Orthodoxy with the observance of Tenebrae services . Even some business establishments close their places of business between 12 a.m. and 3 p.m. Easter is also observed in the various churches as a day of joy and rejoicing, even though the reason differs in some churches who emphasize the rejuvenation of spring instead of concentrating on Christ's corporeal resurrection. Again the pagan world makes much of Easter, but they emphasize the Easter bunny, Easter eggs, egg hunts and the wearing of new apparel.

How different, however, it is with the observance of Ascension, on which traditionally all Christian churches recalled the triumphant Ascension of Christ. Not too many Christian communions have services on the 14th day after Easter, on a Thursday, a day called in one denomination "Holy Thursday."[2] Although the Sunday after Ascension gives opportunity to speak about the Ascension, this opportunity is often ignored. One Lutheran liturgiologist in 1939 lamented "that the high Feast of the Ascension unhappily is so little observed."[3]

The Importance and Meaning of Christ's Ascension

Christ's Ascension has been called Christ's Coronation Day, because it represents the completion of Christ's redemptive mission on earth. In a sense Good Friday was the darkest, most pessimistic day in human history. Had Good Friday been the last word, then the verdict of history would have been the last, then the verdict would have to have been that justice and truth, righteousness, mercy, love, grace and hope were dead. It would have meant that injustice, falsehood, godlessness, hate and despair would have triumphed.[4]

Easter morning, however, gave lie to the philosophy of defeatism and despair. The powers of darkness as represented by the Devil and Christ's enemies would have had their day on April 7, 30 A.D. The powers of darkness triumphed temporarily. They are to bound in a world where Satan and his minions are active. God's plan for the salvation of man could not be frustrated. By the Ascension of Christ the Divine approval was placed on the whole saving ministry of God's Son.[5]

The Feast of the Ascension Celebrated for Many Centuries

For at least 1700 years Christendom has celebrated the glorious and triumphant victory of Christ, when the Light of the World left the earth, on which he had spent over 33 years. While the Ascension observation is first mentioned in the Fourth Century,[6] but spoken in such a manner to allow one to think it was already established and widely observed. History reveals that Ascension was celebrated in Augustine's time (A.D. 354-430) and was universally observed and the Feast ranked with Easter and Pentecost. "The Pilgrimage of Silva," dated around A.D. 385, is supposed to have stated that in Jerusalem there was a solemn procession on Ascension day to the Mount of Olives, where the Empress Helena, born in York, England, had built a memorial on the Mount of Olives. Bede, the English historian, in the eighth-century speaks of its celebration as almost as solemn as that of Easter.[7] In the Episcopalian Prayer Book, Ascension is called "Holy Thursday."[7a] The Greek Orthodox Church denominated it. "Taking up," and the Germans call it "Himmelsfahrt." Ephraim, one of the greatest hymn writers of the Greek Church, called the Nativity, Easter and Ascension "the three Great Feasts of the Godhead."[8] In some sections of the Church, notably in the East, it was customary to celebrate the services in the open, either in the fields, if there was no mountain side or in the cemeteries.

The Biblical Data for the Doctrine of Christ's Ascension

Already in the Old Testament it was predicted that Christ would ascend into the heavens. The Propers for the Festival of the Ascension lists Psalm 47:5 and Psalm 68:18 as passages predicting Christ's Ascension.[9] During His public ministry Jesus informed His disciples concerning His return to heaven by virtue of the Ascension. Most of the references of His Ascension are found in the Gospel of John, which contains about 50 per cent of the Jesus sayings in the Gospels as reported by the Biblical writ era. Thus to Nicodemus Jesus said: "No man has ascended into heaven, but he that descended out of heaven, even the Son of man, which is in heaven" (John 3:13). To his disciples Jesus said: "What if you see the Son of Man ascend where he was before?" (John 6:62). The Savior assured His Apostles: "I shall be with you a little while and then I go to Him who sent me" (John 7:33-34). "On the Passover evening, Jesus knowing that the Father had given all things into His hands and that He had come from God, was going to God, arose from the supper, laid aside his garments, took a towel and girded Himself (13:3-4). In the beginning of His Farewell Discourse Jesus said to those with whom He was walking on the way to Gethsemane: "And I go to prepare a place for you" (14:2). In the same Chapter of John, Jesus reminded His disciples: "And now I have said to you I am going away and coming back to you."

There are no less than nine distinct references by Christ in His Farewell Address (Chapter 41:1-17:26) to His departure from this earth. They are 14:2-4; 14:12; 14:28; 16:5; 16:10; 16:16-19; 16:28; 17:11.

Post-Resurrection Statement About the Ascension

To Mary Magdalene the Risen Christ said: "Do not cling to me, for I have not yet ascended to My Father, and your Father and to My God and your God" (John 20:17).[10]

Mark and Luke's Accounts of the Ascension

At the end of Mark's Gospel, as recorded in a number of manuscripts (Textus Receptus), it is asserted: "So then Jesus after He had spoken unto them (the Apostles), He was received up into heaven and sat down at the right hand of God (16:19)." Luke gives two accounts, one at the end of his Gospel and the other as a part of the introduction of the Book of Acts. The Gospel account in Luke 24:51 states: "While he blessed them, he departed from them." Acts 1:7-11 gives more information about the events that occurred before, during and after the Ascension .

The Ascension In the Epistles of the New Testament

The writings of the New Testament as represented by the writings of Peter and the Epistle to the Hebrews all testify to the Ascension of Christ. Paul in the Ephesian Letter, probably a circular letter to the congregations of Asia Minor, chapter 1:17, writes about Christ's Ascension and its results as follows: "And raised him from the dead and set him at his own right hand in heavenly places." The Apostle Peter in his letter to the congregations of Asia Minor asserted:

"Who is gone into heaven, and is on the right hand of God; angels and authorities being made subject unto him (3:22)." The anonymous writer to the Hebrews is speaking about Christ's high-priesthood, confessed: "Seeing that we have a great high priest, that is passed into the heavens, Jesus the Son of God, let us hold fast our profession

(4:14)." Again in describing the saving work of Christ, the same writer taught: "For Christ is not entered into the holy place made without hands, which are of the true, but into heaven itself, now to appear in the presence of God for us."

The Manner of the Ascension As Reflected In
The Greek Verbs of the Various Ascension Accounts

The Greek text of the New Testament uses thirteen different words to describe the manner of the Ascension.

anabaino (John 3:13; 6:62; 20:17) "To arise" with up.

analambano (Mark 16:19; Acts 1:11), "to take," with up.

analepsis (Luke 9:51, only occurrence in the New Testament) "to receive ," with up.

ana-phero (Luke 24:51), "to bear," with up.

ap-archomai (John 16:7, cf. 20:10), "to go from one place to another," with from .

di-istemi (Luke 24:51), "to put apart."

eis-erchomai (Luke 24:26), "to come, or enter," with in

epairo (acts 1:9), "to raise or lift up."

erchomai (John 17:11), "to come."

hupago (John 7:33; 13:3; 13:3; 14 :4,28; 16 :5,10), "to go away."

hupo-lambano (Acts 1:9), "to take from under," "to receive up."

hupsoo, (John 12:32) "to raise on high," "to elevate."

poreuo (John 14:2,3, 12:16:28; Acts 1:10-11, "to depart," "to journey."

The Physical Ascent Heavenward Denied and Rejected

The Ascension of Christ did not occur in secret but in the open, on a mountain. It was a visible event. One of the angels suddenly present at the Ascension said to the disciples: "He shall come again as you saw him go into heaven (Acts 1:11)." The Ascension of Christ was as historical an event just as the Incarnation, Death and Resurrection were. It was a historical act that occurred in space and time, it was not a sudden disappearance or an evaporation. The Ascension was spatial; it was a majestic going toward the heavens, and was affected by Christ's own power and the going on up or ascent was gradual.[12]

The attending circumstances were these: it took place on the Mount of Olives, the place of Christ's Suffering on the night before His crucifixion. Its witnesses were the Eleven disciples. A cloud received him out of their sight while angels were present announcing the **Parousia**, the Second Coming of Christ, a return to this earth, from where He was leaving on the fortieth day after Easter.

The manner of Christ's Ascension has been and is rejected by liberal theology, which rejects the account in Acts 1:4-12 as factual history,[13] because liberal theology has Christ dead and rotting in Joseph of Arimethea's grave. The resurrection and the ascension would require two distinct miracles and liberalism rejects the whole concept of the supernatural. While Neo-orthodoxy does not subscribe to many views of theological liberalism, it likewise does not accept the factuality or historicity of the Ascension of Christ. Bultmann, who has had a great effect on twentieth century theology, does not believe in Christ's resurrection and consequently in the Ascension. According to the Bultmannians the New Testament contains "myth" which must be demythologized. It is significant that Ramm in setting forth the major themes and theological positions of such men as Kierkegaard, Barth, Brunner, Bultmann, Tillich, Reihold Niehbuhr, Richard Niebuhr, Cullmann, Baar, Richardson, Aulen, Buber, finds nothing about the Ascension to report and discuss in his *Handbook of Contemporary Theology*. [15]

One Lutheran Church which has been influenced by modern theology in its denial or reinterpretation of Christ's Ascension is The Evangelical Lutheran Church in its new **Catechism** and two-volume *Christian Dogmatics*, the former intended for the laity and the latter for theological students and pastors.

Thus the American Edition of the *Evangelical Catechism* states: "The 'ascension' refers to the last appearance of the resurrected Christ to his disciples.[16] The record of the text distinguishes, however, between Christ's tenth appearance and His Ascension, His slowly leaving the Earth and a cloud receiving Him. The Catechism claims Jesus did not take Himself to outer space, where an astronaut could see him."[17] "Heaven is not to be misunderstood a geographic place."[18] If there is no place called "heaven" where did the soul of the dying thief go? Jesus promised this repentant sinner: "Today you will be with me in paradise." Where are those mansions Christ said He would go to prepare for his disciple ? Where is the "place" Jesus would get ready for His followers?

Christian Dogmatics, written by Carl Braaten, Gerhard Forde, Philip Herner, Robert Jenson, Hans Schwan and Paul Sponheim, in its discussion of the Ascension shows the influence of Bultmann.[19] Thus Braaten wrote: "The mythical features of this trajectory of exaltation are obvious the moment we ask where Jesus went when he ascended into heaven."[20] "The need to demythologize the story should not, however, weaken our sense for the deeper message it contains."[21] The denial of the perspicuity of Acts 1:4-11 is made when Braaten wrote: "The end of Jesus' time on earth is like the beginning. It is a mystery clothed in the language of myth and symbol. History does not give us a key to it."[22] The same ELCA dogmatician claimed that while in the church year Easter and Ascension are separated by forty days and thus depicted as two separate events, "that dogmatics would be hard pressed to justify these distinctions with sound historical arguments."[23] Braaten opined that the resurrection and the ascension both testify to the exaltation of Christ and are actually the same event. In support he cited Acts 2:33; 5:30-31; Phil. 2:9.[24] How different from the Biblical understanding of the Ascension given by Reu in his *Lutheran Dogmatics*,[25] by Hove's *Christian Doctrine*,[26] or Stump's *The Christian Faith*,[27] or Schmidt's *The Doctrinal Theology of the Evangelical Lutheran Faith*,[28] reissued by the Augsburg Publishing House in 1961. All these dogmatics were by members of denominations now part and parcel of ELCA.

The Witness of the Disciples to the Actuality of the Ascension

In going forth from earth to heaven, Christ was taken, was received, was borne, was lifted up, arose, went, was raised, was separated. Christ's disciples did not witness the resurrection but they did see Him ascend into heaven. It was not necessary for His disciples to see the stone removed from Christ's grave and Christ being made alive by the Father, Son and Holy Ghost, but it was important to witness and be able to testify to Christ's Ascension into heaven . In one case they saw the effect (in 10 appearances of the risen Christ), but it was important to be able to witness to His physical departure from this earth. "In one case the disciples saw the effects, but not the act; in the other case they saw the act but not effect."[29]

The Necessity of the Ascension

The Ascension was the climax to the whole work of Christ, His Birth; Life, Suffering. Death would be meaningless had Christ not risen from the dead and spent 40 days in giving His Apostles instruction and prepared them for their future Gospel ministry and then 40 days later ascended far above all heavens and returned to the glory He had left around 5 or 4 B.C.[30] The Ascension proves the Resurrection and was required by it. If Christ, truly alive, seen by at least five hundred believers at one time, did not ascend, where is Christ now?

Some have denied the historic physical fact of the ascension, claiming that the textual statement: "He ascended up," would mean down in other parts of the earth. Mark and Luke simply state that Christ ascended from the Mount of Olives in Palestine and not in South Africa nor at the North or South poles. The Ascension of Christ, in relationship to the laws of nature, presents no more difficulty than do the Incarnation or Resurrection of Jesus of Nazareth. Christ's departure from the Earth was affirmed in a number of different ways in Luke's account of the third step in the state of humiliation. Luke, a doctor, recorded: "When he had said this, and while they were looking at him, he was lifted up, and a cloud received him up out of their sight. While they were gazing into the sky as he was going up, suddenly there were two men in white garments standing by them, and they said: 'Men of Galilee, why do you stand gazing into the sky? This same Jesus who has been taken up in just the same way as you have seen him going into the sky.'" Compare this with John's statement in Revelation: "Behold, he is about to come among the clouds, and every eye will see him, even those who pierced him, and all the tribes of the earth will mourn over him." (1:7)

The Results of the Ascension for Christ

The Ascension was the culmination for Christ's redemptive work and it is also the point of contact between the Christ of the Gospels and Christ of the Epistles.

The Ascension represents the victory of Christ over His enemies. The Ephesian Letter of Paul cited Psalm 68:19: "When he ascended, he led captivity captive and gave gifts to men (4:8)." Because of his victories over principalities and powers, Jesus was able to ascend as a victorious general. The Ascension was the final stone in the Christian structure for without the Ascension one would have a tower without a top. It is proof that mankind's redemption is a reality.

It was necessary for Christ so that he could keep His promise to send the Holy Spirit, which occurred on the day of Pentecost.

As result of the Ascension Jesus was able to take his seat at the "right hand of God" and fill all things.

The Results of the Ascension for Christ's Followers

As our Substitute Jesus paid the penalty for mankind's sins and has freed Christians from the control of all their enemies, sin, the Devil, the fear of death and death itself. The Ascension of Christ constitutes a victory for all believers.

Heaven has now been opened for the followers of Christ. We now can believe the promise of Christ that He has gone to prepare a place for His followers. We can now trust his statement: "I go to prepare a place for you. Where I am, there you also shall be."

The Sending of the Holy Spirit a
Blessed Outcome of the Ascension

As a result of the coming of the Holy Spirit promised to His followers in the ten days between the Ascension and Pentecost, was the outpouring of unique blessings on the first-century church and on the church in the centuries to follow.

The accomplishments of the early church were due to the presence of the Holy Spirit sent by Christ as He had announced before his Resurrection and Ascension. The Book of Acts could really be called "The Acts of the Holy Spirit." Christ's Ascension was necessary that the coming of the Spirit of God, as foretold in Joel 3:1-4, (Hebrew text) could occur. Another blessing given the Church as a benefit of the Ascension is that His followers would be able to do greater works than Jesus Himself did. In the Farewell Discourse Jesus promised; "Truly, truly I say to you, he who believes in me will also do the works that I do, and greater works than these will he do, because I go to the Father (John 14:21)." The spiritual conquests of the Christian church have been in one sense "greater works" than the miracles of Christ, for Christ's were temporal, but the Churches were spiritual. Christ's works were local, those of His followers were universal.[31]

Ascension In the "Narrower" Versus Ascension
In the "Wider Sense"

John Theodore Mueller claimed that a Bible student could speak of the Ascension of Christ in a narrower sense, which embraced only the visible elevation of Christ (Luke 24:51; Acts 1:9-11) or in a wider sense, including His sitting at the right hand of God (Acts 2:33,34; Eph. 4:10).[32]

The Blessings for Christians Flowing from Christ's Session

Popular Symbolics of 1934, the product of four outstanding LCMS theologians, asserted: "Christ's Ascension to heaven and His session, at the right hand of God (Mark 16:19; Eph. 1:20; Heb. 1:3) mean that he assumed, according to His human nature, the full exercise of the infinite power and universal divine dominion belonging to it by virtue of the personal union (Ascension, Session) Eph. 1:20-22; Ps. 110:1; Matt. 26:18; John 17:5; Heb. 1:13; 2:8; I Pet. 3:22)."[33] On the basis of Holy Writ J.T. Mueller asserted: "Christ's session at the right hand of God is therefore His exaltation, according to His human nature to the sovereign lordship and rule over all things, Eph. 1:20-23; 4:10; 1 Pet. 3:22, Acts 3:21."[34] The session of Christ does not mean that Christ, according to His human nature, withdrew His presence from this earth and is confined in heaven, as the Reformed teach, who deny in line with their denial of the communication of attributes, that Christ is present everywhere and rules all things according to His human nature. The "right hand" of God is not a circumscribed locality in a spatial heaven, but the infinite power of God, filling in all and ruling all things, Ex. 15:6; Ps. 118:16; 139:7-10; Is. 48:13; Matt. 26:64. So, Christ, who ascended up on high according to His human nature, Eph. 4:8, fills all things and is with us here on "earth according to His human nature, Matt. 28:20; Eph. 4:10.[35]

The Christian's Comfort Flowing from Christ's Session

The Synodical Catechism in its explanation of Luther's Small Catechism asks: "What comfort do you derive from Christ's sitting at the right hand of God," God responds:

A. As our Prophet sends men to preach the Gospel of redemption, and cites as Scriptural proof, Ephesians 4:10-12.

B. As our Priest intercedes (pleads) for us before God and gives as Biblical proof: "If any man sin, we have an Advocate with the Father, Jesus the righteous," and Romans 8:34: "Christ is even at the right hand of God, who also maketh intercession for us."

C. As our King, governs and protects His Church and as Head of the Church rules the world in the interest of the Church, and gives as proof the statement and prophecy of David: "The Lord said unto my Lord, Sit thou at my right hand till I make Thine enemies Thy footstool," repeated by Christ as David was speaking about Him.[36]

Footnotes

1 James Brauer, "The Church Year," In Fred Precht (editor), *Lutheran Worship* (St. Louis: CPH, 1993) pp. 166-160.

2 Walter Gwynne, *The Christian Year, Its Purpose and Its History* (New York: Longman, Green and Company, 1915), p. 69.

3. Paul Zeller, Strodach, *The Collect for the Day* (Philadelphia: The United Lutheran Publication House, 1939), p. 137.

4. R.E. Golladay, *The Challenge of A New Day* (Columbus, Ohio. Published by The Lutheran Book Concern, no date), p. 180, beginning of an Ascension Day Sermon.

5. **Ibid.**, p. 181.

6. Paul Zeller Strodach, *The Church Year*, (Philadelphia: The United Lutheran Publication House, 1924), p. 169.

7. **Ibid.**, p. 169; A. A. McArthur, "Ascension Day," in J.G. Davies' *The Westminster Dictionary of Worship* (Philadelphia: The Westminster Press, 1972), p. 41.

7a. Gwynne, **op. cit.**, p. 69.

8. Cited by Strodach, *The Church Year*, **op. cit.**, p. 169.

9. Luther D. Reed, *The Lutheran Liturgy* (Philadelphia: Muhlenberg Press, 1947), p. 468.

10. Alfred Jeremias, (Leben im Kirchenjahr Leipzig: Adolpf Klein Verlag, 1928), p. 60 claims: this address to Mary Magdalene is "ein Welterklaerungtext, nicht ein Himmelsfahrttext."

11. W. Graham Scroggie, *A Guide to the Gospels* (London: Pickering & Inglis, 1948), p. 619.

12. Francis Pieper, *Christian Dogmatics* (St. Louis: CPH, 1951), II, p. 324.

13. Lowther Clarke, *Concise Bible Commentary* (New York: The Macmillan Company, 1953), pp. 768; 800.

14. Bernard Ramm, *A Handbook of Contemporary Theology* (Grand Rapids: William B. Eerdmans Publishing Company, 1966), would have been on p. 16.

15. *Evangelical Catechism. Christian Faith in the World Today*. American Edition (Minneapolis: Augsburg Publishing House, 1982), p. 194.

16. **Ibid.**, p. 196.

17. **Ibid.**, p. 196.

18. **Ibid.**

19. Carl E. Braaten, *Christian Dogmatics* (Philadelphia: Fortress Press, 1984) I, pp. 528-530.

20. **Ibid.**, p. 552.

21. **Ibid.**, p. 562.

22. **Ibid.**, p. 553.

23. **Ibid.**, p. 563.

24. **Ibid.**, p. 552.

25. M. Reu, *Lutheran Dogmatics* (Dubuque: Iowa; Wartburg Theological Seminary, 1951), Revised Edition, pp. 233ff.

26. E. Hove, *Christian Doctrine* (Minneapolis: Augsburg Publishing House, 1936), pp. 203-204.

27. Joseph Stump, The Christian Doctrine. A System of Christian Doctrine (New York: The Macmillan Company, 1932), pp. 178-179.

28. Heinrich Schmid, *Doctrinal Theology of the Evangelical Lutheran Church* (Third Edition Revised by Charles A. Hay and Henry Jacobs, Minneapolis: Augsburg Publishing House, 1961, originally published 1975 and 1989, pp. 401-403.

29. Scroggie, **op. cit.**, p. 620.

30. **Ibid.**, p. 620.

31. **Ibid.**, p. 621.

32. John Theodore Mueller, *Christian Dogmatics* (St. Louis: Concordia Publishing House, 1955), p. 299.

33. Th. Engelder, W. Arndt, Th. Graebner and F.E. Mayer, *Popular Symbolics* (CPH, 1934), p. 51.

34. Mueller, **op. cit.**, p. 300.

35. Popular Symbolics, **op. cit.**, p. 51.

36. Dr. Martin Luther's *Small Catechism, A Short Explanation* (St. Louis: CPH, pp. 119-120; Cf. also Doctor Martin Luther's *Small Catechism. Explained for Children and Adults.* Originally edited by C. Gausewitz (Milwaukee: Northwestern Publishing House. 1956), pp. 127-129.

Questions

1. What does the pagan world emphasize about Easter? ____
2. The Ascension has been called Christ's ____.
3. Did the Ascension of Christ occur in secret? ____
4. What is the Parousia? ____
5. Neo-Orthodoxy along with liberalism does not accept the ___ of the Ascension.
6. What does the American edition of the Evangelical Catechism teach about the Ascension? ____
7. The Ascension constitutes ____ for all believers.
8. What are the "greater works" Christians will do? ____
9. Who teaches that Christ according to his human nature is confide in heaven? ____
10. What is "the right hand of God"? ____

The Doctrine of the Trinity
in the Old Testament
(A Study for the Trinity Festival)

Christian News, August 7, 1995

Mohammedanism, Judaism, Zoroastrianism and Christianity are spoken of as the monotheistic religions of the world.[1] This may be true of Islam, Judaism and Zoroastrianism, but is not correct of Christianity. Mohammed, in the Quran in a number of passages, accused Christianity of believing in three Gods and therefore being guilty of polytheism.[2] Zoroastrianism begins its doctrine of God with a Good God and Evil God, who existed side by side from eternity and therefore is dualistic in its doctrine of God.[3] Judaism has vigorously rejected the Christian doctrine of the Trinity and repudiated the fact of the Trinity of the Godhead.[4] Those passages in the Old Testament which speak of the Son and the Spirit of God are at best explained in a modalistic manner.[5]

Christian theology from Apostolic times on has taught that God is one, but has manifested Himself as the Father, other times as the Son, and yet at other times as the Holy Spirit. The word Trinity, not used as a word in the Bible, merely expresses the truth that God is three in person and one in divine essence. Opined J. T. Mueller: "From this it is clear that the Term Trinity just as other terms used in explaining the doctrine of God, has not been coined to satisfy reason, but only to express the doctrine of Scripture concerning the true God."[6] Human reason must not be used to judge and reject the Christian doctrine of God, and the Biblical reader must choose between Unitarianism or Tritheism; in other words, it must either deny the three divine Persons (Monarchianism) or the one divine essence (Tritheism, Subordinationism). For this reason the Christian theologian must a **priori** desist from presenting the doctrine or the Holy Trinity in such a way as to make it comprehensible to reason."[7]

God is unchangeable. Through the Prophet Malachi He said: "I the Lord, I change not." God is eternal and is infinite. In Hebrews the reader is informed about Christ: "Jesus Christ, the same yesterday, today and forever."

The New Testament clearly shows that God from eternity has been one divine essence, manifesting itself in three distinct persons. The Father in eternity begot the Son (Psalm 2:7), so also John 1:14, while the Father and the Son have spirited the Holy Spirit (John 14:26; 15:26). The divine acts of generation and spiritation are termed personal acts, but are not common to the three Persons, but belong to, and distinguish, the individual Persons in the Godhead. To the Father Holy Scripture ascribes the act of generation, Psalm 2:7 (John 1:14), by which He communicated to the Son the fullness of the Godhead, or the entire divine essence (Col. 2:3,9). Hence the Father possesses the divine unbegottenness (agenethos), while the Son possesses it as begotten (gennethos). Through the spiration the Holy Spirit received the entire divine essence (Matt.

998

28:19; Acts 5:3-4), so that He is from eternity true God with the Son.[8]

It was in eternity that the decree of predestination look place. It was in eternity that the decree or redemption was made by which the Son agreed to come to this earth and redeem mankind by His suffering and death. Peter described Christ as "the Lamb slain from before the foundation or the earth" (1Peter1:20). Since God has been the Triune God from all eternity, would it not be strange that the entire time period from Creation to the appearance of John the Baptist in A.D. 26 would ignore such a fundamental truth, especially since the entire plan of salvation was intimately connected with distinctive acts of God? We of course recognize that certain truths were a part of the mystery that God first revealed in the New Testament. For instance, that the Gentiles were to share equally with the Jews the blessings of salvation (Ephesians 3:8-10). But in the Old Testament there are so many indications of the Trinity that it is difficult to see how certain scholars cannot find God's Son (The Messiah) and the Holy Spirit active in Old Testament times!

The Ignoring or Rejection of The Trinity by Old Testament Critical Scholarship

Although the field of The Theology of the Old Testament has existed for two hundred years, and since that time many Old Testament theologies have been written, very few have even suggested that the God of the Old Testament is the Triune God.[9]

The School of Comparative Religions depicts the Old Testament concept of God as being influenced at different times by Babylonianism, Egyptianism, or Canaan anitism. They totally reject Old Testament Trinitarianism.

Others, who even claim to be Christian and Lutheran in their Biblical theologies, portray God in the Jewish manner as strictly monotheistic. Gerhard von Rad in his voluminous two-volume opus on *Old Testament Theology* never speaks of the doctrine of the Trinity, never suggests that the Messiah is Christ or refers to the deity of the Holy Spirit.[10] Eichrodt, with whom a new era in the writing of the theology of the Old Testament is supposed to have begun in his two-volume *Theology of the Old Testament*, says very little about a Trinity in the Old Covenant Scriptures. His organizing principle was the "covenant" concept.[11] Baab, *The Theology of the Old Testament*, in the chapter dealing with God, pp. 23-53 never hints at the possibility of the Trinity in the Old Testament.[12] Knight's *A Christian Theology of the Old Testament* ignores the fact that there are in the Old Testament three distinct Persons, whom be does not distinugish.[13] How can an Old Testament Theology be Christian and fail to recognize the existence of God, the Father, God the Son, and God the Holy Spirit? He stresses the idea of the unity of God but not that of the Trinity. The Lutheran Koehler in *Old Testament Theology* devoted seventeen chapters to "God," but no hint is given of theTrinity.[14] The Dutch scholar Vriezen in his *Outline of Old Testament Theology*, like the volumes just discussed, ignores the concept of the Trinity in the Old Testament.[15] The Lutheran Westermann emphasized that the "oneness of God," that which make context possible, but no suggestion of the importance of the Trinity for Old Testament Biblical theology.[16] Another pundit, in his *The Self-Revelation of God* never suggests even the possibility of God having revealed Himself as Father, Son, and Holy Ghost.[17] Dyrness, *Themes in Old Testament Theology* has a chapter "On the Nature of God," but like all mentioned thus far, knows of no Trinity in the Old Testament.[18] Dyrness has a chapter dealing with the Spirit claimed: "The person of the Holy Spirit, while implicit in OT developments, does not come into full view until he is introduced by Christ in John 14-16 and poured out in his people in Acts 2."[19] Unfortunately, he has no chapter on the Messiah, whom the New Testament identifies with Christ.[20] Marten's *God's Design, A Focus on Old Testament Theology*, has considerable to say about Yahweh but very little about the Spirit of God.[21] His views about Jesus, the Messiah are not altogether correct. Again no hint of the Trinity in Cate's *Old Testament Roots for New Testament Faith* and in his chapter treating of God says nothing about the place of the Trinity in the Old Testament.[22] The coming of Messiah was a future event and belief in Him was not demanded by Old Testament believers. The Holy Spirit is not discussed at all. The Trinity is not part of the Old Testament roots for the New Testament faith. H.H. Rowley, outstanding British Old Testament scholar, has a very comprehensive chapter on the nature of God, but nowhere thinks that there was a Trinity in the Old Testament. [23] The same holds true of Brevard Child's *Old Testament Theology in A Canonical Context*.[24] The German Old Testament professor, Werner Schmidt in his *Faith of the Old Testament*, paid a lot of attention to God,[25] mentions the Spirit of God but does not treat of the Messiah, the heart of Old Testament theology.[26] The liberal Yale professor, Millar Burrows, produced *An Outline of Biblical Theology*, covering both testaments and rejects the contention that the Old Testament teaches a Trinily.[27] Paul Heinisch in *Theology of the Old Testament* has this to say about the doctrine or the Trinity: "The OT teaches God is one. It was reserved for the incarnate Son of God to reveal to mankind the mystery of the three Persons in one God. Such teaching would hardly have been intelligible to the Israelites, and because of their polytheistic leanings would have occasioned the worship of three Gods. Nevertheless the greatest mystery of the Christian faith should at least have been foreshadowed in the OT. By this however we are not referring to expressions which some Church Fathers and certain theologians have applied to the Blessed Trinity in the light of N.T."[28] An eighteenth-century conservative Old Testament exegete, Oehler stated: "Though we must not read the New Testament doctrine of the Trinity into the Old Testament, it is yet undeniable that we find the way to the economic Trinity already prepared in the doctrine of the Malakh and of the Spirit."[29] Chesnut, in his *The Old Testament Understanding of God* warned: "What the Christian must be more careful about is the tendency of reading into Old Testament a specifically Christian content."[30] No Trinity in Old Testament is the inevitable result of a such a position. Ronald Youngblood, in *The Heart of the Old Testament*, declared: "At any rate, God did not reveal Himself prematurely in clearly defined Trinitarian terms in the Old Testament Scriptures. To have done so would have been to provide needless temptations to polytheism in the light of the cultures of that day."[31]

Gerhard Hase, Seventh Day Adventist scholar, in the revised edition of *Old Testament Theology, Basic Issues in the Debate*, surveyed all OT Testament biblical theologies between Gabler's views 1787 and 1972 and asserted: "Old Testament theology today is undeniably in crisis. Recent monographs and articles by European and American scholars show that the fundamental issues and crucial questions are presently undecided and matters of intense debate. Though it is centuries old, OT Theology is now uncertain of its true identity."[32] The Biblical Theology Movement was placed in opposition to systematic theology, which organized the doctrines of God's Word under "loci" and used the entire Bible, Old and New Testaments, as the source for the setting forth of doctrines God revealed, doctrines not of man's creation but inspired by the Holy Spirit.[33]

The Trinity In the Age of the Reformation and Orthodoxy

Luther believed that the doctrine of the Trinity in OT was not revealed so clearly as the New Testament.[34] Nevertheless, the Wittenberg Reformer held that the Trinity was clearly set forth in the Old Testament.[34] In his comments on Genesis 35:7 he observed that the greater part of the Jew of course did not believe this doctrine, just as the Turks and the Jews rejected it.[35] At the close of his comments on the Ecumenical creeds, Luther declared that while the doctrine of the Trinity is not brought out so clearly in the Old Testament as it was in the New, it is nonetheless emphatically emphasized. Martin Chemnitz in his *Loci Theologici* Vol. I defends the doctrine of the Trinity as being taught in the Old Testament.[36] In the subsequent centuries Luther's views about the doctrine of the Trinity in the Old Testament have influenced Lutheranism. This view was generally held by the theologians of the sixteenth and seventeenth centuries.[37] They believed that the three persons of the Holy Trinity were revealed to such an extent that they could be perceived. Not all Lutherans agreed with Luther and those who accepted and propounded the Reformer's views. The Helmstedt school of George Calixt, however, was of the opinion that "the mystery of the Trinity was not contained in the Old Testament, but was given to the Patriarchs and the Prophets by immediate and special revelation, that neither the Old Testament believers nor we today could learn it without the help of the New Testament, that the Old Testament contains only vestiges or intimations but not clear and convincing statements of the doctrine, but it is from the New Testament that we learn of the Person of Christ and the person of the Holy Spirit in the Old Testament."[38]

In the nineteenth century the theologian Luthardt declared: "The Old Testament at best only prepares for the Trinitarian knowledge of God, because it contains only the germ of Trinitarian knowledge because it alone contains the Trinitarian revelation."[39] Luthardt rejected the explanations of Luther, Chemnitz, Baier, Gerhard and others, by asserting: "It rests mostly upon a false and forced exegesis and in general an unhistorical approach, which ignores the gradual and progressive develop-ment of revelation." Another scholar, Kirn, claimed that no theologian will turn to the Old Testament for proof texts in support of the doctrine of the Trinity.[40]

Twentieth Century Lutheranism and the Trinity

In the Old Testament as one surveys Lutheran scholarship on the Old Testament the student will find that 1). Lutherans that are liberal reject the view that the Trinity as existing in the Old Testament; 2). Others hold that there are forgleams or adumbration of the Trinity in the Old Testament, and 3). There are those who believe that the doctrine is clearly revealed. Various views now are given as found in the twentieth-century theological literature. Thus Stump wrote: "The doctrine of the Trinity is not explicitly taught in the Old Testament. It is a New Testa-ment doctrine.

When it has been learned from the New Testament, traces and impli-cations may be found in the Old Divine revelation was progressive.[41] Reu, in his *Lutheran Dogmatics*, makes this judgment: "The Old Testament, indeed, contains hardly more than anticipations of this revelation, if the pertinent statements are interpreted, not in the light of the New Testa-ment but historically, i.e., the way in which the Old Testament believer understood them, who did not enjoy the fuller New Testament revela-tion."[41a] Lindberg, in his *Lutheran Dogmatics*, uses passages from both testaments when dealing with the inner relationship of the Three Persons to each other, or when speaking of their Activities (Opera ad extra). How-ever, he makes no specific statement whether or not the Holy Trinity is found in the Old Testament as a doctrine.[42] Revere Weidner asserted: "Though we must not read the New Testament doctrine of the Trinity into the Old Testament, it is yet undeniable that we find the doctrine of the Trinity really and plainly implied in the Old Testament."[42a] Henry Eyster Jacobs, in his *Summary of Christian Doctrine*, on page 41 asked the question: "It is taught in the Old Testament? And the answer given was: "It is suggested there but not expressly taught. When the doctrine has been learned from the New Testament, it can faintly be traced in the Old."[43] Hove in his Christian Doctrine has no statement on the Trinity in the Old Testament, but his presentation of the Trinity accords Old Tes-tament texts the same authority as are assigned to the New Testament.[44]

The Braaten-Jenson *Christian Dogmatic* makes no statement about the Trinity in the Old Testament. Finding the Trinity in the Old Testa-ment is ascribed to post-apostolic writers. Jenson has a section in which he argues that the Hebrew Scriptures were the root for Trinitarianism (Vol. 1, pp. 102-103).

The LCMS and the Doctrine of the
Trinity In The Old Testament

From its very inception in 1847 the LCMS has held that the doctrine of the Trinity was clearly set forth in the Old Testament. A perusal of Eckhardt's *Homiletisches Reallexicon nebst Index Rerum* on the topic of

"Dreieinigkeit" will show that between 1847 and 1912 many books also articles in the theological journal *Lehre und Wehre* emphasized and defended the doctrine of the Trinity as a clearly revealed doctrine of the Old Covenant Scriptures.[45] Baier-Walther,[46] F. Pieper,[47] Dau,[48] J.T. Mueller,[49] Koehler,[50] the essay in *The Abiding Word*,[51] all defend the existence of the Trinity in the Old Testament. In the WELS, Hoenecke agreed totally with the theologians of the LCMS relative to the Trinity in the Old Testament.[52]

In Conservative German Lutheranism

Wilhelm and Hans Moeller in Biblische Theologie des Alten Testaments in heilsgeschichtlicher Entwickelung show bow the Trinity was revealed to Israel during the period of Old Testament times.[52a]

Reformed Dogmaticians and Old Testament Trinity

A number of theologians that belonged to the Reformed persuasion held that the doctrine of the Trinity was only foreshadowed. Thus Bavick, a Dutch theologian, wrote: "The Old Testament contains adumbrations, the nucleus of the doctrine Trinity."[53] He contended that the Apocryphal literature and in Philo the Truth of this doctrine is buried beneath a load of heathen speculations. In the New Testament it is clearly revealed. Scripture reveals to us the relations between the Father, Son and Holy Spirit. In another book Bavick asserted: "Thus the Old Testament itself points out the full revelation of His triune Being."[54] Berkhof disagreed with the early Church Fathers that the Trinity was revealed completely in the Old Testament. The Socinians end Armenians rejected totally the Old Testament having the Trinity as doctrine. But Berkhof claimed both were mistaken, asserting: "The Old Testament does not contain a full revelation of the Trinitarian existence of God, but it does contain several indications."[55]

Payne, a conservative Reformed theologian, held that the Old Testament placed a special emphasis on the unity of God and at this early stage in human thought might have led to polytheism and trinitarianism depended upon in any event on the incarnation of Christ for its demonstration.[56]

Both Judaism and Mohammedanism have rejected the doctrine of the Trinity, contending that the teaching of the Trinity of God violated the unity of the Godhead. Bromley, claimed that "the main contribution of the OT to the doctrine is to emphasize the unity of God. God is not himself a plurality, nor is he one among many others."[56a] The British translator of the massive volumes of Barth's *Dogmatics*, believed that the value of the Old Testament is the rejection of tritheism. Yet he admitted "even in the OT we have clear intimations of the Trinity."

The Trinity in the Old Testament

J. Gerhard rejected the judgment that the doctrine of the Trinity is not found in the Old Covenant Scriptures. Thus he wrote: "We do not say that in the Old Testament there is the same clearness and evidence of the testimonial concerning the Trinity as in the New Testament; but we assert that from the Old Testament some testimonies, in exhibiting the doctrine of Trinity both can and ought to be cited, since God always from the beginning revealed Himself thus in order that the Church at all times might acknowledge worship Him and praise Him, as three distinct Persons in one essence."[57]

The Stance of the Old Lutheran Dogmaticians

Preus, an authority of Post Reformation Lutheran theology, asserted: "Fully as much labor was exerted by the orthodox Lutheran theologians proving Trinity from the Old Testament as from the New. Such procedure was deliberate and should not surprise us. All these theologians believed in the continuity of truth: God does not change, and the same God who has revealed Himself in the life of Christ and in the New Testament was the God of the Old Testament. Therefore it is quite in order to read the theology of the New Testament which is Christ's theology into the Old, or, more accurately, to read the Old Testament in the light of the New. For the New Testament was really a commentary on the Old in terms of fulfillment. Moreover, Lutheran theology believed in the unity of Scripture and believed that this unity to be Christological. Christ was the center of all Scripture, New and Old Testament alike, and all Scripture must be read and interpreted from a Christological perspective. This Christological unity of Scripture implies also a doctrinal unity, and this idea of unity becomes a hermeneutical norm as the old Lutherans interpret the Scriptures. It is therefore not at all surprising to find them ranging all over Scripture as they trace any theological motive, from the doctrine of God to eschatology. All this does not imply that the Old Testament will present a given article of faith with the same clarity or fullness as the New. The theology of the New Testament is often prefigured in the Old in terms of shadows and types. And such differences due to time must not be overlooked by the exegete. But at bottom the theology of all Scripture is one, even as God is One. And so the Lutheran theologians felt free to go to every possible information of the Trinity in the Old Testament and draw out all its implications in terms of all the New and Old Testament parallel evidence. It was the conviction of J .T. Mueller that the Old Testament contains not only 'indications' of the Holy Trinity, but clear passages, in which the doctrine is unmistakably set forth."[59]

Old Testaments Proofs for the Trinity

1. Passages in which God speaks of Himself in the plural number.[60] Thus in Genesis 1:16 the Members of the Godhead said: "Let us make man in Our image." The only explanation for this plural is the Trinitarian explanation. Others are unsatisfactory: Such as that "Us" is a plural of majesty or a plural of plenitude.[61] There are those who interpret the "Us" as God having intercourse with the angels. Knight understood the plural "Us" as a collective allusion to God and His family of creatures.[62] The Lutheran scholar Leupold remarked about the phrase "Let Us Make": "Though almost all commentators of our day regard the view that this is

1004

to be explained in connection with the truth of the Holy Trinity and treat this so-called Trinitarian view as a very negligent quantity. Yet rightly considered, this is the only view that can satisfy."[63]

2. The plural of Elohim testifies to the Trinity. The Hebrew language has linguistic forms for the singular, the dual (objects existing in pairs) and endings (im, and oth) to indicate three and more. Elohim is the plural form of El, Eloah (the poetic form). Elohim occurs 2,550 times, which is only second to frequency to the covenant name Yahweh (Jehovah)[64] Elohim is employed of both the true God and of false Gods. The context has to decide which of the two is meant. When used of the true God, the verbs and adjectives used with Elohim are in the singular, showing that though having one Divine Essence, God is One. The unity is Trinity is set forth by Moses: "Yahweh (LORD) our Elohim is one Yahweh." The plural of Elohim fits in with the verb form, when describing God, saying: "Let Us make man."[65]

3. The Use of Two LORDS (Yahweh) in Genesis 19:24.[66] Thus in the Mosaic Book of Genesis the Scriptures read: "And Yahweh (LORD) rained upon Sodom and Gomorrah sulphur from Yahweh (LORD) from heaven" (19:24). For a number of exegetes this has been a problem. Leupold contends that the view that the church held is still the simplest. The Vulgate translated as follows: "Pluit Deus filius a Deo patre, i.e." "God the Son brought down the rain from God the Father," as the Council of Sirmium worded the statement. Averred Leupold: "We believe the combined weight of this passage including 1:1,2 makes the conclusion inevitable that the doctrine of the Holy Trinity is in a measure revealed in the Old Testament and especially in Genesis. Why should not so fundamental a doctrine be made manifest from the beginning? Luther wrote of Genesis 19:24. "This expression indicates two persons in the Godhead."[67]

4. Passages in Which Christ Is Called "Son of God" indicate the Trinity Psalm 2:7 expressly addresses the Second Person of the Trinity as "Son." Thus David, was caused to write by the Holy Spirit: "Thou art My Son, this day I have be gotten Thee." The Epistle to the Hebrews cited Psalm 2:7 as proof for the deity of Jesus.[68]

5. The Trinity is evident from those passages in which the Three Persons of the Godhead are distinguished.[69] The Biblical reader will discover verses that speak of God as Father, passages in which the Second Person is described in different ways by being called "The Messiah," "the Angel of the Lord,"[70] and the Holy Spirit is described as empowering people and filling the Godman with a sevenfold blessing. Consult the following verses: Gen. 1:1-3 where the Father and Holy Spirit are active in creation. The Son of God, the Word, was the medium through which creation was effected (Cf. John 1:1-3). Passages worthy of special study would be 2 Sam. 23:2; Ps. 33:6; Is. 42:1; Is. 48:16-17; 61:1. David in his last will and Testament, wrote about Christ. "The Spirit of Yahweh (LORD) spoke by me and His Word was on my tongue," here the first and third Persons of the Godhead are distinguished. David in Psalm 33:6 was caused to proclaim: "By the word of the LORD the heavens were made and all the host of them by the Spirit of His mouth." Again one notes a distinction be-

tween two different Persons of the Godhead. The prophet Isaiah in his four Servant passages distinguishes between Yahweh and His Messiah (42:148:16-17; 61:1).[71]

6. The Holy Trinity manifests itself in passages in which the name of Yahweh is repeated three times , as in the Aaronic Blessing (Numb. 6:24 -26); Psalms 42:2; Isaiah 33:22; Jeremiah 33:2; Daniel 9:19).[72]

7. The Holy Trinity is manifest in the TRISHAGION (TER SANCTUS) of the angels, who sang: "Holy, holy, holy is the LORD of Hosts, the whole earth is full of His glory."[73]

8. The Second person of the Trinity is evident from those passages that have the ANGEL of the LORD, different from Yahweh, the Father. The Maleak Yahweh is identified with God. Pieper has presented an extensive and thorough discussion of the Maleak of Yahweh in his *Christian Dogmatics*, vol. 1, pp. 395-397. Payne traced the teaching about "The Angel of the LORD" throughout the various historical periods of the Old Testament.[74] This name for God's Son is found beginning in Genesis, with 22:11-12 and ending with Malachi 3:1. Thus in Genesis 48:18 Jacob blessed his son Joseph and testified: "The Angel who has redeemed me from all evil bless lads etc." In Exodus 3:1-7 the Angel of the Lord appeared unto Moses in a flame of fire, and when Moses saw the burning bush and when God saw that Moses turned He said: "I am the God of your fathers, the God of Abraham, the God of Isaac and the God of Jacob" and later the Angel of the Lord is identified with God. Caemerer noted: "The Son of God moved among the people of God also during the years of the Old Testament. As the Angel of the Lord is identified in many places with God Himself, carrying out specific and important representations of God toward man (Gen. 22:11-18; Ex. 3:1-15; Gen. 16:7-14; 18:19; 21:17-19; 31:11-13; 28:11-22; 33:25-30; and Hos. 12:5; 48: 15f.; 41:19; 23:20: 33:14; Josh. 5:13; 6:2; Judg. 6:11-24; 13:3-25; ls. 63:8-9; Zech. 3:1; Mal. 3:1)".[75] Concerning the Angel of the Lord Vos wrote: "The Angel Is truly divine for otherwise He could not have discharged the sacramental function of assuring man that God was with him ... In the incarnation of our Lord we have the supreme expression of this fundamental arrangement."[76]

9. The Trinity of the Godhead in the Old Testament is shown also by the "Wisdom of God" depicted in the Book of Proverbs in chapter 8:22-31. Throughout Proverbs (chapter 1-9) there appears a personification of "wisdom," in Hebrew **chochmah**. Payne states: "Wisdom appears further to be more than an attribute and to become actually objective to God. On the one hand throughout Proverbs 1-9 there recurs a persistent personification of wisdom that is unique in Scripture."[77]

In Proverbs 1:20-33 and 8:22 Chochmah passes the limits of even the most elaborate personification and is actually hypostatized by the divine writer, Solomon.[78] In 8:22-36 "Wisdom" is said to have existed objectively as a person before the world began and therefore is not a created thing. "Wisdom" lives as One eternally possessed by God (The Hebrew kanah in v. 22 means "possess" and not "created" as found in modern translation). "Wisdom" was God's master workmen: "Chochmah" says: "When

He established the heavens I (a distinct Person) was there (8:27)." "Wisdom" rejoiced before God and was His delight (8:30). But for "Wisdom" men were His delight (8:30).[79] Payne concluded on the hasis of the Proverbs teachings: "Since He is contrasted with the Spirit (1:23), He must Himself be the only begotten Son of the Father, Jesus Christ, the Second Person of the Trinity. Our Lord used the phrase 'the wisdom of God' as interchangeable reference to Himself (Luke 11:9; Matt. 23:34."[80] The Apostle Paul taught the Colossians that in Christ all wisdom was found (2:3) and in his first Corinthian Epistle (1:24,30) called Christ the "Wisdom of God." The most direct New Testament reference to the teachings of Proverbs 8:22 ·36 is found in John 1:1-18.

10. Christ's references to Old Testament to His Deity Supports the Old Testament Doctrine of the Trinity. Jesus gave his enemies who opposed Him proof for His Deity and divine Personality by citing Matthew 22:41-46. Psalm 110:1 was quoted by Jesus to prove His Deity to the scribes and Pharisees. No person has ever been saved who did not believe in the true God and the true Savior of the World (the Second Person of the Trinity). Since the New Testament clearly enunciates this truth (Acts 4;1:1; John 5:23; John 2:23).[81]

11. Trinity Seen In the Old Testament From the Presence and Activity of the Holy Spirit.

The word for "Spirit" is ruach, in Greek "pneuma." Ruach is employed frequently in the Hebrew Old Testament to designate the Holy Spirit.

An excellent presentation of "The Holy Spirit in the Old Testament" can be found in Griffith Thomas's volume The Holy Spirit.[82] In chapter 2 there is contained a comprehensive summarization of the teachings of the Old Testament on the Holy Spirit. Wrote Thomas: "The subject is naturally not so prominent in the Old Testament as in the New, but there are said to be EIGHTY-EIGHT DIRECT REFERENCES To The Spirit in the Old Testament. It is clearly mentioned in about half of the thirty-nine books, though in sixteen of them there is no direct reference. And whatever date we may assign to Genesis, the fact remains that the idea of the Spirit is mentioned in Ch. 1.2 as though quite familiar, just as in Matt. 1."[83]

An examination of all the "spirit" passages will show that the Holy Spirit was a Person, who was active as Creator, Sustainer, Empowerer of the saints, and whose coming in a unique way was predicted by Joel 3:1-4 (Hebrew text), 2:28-32 (English text). Benjamin Warfield has demonstrated in a scholarly and effective manner the Deity of the Holy Spirit in the Old Testaments. The latter summarized his presentation by writing: "The Spirit of God in the Old Testament, is not merely the immanent Spirit, the source of all the world's life and all the world's movement.... He is as well the indwelling Spirit in the hearts of God's children."[85]

Peter told the Christians of Asia Minor: "For prophecy never came by the will of man, but holy men of God spoke as they were moved by the Holy Spirit (2 Peter 1:21)." Paul told pastor Timothy of Ephesus: "All Scripture is **theopneustos**," that is "Spirit-breathed," which means that

1007

the Old Testament came forth from the Holy Spirit just as the breath comes forth from a man. So the Holy Spirit produced the Old Testament Bible. Paul in speaking to the Jews of Rome in A.D. 60: "The Holy Spirit rightly spoke through Isaiah" and cited Isaiah 6:9-10. The author of Hebrews declared that it was the Holy Spirit who was the author of Psalm 95:7-11.

The British scholar Davidson contended in his Theology of the Old Testament that the Old "Testament readers before Christ's time did not understand a single passage in Old Testament as referring to the Holy Spirit."[86] In Acts 1:16 and 2:16, Peter the spokesman, concluded that the Holy Spirit was indeed active during the Old Testament. Unfortunately, many theologians interpret the Old Testament in the light of how they think Israel interpreted their Scriptures. But the real question is: What did God reveal and what did the Holy Spirit intend to set forth as the true and correct sense? The Old Testament is not to be interpreted as documents revealing that beliefs or misbeliefs of the Israelites, but what God intended to make known. So if the Holy Spirit now means by the language of Holy Writ to teach about the reality of His own distinct Person, He doubtless meant no less a view of Himself when He spoke in Old Testament days.[87]

12. The Holy Trinity Is Shown by Those Passages Distinguishing the Three Persons of the Godhead.

There are a number of places in the Old Testament revelation where a distinction is made between the Three Persons of the Godhead.[88] Thus Genesis 1:1-3, where Elohim is said to have created the world, the Spirit of God moved over the face of the waters and God said etc. The Three Persons of the Trinity are here referred to: God, the Father, the Son speaking (=the Word of John 1:1-3) and the Spirit "brooding" upon the waters. Thus the Old Testament begins with the Trinity in action. In Psalm 33:6 a distinction is made between Yahweh (LORD) and His Spirit, who made the host of heaven. In Isaiah the first Servant Song we have the three Persons distinguished. Thus in 42:1 it reads: "Behold! My Servant (Jesus Christ) Whom I uphold, My Elect One in Whom My Soul (Yahweh) delights. I (Yahweh) will put My Spirit (third Person of the Trinity) upon Him (Christ, the Messiah)" (Cf. also 48:16; 61:1). In Proverbs Wisdom (Christ) predicts: "I will pour out My Spirit unto you (Prov. 1:23-29)." In Isaiah 63:9-10, three Persons are distinguished, when the Evangelical Prophet Isaiah wrote: 'The Angel of His Presence (Jesus Christ) saved them, in his pity. He (Yahweh) redeemed them but they rebelled and vexed His Holy Spirit."

The Biblical Plan of Salvation

The plan of salvation which is taught in the New Testament is not different from that taught in the Old Testament, Rom. 3-21-24; 4:1-3.[89] This writer holds that the doctrine of the Holy Trinity is so clearly set forth in the Old Testament that the believers in the Old Testament most assuredly had a true knowledge of God and of the promised Savior, His beloved Son.[90]

1008

Footnotes

1. Iris Culley, "Montheism," *The Dictionary of the Bible and Religion*, Editor William H. Gentz, (Nashville: Abingdon Press, 1986), p. 827.
2. N. J. Dawood, *The Koran* (Baltimore; The Penguin Books, 1974), p. 395.
3. W. G. Oxtoby, "Zoroastrianism," *The Dictionary of Bible and Religion*. **op. cit.**, p. 1142a.
4. "Judaism," Ibid, p. 387.
5. K. Koehler, *Jewish Theology* (New York: The Macmillan Company, 1918), pp. 82-89.
6. John Theodore Mueller, *Christian Dogmatics* (St. Louis: CPR, 1955), p. 155.
7. **Ibid.**, p. 115.
8. A. L. Graebner, *Outlines of Doctrinal Theology* (St. Louis: CPH. 1910), pp. 20-22, 41-42, 46.
9. Robert C. Dentan, *Preface to Old Testament Theology*, (New York: The Seabury Preaa, 1963), pp. 15-86; Gerhard Hasel, *Old Testament Theology: Hasic Issues in the Current Debate* (Grand Rapids: Wm. Eerdmans Publishing Company, 1975), pp. 15-34.
10. Gerhard von Rad, *Old Testament Theology*, Translated by D.M.G. Stalker (New York: Harper & Row, 1962-1965), I, (483 pp.) and II, (355 pp.).
11. Walter Eichrodt, *Theology of the Old Testament*. Translated by J. A. Baker (Philadelphia: Westminster Press, 1916-1967), I (1961), II (1967).
12. Otto J. Baab, *The Theology of the Old Testament* (Nashville: Abingdon Press, 1949), p. 2352.
13. George F. A. Knight, *A Christian Theology of the Old Testament* (Richmond: John Knox Press, 1949).
14. Ludwig Koehler, *Old Testament Theology*. Translated by A.S. Todd (Philadelphia: Westminster Press, 1953), p. 19-58.
15. Th.C. Vriezen, *An Outline of Old Testament Theology* (Oxford: Hasil Blackwell, 1968), agrees with Jewish rejection of Trinity, p. 176.
16. Claus Westermann, *Elements of Old Testament Theology*. Translated by Douglas W. Stoll (Atlanta: John Knox Press, 1982), pp. 1-34. Cf. also Westermann's *What Does the Old Testament Say About God?* (Atlanta: John Knox Press, 1979).
17. J. Kenneth Kunz, *The Self-Revelation of God* (Philadelphia: Westminster Press, 1957).
18. William Dyrness, *Themes in Old Testament Theology* (Downers Grove, Illinois: InterVarsity Press, 1979), pp. 41-62; 201-210.
19. **Ibid.**
20. **Ibid.**, pp 201.210.
21. Elmer A. Martens, *God's Design, A Focus on Old Testament Theology* (Grand Rapids: Wm. B. Eerdmans Publishing Company, 1981), his views about God are given in pp. 18-19; 21,23, 28-29: 81-96, 123, 167-174; 193; 224-226,252,257-258.
22. Robert L. Cate, *Old Testament Roots for New Testament Faith* (Nashville: Broadman Press, 1982), cf. chapters 1-5; pp. 27-157. No Holy Spirit discussed; no Trinity referred to.
23. H. H. Rowley, *The Faith of Israel* (Philadelphia: Westminster Press, 1956) pp. 48-73.
24. Brevard S. Childs, *Old Testament Theology in a Canonical Context* (Philadelphia: Fortress Press, 1985), pp. 28-42, cf. especially p. 41.

25. Werner H. Schmidt, *The Faith of the Old Testament, A History* (Philadelphia: Westminster Press, 1983), Cf. pp. 14, 48-52; 81f.; 112f.; 154; 210-213.

26. **Ibid.**, pp. 198-200.

27. Millar Burrows, *An Outline of Biblical Theology* (Philadelphia; Westminster Press, 1946), pp. 21,78.

28. Heinisch-Heidt, *Theology of the Old Testament* (Collegeville, Minnesota, 1950), p. 105.

29. Gustav Friedrich Oehler, *Theology of the Old Testament*. Revision by George E. Day (New York: Funk & Wagnalls, 1883), p. 133.

30. J. Stanley Chesnut, *The Old Testament Understanding of God* (Philadelphia: Westminster Press, 1968), p. 24.

31. Ronald Youngblood, *The Heart of the Old Testament* (Grand Rapids: Baker Book House, 1971), p. 15.

32. Gerhard Hasel, Old Testament Theology, **op. cit.**, p. 9.

33. Brevard S. Childs, Biblical Theology in Christ (Philadelphia: Westminster, 1970), p. 13.

34. D. Martin Luthers Saemmtliche Schriften, ed. Johann G. Walsh, in modern German (St. Louis; 1880-1910), X, 1019.

35. **Ibid.**, II, n p. 540.

36. As cited by Schmid, op. city., p. 137.

37. Cf. Robert D. Preus, *The Theology of Post-Reformation Lutheranism* (St. Louis and London: CPH, 1972), pp. 231-163.

38. Pieper, *Christian Dogmatics*, **op. cit.**, I, p. 394.

39. Luthhardt, *Kompendium*, 10th edition, pp. 111-112.

40. Kirn, Realenencyklopedier, 3rd edition, Vol. XX, p. 112.

41. Joseph Stump, *The Christian Faith* (New York: The Macmillan and Company, 1932), p. 47.

41a. M. Reu, *Lutheran Dogmatics* (Decorah: Iowa: Wartburg Theological Seminary, 1951), p. 28. Revised Edition.

42. C.E. Lindberg, *Christian Dogmatics* (Rock Island, Illinois: Augustana Book Concern, 1928), pp. 75,77.

42a. R. Weidner, *The Doctrine of God* (Chicago, Flemming Revell, 1904), p. 41.

44. E. Hove, *Christian Doctrine* (Minneapolis: Augsburg Publishing House, 1930), pp. 56,66.

45. Published by the Author (St. Louis Success Printing Co., 1912), pp. 580-590.

46. *Joh. Gillielmi Bageri, Compendium Theologiae Positive*, edited and amended by Guil. Walther (St. Louis: Concordia Verlag, 1889), p. 45.

47. Francis Pieper, *Christian Dogmatics* (St. Louis; CPH, 1950), I, pp. 393-397.

48. W.H.T. Dau, *Lectures on Dr. Graebner's Outline of Christian Doctrine* (St. Louis: Concordia Mimeo Company, 1929), p. 54.

49. J. T. Mueller, *Christian Dogmatics* (St. Louis: CPH, 1955), pp. 158-160.

50. E.W. A. Koehler, *A Summary of Christian Doctrine* (Detroit and Oakland: L. Koehler and A. W. Koehler, 1939), p. 3.

51. R.R. Caemmerer, "The Nature and Attributes of God," in *The Abiding Word*, edited by Theodore Laetsch (St. Louis: CPH, 1947) II, p. 75.

52. A. Hoenecke, *Dogmatik* (Milwaukee: Northwestern Publishing House, 1909), II, pp. 157-161.

52a. Wilhelm and Hans Moeller, *Biblische Theologie des Alten Testaments in heilgeschichtlicher Entwickelung* (Saxen: Johammes Hermann, 1938), p. 522.

53. Herman Bavinck, *The Doctrine of God*. Translated and edited by William Hendricksen (Grand Rapids: Eerdmans Publishing Company, 1955), p. 255.

54. Herman Bavinck, *Our Reasonable Faith* (Grand Rapids: Eerdmans Publishing House, 1956), p. 151.

55. L. Berkhof, *Systematic Theology* (Grand Rapids: Eerdmans Publishing Company, 1941), p. 85.

56. Payne, **op. cit.**, p. 166.

56a. "The Trinity," *Baker's Dictionary of Theology* (Grand Rapids Baker Book House, 1960), p. 531.

57. Johan Gerhard, *Doctrinal Theology*, as cited by Mueller, **op. cit.**, p. 159.

58. Preus, *The Theology of Post-Reformation Luthernism*, **op. cit.**, pp. 131-133.

59. Mueller, *Christian Dogmatics*, **op. cit.**, p. 159.

60. Preus, **op. cit.**, p. 133; Mueller, **op. cit.**, p. 159.

61. Reu, **op. cit.**, p. 28.

62. G. F. Knight, *A Christian Theology of the Old Testament* (Richmond: John Knox Press, 1959).

63. H. C. Leupold, *Exposition of Genesis* (Grand Rapids: Baker Book House, 1942), pp. 85-87.

64. Ludwig Koehler and Walter Baumgartner, *Lexicon in Veteris Testamenti Libros* (Leiden: E. J. Bril, 1958), p. 50; cf. also Herbert Stevenson, *Titles of the Triune God* (Westwood: Fleming H. Revell Co., 1956), pp. 20-24.

65. Preus, **op. cit.**, p. 159.

66. Mueller, **op. cit.**, p. 159.

67. Leupold, **op. cit.**, p. 570; C.K. Lehman, *Biblical Theology*, Volume I Old Testament (Scottsdale, Herald Press, 1971), pp. 92, 371.

68. Mueller, **op. cit.**, pp. 394-395; Preus, **op. cit.**, p. 239.

69. Pieper, **op. cit.**, I, pp. 394-395.

70. Payne, **op. cit.**, pp. 167-168.

71. Cammerer, **op. cit.**, p. 75.

72. Mueller, **op. cit.**, p. 159.

73. Pieper, **op. cit.**, p. 395.

74. Payne, **op. cit.**, pp. 167-170.

75. Caemmerer, **op. cit.**, 75.

76. Gerhardus Vos, *Biblical Theology, Old and New Testaments* (Grand Rapids: Eerdmans Publishing Company, 1959), p. 88.

77. Payne, **op. cit.**, p. 170.

78. Eugene P. Kauffeld, *Divine Footprints. Christ in the Old Testament* (Milwaukee; Northwestern Publishing House, 1983), pp. 185-196.

79. Payne, **op. cit.**, p. 171. Cf. also Charles T. Fritsch, "The Gospel in the Book of Proverbs," *Theology Today*, 7:2 (July, 1950), pp. 169-183. A concluding section recognized the Person of the Christ in Prov. 8.

80. Payne, **op. cit.**, p. 171.

81. Mueller, **op. cit.**, pp. 159-106.

82. W. H. Griffith Thomas, *The Holy Spirit* (Grand Rapids: Kregel Publications), pp. 9-17.

83. **Ibid.**, pp. 10-11.

84. B. B. Warfield, *Biblical and Theological Studies* (Philadelphia: The Presbyterian

and Reformed Publishing Company, 1952).

85. **Ibid.**

86. A. B. Davidson, *The Theology of the Old Testament* (New York: Charles Scribner's Sons, 1904), p. 127.

87. Payne, **op. cit.**, pp. 172-173.

88. Preus, **op. cit.**, pp. 138-163; Pieper, **op. cit.**, pp. 394-395; Wilhelm and Hans Moeller, *Biblische Theologie des Alten Testaments in helisgeschlicher Entwickelung* (Zwickau, Saxen: Johanned Hermann, 1938), p. 522.

89. Martin Chemnitz, *Loci Teologici*. Translated by J.A.O. Preus, (St. Louis: CCPH, 1989), p. 66.

90. Howard Hanke, *Christ and the Church in the Old Testament. A Survey of Redemptive Unity in the Testaments* (Grand Rapids: Zondervan Publishing House, 1957, pp. 7-12. How different from Walter C. Kaiser, *Toward an Old Testament Theology* (Grand Rapids: Zondervan Publishing House 11978, where the Trinity is not discussed where the idea of a different organizing principle is sought for and advocated).

Questions

1. Which religions are spoken of as monotheistic? ____
2. The Quran accuses Christianity of believing in ____.
3. The word Trinity expresses the truth that ____.
4. Is the doctrine of the Trinity comprehensible to human reason? ____
5. Who rejects Old Testament Trinitarianism? ____
6. Who are some scholars who claim to be Christian and Lutheran who deny that the Trinity is taught in the Old Testament? ____
7. Millar Burrows rejects the contention that ____.
8. What did Luther teach about the Trinity in the Old Testament? ____
9. The Braaten-Jenson Christian dogmatics makes no statement about ____.
10. From its inception in 1847 the LCMS clearly taught that ____.
11. Robert Preus taught that Jesus Christ was at the center of both ____.
12. What was the conviction of J. T. Mueller? ____
13. What are some Old Testament proofs of the Trinity? ____
14. Where is the Trinity predicted in Proverbs? ____
15. The Old Testament begins with the ____ in action.
16. The plan of salvation taught in the New Testament is not different from ____.

Thanking God

Jesus Christ's and St. Paul's Directives for a God-Pleasing Observance and Celebration of America's Day of Thanksgiving

Christian News, November 20, 1995

America's National Day of Thanksgiving is observed by Americans in different ways. For millions of Americans November 23 will be celebrated by traveling to be with friends and relatives, by feasting and drinking, by the viewing of football games, by the looking at Macy's Thanksgiving Day Parade or the mummer's parade held annually in Philadelphia. Those who daily go to work will enjoy freedom from the daily business routine. But thanking God will not be a part of their agenda. On the other hand, numerous Christians will engage in most of the activities just alluded to (except heavy drinking), and especially they will thank the Father of Lights and Jesus Christ and the Comforter, the Holy Spirit, for the blessings they have received from the Giver of all good things and which He has bestowed on America since the last Thanksgiving Day. Furthermore, these Christians will gather in God's house for a special Thanksgiving service.

Christians will gather in God's house to praise and thank God, for this is the will of God, who especially in the book of Psalms has given many commandments for his followers to publicly acknowledge what God has done for them by supplying sunshine and rain who kept His promise to Noah that seedtime and harvest would not cease (Genesis 8:22). What the Old Testament urges in many passages, the Lord Jesus Christ and His Apostle St. Paul likewise do in the Gospels and in the Epistles respectively.

It is for remembrance of God's mercies and kindnesses, as well as for the sake of inspiration and for purpose of motivation, that Christ, God's only begotten Son, the Revealer of the Father's will, and St. Paul as Christ's spokesman, have left directives and commandments for Christians to follow relative to the giving of thanks. It is in response to what Christ and Paul as our exemplars did and carrying out the instructions on thanksgiving and thanksgiving that Christians in Canada assembled on October 9th (Canadian National Thanksgiving) and American Christians will gather on November 23rd in their respective houses of worship.

The Lutheran Tradition of Thanksgiving

The Lutheran Churches have included the fourth Thursday in November as a special day in their ecclesiastical year.[1] Historically Lutherans in Europe and America observed a Harvest Home Festival, at which they thanked God for the crops and grain they were enabled to gather in. *The Lutheran Hymnal* had propers for "The Festival of Harvest." The suggested Epistle was Deuteronomy 26:1-11 and the Gospel: Luke 12:13-21.[2] The observance of the Festival of Harvest was yearly held especially in agricultural congregations. Lutheran Christians were glad to respond to the suggestion of the President of the United States to hold a national day of thanksgiving, to be observed the fourth Thursday in November.[3]

The Lord Jesus Christ and Thanksgiving

While there are not numerous instructions by Christ, he has left us enough to aid us in wanting to follow Him and carry out his directives concerning the giving of thanks and showing our appreciation by helping our less fortunate brothers and sisters.[3a] In studying Jesus' teaching on the giving of thanks, it is clear that Jesus gave His Father thanks for both material and spiritual gifts. Before distributing the bread and fish in both the feeding of the five thousands and the four thousand,[4] Jesus blessed them, thanking God for them. Christ did the same on Maundy Thursday evening when instituting the Lord's Supper, known also as the Eucharist, so called because in the Greek account of the celebration the verb is **euxaristeo**, which means "to give thanks."

The example of giving thanks to the Father for bread and fish, unleavened bread and wine should suggest that Christ's followers will imitate their Savior and thank the Triune God for material things as food and drink. It has always been a Christian custom to thank God at meal time. For this reason Luther included in his *Small Catechism* two prayers of thanksgiving, one to be spoken before mealtime and the other after the meal's conclusion.[7] Both of these suggested prayers are from the Psalms.

The Gospels report two other occasions when Christ gave thanks. On one occasion Jesus thanked His Father that he had withheld a true understanding of His teaching from those who were rejecting His divine instructions.

After upraising the cities of Galilee, Jesus declared: "I thank thee Father, Lord of heaven and earth, that thou hast hidden these things from the wise and intelligent and revealed them to babes (Matthew 11:25)." John reported that when Jesus stood at the tomb of Lazarus Jesus thanked His Father that He heard His prayer (John 11:41). Jesus expressed great disappointment at the ten lepers he had healed, that only one, a Samaritan, had returned to thank his benefactor. Surely, if a person has survived a great illness or even escaped death because of medical skill, he ought to give thanks to the doctor or surgeon, and especially then God who has endowed men with the mind and capability to perform the surgery that they are able to utilize. How fortunate are the people of Canada and the United States where by means of governmental and church (The Concordia Health Plans) plans they are enabled to meet costly medical bills and hospital stays which are beyond the ability of most individuals to finance. Again, most Americans and Christians are fortunate to live at a time when life-extending, death-preventing drugs are available. Surely, these are gifts, and the grateful Christian will thank God for their availability.

The Apostle St. Paul on the Giving of Thanks

The Apostle Paul has in his writings considerable to say about thanksgiving and thanksliving,[8] as well by his own conduct as revealed in the book of Acts has demonstrated his beliefs concerning thanksgiving. Luke, a companion of the apostle to the Gentiles, reported that Paul on his sea journey taking him to his first Roman imprisonment was shipwrecked after leaving the island of Crete and it appeared that the 276 persons on board would drown. It was on the fourteenth day when they were drifting through the Adriatic Sea, Paul encouraged the passengers to eat, for the latter had abstained from food for a long time. Luke reports that Paul took bread "and thanked God in the presence of all, he broke it and began to eat (Acts 27:35)." Then later on his way to Rome, he gave thanks to God when Christian brethren came to meet him at Appian Forum and the Three Taverns (Acts 28:15).

Paul Directives on Thanksgiving in His Epistles

Paul has considerable instruction in a number of his congregational letters and a few in his personal letters to individuals. House has listed in his *Historical and Chronological Chains of the New Testament* 38 distinct prayers (this includes also doxologies) in the Pauline corpus and as a part of some of them one finds expressions of thanksgiving for the following: (l) proclamation of the faith (Romans 1:8; I Cor. 1:3f; I Thess. 1:2; cf. Eph. 1:15f; (2) grace bestowed; I Cor. 1:4; II Cor. 1:11; 4:15); (3) acceptance of the word preached I Thess. 2:13; (4) fellowship in the Gospel's progress (Phil. 1:3-5); (5) growth in grace (II Thess. 1:3); (6) knowledge of election (II Thess. 2:13; (7) spiritual blessings Col. 1:12; (8) liberality in giving (II Cor. 9:1ff); (9) joy over converts (I Thess. 3:9).[9]

Paul's Thanksgiving for Personal Benefits

Not only did Paul expect others to give thanks for material and spiritual gifts but he also in the course of penning his letters to others gave thanks for benefits bestowed on others as well as upon himself. Here are those spoken of and acknowledged by Paul: (1) deliverance from bondage (Rom. 7:25); (2) sacrificial labor of other people (Rom. 16:4); (3) non-commission of certain acts (1 Cor. 1:14); (4) gifts bestowed upon him (1 Cor. 14:18); (5) friend's spiritual growth (Phil. 4f).

In his practical section in Ephesians Paul suggested: "Giving thanks for all things unto God and the Father in the name of our Lord Jesus Christ" (Eph. 5:20). That is certainly a comprehensive statement. A suggestion as to what is involved in "giving thanks for all," is listed by Luther in his explanation, in his discussion of giving thanks for "daily bread," in setting forth rather comprehensively: "What is meant by daily bread?" In which he listed at least 20 blessings God bestows on Christians and their unbelieving neighbors.[10] Since this was written in 1529 many new blessings and benefits could be added. Think of all the timesaving devices now available to take away the drudgery which certain aspects of human living bring with them. Think of the miracle drugs now available and the medical and surgical procedures, all designed to lessen pain and prolong life.

Wick Broomall in an article dealing with thanksgiving concluded by discussing the characteristics of thanksgiving as follows: Thanksgiving is acceptable according to God's will (I Thess. 5:18); its neglect is always sinful (Luke 17:16; Rom. 1:21); it will always be a dominant feature of heaven's praise (Rev. 4:9; 7:12; 11:17); Christians should render thanks continually (I Cor. 1:4; Col. 4:2), under every circumstance (Phil. 4:6), to God through Christ (Col. 3:17) and as an antidote to sin (Eph. 5:4).[11]

A Thanksgiving Prayer

O Almighty and Everlasting God, who hast given unto us the fruits of the earth in their season: We thank Thee for all these Thy blessings which Thou hast provided for the nourishment of our bodies; and we pray Thee to grant us grace ever to use the same to Thy glory, to the relief of those who are needy, and, thankfully, to our own comfort; through Jesus Christ, our Lord. Amen.[12]

Footnotes

1. *Lutheran Worship* (St. Louis: CPH, 1982), p. 122.
2. *Lutheran Hymnal* (St. Louis: CPH, 1941), p. 84, in *Lutheran Worship.*
3. **Op. cit.**, there are selections for the One-Year Series and also for the Three-Year Series, p. 120.
3a. Cf. Lawrence O. Richards, *Expository Dictionary of Bible Words* (Grand Rapids: Zondervan Publishing House, 1985), "Thanks/Thanksgiving," pp. 575-596.
4. John 6:3-13; Matt. 14:14-21; Mark 6:34-44; Luke 9:11-17.
5. Matthew 15:32-38; Mark 8:1-9.
6. George G. Tappert, *The Book of Concord* (Philadelphia: Fortress Press, 1959), "The Small Catechism of Luther," p. 383, VIII: Grace at Table.
7. **Ibid.**, pp. 353-354.
8. Richards, **op. cit.**, p. 596.
9. H. Wayne House, *Chronological and Background Charts of the New Testament* (Grand Rapids: Zondervan Publishing House, 1981), pp. 38-39.
10. Tappert, **op. cit.**, p. 347.
11. Wick Broomall, "Thanksgiving," E. F. Harrison, Editor-in-chief, *Dictionary of Theology* (Grand Rapids: Baker Book House, 1960), p. 517.
12. Prayer Number 342—*Thanksgiving, in Collects and Prayers for Use in Church* (Philadelphia: The Board of Publications of the United Lutheran Church in America, 1935), p. 156.

Questions

1. Millions of Americans celebrate Thanksgiving Day by ____.
2. The verb **euxaristeo** means ____.
3. Since 1529 what are some new blessings which can be added to Luther's explanation of giving thanks? _____

The Theological Teachings of Christ's Miraculous Transfiguration

(A Study for Transfiguration Sunday)

Christian News, February 12, 1996

In both the *Lutheran Hymnal* and *Lutheran Worship* the last Sunday of the Epiphany season is observed as "Transfiguration Sunday." Christ's glorification on a mountain was an unusual historical event in the earthly life of Christ. Three of His disciples Peter, James, and John were chosen to witness Christ's greatest glorification on earth before the resurrection. The glorification of the Son of God took place on a mountain, which tradition believed it was to have been Mt. Tabor in Galilee, or Mount Panius, near Caesarea Philippi, or Mount Hermon, in the Anti-Lebanon range.[1] On Mt. Tabor three churches have built in commemoration of the event, but these do not establish that Mt. Tabor was the transfiguration mountain. Holy Writ just calls the place "a high mountain."[2]

The three disciples chosen to witness this historic and unique event of Christ's life were probably those upon whose understanding and sympathy He could rely. They were to become witnesses of His glory before the whole world. John states in his prologue to his Gospel: "We beheld His glory, the glory as of the only-begotten of the Father" (John 1:14), and Peter in his second epistle refers to this experience (2 Peter 1:16-18).

These three disciples who alone witnessed other important events in Christ's life,[3] were asked in an evening hour to have a vigil of meditation and prayer far above the tyranny of this world. While Jesus prayed, his three companions fall asleep.

They were probably tired from climbing the mountain and the cold mountain air. Toward dawn they awoke and saw Christ transfigured.[4] The three disciples saw something no person had seen before. Though Jesus was in the form of a servant, they saw the glory of His Divinity (Phil. 2:6).

On the mountain a most peculiar, miraculous phenomenon occurred: While Jesus was praying. He was transformed, transfigured, before them. His physical body, being transfused and glorified with spirituality, a foretaste of His future glorification. Not only did His face shine like the sun itself, with a luster not of this earth, but His clothing became as white-glistening as snow, as the essence of light itself, beyond the power of any fuller on earth to give them pure spotlessness. All this was visible to them as the disciples gazed in stupefied wonder. His divine glory, which He always bore in Himself, but which was usually hidden or manifested only occasionally in word or miracle, Christ here was transformed and shone through His outward form and person: An unsurpassed revelation of His glory before their eyes. It was an incontestable proof of the fact that He was truly the Son of God; it was visible evidence of his entering through suffering after death to glory. The face of Christ was transformed and shone just as after His ascension and glorification as

1017

revealed in the book of Revelation and His raiment was white as snow (cf. Rev. 1:14-16). The glory which the Son of God possessed in His own light returned for a moment to enshroud Him. In addition Moses and Elias appeared unto them and talked with Jesus. As their bodies had been preserved from destruction, so Jesus' body would not experience decay (Ps. 16:10; Acts 2:27ff.)

The Effect of the Vision

The effect of the vision created terror in the hearts of Peter, James and John, yet they were overjoyed by what they saw and heard. Peter expressed the wish to live there permanently and expressed the desire to have three huts built, one for Christ, one for Elias, one for Moses and forget to suggest one for the three disciples. They also heard the Father speaking out of heaven, saying:

"This my beloved Son, hear ye Him." These are the same words the Father uttered at the Baptism of Jesus. They also saw Moses and Elijah and the conversation was about Christ's suffering and death in Jerusalem. Dean Farrar, in writing about the effect of this vision and happening, said: "Not in a cloud of glory or in a chariot of fire was Jesus to accomplish His work, but with His arm outstretched on a cross; not between Moses and Elias, but between two thieves who were crucified with Him. The disciples had heard heaven's conversion and tasted angels' food."[5]

The Theological Teachings or Theology of The Transfiguration

The occurrence on the Mount of the Transfiguration contains a whole body of divine teachings. In that which follows the various theological teachings will be adduced and commented upon.

I. The Holy Doctrines of The Transfiguration
1. About God

The transfiguration happening teaches the existence of God and thus rules out agnosticism and atheism. The same Triune God who spoke earlier at the Baptism of Christ was the Father, who spoke, the Son, the object of baptism and the Holy Spirit resting on the Son.[6] At both the transfiguration and the baptism God said: "You are my beloved Son, hear ye Him." The Father spoke and a Son presupposes having a Father. Associated with this Person who revealed Himself is the concept of God's preservation of the world and His care for individuals, or His general and special providence. If one grants that God exists, it is not difficult to reason back to special creation for a God of evolution would not exercise such special and individual oversight.[7]

The Scene on the Transfiguration Mountain Also Teaches
2. Special Revelation

In the Old Testament God reveals Himself by direct word, angel of the Lord, vision, dream, mighty acts and by His different names, each of which taught something specific about God. God has also revealed Himself through the inscripturated revelation in the Old Testament Biblical books.[8] Here during the Galilean ministry He revealed Himself to the three disciples and His Son by vision and by the spoken word. If God revealed Himself and his will to people, it was important that this revelation be permanently kept in written form, just as this was done in Old Testament times, so the God of revelation caused holy men to record the twenty-seven books of the New Testament. From the appearance of God here and at other places and times, one logically can infer the transcendence and immanence of God.[9]

The appearance of Moses and Elijah was very significant. Moses was the great lawgiver of Old Testament times. Moses lived from 1525-1406 B.C., while Elias or Elijah was an outstanding prophet who castigated various kings of Judah and Israel. He opposed Ahab and Jezebel, who were promoting the pagan, anti-Yahweh fertility cult. Moses and Elijah had direct contact with God, to whom Yahweh gave revelations and command. Here it is evident that the Old Testament and the New Testament are combined. Moses and Elijah prepared the way for the coming of the Messiah.

3. Teachings About Christ and Redemption (Christology and Soteriology)

In this pregnant incident everything is wrapped up in Jesus. The Father spoke from heaven: "This is my beloved Son, in whom, I am well pleased: hear ye Him" (Matt. 17:5). A son presupposes a father and that means the voice that spoke was not a mother and that one cannot ascribe femininity to God, as the feminist movement today does. The genealogies speak of "the son of the father," as in (Genesis 5, Matthew 1:18). What the Father said amounts to a divine endorsement of Christ carrying with it the incarnation, obedience and sacrifice of Christ—in short the whole redemptive work of Christ. The death of Christ offered as an expiation for mankind's sins is explicitly set forth, for Christ, Moses and Elijah were talking about His coming decease at Jerusalem. The chief topic of conversation between Christ and His heavenly visitors concerned Christ's coming death at the hands of the scribes, Pharisees and Sadducees. Moses and Elijah did not say: "We are saved not by the death of Jesus, but by his life and deeds."

No, the death of Christ was the pivot of His redemptive grace and power. The doctrine of Christ's death carries with it the doctrine of men's sinfulness, indeed, of his depravity, for man could not have saved himself, otherwise no atonement would have been necessary. His death on the cross would have been redundant.[10]

Men and women and children by their own intelligence cannot comprehend the mysteries of God. Declared the Father: "Hear ye Him." (Prophetic office) This shows that human beings need enlightenment. Christ fulfilled the law and the prophets, this is shown by the transfiguration.

4. Person and Work of Christ

That Christ was both man and God is shown by the fact that Jesus had a body and face. His fleshly character is shown by the clothes He wore, by the human speech He employed. His divinity and glory shown forth from His person so that His face glowed like the sun; his clothing so bright that it nearby, blinded the three disciples. Although He humbled Himself (State of humiliation) for some thirty-three years, there were occasions when His divinity shown forth. For the most part His divinity was hidden during the state of humiliation, but here on the mountain He was permitted to give evidence of it. With the aid of other Scriptures, one might say that what happened on the Mountain of Transfiguration is also an earnest and prophecy of the glorified state of Christ, when at His exaltation to the right hand of God, He was filled with all divine fullness, and we are going to be like Him. We have also a glimpse of the glory which shall be revealed in us, when we shall see Him as He is.

5. Information about the State of the Dead

The appearance of Moses and Elijah testifies to the existence of a life beyond the grave. Moses died about 1405 B.C. and Elijah was taken alive into heaven on a chariot of fire (2 Kings 1:11). Both Moses, the author of the Five Books of Moses (the Pentateuch), great leader and lawgiver of Israel and Elijah, the opponent of the Baal worship in Israel, were alive at Christ's time. They were two of the greatest of the old order. Moses was buried on Mt. Nebo by Yahweh Himself and for his body the devil fought with Michael (Jude 9), the archangel. The prophet Elijah, in the presence of Elisha, was taken alive on a chariot of fire into heaven.[11] Both of these men spoke with Jesus on the Mount of Transfiguration. The topic of conversation was the coming suffering and death of God's Son, the promised Messiah of the Old Testament. They appear to have been on most familiar terms with Christ.

6. The Intermediate State

When a person dies his spirit goes either to be with God or with the condemned in hell. The spirits of men and women enter the intermediate state between death and the resurrection.[12] The soul does not sleep nor does not sleep between death and resurrection, as some religious groups hold. Although Moses was buried by God, he did not decompose. Yet here on the Mt. of Transfiguration Moses appears in bodily form, constituting proof that God could give a disembodied spirit a body. There is no distinction made between the body of Moses and that of Elijah. Here, in connection with Christ's metamorphosis, Bible readers are given glimpses of a wonderful eschatological teaching-resurrection and eternal glory for both body and soul.

7. *Recognition in the Hereafter*

The four transfiguration accounts (Math. 17:1-ff.; Luke 9:28ff.; Mark 9:2ff; II Peter 1:16-18) reveal that Christ, Moses and Elijah knew one another; yes, even the three disciples recognized Moses, then lawgiver and Elijah, the great apologete for the God of Israel, whom they had never seen on earth. This would suggest the Christians will recognize one another in heaven.

8. Thoughts about Glorified Material

Leander S. Keyser, an apologete for Biblical Christianity, in commenting on the Transfiguration narrative remarked: "We may also learn some things about the Biblical doctrine of material substance in glorified form. While Christ still retained the essence of His corporeal nature and while that of His garments still remained intact, yet both became too glorious for earthly vision to endure. His face and His clothing shone more brightly than the sun. The transformation scene, therefore, foreshadowed the coming estate of glorification of material substance. So we need not stumble over the doctrinal teaching of a literal resurrection of our bodies. The events that transpired on the Mountain of Transfiguration prove "that in glorification the essence of the body is not destroyed, but its character and form are simply transfigured with divine beauty and glory."[13] John has assured Christians: "We shall have a resurrection both like unto His own glorious body!" (1 John 3:2)

II. The Inspiring Lessons of the Transfiguration Doctrines
1. It Gives Assurance and Hope

The purpose of Christ's transfiguration was to give the three disciples a foregleam of Christ's coming glory when he would ascend to the "right hand of the Majesty on high." After the ascension the leaders of the early church could reason that if their Lord was transfigured for a short time in His State of Humiliation, what must Christ's glory be now that after His ascension He has resumed the glory He had with the Father before assuming man's flesh and blood (John 17:5). Would not such thinking give them courage, when thinking of His power, grace and glory. Christians today can have the same confidence in Christ that Peter, James and John did.

2. It Gives Strength for Everyday Work

Peter wanted to build three tabernacles or huts, so he could keep Christ and the heavenly visitor as long as possible. The dead will only be awakened by Christ at His Second Coming and so the appearance on the Mountain of Transfiguration was a temporary reminding of the arising in connection with the death of Christ (Matthew 27:52-53).

Peter wanted to remain on the Mount of Transfiguration, in enjoyment of the ecstasy of feeling. But this could not be. They had years to live in which they needed to proclaim the Good News and lay the foundation of the Christian Church as is evident from Acts 1-12.

At times Christians have mountainside spiritual experiences but they do not last for every day duties call Christians to action and live a life of sanctification.

Besides Christ's passion being foretold in the Old Testament, on the Mount of the Transfiguration it was the great topic of conversation. Connecting both the Old Testament and the New Testament, Killen asserted: "Thus His passion was foretold as typified by the OT Exodus from Egypt, Moses and Elijah were alike in that each had a vision on a mountain, Moses on Sinai (Ex. 24:15ff.), Elijah on Horeb (I Kings 19:8ff.); each had no known grave (Deut. 34:6; II Kings 2:11); each was mentioned in the closing verses of the Old Testament (Mal. 4:4-6)."[14]

The Gospel of the Transfiguration is a good link between the last Sunday of the Epiphany season and the six Sundays of Lent in *Lutheran Wor-*

ship or a connecting link between the three pre-Lenten Sundays in *The Lutheran Hymnal.*

Footnotes

1. Allen R. Killen, "Transfiguration of Christ" *Wycliffe Bible Encyclopedia* (Chicago: The Moody Press, 1975), 1731.

2. Adam Fahling, *The Life of Christ* (St. Louis: CPH, 1936), p. 378. Fahling claims the summit of Tabor was occupied at the time of the transfiguration of Christ. Afterward it was fortified by Josephus. Cf. Schuerer, I, ii, p. 215, Josephus Wars IV 1, 7-8.

3. Peter, James and John constituted an inner circle. They were with Christ in the house of Jairus, Mark 5:37; Luke 8:51. The three were further privileged to witness the transfiguration, (Matt. 17:1; Mark 9:2; Luke 9:28, and the agony Gethsemane (Matt. 26:37).

4. The Greek *metamorphoo* means to "change into another form."

5. F.W. Farrar, *The Life of Christ*, II, p. 225.

6. A. L. Graebner, *Outlines of Biblical Theology* (St. Louis: CPH, 1905), p. 19.

7. L. S. Keyser, *In the Redeemer's Footsteps,* (Burlington, Iowa: The Lutheran Literary Board, 1918), p. 93.

8. James G.S.S. Thomson, *The Old Testament View of Revelation* (Grand Rapids: Wm. B. Eerdmans Publishing Company, 1960), pp. 9-80.

9. Keyser, **op. cit.**, p. 93.

10. **Ibid.**, p. 94.

11. R. E. Nixon, "Transfiguration, of Christ," J.D. Douglas, Editor, *The New Bible Dictionary* (Grand Rapids; Wm. B. Eerdmans Publishing Company, 1962), p. 1291.

12. Keyser, **op. cit.**, p. 94.

13. **Ibid.**, p. 95.

14. Killen, "Transfiguration of Christ," **op. cit.**, p 1731.

Questions

1. When is Transfiguration observed in both the *Lutheran Hymnal* and *Lutheran Worship*? ____
2. Who witnessed the Transfiguration? ____
3. What did God say at both the baptism and transfiguration of Jesus? ____
4. Moses lived from ____ to ____.
5. One cannot ascribe ___ to God.
6. What is the state of humiliation? ____
7. How did Elijah get to heaven? ____
8. Will Christians recognize one another in heaven? ____
9. John assured Christians that we shall have a resurrection both like ____.

The Foundation Truths
The Origin, Purpose of Lent and the New Concept of the Three Pre-Lenten Sundays

Christian News, March 4, 1996

The Lenten season of the Church Year probably is that time when Christians focus more on the foundation truths of the Christian faith than any other time of the Ecclesiastical Year. While in the days of the Old Covenant believers were required to follow a divinely given Church Year, this was not the case in New Testament times. However, the early Christians were aware of the Passover, Pentecost, Feast of Tabernacles, Rosh Hashanah, Yom Kippur. Jesus observed all commanded festivals of the Old Testament as did His disciples.[1] They attended the Temple and its worship and also went to the synagogue.[2] In the times immediately after the Resurrection, Ascension and outpouring of the Holy Spirit the early apostles continued to observe some of the religious cultic teachings of Judaism.[3]

The Apostle Paul made it a point to observe Jewish laws and arranged one of his missionary journeys that he would be back for Pentecost.[4] Wilson has remarked: "All of the Apostles were Jews, trained in the traditions of the synagogue and accustomed to more elaborate worship of the temple. The first converts were Jews with a similar background. The record of Paul's missionary journeys tells how in every community he visited, his first appeal was made invariably in the local synagogue.[5] Therefore, it is not surprising that in the beginning Christian worship should have been largely colored by Jewish antecedents. The Sabbath, cornerstone of Old Testament worship was at first observed, later then, Sunday, the first day of the week, took its place. Sunday was recognized as our Lord's Day, on which he rose from the dead.[5a] The main elements of Jewish worship were carried over into Christian worship including Scripture readings, psalms,[6] prayers, and some sort of sermon. The most notable change and addition was the celebration of the Lord's Supper, or Eucharist which replaced the Passover, which had served its purpose when Christ was crucified, as "the Lamb that takes away the sins of the world (John 1:29)."

The Christians had no church structures till after the decree of liberation in A.D. 312, issued by Constantine.[7] At first they met in private homes (Colossians 1:2). In Corinth they held "agapes," or love feasts before the celebration of Holy Communion which were held for a while but because of abuse were abandoned. The Eucharist became a central part of Apostolic worship (Acts 20:7).

It did not take too long for a liturgy to develop in Christian gatherings. No copy of these early liturgies have survived. However, references in the Apostolic Fathers do appear. Around A.D. 112 Pliny, a pagan Roman writer, gave a brief description to the emperor Trajan. Justin Martyr around A.D. 150 wrote a defense of Christianity, giving a careful descrip-

1023

tion of the Lord's Supper.[8] From Paul's first letter to the Corinthians one can infer that the early Christians observed Good Friday, because Paul wrote: "Christ our Passover lamb has been sacrificed for us." There was, however, a great difference between the Jewish Pascha and the Christian observance of Good Friday, "for unlike the Jewish Passover the lamb that was sacrificed was not revived, while Jesus as God's Lamb was raised from the dead and thereby called the Son of God (Romans 1:4)."

The Date of Easter Controversy

One of the controversies to divide the Christian Church was the Easter Controversy, which occurred around A.D. 160. This arose from the lack of unification of the time the Passover should be celebrated. The Eastern Church commemorated the death of Christ on the 14th of Nisan, hence "Quartodecimas," from the Latin "14th," and as a result, any day of the week it could be celebrated; the West commemorated the death of Christ on a Friday and the Resurrection of Christ the following Sunday. The Eastern position emphasized Christ's death, the Western, His resurrection. Discussion pertaining to this matter had caused Aniceta and Polycarp to discuss it. Victor I witnessed a schism relative to this dating. The Council of Nicea in A.D. 325 declared itself against the Quardeciman stance and decided that Easter should be celebrated on the first Sunday following the full moon, which happened next after the vernal equinox (March 21st), but if a full moon is on a Sunday, Easter should he celebrated on the Sunday after.[10] This rule meant that Easter could not be celebrated before March 23rd and no later than April 25th. Easter was the first festival to be celebrated by the Eastern Church.

The Early Origin of Easter As a Church Festival

Irenaeus (died 202) of Lyon mentioned Easter as the festival for which the church needed to prepare itself. Tertullian, a priest, mentions Easter's observance, Tertullian died in A.D. 220. However, there was a great variation how long the preparation for Easter should be. Irenaeus speaks of it variously as one day or forty hours. Socrates, an ancient church historian, speaks of a fast of three weeks, while Sozomemus, who wrote down till A.D. 440 refers to the Lenten fast enduring six weeks. Duchesne stated: "The observance of forty days is first distinctly mentioned in the fifth canon of Nicea."[11] Gregory the Great at the end of the sixth century, fixed the beginning of Ash Wednesday as occurring 46 days before Easter. This meant that the Lenten season was of 40 days duration, not counting the six Sundays of Lent as fast days, thus these Sundays were "in Lent," but not "of Lent."

The Origin of the Word "Lent"

The word Lent is derived from the Anglo-Saxon "Lencten," which means spring, the days when the days lengthen.[12] The Latin name is "Quadragesima," which signifies "fortieth." The Christians remembered with special devotion the forty hours during which the Savior lay in the tomb of Joseph of Arimethea. Then the period of commemoration was extended to two weeks, and then to forty days, not Sundays, considered as fast days.

The Primary Purpose of Lent

"The primary purpose of a fast before Easter," wrote Blunt, "was doubtless that of perpetuating in the hearts of Christians the sorrow and mourning which the Apostles and Disciples felt during the time that the Bridegroom was absent. This sorrow had been turned into joy by the Resurrection, but no Easter joy could ever erase from the mind of the Church the memory of those awful forty hours of blackness and desolation which followed the last sufferings of the Lord, and the Church lives over yearly the time from the morning of Christ's Good Friday to the morning of the (first) Easter Day, by a representation of Christ "evidently set forth crucified among us,"[13] (Gal. 6:14). This probably was the earliest idea of a fast before Easter.

It almost necessarily followed that sorrow concerning the death of Christ should be accompanied by sorrow for the cause of that death. Therefore, the Lenten fast became a period of self-discipline, and that was the case from its first institution in apostolic times. Probably the Early Church looked upon the pattern of Jesus who fasted forty days in the wilderness after having been tempted by the Devil. There was also the Old Testament of Moses being on Sinai (Deut. 10:10) forty days and forty nights and Elijah travelling for 40 days and 40 nights on a meal given him by the Angel of the Lord (I Kings 19:8).

The Pre-Lenten Cycle

The Christmas cycle concluded with the last Sunday after the Epiphany. The pre-Lenten cycle began with the Sunday Septuagesima. In 1970 four major Christian Churches, the Roman Catholic, the Presbyterian, the Protestant Episcopal and various Lutheran denominations adopted a revised Church Year.[14] This new arrangement extended the Epiphany season by making the traditional pre-Lenten Sundays the last three Sundays of the Epiphany, with the last Epiphany Sunday being the Sunday of Christ's Transfiguration.[15] Thus the traditional Sundays of Septuagesima, Sexagesima and Quinquagesima were eliminated, and were set forth as concluding the Epiphany season. Formerly, the number of Sundays after Epiphany depended on the date on which Easter fell. If Easter is very early, there was only one Sunday after Epiphany, on the other hand if Easter occurs as late as possible, there are six Sundays after Epiphany. The Second Sunday after Epiphany was known as the Festival of the Name of Jesus.

The Three Sundays before Ash Wednesday traditionally were designed to prepare for the Lenten season (a penitential season).[16]

Sunday Septuagesima

P.E. Kretzmann claimed that the time of fasting, began with Septuagesima, the ninth Sunday before Easter. The time from Septuagesima till Ash Wednesday is known as the pre-Lenten Sundays (Vorfasten in

German), and the clergy began fasting on this Sunday.[17] The days from Quinquagesima till Ash Wednesday were known as Carnival Days and given over to all manner of activities, marked by processional and theatrical exhibitions.

Alfred Jeremias called the Sundays between Epiphany and Invocavit, the first Sunday in Lent, as "die leere Sontage."[18] The three Sundays of the pre-Lenten cycle are prosaic numerals for seventy, sixty, and fifty respectively, thus meaning that the three pre-Lenten Sundays fell within a period of seventy, sixty and fifty days respectively before Easter. After Transfiguration Sunday the Church sets its face to go up to Jerusalem (Luke 9:54), there again to behold all that came to pass for us men and for our salvation. From the transcendence of the Transfiguration Mount the Church descends to the depths of sorrow; from glory to shadows and gloom; from the Mount of Light to the valley of Suffering and then on to the Hill of the Cross.[19] This is what happens after the Transfiguration observance. Jeremias noted that with the Sunday Septuagesima priests in the Roman Church began their fasting and for this cause the people named it "das Herrenfest" (The Feast of the Lord), in distinction from the 40 days beginning with Ash Wednesday.[20]

Ash Wednesday, the Beginning of Lent Proper
Ash Wednesday was the signal for the beginning of the Lenten fast. The custom of placing ashes upon the forehead of the attendants at church services, preceded by appropriate ceremonies, goes back to the eleventh century. The ashes used were acquired by ashes made from the palm distribution on Palm Sunday of the preceding year and the clergy signing the cross with them on the heads of those before him, while he said: "Remember man, that thou art dust, and unto dust shalt thou return."[21]

Shrove Tuesday
The day before Ash Wednesday is known as Shrove Tuesday because in medieval days penitents were accustomed to go to private confession on that day and to be shriven, that is, absolved for sins and thus prepared for a proper observance of Lent. In Shakespeare's time it had become the equivalent of Italian **carnival**, which means farewell to flesh in reference to giving up flesh-meat during Lent.[22]

The Sundays of Lent are not counted as fast days, it may be worthy of note that the fourth Sunday in Lent was known as Mid-Lent Sunday, in French (Mi-Careme) and also termed Refreshment Sunday on account of the Gospel selection was the Miracle of the Feeding of the Five Thousand.[23]

In the old Church Year and its pericopes the six Sundays of Lent were named after the first word of the Introit: They were known as 1. Invocavit (Ps. 25:6), 2. Reminiscere, 3. Occuli (Ps. 25:15), 4. Laetare (Is. 66:1). 5. Judica and Passion Sunday.

These Latin names have been abolished in the revised Church Year and instead we have 1st, 2nd, 3rd, 4th, 5th Sundays in Lent, the objection to the old names was no doubt that people did not understand Latin and thus an obstacle to effective communication was removed, thereby it is hoped furnishing a better understanding of the Lenten season.

Passion Week or Holy Week

It is a common mistake to speak of the last week of Lent as Passion Week. The name properly belongs to the preceding week. The fifth Sunday is Passion Sunday[24] when the Epistle for the day begins to tell of the great sacrifice (Hebrew 9:11-15). The correct name for the last week before Easter is **Holy Week**. The German name for this week is: Stille Woche or Silent Week.[25] The Orientals called it "the Great Week" by Chrysostom, so called because of the great events which occurred during this week.

Palm Sunday, The Beginning of Holy Week

The first day of Holy Week is Palm Sunday, that being the day of our Lord's entrance into Jerusalem, by means of which He proclaimed His Messiahship.[26] It happened in fulfillment of the prophecy of Zechariah 9:9. The Pilgrimage of Sylvia gives an account of the ceremonies of Holy Week in Jerusalem in the fourth century A.D. She also reported that there were processions of palm-bearers in imitation of the fact that as Jesus entered Jerusalem on a donkey (a royal animal) that the people strewed palm branches in the way of Christ as He rode into the Holy City.[27] The account of the triumphant entry is recorded by all four Evangelists. To record the same event four times does not happen very often in the Gospels. Since the Holy Week was the last week of Christ's State of Humiliation and since it preceded His condemnation, crucifixion and death, it surely will be profitable to take note of the events of the three days following Palm Sunday. For this reason the Church Year considered each day of Holy Week worth remembering.[28] Just as on Palm Sunday it became customary for the faithful to assemble on the Mount of Olives and from there went in procession to the city of Jerusalem, carrying olive branches and singing, while the bishop rode in their midst sitting on a donkey, similarly other events in the days preceding the crucifixion were dramatized in the later services of the week. It was only in the sixth century that services in the West included a procession with palms.

It is significant to note that about one-fourth of the 89 chapters which compose the content of the Four Gospels are concerned with the events of Holy Week. In Mark, chapters 11:1-15:15:47, deal with happenings of Silent Week.

Holy Monday

Every day of Holy Week except Saturday is given a full set of Propers.[29] During three of the days of the week, three Messianic prophecies from the prophecy of Isaiah are used.[30] On the way to Jerusalem Jesus pronounced His judgment on the barren fig-tree as a type of the Jewish Church. He cleared the Temple for the second time, the first occurring in the early Judean ministry (John 2:13-17), driving out the sellers and buyers from its courts. The chief priests and the scribes took counsel to put Jesus to death.

Holy Tuesday
Christ teaches in the temple and answers questions put by His enemies. Jesus speaks a number of parables and denounces the scribes and Pharisees. Jesus sits with His disciples on the Mount of Olives overlooking the city and foretells its destruction (Mark 11:20). The last days of His public ministry take place.[31]

Jesus foretells His betrayal by Judas. The chief priests agree with Judas for thirty pieces of silver to have Judas betray the Lord (Luke 23:1-7).[32]

Maundy Thursday
This is the day on which Jesus instituted the Lord's Supper, when He first prepared with His disciples to eat the Passover. He ate with His disciples the Passover on the evening before His death, but it was on the commencement of Good Friday according to Jewish reckoning that Christ both celebrated for the last time the Passover and instituted the Lord's Supper, took the unleavened bread and wine used at the Passover celebration. According to John 13 Jesus washed the feet of His disciples and gave the "new command," that His followers should love one another." Because of this commandment to love, Holy Thursday is known as Maundy Thursday, **Dies Mandatum**. The German also call this Thursday "greener Donnerstag," i.e. "Green Thursday."[33] It was also called **Dies Natalis Calicis** (the Birthday of the Eucharist), **Dies Panis** (the Day of the Bread), **Dies Mysteriorum** (of the Sacred Mysteries). The Greek called it **The Great Fifth Day**.[34]

Good Friday
The earliest name for this day, **"Pascha,"** referred to the Jewish Passover celebrated at this time. Other names were: "Day of the Lord's Passion," "Day of the Absolution," and "Day of the Cross," and also in early times also **Pascha Staurosimon** (The Paschal, Day of the Crucifixion) as Easter was called **"Pascha Anastasimon,"** (Paschal Day of the Resurrection). Later it became the Great Friday (Parasceves) and the Dies Dom. **Passionis** (The Day of the Lord's Passion).[35] The German Name is **Karfretag, Trauerfreitag**. The name "Good Friday" is a peculiarly English expression. Says Reed: "It reflects the joy of completed redemption and protests against superstitious notions that all Fridays are unlucky" and that this peculiar Friday must be shrouded in funeral gloom."[36]

Through the process of time through ritual and custom the Western church came to emphasize the solemn character of the day. Strodach noted: "A most strict fast was enjoined (sick and aged were excepted). Works of charity and gifts of love were urged. All notes of joy were scrupulously hushed: The Glorias had already been excluded at the beginning of the week; now the bells were silenced; no kiss of peace was given at the Communion; all altar ornaments and coverings were removed; the vestments were black; lamps and candles were gradually extinguished; a long series of intercessory prayer distinguished one of the devotions. The Passion account of St. John was read, forming the center of the Church's devotions, but probably the most conspicuous ceremony was the Adoration of the Cross; during this the Reproaches and the hymns "Pange, lingua gloriosa," "Sing, My Tongue, the Glorious Battle, and **Vexilla regis**." The Royal Standard Forward Goes were sung. It is surprising to what lengths people in different countries did go to emphasize the sufferings of Christ. In Spain churches were closed, in all churches on Good Friday no services were held.[37]

The Church of the Reformation and Good Friday
Strodach claimed: "The appointments of the Church of the Reformation look to use the Day as one of the most high and solemn praise. They presuppose a Celebration of Holy Communion, a distinct heritage of the Reformation, and what better day than this on which to unite in the Memorial of the Passion! (I Cor. 11:26). The altars were draped in black, and carried the silent message of invitation and participation.[38]

Saturday of Holy Week
Saturday of Holy Week was termed the **Great Sabbath, Holy Sabbath** dating back to post-apostolic times. In the literature the day before Easter was denominated the **Vigils of Easter, Holy Saturday, Easter Eve** and in **German Karsamstag.**[39] The day was considered a fast day, but as the day continued sorrow was turned into joy, as the Christian congregation awaited the resurrection of Christ from the dead. Strodach claimed: "The ceremonies of the day included the Blessing of the New Fire, and the Paschal Candle and the Water of Baptism, and at one time the Baptism of the Catechumens. The Alleluia appeared in Communion and white vestments were used. Naturally, the services grew in importance toward the close of the day and continued until after midnight to welcome the early dawn."[40]

Saturday Evening of Holy Week
The Lutheran Hymnal has an Easter Evening or vespers, for which there are the Propers: Psalmody, Scripture readings, Antiphon and Collects.[41] The ancient Epistle for Saturday was Colossians 3:1-4 and the Gospel Matthew 28:1-7. By contrast *Lutheran Worship* gives Matthew 27:57-66, a text appropriate for the day preceding Christ's physical resurrection from the dead.[42] In ancient time catechumens were baptized on this day. Even when services were held on Saturday Eve, the custom was to read the seventh part of the History of the Passion.[43]

If the Lenten hymns and the Scriptures that treat of Christ's suffering and death are not explained away and they are allowed to declare their clear messages, these can also in liberal churches set forth the great central doctrine of our salvation, namely that God was in Christ reconciling the world to Himself and not imputing their sins to them and now has given the world the message: "Be ye reconciled to God" (2 Cor. 5:18-20).

Footnotes

1. Jesus and His Disciples kept the ceremonial law by keeping all the festivals commanded by the law of Moses.
2. Peter and James did not at first radically depart from observing Jewish religious practices, cf. Acts 2:1; 3:1; 15:29.
3. Acts 15:29.
4. Acts 20:6; 20:16 (Paul planned to be present for Pentecost).
5. Acts 13:14; 14:1; 17:17; 18:4, 19; 19:8.
5a. Acts 20:7.
6. Ephesians 5:19; Colossians 3:16; 13:16.
7. Frank E. Wilson, *An Outline of the Prayer Book* (New York: Morehouse-Gorham Company, 1936); pp. 9-10.
8. **Ibid.**, p. 10.
9. Walker Gwynne, *The Christian Year* (New York: Longmans, Green and Company, 1915), p. 32.
10. William Pauck, "Easter," in Vergilius Ferm, Editor, *An Encyclopedia of Religion* (New York: The Philosophical Library 1945), p. 239; Alfred Jeremias, *Leben im Kirchenjahr* (Leipzig: Adolf Klein, Verlag, 1928), p. 50.
11. Duchesne, p.365 as cited by Gwynne, **op. cit.**, p. 107, A. A. MacArthur, "Lent," in J.C. Davies, *The Westminster Dictionary of Worship* (Philadelphia; The Westminster Press, 1972), pp. 212-213.
12. MacArthur, **op. cit.**, p. 212.
13. As cited by Gwynne, **op. cit.**, p. 108.
14. *The Lessons. Series A, B, C. Contains the First Lesson, the Second Lesson and Gospel readings for the three-year lectionary* prepared by the inter-Lutheran Commission on Worship: Minneapolis: Augsburg Publishing House, no date).
15. Cf. *Lutheran Worship* prepared by The Commission on Worship of the Lutheran Church, Missouri Synod, 1982), p. 8a.
16. Paul Zeller Strodach, *The Church Year* (Philadelphia: The United Lutheran Publishing House, 1924), p. 90.
17. P.E. Kretzmann, *Christian Art in the Place and in the Form of Lutheran Worship* (St. Louis; Concordia Publishing House 1921), p. 355.
18. Jeremias, **op. cit.**, p. 37.
19. Paul Zeller Strodach, *The Collect for the Day* (Philadelphia: The United Lutheran Publication House, 1924), p. 71.
20. Jeremias, **op. cit.**, p. 37.
21. Luther Reed, *The Lutheran Liturgy* (Philadelphia: Muhlenberg Press, 1947), p. 453.
22. Wynne, **op. cit.**, p. 109.
23. **Ibid.**, p. 109.
24. Paul Zeller Strodach, *The Church Year. Studies in Introits, Collects, Epistles and Gospels* (Philadelphia: The United Lutheran Publication House, 1924), p. 126.
25. Reed, **op. cit.**, p. 460.
26. Saint John 12:13.
27. Reed, **op. cit.**, p. 458.
28. Wynne, **op. cit.**, pp. 110-111.
29. Cf. Lessons A, B, C, **op. cit.**, pp. 39-48.
30. *Lutheran Worship* (St. Louis: Concordia Publishing House, 1982), pp. 41,42,43,45.

31. Adam Fahling, *Harmony of the Gospels* (Grand Rapids; Zondervan Publishing House, no date), pp. 171-179.

32. The Gospels do not record anything happening on Wednesday of the crucifixion week. Tuesday was a very full day.'

33. Strodach, *The Church Year*, **op. cit.**, p. 141.

34. **Ibid.**, p. 141.

35. **Ibid.**, p. 144.

36. Reed, **op. cit.**, p. 462.

37. Strodach, *The Church Year*, **op. cit.**, p. 145.

38. **Ibid.**, p. 146.

39. **Ibid.**, p. 147.

40. **Ibid.**, p. 147.

41. *The Lutheran Hymnal*, **op. cit.**,
pp. 45-46.

42. **Ibid.**, p. 46.

43. Strodach, *The Church Year*, **op. cit.**, p. 145.

Questions

1. During the Lenten Season of the Church, Christians concentrate on ____.

2. The main elements of Jewish worship were ____.

3. The Christians had no church structures until ____.

4. The Council of Nicaea in A.D. 325 decided that Easter should be celebrated ____.

5. The word Lent is derived from ____.

6. When did four major denominations adopt a revised Church Year? ____

7. What was eliminated? ____

8. Ash Wednesday was the signal for ____.

9. What does the Italian carnival mean ?____

10. What is the difference between Passion Week and Holy Week? ____

11. About one-fourth of the Gospels are concerned about ____.

12. Why is Holy Thursday known as Maundy Thursday? ____

13. On Good Friday the altars were draped in ____.

The Eschatological Emphasis of the Lutheran Church Year

Christian News, December 2, 1996

Where did the universe come from? What are mankind's origins? What is the purpose of human existence? What will be the man's personal end? Will there be an end for the universe? These are the great questions asked by philosophy and theology. All these questions are answered by God's Word and are given in the course of the Church Year in the selections found in Old Testament texts, in Epistle periscopes and in selections from the four Gospels, appointed to be read and preached on different Sundays of the Ecclesiastical Year. It will be found that the Church Year as used by liturgical churches presents the worshippers with a balanced spiritual diet, stressing all the basic doctrines basic to Christianity's plan of salvation.

The Lutheran Church Year originally cleansed by Martin Luther,[1] consists of two parts: The festival and non-festival halves. The first half (26 Sundays) proclaims the work of the Triune God done for mankind's salvation. The doctrine of the Incarnation of Christ His suffering and death, crucifixion burial, resurrection and bodily ascension and the outpouring of the Holy Spirit sent by Christ after His Ascension constitute the substance of the first half of the Church Year.[2] All three persons of the Godhead are depicted as involved in mankind's eternal salvation. Christmas teaches believers that it was God the Father, who out of love sent his Son (John 3:16), so that Christmas is also the Festival of the Love of God in addition to teaching the great truth that God assumed human nature. Easter is the festival of God the Son's resurrection from the dead, followed by the Festival of the Ascension celebrating the God-Man Jesus' resuming the glory He had with the Father from all eternity. The Festival of Pentecost commemorates the sending of the Holy Spirit in Jerusalem resulting in the Holy Spirit converting three thousand Jews to believe in Christ Crucified as their Savior and Redeemer. The Trinity Festival, although it comprehends all teaching of the first half of the Church Year, caps them all as an all-embracing climax differs radically from all other festivals in the year. The Church Year is an annual observance of historic events.[3] The festival of the Trinity, on the other hand is an expression of a great Doctrine by the Church, and her adoring worship of the Father, Son and Holy Spirit, centralized in this unique expression on this Day as the climax of the Year. In 1332 it obtained formal authorization.

The last 26 Sundays of the Church Year were traditionally divided as follows: 1. The Sundays from Trinity or Pentecost to St. Peter and St. Paul's Day (June 29); 2. The Sundays from St. Peter and St. Paul to St. Laurentius Day (August 10); 3. The Sundays from St. Laurentius Day to St. Michael (September 29); 4. The Sundays from St. Michael to St. Andrews Day (November 30).[4] The last three Sunday of the Trinity or the last three Sundays after Pentecost have an eschatological emphasis, as does the Second Sunday in Advent.

Apocalyptics constitutes an important element in the revelational data of the Old and New Testaments.[5] The subject of the Last Things (eschatology) is an important component of Biblical apocalyptics. In the Old Testament especially the following Scriptures portions are apocalyptical in nature: Joel 2:28-32; Isaiah 24-27; 34-35; also Is. 65-66; Ezekiel 38-39; 40-48; Daniel 2, 7-12; Zechariah 9-14. In the New Testament Matthew 24-25; Luke 23; Mark 13 ("The Little Apocalypse"); 2 Thessalonians 3:7-14 and large portions of Revelation. Scattered throughout Holy Writ are verses that are apocalyptical, thus showing the importance of Biblical eschatology as revealed as a vital teaching, given in a number of doctrines dealing with the questions: "What will be the end of this age like? What will happen to the universe? What will happen to mankind, composed of babies, children, adolescents middle-aged people and the senior members when they die and those living at the end of the age?"

The discipline of eschatology in Christian theology deals with questions like this: Will death end all? Is there an after-life? Is there a heaven or a hell? Will there be resurrection to eternal life for those who have died with faith in Christ? Will there be a resurrection of all people who have lived since Adam? Will there be a judgment besides the personal and individual which occurs immediately upon death?

The Lutheran Hymnal and *Lutheran Worship* and Their Contribution to Biblical Eschatology

Since both *The Lutheran Hymnal*[6] and *Lutheran Worship*[7] are used by congregations of The Lutheran Church-Missouri Synod, and have many Scriptural texts in common, they will be the subject of this presentation. A perusal of Old Testament texts, New Testament selections, and various propers give answers to the major teachings of eschatology. This study will limit itself to the Scriptures of the Old and New Testaments and not discuss the Propers: Such as the Collects, the Versicles, Graduals or any other which they are employed.

The Apocalyptic Teachings of *The Lutheran Hymnal* Enunciated on the 25th Sunday After Trinity

Already on the 22nd Sunday after Trinity the teaching is expressed: "Our citizenship is in heaven." On the 25th Sunday after Trinity the Reformers selected as the Epistle of 1 Thessalonians 4:13-18. In this portion of Paul's first Thessalonian Letter he informs believers that the Christians who have fallen asleep in Christ will be raised, just as Christ was raised from the dead. The early Church constantly lived in expectation of Christ's visible return.

Because of the emphasis on the Second Coming (Greek: the Parousia) the two Thessalonian Epistles have been called "The Eschatological Epistles."[8] Each chapter of 1 Thessalonians ends with a statement about Christ's Second Coming (cf. 1:10; 2:19; 3:13; 4:4; 16:5, 23).

Both the Epistle and the Gospel tell of Jesus' return. The extensive text for the 25th Sunday after Trinity 1 Thessalonian 4:13-18 is unique among New Testament eschatological those will be raised, who believe in Christ's resurrection, Christ being the first fruit of them to be raised from the dead. Paul's argumentation means that the place of believers in the Lord will be raised and be with Him when He comes.

Paul informs the Thessalonians: "This we say unto you by the word of the Lord." Paul's argument does not mean that Paul received a special word from Jesus about Christ's return but that he is teaching what is based on what Jesus had spoken as recorded by the three evangelists (especially Matthew 24-25). There are sayings in the Gospels which have a striking resemblance to Paul's as is the case in Matthew 24:31 and John 6:33. When He would again appear Jesus assured His followers, that the dead believers and the living believers would share in His kingdom. Paul then reveals a remarkable happening, namely that as the Second Coming of Christ (the Parousia) dead and living would meet the Lord in the air. The New Testament scholar P.E. Kretzmann claims that in 1 Thessalonians 4:13-18 the sequence of events on the last day are given. Thus he wrote: "Because the Lord Himself will descend from heaven with a loud summons with the voice of the archangel and with the trumpet of God, and the dead in Christ shall rise first. Thereupon we, the living ones, who remain over will be caught up together with them in the clouds of heaven to meet the Lord in the air, and so shall we always be with the Lord."[9]

The Gospel selection for the 25th Sunday after Trinity in *The Lutheran Hymnal* is Matthew 24:15-28, a part of the Mount Olivet Discourse. This sermon is the most complete eschatological section of the New Testament. The Mount of Olivet Discourse refers to two coming destructions: The destruction of Jerusalem in A.D. 70 and the future end of the world. Strodach wrote about the Epistle and Gospel for the twenty-fifth Sunday after Trinity as follows: "The one definitely, the other may we say?—Pictorially: For the doom of Jerusalem and her terrible visitation and judgment, the Church has always considered a type of the Final Things. Herein, when this prophecy of the Abomination of Desolation and the warning against "false Christs" (let us not forget WHO spoke these words of this Gospel!)—Are not only lessons stern and terrible but anxious and loving anxiety that the believer continue steadfast even unto the end, unswerving in his allegiance; in all, through all, clinging to that one great hope in his only Lord, Master and Savior.[10]

Lutheran Worship's 3rd Last Sunday
(25th Sunday After Pentecost)

Matthew 24:15-28 is the Gospel selection for the twenty-fifth Sunday after Pentecost or the 3rd last Sunday of the Church Year. This is the reading for the 3-Year Cycle and the LCMS's one year Cycle. Although verses 15-26 speak of the destruction of Jerusalem by the Roman armies in A.D. 70, verses 27-28 shift the attention to Christ's Second Coming. "For just as the lightning flashes from the east, and is seen even to the west; so will be the coming of the Son of man wherever the corpse lies, there will be the vultures flock together" (Matthew 24:27-28).

Matthew 25:31-46 is the Gospel Lesson for Twenty-Sixth Sunday after Trinity in *The Lutheran Hymnal* as well as the Gospel reading for the 2nd Last Sunday of the Ecclesiastical Year in both the 3-Year and 1-Year Cycle of *Lutheran Worship.*

Matthew 25:31-46 constitutes the closing scene of the Mount Olivet Discourse. These concluding verses might be called "The Throne of the Son of Man." This sublime scene is a portrayal of the power and glory of Jesus. Here Christ is depicted as King of Kings, who now no longer acts in the capacity of Redeemer, but as Judge of all mankind. This scene is not intended to give the program of judgment but rather to set forth the nature and principles of judgment. During the present age Jesus is manifested as Savior: Then He will be shown as King and Judge.

Jesus, the Son of God is depicted as sitting on the judgment throne, attended by hosts of angels, the whole human race before Him awaiting His verdict. These tremendous words were spoken within a few days of His Cross. In verses 34-45 Christ explains and illustrates His method of judgment and He will act as the representative Man who by His atoning death, has paid for the sins of the world and He will proceed on the principles manifested in his redemptive work. Only two classes of men will be recognized. They will be distinguished by their attitude to Jesus. The Lord identifies Himself with His disciples. Their attitude toward Him is judged by the way they treat His followers. Only those who have accepted Jesus and have been justified by faith can perform deeds which show that their faith is genuine. Faith without works is dead. The separation which Christ makes will be final and unalterable eternal punishment for those who rejected Christ and eternal life for those who had accepted Christ as their Savior and Redeemer.

The Epistle Selection for The 26th Sunday
After Trinity of *The Lutheran Hymnal*

The Luther Hymnal lists two Epistle Texts: 2 Peter 3:3-14 or I Thessalonians 1:3-10, both of which are rich in eschatological teachings.

2 Thessalonians 1:3-10

In the Thessalonian selection Paul, an Apostle of Jesus Christ, assures the Thessalonian congregation that their troubles are an evidence of the righteous judgment of God, who will count you worthy of his kingdom, in behalf of which you are suffering. At the end of the five chapters of I Thessalonians Paul makes a statement about the Parousia. Unfortunately, the Thessalonians misunderstood certain aspects of Christ's Second Coming. One misconception was the idea that departed Christians would not participate in the Second Coming of Christ. Paul assures the Thessalonians, that God would do justice to those who had fallen asleep in Christ. Paul's assuring words: "For truly God's justice must render back trouble to those who are troubling you, and give to you who are now troubled, and along with me at the unveiling 'apocalypse' of the Lord Jesus from heaven, with his mighty angels, in flaming fire. Then shall he take vengeance on those who know not God, even on those who do not obey the Gospel of our Lord Jesus. They shall suffer punishment, even an eternal destruction from the presence of the Lord, and from the brightness of his glorious majesty, when he comes to be glorified in all his saints, and to be wondered at in all believers, on that Day (for you also believed our testimony)" 2 Thessalonians 2:6-10. This Pauline Second Thessalonian Scripture is rich in eschatological teachings.

It should be noted that 2 Thessalonians 1:3-10 is one of the Epistle selections for the Second Last Sunday of *Lutheran Worship* in the Three-Year Series.

2 Peter 3:3-14 of *The Lutheran Hymnal*

Both the Three-Year-Cycle and the One-Year Cycle of *Lutheran Worship* have readings from 2 Peter 3, limit the selection to verses 3 and 4. In *The Lutheran Hymnal* the Petrine reading is the alternate to 2 Thessalonian 1:3-10.

The Apostle Peter informed the congregations of Asia Minor that he was giving them instruction and facts revealed to the prophets and apostles. In the future people will question the factuality of Christ's Second Coming, ridiculing the Parousia. The objections to this apocalyptic teaching was based on two reasons. In verses 3-4 Peter cites that one reason is that so much time has elapsed between Christ's proclamation of the Second Coming and the time before the appearance of this Petrine Letter between A.D. 63-68, (the year of Peter's death). The opponents also cited the fact of natural law, "all things continue as they were." Under the guidance of the Holy Spirit Peter answers these objections. Regarding the uniformity of nature, there was intervention in nature in the days of Noah. In the latter's time people also mocked when Noah warned his contemporaries of the coming of a flood. With regard to the passage of time before the announcement of Christ about His *Parousia*, Peter reminds the readers that God is not affected by the passage of time. To God, a day is like a thousand years and a thousand years are like a day.

In verses 10-13 Peter describes fact about the final judgment. The Day of Christ will be like the coming of a thief, who does not give his victim notice of his planned theft. Thus the Second Coming will occur suddenly. Then Peter gives this further information about the end of the universe: "But the heavens and the earth that now are, by the same word of the Lord (which word of God formed out of water and through water) would cause the heavens to crash, and the heavenly bodies will melt with fervent heat, and the earth with it will be burned up." This picture of elements being consumed, reminds us of the destructive power of both the atomic bomb and of the hydrogen bomb.

The purpose of Peter's penning the eschatological teachings in chapter 3:1-13 was practical. His readers are urged to live blameless lives and preserve a quiet confidence. He reminds the congregations of Asia Minor what his fellow-apostle Paul wrote about the Lord's long-suffering as giving further opportunity of salvation (vv. 14-15).

The Twentieth-Seventh Sunday After Trinity in *The Lutheran Hymnal*

For this last Sunday of the Church Year the Epistle selection is found in I Thessalonians 5:1-13. It is only occasionally that the congregation of worshippers ends the Church Year with a twenty-seventh Sunday after Trinity. The length of the Season varies accordingly as the Easter date falls early or late; early, a longer season and more Sundays after Trinity; late, a shorter season and fewer Sundays after Trinity. Since the range of the Easter date is limited to a certain limit of days, the variation in the number of days after Trinity is also limited to a few weeks only. The longest period has been referred to. The shortest is one which ends with the twenty-third Sunday after Trinity. When using *Lutheran Worship* it should be noted that Trinity Sunday is the first Sunday after Pentecost. Thus there is also a difference of one number in referring to the Sundays after Trinity versus the numbering of Sundays after Pentecost.

This year *Lutheran Worship* has twenty-three Sundays after Pentecost, followed by Sundays called 3rd Last, Sunday, 2nd Last Sunday and last Sunday of the Church Year, or the "Sunday of Fulfillment." Again the number of Sundays after Pentecost will be determined by the date of Easter.

The Last Sunday of the Church Year in *The Lutheran Hymnal* has as Gospel Lesson Matthew 25:1-13. Chapter 25 of Matthew, a part of the Mt. Olivet Discourse, begins with two parables of final destiny. The first parable depicts the virgins waiting for the bridegroom. The parable teaches the lesson of vigilance and patient waiting and the need for inward preparation. This consists in the possession and cultivation of spiritual life. The ten virgins were all alike in outward profession: They all carried lamps. The two groups differed in the matter of oil, which may be the symbol of the Holy Spirit. The wise virgins who took oil to supply their lamps, represent those whose lives are fed by the inward presence of the Spirit (Rom. 8:9). The lamps of the others went out when the crisis came. The true believers at all times are ready for the Coming of the Lord.

The Epistle for the Last Sunday of the
Church Year According to *The Lutheran Hymnal*

The Reading is from Paul's eschatological Epistle, I Thessalonians, chapter 5:1-13. The main thought of this pericope is the admonition: "Live as children of light." This is done by Christ's followers when they follow the instructions God gives them through St. Paul. Jesus already had taught his believers that His coming would be like a thief coming unexpectedly at night (Matt. 24:43). Christ tells his devotees that His Coming will be unexpectedly bringing sudden destruction. The prophets in the Old Testament and certain New Testament writers like Paul speak about "the Day" of the Lord. In the Old Testament "the Day of the Lord" often refers to the supreme manifestation of the Lord's power, which is to be ushered in by the Second Coming. Christians are described as being sons of light and not of darkness, when people sleep and are unaware as to what was happening. On the other hand, Christ's followers are to be alert and do this when they put on the breast-plate of faith, and for a helmet, the hope of salvation. God has not appointed believers for wrath, but to win salvation through our Lord Jesus Christ.

The Last Sunday of the Church
According to *Lutheran Worship*

In The Lutheran Book of Worship, published 1978, this Sunday was called "Christ the King," but in the 1982 *Lutheran Worship*, called "the Sunday of Fulfillment."[11] In *Lutheran Worship*, in 3-Year Cycle for 1996, 2 Peter 3:3-4, 8-10a, 13 is given, which is also recommended in the 1-Year Series. 2 Peter 3:3-14 has already been discussed.

An Alternative Epistle Selection for the
Last Sunday of *Lutheran Worship*

I Corinthians 15:20 is also recommended for the Sunday of Fulfillment. This pericope is taken from "The Great Resurrection chapter of the New Testament." The Gospel of Christ's resurrection implies the resurrection from the dead, because if the dead do not rise then Christ is still dead. It would further mean that the Gospel preaching is useless and the apostles are false witnesses. If Christ be not raised, then faith in Him is empty, Christians are yet in their sins, those who have believed in Christ have perished, and the Christian life is a delusion.

The Old Testament Selection for the
3-Year Cycle of *Lutheran Worship*'s Last Sunday

Isaiah 65:17-25 is also the reading for the 1-Year Series of *Lutheran Worship*. This selection is taken from chapter 65, which together with chapter 66, is considered eschatological. Isaiah 65:17-25 is the answer to the prayer of Israel (cf. 63:7-64:12). In answer to Israel's prayer, the Lord declares that those who have rejected His gracious invitation and provoked Him by persisting in their abominable idolatries are to be punished and destined to destruction (vv. 1-7). Those who have been faithful to Him— "my servants" are to be saved. As the true seed of Jacob, the chosen remnant of Judah, they are to inherit the restored land of blessing (vv. 8-10). But those who have forsaken the Lord for false gods and do not respond to his call are to be given over to destruction (vv. 11-12). A final separation is to be made to the two classes, and their diverse fate is drawn out in five striking contrasts (vv. 13-16).

Then the Lord announces His creation of a new heaven and a new earth, in which there will be a new Jerusalem for His people, where He and they will rejoice together and there will be no sound of mourning. An idealized description will be given of what life will be like in the new Jerusalem. In this city, there will be people living a long time and the saved will enjoy all manner of blessings.

The Second Coming Proclaimed by Advent Reading
First Sunday of Advent According to Lutheran Worship

In the 3-Year Series Matthew 24:37-44 is one of the Gospel pericopes. This part of the Mount Olivet Discourse announces that the coming of Christ will be like the lightning flame flashing in the east and is seen in the west. After the tribulation of those days with extraordinary events occurring with sun, moon and stars, then the Son of Man will appear in the clouds of heaven. Then all the tribes of the earth will see the Son of Man and lament. Thereupon Jesus will send forth His holy angels to gather the elect together from the four corners of the earth. No person knows the day or time when the Son of Man will appear with a great trumpet sound. Christ's coming will occur when men least expect it. The admonition of our Lord is: Be ready and do not be surprised when Jesus suddenly appears.

The Second Coming Predicted in
The Lutheran Hymnal for Advent 2

The Gospel is Luke 21:25-36. This Gospel selection parallels Matthew 24:37-44, the Matthean text and the Luke 21:25-26, incorporates a number of parables used to illustrate the eschatological teaching of Christ. With the Second Coming of Christ, there will be inaugurated the Kingdom of God. Though the heavens and the earth will be destroyed, the Lord assures His followers: "Heaven and earth will pass a way, but my words shall never pass away (Luke 21:33)."

Advent teaches Christ's Church that there are three comings of Christ. His first coming in the flesh at Bethlehem will have been useless if Christ does not enter the human heart. Only if a person accepts the purpose of the Incarnation will he lead a God-pleasing life and been abled joyfully to look the Second Coming to Judgment.

It is thus apparent that the Second Coming is remembered at the beginning of the Christian Church Year just as the *Parousia* concludes the last Sundays of the Ecclesiastical Year.

Footnotes

1. "Liturgies," in L. Fuerbringer, Th. Engelder and P.E. Kretzmann, *The Concordia Cyclopedia* (St. Louis: Concordia Publishing House, 1927), p. 412b.
2. Paul Zeller Strodach, *The Church Year* (Philadelphia: The United Lutheran Publication House, 1924), pp. 182-183; Luther D. Reed, *The Lutheran Liturgy* (Philadelphia: Muhlenberg Press, 1947), pp. 472-473.
3. Strodoch, **op. cit.**, p. 183.
4. **Ibid.**, p. 183.
5. George R. Crooks and John Hurst, *Library of Biblical and Theological Literature*, Vol. II. Biblical Hermeneutics (New York: Eaton and Mains. New Edition Thoroughly Revised, 1890), pp. 338-339; Milton S. Terry, *Biblical Hermeneutics* (Grand Rapids: Zondervan Publishing House, 1974), pp. 427-437; 438-453; 454-464.
6. *The Lutheran Hymnal*. Authorized by the Synods Constituting The Evangelical Lutheran Conference of North America (St. Louis: Concordia Publishing House, 1941), 858 pp.
7. *Lutheran Worship*. Prepared by The Commission on Worship of The Lutheran Church-Missouri Synod (St. Louis: Concordia Publishing House, 1982), 105 pp.
8. W. Graham Scroggie, *Know Your Bible*. Volume II Analytical. The New Testament (London: Pickering & Inglis, No Date), pp. 104-105.
9. Paul E. Kretzmann, *Popular Commentary of the Bible* (St. Louis: Concordia Publishing House. 1923). N.T., II, p. 353.
10. Strodach, **op. cit.**, 261.

11. *Lutheran Book of Worship*. Prepared by the churches participating in Inter-Lutheran Commission on Worship, Lutheran Church in America, The American Lutheran Church, The Evangelical Lutheran Church of Canada, The Lutheran Church-Missouri Synod (Minneapolis: Board of Publications and for Publication Board, Lutheran Church in America, 1978), p. 30.

Questions

1. The Church Year as used by liturgical churches presents ____.
2. What constitutes the first half of the Church Year? ____
3. The Church Year is an annual observance of ____.
4. The discipline of eschatology deals with ____.
5. The early Church constantly lived in expectation ____.
6. What is the Parousia? ____
7. Faith without works is ____.
8. To God a day is like ____.
9. The elements being consumed remind us of ____.
10. The true believers of all time are ready for ____.
11. No person knows the ____ when the Son of Man will appear.
12. Advent teaches Christ's church that there are three ____.

The Holy Day of Lights and Christ the Light of the World

Christian News, January 6, 1997

In 1997 the Epiphany season of the Church Year will be shorter then it was in 1996, because Easter comes as early as possible. This year Easter will be commemorated on March 30, with Ash Wednesday, the first day of Lent, being observed on Lincoln's Birthday, namely, February 12th.[1] This means that three Sundays in January and the first two Sundays of February according to *Lutheran Worship* will be Epiphany Sundays. The Transfiguration of Christ will be remembered on February 9th. CPH's *Pocket Diary* suggests that Sunday, January 5th, be used to celebrate the Epiphany festival, this Sunday preceding Epiphany one day before.

Relative to the length of the 1997 Epiphany season, there is a difference between the Synodical Conference's *Lutheran Hymnal*[2] and *Lutheran Worship*. The *Lutheran Hymnal*, still used in some LCMS congregations, has only two Sundays after Epiphany,[3] while *Lutheran Worship* will have five.[4] After the Epiphany Season the *Lutheran Hymnal* has three Sundays, known by the Latin names of Septuagesima, Sexagesima, and Quinqugesima, a cycle of three Sundays to act as a bridge between Epiphany and Lent.[5] *Lutheran Worship* has eliminated the pre-Lenten Sundays and added them to the last part of the Epiphany season.[6] This change and reassignment of the three pre-Lenten Sundays was made by the committee in 1970. However, in both hymnals the Transfiguration of Christ is the Sunday before Ash Wednesday,[7] which inaugurates the forty-six days between Ash Wednesday and Easter.

Different Names for Epiphany in Liturgical Traditions

"Epiphany" means "manifestation of Our Lord."[8] It is also called "Theophany" or "Manifestation of God."[9] In Germany Epiphany (Epiphanien) was known as "The Feast of the Three Kings" (Dreikoenig Tag). In England it was called Twelfth Day[10] the English designation links Epiphany with the Christmas Cycle, since the coming of the Wise Men was the Gospel for Epiphany. Strodach, the Lutheran liturgiologist, observed: "The association with Christmas is natural, bringing as it does one of the precious Gospels of the Holy Infancy."[11] Epiphany has the distinction of being one of the oldest festivals observed by the Christian Church Year. The Liturgical Year did not come full blown into existence but went through a varied evolution during a period of hundreds of years, during which it evolved in the Eastern and Western Churches. This holds true especially of the two festivals: Christmas and Epiphany. While the Western Churches celebrated December 25 as Christ's Natal Day, the Eastern Churches observed January 6 as the day of Christ's birth.[12]

The History of the Origin of the Epiphany Festival

McArthur contended: "We must free ourselves from the western tradition which understands the festival in terms of the magi's coming. Its significance as Epiphany or Manifestation conveys primarily and normatively, not the manifestation of Christ to the gentiles as such, but rather the manifestation, the revelation to the world of Jesus Christ."[13] According to the researches and conclusions of McArthur, the celebration of Epiphany on 6 January to Christmas, 25 of December is a complicated one. He claimed that a true solution of the problem depends on an awareness of the fact, that before Christmas came into being in the fourth century, there was already in the Eastern Empire, an ancient festival commemorating in unitive fashion the manifestation of God, both in the birth and baptism of Jesus Christ. McArthur further contended that 25 December acted as a reagent, so that in the East the dual significance of Epiphany resolved itself into distinct elements. Thus 25 December was established as the Day of the Incarnation and 6 January as the date of Christ's Baptism.[14]

John Cassian, in his *Conferences*, indicated that in Egypt between 380-400, Epiphany was a unitive festival, commemorating both the incarnation and the baptism of Jesus. According to McArthur's interpretation of liturgical history during the years 325 to 400, Christmas acted as a reagent on the original celebration of Epiphany in the geographical area of Constantinople, Asia Minor and Antioch.[15] Sermons of Gregory Nazianzen of Constantinople show that in Byzantium Christmas was celebrated there by 380 and was called Theophany or the Birthday. The celebration of the Incarnation feast was also concluded with the account of the adoration of the Magi. The festival observed on 6 January was Epiphany, the Feast of Lights or The Day of Holy Lights, commemorating Jesus' Baptism. So McArthur observed: "Thus it seems obvious that before Christmas was introduced, the Church of Constantinople must have had on 6 January a festival commemorating both the birth and baptism of Jesus and called Theophany, Manifestation of God, clearly a synonym for Epiphany. When the primary theme, the incarnation was transferred to 25 December, the title was also taken reading of the Sermons of Gregory of Nyssa shows in an Epiphany sermon that in Asia Minor the situation was the same as in Constantinople.[16]

McArthur claimed that in a sermon preached on Whitsunday in 386, Chrysostom makes reference to Epiphany as the first Christian festival, commemorating the appearance of God on earth. By the end of 586 the situation had changed and Christmas was being celebrated for the first time. The latter was described as the festival upon which all others depended. As in Constantinople, the birth of Christ included the adoration of Christ by the Wise Men. Unlike Gregory Nazianzus, Chrysostom used the term "Theophany" and did not apply it to Christmas. McArthur concluded his discussion by saying: "There can be no doubt that in Antioch, towards the close of 386 and the beginning of 387, 25 December now signified the birthday and January 6 the Baptism of Jesus. The simple and brilliant pattern characteristic of Antioch did not repeat itself in other parts of the different regions of the Eastern and Western Churches. It is possible that in fourth-century Jerusalem that Jerusalem celebrated on

Epiphany the incarnation alone.[17]

In the fifth-century the coming of the Magi was only remembered in Rome, and with Rome's ascension to a prominent place in Latin Church life, the Roman position was generally adopted.

The lectionary of Luxeuil showed that toward the beginning of the eighth century the Baptism of Jesus was commemorated at Epiphany.[18]

The Lutheran Church in its use of the Church Year followed that form in which the Reformer had been raised in and this fact determined the liturgies of Lutheranism for over four hundred years. Luther, however it should be noted, cleansed the Roman Year of all unbiblical elements and practices.[19]

The Holy Day of Lights or Day of Holy Lights, Commonly Called Epiphany

The Epistle for Epiphany is Isaiah 60:1-6 and the Gospel is Matthew 2:1-12. In both of the Biblical selections Christ is identified with the concept of "light." It was the light of an unusual star that led the Magi to Palestine, first to Jerusalem and then to the place in Bethlehem where the Holy Family was residing. The coming of Christ to this earth had been predicted by the prophet Isaiah who in chapter 60 declared: "Arise shine for thy light is come. This is one of a number of Scriptural references in which Christ is called "Light." The Evangelist wrote concerning Christ's opening portion of His Galilean ministry that Jesus withdrew into Galilee and settled in Capernaum and settled in Capernaum-by-the-Lake, near the border of Zebulun, land of Naphthali, in order that Isaiah's prophecy might be fulfilled the "the land of Zebulun and Naphthali, road by the lake. The people who were sitting in darkness have seen a great light and those who were dwelling in the land of the shadow of death the light has dawned" (Isaiah 9:1-2).

John in his prologue speaks of Christ before His incarnation: "In Him Was life and the life was the light of men. The light is shining in the darkness and the light has not overwhelmed it (1:4)." John the Evangelist describes the ministry of John the Baptist as being a witness for the Light so that men might believe through Him. John the Baptist informed his first-century hearers that he was not that Light, but it was his duty to bear witness concerning the Light. It was his commission to inform people that Christ was that Light which enlightens every person who then was coming into the world.

The Apostle John frequently refers to Christ as the "Light." Rejection of Christ as the Light brought condemnation for those refusing to accept It (3:19). Everyone who comes to the truth is said to accept the Light. Every human being (3:21) who does evil hates the Light. John describes Jesus as a burning light and true believers rejoice in it (5:35).

John's Gospel has seven sayings, each one begins with the phrase "I am," and in these "I am's" Jesus makes claims which only God could make and only are applicable to deity. One of these remarkable assertions was the one found in chapter 8:12, namely, "I am the Light of the world" Jesus informed the Jewish crowd in connection with healing a blind man: "I must work the works of Him that sent Me while it is day, night cometh when no man can work. While I am in the world I am the Light of the world (v. 12)." In chapter 12 Jesus warned his fellow countrymen: "The Light is among you a little longer. Walk while you have the Light, lest darkness overtake you. He who walks in darkness does not know where he is going. While you have the Light, believe in the Light, so that you may become the sons of light (12:35-36)."

The Appropriateness of Calling Christ "The Light of the World"
1. Christ as Light, a Scriptural Designation
The promise of Christ was: "I am the Light of the world; he that followeth shall not walk in darkness but have the light of life 8:12)." The circumstances under which these words were uttered are worthy of special mention. Christ spoke this "I am" at the Feast of Tabernacles. At nightfall, on the first night of the feast the two golden lamps which stood on one sight of the altar in the Temple court, were lighted and poured their light over the Temple and city, while far into the night troops of rejoicing worshippers held a sacred dance, accompanied by vocal and instrumental music. It was on this occasion while people were bathed in this artificial light, that Jesus said before the attending people: "I am the Light of the world." The lights by the altar and the pillar of fire were the visible vehicles of God's presence. The Book of Exodus states: "The Lord went before them in a thick cloud (Ex. 19:9)." "The Lord looked through the pillar." Another expression in Exodus reads: "The Lord came down in the cloud and spoke with Moses." In this manner Yahweh showed that He was present with Israel: At all times there was hovering over them a pillar of cloud by day and a pillar of fire by night. By means of these two different pillars God controlled all movements of Israel after they left Egypt and controlled all moves of the Israelites in the wilderness.

Under David Israel controlled all of Palestine from the river of Egypt to northern Mesopotamia.

With Solomon's success the twelve-tribe kingdom reached the peak of its glory, but toward the end of Solomon's reign disintegration set in. With his son Rehoboam the kingdom was divided, with ten tribes breaking away and forming the Northern Kingdom.

Two rival kingdoms, the Northern and Southern, fought each other and the Southern was influenced by Yahweh-denying rulers of the Northern Kingdom. Because of religious apostasy and defection both kingdoms were punished by the Assyrians and Babylonians, as various prophets of God had warned and were destroyed. Thus the Old Testament records that the Northern Kingdom ceased and its people were taken into the Assyrian captivity. The Southern was punished by Assyria and eventually the Babylonians ended the existence of the Davidic Kingdom and took the Judeans into the Babylonian Captivity (586-538 B.C.). This was followed by the Persian domination (539-331 B.C.). Successively the returning Israelites and their offspring came under the rule of the Ptolemies (323-198 B.C.), followed by that of the Seleucids (198-63 B.C.). In 63 B.C. Rome conquered Palestine.[22] In the times of Christ the light had departed from Israel as one poet wrote:

So fallen, so lost
The Light withdrawn,
The Glory gone forevermore.

Thus the Jews in Christ's day (6 B.C.-33 A.D.) had only two lamps to remind them of the glory that once the twelve-tribe nation had enjoyed. The Jews in Jesus' days could truly say "Ichabod," "the glory is gone." Despite this gloomy situation the Hebrews could remind themselves of Isaiah's prophecy: "The people that sat in darkness have seen a great light (9:2)." Later on Zechariah the priest and husband of Elizabeth, in his hymn of thanksgiving, the Benedictus, referring to this light as "the day spring from on high hath visited us to give light to them that sit in darkness." Simeon, forty days after Christ's birth, exultingly proclaimed "Lord, now lettest Thou thy servant depart in peace, according to Thy word, for mine eyes have seen thy salvation, which thou hast prepared before the face of all people, a light to lighten the Gentiles, and the glory of Thy people Israel. In the year 26 of 27, the Lightbearer appeared before the people when He declared: "I am the Light of the world."

2. Light is Extremely Pure

How well the designation Light applies to Christ. Light is the purest and most untarnished substance in the world. Snow is pure, as is water and air, but each of these will admit of defilement and may be marred and polluted. It is not so with light. Man's hand cannot soil it. No corruption can defile its rays or attach pollution to its beams.

Babies and children, young people, people beyond thirty years have inherited original sin from their progenitors. All men are conceived in sin and are born as sinners. By contrast Jesus was not conceived in sin nor was he a sinner when Mary, mother of God, gave birth to Him. Jesus spent thirty-three years in a sinful world and left it unsullied. The Biblical writer testified: "He did no sin, neither was guile found in His mouth." Pilate stated before His enemies: "I find no fault in Him at all." The male factor on the cross remonstrated with his partner in crime: "The man has done nothing amiss." Judas Iscariot, Christ's betrayer, exclaimed before Jewish leaders, as he threw their blood money on the floor: "I have sinned in that I have betrayed innocent blood." The centurion, a spectator to the crucifixion of Christ, cried out: "This certainly was a righteous man and the Son of God." Christ challenged His enemies: "Which of you convincest Me of sin?" Truly, Christ was pure, for like light he was pure all His earthly life.

3. Life Is Free

Light on earth comes without cost and appears everywhere. No poverty is so great as to bar a person from enjoying its blessings. There is not a nook or corner in this wide world into which the light refuses to come. The palaces of the great and the huts of the humble alike does it guild, and without money or paying a price does it come to every human being. Light is free and so is Christ and His salvation. It was the desire that His Heavenly Father wanted all people to enjoy the results of the suffering, death and resurrection of Christ. Jesus, before His leaving this earth said on a mountain in Galilee: "Go you into all the world and preach the Gospel," the Good News, how salvation is available for mankind. There is no palace or domicile into which Christ does wish to enter and be welcomed and accepted as Savior and Redeemer. Jew and Gentile, male and female, slave or free, black, yellow or white are offered the blessings of heaven on the same terms of grace. Yes, Christ is the Light of the World and is ready to lighten every human individual that comes into the world and sees the light of day.

4. Light Is Revealing

Another quality pertaining to light is, that it is revealing. In Holy Writ, "light" and "darkness" are opposites. Darkness obscures facts, causes and people. Where there is no light, a pit may gap at one's feet, a murderer may be waiting in our path with a dagger aimed at the heart. The darkness hides danger in certain situations but is apparent when the light shines on them. Thus it is also in the spiritual world, where Christ is the Great Revealer. It is only through Christ that we come to know God and the nature of ourselves. From Christ we learn who we are, what our needs are, and how to relieve them. One of the most difficult matters when preaching the Word of God is to convince human beings that they are guilty before God. Such people are living in darkness and need the light to show them how reprehensible they are in God's sight. Christ is the Light who wants to show them their need and the help He can give them.

5. Light Is Life-giving

Not only does light dispel darkness but simultaneously it gives life. Without Christ the Light of the world the world is spiritually dead. Look upon the Classical World, which shows how Greece and Rome practiced idolatry and debauchery, where human beings (slaves) were treated worse than animals. Consider the Egyptians who worshipped and adored bulls, crocodiles, reptiles, bugs and birds as gods. Think of the Chinese, Japanese and Hindus of the past and present with their hopeless concepts about life and the after-life. These were all in existence in Christ's day. All these and many systems of religion today do not satisfactorily answer the question: "What shall I do to be saved?" They fail at a point where they are most needed. By contrast to all non-Christian religions, Christianity assures all people: "The blood of Jesus Christ, the Son of God cleanses us from all sins (John 1:29)." "He that believeth and is baptized shall be saved (Mark 16:15)."

A convert told a missionary: "I cannot argue religion, but I know this, that when I was a man of evil character, Jesus got hold of me and made me over." Yes, Christ makes men of character.

He makes them strong and courageous, people who are loving and charitable, self-controlling people. Christ energizes His followers to fight the good fight, to finish the course, to keep the faith unto the end. Yes, Christ, who dispels darkness, also gives life now and hereafter eternal life, which begins with conversion and will extend through out all eternity.

Footnotes
1. CPH's *Pocket Diary for 1997* (St. Louis: Concordia Publishing House, 1997), p. 3.

2. **Ibid.**, p. 12.

3. *The Lutheran Hymnal.* Authorized by the Synods Constituting the Evangelical Synodical Conference (St. Louis: Concordia Publishing House, 1941), pp. 58-59.

4. *Lutheran Worship.* Prepared by The Committee on Worship (St. Louis, Concordia Publishing House, 1984), pp. 21-25; 30-36.

5. *Lutheran Hymnal*, op. cit, pp. 60-61.

6. Arthur C. Piepkorn, "Church Year," Erwin Lueker, *The Lutheran Cyclopedia* (St. Louis: Concordia Publishing House, 1975), Par. 18, p. 180.

7. **Ibid.**, Par. 4, p. 179.

8. Walker Gwynne, *The Christian Year* (New York: Longmans, Green, and Co., 1915), p. 60.

9. Paul Zeller Strodach, *The Church Year* (Philadelphia: The United Lutheran Publication House, 1924), p. 60.

10. **Ibid.**, p. 60.

11. **Ibid.**, p. 60.

12. Alfred Jeremias, *Leben im Kirchenjahr* (Leipzig: Adolf Klein Verlag, 1928), p. 31.

13. A. A. McArthur, "Epiphany," J.G. Davies, Editor, *The Westminster Dictionary of Worship* (Philadelphia: The Westminster Press, 1972), p. 170a.

14. **Ibid.**, p. 170b.

15. **Ibid.**, p. 170b.

16. **Ibid.**, p. 170b.

17. **Ibid.**, p. 171a.

18. **Ibid.**, p. 171a.

19. Cf. P. E. Kretzmann, *Christian Art in the Place and in the Form of Lutheran Worship* (St. Louis: Concordia Publishing House, 1921), pp. 275-283.

20. Cf. Strodach, **op. cit.**, pp. 60-65.

21. Cf. "Light," in *The Zondervan Expanded Concordance* (Grand Rapids: Zondervan Publishing House; 1968), pp. 797-798; F. Baudraz, "Light," J. J. Allmen, *A Companion to the Bible* (New
York: Oxford University Press, 1958), p. 238a-b.

22. For the latter years of Jewish history cf. Charles F. Pfeiffer, *Old Testament History* (Grand Rapids: Baker Book House, pp. 351-378; 385-535; 555-584.

Questions

1. "Epiphany" means ____.
2. The Eastern Churches observed ____ as the day of Christ's birth.
3. It was the duty of John the Baptist to ____.
4. John describes Jesus as ____.
5. Under David, Israel controlled ____.
6. Why were both kingdoms destroyed? ____
7. Who took the northern Kingdom into captivity? ____
8. When were the Judeans taken into Babylonian captivity?____
9. Rome conquered Palestine in ____.
10. Ichabod means ____.
11. What is the purest and most untarnished substance in the world? ____
12. All men are born ____.
13. Christ makes men of ____.

Ascension Day

The Ascension and Enthronement of Christ: Its Significance for the God-man Jesus and His Followers

Christian News, May 5, 1997

The festival half of the Church Year reaches its zenith on the fortieth day after Easter, with Christ's ascension.[1] It is one of the movable feasts of the church calendar, together with Lent, and the Trinity, Pentecost and Trinity festivals.[2] The thirty-three years of Christ's life began with his bodily assumption of life in the womb of the Virgin Mary of Nazareth and ended with his bodily ascension from the Mount of Olives, near Bethany.[3] Ascension is a festival which ought to be an occasion of great joy and jubilation. The truth, however, is that it is a day which is nearly forgotten in Protestant liturgical churches. Ascension falls on a Thursday and is treated as if nothing significant had happened on the second Thursday preceding Pentecost.

There is no fanfare or anticipation of this climactic day in Christ's earthly life. Christmas and Easter are two days when the materialistic world celebrates Christmas and Easter. The former is observed with the giving of gifts, caroling, emphasis on Santa Claus, family visiting, placing house outside decorations, while Easter is celebrated because of the Easter bunny, egg hunting, wearing of new apparel and fashion parades. The pagan world has succeeded in de-christianizing Christmas and Easter. The world knows nothing of Christ's ascension. The Roman Catholic and Eastern Orthodox Churches, while having services in their respective churches, in some respects may be classified with Protestant liturgical services in making no special preparatory efforts to focus their membership on Christ's enthronement and point out its significance for Christ and what it means for Christ's true believers and followers.

The History of the Origin of the Liturgical Observance of Ascension

Ascension is a church festival which appears to have been observed early in the history of the Church's worship.[4] Late in the fourth Christian century Etheria has allegedly been described as seeing a service held in Jerusalem in the Church of the Nativity on the fortieth day after Easter.[5]

MacArthur has thoroughly examined **The Pilgrimage of Silvia,** dated about A. D. 385, and claimed that the account of Etheria does not actually testify to an ascension service, as some have contended.[6] However, the holding of an ascension is attested to in **The Apostolic Constitutions,** according to which ascension was clearly celebrated in the spirit of joy and of the giving of thanks for the completion of Christ's earthly life.[7]

Reed claimed that the Roman Catholic Church on ascension day employs a symbolic ceremony. After the reading of the Gospel, a Pascal candle, whose light during forty days had represented the presence of the

Lord in the midst of His disciples, is extinguished. Sermons by Augustine (354-439) and Chrystomos and other early fathers, show that in their day the ascension festival was observed. In Patristic literature ascension was looked upon as a "Major" or a "Great" festival. The Greek Church called it "Taking Up." It is also referred to as "Holy Thursday."[8] Ephraim, one of the greatest ecclesiastical Greek writers, called the Nativity, Easter and Ascension "the three feasts of the Lord, Godhead."[9] The same section of the Eastern Church also had a custom of celebrating festivals in the open, either in fields, if there was no mountainside or in cemeteries.[10]

The Historicity of the Ascension Attacked

Those who make reason the norm for the evaluation of miraculous events, categorically reject the ascension of Christ as an actual historical happening. Thus the Jesus Seminar asserted about the Lucan ascension account: "Luke's commission, like those found in Matthew and John, are the work of individual evangelists or communities in which they lived. They express the goals of the emerging Christian movement. They look back upon Jesus from a great distance, for them Jesus had become the object of a new faith, soon to become a world religion; Jesus himself is a tiny historical dot on the distant horizon, nearly discernible as a real purpose..."[11] As far as Funk, Hoover and the Jesus Seminar members the account was not written by Luke and the ascension is a story created by later individuals, who wanted to make something of Jesus, who "was only a tiny historical blot on the distant horizon." Like Thomas Jefferson, and David Strauss, to whom the volume is dedicated, the latter did not belief in a supernatural Christ, which meant the ruling out of the miraculous. Today mankind is living in an age when the deity of Christ is so frequently attacked by supposedly Christian scholars and needs to be defended and when the miraculous nature of the ascension must be emphasized.

The Jesus Seminar fails to acknowledge the fact that the ascension of Christ was foretold in the Old Testament, the fact that the Gospels, the Pauline Epistles, the Book of Acts and Revelation, all assume the historicity of the resurrection and of the ascension and build significant aspects of Biblical theology on the doctrines of Christ's resurrection and his bodily ascension.

Biblical References to the Ascension in the Gospels

Mark, Luke and John all have declarations about Christ's ascension.[12] Mark in 16:19 listed the ascension as the last appearance of Christ before leaving the earth, where Jesus had spent over thirty-three years. This verse refers both to the ascension and to the session of Christ at God's right hand. Luke in 9:51 spoke of the ascension as a future event. On a Palestinian road Jesus said to Cleophas and his friend: "Beloved is not the Christ to suffer these things and enter into his glory?" Saint Luke concludes his writing to Theophilus: "He (i.e. Jesus) led them (the Apostles) out until they were over against Bethany; and He lifted up His hands, and blessed them. He parted from them, and was carried up into heaven (Luke 24:26)."

Many Allusions in John's Gospel

Jesus in His conversation with Nicodemus asserted: "No man has ascended into heaven, but He that descended out of heaven, even the Son of Man which is in heaven (3:31)." In the Bread of Life Sermon spoken in Capernaum, after the feeding of the five thousand, Jesus said to his disciples: "Does this displease you? What then if you see the Son of Man ascending where He was before? At the feast (probably a Passover) Jesus asserted to the high-priest and Pharisees' officers: "Still for a little longer I am with you, and then I go to Him who sent me. You will search for me and will not find me, where I am going you cannot come (7:33-34)."

Chapters 12 to 24 in John's Gospel Treat of the Last Fifty Days in the Life of Jesus!

There are at least twelve references to Christ's leaving this world, where He had spent over thirty-three years. During the third Passover attended by the Lord, the latter asserted on what now is known as Palm Sunday, after a voice from heaven said, "I will glorify it again" (12:29), "And I, if I be lifted up from the earth will draw all men unto myself."

John 13:1-10 describes Jesus washing the feet of His disciples and this unique chapter begins like this: "Now just before the Feast of the Passover, Jesus knowing that His hour was come when He would leave this world and go to the Father." Thus Christ asserted that after some time He would return to the glory which He had with the Father going back into eternity in which He left, when He assumed man's nature in taking on flesh and blood in the incarnation.

John, chapters 14-17, contains the important "Farewell Discourse" of the Master, a block of chapters only found in the Johannine Gospel.[13] What a treasure would have been lost had these chapters not been preserved by John. In a very comforting opening paragraph of chapter 14, Our Lord promised his disciples that He was going to prepare a house for them. Jesus assured His disciples: "If it were not so, I should have told you, for I am going to prepare a place for you. In my Father's house there are many mansions" (14:6). The Lord of Life assured His disciples: "I am the Way, and the Truth. No man comes to the Father but by me." Believing in Christ meant also knowing the Father. Christ claimed to be in the Father and the Father in Christ. Having stated that informative truth, Christ declared: "I tell you solemnly that he who trusts in Me shall himself do the works that I do, because I am going to the Father (14:12-13)." In the last paragraph of chapter 14 (23-31) Jesus clearly declared: "I am going away and yet I am coming to you. If you loved me you would have been glad, because I said 'I am going to the Father, for the Father is greater than I.' And now I tell you before it happens so that when it happens you may believe (14:28-29)."

John 16 and the Frequency of References to Christ's Departure

John 16 has seven references to Christ's leaving this earth and His return to heaven. Chapter 16 is essentially significant because of its teachings about the Holy Spirit's part in the life of the Church and in the individual Christian's life. The coming of the Holy Spirit would only occur if the Son of God would return to heaven and thereafter would keep His promise to pour out the Holy Spirit upon his followers and those who accepted Christ as Savior and Redeemer. At first Jesus withheld certain truths from the disciples, but on the night before His death He promised: "But now I go my way to Him who sent Me, yet none of you asks me, 'Where are you going?'" As the disciples together with Jesus were crossing over the brook Kidron on their way to the Gethsemane, Jesus told His Apostles: "Yet I am telling you the truth—my going is for your good. For unless I go away the Comforter (Greek: paraclete) will not come to you, but if I depart, I will send him to you (16:7)." According to Jesus' teaching the work of the Holy Spirit will involve his convicting the world of righteousness, "because I am going to my Father, and you will no longer see Me (16:9-10)." According to the Johannine account the disciples did not understand or comprehend Jesus' statement about his departure from the earth and His return to the Father (16:16-18). In encouraging his disciples to pray to the Father in Christ's name, He asserted "I have come from God. I came forth from the Father, and am come into the world: Again, I am leaving the world, and am going to the Father (16:28)."

In Christ's high priestly prayer he again repeated the fact that he was leaving this world and returning to the Father.[14] Among other things Jesus declared: "I am no longer in the world, but these are in the world. And I come to thee (17:11)." The assertions in chapters 14-17 were spoken during the state of humiliation, but the same prediction of His imminent return was also made during the state of exaltation. In chapter 20, the resurrection chapter of John's Gospel, the evangelist has recorded the resurrected Christ's meeting with Mary Magdalene, out of whom he had driven out a number of evil spirits. After the Resurrection, the Messiah revealed Himself to her, she wanted to touch Him but the Master discouraged her, saying: "Cease clinging to me, for I am not yet ascended to the Father. But go to my brethren and say to them: "I am ascending to my Father and Your Father, to my God and your God."[15] In obedience to this command she went and told the apostles the message that Christ truly had been raised from the dead.

Luke's Accounts of the Ascension

Luke, by profession a doctor and an educated person by first century standards has given the world two different accounts of Christ's Ascension into heaven.

His life of Christ's memoirs with the assertion: "And he led them out until they were over against Bethany, and he lifted up his hands and blessed them. And it happened while He was blessing them, that He departed from them and was carried up into heaven" (Luke 24:50-51). In his missionary history, relating the growth of the Christian Church in Jerusalem, Samaria, Judea, Asia Minor, Greece, Illiricum, Italy, and Spain, Luke begins The Book of Acts, A. 30, with the record of the Ascension. In fact, the account in Acts is the most complete one about the

Ascension in New Testament literature. His historical account, written to Theophilus, reads like this: "My first account, O Theophilus, dealt with all that Jesus began doing and teaching down to the day when, after giving instruction through the Spirit to the apostles whom he had chosen, he was taken up to heaven" (1:1-2). After commanding the disciples not to leave Jerusalem until the Holy Spirit had been poured out upon them and after giving them the great commission (v. 8), He was lifted up and a cloud received Jesus out of their sight. While they were gazing heavenward, suddenly two men in white stood with them and announced to them that "this same Jesus who has been taken up from you into the sky, will come both in the same way as you have seen him going up into the sky" (1:1-11).

Other Scriptures state that Christ sits at the right hand of God and these verses teach what Christian theology has called "the session."[16] Christ's session presupposes his prior Ascension. In Colossians Paul encourages the Christians at Colosse: "If you then are risen with Christ, seek those things which are above, where Christ abides, seated at the right hand of God. Set your heart on things above, not on earthly things; for you have died and your life is hidden in God. When Christ our life appears, then will you also appear with him in glory" (3:1).

The Epistle of the Hebrews Presupposes the Ascension

There are a number of passages that speak of Christ's session, which presuppose the ascension of Christ. The opening paragraph of Hebrews chapter one makes a number of significant statements about Christ (1:1-3) and concludes with this information: "And upholding the universe by the utterances of his power, after by himself making purification of our sins, has taken His seat at the right hand of the Majesty on High." In speaking about the high-priesthood of Jesus, the author of Hebrews declared: "The sum of all that we have been saying is this; we do have such a High Priest, and he has taken his seat on the right hand of the throne of Majesty in the heavens, a minister of the sanctuary and of the tabernacle, which the Lord pitched, not of man (8:1-20)." In chapter 10, in which the way into the holiest is described; the writer of Hebrews wrote: "For while every priest stands day after day, at his ministrations, and many times repeats the same sacrifices, which can never take away sins, this Priest, after offering one Sacrifice for sins, sat down forever on God's right hand; henceforth waiting until his enemies be put at the footstool of his feet. For by one single offering he has perfected forever those whom he is sanctifying" (10:11-14).

The Greek Vocabulary Describing the Ascension

Scroggie has pointed out that thirteen different verbs are employed by Mark, Luke and John in their Ascension accounts. An analysis of these verbs clearly shows that the New Testament clearly teaches Christ's leaving this earth. These verbs are the following:

1. **ana-baino,** meaning to arise up (John 3:13; 6:62; 20:17).
2. **ana-lambano,** meaning to take, with up (Mark 16:19; Acts 1:11).

3. **ana-lepsis,** meaning to receive up (Luke 11:51, only occurrence in T.T.)
4. **ana-phero,** meaning to bear, with up (Luke 24:51).
5. **ap-erchomai,** meaning to go from one place to another, to return (John 16:7; c f 20:10) the verb with from.
6. **di-istemi,** meaning to put apart (Luke 24:51).
7. **eis-erchomai,** meaning to come, enter, within Luke 24:26).
8. **epairo,** meaning to lift or raise up (Acts 1:9).
9. **erchomai,** meaning to come (John 17:11).
10. **hypago,** meaning to go away (John 7:33; 13:3; 14:4; 14:28; 16:5,10.)
11. **hypolambano,** meaning to take from under, to receive up (Acts 1:9).
12. **hypsoo,** meaning to raise on high, to elevate (John 12:32)
13. **poreuo,** meaning to depart, to journey (John 14:2,3,12; 16:28; Acts 1:10,11).[17]

The Difference Between the Resurrection and Ascension's Occurrences

Christ's disciples did not see Jesus bodily being resurrected from the dead, but they did see Him arise into heaven, where in their sight a cloud received Him. It was not necessary to see Jesus come forth from the tomb, because after the third day after His crucifixion, death and burial, he was seen alive by different individuals, men and women, on one occasion by five hundred people who were still living when Paul penned His first Corinthian Epistle. In a glorified body Jesus appeared over a forty-day period, in different localities.[18] But it was necessary for his disciples to see Jesus leave Palestine and thereafter was nowhere to be seen in His physical body. In the case of the resurrection, the disciples saw the effect, but in the case of the Ascension it was necessary for the disciples to be participants in the viewing of Jesus corporeally ascending upward and forever to be absent from the earth. In the Gospels Jesus told His disciples that he was to leave them as never before. It is as Scroggie remarked: "Up or down, indicating direction will not bear scientific scrutiny, but that which matters is plain, that He Who came into the world went from it, and never since has been physically in it."[19] Lutherans believe that Christ is sacramentally present in the Lord's Supper, that with the bread and with the wine as the words of institution are spoken, the communicant receives the body and blood of Christ in a supernatural manner.

The Significance of the Ascension for Christ, The God-man

With the Ascension of Christ there occurred the culmination of the Incarnation and it was the reward for His suffering and death. The Ascension placed the stamp of approval on Christ's resurrection from the dead. The resurrection and the Ascension fall together. If Christ was not corporeally resurrected, then the Ascension would have been impossible. However, since Christ was seen alive by many witnesses over a forty-day period, where is he now, but in heaven?

The Ascension of Christ is the counterpart to His coming to this earth, celebrated by the Christians at Christmas or at Epiphany as is done by the Orthodox Eastern Church. Christ having completed His redemptive work for the salvation of mankind, returned to the Father and the Holy Spirit. Paul told the Christians of Asia Minor that in Psalm 68:18 the Ascension of Christ had been predicted. Thus the apostle wrote: "Now surely this 'he ascended' implies that he also descended into the lower parts of the earth. He who descended is he who ascended above the highest heaven, that he might fill the universe" (Eph. 4:9-10).[20] The theologian Stump correctly remarked: "The Ascension is not to be understood as a removal from earth to some other part of the physical universe, but the transition of Christ into another relationship to the visible world." The Ascension was to the abode and presence of the Father in heaven."[21]

What took place after a cloud received Jesus Holy Scripture does not describe. One cannot conceive that this upward motion continued indefinitely. We do not know what Heaven really is. However, God's Word has indicated that Heaven is a mode of existence different from our earthly temporal existence. Into this mode of existence it is that Christ passed. Christ ascended, as Paul declared, that "he might fill all things (Eph. 4:10)."

The withdrawal of Christ's visible presence does not mean that He ceased to be present in this world. On the contrary, Jesus is present everywhere in this world, not in a visible, yet in a real and effective manner. Before His Ascension, Christ promised his followers, "And lo, I am with you always, even unto the end of the age (Matt. 28:2)." In a passage dealing with an erring brother Jesus said: "For wherever there are two or three in my name, there am I among them (Matt. 18:20)."

The immediate Ascension into heaven resulted in His sitting at the right hand of God. The Session of Christ was the direct result of the Ascension. Mark averred: "He was received into heaven and sat at the right hand of God." The Session was the forth stage in the exaltation of Christ.[22] It meant that Christ, according to His human nature, also assumed the full use of divine power and majesty which belonged to it by reason of the personal union. The Session of Christ means that Christ now as man and as Second Person of the Trinity participates in the omnipotent government of the world. The ascended Lord sits at the right hand of the Father (I Peter 3:22). The phrase "on the right hand of God" is a figurative expression for God's power. God being a spirit has neither a right hand nor a body, which hears with ears, or eyes with which He sees, or feet with which he walks. But the term "right hand of God" is an anthropomorphism to denote His might and majesty (Ex. 15:6; Psalm 89:13). Hebrews speaks of the right hand of power (Heb. 1:3), the right hand of the throne of majesty (Heb. 8:1), and the right hand of the throne of God (Heb. 12:2).

Christ now according to His human nature participates in God's rule over all things in heaven and earth. He no longer exercises full sway simply according to His divine nature, as he did during the period of humiliation, but He now exercises a full sway according to his human nature.[23] He rules as the God-man over all things in mediatorial reign designed to further the kingdom He founded by His redemptive work on earth. It was necessary for Christ to ascend into heaven and begin His session at God's right hand in order to keep His promise to send the Holy Spirit to His Church and thus inaugurate the great missionary activity that has occurred in the world for the last nearly two thousand years. By sending forth the Holy Spirit to work in the hearts of people, He calls, enlightens, gathers, sanctifies the believers unto eternal life.

As a part of His session, He exercises, his High Priesthood, His Prophetic office and also His Kingly Office.[24]

The Exercise of the High Priestly Office

The author of Hebrews assures believers: "We have such a high priest, who is set on the right hand of the throne of the Majesty in the heavens." Paul taught the Roman Christians: "Who is he that condemneth? It is Christ that died, yea, rather is risen again, who is even at the right hand of God, who also maketh intercession for us."[25] The Apostle John comforts his readers with the promise: "If any man sin, we have an advocate with the Father, Jesus Christ the righteous: And he is the propitiation for our sins: And not for ours only, but also for the sins of the whole world" (I John 2:1-2).

Christ Exercising His Prophetic Office as Ascended Lord

As our Prophet Jesus sends men to preach the Gospel of redemption.[26] Paul gave this informational statement: "He ascended up far above all heavens that He might fill all things. And he gave some apostles, and some prophets; and some evangelists; and some pastors and teachers; for the perfecting of the saints, for the work of the ministry, for the edifying of the body of Christ" (Eph. 4:10-12). The great commission assigned the Church the obligation to preach the Gospel to all people in the world (Matt. 28:18-20).

Christ Exercising His Kingly Office as Ascended Lord

Stump claimed: "The kingship of Christ shall last during the entire mediatorial era, that is, during all that time in which Christ applies to all men through the Gospel the blessings of redemption which He has accomplished, and assigns to them their eternal destiny. With the second coming of Christ and the final judgment, the mediatorial era will come to an end. God's efforts to save all men will then have exhausted all resources of grace, and the fate of all men, good and bad, will be fixed forever."[27]

* * *

With The Venerable Bede (died 735) we sing:
O risen Christ, ascended Lord,
All praise to Thee let earth accord,—Alleluia!
Who art, while endless ages run,
With Father and with Spirit One—Alleluia!
Hymn 212, verse 7 in *The Lutheran Hymnal*

1055

Footnotes

1. Paul Zellar Strodach, *The Collect for the Day* (Philadelphia: The United Lutheran Publication House, 1939), p. 137.

2. Walter Gwynne, *The Christian Year. Its Purpose and History* (New York: Longmans, Grees and Co., 1915), pp. 64-74.

3. Adam Fahling, *The Life of Christ* (St. Louis: Concordia Publishing House, 1936), p. 710.

4. Luther D. Reed, *The Lutheran Liturgy* (Philadelphia: Muhlenberg Press, 1947), p. 469.

5. Gwynne, **op. cit.**, p. 69.

6. A. A. McArthur, "Ascension Day," in J.C. Davies, *The Westminster Dictionary of Worship* (Philadelphia: The Westminster Press, 1972), p. 41.

7. Paul Zellar Strodach, *The Church Year* (Philadelphia: The United Lutheran Publication House, 1924), p. 169.

8. Reed, **op. cit.**, p. 469.

9. Strodach, *The Church Year*, **op. cit.**, p. 169.

10. **Ibid**.

11. Roland W. Funk, Roy W. Hoover, and *The Jesus Seminar. The Five Gospels. What Did Jesus Really Say?* (San Francisco: Harper, 1993), p. 400.

12. Cf. the exposition by Fahling, **op. cit.**, pp. 709-711; John Ylvisaker, *The Gospels* (Minneapolis: Augsburg Publishing House, 1932), pp. 575-788.

13. Charles R. Erdman, *The Gospel of John* (Philadelphia: Westminster Press, 1944), pp. 130-131.

14. John 17:1-26.

15. John 20:17, in *The New Testament in Modern Speech. The Centenary Translation* (Philadelphia: The Judson Press, 1924), p. 305. The Scripture translations in a number of places in this essay are taken from *The Centenary Translation*.

16. Theodore Mueller, *Christian Dogmatics* (St. Louis: Concordia Publishing House, 1955), pp. 300-301; Heinrich Schmid, *The Doctrinal Theology of the Evangelical Lutheran Church*. Third Edition, revised by Charles A. Hay and Henry E. Jacobs, 1875 Edition (Minneapolis; Augsburg Publication House, 1961), pp. 403-407.

17. W. Graham Scroggie, *A Guide to the Gospels* (London: Pickering & Inglis, 1948), p. 619.

18. **Ibid.,** pp. 608-609.

19. **Ibid.,** p. 620.

20. *The Centenary Translation*, **op. cit.**, p. 518.

21. Joseph Stump, *The Christian Faith* (New York: The Macmillan Company, 1932), p. 178.

22. A.L. Graebner, *Doctrinal Theology* (St. Louis: Concordia Publishing House, 1910), pp. 131-133.

23. M. Reu, *Lutheran Dogmatics* (Dubuque: Iowa; Wartburg Theological Seminary, 1951), Third Edition, pp. 235-236; Stump, **op. cit.**, p. 179.

24. *A Short Explanation of Dr. Martin Luther's Small Catechism. A Handbook of Christian Doctrine* (St. Louis: Concordia Publishing House. Question and Answer No. 155, pp. 119-120.

25. Reu. **op. cit.**, p. 238.

26. Martin Luther's *Small Catechism*, **op. cit.**, p. 119; Edward W. A. Koehler, *A Summary of Christian Doctrine*. Second revised Edition, prepared by Alfred Koehler

(Detroit, Michigan, and Oakland, California, 1932 and 1951), pp. 109-110.

27. Stump, **op. cit.**, p. 202; Koehler, **op. cit.**, p. 118.

Questions

1. Ascension is a day which is nearly ____.
2. The Greek Church called Ascension ____.
3. What does the Jesus Seminar say about Luke's account of the Ascension? ____
4. Today ____ must be defended.
5. Chapters of John 14-17 contain ____.
6. The Epistles of Hebrews presupposes the ____.
7. How many Greek verbs are employed by Mark, Luke, and John in their Ascension accounts? ____
8. On one occasion Jesus was seen by ____.
9. The Ascension of Christ is not to be understood as a removal of Christ from earth but a ____.
10. Heaven is a mode of existence different from ____.
11. The Session of Christ means that Christ now ____.
12. The term "right hand of God" is ____.

The Holy Spirit

*The Names and Titles of the Holy Spirit
in the New Testament
(A Study for Pentecost Sunday)*

Christian News, May 12, 1997

Holy Scripture depicts the Holy Spirit as present and active on the first day of creation. While the Holy Spirit is not mentioned so frequently in the Old Testament, the Holy Spirit was active from the beginning of human history and will be until the end of the world.[1] "Three in One" is never revealed specifically in the Old Testament—but it is implied.[2] The Spirit of God has been designated the Third Person of the Holy Trinity. What Bible readers know of God the Holy Spirit has been made known to them by the Spirit of God for as St. Paul informed the Corinthian Christians: "The things of God knoweth none save the Spirit of God (1 Cor. 2:11, Revised Version)." Various passages in the Old Testament show that the Holy Spirit was active between Genesis 1:2 and the coming of Christ.[3] Since the writer in an earlier study has written on the Holy Spirit in the Old Testament, this presentation will treat the names and titles of the Holy Spirit in the New Testament.

J. Elder Cummings wrote: "What does the great variety of names by which the Holy Ghost is known in the New Testament import?" One thing is, the fullness of revelation about in the Word, each name telling something more than the rest of what the Spirit is. Indeed, were there nothing more told than His names, we should have in them alone a rich revelation concerning Him. Another thing which these names set before us is our own spiritual need in its unspeakable depth and breadth, and His blessed sufficiency to meet that need on all sides, for every one of these names has a practical bearing on our souls."[4]

Andrew Murray observed many years ago: "The distinctive glory of the dispensation of the Spirit is His divine personal indwelling in the heart of the believer, there to reveal the Father and the Son."[5] There are many passages that describe the nature of God, that make known the glory and grace of God the Father and the Lord Jesus Christ. So several names and titles are ascribed to the Third Person of the Trinity. Biblical titles of the Holy Spirit express His deity, His attributes, His ministry among men, and the gifts which He bestows.[6] Henry Barclay Swete has written a very helpful book about **The Holy Spirit in the New Testament**.[7] In this volume the British prelate did not attempt to demonstrate the truth of Catholic doctrine of the Holy Spirit by an appeal to the New Testament, but endeavored to assist New Testament readers to realize the position of the First Christian readers in what they recorded about the Holy Spirit in connection with the history of their times or out of their own experiences of spiritual life.

The Holy Spirit plays a prominent role in the Gospels, in the history and building up of the Christian Church in Acts. In his 13 Epistles there are a great deal of references to the varied activity of the Holy Spirit.[8] There are a few books of the New Testament canon which do not mention some aspect of the doctrine of pneumatologv. This essay will limit itself to the names and titles of the Holy Spirit. A study of the descriptive names of the Third Person of the Godhead will show that some of the same gifts and graces ascribed to the Son of God, the Second Person of the Holy Trinity, are also predicated of the Holy Spirit.[9]

Bishop House wrote: "Thus the believer lives by the Spirit (Ga. 5:25) and lives by faith in him (Gal. 2:20). The Spirit dwells in him (1 Cor. 3:16), and Christ dwells in his heart by faith (Eph. 3:16,17; cf Rom. 8:8-9). The Spirit sanctifies the believer (1 Pet. 1:1-2) and Christ is made unto him sanctification (1 Cor. 1:30).[10]

The New Testament shows that the Spirit — the Spirit of God (as stated in Matt. 3:16; 1 Cor. 6:11; 2 Cor. 3:3) has a relationship to men and women as members of Christ's body.

1. **The Spirit of Christ,** for Paul in Romans 8:8-9 wrote: "But you are not in the flesh but in the Spirit, if indeed the Spirit of God dwells in you. Now anyone who does not have the Spirit of Christ, he is not His."

2. **The Spirit of Jesus.** In speaking about his imprisonment Paul assured the Philippian congregation: "For I know that this will turn out for my salvation through your prayer and the supply of the Spirit of Jesus Christ." The Roman congregation was assured by the Apostle to the Gentiles: "And if Christ is in you, the body is dead because of sin, but the Spirit is life because of righteousness, but if the Spirit of Him who raised Jesus from the dead dwells in you, He who raised Christ from the dead will also give life to your mortal bodies through His Spirit who dwells in you" (Rom. 8:8-9). The fact that in Romans 8:9 the Spirit is called both the Spirit of God and the Spirit of Christ, shows their equality and functions of the one Godhead. The New Testament depicts the Father as the Source of all grace; the Son, as the Channel, and the Spirit proceeding from the Father and the Son, as the Agent. The New Testament writers never portray the Holy Spirit as an agent of God as do monotheists and deniers of the Trinity of God. The Father and the Holy Spirit are referred to in various passages as distinct from each other. The Holy Spirit is no subordinate representative of the Godhead.[11]

3. The Lord the Spirit (2 Cor. 3:18)

In the last verse of chapter three of Second Corinthians, Paul alludes to the Holy Spirit and bears witness to His essential Deity and co-equality with the Father and the Son. Griffith Thomas in his study of the Holy Spirit wrote: "The Holy Spirit is closely related to God (Rom. 8:9), is regarded as possessing personal activities; and is intimately bound up with (Christ (Rom. 8:9)." Stevenson averred: "The activity of Christ as Redeemer and Head of the Church is regarded as continued by the Holy Spirit, and yet with all this intimacy of association they are never absolutely identified."[12]

4. The Eternal Spirit (Heb. 9:14).

In writing about the Heavenly sanctuary whither Christ has ascended and where Christ will exercises His mediatorship,[13] the Author of Hebrews declared: "For if the blood of goats and calves and the ashes of a heifer, sprinkling the unclean, sanctifies for the purifying of the flesh, how, much more shall the blood of Christ, who through the eternal Spirit offered Himself without spot to God, purge your conscience from dead works to serve the living God?" It should be noted that some scholars understand verse 18 to refer to the Holy Spirit.[14] Westcott and some scholars render: Christ through the eternal Spirit offered Himself etc., claiming that the absence of the articles from **pneuma aionion** depicts the spirit here a power possessed by Christ, Spirit. But it should be remembered that no man's spirit can properly be called eternal, but Christ's Spirit is in virtue of His Divine Personality eternal. Even if the Third Person of the Godhead is not spoken of as eternal, there are other Biblical passages which call the Holy Spirit as eternal.

5. The Seven Spirits of God

The title is used in Revelation 1:4 and 3:1.

The number "seven" is frequently used symbolically to denote the idea of perfection, completeness. This designation of the Holy Spirit is variously interpreted by Biblical scholars. One view is that John is called the Holy Spirit the Spirit of fullness. Still another view proposed is that it alludes to the Spirit in the perfection of His operation. Yet another proposal is that the title expresses perfect spiritual endowment (cf. Is. 11:1; Rev. 5:6). Stevenson believed that the Seven Spirits of God is a phrase which is highly symbolical, expressing absolute perfection of the Spirit in all his attributes.[15]

In relationship to the Christian Church, He is the Spirit of Christ (1 Pet. 1:11), John 15:26:7.[16] In Revelation Jesus is described as "He that hath the Seven Spirits of God," that is, has the fullness of resources to meet every need for the "seven" stars and all its people.

6. The One Spirit (Eph. 4:4)

In all the different titles revealed by Holy Writ, the product of the activity of the Holy Spirit, in the manifold ministries among people the Spirit is "one Spirit of God who made Mary pregnant, came down upon Christ at His baptism and lives in the Christian's heart. He is the Giver of all spiritual gifts bestowed upon Christ's followers."[17]

7. The Holy Spirit (Matt. 1:18; 28:19)

Holy Spirit is one of the distinctive names by which the Third Person of the Trinity is known in New Testament and in the early Literature of the Christian Church. Holiness is an attribute which essentially belongs to God. In John chapter 14, verse 26, Jesus promised to give His disciples the Paraclete, defined as: The Holy Spirit, whom the Father would send in the name of Christ. Not only is the Third Person of the Godhead holy, through Word and Sacrament He makes the true believers holy and helps to fulfill the command of God: "Be ye therefore holy, as I the Lord, your God am holy" (Lev. 119:1). The Holy Spirit is also called "The Spirit of Holiness" (Rom. 1:4). It is a Biblical teaching that while we are by nature sinful and corrupt, and not holy, may by the grace of God be made holy by the Holy Spirit's activity through the application of the means of grace (i.e. Word of God and Sacraments).[18]

8. The Spirit of Holiness (Rom. 1:4)

Stevenson in his excellent book, *The Titles of the Triune God,* in his discussion of the titles used of the Holy Spirit, considered "the Spirit of Holiness" as describing an attribute of the Holy Spirit.[19] Paul in the opening paragraph of Romans described the good news as promised in the Prophets of the Old Testament and that the Gospel "is about His Son, who was born a descendant of David, in terms of human birth, but according to his spirit of holiness, was declared to be the mighty Son of God by His resurrection" (11-40). Arndt argues that "according to the Spirit of holiness," does not refer to the Holy Spirit, but the phrase "according to the Spirit of holiness" responds "according to the flesh" in v. 3. According to Arndt, it refers to the divine nature of Christ. God is a Spirit, and therefore the expression "Spirit" is employed here, and to make it clear that the divine nature is pointed to, the genitive "of holiness" is added. On the use of the term Spirit with reference to Jesus cf. 2 Cor. 3:17. That not the Holy Spirit is meant here, the third Person of the Trinity, is evident from the fact that the Holy Spirit is always referred to differently, simply as "Spirit," or as "Spirit of God," or as "Holy Spirit."[20] The expression which we find here is never employed by Paul, or anybody else in the New Testament to designate the third Person of the Trinity. Romans 1:4 is one of the most important Christological portions of the New Testament.

9. The Spirit Wisdom (Eph. 1:17)

There is a difference among scholars whether or not the Holy Spirit is meant by Paul.

A.T. Robertson calls attention to the fact that the Revised Version does understand the Greek **pneuma** as referring to the Holy Spirit, but Robertson claims it is open to the question if it is possible to attain wisdom and revelation apart from the Holy Spirit.[21] Vincent in his Word Studies of the New Testament believes that the Holy Spirit being spoken about as giving wisdom and revelation.[22] Averred Vincent: **"Spirit** has not the article, but the reference is the Holy Spirit. Compare Matt. 12:28; Luke 1,15,35,41; Rom. 1:4; 1 Pet. 1:2. The Holy Spirit imparts general illumination (wisdom) and special revelations of divine mysteries."[23] Paul informed the congregations of Asia Minor that Christ has been made unto as wisdom (1 Cor. 1:30) and abides in us by His Holy Spirit (Gal. 2:20): All holiness we can ever know is the very life in us, the power of the resurrection (Phil. 3:10). The holiness in life which Christians should exhibit is not of their own doing, but the result of the Spirit of God.

10. The Spirit of Truth (John 14:17; 16:33)

Jesus claimed to be the truth (John 14:6). What God and the Son are as being the truth, that one would expect also the Holy Spirit to be. In His Farewell Discourse Jesus told the disciples:

"If you love, you will obey my commandments, and I will pray the Father, and he will give you another Comforter to be with you forever, the Spirit of Truth" (John 14:15-17). In the course of this discourse Jesus also declared: "I have yet many things to say to you, but you cannot hear them now. But when he is come, that Spirit of Truth, he will guide into the

1061

truth" (16:12-13). The Holy Spirit will guide to a correct understanding of the Word of God, which he caused holy men of God to record. The Spirit of Truth imparts to the believers the very life of Christ Himself The Holy Spirit as the Spirit of truth has caused to be recorded the truth about the true way of salvation, about origin and purpose of human existence.

11. The Spirit of Faith (2 Cor. 4:13).

Stevenson lists the same spirit of faith of 2 Corinthians as referring to Holy Spirit.[24] In support of this interpretation he wrote: Faith is the one factor of our salvation, the one quality in us which God requires, in response to the redemption He has provided in Christ: And of that **we cannot boast,** for it is not of ourselves, but it is a gift of God by His Spirit (Eph. 2:8). But again we must stress that faith is not just a mere **gift,** it is an activity of God in the heart, by His Spirit. And the Spirit who quickened faith in us unto salvation will lead us "from faith to faith" (Rom. 1:17); the life begun in an act of faith continues in a constancy of faith. And for every need, every demand of this life of dependence has given us "the Spirit of faith."

Vincent in His **Word Studies in the New Testament** contends that "the same spirit of faith and refers to what follows after verse 13." Opined this scholar: "Spirit of faith: Not distinctly the Holy Spirit, nor, on the other hand, a human faculty or disposition, but blending both; faith as a gift of the Spirit of God."[25]

12. The Spirit of Grace (Heb. 10:29).

Alford believed that grace characterized the Spirit, thus it would be proper to list "Spirit of Grace as describing the Third Person of the Godhead."[26] This title sums up what God has caused to work in human hearts. One passage of Paul sets forth the importance of God's grace: "By grace are you saved and that not of yourselves, it is a gift of God." The willingness for the Holy Spirit to convert and sanctify people is prompted by "grace." As Paul also stated it in Romans 8:34: "With Christ he freely gives us all good things."

13. The Spirit of Adoption (Rom. 8:15)

As a result of Christ fulfilling the demands of the law for mankind, and paying the penalty of mankind's sins, and through conversion, regeneration and justification the elect of God have become "sons of God." In Romans 8, in which the glorious freedom of the Gospel is described, Paul declares: "And because you are sons, God hath sent forth the spirit of His son into your hearts, crying, 'Abba Father.'" Paul also assured the Roman Christians "For only those are sons of God who are led by God's Spirit. For you have not received a Spirit of slavery in order that you should be afraid, but you have received the Spirit of adoption in order that you be no more afraid, but you have received the spirit of adoption in which we cry out: My father, my dear Father."[27] "For His Spirit himself bears witness to our spirit, that we are the children of God (Rom. 8:16)."

The Spirit of adoption leads believers in a privileged relationship and thus—

14. The Spirit of Your Father (Matt. 10:20)

Jesus told His disciples that in their salvatory work they would meet with opposition and persecution. When they are brought before Jewish and Roman authorities, they should not worry: "For it will be given you in that very hour, for it will not be you as speaker but the Spirit of your Father who speaks in you (Matt. 10:20-21)." Every good gift comes from God (James 1:17) who hath blessed us with all spiritual blessings in heavenly places (Eph. 1:3). It is the Holy Spirit bestows all blessings on the children of God.

Further the Spirit is—

15. The Spirit of Life (Rom. 8:2; Rev. 11:11)

On Maundy Thursday evening Jesus told His disciples: "I am the way, the truth and the life" (John 14:6). In his first epistle John declared: "He that has the Son has life (5:12)." As a result of the Spirit's indwelling, eternal life has begun. It is the Holy Spirit who produces new life in sinners, dead in trespasses, by opening up the fountains of life. In one of His discourses Jesus promised His followers: "He that believeth in me, as the Scripture says, out of his belly (Inner man) shall flow rivers of living water." John informs his readers "This spake He of the Spirit, which they that believe on Him should receive: For the Holy Spirit was not yet given, because Jesus was not yet glorified (John 7:37-38)." The Holy Spirit causes the perennial welling up of grace within the hearts of believers.

16. The Comforter (John 14:16; 15:26).

On His way to the Garden of Gethsemane the Savior assured his disciples: "If you love me, you will obey my commandments. And I will ask the Father, and He will give you another Advocate to be forever with you — the Spirit of truth. That Spirit the world cannot receive, because it does not see Him or know Him. You know Him, because He remains by your side." The word "counsellor" found in the King James Version does not completely reproduce the Greek "paracletos." The New King James renders "paracletos" as "Helper." The Greek word means "called to the side to help." Inexhaustible wealth of promise is contained within that word. Stevenson claims: "It means that He is **ever present** with the believer; and ever present to help, to be all that Christ in His wondrous grace is. The Spirit brings the presence, the resources, of the Lord Himself." [28]

Only the Christian religion has such a comforting doctrine of the person and work of the Holy Spirit. Murray has well sized up the importance of the Holy Spirit when he wrote: "The destructive glory of the dispensation of the Spirit is His divine personal indwelling in the heart of the believer, there to reveal the Father and the Son."[29]

Footnotes

1. Leon J. Wood, *The Holy Spirit in the Old Testament* (Grand Rapids: Zondervan Publishing House, 1956), p. 17; H. G. Leupold, *Exposition of Genesis* (Grand Rapids: Baker Book House, 1942), I, p. 49.

2. Herbert F. Stevenson, *Titles of the Triune God* (Westwood, N. J., Fleming H. Revell Company, 1956).

3. W. H. Griffith Thomas, *The Holy Spirit* (Grand Rapids: Kregel Publications, 1986). Reprint of 1913, published by W. Eerdmans Publishing House, Grand Rapids;

Wood, **op. cit.**, pp. 23-24.

4. Stevenson, **op. cit.**, p. 170.

5. Cited by Stevenson, **op. cit.**, p. 170.

6. *A Short Explanation of Dr. Martin Luther's Small Catechism* (St. Louis: Concordia Publishing House, 1943) pp. 124-125.

7. Henry Barclay Sweet, *The Holy Spirit in the New Testament* (Grand Rapids: Baker Book House, 1976). Reprint of 1910 edition, issued in London, 417 pp.

8. George Johnston, "Spirit: in Alan Richardson, *A Theological Word Book of the Bible*, Alan Richardson, editor (New York: The Macmillan Company, 1950), pp.237-287a.; Joseph Haroutunian,

"Spirit, Holy Spirit," Alan Richardson, *A Dictionary of Christian Theology* (Philadelphia: Westminster Press, 1969), pp. 318-327.

9. Stevenson, **op. cit.**, p. 175.

10. Cited by Stevenson, p. 177.

11. Griffith Thomas, **op. cit.**, p. 33.

12. Stevenson, **op. cit.**, p. 177.

13. Marvin R. Vincent, *Word Studies in the New Testament* (Grand Rapids: Wm. B. Eerdmans Publishing Company, 1975, a reprint of 1887 edition IV, pp. 483-484.

14. Cf also Kenneth S. Wuest, Wuest's *Word Studies From the Greek New Testament* (Grand Rapids, Wm. B. Eermans Publishing Company, II., pp. 161-162.

15. Stevenson, **op. cit.**, p. 177.

16. **Ibid.**, p. 177.

17. Cf. Henry Alford, *The New Testament for English Readers* (Chicago: Moody Press, no date), p. 1228.

18. E.W.A. Koehler, *A Summary of Christian Doctrine* (Oakland, Calif.; 1952), pp. 128, 190-191.

19. Stevenson, **op. cit.**, p. 178.

20. William Arndt, *Mimeographed Lecture Note on Romans* (St. Louis: Concordia Seminary Mimeograph Company, 1931), pp. 1-2.

21. A. T. Robertson, *Word Pictures in the New Testament* (Nashville: Broadman Press, 1930), IV, p. 520.

22. Vincent, *Word Studies in the New Testament*, **op. cit.**, p. 370.

23. **Ibid.**, p. 371.

24. **Ibid.**, p. 179.

25. Vincent, **op. cit.**, III, p. 313.

26. Alford, **op. cit.**, p. 1109.

27. Translation of Helen Barrett Montgomery, *The New Testament in Modern English. The Centenary Translation* (Philadelphia: The Judson Press, 1924), p. 415 (Rom. 8:14-15).

28. Stevenson, **op. cit.**, p. 181.

29. Andrew Murray as cited by Stevenson, **op. cit.**, p. 170.

Questions

1. Holy Scripture depicts the Holy Spirit as present and active on ____.

2. Some of the same gifts and graces ascribed to the Son of God are also predicated of ____.

3. The New Testament never portrays the ____ as an agent of God as do the ____.

1064

4. Is the Holy Spirit a subordinate representative of the Godhead? ____
5. The title "seven" is frequently used to denote ____.
6. Who made Mary pregnant? ____
7. Who is the Paraclete? ____
8. The holiness of life which Christians should exhibit is the result of ____.
9. The Comforter is the Spirit of ____.
10. Faith is not just a mere gift but it is ____.
11. The willingness of the Holy Spirit to convert and sanctify people is prompted by ____.
12. Jesus told his disciples that in their salvatory work they would meet ____.
13. Who produces new life in sinners? ____
14. The Greek word "paraclete" means ____.

Thanksgiving

The First Public and Most Famous of Thanksgiving Services in World History and Its Relationship to the 1997 Thanksgiving Observance

Christian News, November 24, 1997

Each year the President of the United States calls on the citizenry of the land to give thanks to God for the blessings God has bestowed upon the fifty states the past year. Christians are glad to respond to this presidential proclamation, and would otherwise in some manner give thanks to the Triune God for the past year's blessings.

In Lutheranism it has been customary for congregations to observe The Festival of Harvest, thanking the Almighty for the fruits of the harvest so necessary for human existence.[1] In Germany and other lands it was customary to celebrate the Harvest Festival on a Sunday after the harvests had been gathered in.

Many sixteen-century Lutheran Orders (Calenberg, 1542, Osnabrueck 1543, Hilderheim, 1544, Prussia 1558) combined it with Saint Michael's Day (September 29). Others celebrated Harvest Home on either the Sunday before or after Saint Michael's Day. This custom was brought to America from Europe before the various presidential proclamations, as George Washington did in 1789 and President Madison in 1812, or in 1858 when twenty-five governors annually appointed thanksgiving days or President Lincoln in 1863 who appointed a National Day of Thanksgiving. Since that time each president followed suit and designated the last Thursday in November as a day of thanksgiving.[2]

Thanksgiving God's Will According to the Old and New Testaments

Christians who consider and believe that the Bible is God's Word, if they obey it, and direct their lives by its teachings, can hardly miss the many references to the giving of thanks which God expects of his followers. Each Testament has a special thanks vocabulary.[3] In the Hebrew Old Testament **"adah"** and **"yada"** are the usual words, found over sixty times in various books of the Old Covenant Scripture.[4] There are many exhortations in twenty-six different Psalms to give thanks.

The noun for thanksgiving is **"todah."** One of the sacrifices commanded by God, the meal offering was a sacrifice of thanksgiving (Lev. 2).

The New Testament uses a number of different words for giving thanks, such as **eucharisteo** "to thank," **ekshomolgeomai** "give glory to," "echo charin," "to have favor."[6] Besides direct commands to give thanks, there are also the examples of Jesus and Paul on different occasions giving God thanks. There are over a hundred Biblical passages encouraging followers of God to express appreciation for blessings bestowed.

The World's First Public Thanksgiving Service

The earliest example of a public thanksgiving is recorded in Genesis 8:20: "And Noah built an altar to Yahweh, and he took of all clean cattle and of all clean birds and offered a burnt offering upon the altar." Many commentators do not consider this sacrifice an expression of gratitude of the people who had been spared a watery death.[7] This was more than simply an ordinary sacrifice. This was an occasion, when Noah in the presence of the seven others who had been preserved alive, was expressing deep felt thanks and appreciation for the gift of life. Correctly Leupold observed: "In view of the whole preceding situation and the natural feelings of gratitude that must have possessed the heart of any one or any group, that they alone have been spared in a universal catastrophe, we find the ruling out of the idea of thanksgiving in connection with sacrifice to be preposterous. The purpose of thanksgiving and of propitiation blend in this sacrifice."[8]

This is the first reference to an altar in the Bible. Genesis 4:26, which reads: "Then men began to call on the LORD (Yahweh)," but it does not mention an altar. Possibly Enosh may have used his father's altar. We do not know when altars originated, whethering in Adam's time or Noah's. The Hebrew word for altar was "Mizbeach," and strictly means "the place of slaughter."[9] This altar was raised to Yahweh, because Noah is mindful of the gracious fidelity which God so mercifully displayed.

Leupold contends that this is another supporting argument that Noah's offering was an offering of thanksgiving. Noah, his wife, Ham, Shem and Japheth and their three wives—eight people—were the first participants in the public service of thanksgiving, a unique occasion in the early history of mankind.

The Historic Occasion For the Giving of
Thanks By Noah and His Family

These eight people accepted God's invitation to enter the ark, built by Noah, who after one hundred and twenty years of grace had elapsed and Noah's preaching to his generation had failed, God caused them to enter and closed the ark's door. According to Genesis 7:2 "the fountains of the great deep were opened and the windows of heaven were opened." It rained upon the earth forty days and forty nights. The water prevailed upon the earth one hundred and fifty days. After the one hundred and fifty days the water began to decrease. Then the ark rested the seventeenth day of the month on the mountains of Ararat (8:4).[10] On the tenth month, on the first day of the month, the tops of the mountains were seen. Forty days later Noah sent out a raven from the ark after having opened the window of the ark. Because the raven could not find a resting place it returned to the ark. Then after some time another raven was sent forth. The third time this bird found a resting place and did not return (7:8-12). After fifty seven days Noah was commanded by God to go forth from the ark.

Noah's Sacrifice of Thanksgiving and God's Response

Noah offered clean beasts and clean fowl and the post-flood report of Moses was to the effect that they were accepted by Yahweh. Wrote Leupold: "This sacrifice presents one of the most solemn scenes of all history: Round about, the earth which is rapidly rejuvenating: The background the most awful catastrophe in the annals of mankind; above the true and faithful Yahweh, who is man's only Hope."[11]

The participants in this first public thanksgiving soon found out how God reacted to Noah's sacrifice offered on behalf of the eight people for whom a second beginning for the continuance of the human race was being made. Moses has recorded the manner in which God responded to Noah's offering of clean beasts and clean birds. "When Yahweh smelled the pleasant odor. He said within his heart: Never again will I curse the ground for man's sake, because the imagination of man's heart is evil from his youth; never will I smite all living things as I have done (8:22)." The Lord regarded Noah's sacrifice of thanksgiving as "a sweet savor" or more literally a "smell of satisfaction." God promised that never again would there be a universal destruction of the whole earth by a flood (v. 22: cf. 9:9-17). As has been pointed, if Noah's flood was merely a local flood, then the Lord has not kept His promise for there have been many local floods. One of the most catastrophic floods in the history of America was the Johnstown flood of 1889. Rehwinkel in his book *The Flood* has listed a number of them.[12]

God's Covenant with Noah about the Future

To this initial promise of verse 21, God ties up several more, all in the spirit of the first and displaying the generous measures the same grace that He had promised in the first. At this first great thanksgiving celebration God promised Noah, "that as long as the earth shall stand, seed time and harvest, summer and winter, cold and heat, and day and night shall not cease (v. 24)." This promise has been kept by God in His dealings with mankind. What wonderful promises God made at the first universal thanksgiving service to this audience of eight. They were told as God's creatures they needed not to fear such a great tragedy as that produced by the Deluge, whose evidences remained on all sides. Noah's descendants and their descendants could depend on several regular features as long as the earth would remain. A knowledge of this fact makes for a stability of life and creates peace of mind. Leupold believed that the regular variation of times and seasons is not regarded as merely natural, fixed by nature's but as an outgrowth of God's specific promise.[13] Yahweh promised "seedtime" and "harvest" which are necessary to sustain life on planet earth. "Cold and heat" are next mentioned, because of the part they play in "seedtime" and "harvest." "Heat and cold" are found in "summer and winter." Finally God promised the alternation of "day and night." If there were no daytime when the sun could be active there would be no growth and food for animals and men and women. What God promised in verse 24 are needful for the survival of mankind and for the animals of whom it depends.

The Relation to the Noahic Promise and Today's Thanksgiving

The first public thanksgiving held at the conclusion of the worldwide Deluge[14] is related to our celebration in 1997, because intermittently the promises given to Noah have occurred and the harvests that have been realized throughout the world could not have happened had not the promises given at the first national thanksgiving been promised by God. In certain continents, like Africa, God has withheld rain so that there could be no real seedtime and the resultant harvests could not occur. Some continents have been receiving too much rain, again making impossible seedtime and harvest. While many rule out God from working through nature and controlling its forces, let us recognize that God not only has created the universe but also that he preserves it.[15]

The many teachings about the providence of God are completely ignored. If for our readers there has been seedtime and harvest, summer and winter, day and night, we have much to thank the giver of all good things, and recognize Him as our only hope for healthy living, as the spiritual blessings which God has made available to those who believe in Him and trust Him.

Footnotes

1. Luther D. Reed, *The Lutheran Liturgy* (Philadelphia: Muhlenberg Press, 1947), p. 513.
2. **Ibid.**
3. Robert Young, *Analytical Concordance to the Bible*. Twentieth Edition by Wm. Stevenson (New York: Funk and Wagnells Company, No Date), pp. 969-970. Zondervan Expanded Concordance
(Grand Rapids: Zondervan Publishing House, 1968), pp. 1411-1412.
4. William Wilson, *Old Testament Word Studies* (Grand Rapids: Kregel Publications, 1978), p. 443.
5. Ludwig Koehler and Walter Baumgaertner, *Lexicon in Veteris Testamenti Libros* (Leiden: E. J. Brill, 1950), p. 1020.
6. Young, **op. cit.,** pp. 969-970.
7. Charles Pfeiffer, *The Book of Genesis* (Grand Rapids: Baker Book House, 1959), p. 83; Leon Wood, *Genesis - Bible Study Commentary*, 1975), p. 50; Charles T. Fritsch, *The Book of Genesis* (Richmond: John Knox Press, 1959), p. 44; Derek Kidner, *Genesis* (Chicago: Inter-Varsity Press, p. 109); Francis Schaeffer, *Genesis in Space and Time* (Downers Grove: Inter-Varsity Press, 1972), p. 145; Alan Richardson, *Genesis I to XI* (London: SCM Press, 1953), p. 104.
8. H.C. Leupold, *Exposition of Genesis* (Grand Rapids: Baker Book House, 1942), p. 321.
9. **Ibid.,** p. 321.
10. For a time schedule of the events connected with the Flood, cf. Wood, **op. cit.,** p. 49.
11. Leupold, **op. cit.,** p. 322.
12. Alfred M. Rehwinkel, *The Flood, In the Light of the Bible, Geology, and Archaeology* (St. Louis: Concordia Publishing House, 1951), p. 330.
13. Leupold, **op. cit.,** p. 324.
14. John Whitcomb and Henry Morris, *The Genesis Flood* (Philadelphia: Presbyterian

and Reformed Publishing House, 1961), pp. 1-35; Arthur C. Custance, *The Flood: Local or Global* (Grand Rapids: Zondervan Publishing House, 1963), pp. 28-43.

15. Cf. John T. Mueller, *Christian Dogmatics* (St. Louis: Concordia Publishing House, 1955), pp. 189-191.

Questions

1. Who appointed a National Day of Thanksgiving in 1858? ____
2. What does eucharisteo mean? ____
3. What is the first reference to an altar in the Bible? ____
4. Who were the first participants in the first public thanksgiving service? ____
5. "The imagination of man's heart is ____.
6. What makes for stability of life and creates peace of mind despite all talk about Global Warming? ____

The Advent and Christmas Hymns of Luke's Gospel

Christian News, December 15, 1997

There is an interesting parallel to be found between the Advent, Christmas and post-Christmas events celebrated in Christian liturgies of the Advent, Christmas and Epiphany seasons and the first and second chapters of Luke's Gospel. Luke 1 parallels the liturgical propers used in the Advent season. Luke 2 records the fulfillment of the prophecy of chapter 1 that Mary would give birth to a Son. The third Gospel records the happenings that occurred in connection with Christ's birth. His presentation in the Jerusalem Temple, His visit to Jerusalem at the age of twelve, and a summary statement of Jesus' life between his twelfth and thirtieth birthday.

All the Bible readers know about the first thirty years of Christ's life are found in the first two chapters of Matthew's Gospel and the first two chapters of Luke's Gospel.[1] In the accounts of John the Baptist's birth, Mary's receiving the message other future Virgin Birth. Christ's birth and presentation in the Temple are imbedded in five hymns (including the Hail Mary). Because of these hymns Luke has been called "the Hymnologist of the Christian Church."[2]

The following are the five hymns of Luke, chapters 1 and 2: 1. At the annunciation (the Hail Mary), the Magnificat of Mary, the Benedictus of Zecharias, the Gloria in Excelsis of the angel chorus and the Nunc Dimittis of Simeon. These five hymns have influenced the liturgies of the Eastern Church, the Greek Orthodox Churches, the Roman Catholic, the Episcopalian, the Lutheran Church and the Methodist Episcopal Church. The Eastern and Western Churches have adopted all five, the Protestant Churches four of them. The Ave Maria (Hail Mary) is a Roman Catholic prayer to Mary consisting of Luke 1:28, 42 and a precatory sentence: "Holy Mary, mother of God. Pray for us sinners now and in the hour of our death" added in the 15th century. Paul V ordered its daily use in 1568. Together with the Credo and Pater Noster the Hail Mary was to be spoken each day and is the repeated prayer of the Rosary and the Angelus.

Advent and Christmas In the Lutheran Ecclesiastical Year

Advent begins on November 30 (St. Andrew's Day) or thereafter and has four weeks with four Sundays.[3] The Advent season is designed to prepare the faithful for a worthy celebration of the feast of the Incarnation.[4] The great design of Advent is to create the spiritual conditions and attitudes for a God-pleasing celebration of the fact that the Word became flesh (John 1:14).

Other comings of Christ are also recalled by means of the different propers of the Advent services.[5] Christians are reminded that they are strangers and pilgrims upon earth and that Jesus will again come a second time and that Jesus will gather His flock and also hold a general judgment. Christmas, however, will be meaningless. If those who wish to be with the Lord have not accepted Jesus as their personal Savior, Advent is considered a penitential season, during which Christians should take stock of their lives and repent of their sins, those both of omission and commission.[6]

December 24, 6 p.m.
Christmas Begins
The Advent season technically ends on December 24, 5:59 p.m. and at 6 p.m. Christmas begins with Christmas Eve service. Thus it may be said that Advent glides silently into Christmas.

As far as the Gospel of Luke is concerned the historic events of chapter 2 follow immediately after chapter 1, and thus one might say that the happenings of chapter 1 glide into chapter 2. Chapters 1 and 2 constitute a unity. Chapter 2:1-20 gives the account of the fulfillment of Genesis 3:15; Isaiah 9:5-6; and Micah 5:2, also validating the message of Gabriel to Mary in Nazareth.

An Analysis of the Contents of Luke
Chapters 1 and 2
In chapter 1 John the Baptist receives considerable attention in w . 8-27; and w. 57-63. In verses 8-27 it is the angel Gabriel who is the speaker, while in v. 57 it was John's father, the priest Zecharias. In both chapters land 2 the supernatural and miraculous dominate in terms of the appearance of the angel Gabriel who brought Zecharias and Mary of Nazareth messages. In chapter 2 Luke records the miraculous virgin birth of Jesus, the appearance of an angel to shepherds and the heavenly appearance of a host of angels.

Chapter 1 records two different responses to the messages of the angel Gabriel. When Zecharias was told that his wife Elizabeth in her old age was to have a son, he questioned and doubted it. Because of his doubt he could not speak until the day of the circumcision and naming of his son John. Mary on the other hand was surprised by the message that, even though not married, she was going to bear a son. She wondered how this possibly could be, but believed the angel Gabriel. She accepted the fact that the Holy Spirit would come over her and cause her pregnancy and on a visit to Elizabeth conveyed the message that she was to bear Him "who would redeem His people from their sins."[7]

The Fulfillment of Gabriel's Prophecy
Luke records the fact that Elizabeth, no longer of childbearing age, became pregnant and was visited by Mary, who when Mary greeted her, the babe in Elizabeth's womb leaped for joy. The last part of chapter 1 informs the reader that John the Baptist was circumcised and named. At the latter ceremony Zecharias received his speech back. All that the Biblical readers know of the childhood, adolescence and growing to manhood of John is given in verse 80: "and the child grew continually, and became strong in the Spirit, and remained ever in the desert till the day

of his showing to Israel."

Mary's Magnificat

Mary's song breathes a calm deep, inward response and a sense of profound gratitude (w. 46-51). It is modelled on Hannah's song of praise and contains several sentences from the Psalms. It seems that Mary was familiar with the Old Testament Scriptures. She was acquainted with the Messianic prophecies, as is shown by the conclusion of her hymn of praise, "as he spoke to our forefathers, to Abraham, and his offspring forever" (v. 55).

The Canticles of the Liturgy

The Magnificat is one of the canticles that was adopted and developed in the liturgical churches. *The Concordia Cyclopedia* defined a canticle as "non-metrical spiritual songs, psalms, or hymns, taken directly from Scripture and used in the Church from the earliest times, usually chanted at the prescribed place in the services."[8] In some instances the Bible-text has been paraphrased to some extent; in others it has been retained practically unchanged.

The following are those used:

1. **Gloria Patri**, "Glory to the Father and the Son and the Holy Ghost," based upon the baptismal formula (Matt. 28:19), a paraphrase in use since the first century, also known as the Lesser Doxology;
2. **The Gloria in Excelsis**, or song of the angels, Luke 2,14, enlarged into a hymn of adoration celebrating the glory and majesty of God as manifested in the merciful gift of His Son;
3. **The Tersanctus**, or hymn "Holy, Holy, Holy," a combination of the hymn of the seraphim before the throne of God, Is. 6,2,3 and of the multitudes that went forth at the time of His triumphal entry into Jerusalem, Matt. 21,9, the section chanted by the people being taken from the great Hallel of the Jewish festival season, Ps. 118, 25,26.
4. **The Nunc Dimittis** of the aged Simeon, sung at the Communion Service as well as Vespers;
5. **The Te Deum Laudamus**, a hymn of praise, whose authorship is ascribed either to Athanasius or Ambrosius, which includes praise, confession of faith, and petition, sung in the morning service, or matins;
6. **The Benedicte**, beginning "O all ye works of the Lord bless ye the Lord," from the Song of Three Holy Children, in the Apocrypha;
7. **The Magnificat**, beginning "my soul doth magnify the Lord," the song of praise of the Virgin Mary, Luke 1,46-55;
8. **The Benedictus**, "blessed be the Lord God of Israel," the song of praise intoned by Zecharias, 1,68-79, used especially in festival services at Christmastide.

The Liturgical Use of The Magnificat

The Magnificat and The Nunc Dimittis are regularly appointed for Vespers.[9] The use of The Magnificat is proper on all festivals and may also be employed at other times. Reed claims that the Christian emphasis also appears in the use of the Gloria Patriat the end of the canticle.

This specifically recognizes the fact that He Who lives and reigns with the Father and the Spirit forever and ever is our Mediator and that as St. Paul says, it is right for us "to give thanks always for all things on to God and the Father in the name of our Lord Jesus Christ" (Eph. 5:20).

The use of the Gloria Patri here incorporates Mary's specific thanksgiving into a more general thanksgiving. [10]

The Benedictus of Zechariah

Zechariah spoke his hymn of praise at the birth of his son John (1:57-80). The Song is based on the Old Testament Messianic prophecies and is full of the idea of redemption. McNichol claimed:

"It shows that the spiritual significance of the Messianic age which was now being ushered in was well understood by the devout souls in Israel. He gives thanks for the coming of the Messiah, which implies that Zecharias knew of the incarnation and looked for the deliverance which His presence is about to procure for Israel (67-75). Then he expressed the joy at the part his son was assigned and the song overflows with a closing thanksgiving for the Messianic salvation (76-79)."[11] Zechariah announced his Son would be the way preparer for the Messiah. The priests Zechariah called Jesus the Dayspring on high who would be born to give light to those sitting in darkness and to guide his followers into paths of peace. The Benedicttis is Zechariah's song of thanksgiving and is cast in Jewish form, though its sentiment is truly Christian. The Benedictus is one of the three New Testament canticles which commemorates the incarnation. The other two are the Magnificat and The Nunc Dimittis. As early as the fourth century these three hymns were appended to the Book of Psalms, the hymn book of the early Christian Church.[12]

In the West the Benedictus was sung every morning after the Lesson (The Chapter at Lauds), which was spoken at dawn in thanksgiving of the coming of the world's redeemer and also because of the reference to The Dayspring on High who has visited His people.[13] The Benedictus came into the liturgy of the Lutheran Church at the time of the Reformation.

Liturgically speaking, the Benedictus is proper for the four Sundays of Advent, and from Septuagesima till Palm Sunday. It may be used at any time and sometimes is employed as an alternative for the **Te Deum**.[14]

Chapter 1, the Advent chapter, ends with a summary statement about what happened after John's birth, circumcision and naming till at the age of thirty he began to preach in the Judean wilderness: "Repent, for the kingdom of God has come." Thus verse 80 reads: "And the child grew continually, and became strong in the Spirit, and remained in the desert till the day of his showing to Israel."

Luke 2—The Christmas Chapter and Certain Post-Christmas Events

One of the outstanding passages in world literature is the Lukan account of Christ's birth (w. 1-20). Its rendition in The Authorized Version in English is in inimitable prose. Luke's account begins with a historical note (w. 1-3), with the decree of Caesar Augustus for a worldwide Roman census. The imperial decree necessitated Joseph and Mary, both of the house and lineage of David, to go to Bethlehem, where David once lived. The prophet Micah in 5:2 had predicted that the Messiah was to be born in Bethlehem, in Judea. Under the most humble circumstance the Lord of the world was born. At His birth an angel host was heard singing: "Glory to God in the highest and peace on earth to men of good will." This verse, the basis for the Canticle, called "The Glory in Excelsis" has been rendered differently. The Authorized Version translated: "Glory to God in the highest and on earth peace, good will to men." The *Revised Standard Version* has: "Glory in the highest, and on earth peace among men with whom he is pleased." According to Alford a reading favored by the Alexandrine, Vatican, and Sinaiticus is "among men of good pleasure."[15] The latter are the elect of God's people. The song of the heavenly chorus occurred after an angel appeared to the shepherds on Bethlehem's field and informed these men that the Savior had been born. Thus the miraculous dominates the account of Christ's Incarnation.

The Gloria in Excelsis

The song of the angel choir became the introduction to a larger hymn of praise, "The Gloria in Excelsis." Reed contends that "in its original form the Gloria in Excelsis was a private Psalm, sung in Greek in the morning office but not as a part of the Mass. It is considered to be of Eastern origin."[16] It is seen by liturgiologists as the only surviving complete example of compositions improvised in the early Christian assemblies as expression of fervid devotion. In spirit it is akin to the Magnificat and the Benedictus.

For the Wording of The Gloria in Excelsis the reader should consult *The Lutheran Hymnal*, or *The Lutheran Book of Worship*. The Gloria in Excelsis follows the Kyrie and changes the mood of the worshipper.[17] It is an outburst of joy and praise to the Holy Trinity and lifts the worship from thoughts of self to contemplation of the Divine and from consciousness of human need to glorification of God's majesty, power and holiness.

Scholars like Parsch believe that the middle part of the Gloria in Excelsis was the earliest form, and that it consisted of a series of acclamations addressed to Christ and that the address to the Father was added later and the opening verse: "Glory to God on high and on earth peace, good will toward men" last of all.[18] Besides being a hymn of praise to the Father, it is especially a hymn of redemption. Thus early in the service it grounds the participants' worship and faith.

'The Gloria in Excelsis is omitted during Advent and from Septuagesima till Easter, because the Advent and Lenten Sundays are considered to be penitential seasons.[19]

The Second Christmas Hymn of Luke 2

The Nunc Dimittis is the second Christmas hymn in chapter 2 of the Lukan Gospel. It is the last of the New Testament Evangelical Canticles.

This hymn is taken from the Latin words of the Vulgate, "Lord now lettest Thou thy servant depart in peace." The word peace occurs in both Christmas Canticles and is used in two different senses, the first relates to the fact that the warfare between God and His creation would be eliminated by the Savior and the second refers to the feeling of complete happiness and contentment Simeon felt because he knew that God had kept His promises of old and he could come to God in death as a forgiven sinner. The Nunc Dimittis is also known as "The Song of Simeon."

The occasion for the utterance of these words was on the fortieth day after Christ's birth when Mary presented herself for purification because of being unclean which would not agree with Roman Catholic teaching of Mary's Immaculate Conception. Simeon, an old man, was looking for the redemption of Israel and by the Holy Spirit was caused to go to the temple where Joseph and Mary complied with the Law of Moses about births of male infants and Simeon took the Christ Child in his arms and made a pronouncement that set forth a number of facts; 1. He was privileged to See the Christ, the Salvation-bringer, and 2. this salvation was also to be for the Gentiles and, 3. would rebound to the glory of Israel. Simeon, under inspiration of the Holy Spirit, predicted Jesus would be a source of blessing for those accepting Him and a reason for downfall for those rejecting Him. Simeon's address to Mary (vv. 33-35) showed that he had insight of the meaning of the prophecies which foreshadowed the sufferings of the Messiah. The great suffering of Christ on Holy Thursday and Good Friday was predicted by Simeon.

Anna, the aged prophetess, who in some respects confirmed Simeon's prophecies, gave thanks to *God* for Christ and the salvation he would effect. Her words (w. 36-38) showed that she was one of a group of individuals looking for the coming of the Messiah. Anna proclaimed her faith in Jesus and encouraged others to accept the Messiah. Like the Magnificat, the Nunc Dimittis contains allusions to the Old Testament (Is. 52:10; Psalm 98:2; and Is. 42:6).

The Liturgical Use of Nunc Dimittis

The Nunc Dimittis is one of the eight canticles developed and employed in worship of the Eastern and Western Churches. Later in the days of the Reformation the Anglican and Lutheran Churches also included it in their liturgies. Relative to its employment in church services, Reed wrote: "There is a fine appropriateness in the use of this Canticle for Vespers. Bright morning hymns and the jubilant Te Deum belong to the Matins. The quieter evening hymn, and this, the shortest and tenderest of the Canticles belongs to the close of day. It is a hymn of parting and a prayer for peace and rest, in view of the end of the day and the close of life, sleep being a type of death. Its opening words suggest the figure of a sentinel who seeks permission to depart after a long vigil; or more agreeable with oriental usage, the figure of a guest departing after a visit. Like the Magnificat, it contains allusions to the Old Testament (Is. 52:10; Ps. 98:2; Is. 42:6). In our own use of it, we like Simeom appropriate God's salvation in Christ and affirm our belief that God's promises in Him are meant for the whole world."[20]

Freeman in his book, *The Principles of Divine Service*, asserted about the relationship of The Nunc Dimittis to the Incarnation, the Holy Communion and The Evening Office as follows: "It originally occurred in an office (the Eastern Vespers) in which the True Light had symbolically been brought in, in the form of the Gospels; the summary of the Eucharistic Epistle read; and other features of the great Rite imitated or paralleled. It was a thanksgiving, therefore, not for the incarnation only, but for Eucharistic consummation . . . and for the Apostolic announcement to all nations of the finished work of salvation.... These great topics then, associated with the Eventide of the world and of the day, may well be in people's thought when reciting The Nunc Dimittis."[21]

Earliest History of the Usage of The Nunc Dimittis

Luke 2:25-32, it is believed, was a Canticle used in the ancient Office of Lights. The Apostolic Constitutions of the fourth century (Book VII: 48) mention The Nunc Dimittis. Though the Canticle was used in Eastern Church at Vespers, it eventually entered the Western Church through the Benedictine Office of Compline. In the Feast of the Purification it was rendered with great solemnity.[22]

The Nunc Dimittis in the Lutheran Liturgy

When Luther cleansed the church year and the liturgy of all unscriptural elements, the Lutheran Orders introduced this Canticle from Compline and appointed the Nunc Dimittis as an alternate for The Magnificat. It was also given as an additional Canticle to be sung at the close of Vespers.[23]

Footnotes

1. Adam Fahling, *Harmony of the Gospels* (Grand Rapids: Zondervan Publishing House, No Date), p. 77; 17-26.
2. D.A. Hayes, *The Synoptic Gospels and the Book of Acts* (New York: The Methodist Book Concern, 1919), pp. 260-261.
3. James Brauer, "The Church Year," Fred L. Precht, Editor, *Lutheran Worship* (St. Louis: CPH, 1993), pp. 156,161.
4. Paul Zellar Strodach, *The Church Year* (Philadelphia: The United Lutheran Publication House, 1924), p. 26; Walker Gwynne, *The Christian Year* (New York: Longman Green & Co., 1915), p. 54.
5. Alfred Jeremias, *Leben im Kirchenjahr* (Leipzig: Adopf Klein Verlag, 1928), p. 17.
6. **Ibid.**, p. 18.
7. For a brief discussion of Luke, chapters 1-2, cf. Charles R., *The Gospel of Luke*, 1931, pp. 21-45.
8. "Canticles," in L. Fuerbringer, Th. Engelder and P. E. Kretzmann, *The Concordia Cyclopedia* (St. Louis: Concordia Publishing House, 1927),pp. 110-111.
9. Luther P. Reed, *The Lutheran Liturgy* (Philadelphia: Muhlenberg Press, 1947), p. 415.
10. **Ibid.**, p. 415.
11. John McNichol, *Thinking Through the Bible* (Grand Rapids: Kregel Publications,

1976), p. 190.

12. Reed, **op. cit.,** p. 396.

13. **Ibid.,** p. 396.

14. **Ibid.**

15. Henry Alford, *The New Testament for English Readers* (Chicago: Moody Press, No Date), p. 304.

16. Reed, **op. cit.,** p. 258.

17. **Ibid.,** p. 256.

18. Pius Parsch, *The Liturgy of the Mass* (St. Louis: Herder, 1939), p. 99.

19. Reed, **op. cit.,** p. 259.

20. **Ibid.,** p. 417.

21. Philip Freeman, *The Principles of the Divine Service* (London: Henry, 1866), Vol. 1, pp.

22. Reed, **op. cit.,** p. 417.

23. **Ibid.,** p. 417.

Question

1. Luke has been called the ____.
2. Advent begins on ____.
3. The Advent season is designed to ____.
4. Christians are ____ and ____ on earth.
5. Advent is considered a ____ season.
6. Christmas begins with the ____.
7. What happened to Elizabeth when Mary greeted her? ____
8. Who is the author of the Magnificat? ____
9. What is a canticle? ____
10. What is the Gloria in Excelsis? ____
11. When is the Nunc Dimittis used? ____
12. When may the Magnificat be used?____
13. The Benedictus came into the liturgy of the Lutheran Church at the time of ____.
14. What dominates the account of Christ's Incarnation? ____
15. When is the Gloria in Excelsis omitted? ____
16. The Nunc dimittis is also known as ____.
17. What does not agree with the teaching of Mary's Immaculate Conception? ____
18. Simeon predicted ____.

Advent and Christianity

Dear Pastor Otten:
You may possibly use the enclosed essay as spiritual and devotional reading for Advent and Christmas.
Enclosed please find a presentation:
"Advent and Christmas Prophecies in Isaiah and Micah, Two Eighth Century G.C. Prophets."
Yours in Christ,
Raymond Surburg

A Study for the Feast of the Circumcision and Naming of Christ (January 1)
The Name Above Every Name: Jesus

Christian News, December 29, 1997

When Jesus was circumcised on the eighth day. He was given the name of Jesus (Luke 2:21). Stevenson correctly has asserted: "Of all names ascribed to our Lord Jesus Christ, the best beloved by Christians, is the simplest— the human name of JESUS."[1] The name of Jesus was determined by God's messenger Gabriel, who told Mary that she was going to have a Son, who shall be called Jesus. He shall be great and shall be called the Son of the Most High (Luke 1:31). An angel appeared unto Joseph while Mary was with child and announced to him: "Do not be afraid to take Mary your wife home, for what is begotten in her was by the Holy Spirit, and she shall bear a son, and you shall call him Jesus, for he will save His people from their sins" (Matthew 1:21). It is the name appointed by God the Father, not only for the brief time Jesus was to spend on earth but as the name by which He shall be worshipped forevermore (Philippians 2:10-11). It is the name that is to set the tone for everything a Christian does. "Whatsoever you do in word or in deed, do all in the name of the Lord Jesus, giving thanks to God the Father through Him (Colossians 3:17)." As Paul told the Philippians: "It is the name at which every knee will bow, of those in heaven, and those on earth, of those under the earth, and every tongue confess that Jesus is Lord to the glory of God the Father" (2:10-11): The name of Christ enshrines and expresses the mystery of His person and wonder of His redeeming love Jesus, name of matchless splendor! Name of all other names above Glorious Son of God incarnate King of Kings and Lord of love.[2]

The New Testament uses the name JESUS for three different persons: 1. For Mary's Son; 2. For Joshua, son of Nun (Acts 7;45; Heb. 5:4) and 3. For Justus, a Christian who was with Paul in Rome and with the apostle to the Colossians (Col. 4:11).[3]

The Frequency of Use of Jesus' Name in the New Testament

Jesus is the name which is most frequently employed in the New Testament of the Second Person of the Godhead. The name of Jesus occurs hundreds of times in the New Testament.[4] Its most frequent use is found in the Four Gospels, where there are over four hundred references. In the Book of Acts, the great missionary book of the New Testament, showing how the Word of God spread between A.D. 30 and A.D. 60, Luke employed the name 49 times. The Apostle Paul has references to Jesus in nine of his Epistles: Romans (five times), I Corinthians (five times), II Corinthians (seven times), once in Galatians, twice in Ephesians, twice in Philippians, once in Colossians, six times in I Thessalonians, once in II Timothy and once in Philemon. The Epistle to the Hebrews, which is a Christological epistle, has nine references to Jesus. Other General Epistles: II Peter one time, in I John four times and in Revelation seven times.[5]

The Apostles Never Addressed Mary's
Son by The Name of Jesus

Although there existed great intimacy and familiarity between Jesus and His Apostles, the latter never addressed Him as Jesus, but they accosted Him by such titles of respect as "Lord" and "Master." But it was different with the people of Nazareth, Jesus' home town, who did not recognize the person they had grown up with, as the Messiah, whose coming and activity was foretold in many Old Testament prophecies. The people of Nazareth referred to Jesus as Jesus, son of Mary, but on their lips it had no such significance as that which the Early Church ascribed to God's Son. People of first-century Palestine spoke of Jesus of Nazareth as the "prophet from Galilee" or as Jesus of Nazareth or "the Nazarene," "Jesus, David's Son (Luke 23:42 RSV)."

The Name "Jesus" Born
By Many First Century Palestinian Jews

When Jesus walked the land of Palestine in the first century, the name of Jesus was the name of many male Jews, just as today the name **Hesuh** is the first name of many males hailing from various Latin countries like Spain, Portugal, Italy, Cuba, Central America, and South American countries. Among New Testament Christians the only one to address the Lord as Jesus was the repentant thief on the cross (known as Dysmas), when he said: "Jesus, remember me when you come into your kingdom" (Luke 23:42).

Name of Jesus Linked to the Old Testament Joshua

The Greek IESOUS is a rendering of the Hebrew Joshua, "Jehovah Is Salvation."[6] Tracing the origin of Joshua, it is found that the son of Nun, Moses' servant was called Hoshea or Oshea, meaning "salvation." But Moses renamed him Jehoshua (Num. 13:16). Possibly in anticipation of the work for which God had appointed him, as a testimony of the salvation or deliverance to be brought for Israel by Jehovah. Stevenson made this comparison between Joshua and Jesus of Nazareth: "As born by Joshua this name was an expression of faith in God and testimony to God; in Jesus the true deep significance of the name was fulfilled.

God had visited His people in the Person of His Son, to serve them. The name of Jesus declares His redeemed intent toward sinful men, it contains with the very essence of the Gospel.[7]

The name Joshua comes from the verb **yasha** "to save."[8] The first use of this Hebrew verb is found in Exodus (14:30) and there embraces all that the verb later on was to signify in Holy Writ. Wilbur Smith concluded about the use of Yasha: "This testifies to that great truth that the first occurrence of any major work in divine revelation is the acorn out of which all that pertains to it was ultimately to grow."[9]

A New Significance Attributed to Jesus' Name

In New Testament times the name of Jesus took on new significance, once used as an ordinary Name of Jewish individuals, became a distinctive and extraordinary name, one apart from other designations for Christ. Warfield, professor of Princeton Theological Seminary (1851-1921), in his book **The Lord of Glory** has stressed the fact which applies to all of Christ's names, that the man of Nazareth, imparted to the names of God's Son a new content of meaning.[10] As time passed on the Jews refrained from giving his name to their sons, because Jesus had been crucified allegedly as a criminal, while Christians felt that the name of Jesus was too sacred to give their offspring. As time passed on the name became unique—His alone. Still there is the strange paradox that although the name was avoided when bestowing a surname on a child the name of Jesus evoked the most heartfelt response of faith and love and stirred the utmost devotion. Warfield aptly has remarked: "For Jesus is the name of Him who became MAN it declares His true humanity, it expresses all that was contained within the Old Testament's 'Immanuel.'"[11]

Jesus, the Answer to Mankind's Needs

When Jesus was circumcised he placed Himself under the Law which He had come to fulfill for every human being who ever lived. The requirements of God's laws which all human beings have broken He came to keep. Circumcision was the beginning of this work of Jesus. After he had been circumcised He was given the name of Jesus. Jesus came down from heaven to meet the needs of sinners and all people, sinful by virtue of their original sins and actual sins. Moses once asked Yahweh: "Show me Thy glory." This God has done in the person of his only-begotten Son. The author of the Hebrew Epistle asserted; "God who in ancient days spoke to our ancestors in the prophets, at many different times and by various methods, at the end of these days has spoken to us in a Son whom He pointed the heir of all things 1:1."[12] The unclouded revelation of God is given mankind in Jesus, the fullness of divine grace has and is being bestowed on people.

1081

The Great Significance of Jesus' Name for Believers

Immeasurable is the comfort which is to be found in the name of Jesus. In the Old Testament the Psalmist assures the believers that "he knowest" our frame: He remembers that we are dust (Psalm 103:14). "During Christ's three year ministry on earth, Jesus performed many miracles of healing and showed compassion to the demon-possessed, the lame, the blind, the deaf, performing many miracles of healing for people afflicted with many kinds of diseases. Above all, Jesus had come to provide for the eternal happiness of mankind by bearing as mankind's substitute their sins, which separated mankind from the Heavenly Father, by His sacrificial death Jesus demonstrated a love "that passeth all human understanding," and by his vicarious death and by His victorious rising from the dead, Jesus made John 3:16 the most comforting text in the Bible.

After His victorious resurrection, Jesus ascended on high where He now makes intercession constantly for His followers. In the heavenlies Christ is now available as the Christian's Advocate and Intercessor and still bears the name "Jesus" before which every knee will someday bow. A poet expressed it this way:

Where High the heavenly temple stands
The house of God not made with hands
A great high priest our nature wears
The guardian of mankind appears.[13]

"Christ" Combined With Jesus' Name

The New Testament Scriptures frequently writes of "Jesus Christ."[14] This combination of "Christ" with Jesus occurs in significant places in the theology of the New Testament. Stevenson has pointed out that while Jesus is the personal name of the Son of God, so "Christ" is His official title.[15] The Greek **Christos** (Christ) is the equivalent of the Hebrew and Aramaic **Meshiach** or "Anointed One."[16] In the history of Old Testament religion it is found that prophets, priests and kings were anointed for their respective tasks.[17] That is the way God directed Israel to proceed as these three different classes of Jews were inducted into their assigned offices. The fact that Jesus is called the Anointed One shows, as may be seen from many examples, that He was anointed to the prophetic, the priestly and kingly offices. The Israelites were taught the fact of the different types of work their Redeemer was to be involved in and performed by Him.

On a visit to the synagogue in Nazareth, Jesus declared: "The Spirit of Jehovah is upon me, because He has anointed me..." (Luke 4:18). After Christ's ascension Peter declared to Cornelius and his household that "God has anointed Jesus of Nazareth with the Holy Ghost" (Acts 10:38). The Hebrew people and their leaders believed that the **Meshiach** would deliver them from their enemies and restore the glory of Israel. The rabbis entertained the concept of "David's greater son" as freeing the Jews from the Roman yoke, even though their concept of the Messiah was wrong, that does not invalidate the correct understanding of the Old Testament **Meshiach,** whose spirituality is correctly set forth in the Old Covenant Scriptures.

Matthew in his genealogy of Jesus in his enumeration of Jesus' ancestors asserted: "And Jacob, of Joseph, the husband of whom was born Jesus, who is called Christ" (Matt. 1:16). The angel who appeared to the shepherds on Bethlehem's fields, announced to them that Christ had been born (Luke 2:11). Simeon in the Temple at the Presentation called the Son of God 'the Lord's Christ' (Luke 2:26). When wise men came from the East looking for the King of the Jews, Herod asked the Scribes and priests where Christ should be born (Matt. 2:4). When John the Baptist began his ministry he told the Pharisees: "I am not the Christ" (John 1:20), but pointed to Jesus, clearly asserting that Jesus of Nazareth was the Christ. At once a number of John's disciples left him and followed Christ.

The Occurrence of the Name of Christ in the Four Gospels

The name of Christ is found 13 times in Matthew; 6 in Mark. 12 in Luke, 18 in John's Gospel.[18]

An analysis of these passages will reveal that together with the name of Jesus, the Christ passages give us practically all that Divine Revelation wanted the followers of the Nazarene to know about His ministry, set forth in His activity and teachings.

Jesus - Self-Testimony About Being the Messiah or Christ

Jesus of Nazareth never used the title "Christ" concerning Himself. However, when the Samaritan woman said to him: "I know that when Messiah cometh, which is called Christ," Jesus replied to her: "I that speak unto thee am He (John 4:25-26)." At Caesarea Philippi Peter made a great confession, exclaiming: "Thou art the Christ, the Son of the living God," to which Jesus responded: "Blessed art thou, Simon Bar-jona: for flesh and blood hath not revealed it unto thee but My Father which is in heaven" (Matthew 16:16-17).

At the trial of Jesus before the Sanhedrin the high priest asked Jesus: "I adjure Thee by the living *God* that Thou tell us whether Thou be the Christ, the Son of God (Matthew 26:31)." Jesus replied openly and unequivocally: "Thou sayest I am." Because of this claim the Jewish Sanhedrin condemned Jesus to death and delivered Him to be crucified by Pontius Piliate and the Roman soldiers.

At Pentecost, the keynote of Simon Peter's sermon was: "God hath made the same Jesus, whom ye have crucified, both Lord and Christ (Acts 2:36)." Paul reasoned on his missionary activities in many Jewish synagogues, by showing the Jews out of the Old Testament Scriptures contending that Christ needs to have suffered and risen from the dead; and that Jesus, whom I preach to you is Christ (Acts 17; 3; cf. 26:23). The name of Christ occurs with considerable frequency in his writings, in his 13 epistles addressed to churches in Asia Minor and Europe and to three individuals. Thus the **Concordances** show that Paul uses Christ alone in Romans 35 times. Forty-five in I Corinthians, 37 in II Corinthians, 24 in Galatians, 27 in Ephesians, 18 in Philippians, 19 in Colossians, 5 in 1 and 2 Thesalonians, 3 in 1 and 2 Timothy, 1 in Philemon.[19]

An interesting Pauline theology could be constructed alone from his "Christ" passages apart from what could also be deducted from the "Jesus" passages."[20]

The writers of the General or Catholic Epistles, such as Peter, John, Jude, James, as well as the anonymous writer of Hebrews have employed the name of Christ singly the following times: Nine in Hebrews, 10 in 1 Peter, 4 in 2 and 3 John, and 4 in Revelation. Because of the great importance of the dual title "Jesus Christ" there was also added the designation of "Lord."[21] New Testament Christians, as well as modern Christians, enjoy speaking about their Savior as "our Lord Jesus Christ."

Jesus Christ as "Lord"

The names "Jesus" and "Christ" during the lifetime when the Word become flesh, assumed a fuller and more meaningful nature. This is also time of the title "Lord" applied in the New Testament to the Second Person of the Trinity. Averred Stevenson: "At first it was a mere respectful address, the equivalent to 'Sir,' but before the New Testament closes the title has come to possess all the weight of Deity."[22]

The Greek word for "Lord" is **kurios.** In the linguistic usage of the New Testament it has a wide range of meanings. Sometimes in the literature of the New Testament it is used for "owner," "lord," or "master.""" In the Septuagint **Kurios** was employed to designate the divine titles of **Adonai** and **Jehovah.**[23] At first when Jesus' disciples addressed Jesus it was a term of respect, which in the course of their lives, came to mean the same as the Greek Old Testament's usages of **Kurios.**

Like the names of "Jesus," "Christ," the name **Kurios** was given Jesus at His birth. The angel said to the Bethlehem shepherds: "Unto you is born . . . Christ the Lord" (Luke 2:11). When John the Baptizer began his ministry in the Judean wilderness he called his nation to "Prepare ye the way of the Lord" (Luke 3:4). In both these references the name **Kurios** is the equivalent of Jehovah (or Yahweh). In the course of their theological apprenticeship the disciples learned the true meaning of the designation "Kurios." Thus Peter after witnessing the draught of fishes, exclaimed: "Depart from me; for I am a sinful man, O Lord" (Luke 5:8). While prior to Holy Week Jesus did not define the title "Lord," but did use it authoritatively in the synagogue of Capernum, by asserting "the Son of Man is Lord of the Sabbath" (Mark 2:28). During the week before His crucifixion He employed the title and applied it to Himself On Palm Sunday Jesus sent his disciples to fetch an ass and its foal by saying: "The Lord hath need of them" (Matt. 21:3). On Tuesday of Holy Week in his disputations with the Pharisees He asserted that was David's Lord (Matt. 22:41-46). In the Mount Olivet Discourse, in which Jesus Christ outlined conditions before His Second Coming, exhorted the disciples to "watch ... for ye do not know what hour your lord doth come" (Matt. 24:42; cf v. 46; 25:13). In the Upper Room, where Christ instituted the Holy Communion, he said to the apostles: 'To call me Master and Lord: and ye say well; for so I am" (John 13:13). After His resurrection, Thomas, a week after the Resurrection event, when Christ gave him the physical evidence for his resurrection, exclaimed; "My Lord and my God." From that time forward the name of "Lord" became a name setting forth His Deity and has the meaning of Jehovah of the Old Testament.

The Lord in the Book of Acts

The writer of Acts, doctor Luke, in his history of the spread of Christianity from Jerusalem,Judea, Samaria, Damascus, Roman and Asia Minor, Europe and as far as Spain had occasion to employ the name "Lord" about one hundred times. In Acts "Lord" is the most frequently used name and it has replaced "Jesus" as the narrative name. Stevenson suggested: "Use of the personal name Jesus would doubtedly now be considered too great a familiarity; and 'Christ' was too formal. So the 'Lord' took on the quality of a name rather than a title: But one tinged with respect which was recognized to be His due."[25]

The Lord in the Pauline Epistles and in the Catholic Letters

In his Letters Paul presents many truths that flow from the meaning and position of Christ's lordship. In Romans Paul shows that Jesus is Lord not only of the saved, but also of all created things (Rom. 14:9; Heb. 1-3-6). In his address to Cornelius' household, Peter declared that Jesus of Nazareth was "Lord, of all" (Acts 10:36). In the work of redemption, Paul taught that "no one can call Jesus Lord, except by the Holy Spirit" (1 Cor. 12:3). In his swan song epistle, Paul claims Christ is King of Kings and Lord of Lords (1 Tim. 6:15). The Philippian Christians were informed that Jesus Christ is "the Lord, to the glory of God the Father" (Phil. 2:11). Peter calls upon all Christians to "sanctify in your hearts Christ as Lord" (I Peter 3:15). It is necessary to believe in Jesus Christ as Lord, for Paul assures Christ's followers: "No man can call Jesus Lord, except for the Holy Spirit." The Lord of glory is our Lord and our God. The last book of the Bible states: "He who testifies to these things say, 'Surely I am coming soon.' Amen, Come Lord Jesus! The grace of our Lord Jesus be with all the saints. Amen" (Rev. 22:21-22).

Footnotes

1. Herbert F. Stevenson, *The Titles of the Triune God* (Westwood, N.J.: Fleming H. Revell Company, 1956), p. 110.
2. As cited by Stevenson, **op. cit.,** p. 110.
3. Abbott-Smith, *A Manual Greek Lexicon of the New Testament* (New York: Charles Scribner' Sons, 1929), p. 215.
4. Robert Young, *Analytical Concordance to the Bible*. Twentieth Edition. By Wm. B. Stevenson (New York: Funk and Wagnalls, No Dates), pp. 165-166.
5. **Ibid.,** p. 166.
6. "Iesous," im G. Abbott-Smirth, *A Manual Greek Lexicon of the New Testament* (New York: Charles Scribner's Sons, 1929), p. 215.
7. Stevenson, **op. cit.,** p. 111.
8. "Yashan," Ludwig Koehler, and Walter Baumgartner *Lexicon in Veteris Testament*

(Leiden: E . J. Brill. 1958), pp. 412-413.

9. Stevenson, **op. cit.,** p. 111.

10. B. B. Warfield, *The Lord of Glory* (London: Hodder & Stoughton, 1907), p. 105.

11. **Ibid.**, p. 108.12. *The New Testament in Modern English*. The Centenary Translation (Philadelphia: The Judson Press, 1924), p. 593.

13. As cited by Stevenson, **op. cit.,** p. 113.

14. Young, **op. cit.,** p. 543-544. *Zondervan Expanded Concordance* (Grand Rapids: Zondervan Publishing House, 1968), pp. 185-186.

15. Herbert Stevenson, **op. cit.,** p. 114.

16. Abbott-Smith, **op. cit.,** p. 484.

17. **Ibid.,** 485.

18. Stevenson, **op. cit.,** p. 115.

19. Young-William Stevenson, **op. cit.,** p. 166.

20. Young-Stevenson, **op. cit.,** p. 166; James Strong, *Exhaustive Concordance,* Complete and Unabridged (Nashville: Broadmand Press, 1979), p. 192.

21. Young-Stevenson, **op. cit.,**pp. 620- 621.

22. Zondervan *Expanded Concordance*, **op. cit.,** p. 710.

23. F. Wilbur Gingrich, *Shorter Lexicon of the Greek New Testament* (Chicago University of Chicago Press, 1965), p. 123.

24. *Handy Concordance to the Septuagint* (London: Samuel Bagster and Sons, 1970). A Reprint pp. 145-146.

25. Herbert Stevenson, **op. cit.,** p. 118.

Questions

1. Who determined the name Jesus? ____
2. In the four Gospels there are over ____ references to Jesus.
3. How did the Apostles refer to Jesus? ____
4. The only New Testament Christian to address the Lord as Jesus was ____.
5. Jesus provided for the eternal happiness of man by ____.
6. Jesus made ____ the most comforting text in the Bible.
7. The Hebrew believed that ____ would deliver them from their enemies.
8. Why did the Jewish Sanhedrin condemn Jesus to death? ____
9. The Greek word for Lord is ____.
10. When was the term Kurios give to Jesus? ____
11. What term for Jesus is most frequently used in Acts? ____

The Epiphany Season

The Lesser Festivals of the Lutheran Church Year Occurring in the Expanded Epiphany Season (January 6 till February 24, 1998)

Christian News, January 26, 1998

The Lutheran Church Year may be divided into two parts: The festival half and the non-festival.[1]

The festival half is organized around the great salvatory acts of the Triune God. The part without festivals is concerned with the promotion of directives for the living of a sanctified life, flowing from a living and justified faith. Christ is the heart of both parts of the Ecclesiastical Year. There are two kinds of festivals observed during the festival and non-festival halves of the Church Year: Major or Minor. The Major festivals observed in the course of the 52 Sundays comprising the Year of Our Lord are found in the first half of the Church's religious year, although since the Reformation the Lutheran Church has added the observation of Sundays like Reformation Festival (October 31), anniversary of Luther's death, Harvest Home and Thanksgiving. The festivals of the first half of the Church Year occur between the beginning of December and June, while the Lesser festivals are scattered over the whole year. The Major festivals are celebrated in a congregation's regular worship services, while the Lesser or Minor are observed in the chapel services of the Lutheran Church-Missouri Synod's two theological seminaries and possibly also in the chapel services of the colleges and universities supported by The Concordia University system.

The Lutheran Hymnal[2] and *Lutheran Worship*[3] do not have the same arrangement in their respective Church Calendars, although both distinguish between Major and Minor Festivals.

Lutheran Worship included the changes made by a commission of the Roman Catholic Church, the Episcopalian, the Presbyterian and Lutheran Churches adopted 1970 which extended the Epiphany Season till Ash Wednesday, and eliminated the three pre-Lenten Sundays of Septuagesima, Sexagesima and Quinquagesima, three Sundays said to be found occurring with a cycle of 70,60 and 50 days before Easter.[4] The 1970 commission also recommended of speaking of the Sundays after Pentecost, in place of "Sundays after Trinity." In fact Trinity Sunday is called the First Sunday after Pentecost. This means there are therefore more Sundays after Pentecost than there were Sundays after Trinity. In the post 1970 revision there is a longer Epiphany Season. In 1998 there are six Sundays after Epiphany and thus this represents a longer Epiphany Season than the one found in *The Lutheran Hymnal*.

Dr. Piepkorn said that the church calendar in use in general in the Lutheran Church may be said to include the following Sundays, festivals and days: A Movable: The Sundays in Advent; Septuagesima; Sexages-

ima; Quinquagesima; the Sunday after Epiphany ending in the Transfiguration (also kept on the 6th of August); Ash Wednesday; Invocavit;
Reminiscere; Occuli; Laetare; Judica; Palm Sunday; Monday, Tuesday,
Wednesday of Holy Week; Maundy Thursday; Good Friday; Holy Saturday; Easter, and two days following; Quasimodogeniti, Misericordia (s);
Domini; Jubilate; Cantate; Rogate; Ascension; Exaudi; Pentecost; Trinity
and Sundays after Trinity.[5]

The Fixed Festivals

St. Andrew (November 30); St. Thomas, December 21; Christmas (De-
cember 25); St. Stephen, December 26; St. John the Evangelist, December
27; Holy Innocents, December 28; Circumcision and Naming of Jesus,
January 1; Epiphany, January 6; Conversion of St. Paul, January 25;
Presentation and Purification, February 2; St. Matthias, February 24;
Annunciation; March 25; St. Mark, April 25; SS. Philip and James the
Less, May 1; Birth of John the Baptist, June 24; SS. Peter and Paul, June
29; Visitation, July 2; Mary Magdalene, July 22; St. James the Elder,
July 25; St. Bartholomew, August 24; St. Matthew, September 21;
Michelmas, September 29; SS. Simon and Jude, October 28; Reformation,
October 31; All Saints, November 1. Piepkorn omitted The Commemora-
tion of Pastors and Confessors: Timothy and Titus (January 24 and 26,
respectively) in his listing of Lesser Festivals.[6]

Other Days Commemorated in the History of Lutheranism

Piepkorn in his article on "the Church Year" listed the following as
commemorations observed in different parts of world Lutheranism: St.
Nicholas, December 6; Christmas Eve, December 24; the Baptism of Our
Lord, Sunday after New Year; St. Gregory I (the Great), March 12; the
Presentation of the Augsburg Confession, June 25; St. Lawrence, August
10; the Beheading of St. John the Baptist, August 29; Holy Cross Day,
September 14; St. Martin, November 11, St. Catherine of Alexandria, November 25; the Festival of Harvest is often kept on the Sunday of Michelmas; Thanksgiving on the 4th Thursday in November and the
commemoration of the departed Faithful; All Souls' Day, November 2.[7]

Present-Day Practice Relative to the Lesser Festivals

Liturgiologists also use the terminology of Major and Minor in describing the festivals found in the liturgical year. The Major Festivals are observed in the regular church services, while the Minor are probably only
celebrated in the worship services at our two theological seminaries and
in the chapel services of the colleges and universities supported by the
Concordia University System of the Lutheran Church-Missouri Synod.
While the average Lutheran only participates in the commemoration of
the Major Festivals as observed in their houses of worship, it would be
profitable for devout Lutheran to use their hymnals and take note of
these lesser festivals, which call attention to martyrdoms of the Apostles
or the acts of Mary directly connected with Christ's life or with events
that recall certain events in the life of Jesus Christ and those individuals

He chose to carry out the Great Commission. Concordia's Devotional booklets regularly allude to these lesser festivals in their giving the date of the day of the week as they proceed through each month.[8] *Lutheran Worship* has a number of hymns in which the average churchgoer may gratefully remember the specific event that deals with the Apostles and St. Paul.[9] The possessor of *Lutheran Worship* will find the liturgical portion, pp. 94-117, helpful in reading the Collects, the Scripture Readings, Introits and Verses, as a part of the Christian's daily devotional readings for the Minor Festivals.

It is the purpose of this presentation to take note of the Lesser Festivals occurring during the expanded Epiphany Season, January 6 till Ash Wednesday (February 24).

Epiphany, January 6

This sixth day of January ushers in the Epiphany season which ends now (1998) with the day before Ash Wednesday. Epiphany is known as "The Epiphany," "Manifestation of God." It has been called The Festival of the Three Kings, in England Twelfth Night. Historically, Epiphany antedated December 25 as commemorating the Nativity of Christ. In the Eastern Churches Epiphany is their Christmas. Two Epiphanies were observed in the Eastern Church: The Baptism and Birth of Christ.

Epiphany has also been remembered for its missionary message, wise men coming from the East to worship the Christ Child. In the Sundays following Epiphany a number of Epiphanies have been added, such as the First Miracle, also Bethphania, the place where the miracle took place.[10]

The Confession of St. Peter (January 18)

The Third Withdrawal (Matt. 16:13-20) saw Jesus withdrawing into the northern most district of Galilee, the parts, of Caesarea Philipi.[11] Here took place Peter's great confession of Christ. Christ asked His disciples what opinions the general public held about Him. After hearing the different views Christ asked the disciples. Who do you say I am? Peter immediately answered: "You are Christ the Son of the Living God." Jesus told Peter that that confession had been inspired by God the Father and was not the result of his thinking. The significance of this confession which brought Jesus joy as His commendation to Peter shows, lies not only in the recognition in Him the promised Messiah but also recognizing in the Messiah, the Divine Nature, Jesus was more than the best and greatest of men; He was God,[12] come down from heaven among men, God manifest in the flesh.

Propers of the Confession of St. Peter

Scripture reading for the One year series: Psalm 23, Acts 2:22-24,32-33; I Peter 1:3-5; Matthew 16:13-19. In the Three-year Series: Psalm 18:1-7; 16-19; Acts 4:8-13; I Cor. 10:1-5; Matthew 16:13-19.[13]

Collect for the Day

"Dear Father in heaven, as you revealed to the apostle Saint Peter the blessed truth that Jesus is the Christ, the Son of the living God, strengthen us in the same faith in our Savior that we may joyfully confess that there is no salvation in no one else; through Jesus Christ our Lord, who lives and reigns with you and the Holy Spirit, one God now and forever."[14]

Three days toward the end of our secular January there are three Lesser Festivals observed, Timothy (January 24), the Conversion of St. Paul (January 25), and Titus (January 26).

St. Timothy, Pastor and Confessor (January 24)

Timothy (Greek: 'honoring God') was the closest companion and messenger of the Apostle called Timothy his "dear and faithful child in the Lord," "his brother" or "fellow-worker." Timothy of Derbe was entirely at Paul's disposal from Paul's visit to Lystra in the Second Missionary Journey until the time of Paul's death in Rome, a period of about 17 years.

Timothy was by nature timid and reserved. Paul mentioned Timothy a number of times in his Epistles in his correspondences to the Corinthians, Thessalonians, Philippians. To the Corinthians Paul wrote: "When Timothy comes, see that you put him at ease or he is doing the work of the Lord as I am. So let no one despise him. Speed him on his way in peace, that he may return to me; for I am expecting him with the brethren (I Cor. 15:10,11)." Still Paul sent Timothy to strengthen the recalcitrant Corinthian members in their faith and loyalty. The Apostle wrote similarly to the Thessalonian congregation: "We sent Timothy our brother and God's servant in the Gospel of Christ to establish you, that no one be moved by these afflictions. You yourselves know this is to be our lot" (I Thess. 3:2,3).

Although Timothy was shy, Paul entrusted him with many of his spiritual concerns taking place in many of the congregations he supervised. In prison Paul wrote the Philippians: "I hope in the Lord Jesus Christ to send Timothy to you soon so that I may be cheered by news of you. I have no one like him, who will be genuinely anxious for your welfare. They all look after their own interests, not those of Jesus Christ. But Timothy's worth you know, how as a son with a father he has served me in the Gospel" (Phil. 2:19-22). Although Timothy may have been subject to "frequent ailments" (I Tim. 5:23), he seems to have been constantly sent on dangerous and difficult assignments. Timothy was a man of courage and according to tradition became a martyr.[15]

The Early Life of Timothy

Timothy was a native of Lystra, the son of a Greek father and a Jewish mother, named Eunice, and a grandmother Lois.[16] When Paul returned to Lystra, where on his first journey he had been stoned, he found Timothy as a member of the congregation together with his grandmother and mother. They had trained him in the Old Testament Scripture which he knew from childhood. So on Paul's Second Missionary Journey Paul decided to take Timothy along as a Gospel-helper, and because he had not been circumcised, had him circumcised so that he would present no obstacle in Paul's missionary work among Jews. Timothy joined Paul, Silas in their journeys over European Macedonia. Somehow Timothy escaped the episode when the Jews were incensed and drove Paul out of the city, nor was he involved in the jailing of Paul and Silas in Philippi. When Paul visited Athens, Silas and Timothy remained in Berea and Thessalonica before joining Paul in Corinth. When Timothy was ordained by the laying of the hands of the Presbytery is not clear. Whether presbyter Timothy joined the Apostle in Antioch between the Second and Third Missionary Journeys is not clear.

It is known that Erastus and Timothy were helping Paul during the Apostle's longest teaching ministry in Ephesus. It was from Ephesus that Timothy carried Paul's Corinthian correspondence.

Timothy's name is also found in Thessalonian, Colossian and Philippian Letters. At the conclusion of the Third Missionary Journey Timothy met Paul at Troas the night Eutyches fell from the third story and Paul revived him. If Paul wrote the Captivity Letters from Rome, then Timothy was with him.

Timothy was the recipient of two epistles sent to him by Paul, known as I and II Timothy. It appears that Paul sent Timothy to Ephesus where he became the pastor of the Ephesian Church. While in Rome during his second Roman Imprisonment Paul expected the executioner soon and he asked Timothy to bring to him his scrolls and a coat he had left at Troas before winter came which the Apostles greatly needed because of the damp condition of the prison in which he found himself. The author of Hebrew (according to the Vulgate: Paul) wrote the Jewish Christians, the recipients of the Hebrew Epistle: "You know that our Timothy has been set free," which would imply that Timothy had been in prison (13:22).

Timothy in Early Christian Tradition

Eusebius the 4th century Christian historian, reports that Timothy was the first bishop of Ephesus. An apocryphal Acts of Timothy depicts Timothy being martyred on January 23, as he protested the licentious activities in honor of Diana of the Ephesians.[17]

The Propers for St. Timothy in *Lutheran Worship*

Scripture readings in the Three-Year Cycle: Psalm 84; Ezek. 34:11-16; or Acts 20:17-35; I Peter 5:1-4; or Ephesians 3:14-21; John 21:15-17 or Matthew 24:42-47.[18]

Collect: "O almighty God, by your Son, our Savior, you have always given to your Church on earth faithful shepherds to guide and feed your flock. Therefore we pray, make all pastors diligent to preach your holy Word and minister your means of grace and grant your people wisdom to follow in the way that leads to eternal life; through our Lord Jesus Christ, who lives and reigns with you and the Holy Spirit, one God, now and forever.[19]

The Conversion of St. Paul (January 25)

The conversion of St. Paul must be proclaimed as one of the greatest historical happenings of the last two thousand years. Paul was the great interpreter of Jesus Christ as may be seen from his 13 Epistles. Luke, the evangelist and author also of the Book of Acts, was a personal friend of Paul and has given his account of the conversion of Saul of Tarsus (Acts 9:1-22). Paul has also given an account to the mob in Jerusalem who wanted to lynch him and kill him (Acts 22:1-16).[20] Paul claimed that in the year A.D. 33 he was on his way to Damascus to search out Christians to have them persecuted. As he approached Damascus, suddenly a light shone from heaven and he was confronted by Jesus of Nazareth and miraculously accepted Christ as His Savior and Redeemer. From Christ he received the assignment to bring the Gospel to the Gentiles. He whom he hated with every fiber of his being to whom he now became devoted and was willing, as happened in Rome, to die for Him.

Paul, humanly speaking, outdistanced Peter, and embarked on three missionary journeys, in the course of which he founded many congregations in Asia Minor, Greece, Dalmatia and Italy. He probably also extended his missionary activity to Spain. The land around the Mediterranean experienced the promulgation of a new religion which after three hundred years conquered the mighty Roman Empire. Of the 27 Books of the New Testament Paul definitely wrote 13 and if Hebrew is Pauline, 14. He had contact with a number of pastors, Timothy and Titus especially.[21]

Propers for the Conversion of St. Paul

The Scripture readings are: Psalm 67; Jeremiah 1:4-10; Acts 90-1-22; and Matthew 19:27-30 in the One-Year Series. In the Three-Year Series: Psalm 67; Acts 9:1-22; Galatians 1:11-24; Luke 21:10-19.[22]

The Collect reads: "Almighty God, as you turned the heart of him who persecuted the Church and by his preaching caused the light of the Gospel to shine throughout the world, grant us ever to rejoice in the saving light of your Gospel and to spread it to the uttermost parts of the earth: Through Jesus Christ, your Son, our Lord, who lives and reigns with you and the Holy Spirit, one God, now and forever."[23]

The Feast of Titus, Pastor and Confessor (January 26)

Of the conversion of St. Paul the Church remembers the person and work of Titus. The Greek name for the English Titus is **Titios**, a praenomen only, the surname is not given in Holy Writ.[24] He was a Greek Christian and for nearly 20 years an associate of St. Paul, for whom he acted in Corinth. The New Testament shows that Titus was active in Achaia, Dalmatia on the Adriatic and finally on the island of Crete. Strangely Luke in the Acts never mentions Titus, but Paul does in his correspondences in I Corinthians and in his "Swan Song" Epistle to Timothy (II Timothy 4:14). Paul also addressed to his representative on Crete the Epistle to Titus, one of the three Pastoral Letters.

The first mention of Titus in the New Testament appears in Galatians

2:1 as a person on the delegation from Antioch who was with Paul and Barnabas on a journey to Jerusalem around A.D. 40. Different opinions exist among Pauline specialists whether this was the visit recorded in Acts 11, or that in Acts 15, the holding of the Apostolic Council. Titus was taken along to this first great church council in the history of Christianity to show that a Gentile Christian did not need to be circumcised, Titus being uncircumcised. The Jewish Christian party insisted that Gentiles had to be circumcised and hold all requirements of the Mosaic Law. Paul refused to have Titus circumcised as a matter of theological principle.

During Paul's Third Missionary Journey the Apostle Paul was apprised of the existence of four different factions in the Corinthian Church. Besides this, there were doctoral problems and ethical principles were being violated. Paul wrote I Corinthians to correct the situation in Corinth.[25] The letter, written in A.D. 55, went by sea and Timothy at the same time made a personal visit to Corinth. Neither Paul's Letter or Timothy's visit corrected the problems. Paul left for Ephesus and wrote a severe letter, believed to be found in II Corinthians, chapters 10-13, which was brought by Titus, older and more experienced than Timothy. II Corinthians has a number of passages referring to Titus (Cf. 2:13; 7:6,13-14; 8:6-23; 12:18).

The last reference to Titus is to be found in Paul's last letter, II Timothy. Paul had been arrested, condemned and was expecting the executioner and was depressed by the scattering of congregations throughout the Mediterranean world. At Paul's request Titus had gone to Dalmatia on the east coast of the Adriatic, probably to Nicopolis. Between Paul's First and Second Roman Imprisonments Titus was sent to Crete, where he supervised church life. While in Crete Paul sent him the letter, now known as The Epistle to Titus,[26] one of the three Pastoral Epistles.

Eusebius in his Ecclesiastical History reported that Titus became the first bishop of Crete. His traditional burial place is at Gortyna, the ancient capital of Crete, though his head is venerated as a relic at St. Mark's, Venice.[27]

The Propers for the Feast of Titus
The Collect, Introit and Scripture readings are the same as those appointed to be used in connection with the observance of St. Timothy.

The Presentation of Our Lord (February 2)
Luke in chapter 2:22-33 reports the fact that the Holy Family went to the Jerusalem Temple on the fortieth day after Christ's birth. Mary went there to be purified as required by the Law of Moses, as found in Leviticus 12:8. It was on this occasion that Simeon took the Christ child into his arms and uttered the words of the Nunc Dimittis. The prophetess Anna testified concerning Mary's Son that He was the Messiah people were eagerly expecting. Roman Catholics treat this Feast as a Marian festival, while Lutherans consider it an occasion honoring Jesus. Mary's need for purification does not support the teaching of the Immaculate

1093

Conception, a doctrine of Roman Catholicism. The first mention of this lesser festival is found in a letter of Sylvia, who stated that this day was observed in Jerusalem at the end of the fourth century. Its earliest name was Hypapante (Greek for "Meeting") and had reference to Simeon's meeting Christ in Mary's arms. It became customary to bless candles on this day, stressing the Presentation of Christ, rather than Mary's purification. As the cult of Mary grew, February 2 came to be known as "The Purification of Mary," a name strikingly incongruous with the teaching that Mary was sinless from conception in her mother's womb. Both Lutherans and Episcopalians regard February 2 as a festival honoring Christ. The 40 days between Christ's Birth and His Presentation was performed according to the Mosaic Law, demanding that a sacrifice should be offered for every child. During the Middle Ages February 2 was called Candlemas, referring to the blessing of the candles used in the worship service of that day.[28]

Propers for the Presentation of Our Lord
The Introit is taken from Psalm 48,1,8a. The Scripture Readings of the One-Year Series are: Psalm 84, Malachi 3:1-4; Hebrew 2:14-18; Luke 2:22-32. The Three-Year Series suggests: Psalm 84; I Samuel 1:21-28; Hebrews 2:14-18; Luke 2:22-40.[29]

The Collect
Almighty and ever-living God, grant that as your only begotten Son was on this day presented in the temple in the substance of our human flesh, so by him we may be presented to you with pure and clean hearts; through Jesus etc.[30]

Martin Luther Doctor of the Church (February 18)
The Lutheran liturgy is unique among the churches of the world in appointing two of its days in the Ecclesiastical Year to Martin Luther, namely, October 31, recalling the nailing of the 95 theses on the church door of Wittenberg, signaling the beginning of the Protestant Reformation,[31] and the day of his death, February 18, 1546, in Eisleben, Germany.[32]

Conservative Lutherans have recognized that Christ used the Wittenberg Reformer as the instrument for the restoration of apostolic Christianity. Luther's emphasis on Sola Scriptura, Sola Gratia, Sola Fidei and Solus Christ showed the inadequacy of the theology of Roman Catholic Church and became the heart of Protestantism. Not only did Luther restore the true plan of salvation, but removed the uncertainty that characterized the complicated theology of Rome.

The Lutheran Church-Missouri Synod commemorates two doctors of the Church, Martin Luther and C. F. W. Walther.

The Propers for the Commemoration of the Doctors of the Church
The Introit is based on Psalm 46:1-3,7. The Readings in the One Year

1094

Series are: Psalm 26; Isaiah
55:6-11; Romans 10:5-17; John 15:1-11.[33]
The Gradual is based on Psalm 146:5; 149:4.

The Collect of St. Martin's Day

O Lord God, heavenly Father, pour out your Holy Spirit on your faithful people, keep them steadfast in your grace and truth, protect and comfort them in all temptations, defend them against all enemies of your Word, and bestow on Christ's Church Militant your saving people.[34]

The Feast of St. Matthias (February 24)

This year, 1998, the Lesser Feast of St. Matthias occurs on the day before the beginning of the Lenten season (February 25, Ash Wednesday). According to Luke's account in Acts 1:15-26, one of the first actions undertaken by the Eleven Apostles, under the leadership of Peter, was to make a replacement for Judas Iscariot who had committed suicide. In church tradition it was speculated that the selection of Matthias was premature and that Paul was selected by Christ to fill the place of Christ's betrayer as the "twelfth Apostle." The Feast of St. Matthias has not been found in the early sacramentaries before the year 1000.

All rites have the same Lesson: Acts, as the Epistle Reading, recounts "giving of lots." Names were written on wood parchment and placed in a bowl which was shaken.[35] Of the two names placed in the bowl, namely those of Joseph, called bar-Sabbas (surnamed Justus) and Matthias, the latter's name fell out after the bowl had been shaken, preceded by prayer of those present in the Upper Room (Acts 1:26).

The Propers for the Feast

Scripture readings in the One-Year Series: Psalm 16; Acts 1:15-26; I John 2:15-17 and Matt. In the Three-Year Series: Psalm 133; Isaiah 66:1-2; Acts 1:15-26; Luke 6:12-16.[36]

The Collect

Lord God, heavenly King, whose chosen apostles have witnessed to us regarding your resurrection, grant that your Church, even preserved from false teachers, may praise your wonderful works and walk in the power of your resurrection; for you live and reign with Father and the Holy Spirit, one God, now and forever.[37]

Footnotes

1. Paul Zellar Strodach, *The Church Year* (Philadelphia; The United Lutheran Publication House, 1924), p. 182; Walter Gwynne, *The Christian Year and Its Purpose* (New York: Longmans, Green and Company, 1915), pp. 52-57; 64-69; 70-74; Alfred Jeremias, Lebenim Kirchenjahr (Leipzig: Adolf Klein Verlag, 1928), pp. 12-13; Fred L. Precht, *Lutheran Worship* (St. Louis: CPH, 1993), pp. 146-174.
2. *The Lutheran Hymnal.* Authorized by the Synods Constituting the Synodical Conference of North America (St. Louis: Concordia Publishing House, 1941), p. 3.
3. *Lutheran Worship.* Prepared by the Commission of Worship of the Lutheran

Church-Missouri Synod (St. Louis: Concordia Publishing House, 1982), pp. 8-9.

4. A.C. Piepkorn, "Church Year," in Erwin Lueker, *Concordia Cyclopedia* (St. Louis: Concordia Publishing House, 1975), p. 179,13.

5. Piepkorn, **op. cit.**, p. 180; P. E. Kretzmann, *Christian Art in the Place and in the Form of Lutheran Worship* (St. Louis: Concordia Publishing House, 1921), p. 374.

6. Piepkorn, **op. cit.**, p. 180.

7. **Ibid.**

8. Cf. *Portals of Prayer*, January-March, 1998, 2,7,19,24.

9. Cf. Hymn Numbers 180-195 of *Lutheran Worship*.

10. Strodach, **op. cit.**, pp. 60-61.

11. John C. McNichol, *Thinking Through the Bible* (Grand Rapids: Kregels Publications, 1976), p. 172.

12. **Ibid.**

13. *Lutheran Worship*, **op. cit.**, p. 96.

14. **Ibid.**, p. 96.

15. For the Life of Timothy cf. Ronald Brownrigg, *Who's Who in the New Testament* (New York: Pillar Books, 1977), pp. 566-569.

16. Alexander Renwick, "Timothy," *Wycliffe Bible Encyclopedia* (Chicago: Moody Press, 1975), II, pp. 1713-1714.

17. Brownrigg, **op. cit.**, p. 569.

18. *Lutheran Worship*, **op. cit.**, p. 104.

19. **Ibid.**

20. For a discussion of the two accounts of Paul's conversion, cf. William Arndt, *Bible Difficulties and Seeming Contradictions*, Revised by Robert G. Hoerber and Walter H. Roehrs (St. Louis: Concordia Publishing House, 1987), p. 129.

21. For a life of St. Paul cf. Brownrigg, **op. cit.**, pp. 398-424; Walter Dunnett, "Paul," *The Wycliffe Bible Encyclopedia* (Chicago: Moody Press), II, pp. 1291-1300.

22. *Lutheran Worship*, **op. cit.**, p. 96.

23. **Ibid.**

24. For the life of Titus, cf. Brownrigg, **op. cit.**, pp. 573-576; H. A. Hanke, "Titus," *The Wycliffe Bible Encyclopedia*, **op. cit.**, II, p. 1719.

25. D. Edmond Hiebert, *An Introduction to the Pauline Epistles* (Chicago: Moody Press, 1954), pp. 111-112.

26. F.A. Stroth, *Die Kirchen-Geschichted es Eusebius von Caesare. Aus dem Griechichen uebersetzt* (St. Louis: Verlag von L. Volkening, 1904), p. 63.

27. Brownrigg, **op. cit.**, 576.

28. Luther D. Reed, *The Lutheran Liturgy* (Philadelphia: Muhlenberg Press, 1947), p. 499.

29. *Lutheran Worship*, **op. cit.**, 107.

30. **Ibid.**

31. **Ibid.**, p. 115

32. **Ibid.**, p. 109

33. **Ibid.**, p. 110.

34. **Ibid.**

35. Brownrigg, **op. cit.**, pp. 379-380.

36. *Lutheran Worship*, **op. cit.**, p. 96.

37. **Ibid.**, p. 96.

Questions

1. The Lutheran Church year may be divided into ____.
2. Who is the heart of both parts of the Ecclesiastical Year? ____
3. *Lutheran Worship* included the changes made by ____.
4. The 1970 commission recommended speaking of the Sundays after ____ rather than after ____.
5. The presentation of the Augsburg Confession is celebrated on ____.
6. It may be profitable for devout Lutherans to use their hymnals for ____.
7. Epiphany has been called ____.
8. Jesus was more than ____, He was ___.
9. Timothy was a man of ____.
10. The name of the mother of Timothy was ____ and the name of his grandmother was ____.
11. According to the Vulgate Paul wrote____.
12. What does Eusebius report about Timothy? ____
13. The conversion of St. Paul must be proclaimed as ____.
14. What conquered the mighty Roman empire? ____
15. Eusebius reported that Titus became ____.
16. Mary's need for purification does not support ____.
17. When did Luther die? ____
18. What shows the inadequacy of Roman Catholic theology? ____
19. What other doctor of the Church does the LCMS commemorate besides Luther? ____
20. In church tradition ____ was subjected by Christ to fill the place of ____.

The Implications of the Resurrection of Jesus Christ

(Easter 1998)

Christian News, April 13, 1998

On April 12, the Christian world will celebrate the 1,967[th] anniversary of the corporal resurrection of Jesus Christ, which possibly occurred in 31 A.D.[1] From the New Testament it is apparent that this historical and world-shaking event was celebrated in the thirties or forties of the first Christian century in Asia and European churches, for Paul indicates this in I Corinthians 15, when he wrote: "Let us celebrate the festival, not with the Old leaven, but with the unleavened bread of sincerity and truth" (I Cor. 5:6-8.)[2] The day of our Lord's resurrection is known by different names in the Christian Church.[3] The English Easter is supposed to be derived from the pagan goddess **Eostre** or **Ostera**, whose festival was celebrated at the time of the vernal equinox. Some philologists, being unhappy with the pagan derivation of Easter, have proposed that Easter could be derived from the old German **urstan** "to rise," and **urstand**, "resurrection." The modern name in the Greek is **Lampra**, Bright Day. Unfortunately, there arose in A.D. 136 a discussion as to whether the feast should be kept on the same day as the Jews kept the Passover, namely, the 14th day of Nisan, no matter on what day of the week it happened to fall, or else on the Sunday following. Those who insisted on the 14th of Nisan were called Quartodecimanians,[4] from the Latin word for fourteen, those holding Easter on Nisan 14 were chiefly or solely Eastern Christians, especially in the region of Ephesus, where it was claimed the Apostle John had been active. The Western Churches, however, held that the better day was the Sunday after the full Paschal moon, that being the day of the week which our Lord Himself had sanctified by His rising from the dead. The differences here stated were already discussed by Polycarp of Smyrna and Annicetus of Rome (ca. 155). Under Victor of Rome, about a generation later it led to a schism. The Council of Nicea declared itself against the Quartodecimanians who were henceforth treated as heretics.[5]

The date when Easter falls varies from year to year, and this variation in date has a far reaching effect upon the whole church year. Just as the date of Easter spawned the Paschal Controversy, so much difficulty developed in connection with the determining of the Easter date. The question arose: should Jewish computations be used (the close connection between the Jewish Passover and Easter) or should the mathematical calculations of Alexandrian scholars be used. The West depended in great part upon the Alexandrian efforts.[6]

Some Hymnals give a table of the days in which Easter will fall, as does *The Lutheran Hymnal* on page 158, giving "Table of the Days on which Easter will fall from 1941-2000."

Gwynne claimed: "The intense feeling which the Pascal Controversy occasioned was apparently so trifling, testifies to the importance the Early Church ascribed to the historic reality of the Resurrection.[7] On this single fact they knew, rested all else of the Christian faith, for if Christ's body never arose from the dead, their faith in Him was all vain (See Rom. 1:9; 1 Cor. 15:14-20). It was because of this that the Eastern Church gave Easter the name of "the Feast," as that feast which out ranks all others and that the Western Church regarded it as "the Queen of the Festivals."[8]

The Priority of Easter in the Christian Church Year

The priority of Easter in the Christian Church Year is shown by the fact that all other festivals are dependent upon its occurrence. Of what value would the Incarnation of Christ be if He had remained in the grave? There, of course, could not have been an Ascension event, because only a living Christ, and not a dead One, could arise into heaven. Without the Ascension there could not have been a Pentecost festival, for Jesus, while on earth, had promised to send upon His disciples the Holy Spirit. Thus no resurrection of Christ, no Pentecost. If Christ had not been raised from the dead, He would not have been declared to be the Son of God. Thus the Trinity Festival would be meaningless without the deity of God's Son. Events celebrated before Easter and events after Easter are depended upon Christ's corporal resurrection in historic time.

The resurrection of Jesus Christ was a part of the ABC's of the Christian proclamation, as may be seen by the numerous references to this event in the books of the New Testament. A perusal of the Book of Acts shows that the apostles emphasized it. Paul in his Epistles showed its importance. In I Corinthians 15 he showed the Corinthians how everything, their future salvation as well as the destiny of the Christians who have already died were greatly dependent upon the reality of Christ's corporeal resurrection from the dead.

Because of the historicity and reality of Christ's resurrection, the Biblical readers may now assume that certain implications flow from Christ's rising from the dead.[9] These deductions of benefits resulting from this central and foundational truth of the Christian religion will now be set forth.

The doctrinal fact of Christ's resurrection testifies to the unity of the sixty-six books of Holy Writ. The doctrine of Christ's resurrection is asserted in both Testaments, the Old and the New. The prophet Isaiah, in his great Fourth Servant Passage, has Isaiah predicting: "He shall see His seed, He shall prolong His days," (v. 10b). The Apostle Paul told the Corinthians "that Christ died and arose again according to the Scriptures (I Cor. 15:3)." In the Gospel the Holy Spirit has occasioned four different writers to describe what happened on the third day after Christ's crucifixion, death and burial. Christ, before His crucifixion, announced a number of times the purpose of His mission was to give His life a ransom for many. He told His disciples a number of times that He had to go to Jerusalem, to be captured and die, so that the Scriptures might be fulfilled.

In connection with Christ's resurrection the believer finds the existence of the phenomenon of prophecy and fulfillment, thus pointing to the unity of the Bible. The Old Testament is incomplete without the New Testament. Judaism bases its religious teachings solely on the Old Testament and the Talmuds but rejects the New Testament. Both Testaments proclaim the same plan of salvation. The New Testament cannot be understood without the Old, which is quoted hundreds of times and cited as inspired Scripture. Without the New Testament the Old would be incomplete and leave the readers with predictions, concerning which one would not know whether they had been fulfilled.

The Implication of the Resurrection for Jesus Christ's teaching, especially concerning His Person and work.[10] The resurrection testifies to the truthfulness of Christ's teaching. Jesus had predicted that it was necessary for Him to go to Jerusalem, where the Jewish leaders would have Him seized, condemned to death and die in Jerusalem and also that He would rise again. The fact these remarkable predictions came true, would also support the truthfulness of His teachings, such as that His blood was shed for the remission of mankind's sins, that He had come down from heaven, that He proclaimed the words of the Father, that He and the Father were one, that He was the Son of God and that individuals believing in Him would have eternal life and their rejection of Him would cause them to be eternally lost (John 3:35-36). The empty tomb and the fact that various men and women saw Christ alive (Matthew 28; John 20; Mark 16; Luke 24) and on one occasion by five hundred people, should assure Christians of the corporeal resurrection of Christ.

The Implication for Christ's atoning death. In the beginning of his Letter to Rome, Paul declared that Christ was declared to be the Son of God with power, according to the Spirit of holiness by the resurrection from the dead (Rom. 1:4-5). Paul gives a precise statement for the belief of the church in the years following Jesus' earthly life—that Jesus, David's son, was both human and divine and especially the Son of God, a divine being. Paul asserted that Jesus of Nazareth was declared to be God's Son by the resurrection from the dead.

The third implication flowing from Christ's bodily resurrection was the fact that Christ was raised again for our justification (Romans 4:25) and that could only have been accomplished by a Person who was God.

Another implication of Christ's resurrection is the fact that it testifies to Christ's omniscience. Before Christ's seizure, condemnation, death, burial and resurrection Jesus knew that these events were going to transpire. At His first attendance of a Passover festival, the Jews demanded a sign of Jesus after He had cleansed the Temple, and Jesus responded: "Destroy this temple, and in three days I will raise it up" (John 2:19). Only God could make a prediction like that after the third day, after His crucifixion, He would be alive again. The fulfillment of the prophecy of Christ made years before His resurrection is confirmed by the four Gospel accounts, as found in Matthew 28; Mark 16, Luke 24, and John 20 and Paul's account in I Corinthians 15:1-11 and numerous statements in the Book of Acts.[11]

Still another implication of Christ's resurrection is shown in the effect this historical happening had on the 12 Apostles and later on St. Paul. Before Christ's resurrection the disciples of Christ were afraid for their lives and went into hiding. But after the resurrection of Jesus their cowardness was turned into great boldness and they fearlessly proclaimed that Jesus of Nazareth was the promised Messiah of Old Testament prophecy and boldly testified that He was the Savior of the world. A profound and permanent change took hold of Peter, John and the rest of the Apostolic Band. Everywhere they traveled, they intrepidly proclaimed His death and resurrection. Later on, their enemies claimed that they had turned the world upside down. For this resurrection they suffered scourgings and imprisonment. All the Apostles, save John, suffered martyrdom somewhere in the Roman Empire, in Europe and in Asia. This may be seen by reading the Acts of the Holy Spirit as recorded by doctor Luke in Acts and by reading the annals of church history as reflected in the *Apostolic Fathers*[12] and the *Church History of Eusebius*.[13] The resurrected Christ appeared to Saul of Tarsus on the Damascene Road and changed him from a violent persecutor of the Christian Church to the greatest missionary of the Early Church. In 2 Corinthians Paul listed what he had suffered during his ministry up till the time of the writing of the Second Corinthian Epistle (about 55 A.D.). Thus he informed the Corinthians: "In labors more abundant, in stripes above measure, in prisons more frequently, in deaths often, from the Jews five times I received forty stripes minus one, three times I was beaten with rods; once I was stoned; three times I was ship-wrecked; a night and a day I have been the deep, in journeys often, in perils of waters. In perils of robbers, in perils in the sea, in peril among false brethren, in sleeplessness often, in fastings often, in cold and nakedness." (2 Cor. 11:23-26) and finally martyred by beheading in Rome.

Another implication flowing from Christ's bodily resurrection was the relationship of this event to the believer's life. The Apostle Peter began his epistle of Hope like this: "Blessed be the God and Father of our Lord Jesus Christ, who according to his abundant mercy has begotten us again to a living hope through the resurrection of Christ from the dead, to an inheritance incorruptible and undefiled and that does not fade away, reserved in heaven for you" (I Peter 1:3-4). It is faith in the atoning work of Christ which gives this living hope, in a Person, who faced death, conquered it and as a result was able to promise by Paul to his believers "that He who raised Jesus from the dead shall raise up us with Jesus" (2 Cor. 4:14).

Paul in his great resurrection chapter, I Corinthians 15 declared that if Christ had not been raised, then those who had fallen asleep in Christ would not live again, however, the Apostle triumphantly declared: "But now is Christ risen and become the first fruits of them that slept. For since by one man death came, by man also the resurrection from the dead. Christ the first fruits, then they that are Christ's at His coming" (I Cor. 15:20-21).

While on earth Jesus promised His disciples: "Because I live you shall live also" (John 14:19). Jesus promised Martha: "I am the resurrection and the life, he that believeth in me, even if he has died shall live and whosever believeth on me shall never die" (John 11:25-26). On the evening before His death the Lord assured his disciple: "I go to prepare a place for you, and I will come again and receive you to myself, that where I am you may be also" (John 14:2-3).

Another implication of the resurrection is to be seen from early apostolic history, years 30-60 A.D.[14] In carrying out the great commission (Matt. 28:20; Acts 1:8), namely to evangelize the whole world by baptizing and instructing people, Luke records how the Gospel was spread and accepted in Palestine, Asia Minor, southern Europe. Christ's death and resurrection was the message that caused many churches to be established. It was the proclamation of Christ's resurrection that caused people to believe and have hope for this life as well as for the life to come.

Another implication flowing from the resurrection of Christ was the substitution of the Lord's day, the first day of the week, for the Sabbath, the seventh day of the week,[15] **which had been in force since the giving of the Decalogue on Mount Sinai till the time of the death of Christ on Calvary.** Early apostolic Christians substituted the first day of the week, as a weekly anniversary of Christ's resurrection event for the Sabbath. Ever since the early thirties of the first Christian century Christians have worshipped on Sunday, while Judaism held on to the seventh day as the day of worship. Mohammedanism recognizes neither Sunday or the Sabbath as its holy day, but worship their Allah on Fridays.

The Implication of the resurrection of Christ on the believer's present life.[16] A Christian is a person who manifests in his daily living day by day the power flowing from the resurrection of Christ, as outlined in Romans, chapter 6. Paul stated the essence of the Christian life in vs. 4-5: "we were buried therefore with Him through baptism into death, that like as He was raised from the dead through the glory of the Father, we shall also walk in newness of life. For if we have been united with Him in the likeness of the resurrection." Because of this fact Paul concluded: "Present yourselves to God, as alive from the dead" (vs. 11,13; Col. 2:13; 7:4; Rom. 8:11; Eph. 1:18-20; Phil. 3:10-11; Col. 2:13).

Another theological implication of the bodily resurrection of Christ is the fact that God accepted the atoning sacrifice of His Son for the sins of the world. By his death Christ has paid the penalty mankind deserved for its sins. In I Corinthians 15, one of the greatest chapters of the New Testament Paul declared that Christians would be still guilty and their faith would be vain if Christ remained dead. But the Apostle to the Gentiles comforted the Corinthian Christians: "Now Christ has been raised,"[17] thus establishing all the claims and promises given while on earth and also the many promises given the world through various inspired New Testament writers.

The Roman Christians were told: "Christ was delivered for our offenses and raised again for our justification (Rom. 4:25). Dressed in Christ's righteousness the Christian believer may now appear before God as a person who has been declared righteous and who does not have to fear the wrath of God.

Another implication flowing from the resurrection is the fact that the Ascension of Christ, the God-man, was possible. The Ascension of Christ was the ultimate goal of Jesus Christ, who returned to the glory which He had with the Father before His Coming to this earth to assume human nature and to redeem them that were under the law (Gal. 4:4). Christ's life would have been a failure if He had not returned to the Father, because as the ascended Lord He now exercises in heaven his threefold offices as Prophet, Priest and King. Jesus ascended into heaven as our forerunner (Hebrew 6:20). With the Ascension the divine-human Christ now permanently sits at the right hand of God. One of the purposes of the Ascension was to keep His promise to His followers: "Father, I will that they whom Thou hast given Me be with Me where I am, that they may behold My glory (John 17:24) or the promise, "where I am, there ye maybe also" (John 14:3).

Another implication of the resurrection was that it made possible Christ's Session at God's right hand.[18] This sitting is explained by Paul in Ephesians (The Epistle of the Heavenly Places) "God set Him (Christ) at His own right hand in heavenly places, far above all principality and power and might and dominion and every name that is named, not only in this world, but also in the world to come; and hath put all things under His feet and gave him to be Head over all things to the Church, which is His body, the fullness of Him that fulleth all in all" (Eph. 1:20-23).

The Session began on the fortieth day after Christ's resurrection. The Old Testament portrays God as sitting on the throne of the universe, thereby signifying sovereignty (I Kings 22:19; Ps. 2:4; 99:1), holiness (Psalm 47:8) and majesty (Is. 6:4). In Psalm 110:1 the Messiah is invited to occupy the place of honor at God's right hand (Mark 12:36; Acts 2:3; Heb. 1:13). His throne is to be one of sovereignty and priesthood (Ps. 110:1,4; Zech. 6:12-13) and of judgment (Mal. 3:3).[19] The Hebrew word for sitting is **Yashab**.

Only after the resurrection could God exalt Jesus as the Ascension (Phil. 2:9-11; Eph. 1:10-23). As a result of Christ's bodily resurrection, Ascension and Session Christians derive great comfort for they know from Holy Writ that Jesus is now exercising His threefold offices of Prophet, Priest and King. As our Prophet he sends men to preach the Gospel of redemption (Eph. 1:20-23), as our High Priest intercedes (pleads) for us, as John has assured us: "If any man sin, have and Advocate with the Father, Jesus Christ, the Righteous," or as Paul was instructed to write: "Christ is even at the right hand of God, who also maketh intercession for us (Rom. 8:34) and as our King governs and protects His church and as Head of the Church rules the world in the interest of the Church (Ps. 10:1; Matt. 22:24).[20]

Because Christ arose from the dead, the Bible also teaches that it will

1103

be the resurrected Christ who is fitted and ordained at the end of the age (Rev. 5:1-7) and to be the final judge of man (John 5:21-22; Acts 10:42; 17:31).

The final implication of Christ's bodily resurrection is of an eschatological nature, for the resurrection bespeaks the final complete victory over death and over their effects on both man and creation.[21] Because Christ arose believers shall also arise with a resurrection body (I Cor. 15). Because Christ arose, nature too will be freed from the curse. This is the explanation of the fact that the resur- rection of the believer or the manifestation of the sons of God "through the redemption of the body," and the removal of "the bondage of corrup- tion" at Christ's second coming are spoken of as occurring simultaneously (Romans 8:18-23).

The Validity of Christ's Resurrection

Killen claims that "the validity of the resurrection of Christ rests upon the certainty of Jesus's death and burial and sealing of the tomb, the displaced stone and empty tomb, the undisturbed condition of the grave clothes, and on the record of ten different physical appearances of the risen Jesus. The appearances are attested in six accounts—all in all four Gospels, in Acts and I Cor. 15."[22] In fact, the resurrection of Christ is the best attested historical event of the ancient history. It is as Merrill Tenney has written: "The resurrection is relevant to the human need for purpose and assurance. . . . The event is fixed in history, the dynamic is potent for eternity."[23]

Footnotes

1. H. Wayne House, *Chronological and Background Charts of the New Testament* (Grand Rapids: Zondervan Publishing House, 1981), p. 118.
2. I Corinthians was probably composed in Ephesus in A.D. 54.
3. Luther D. Reed, *The Lutheran Liturgy* (Philadelphia: Muhlenberg Press, 1947), pp. 463- 464.
4. C.C. Thorne, "Quartodecimanians," J.D. Douglas, editor, *The New International Diction ary of Church History* (Grand Rapids: Zondervan Publishing House, 1974), p. 817.
5. L. Fuerbringer, Th., Engelder, P. E. Kretzmann, *The Concordia Cyclopedia* (St. Louis: Concordia Publishing House, 1927), pp. 438-439.
6. Millard Scherick, "Pascal Controversies," *International Dictionary of Church History*, **op. cit.**, p. 750.
7. Walker Gwynne, *The Christian Year* (New York: Longmans, Green & Co., 1915), p. 15.
8. Reed, **op. cit.**, p. 464.
9. Wilbur Smith, "Resurrection," in Harrison, Editor-in-Chief, *Baker's Dictionary of Theology* (Grand Rapids: Baker Book House, 1960), pp. 453-454.
10. **Ibid.**, p. 453.
11. Statements about the bodily resurrection of Christ in Acts are found in 2:24; 2:38; 13:37; 37-38. Also 2:32; 3:15; 5:32; 10:39; 13:31-32; 10:39; 13:31-32; 26:16.
12. K. Lake, *The Apostolic Fathers* (London: Heineman, 1925 and 1930), 2 vols.
13. K. Lake, *The Ecclesiastical History* (New York: G.E. Putnam Sons, 1926), I, pp. 1-425.
14. Smith, Resurrection, *Baker's Dictionary of Theology*, **op. cit.**, p. 453.
15. Colossians 2:16; Rom. 14:5; *Augsburg Confession*, XXVIII, pp. 51-60. Cf. also "Lord's Day," *Wycliffe Bible Encyclopedia* (Chicago: Moody Press, 1975), p. 1049.
16. *Baker's Dictionary of Theology*, **op. cit.** p. 453.

17. For a brief discussion of I Corinthians 15, cf. Charles R. Erdman, *The First Epistle of Paul to the Corinthians* (Philadelphia: The Westminster Press, 1956), pp. 153-168; F. Godet, *Commentary on St. Paul's First Epistle to the Corinthians* (Edinburgh: T.& T. Clark, 1893), II, pp., 103-171.
18. Allen Killen, "Resurrection of Christ," *Wycliffe Bible Encyclopedia* (Chicago: Moody Press, 1975), p. 1458; *Exposition of Lutheran Small Catechism* (St. Louis: Concordia Publishing House, 1943), pp. 119-120.
19. David H. Wheaton, "Session," *Baker's Dictionary of Theology*, **op. cit.**, p. 482.
20. Cf. John Theodore Mueller, *Christian Dogmatics* (St. Louis, Concordia Publishing House, 1975, pp. 304, 305, 313-314,315-317).
21. Allen Killen, "Resurrection of Jesus Christ," *Wycliffe Bible Encyclopedia*, **op. cit.**, p. 1458.
22. Killen, **op. cit.**, p. 1439.
23. Merrill C. Tenney, *The Reality of the Resurrection* (Chicago: Moody Press, 1972), p. 19.

Questions

1. The English Easter is supposed to have been derived from____.
2. The modern name in the Greek is____.
3. The Western Church regarded Easter as____.
4. The Trinity Festival would be meaningless without____.
5. Do both the Old and New Testament proclaim the same plan of salvation?____
6. Christ was raised again for our ____.
7. What effect did Christ's resurrection have on the 12 Apostles____.
8. All the Apostles except John suffered____.
9. Jesus told His disciples "Because I live ____."
10. What was the message that caused many churches to be established? ____
11. What became of the Lord's Day? ____
12. When do Mohammadens worship Allah?
13. God accepted the atoning sacrifice of His Son for____.
14. One of the purposes of the Ascension was to ____.
15. Jesus is now exercising His____.
16. What is the best attested event of ancient history? ____

Ascending to Glory
The Significance and Blessings of Christ's Ascension Into Heaven

(A Study for Ascension)
Ascension Day, May 21, 1998

Christian News, May 18, 1998

On the fortieth day after Easter the glorification of the Son of God occurred, Jesus ascended to the glory which He had with the Father when Jesus had left; some thirty years before and assumed human nature in the body of His mother Mary. He spent most of His earthly life in the State of Humiliation except the time He was made alive on Easter morning in the tomb of Joseph of Arimathea and then proceeded to show those in Hades (hell) that He was victorious over sin, death, the Devil and all enemies till the day of His ascension. The latter event occurred on the Mount of Olives, near Bethany (Luke 24:50 and Acts 1:12). Luke tells his readers that a cloud received Jesus. Whether that was the Shekinah or a natural cloud of vapor the record does not make clear.

The Ascension was anticipated in the Old Testament in Psalm 68:18 and in Psalm 110:1, and Jesus Himself spoke if it prophetically in John 6:62 and 20:17.

The Ascension is the fourth step in the State of Exaltation, being preceded by the descent into Hades and the corporeal resurrection from the dead and the forty glorious post-Easter days. Unquestionably the Ascension of Christ was the climactic and crowning event of His earthly life, during which Jesus, the God-Man, accomplished something which God only could have done, namely, effecting the reconciling of God to the world, through His active and passive obedience.

The Ascension of Christ has been a stumbling block for opponents of the miraculous and the supernatural as given in the Bible. Unbelievers reject the historicity of the Ascension event and claim that what Luke has reported about Christ's departure from the earth was only to be considered as symbolical, was asserting that He now is no longer on earth and somehow is found in heaven. One scholar has asserted about this denial: "That it is an attempt to retain the spiritual value of the Ascension without sacrificing the concept of the natural world system susceptible to the supernatural."[1] The Ascension of Christ, followed by the Session at God's right hand, makes possible the fact that the Ascension has a particular meaning for Jesus Christ and also for His followers and has also resulted in blessings being bestowed on His Church and its members.

The Significance for Christ and His Devotees
Luke describes Christ's leaving this earth for heaven in Luke 24:51, and more fully in Acts 1:9.

Ross contends that even though the words "And was carried into heaven" are probably not a part of the original text of Luke 24:51,[2] these doubtful words in Luke 24:51[2] expresses what was in Luke's mind.[3] In accordance with oral testimony of the Apostles, Luke carried on his story of the life of Jesus as far as the day He was taken up (Acts 1:2).

According to the testimony of the Apostle John, Jesus is reported on three occasions as referring to His coming Ascension (John 3:13; 6:62; 20:17). Paul speaks of Christ as "having ascended far above all heavens" in order to permeate the whole universe, with His presence and power (Eph. 4:11). The following expressions assume the fact of Christ's Ascension: "received into glory" (I Tim. 3:16), "gone into heaven" (I Pet. 3:22) and "passed through the heavens" (Heb. 4:14). Paul called upon the Colossians to seek the things that are above where Christ is seated at the right hand of God. All New Testament references to the Session presuppose that act that leads to the sitting at God's right hand, namely, the Ascension.

The Meaning for Christ and His Followers

When Christ left this earth in Palestine, there were terminated the post-resurrection appearances, that time period during which Jesus by many infallible proofs gave evidence of His bodily resurrection. It was all the time during which Christ gave His disciples instruction about the kingdom of God (Acts 1:3). When the people present on the Mount of Olives saw Jesus ascending on high and disappearing from their view were no longer to see Him visibly as had Jesus' Jewish contemporaries, the Twelve Apostles and followers whom He had converted during His ministry, also some Romans and Phoenicians, and the cities of the Decapolis. Although Christ's visible presence would be removed, Jesus nevertheless promised that His followers would experience His presence in a different way. In His great Commission assignment He assured them "that He would be with them unto the end of the age" (Matt. 28:20). He also promised that "where two or three were gathered in His name. He would be with them." In the Lord's Supper He taught His followers that they would receive His true body in, with and under the bread, and also with the cup containing wine, His blood shed on Calvary's cross. He also informed His followers that He would remain in heaven until His Second Coming (Acts 3:21).

Another important meaning would be for Christ that He never again would suffer humiliation according to his human nature, but from the time of the Ascension would always share the glory and power inherent in his Divine Nature and that as the God-man Jesus would have all the powers of the Godhead also according to His human nature. When Jesus left His Father in order to suffer and die for mankind. He came down as a Divine Spirit, but as a result of the Ascension sits at the right hand of God with a human nature; it is the God-Man who now fills all things.

Yet another meaning of Christ's Ascension would be that the ascending on high was possible because Christ had successfully accomplished the mission on account of which He had assumed human nature and humbled Himself. As the God-man Jesus had come to redeem those that were under the law and hurdling toward eternal destruction and ever-lasting banishment from God. Jesus, by His vicarious suffering and death upon the cross, had made possible the salvation of those who in pre-crucifixion times had believed in the Messiah's coming atoning death, and those living at Christ's time and those who would believe in Him until His Second Return. Not to have accomplished His mission would have meant that as a failure He was returning to His Father, but as Glorious Achiever of His mission He appeared before His Father and the holy angels who will accompany Him in the clouds of heaven as He returns for the Great Judgment and the taking to Himself those living at His Coming and those believers whom Jesus would resurrect from the dead.

The Meaning of the Ascension for Christ's Followers

The great meaning of the Ascension for Christ's devotees is the assurance that Christ still lives and is available for help and encouragement because now they can pray to the Father through Jesus. They also can address their petitions and requests to Jesus, who as the author of Hebrews says, can be touched with a sense of our infirmities. Since now, we have a great high Priest Jesus, the Son of God, who has passed through the heavens, let us hold fast our confession of faith. For we have not a High Priest who cannot sympathize with our weaknesses, but one who has been tempted in all points like as we are, yet without sin. "Let us then, draw near with glad boldness to the throne of grace, that we may receive mercy, and find grace to help us in our times of need" (Hebrews 4:14-16).

Jesus Will Be Present Through the Holy Spirit

Although Jesus would no longer be visibly with His disciples. He would be with them through His Holy Spirit. Thus He promised His followers: "And I will pray the Father, and He will give you another Helper, that He may abide with you forever— the Spirit of truth, whom the world cannot receive, because it neither sees Him nor knows Him, but you know Him for He dwells within you and will be in you. I will not leave you orphans, I will come to you. Let not your heart be troubled, neither let it be afraid"(John 14:16-18). Through His Holy Spirit Jesus communicates gifts and blessings.

The Exercise of Christ's Threefold
Office as Prophet, Priest and King

According to the Old and New Testament Scripture, as a result of the Ascension and consequent Session, Jesus now exercises a threefold Office; as Prophet, High Priest and King and as a result blessings are bestowed upon the Church and its believing members.[4]

As a Prophet

As a prophet Jesus makes possible the sending forth of men and women to preach the Gospel of Redemption. Paul informed us: "He ascended up above all heavens that he might fill all things. He gave some apostles, and some prophets, and some evangelists for the perfecting of the saints, for the work of the ministry; for the edifying of the body of Christ" (Eph. 4:10-12). To His disciples Jesus said: "He who hears you, hears Me, and he who rejects you, rejects Him who sent Me" (Luke 10:16).

As High Priest

In heaven, Jesus as risen and ascended Lord, intercedes for us when we sin and violate God's commandments. In the presence of His father Jesus intercedes for us on the basis of His one perfect and final sacrifice. Paul asks the question in his great Romans 8 chapter: "Who shall accuse God's elect? God acquits them; who is there to condemn? Will Christ who dies? Yes, and who rose from the dead. The Christ who is also at the right hand of God, and is interceding for us?" (Rom. 8:3-4).

John the Apostle assures the Asia Minor Christians: "If any man sin we have an Advocate (Greek: Paraclete) before the Father, Jesus Christ the righteous (1 John 2:1)." The author of Hebrews has this assuring teaching: "Hence also he is able to continue saving to the uttermost those who are ever drawing near to God through him, seeing that he is ever living to intercede for them" (Heb. 7:25).

As King

Another benefit Christians enjoy as a result of the Ascension and what followed was that as King of Kings and Lord of Lords, Jesus governs and protects His Church in the interest of His Church. David already predicted this in Psalm (110:1) when he wrote "The Lord said unto My Lord, 'Sit thou at my right hand till I make thine enemies Thy footstool.'" (Ps. 110:1, quoted by Jesus in Matthew 22:44).

The Sending of the Holy Spirit

Another blessing for the Christian was the promise of the sending down the Holy Spirit from heaven to dwell in the believer as Divine helper.[5] Thus Christ told his followers on Maundy Thursday evening: "I am telling you the truth—my going is for your good. For unless I go away the Comforter will not come to you but if I depart I will send Him to you; and when He comes He will convict the world of sin and of righteousness, and of judgment, of sin because they do not believe on me; of righteousness, because I am going to My Father, and you will no longer see me; of Judgment because the Prince of this world is judged" (John 16:7-8). In verse 16 later on we have the paradoxical statement of Christ: "In a little while you shall behold me no more, again in a little while you shall see Me because I am going to the Father."

The Ascension signifies for the believer also the identification with Christ in that the Christian believer is seated positionally with Christ in the heavenly (Eph. 2:6; Col. 3:1-3). Paul assured the Christians of Asia Minor: "But God who is rich in mercy, because of the great love with which he loved us, even while we were dead in trespasses and sins, made us live together with Christ, it is by grace you have been saved, together with Him He raised us from the dead, and together with Christ Jesus seated us in the heavenly realm in order that He might show to the ages to come the amazing riches of his grace by his goodness in Christ Jesus" (Eph. 2:4-6).

As a result of the Holy Spirit's presence in His Church, the ascended Lord promised a special spiritual blessing that through the Holy Spirit the latter would bring all things to their remembrance. This happened when the Holy Spirit caused them accurately to recall through preaching and instruction the teachings of Christ spoken while active in Palestine and adjacent lands. It also involved that the Spirit of Truth would cause them to write the story of Christ as given in the Four Gospels and in letters of the New Testament written by Peter, John and James, writer of Hebrews, and later by Paul. Jesus promised that His Holy Spirit would guide them in all truth. Where is that truth to be found? In the 27 books of the New Testament canon.

The Terminus of the Christ's Ascension: The Session at God's Right Hand

It was through the Ascension that Christ, the God-Man, could permanently take His place at the right hand of *God,* usually called "The Session." By this phrase is meant that with the Father Christ occupies a place of honor and distinction. Mark says: "He was received up into heaven and sat on the right hand of God" (Mark 16:19). The right hand of God is an anthropomorphic expression. It is a figurative expression as God has no body. The expression is very often employed and denoted the power of God (Ex. 15:6; Ps. 18:35; 20:6). We also find the expression "the right hand of power" (Matt. 26:64); "the right hand of majesty" (Hebrew 1:3), "the right hand of the throne of the Majesty" (Hebrews 8:1), "the right hand of the throne of God" (Hebrews 12:1). In this connection one should note Paul's statement in the Ephesian Epistle 1:20-23: "When He raised Him from the dead, and set Him at His own right hand in the heavenly places, far above all principality, and power, and might, and dominion and every name that is named, not only in this world, but also in that which is to come; and hath put all things under His feet, and gave Him to be the Head over all things to the church, which is His body, the fullness of Him that filleth all in all." By the Session at the right hand of God "is meant the full exercise of the power and authority given Jesus according to His human nature."

The Ascension and the Second Coming

While the disciples were watching Christ ascend upward, suddenly there were two men in white standing by them and said to them: "This same Jesus who has been taken up from you into the sky will come back in just the same manner in which you have seen Him going in the sky" (Acts 1:11). If Christ did not intend to return, then what would be the purpose of Christ's Ascension for humankind? With his prediction of these men (angels) other inspired writers of the New Testament agree (Matt. 24:30; Heb. 9:28).

The Ascension of Christ As Reflected
in the Hymnody of the Christian Church

A perusal of Christian hymnology as reflected in *The Lutheran Hymnal*, hymns 212-223 and in *Lutheran Worship* No. 148-153 will show how many different hymnologists dating back to Venantius Honorius Fortunatus (530-609) and the Venerable Bede (died 735) and in the centuries following their deaths have accurately related the historic event as set forth by Scriptures and grasped the significance for Christ and His followers and the blessings available for those devotees who die in faith in the resurrected and ascended Christ. In both hymnals, the Ascension hymns set forth the spirit of victory, joy, praise and hope, occasioned by the Ascension and Session of Jesus Christ, the God-Man. Appropriately this presentation of Christ's Ascension the writer concludes with stanzas 1, 4 and 5 of Friedrich Funke's "Draw Us to thee," *The Lutheran Hymnal*, No. 215:

Verse I: Draw us to Thee,
For then shall we
Walk in Thy Steps forever
And hasten on
Where thou art gone
To be with Thee,
Dear Savior.

Verse 4: Draw us to Thee
That also we
Thy heavenly bliss inherit
And ever dwell
Where sin and hell
No more can vex our spirit.

Verse 5: Draw us to Thee
Increasingly
Into Thy kingdom take us;
Let us forever
Thy glory share.
Thy saints and joint heirs
make us.

Footnotes

1. D.W.Burdick, "Ascension of Christ," *Wycliff Bible Encyclopedia* (Chicago: Moody Press, 1975), I, p. 157.
2. Bruce M. Metzger, *A Textual Commentary on the Greek New Testament* (London-New York: United Bible Societies, 1971), pp. 189-190.
3. Alexander Ross, "The Ascension of Christ," Everett F. Harrison, Editor-in-Chief, *Baker's Dictionary of Theology* (Grand Rapids: Baker Book House, 1960), p. 67a.
4. C. Gausewitz, *Doctor Martin Luther's Small Catechism* (Milwaukee: Northwestern Publishing House, 1956), pp. 128-129.

5. Cf. W. H, Griffith Thomas, *The Holy Spirit* (Grand Rapids; Kregel Publications, 1986), Chapters 21-24, pp. 164-192.

Questions

1. When did the Ascension of Christ take place? ____
2. Jesus spent most of his earthly life in the State of ____ .
3. Where was the Ascension anticipated in the Old Testament? ____
4. Unbelievers say that the Ascension should only be considered ____ .
5. All New Testament references to the Session presuppose ____ .
6. What terminated when Christ left the earth? ____
7. Jesus promised that where two or three are gathered together ____ .
8. The great meaning of the Ascension for Christians is ____ .
9. The threefold office of Christ is ____ .
10. What is a Paraclete? ____
11. The Spirit of Truth would cause the apostles to ____ .
12. The truth is to be found in ____ .
13. The right hand of God is a ____ expression.
14. The Ascension hymns set forth ____ .

The Holy Spirit

Christian News, May 25, 1998

The Holy Spirit's Use of the Means of Grace
(A Study for Pentecost)

Only liturgically oriented churches yearly commemorate the outpouring of the Holy Spirit which occurred on the fiftieth day of Easter, on the Jewish Pentecost festival. Acts 2 depicts the Holy Spirit as a Person separate from the Father and the Son, who plays the two important roles of establishing and maintaining the faith of the Christian Church and of its constituents.

The matter of the Nature of God has been the subject of debate in the churches since the early centuries and there have resulted erroneous teachings and misconceptions about the Person and Work of the Holy Spirit. In 1963 a Concordia Seminary, St. Louis professor wrote and published a book titled "The Half-Known God."[1] Professor Wunderlich began Chapter 1 this way: "The theology of the Holy Spirit is a neglected one among many Christians."[2] Other theologians have joined this chorus lamenting the neglect of the Biblical doctrine of the Holy Spirit.[3] As a result of Pentecostalism and the Holiness Churches in recent years there has been an emphasis on the Person and Work of the Holy Spirit. Some would even allege that other doctrines of Holy Writ have suffered because of a recent overemphasis on the Holy Spirit and the miraculous gifts that He is supposed even today to bestow on the Church.

The Holy Spirit, An Important Biblical Doctrine

Holy Writ, Old[4] and New Testaments,[5] contain considerable material about the Person and Work of the Holy Spirit. Thus the Spirit of God is depicted as involved in creation, revelation and inspiration of Scriptures and in redemption. The New Testament especially contains significant teachings about the Third Person of the Trinity. Holy Writ portrays the Holy Spirit as God and as a member of the Trinity, establishing and maintaining the Christian Church. Christian theology in its setting forth how the Holy Spirit works shows conclusively that the Holy Spirit works through the Means of Grace, the Word of God, through Law and Gospel and through the two sacraments of Holy Baptism and the Lord's Supper.[6] It is through the Means of Grace that people are converted, born again and maintained and sustained in the Christian Church. In the strictest sense the instrument of grace is one only, viz., the Word of God, since it is the Word which makes a sacrament of Baptism and the Lord's Supper, on account of the emphasis laid upon the Word in the Confessions of the Lutheran Church, the Holy Scriptures have been called the Formal Principle of the Reformation. Not only has Scripture alone normative authority in faith and conduct, but all the regenerative influences of the Holy Spirit operate through the Word, and through the Word alone. The Reformed doctrine of Predestination excludes the idea of the Means of Grace which impart the Spirit and His gift to men; the Spirit works effectively only on the elect, according to the system of Calvin.[7] Hence even in the earliest days (Zwinglian) Reformed theology substituted for the external Word, as means of grace, an "inner word," through which alone the Spirit is believed to work, the lack of emphasis, even in the best of Reformed preaching, is a problem, not considering the divine Word as the vehicle of regenerating grace and on the Sacraments. According to Reformed theology the office of the Word is to point to the way of life, without communicating that which the idea conveys. The Reformed do not deny that Word and sacraments are unnecessary, but that they are only symbols of what the Holy Spirit does immediately and directly.[8] These notions are contained in Zwingl's *Method of Faith*. From this position, in the days of the Reformation it was but one step from the stance of the so-called enthusiasts (Schwaermer) and certain sects who emphasized the "inner light," generally identified "the baptism of the Holy Spirit" and to the necessity of "a second conversion." This led to the emphasis on revivalism, which has characterized Methodist, Pentecostalism and particularly the Reformed doctrine of an immediate operation apart from the Means of Grace.

The Holy Spirit Employs the Means of Grace in His Work

The Spirit of God, the Third Person of the Holy Trinity, operates through the Means of Grace, the Word of God (including Law and Gospel) and through the two sacraments of Holy Baptism and the Lord's Supper. The Holy Spirit, emanating from the Father and the Son, has brought about the existence and perpetuation of the Christian Church. In bringing about the conversion and regeneration of those who are saved by God's grace, the Paraclete employs the Word of God and the Sacraments, because they are the means through which God's grace is brought to men and women, and through which the Holy Spirit works His saving effects.

The Means of Grace are adapted to the nature and purpose of the Holy Spirit's work. Concerning this matter Stump wrote: "In the last analysis, His work is that of drawing and persuading men to believe and to continue to believe. In the broad sense the **Word** is the means of persuasion. In saying this we include the Sacraments along with the Word proper. For essentially the sacraments are the Lord also; God speaks in them. Not only is the Word the principal part of the sacraments, but the sacraments themselves as a whole, including the sacramental action and the words connected with it are meant to convey the very same essential truth as is conveyed by the Word proper. And it is through the **truth** set forth in Word and sacrament, that the Holy Spirit draws and persuades men to believe and are saved."[9]

Different Characteristics of the Two Sacraments

Christian theologians have pointed to this difference in the two sacraments: The Word of God has been termed the audible Word, the two sacraments the visible Word although the audible Word can appear in

1114

print and thus be visible, also when signed to the deaf, by means of visible gestures of the hands.

The Contribution of Acts 2 to the
Doctrine of The Holy Spirit's Work

The historic Pentecost occurrence in Jerusalem in the year A.D. 30 shows how the Holy Spirit operates (Acts 2:1-31). When the Christian Church was born on the fiftieth day after the day of Christ's bodily resurrection, it was not only characterized by the sound of a rushing mighty wind and cloven tongues of flame on the heads of the Apostles which were in evidence but there was a mighty preaching of the wonderful works of God in Christ by the Apostles speaking in many different languages, made possible by the Holy Spirit, but notably a sermon by Peter, who addressed the multitude assembled, calling upon them to repent, to accept Christ as their Savior and to be baptized for the remission of sins (Acts 2:38). As a result of this mighty sermon, the Holy Spirit working upon the hearts of different people from various parts of the Roman Empire in Europe, Asia and Africa caused three thousand people to come to faith in Christ and become Christians and were baptized.

This has been the case ever since, for Christian people have been born again, "not of corruptible seed but of incorruptible by the Word of God, which liveth and abideth forever." St. James expressed it this way: "Of His will begat He us with the Word of truth that we should be a kind of first-fruit of His creatures (James 1:18)."

The Holy Spirit and Baptism

Holy Scriptures repeatedly mention regeneration as being effected through Holy Baptism.[10] This is surely what Jesus had in mind when He said to Nicodemus: "But I say unto you, Except a man be born of water and the Spirit, he cannot enter into the kingdom of God" (John 3:5). It was spoken at a time of John's baptism. Thus Nicodemus was a Pharisee, and the Scribes and Pharisees, to their own condemnation, rejected the will of God that they should be baptized by John (Luke 7:30). Therefore, the Lord speaking to Nicodemus stressed particularly the importance of Baptism as a means by which the Holy Spirit works the new birth in a person and without which an individual, of either sex, could not enter the kingdom of God.

In Titus 3:5 Paul stressed the idea that the Holy Spirit through Holy Baptism effected conversion. "Not by works of righteousness which we have done but according to His mercy He saved us by the washing of regeneration and renewing of the Holy Ghost." Both expressions refer to Holy Baptism. Baptism is the washing by which regeneration is granted to individuals by which people are renewed by the Holy Spirit.

Professor Kramer wrote:

"Without the new birth a man cannot be saved. The new birth consists essentially in this, that a sinner comes to faith in Christ as his Savior. The new birth is wholly a gift of God, or of the Spirit of God. The Holy Spirit gives this new birth through means—through the preaching of the

Gospel and through Holy Baptism."[11]

Why can water do such great things? To many this appears unreasonable that applying water can effect a new life, turn a person's life around. Luther in dealing with this question in his discussion of Baptism wrote: "It is not the water indeed that does them, but word of God which is in and with the water, and faith, which trusts such word of God in the water. For without the word of God the water is simple water and no Baptism. But with the word of God it is a Baptism, that is a gracious water of life and a washing of regeneration in the Holy Ghost, as St. Paul says in Titus, chapter three."[12]

What Happens in Baptism?

In the words of institution, it is stated: "Baptizing them in the name of the Father, the Son and the Holy Ghost (Matt. 28:19)." In Holy Baptism the baptized person is brought into fellowship with Father, Son and Holy Ghost. The name of God is named over the person and henceforth this person belongs to the Triune God as His very own. Therefore, in Baptism an individual is returned to God the Father, his Creator, to God the Son Who loved him and gave Himself for him, to God the Holy Ghost, who would dwell in his heart and henceforth rule every thought and action. Through the new birth a male or female person becomes a child of God.

With the foregoing presentation a number of Bible passages agree. Paul in Galatians 3:27 advised the congregations of Galatia: "As many of you as have been baptized in the name of Christ, have put on Christ." Here it is shown that by Baptism the baptized person puts on Christ as he would put on a garment. His sins are hidden from the eyes of God, who looks at the baptized person now clothed with Christ's righteousness. Paul reminds the Corinthians: "But you are washed, but you are sanctified, but you are justified in the name of the Lord Jesus Christ and by the Spirit of our God (I Cor. 6:11)." In his first Epistle to the churches found in Asia Minor, Peter compares the waters of baptism with the waters of the flood, which drowned a whole generation of wicked people in the days of Noah but saved Noah and seven others with him in the ark and wrote: "So Baptism also now saves us (1 Peter 3:21)."

Paul taught the same thing about the Church: "Christ also loved the church and gave it with washing by the Word (Eph. 5:26)." By Baptism the baptized person becomes a part of the Church, for Paul wrote: "For as the body is one and hath many members and all members of that one body being many, are one body, so also is Christ. For by one Spirit we are all baptized into one body, whether we be Jew or Gentile, whether we be bond or free, and all have been made to drink of one Spirit (1 Cor. 12:12-13)." With Baptism comes a new life. "If anyone be in Christ, he is a new creature, old things are passed away, behold, all things are new (2 Cor. 17)."

Christians who teach that baptism has a regenerating and saving effect are accused of advocating that all that a person needs is to be baptized and this automatically saves him or her. That is neither the teaching of Holy Writ or of the historic Lutheran Church. The fact is that the new life that has been created by baptism needs to be nourished until death occurs. The truth is that the moment a person is a baptized person he leads a God-pleasing life. Concerning this matter Paul wrote: "Shall we continue in sin that grace may abound? God forbid! Shall we, that are dead to sin, live any longer in sin? Know ye not that so many as were baptized into Jesus Christ were baptized into His death. Therefore, we are buried with Him by Baptism into death that like as Christ was raised from the dead by the glory of God the Father, even so we also should walk in newness of life (Romans 6:1-41)."

As baptized into Christ and having been risen with Him, nothing but newness of life avails anything in being a new creature. It is as Paul said to the Galatians: "In Christ Jesus neither circumcision availeth anything, nor uncircumcision, but a new creature. Whoever is born of *God,* and every one that loveth Him that begat loveth also that is begotten of Him (I John 5:11)."

Over and above the Word of God, and the remembrance of Baptism, another additional powerful means for growth in grace and holiness is the Lord's Supper or Eucharist. St. Matthew in chapter 26:23-26 wrote: "As they were eating, Jesus took bread and blessed it, broke it and gave it to His disciples saying: "Take eat this is my body and Drink ye all of it, for this is the blood of the New Testament, which is shed for you for the remission of sins." St. Paul in I Corinthians 11:23-26 repeats the words of institution of the Holy Communion and added the command: "This do in remembrance of Me."

The Lord's Supper has been celebrated since before the middle of the first Christian century and has been a source of great comfort and strength in temptation, in sorrow and in the hour of death. While Baptism is performed once, the Lord's Supper is celebrated frequently. The Bible says that as often as the Lord's Supper is celebrated, the death of Christ is recalled.

The Lord's Supper is a Means of Grace, because through it benefits are bestowed, such as the forgiveness of sins and through it a man is justified, and thus makes possible peace with God. Another benefit bestowed by the Eucharist is that the Holy Spirit unites His followers with other members of the body of Christ (Eph. 1:2-3; 4:15-16). While this takes place through the preaching of the Gospel and through the waters, of Baptism, the body of Christian friendship is mightily strengthened through the Lord's Supper. This is what Paul is referring to in I Corinthians 10:7, where he wrote: "For we being many, are one bread and one body, for we are all partakers of one bread."

When Christians commune about the Lord's Table, they enjoy fellowship in the body of Christ, the Church; the Holy Spirit working by the Means of the Gospel, Baptism and the Lord's Supper unite Christians together as one body.[15] In this fellowship Christians are caused to remember that they are the sons and daughters of God and are given a foretaste of that life that will be theirs in the presence of God. "Beloved, now we are the sons of God, and it does not yet appear that we shall be, but we

1117

know that when He shall appear, we shall be like Him, for we shall see Him as He is (1 John 3:2)."

Footnotes

1. Lorenz Wunderlich, *The Half Forgotten God* (St. Louis: Concordia Publishing House, 1963).
2. **Ibid.**, p. 12.
3. George S. Hendry, *The Holy Spirit in Christian Theology* (Philadelphia: Westminster Press, 1954), p. 4; Pitney Van Dusen, Spirit, Son and Father (New York: Charles Scribner Sons, 1938), p. 13.
4. Genesis 1:2; Ex. 31:1; 35:31; Num. 24:2; I Sam. 10:10,11,16; 19:22; 11 Chron. 15:1; Job 27:3; Ezek. 11:24.
5. John 11:26; 15:26; 16:14; Luke 2:27; 4:1; 10:21; Cf. also Zondervan's Expanded Concordat (Grand Rapids: Zondervan Publishing House, 1968), p. 1326, columns 2 and 3. 6. Cf. "Means of Grace," in Joseph Stump, *The Christian Faith* (New York: The Macmillan Company, 1932), pp. 289-299.
7. Th. Engelder, W. Arndt, Th. Graebner, F. E. Mayer, *Popular Symbolics* (St. Louis: Concordia Publishing House, 1934), p. 77.
8. John Calvin, *Institutes of the Christian Religion*, Translated from the Latin by John Allen Philadelphia: Presbyterian Board of Christian Education, No Date), Part III, Chapter Vol. II, pp. 179fr.
9. Stump, **op. cit.**, p. 289.
10. Fred Kramer, *The Holy Spirit and the Sacraments* (St. Louis: Concordia Publishing House, 1964), pp. 6-7.
11. **Ibid.**, p. 8.
12. Theodore G. Tappert, *The Book of Concord* (Philadelphia: Fortress Press, 1959), *The Small Catechism*, p. 349.
13. *Popular Symbolics*, **op. cit.**, pp. 104.112,179.
14. Ibid, pp. 104-112.
15. Kramer, **op. cit.**, pp. 14-15.

Questions

1. Who wrote "The Half Known God?" ____
2. It is through the Means of Grace that people are ____.
3. What is the formal principle of the Reformation? ____
4. The Reformed maintain that the Word and sacraments are only ____.
5. The Spirit of God operates through ____.
6. The Christian Church was born on ____.
7. Without the new birth a man cannot be ____.
8. "So Baptism also now ____."
9. The Lord's Supper is celebrated ____ Baptism only ____.

The Holy Trinity

Christian News, June 1, 1998

The Doctrine of the Holy Trinity as Reflected In the Three Ecumenical Creeds and Also in Certain Canticles of the Christian Liturgy

(A Study for Trinity Sunday)

The doctrine of the Holy Trinity is well attested in the Scriptures of the Old and New Testaments. This fundamental doctrine is clearly explicated in the Three Ecumenical Creeds and in certain Canticles of the Christian Liturgy, as *The Gloria Patri, the Glory in Excelsis* and the *Te Deum Laudamus.*

The Biblical Basis for The Trinity as Set Forth In the Apostles' Creed, The Nicene Creed and Old Testament:

The Old Testament contains not merely indications of the Trinity, but explicitly distinguishes between the Father, His Son, called the Messiah, and also the Angel of the Lord, in the plurality of the name Elohim and in passages where the three persons are distinguished, as in Genesis 1:1-2; 2 Sam. 23:2; Ps. 33:6; Is. 42:1; 48:16-17; Is. 61:1.[1]

New Testament:

Passages where the Father, the Son and the Holy Spirit are mentioned together: Matthew 3:16-17: "As soon as Jesus was baptized, He stepped out of the water, and now heaven was opened. And He saw God's Spirit coming down on Him as a dove. And a voice from heaven said, 'This is My Son, whom I love and delight in.'"

Matthew 17:5: "He was still speaking when a bright cloud suddenly overshadowed them, and a voice came out of the cloud: 'This is My Son whom I love and delight in. Listen to Him!'"

Romans 8:26-27: Father and Son working together:

"In the same way the Spirit helps us in our weakness, because we do not know how we should pray, but the Spirit Himself pleads for us with yearnings that can't find any words. He who searches our hearts knows what the Spirit means to do, that in God's own way He's pleading for the holy people."

John 10:30: Father and Son are One: Jesus declared: "I and the Father are one."

Matthew 28:19: The Baptismal Command to baptize in the name of the Father, the Son and the Holy Spirit.

John 14:6: The Holy Spirit distinct from the Father and Son: "And I will ask the Father, and He will give you another Comforter to be with you forever." (All three Persons mentioned.)

2 Corinthians 13:11: "The grace of the Lord Jesus Christ, the love of God, and the fellowship of the Holy Spirit be with you all!"

I Peter 1:2: All three Persons are active in redemption:

"Chosen long ago by God the Father to be made holy by the Spirit. Christ and be sprinkled with His blood: God give you more and more."

John 17:5,24: The relationship between Father and Son existed before the foundation of the world:

John 17:5: "And now Father glorify Me at your side with the glory I had with You before the world began." Verse 24: "Father, I want those You gave me to be with Me to see My glory that You gave Me because You have loved Me before the world began."

Truths Taught by All Three Ecumenical Creeds

All three ecumenical Creeds, the Apostles' Creed, the Nicene Creed and the Athanasian Creed, refer to the three different persons of the Holy Trinity, the Father, His Son and the Holy Spirit.

The Apostles' Creed ascribed different **opera ad extra** (divine works) to each of the Three Members of the Christian Godhead.[2] The three creeds are believed to have grown spontaneously from such confessions as found in Matt. 16:16; John 1:49; 6:69; 11:23; 20:28; Acts 8:37; of Jesus and the Father: Matt. 10:32,33; Mark 16:16; Acts 14:15; and of Trinity: 2 Cor. 13:14; I Peter 1:20, the confession of Peter, Matt. 16:16; John 1:49 and the baptismal formula, Matt. 28:19 and these passages most likely influenced the development of the three creeds. Both Ignatius, Ep. and Tral. 9, and Justin Martyr Apol. 1:13,21, have references to the Apostles' Creed.[3] At first the Apostles' Creed was only memorized and not written. It was explained to the catechumens in the last stages of their preparation. The ante-Nicene Fathers referred to it as "the rule of faith," "apostolic tradition," and "symbol of faith." Ireneus, Novatian and Cyprian refer to "rules of faith" in various of their writings.[4]

The Apostles' Creed

The teachings of the Apostles' Creed arose independently in various parts of the Eastern and Western Churches.[5] A very early form of this creed was the Roman Creed: "I believe in God the Father, Almighty, and in Christ Jesus, His Son, our Lord, and in the Holy Spirit, the Holy Church, and Resurrection of the flesh." Ultimately, a longer form became standard in the West. Rufinus gives the complete Latin text and Marcellus of Ancyra, the Greek text.[6] Later there was added: "He descended into Hades," taken from the creed of Aquileja. The word "catholic" was taken from Oriental creeds and "life everlasting" perhaps from Revenna and Antioch.[7] The present form triumphed in the West (6th to 8th centuries) due to the influence of the Church of Rome. In the 12 statements comprising the Apostles' Creed, it may be asserted that the fundamental doctrines of the faith, beginning with creation in the first part, Genesis 1:1-2 and ending with eternal life (Rev. 21-22), are given.

The Nicene Creed (Symbolum Niceno-Constantinopolitan)

The Nicene Creed is believed to represent the Eastern development of the baptismal formula and its formulation was occasioned by the Arian Controversy, when Arius denied the same essence to the Son as he did to the Father.[8] Arius claimed that the Son of God was not of the same ousia, omeousia, and was only like the other, **homoios** namely, of like essence. So the Nicene Creed aimed at safeguarding the Biblical teaching about the deity of Christ.[9] It ended with an anathema against the Arians.

The Niceno-Constantinopolitan Creed is named after the fact that Aetus presented it at the Council of Chalcedon (A.D. 451) and ascribed the creed to the 150 bishops together with Theodosius held at Constantinople against the Pneumatomachians (381).[10] The later view held that the Holy Spirit was merely a creature and inferior to the Son. Macedonius was the leader of the Pneumatomachi and represented the theological position of the Semi-Arians.[11]

The Niceno-Constantinopolitan Creed made a few changes in the Nicene Creed and enlarged the Third Article with the addition of asserting the deity of the Holy Spirit. The additions are said to be similar to the creeds of Epiphanius and Cyril of Alexandria.[12]

There are two forms of the Constantinopolitan Creed: The Western which asserts that the Holy Spirit proceeds from the Father and the Son, while the Greek Orthodox Church holds that the Holy Spirit proceeds from the Father,[13] but not from the Son, known as the **monarchia** (sole rule). The Filioque ("and from the Son") was added by the Roman Church, and as a result a permanent split because of it occurred between these two great church bodies of Christendom.

The Nicene Creed is more theological, polemical than the Apostles' Creed and echoes sharp distinctions, as "coessential," "coequal," "begotten not made," so phrased by the orthodox against heresies.

The Athanasian Creed
(Symbolum Quicunque)
The Athanasian Creed is the third and last of the ecumenical creeds. When it originated is a matter of debate.[14] Since the ninth century it has been ascribed to Athanasius,[15] but this theory has been given up since the seventeenth century. One reason given is: Athanaius did not write in Latin but in Greek.

The contents of the Athanasian Creed presupposes the heresies propounded by Nestorianism and Eutychianism.[16] The Creed appears to have originated in Gaul or North Africa as a commentary on the first four ecumenical councils. Trillhaas claimed that "the socalled Athanasian Creed is a long catalog of statements expounding the Trinity and the Incarnation."[17] According to its very first statement ("whosoever would be saved") salvation and damnation hinges on the acceptance of these statements. It is likely that it contains many quotations from Ambrose and Augustine.[18] In the Athanasian Creed the confessor of this creed will find a doctrine of the Trinity more definite and developed than in the Nicene and Apostles' Creeds. The latter did not give a formulated doctrine of the dogma of the Trinity in the sense of the economic Trinity, but sets forth the Trinity teaching by proclaiming the deity and the Holy Spirit (called imminent Trinity). Neve claimed that in Part I of the Athanasian Creed the doctrine of the Trinity was explicated as it was developed and completed in the West by St. Augustine. Averred Neve: "Here we have put in formula and guarded against any evasion, the doctrine of the one divine Being or Essence and the Tri-personality of the Father, Son and Holy Ghost."[19]

Two particulars should be emphasized as being characteristics of the Athanasian Creed. First, any kind of **subordination** of the Son to the Father, and the Holy Spirit to both are excluded. The Godhead of the Three Persons "is all one." All have equal glory and majesty. The Athanasian Creed asserts: "They are uncreated, incomprehensible, almighty, they are all one God. None is before or after the other; none less than the other. They are coeternal and coequal."[20]

Relative to the word persona, Schaff has observed that **persona** is neither taken in the old sense of a mere personation or the form of manifestation (Greek **Prosopos**, face, mask) nor in the modern sense of an independent, separate being or individual, but in a sense which lies between the two conceptions, and avoids Sabellianism on the one hand, Tritheism on the other,[21] which according to Neve means: "The divine persons are in one another and form a perpetual intercommunication and motion within the divine essence. Each person has all the divine attributes which are inherent in the divine essence but each has also a characteristic individuality of property, which is peculiar to the person and cannot be communicated; the Father is unbegotten, the Son is begotten of the Father and the Holy Spirit proceeding from the Father and the Son."[22]

Part II of The Athanasian Creed

The pre-existence of Christ was especially dealt with in the Nicene Creed and thus secured His Divinity; the Athanasian Creed, in Part II, is concerned with Christ's post-existence and dealt with the problems relating not to eternality, but to the incarnate life and personality of the Savior of mankind. This part of the Athanasian Creed represents a symbolic expression of the Christology set forth at Chalcedon (A.D. 451), which sets forth the orthodox doctrine produced by the Councils of Ephesus (A.D. 431) and Chalcedon (A.D. 451) and also outlined in the famous letter of Pope Leo the Great to Flavian after the so-called Robber Synod (A.D. 449). The Creed of Chalcedon was preceded by a reaffirmation Niceno-Constantinopolitan Creed. Neve claimed that the Creed of Chalcedon was the basis for The Athanasian Creed.

The Christology of Chalcedon

The Athanasian Creed teaches a true Incarnation of God's Son, which did not consist in a conversion or transmutation of God into man, nor of a conversion of man into God and consequently an absorption of one into the other or a confusion (Greek: krasis) nor on the other hand a mere indwelling (Greek: enoichesis, Latin: inhabitatio) of the one into the other, nor an outward transitory connection (Greek: synapheia, Latin: inhabitatio) of one into the other, nor an outward transitory connection (Greek:

synapheia, Latin: conjunctio) of the two factors. Yes, it was an actual and abiding union of the two in one personal life.[24]

The Distinction Between Nature and Person

John in his Gospel called Jesus the LOGOS (1:1) and the latter did not assume a human person, else He would have had two Persons, a Divine and a human. As God He took on human nature, common to all mankind, and therefore was able not just one individual but all humans, as partakers of their nature (Hebrew 2:14).

The God-Man as the Result of the Incarnation

Christ is not a double being, with two persons, as the Nestorians held, nor a compound middle being, a **tertium quid**, neither divine or human, Christ is one person, both Divine and human. The soul is also included in His humanity (against Apollinarius).

The Duality of the Natures

Eutychianism taught that there was a distinction between the Divine nature and human nature, even the Incarnation, without confusion or conversion (Greek: asyncrytos, inconfused and **ateptios**, Latin: immutabilis); over against Nestorianism the assertion is made that between the two natures there was no division or separation (Greek: adiairetos, Latin: inseparabiliter), so that the Divine will always remain Divine, and the human ever human, and nevertheless both the Divine and the human have continually a common life and interpenetrate each other, like the Persons of the Trinity (perichoresis, permatio).[25]

The Unity of the Persons
(kenosis hypostatike, unio hypostatica, later unio personalis)

Neve claimed that the Athanasian Creed sets forth "the union of the divine and human in the one person of Christ is a permanent state resulting from the Incarnation, and is a real, supernatural, personal and inseparable— indistinction from the essential absorption or confusion, or from a mere moral union, or from a mystical, such as holds between the believer and Christ."[26] The two natures constitute one personal life, and yet remain distinct. Lutheran theology, in the interest of the personal union, states the Son of man came down from heaven (John 3:16), while yet the son of God took flesh from the Virgin Mary, and yet on the other hand enemies crucified the Lord of glory (1 Corinthians 2:8). As a human being Christ suffered but not in His Godhead which could not suffer, but in the weaknesses of the human nature. Further Neve contends that the divine nature is the seat of self-consciousness and pervades and animates the human[27] (p. 37).

The whole work of Christ is attributed to both natures. The entire person of Christ is the subject of the work of Christ. Infinite worth is ascribed to His work on earth because the humanity is in the personal union with His Divinity.[28]

The Enhypostasia Denial Of Two Natures in Christ
(Or Anhypostasia of the Human Nature)[28a]
The avoidance of ascribing a double personality the Early Church took the stance that Christ's human nature had no independence of its own, but the Divine took the initiative in the act of the Incarnation and is the root and basis of personality.[29]

Characteristics of the Athanasian Creed
Both parts of the Athanasian Creed undertake to deal with the important teaching truths of the Holy Trinity and the Incarnation by means of speculation and logical deductions. The statements of the Athanasian Creed represent the thinking and theological conclusions of the first five centuries of Christian Church history. It is recognized that dealing with the doctrines of the Trinity and the Incarnation that these two doctrines contain impenetrable mysteries. The Athanasian Creed does not endeavor to solve these mysteries but does try to state the essential elements of these doctrines and defines the boundary lines of error. Schaff said that this creed avoids the Scylla as well as the Charybdis: In the doctrine of the Trinity it avoids tritheism on the one hand, and Sabellianism on the other hand; in the doctrine of the Incarnation it gives the position half-way between Nestorian dualism and Eutychian Monophysitism.[30]

The Athanasian Creed Compared
With the Apostles' and Nicene Creeds
The Athanasian Creed is the most theological of the three ecumenical creeds. It has been called a "musical creed" or a "dogmatic psalm." Among the three creeds the Athanasian Creed resembles the *Formula of Concord* among the symbols or confessions of the Lutheran Church as found in the Book of Concord of 1580.[31]

What About the Condemnatory
Clauses of the Athanasian Creed?
One of the features of the Athanasian Creed, absent from the other two, are its condemnatory clauses, such as: "Whosoever will be saved before all things, it is necessary that he hold the catholic faith which faith except one hold the Catholic faith, which faith except everyone do keep whole and undefiled, without doubt he shall perish everlastingly." In the middle of the text: "He therefore that will be saved must think of the Trinity. Furthermore, it is necessary to everlasting salvation; that he also believe rightly the Incarnation of our Lord Jesus Christ." Finally at the close: "This is the Catholic true Christian faith, which, except a man believe faithfully, he cannot be saved."

For a clarification of these condemnatory clauses Neve called attention to the fact that in the Augsburg Confession there are damnatory or rejectory clauses, namely, in Articles I, II, V, VIII, IX, XII, XVI, XVII, XVIII.[32] However, the ones in the Athanasian Creed claim that he who fails to be orthodox cannot be saved, but the Lutherans do not assert that those who are not orthodox cannot be saved. The *Formula of Concord* has this illuminating statement that not only shall the Biblical position be stated but rejecting the doctrine opposed to it. But the Formula has this declaration: "It is in no way our design and purpose to condemn men who from a certain simplicity of mind, and nevertheless are not blasphemous against the truth of the heavenly doctrine, much less in deed, entire churches, which are either under the Roman Empire, or the German nation or elsewhere."

Neve observed: "There is difference between fully understanding a fundamental doctrine and consciously rejecting, or even blaspheming it."[33]

However, it should be noted that there is a confessional truth in the damnatory clauses of the Athanasian Creed. It cannot be a matter of indifference for a person or church body to reject the doctrinal expressions of the Church. John Gerhard averred: "He who ignores the mystery of the Trinity does not know God."

The Use of the Athanasian Creed by Major Churches of Christendom

The Greek Orthodox Eastern Church lists the Athanasian Creed (without the filioque) as a part of its theological beliefs, but does not employ it in its worship services.[34] The Roman Catholic Church since the time of Pope Gregory IX in 1223 sent it to Constantinople. The Roman Catholic Church uses it during its services during Advent and Lent.[35]

The Lutheran Church has placed it in the Book of Concord, as the third of the Ecumenical Creeds,[36] but does not use it for liturgical purposes. However, there are Lutheran Churches where the congregation on Trinity Sunday reads the Athanasian Creed in place of the Apostles' or Nicene Creed, which is read and confessed on Communion Sundays.

As far as the Reformed Churches are concerned some Reformed bodies have accepted the Athanasian Creed.[37] The Episcopal Church has assumed an ambivalent attitude to this major creed of Christendom. In England, the Episcopal Church used it on certain days. The Protestant Episcopal Church in the United States by a decision of 1876 does not any longer accept the Athanasian Creed.[38] Various denominations among the Reformed are indifferent to using and accepting the theology of the Athanasian Creed, because they are opposed to credal obligations incumbent on a church or individual.[39]

II. Liturgical Canticles Testifying to the Doctrine of the Trinity The Gloria Patri (The Little Doxology)

The Gloria Patri has doctrinal as well as devotional value. It distinguishes the Christian use of the Psalter and comments on Old Testament texts with the later and fuller revelation of the New Testament. Thus it is regularly added to every Psalm, canticle or portion thereof.[40] Reed claimed: "Thus its use in the early church affirmed the orthodox belief in the divinity, equality and eternity of the three Persons, in opposition to Arian and other heresies."[41] The continued use of the Gloria Patri today is more than a memorial of ancient controversies. It is a brief but clear profession of faith in the Holy Trinity and particularly of our Lord. The Scriptural basis for the **Gloria Patri** is found in such passages as Romans 16:27; Ephesians 3:21; Philippians 4:20 and Revelation 1:6.[42]

The Gloria in Excelsis (Glory in the Highest)

In the Gloria in Excelsis the three Persons of the Trinity are addressed. This canticle came immediately after the Kyrie; as a hymn praise, it has the worshippers praising joyfully the fact of God's love in sending of his Son, who as the Lamb of God takes away the sins of the world. While the *Gloria in Excelsis* is a hymn of praise to the Father, it is also a jubilant anthem of redemption.

Asserted Reed: "Thus early in the services it grounds our faith and worship in the incarnation, the atonement and the perpetual intercession of our Lord. For a moment it stops in its flight to involve mercy and help, then swiftly and objectively, as though having glimpsed the glory of Almighty, rises to its final outburst of worship and praise to Christ and the Holy Ghost as most high in the glory of God the Father."[43]

The *Gloria in Excelsis* dates from the fourth century, although it may be older, found in the *Apostolic Constitutions* (vii:47) as does also Athanasius (died in 373).

The second part of the three parts of the *Gloria in Excelsis* anticipates the wording of the **Agnus Dei**, which only entered the Liturgy centuries later. Reed believed that the *Gloria in Excelsis* was introduced into the Eucharistic service in the Western Church in connection with the Christmas Vigil. This was especially fitting because of the reference to the angels' song at Christ's birth. The Incarnation and the Holy Communion "are both manifestations of the real presence of Christ among men."[44]

The Te Deum Laudamus

The Te Deum Laudamus is considered one of the noblest hymns of the Western Church. It combines praise and prayer in exalted strains of rhythmic prose. The affirmations of this canticle are creedal in form (particularly vs. 10-19) and constitute a basis for petitions of universal significance.[45] The earliest reference of the Te Deum Laudamus occurs around A.D. 500. By the time of Benedict (A.D. 530) the Western Church was employing it. According to Dom Morin (1894), possibly Niceta, a missionary bishop of Remesina, in Dacis (A.D. 335-414) was the compiler of the Te Deum Laudamus.[46]

In structural form the *Te Deum* resembles the Gloria in Excelsis and may have influenced the former form. The *Te Deum* has three divisions— two principle parts and an appendix. Part I(vs. 1-13)sounds forth the praise of God the Father (vs. 1-6), and then in full chorus, of the Holy Trinity(vs. 7-13); the second part (vs. 14-21) again, like the Liturgy, commemorates Christ's redemptive work and upon the basis of this asks for divine aid.[47]

The hymn in the beginning is allegedly to most likely ended with the words: "In glory ever lasting." Part III (vs. 22-29) was probably added from one of the suffrages in the form of versicle and response, which anciently concluded certain hymns, in this case the Suffrages which followed the *Gloria in Excelsis* in the Eastern Office. The Gloria had its place as morning hymn in the Greek Office since the fourth century. When it was transferred to the Mass in the Western Church, the Te Deum may have been inserted in the vacant place at Matins. In this manner the eight verses may have become attached to the original text. They are chiefly from the Psalms and lack unity.[48] In 1529 Martin Luther translated into German in a free version of 52 lines as Herr Gott, dich loben wir, arranged for antiphonal singing. It appeared in Spannenberg's Kirchen gesenge.

The Te Deum Laudamus is a morning hymn, as the petition "Vouchsafe O Lord to keep us this day without sin," clearly indicates. The liturgical employment of the *Te Deum* was designed on the Matins of all festivals and all Sundays except in Advent and from Septaugesima to Palm Sunday. It was also used at special occasions as a hymn of thanksgiving. The fact that the Te Deum was used at anniversaries had given occasion to inumerable polyphonic settings for choir.[49]

The Doctrine of the Trinity in Christian Hymnology

Both the *Lutheran Hymnal* and *Lutheran Worship* have hymns setting forth the doctrine of the Trinity. Hymn numbers 237-253 are various hymns explicating the doctrine of the Trinity. Among these are Luther's Versification of the Nicene Creed: "Wir glauben all an einen God," No. 251, and a versification of the *Te Deum Laudamus*, "Holy God, We Praise Thy Name, No. 250. There are a number of hymns that describe poetically The Apostles' Creed, No. 252, 253; in *Lutheran Worship*, hymns 168-175. Many other hymns have references to the Trinity; a listing of these may be found in *The Handbook of the Lutheran Hymnal*.[50]

Footnotes

1. J. T. Mueller, *Christian Dogmatics*, (St. Louis: Concordia Publishing House, 1975), pp. 158-160.
2. A. L. Graebner, *Outlines of Doctrinal Theology* (St. Louis: Concordia Publishing House, 1910), p. 46.
3. J. L. Neve, *Introduction to the Symbolic Books of the Lutheran Church* (Columbus: Lutheran Book Concern, 1926), pp. 44-45.
4. Fernand Cabrol, *Liturgical Prayer, Its History and Spirit* (New York: Kennedy, 1925), pp. 108-110; Neve, **op. cit.**, pp. 47-48.
5. Robert M. Grant, "Apostles," in Lefferts A. Loetscher, *Twentieth Century Encyclopedia of Religious Knowledge* (Grand Rapids: 1955), I, p. 55a.
6. "Apostles' Creed," in L. Fuerbringer, Th. Engelder, P. E. Kretzmann, *Concordia Cyclopedia* (St. Louis: Concordia Publishing House, 1927), p. 32.
7. "The Apostles' Creed" (Philip Schaff, *The Creeds of Christendom* (New York: Harper & Brothers, 1897), I, p. 35.
8. "Nicene Creed," *Popular Symbolics*, **op. cit.**, p. 542.

9. **Ibid.**, p. 542.

10. "Pneumatomachi," *Concordia Cyclopedia*, **op. cit.**, p. 589a.

11. **Ibid.**, p. 589b.

12. Neve, cit., pp. 66-67.

13. Schaff, **op. cit.**, I, pp. 25-26.

14. "The Athanasian Creed," Schaff, *The Creeds of Christendom, I, History of the Creeds*, **op. cit.**, p. 35.

15. Neve, **op. cit.**, p. 72.

16. "Athanasian Creed," Neve, p. 72.

17. Wolfgang Trillhaas. "Creeds," *The Encyclopedia of the Lutheran Church* (Minneapolis: Augsburg Publishers, 1965), I, p. 629b.

18. **Ibid.**, p. 629b.

19. Neve, **op. cit.**, p. 74.

20. "The Athanasian Creed," in Theodore Tappert, *The Book of Concord* (Philadelphia: Muhlenberg Press, 1959), pp. 19-20.

21. Neve, **op. cit.**, p. 74; Schaff, **op. cit.**, I, p. 38.

22. **Ibid.**, p. 74.

23. **Ibid.**, p. 75.

24. **Ibid.**, p. 76.

25. **Ibid.**, p. 77.

26. **Ibid.**, p. 78.

27. **Ibid.**, p. 78.

28. **Ibid.**, p. 78.

28a. Cf. F. Pieper, *Christian Dogmatics* (St. Louis: Concordia Publishing House, 1950), I, pp. 382-384.

29. Schaff, *Creeds of Christendom*, **op. cit.**, I, p. 38.

30. Neve, **op. cit.**, p. 79.

31. **Ibid.**, p. 79.

32. **Ibid.**, p. 79.

33. **Ibid.**, p. 80.

34. Schaff, **op. cit.**, I, p. 40.

35. Neve, **op. cit.**, p. 81.

36. Tappert, **op. cit.**, pp. 19-20.

37. Neve, **op. cit.**, p. 82.

38. **Ibid.**, p. 82.

39. **Ibid.**, p. 82.

40. Luther D. Reed, *The Lutheran Liturgy* (Philadelphia: Muhlenberg Press,
1947), p. 252.

41. **Ibid.**, p. 242.

42. **Ibid.**, p. 242.

43. **Ibid.**, p. 259.

44. **Ibid.**, p. 260.

45. Reed, p. 393.

46. George Barrois, "Te Deum," *Twentieth Century Encyclopedia of Religious Knowledge* (Grand Rapids: Baker Book House, 1955), II, p. 1093.

47. **Ibid.**, p. 393.

48. Reed, **op. cit.**, p. 393.

49. **Ibid.**, p. 393.
50. Compiled by W. G. Polack, *The Handbook to the Lutheran Hymnal* (St. Louis: Concordia Publishing House, 1942), p. 665.

Questions

1. The doctrine of the Holy Trinity is attested in ____.
2. The Greek Orthodox Church holds that the Holy Spirit proceeds from ____.
3. The Nicene Creed is more ____ that the Apostles' Creed.
4. The Athanasian Creed excludes any kind of ____.
5. The Nestorians held that Christ was ____.
6. The whole work of Christ is attributed to ____.
7. Do Lutherans assert that those who are not orthodox cannot be saved? ____
8. John Gerhard said that those who ignore the mystery of the Trinity cannot ____.
9. When do some Lutheran Churches use the Athanasian Creed? ____
10. The Te Deum Laudamus is considered ____.

Music

The Text, Music and Employment of the Bible In Handel's Greatest Oratorio: "The Messiah"
Christian News, December 14, 1981

The yearly singing of Handel's oratorio "The Messiah" has become a tradition which is now of long standing. Each Advent and Christmas season millions of people in the world hear oratorio societies, church choirs, recordings on records and tapes or cassettes render "The Messiah." Even those who do not accept Jesus Christ as the promised Messiah foretold in the Old Testament Scriptures are enthralled by the lovely music of this Handelian oratorio, which has become famous for a number of its outstanding choruses. Paul Lang wrote about the Messiah as follows:

The *Messiah* has become the epitome of the modern oratorio. This is understandable, for it unites choruses, arias, and recitatives into a great hymn and conjured up a Christianity without denominational coloring. But we may misjudge the essence of the Handelian style if we confuse our acquaintance to the one lyric among his thirty-two compositions in that form.[1]

Another musicologist made this statement about the Messiah:

Handel's "Messiah" is most representative of all the works of its class. Not in opera, not in fact in any form of music, does one compo-

1130

sition stand out head and shoulders above its fellows as does this. It is not asserted that it is the first from the viewpoint of the musician, but no other oratorio has enjoyed such enduring popularity—such positive adoration. Many generations have approved of it, and as different as the tastes of the eighteenth and twentieth centuries in most particulars, by this work they both alike have been melted to tears and aroused to higher aspirations.[2]

The oratorio in its modern form is a musical setting of a sacred story or text in style more or less dramatic. Its various parts are assigned to four solo voices and to single or double chorus, with accompaniment of full orchestra, sometimes amplified by the organ. The oratorio like the opera, has its recitative which links together and leads up to various numbers. The name "oratorio" is said to come from the word "oratory," or place of prayer, where these compositions were first performed.[3] The earliest traces of the oratorio in its incipient stages has been traced to the twelfth century. Crescimbeni, one of the earliest musical writers, claimed:

> The oratorio had its origin from San Filippo Neri, who, in his chapel, after sermons and other devotions in order to allure young people to pious offices, and to detain them from earthly pleasures, had hymns, psalms, and such like prayers sung by one or more voices.[4]

According to Upton the oratorio as a musical form went through a number of stages.[5] In its earliest stages of development it began with the moralities, mysteries, and miracle-plays of the thirteenth and fourteenth centuries. It was however, in the time of San Filippo Neri that the real oratorio was born. Neri undertook to compose dramatizations and performances of Biblical stories such as "The Good Samaritan" "The Prodigal Son," and "Tobias and the Angels," accompanied by music written by his friend Giovanni Animuccia. At that time the term "oratorio" came into being. At first the earliest oratorios were crude. A development continued and the conclusion of the first period brings the historian of music to the second stage in the oratorio's evolution, namely, the composing of passion-music, which eventually is regarded as the connecting link between the earlier form created by the Italian composers of the sixteenth and seventeenth centuries and the oratorio as it appeared after it had felt the mighty influence of Handel.[6]

Handel and His Oratorios

George Friedrich Handel (1685-1759) was born at Halle, in Lower Saxony, the son of a barber-surgeon, February 23, 1685.[7] Like many another composer, Handel revealed his musical talents at an early age. Handel received little encouragement from his family in his early years as far as developing his musical talents. It was only after his father's death that he was able to concentrate on music. The Duke of Saxe-Wesenfels recognized Handel's ability and supported Handel's efforts to become a composer and a musician. When nine years old Handel was writing spiritual cantatas; at ten he composed a set of cantatas. At twelve Handel was in Berlin to continue with his music education. After the death of his father,

Handel began to study law, but music had such an attraction for him that he returned to his real love, music. In Hamburg he continued his musical studies and became second violinist in the orchestra. At eighteen he was appointed organist of the Cathedral at Moritzburg. After a year he left his position for Hamburg.

In the opening years of the eighteenth century Handel spent three years in Italy writing operas. Handel also demonstrated proficiency in the playing of the harpsichord. At 19 years of age he composed "The Passion of St. John," a major work. At 20 he wrote the opera "Almira." In 1710 Handel became Kapelmeister in Hanover.

In 1710 Handel visited London where he acquired fame because of his operas. Beginning with 1712 to the year of his death (1759), England became the permanent home of the German Handel. After sometime, people in London became tired of Italian operas in which Handel specialized and the latter went bankrupt producing them. In eight years Handel lost $51,000 on Italian opera. Slanders of various sorts were circulated about him, and his works were no longer well received. In the midst of this adversity, sickness overtook Handel, ending in a partial stroke.

Handel then went to Italy and after sometime there, he returned to England, where after a few more operatic failures Handel devoted himself to the writing of oratorios, with which he made his name famous for all time. Handel once said: "Sacred music is best suited to a man descending into the vale of tears." Handel's first oratorio *Esther* (or Haman and Mordecai), was in reality a masque, while *Semele, Alexander Balus*, and *Susanna* are veritable chorus operas. Hercules, called a "musical drama" by Handel himself, should according to Lang, be considered the highest peak of late baroque music drama. *Deborah, Saul, Israel in Egypt, Samson, Joseph, Belshazzar, Judas, Maccabeus, Joshua, Solomon*, and *Jeptha* are gigantic choral tragedies. The three greatest of Handel's oratorios were *Israel in Egypt, Judas Maccabeus* and the *Messiah*.

The Messiah of Handel

What Klopstock endeavored to accomplish in his epic *Der Messias*, Handel achieved in his greatest creation, "The Messiah." Messiah is unique among the twenty oratorios that Handel composed, in that it is the only one with any connection with the Christian religion.[8] The Messiah represents the ripened product of Handel's genius and reflects on the noblest aspirations and most exalted devotion of mankind. Upton wrote about this oratorio: "Among all his oratorios it retains it original freshness, vigor, and beauty in the highest degree, in that it appeals to the loftiest sentiment and to universal religious devotion, and is based upon the most harmonious, symmetrical, and enduring forms of the art."[9] Sir Thomas Beecham, in an essay written for RCA record album of the Messiah, wrote: "In view of the comparative neglect of Handel's music today, it might seem difficult to substantiate a valid claim for him to be numbered among the few supremely great Masters of music."[10] In volume 1 of his *A Mingled Chime*, Beechem wrote: "Since his time mankind has heard no music written for voices which can even feebly rival his for grandeur of build and tone, nobility and tenderness of melody, scholastic skill and ingenuity of effect."[11] Beechem claims that "the justice of this opinion can easily be confirmedby an honest comparison between his choral writing and that of any other composer from Palestrina down to the present day. In this domain he has no serious rival. When it comes to purely instrumental music it may be freely admitted that this great contemporary of Bach bears the palm, and by excelling in small forms is more accessible to the modern executant."[12]

Handel began the *Messiah* on August 22, 1741 and finished it on September 14 — a colossal work composed in twenty-four days. Handel was 56 years old at the time of the Messiah's writing. The composer of this magnificent oratorio was prepared for its composition by virtue of his broad and mellow philosophy endowed with experience and sorrow. The first part of the Messiah was concluded by August 28th, the second part by September 6, and the third part by September 12th, and the instrumentation was complete by September 14th. The text was taken from the Bible, which was understood literally, and the libretto was arranged by Charles Jennens (1700-1773), who, singularly enough was not satisfied with the music which so greatly has satisfied the world.

At the time of the Messiah's composition Handel was having a trying time in London . Handel, who could be blunt and fear less, also managed to collect enemies, who persecuted him and exposed Handel to "the meanest and most exasperating of tricks and insults." Added to this was the distressing fact that Handel's recent productions were coldly received, and so it was with great relief that Handel accepted the Duke of Devonshire's invitation to come to Ireland. The Duke was the Lord Lieutenant of Ireland and in that capacity he had invited Handel. The latter arrived in Ireland November 18, 1741 with the newly finished score of the Messiah in his travelling bag. In Ireland Handel was well received and his music was held in high honor by the Irish. Handel remained nine months in Ireland.

The First Performance of the Messiah

The first regular performance of the Messiah was given in Dublin, on Tuesday, April 13, 1742. The announcement of the first Dublin performance read:

This day will be performed Mr. Handel's new grand Sacred Oratorio called the MESSIAH. The doors will be opened at Eleven, and the performance begins at Twelve.

The Stewards of the Charitable Musical Society request the Favour of the ladies not to come with hoops this day to the Musick Hall in Fishamble Street. The Gentlemen are desired to come without their swords.

Faulkner's Journal which contained the preceding announcement, dated April 13, 1742, on April 17, 1742 had the following:

On Tuesday last, Mr. Handel's Sacred Grand Oratorio, the MESSIAH, was performed in the New Musick Hall in Fishamble Street; the best Judges allowed it to be the most finished piece of Musick. Words are wanting to express the exquisite Delight which it afforded to the admiring crowded audience. The Sublime, the Grand, and The Tender, adapted to the most elevated to transport and charm the ravished Heart and Ear . . .

The day prior to April 13, a benefit performance was given "For the Relief of the Prisoners in the Several Goals, and for the support of Mercer's Hospital, in Stephen's Street and the Charitable Infirmary on the Inn's Quay" at the Musick Hall in Fishamble Street. The performance of the Messiah was not only praised in *Faulkner's Journal*, but also the *Dublin Gazette* and *Dublin News-Letter* acclaimed the composition as a most finished piece of music. One admirer expressed his appreciation as follows:

> To harmony like His celestial power was given
> To exalt the soul from earth and make of hell a heaven.

The First English Performance of Messiah

The English performance was given at Covenant Garden, March 23, 1743, sometime after Handel's return to London. On this occasion the rendering was not as enthusiastically received as in Dublin the year before. But moved by the "Hallelujah" chorus at this performance was King George II, who was present, stood when he heard the words "for the Lord God omnipotent reigneth." Thus a custom was inaugurated which has become practice at all public renditions of the Messiah. During Handel's lifetime the Messiah was given thirty-four times; in fact the maestro's last public act was to direct the Messiah on April 16, 1759, just a week before his death. In 1784, at Westminster Abbey, a "performance was given which involved an orchestra of two hundred and forty musicians and a choir of two hundred and seventy-five voices." This was considered a great and an outstanding performance. On the anniversary of Handel's death the Messiah was performed at the Crystal Palace with an orchestra of four hundred and sixty and a chorus numbering two thousand and seven hundred.

The Messiah In America

On January 4, 1770 the *New York Journal* announced that:

A SACRED ORATORIO, on the Prophecies concerning CHRIST, and his Coming, being an extract from the late Mr. Handel's Grand Oratorio called the MESSIAH, consisting of the Overture: and sixteen other Pieces, viz. Airs, Recitations, and Choruses Never performed in America.

After New York the MESSIAH was rendered in Charleston, Norfolk, Bethlehem, Pa., Philadelphia and Boston. From Dublin to London, from London to the European continent and to America, Australia and Africa, to Russian Messiah triumphantly marched. In Boston the Messiah had been performed since 1818 by the Handel and Hayden Society eighty times by 1905.

The Organization of the Messiah

The oratorio is divided into three parts. The first depicts the longing of the world for the Messiah, prophesies Messiah's coming, and announces His birth; the second part is devoted to the sufferings, crucifixion, death, resurrection and exaltation of Jesus Christ and also develops the spread and ultimate triumph of the Gospel. The third part is concerned with the declaration of the highest truths of the Christian faith — faith in the existence of God, the certainty of eternal life, the resurrection of all flesh and the attainment of eternal happiness.

PART I: (THE PROPHECY)
The foretelling of the Coming of the Messiah by the Prophets, the celestial announcement of Messiah's birth by angelic heralds and the birth of the Messiah constitute the opening of the oratorio. This is followed by the reception of "the tidings of great joy" by the shepherds:

The Advent Message
I. The Overture
The Messiah begins with an overture, or rather orchestral prelude. One musicologist has described the overture as follows: "The overture begins with a slow movement in dotted rhythm played twice, first loudly, and then softly. A fugal allegro follows in the same minor key as the first, built on a leaping subject that ends with a quaver figure which plays an important part in the subsequent expansion. By all the traditions of the day an air of minuet should close the overture. But instead the major they ushers in the accompanied recitative 'Comfort Ye,' whose orchestra pattern was taken from an earlier Handel work.

II. "Comfort Ye My People:" Recitative (Tenor) Accompanied
Comfort ye, comfort ye my people, saith your God; speak ye comfortably to Jerusalem; and cry unto her, that her warfare is accomplished, that her iniquity is pardoned.

The voice of one crying in the wilderness: prepare ye the way of the Lord, make straight in the desert a highway for our God (Isaiah 40:1-3).

In "Comfort Ye," the beautiful opening bars increase their power and add to their strength under the solo tenor, and conclude in the key of the dominant. Here the recitative style changes, up till then the recitative was "accompanying recitative, but now it becomes **recititatio secco**, in which the accompanying voice is punctuated by chords.[13] The change is directly occasioned by a change in mood.[14]

The tenor recitative of "Comfort, comfort ye" is followed by:

III. Aria (tenor):
Every valley shall be exalted, and every mountain and hill made low, the crooked made straight, and the rough places made plain (Isaiah 40:4).

Following "Every valley shall be exalted" these resounds the first of the mighty choruses of the Sacred Oratorio:

IV. Chorus:
"And the glory of the Lord shall appear and all flesh shall see it to-

gether; for the mouth of the Lord has spoken it." (Isaiah 40:5). The material is a short ritornello after this the voices treats it semi fugally and with much imitation.[15]

Up to this point joy has been the keynote of the text, but with the "Thus saith the Lord" some fearful consideration is introduced.

V. Recitative (Bass):
Thus saith the Lord of Hosts: Yet once in a little while and I will shake the heavens and the earth, the sea and the dry land and I will shake all nations; and the desire of all nations shall come. The Lord, whom ye seek, shall suddenly come to His Temple, even the messenger of the covenant, whom ye delight in; behold He shall come saith, the Lord of Hosts (Haggai 2:7-10; Malachi 3:1).

The prophecy of Haggai is announced, only to be followed by human apprehension in the great aria (Bass).

VI. But who may abide the day of His coming, and who shall stand when he appeareth (Malachi 3:2).
The aria "But who may abide etc." has two thematically independent sections which are repeated, the first shortened, and the second transposed from the first appearance in the major to the minor."[16]

In response to No. VI, in which the approaching Supreme God who knows no compromise and thus strikes the heart of humanity with fear, there now comes the blessed assurance in a chorus:

VII. And he shall purify the sons of Levi, that they may offer unto the Lord an offering in righteousness (Malachi 3:3).
This is a beautiful and remarkably difficult number, here we have a fugued chorus closing in simple harmony.[17]

Once more the prophet Isaiah announces a joyful message:

VIII. Recitative (Contralto):
Behold, a virgin shall conceive and hear a Son, and shall call His name Emmanuel, God with us (Isaiah 7:14).

The reception of Isaiah's prophecy is stated in the sweet melody and chorus:

IX. Air (Contralto) and Chorus:
O thou that tellest good tidings to Zion, get thee up into the high mountain: O thou that tellest good tidings to Jerusalem, lift up thy voice with strength; lift it up, be not afraid: say unto the cities of Judah, behold your God! (Isaiah 40:9).

Arise, shine for thy light is come, and the glory of the Lord is risen upon thee (Isaiah 60:1).

The aria "Thou that telleth" treats the violins in an obbligato manner, and the **de capo** is beautifully altered to bring in the new words "the glory of the Lord is risen upon thee." The chorus then takes the material and treats it partly by imitation and partly homophonically, after which the opening ritorello is heard again in full.[18]

The ominous event of Christ's rejection by the world (John 1:11) casts its shadow before in the bass recitative:

X. Recitative (Bass) accompanied:
For, behold, darkness shall cover the earth, the gross darkness the people, but the Lord arises upon thee, and the Gentiles shall come to thy light, and kings to the brightness of thy rising (Isaiah 60:2-3).

One musicologist in describing this recitative has written: "Here the hearer has an example of Handel's power of form. The simple reiterated pairs of semiquavers rising over the slowly-moving harmonies and changing to quavers in the middle of the movement are an aptly expressive accompaniment describing the change from darkness to light."[19]

The aria, "The people that walketh in darkness," which Mozart draped with delicately elaborate ornamentation,[20] is an aria which has curious but characteristic modulations and leads to one of the most graphic fugued choruses of the whole Messiah:

XI: Air (Bass):
The people that walked in darkness have seen great light; and they shall dwell in the land of the shadow of death, upon them hath the light shined (Isaiah 9:2).

The climax of the first part of the Messiah comes in the impressive chorus:

XII: For unto us a child is born, unto us a son is given, and the government shall be upon his shoulder; and His name shall be called Wonderful, Counsellor, the Mighty God, the Everlasting Father, the Prince of Peace (Isaiah 9:6-7).
The music for "Unto us a child is born" comes from an Italian cantata of Handel's youth on the tricks of the god of love. Only the great invocation of "Wonderful Counsellor" and the rest thrice-repeated are new.

In this great chorus there are interwoven with the violin parts and emphasized with sublime announcements the names of the Messiah in full harmony and with the strongest choral power.[21] This chorus is followed with a Pastoral Symphony.

XIII. The Pastoral Symphony:
After the great burst of sound has died away in the chorus, there then follows a significant pause. To the previous glorious tumult there now comes tranquility. At this juncture Handel inserted an antique pifa of the Calabrian peasants, usually called "the Pastoral Symphony," written for strings. The "Pastoral Symphony" is based on a simple tune which Handel remembered hearing in his younger days at Christmas time in the streets of Rome.[22]

XIV. Recitative (Soprano)
"There were shepherds abiding in the field, keeping watch over their

flocks by night (Luke 2:7).

Some subtle quality places before the hearer the peaceful hillsides of Bethlehem. The hearer is aware that it is night and that the shepherds are watching over their flocks by night. The night sky is studded with stars which shine with great brilliance. By means of a series of graphic recitatives Handel tells of the sudden appearance of the world's SAVIOR. The Messiah's coming is announced by means of:

XV. Recitative (Soprano):

And the angel said unto them, fear not; for behold I bring you good tidings of great joy, which shall be to all people. For unto you is born this day in the city of David, a Savior, which is Christ the Lord (Luke 2:11-12).

The angelic narrative used in the recitative records the apparition in sudden speed and the accompaniment is in the style of Italian opera.

XVI. Recitative (Soprano) accompanied:

And suddenly there was with the angel a multitude of the heavenly host, praising God and saying (Luke 2:13):

XVII. Chorus:

Glory to God in the highest, and peace on earth, good will towards men (Luke 2:14).

The chorus of the heavenly hosts is remarkably expressive, and affords sharp contrasts in the successive clear responses to the fugue. The chorus has trumpets for the first time in the original score.[23]

XVIII. Air (Soprano):

Rejoice greatly, O daughter of Zion! Shout daughter of Zion! Behold, thy king cometh unto thee (Zechariah 9:9-10).

XXIX. Recitative (Contralto):

Then shall the eyes of the blind be opened, and the ears of the deaf be unstopped; then shall the lame man leap as a hart, and the tongue of the dumb shall sing (Isaiah 35: 5-6).

XX. Air (Alto):

He shall feed His flock like a shepherd; and He shall gather the lambs with His arm, and carry them in His bosom, and gently lead them with young (Isaiah 40:11).

XXI. Air (Soprano):

Come unto Him, all ye that labor and are heavy laden, and He will give you rest. Take His yoke upon you, and learn of Him, for He is meek and lowly of heart, and ye shall find rest unto your souls (Matthew 11:28-30).

XXII. Chorus:

His yoke is easy and His burden is light (Matthew 11:30).

The difficult and very brilliant aria for soprano "Greatly rejoice" and the lovely aria "He shall feed his flock" originally written entirely for soprano, find Handel returning to the pastoral style, and a short chorus "His yoke is easy" concludes Part I of the Messiah.[24]

PART II CHRIST'S SACRIFICE, REJECTION, DEATH AND RESURRECTION

In this portion of the Messiah some of the most marvelous musical productions are found. It has been acclaimed as the most impressive part of this great oratorio. As one critic of the Messiah has put it: "Here we find three of the finest choruses ever written by Handel." These are "Behold the Lamb of God," "Lift up your heads," and "The Hallelujah" chorus.[25]

XXIII. Chorus:

Behold the Lamb of God that taketh away the sins of the world (John 1:29). This chorus sets a tragic mood with its dotted rhythm.

XXIV. Air (Contralto):

He was despised and rejected of men, a man of sorrows and acquainted with grief (Isaiah 53:3).

He gave His back to the smiters and His cheeks to them that plucked off the hair: He hid not his face from shame and spitting (Isaiah 50:6).

Milner claims that "He is despised" is "the first **de capo** aria in the Messiah to preserve the full conventional requirements of the form: the middle section uses material different from the first, and the repeat is exact and entire."[26] In this musical piece Handel gives a description of the contumely heaped upon the Son of Man, over whose composition Handel is said to have been in tears. "He was despised" is acclaimed as one of the most pathetic and deeply expressive songs ever composed, for in this song the very key-note is truth.

XXV. Chorus:

Surely He hath borne our griefs, and carried our sorrows; He was wounded for our transgressions; the chastisement of our peace was upon Him. And with His stripes we are healed (Isaiah 53: 4-5).

"And with his stripes" we are said to have a strict fugue whose countersubject provides the main material for its episodes. This in turn leads into:

XXVI. Chorus:

All we like sheep have gone astray; we have turned everyone to his own way (Isaiah 53:6).

And the Lord hath laid upon Him the iniquity of us all (Isaiah 53: 6).

Anthony Milner described this chorus: "All we like sheep" as built over a persistent leaping bass. Its theme is another borrowing from the Italian cantata, but the working out is new. The repetitions of the florid semiquavers on "we have turned" increase in excitement till they are contrapuntally combined, leading to a sudden adagio where the voices enter in imitation for "The Lord hath laid on him" in solemn harmonies."[27] This chorus closes with an adagio of great beauty.

XXVII. Recitative (Tenor) accompanied:

All they that see Him; laugh Him to scorn; they shoot out their lips, and shake their heads saying:— (Psalm 22:7).

A tenor recitative, "All they that see laugh," precedes the choral fugue "He trusted in God," the only movement that may be called dramatic in style, in spite of its fugal form. The tenor solo describes the dissolution of the Passion in a recitative that modulates ceaselessly, beginning in A flat and ending in B major. There is no orchestral ritornello in the short aria "Behold and see."

XXVIII. Chorus:

He trusted in God that He would deliver Him; let Him deliver Him, if he delight in Him (Psalm 22:8).

In this fugal chorus there resounds the hostility of the mob. This latter chorus is accompanied by:

XXIX. Recitative (Tenor) accompanied:

Thy rebuke hath broken His heart; He is full of heaviness. He looked for some to have pity on Him, but there was no man, neither found He any to comfort Him (Psalm 69:20).

XXX. Air (Tenor)

Behold, and see if there is any sorrow like unto His sorrow (Lamentations 1:12).

XXXI. Recitative

He was cut off out of the land of the living, for the transgression of Thy people was He stricken (Isaiah :8).

XXXII. Air (Tenor)

But thou didst not leave His soul in hell; nor didst Thou suffer Thy Holy One to see corruption (Psalm 16:10).

With this air Handel testified to his belief in the resurrection of Jesus Christ, God's promised Messiah.

Handel also believed in the bodily ascension of the Messiah, as may be seen from the next chorus:

XXXIII. Chorus:

Lift up your heads, O ye gates, and be ye lift up, ye everlasting door, and the King of Glory shall come in.

Who is this King of Glory?

The Lord strong and mighty, the Lord mighty in battle.

Lift up your heads, O ye gates, and be ye lift up, ye everlasting doors, and the King of Glory shall come in.

Who is the King of Glory?

The Lord of Hosts, He is the King of Glory (Psalm 24:7-10).

This is the only five-part chorus in the Messiah and it has a welcome spaciousness. The chorus begins with antiphonal dialogue and concludes with spirited counterpoint.[28]

These musical numbers are followed by:

XXXIV. Recitative (Tenor):

Unto which of the angels said He at any time, Thou art My Son, this day I have begotten Thee? (Hebrews 1:5).

This is followed by the chorus:

Let all the angels of God worship Him (Hebrews 1:6).

This is said to be an unusual fugue, "for after its first triumphant statement, the subject is accompanied by its self in diminution (i.e. in smaller note values) wherever it appears."[29]

The previous chorus is followed by:

XXXV. Air (Bass):

Thou art gone up on high; Thou hast led captivity captive, and received gifts for men, yea, even from Thine enemies, that the Lord God might dwell among them (Psalm 68:18).

Handel wrote four different versions of "Thou art gone up on high." Milner claims that "its ritornello has a striking semiquaver figure which the voice does not exploit, an unusual feature."[30]

XXXVI. Chorus:

The Lord gave the word, great was the company of the preachers (Psalm 68:11).

Although this chorus is short, yet it is said to be elaborate in its figuration.

XXXVII. Air (Soprano):

How beautiful are the feet of them that preach the Gospel of peace, and bring glad tidings of good things (Romans 10:15).

Handel set this in six different ways. With this aria begins the triumphant story of the struggle of the Gospel against prejudice and enmity.

XXXVIII. Chorus:

Their sound is gone into all lands, and their words unto the end of the world (Psalm 19:4; Romans 10:18).

In the next selection Handel has depicted the opposition that would occur when the Messiah appeared in the world. Here Handel treats two themes demanded by the textual arrangement in freely-moving imitation.

XXXIX. Recitative (Bass):

Why do the nations so furiously rage together, and why do the people imagine a vain thing?

The kings of the earth rise up and the rulers take counsel together against the Lord and against His Anointed? (Psalm 2:1-2)

This great bass aria gives evidence of elaborate vocal ornamentation; it omits the **de capo** of its first section to lead immediately into the Chorus, "Let us break".

XXXX. Chorus:

Let us break their bonds asunder, and cast away their yokes from us (Psalm 2:3).

About this chorus Milner remarked: "This makes splendid use of close imitation to produce contrapuntal combinations that move rapidly to a grand climax."[31]

XXXXI. Recitative (Tenor):

He that dwelleth in the heavens shall laugh them to scorn; the Lord shall hold them in derision (Psalm 2:4).

Handel's use of Psalm 2 shows that he considered this a Messianic Psalm, a stance also taken by a number of New Testament writers.

XXXXII. Air (Tenor):

Thou shalt break them with a rod of iron; Thou shalt dash them in pieces like a potter's vessel (Psalm 2:9).

In this musical piece the violins are treated in the obbligato manner, and the final ritornello duty for the repeat of the first section. This is followed by the great Hallelujah chorus:

XXXXIII. Chorus:

Hallelujah! For the Lord God omnipotent reigneth (Rev. 19:6). The kingdom of this world is become the kingdom of our Lord, and of His Christ; and He shall reign forever and ever. King of kings, and Lord of lords, Hallelujah! (Rev. 11:15).

Concerning this great chorus Upton wrote: "It opens with the shouts of Hallelujah. Then ensure three simple phrases, the groundwork for the "Hallelujah." These phrases, seemingly growing out of each other, and reiterating with constantly increasing power, interweaving with and sustaining the "hallelujah" with wonderful harmonic effects, make up a chorus that has never been excelled, not only in musical skill, but also in grandeur and sublimity."[32]

According to Milner, Handel explored in the "Hallelujah" chorus the typical Handelian triumphal manner found in such works as *Zadok the Priest* and *Dettingen Te Deum*, thus providing a great climax for Part II of the Messiah.

The listener can appreciate after hearing the marvellous chorus how Handel felt while composing this chorus: "I did think I did see all heaven before me and the great God Himself."[33]

Some musicologists believe that if Handel had ended his oratorio at this climatic point it would not have diminished from the greatness of this oratorio, but Handel added a third part.[34]

PART III: CHRIST TRIUMPHANT

Part III opens with a sublime confession of faith. There is no anti-climax, something which might seem impossible in view of the greatness of the Hallelujah chorus. But, it may be asked, what is more beloved than the following aria:

XXXXIV. Air (Soprano):
I know that my Redeemer liveth, and that He shall stand at the latter day upon the earth; and though worms destroy this body, yet in my flesh I shall see God (Job 19:25).

For now is Christ risen from the dead, the first-fruits of them that sleep (I Corinthians 15: 20).

According to Milner in this aria Handel has produced one of the most original arias that he wrote. He claims that "I know that my Redeemer" has an accompaniment consisting mainly of violins and bass; the violins are treated in the **obbligato** style, in duet with the solo soprano. The second section of the aria with its new theme is not followed by a repeat of the first; instead, it expands its own material in the voice part over the repetition of the first theme in the orchestra. Only when the voice is silent does the opening ritornello return.[35]

This beautiful aria is followed by two quartets in plain counterpoint:

XXXXV. Quartet:
Since by man came death (I Corinthians 15: 21).

XXXXVI. Chorus:
By man came also the resurrection of the dead (I Corinthians 15: 21).

XXXXVII. Quartet:
For as in Adam all men die (I Corinthians 15:22a).

XXXXVIII. Chorus:
Even so in Christ shall all be made alive (I Corinthians 15:21-22).

XXXXIX. Recitative, Accompanied (Bass):
Behold, I tell you a mystery; we shall not all sleep, but we all shall be changed in a moment in the twinkling of an eye, at the last trumpet (I Corinthians 15:51-55).

XXXXX. Air (Bass):
The trumpet shall sound, and the dead shall be raised incorruptible, and we shall be changed (I Corinthians 15: 52).

For this corruptible must put on incorruption, and this mortal must put on immortality (I Corinthians 15:52).

Here we have Handel employing a trumpet obbligato which is a full de capo aria. This aria will always be admired for its beauty and stirring effect.[36]

XXXXXI. Recitative (Alto):

Then shall be brought to pass the saying that is written: Death is swallowed up in victory (I Corinthians 15:54).

This is followed by:

XXXXXII. Duet (Alto and Tenor):

O death, where is thy sting? O grave, where is thy victory? The sting of death is sin, and the strength of sin is the law (I Corinthians 15:55).

This is said to come from an earlier Italian work by Handel.

XXXXXIII. Chorus:

But thanks be to God which giveth us the victory through our Lord Jesus Christ (I Corinthians 15:57).

This is characterized by the typical Handelian mixture of contrapuntal and homophonic textures.[37]

XXXXXIV. Air (Soprano):

If God be for us, who can be against us? Who shall lay anything to the charge of God's elect? (Romans 8:31-32).

It is God that justifieth, who is he that condemneth?

It is Christ that died, yea rather, that is risen again, who is at the right hand of God, who makes intercession for us (Romans 8:33-34).

The air "If God be for us" has the longest ritornello of any movement of the Messiah and disregards the **de capo** form except in the final repetition of the ritornello.[38]

XXXXXV. Chorus:

The final chorus of the Messiah begins with homophony:

Worthy is the Lamb that was slain, and hath redeemed us to God by His blood, to receive power and riches, and wisdom, strength and honor, and glory and blessings (Revelation 5:12).

Blessing and honor, glory and power, be unto Him that sitteth upon the throne, and unto the Lamb, for ever and ever. Amen (Revelation 5:12).

"Worthy is the Lamb" is a piece of smooth, flowing harmony. "Blessing and honor" is a fugue led off by the tenors and the basses in unison, and repeated by the sopranos and altos on the octave, closing with full harmony on the words "forever and ever," repeated a number of times.[39]

One musical historian asserted about these last choruses:

"But the choruses 'Worthy is the Lamb' and the final dignified 'Amen' are an exaltation of the sound in which all creation seems to join the angels about the throne of God. The 'Amen chorus' is a marvelous piece of contrapuntal workmanship, and the last page seems to many musicians to contain the grandest climax to be found in all choral art."[40]

Anthony Milner concluded his discussion of the Messiah with this significant assertion: "After experiencing the sublimities of the *Messiah* the listener may readily agree with Beethoven's estimate of Handel: 'He was the greatest composer who ever lived'."[41]

The Manuscript Sources of the Messiah[42]

Two autographic copies of the Messiah are deposited in the British Museum. One is British Museum RM 20f2. Part I is dated August 22nd, 1741, at the beginning, and 28th August, at the end. Parts II and III are dated, at the end, 6th and 12th September respectively. Two more days were spent on orchestral detail.

Aside from the chorus "Their sound is gone out into all lands and their words unto the ends of the world," this score is completely in Handel's hand. However, it gives evidence of extensive alterations and revisions, and so does not represent the Messiah as first performed in Dublin. The second autographic score is British Museum RM 20g[6]. This copy has two versions of the chorus "Their sound is gone into all the world," the first version is almost identical with version 2, is written for two altos and chorus, and has an introduction altered from the anthem "As pants the heart."

The second version is very different from any existent Messiah version, but appears to be related to an item in "Occasional Oratorio (1746)." It is for soprano and chorus.

During Handel's lifetime a number of copies of the Messiah were prepared that are still extant in various public and private collections. They are:

1. St. Michael's, Tenbury Nos. 346-7 (Ouseley Copy)

This was prepared from the autograph score by J. C. Smith's hand for the first performance, but which has extensive subsequent alterations.

2. British Museum Edgerton 2937 (Granville Collection), written before 1746 by J.C. Smith.

3. British Museum Add. mus MS 5062

Scholars believe that it was prepared by Henry Needler, likely for the 1744 performance of the Messiah by the Academy of Ancient Music to which Needler belonged.

4. British Museum RM 19 a 2 (Aylesford Collection)

This score contains the aria "Who may abide the day of his coming" and the aria "why do the nations furiously rage."

5. British Museum RM 19 d 1.

This is a copy made by Charles Jennens about 1754. It contains an extensively figured and ornamented keyboard transcription, but breaks off before the end of the chorus "Glory to God in the highest."

6. Goldschmidt Copy

It was the property of William Hayes and employed by him for performances at Oxford and other places, now found in an unknown private collection.

7. Dublin Copy

All traces of it are lost, a copy that was sent to a Dublin charity in 1743.

Copies of The Messiah prepared in the eighteenth century after Handel's death:

1. British Museum Add. mus. MS 399774
Date and copy is unknown.
2. British Museum RM 18 b 10.
Prepared about 1765.
3. British Museum RM 18 c 2.
4. Dublin (Library of Archbishop Marsh)
A score prepared by John Matthews (for a Salisbury performance). It contains a number of unique vocal ornaments as employed by Handel during his lifetime.
5. Fitzwilliam Museum (Lennard Collection)
Copyist of this score not known.
6. Foundling Hospital
A score and set of parts (first soprano and instrumental bass missing J representing the work as performed about 1754. The soloists' parts also include the equivalent parts in the choir uses, in which they were evidently required to participate.
7. Hamburg Stadt U. Universitatsbibliothek No. 221
Written in the hand of J. C. Smith and his son, copied about 1762. Chrysander chose this score as the chief source for his edition of the Messiah.
8. King's College Cambridge (Mann Collection)
Although only copied in 1780, it represents the version used at the first London performance.
9. King's College Cambridge (Rowe Collection)

Recordings of the Oratorio "The Messiah"
Ever since the invention of the phonograph and other recording aids the Messiah has been put on records. Over the years all the great companies ,that produce and sell phonograph records, tapes and cassettes have been periodically recording "The Messiah." Since the length of the complete Messiah demands about three hours of listening time, some recordings have been made available to the listening public in a shorter version, usually of two records, while the complete version requires at least three records. The recording companies have also issued records which only contain some of the better known and outstanding arias and choruses.

The Schwann-1. Record and Tape Guide, September 1980 has listed at least seventeen different recordings of Handel's greatest oratorio, of which fourteen are three-record sets and three two-record versions.[42] Conductors like Berstein, Scherchen, Marriner, Richter, Ormandy, Davis, Mackerras, Sargent, Dunn, Leppard, Klemperer, Boult, Bonynge are listed as conductors of Messiah-recordings currently available. If one were to consult earlier catalogues of Schwann, other conductors would be listed. Orchestras like the New York Philharmonic, the Vienna State Orchestra, the London Philharmonic, the Philadelphia Orchestra, the English Chamber Orchestra, the Royal Philharmonic Orchestra, the Liverpool Philharmonic, the Philharmonic Orchestra are some of the great world orchestras who have participated in the electronic reproduction of the Messiah. Also the great choral societies of our day were employed, namely, such as: The Westminster Choir, the Academy Chorus, St. Martin's Chorus, London Symphony Chorus, Mormon Tabernacle Chorus, the Ambrosian Singen, the Austrian Radio Chorus, English Church Chorus, the Huddersfield Choral Society.

Sommerset High Fidelity has produced a recording of the Messiah, directed by Walter Susskind, that was preceded by exhaustive research in 1958 by Dr. Eric Beuman, Wilhelm Willie and D. L. Miller of Miller International Company in London to find a hall or church that had the acoustical requisites for producing the finest Messiah ever recorded.[44] Dr. Beuman stated that they looked for "a location with ethereal acoustics and an organ that can be tuned."[45] The church chosen was that of St. Mary Magdelene in Paddington, a church itself with a rich musical tradition.

The Theological Message of the Messiah and Handel's Understanding of the Old and New Testaments

In his popular oratorio the Messiah Handel has given expression to his religious convictions and beliefs as expressed in the libretto and the recitatives, arias and choruses, many of which have become famous with music listeners. From an analysis of the manner in which Jennens and Handel used Scripture, one may deduce that they employed the following hermeneutical principles of Biblical interpretation. For these two collaborators the Bible was the inspired Word of God, which sets forth a clear plan of salvation for mankind. They considered the Bible, even though existing in two parts, namely, as the Old Testament and the New, as one complete revelation from God . They followed the New Testament hermeneutical principle that the New Testament when properly understood interpreted the Old Testament correctly. For Jennens and Handel the center of the Bible was Jesus Christ, whose coming into the world had been determined in the eternal councils of God. Their employment of the Bible clearly shows that they believed that events concerning the Messiah had been foretold in the Old Testament and were fulfilled in the New. Regarding the interpretation of Messianic prophecy they believed in direct or rectilinear prophecy. They identified Jesus of Nazareth as the Messiah foretold in a number of Old Testament passages.

Isaiah 7:14, which today is understood as referring to a woman of Ahaz's time who was going to become pregnant and bear a son and for some unknown reason would call this child Emmanuel (God with us), was understood as a prophecy of the Virgin-conception and Virgin birth of Christ. The great Christmas prophecy: "Unto us a child is born unto us a son is given, and His name shall be called Wonderful (Hebrew-pele, i.e. the Miracle) Counsellor, the Mighty God, the Everlasting Father" testify to the deity of the Messiah. The doctrine of the vicarious and substitutionary atonement is enunciated by Handel in his use of the Fourth Servant Passage (Is. 52:13-53:12), as clearly taught by Isaiah in chapter 53. The nature of the Messiah's kingship is described in the passage from

1147

Zechariah 9:9. Christ's kingship was of a spiritual nature, the kingdom of grace, in which the Messiah would gather the lambs in his arms.

In the libretto the hearers will become aware, if they know their Bible, that there are passages and clusters of verses taken from both Testaments. From the Old Testament the following verses were appropriated: Job 19:25; Isaiah 7:14; 9:1-2, 6-7; 11:1; 35:5; 40:1-3, 5, 11; 50:6; 52:7; 53:3-6; Psalms 2:1-4, 9; Psalm 16:10; 22:7; 24:7-10; 68:17; 69 :20; Lamentations 1:12; Zechariah 9:9; Malachi 3:1-3. The majority of Old Testament verses are from Messianic Psalms and from Isaiah, called "the fifth Gospel."

The New Testament has supplied the following texts: Matthew 11:28-30; 27:47; Luke 2:7,11-12,14; Romans 5:12; 8:31,39; 10:15; I Thessalonians 4:14; I Corinthians 15:12,21-22,51,52,58; Hebrews 1:1,5; Revelation 5:12; 11:15; John 1:29.

Of all the twenty oratorios composed and produced by Handel the Messiah is the only one employing texts from both the Old and New Testaments.

The manner in which Jennens and Handel have used the Old Testament would indicate that the Lutheran Church as well as the Church of England found Christ foretold in the passages from Job, Isaiah, Psalms, Zechariah and Malachi; the librettist and the musical composer were following the interpretation of these passages as understood by the theologians and exegetes of the eighteenth-century, who were in accord with the exegesis of these verses since New Testament times.

The verses from The New Testament utilized in the Messiah are outstanding, first of all, believing that the Old Testament Messianic predictions were fulfilled when Christ was born in Bethlehem in Judea of the Virgin Mary. The Passion and Suffering of Jesus are faithfully depicted as portrayed in the Gospels. Jennens and Handel taught the deity of Christ by quoting Isaiah 9:6-7 and by also citing the argument from Hebrews 1:5-6. The great "Resurrection Chapter" of the New Testament, I Corinthians 15, used in the second part of the oratorio, testifies mightily to Christ's corporal resurrection and because Christ rose from the dead, His followers also will be raised. Those who are declared righteous because of Christ's vicarious atonement will join the heavenly throng who will sing praise to the Lamb that was slain from before the foundation of the world.

One fact is certain, Handel could never have composed his greatest of oratorios, had he received his theological instruction by pastors who had adopted the presuppositions and conclusions of the historical-critical method. Modern Old Testament hermeneutic repudiates the Christocentricity of the Old Testament. It also rejects the Lutheran principle: "Scripture interprets Scripture," as well as the principle of The Analogy of faith. Modern Protestant hermeneutic repudiates the New Testament's stance that there were Old Testament prophecies about Christ, whose fulfillments are recorded on the pages of the New Testament. Luther emphasized the Christocentricity of the Bible, as did also the authors of the various Lutheran Confessions that are found in the Book of Concord of

1580. Had Jennens and Handel read and accepted the principles of interpretation set forth by Westermann, Mowinckel, Bultmann, Noth, Zimmerli and other European and American scholars the Messiah never could have been composed and thus contributed to the proclamation of the Gospel throughout the world for some two hundred odd years.

Footnotes
1. Paul Henry Lang, *Music in Western Civilization* (New York: W.W. Norton and Company, Inc., 1941), p. 526.
2. Josephine Thrall, *Oratorios and Masses* (New York and Chicago: Irving Square, 1908). p. 93.
3. Cf. "Oratorio," Oscar Thompson, *The International Cyclopedia of Music and Musicians*, (New York: Dodd, Mead and Company, 1958), pp. 1304-1306.
4. As quoted by George P. Upton, *The Standard Oratorios* (Chicago: A.C. McClurg and Company, 1899), p. 9.
5. **Ibid.**, pp. 19-21.
6. **Ibid.**, p. 18.
7. Cf. *Grove's Dictionary of Music and Musicians* (5th edition, edited by Eric Blom; New York: St. Martin's Press, 1959), IV, 37-50.
8. Sir Thomas Beechem, Booklet accompanying the record set of RCA's *The Messiah*, (no date), p . 4.
9. Upton, **op. cit.**, p. 140.
10. Beechem, **op. cit.**, p. 4.
11. Sir Thomas Beechem, *A Mingled Chime*, quoted in his essay of the *Messiah* in the booklet accompanying the RCA record volume, p. 4.
12. **Ibid.**, p. 4.
13. Anthony Milner, in Notes accompanying the London LLA-19, "Handels Messiah," conducted by Sir Adrian Soult.
14. **Ibid.**
15. **Ibid.**
16. **Ibid.**
17. Upton, **op. cit.**, p. 145.
18. Milner, **op. cit.**, Notes for Messiah Recording, London ffrr. LLA -19.
19. **Ibid.**
20. Thrall, *Oratorios and Masses*, **op. cit.**, p. 99.
21. Upton, **op. cit.**, p. 145.
22. Thrall, **op. cit.**, p. 99.
23. Milner, **op. cit.**
24. Upton, p. 146.
25. Thrall, **op. cit.**, p. 99.
26. Milner, Notes on London ffrr. LLA-19 Recording of the Messiah.
27. **Ibid.**
28. **Ibid.**
29. **Ibid.**
30. **Ibid.**
31. **Ibid.**
32. Upton, **op. cit.**, p. 147.
33. **Ibid.**, p. 148.
34. **Ibid.**, p. 148.
35. Milner, **op. cit.**
36. **Ibid.**
37. **Ibid.**
38. **Ibid.**
39. Upton, **op. cit.**, p. 148.
40. Thrall, **op. cit.**, p. 100.

41. Notes for the London recording of "The Messiah," conducted by Adrian Boult.
42. Based on information found in the booklet accompanying Messiah recording Angel, C1, 3657, conducted by Otto Klemperer, p. 12.
43. **Schwann-1 Record and Tape Guide** (Boston: Schwann Record Catalogs, 1980), pp. 90-91.
44. Booklet accompanying Somerset High Fidelity recording or the Messiah, p. 7.
45. **Ibid.**

Questions

1. The yearly singing of "The Messiah" has become a ____.
2. "Oratory" is a place of ____.
3. When did Handel live ____.
4. Handel was born in ____.
5. What became of the permanent home of Handel in 1712? ____
6. Handel's Messiah is his only oratorio connected with ____.
7. Handel composed the Messiah in ___ days.
8. The text of the "Messiah" was taken from ____.
9. At the anniversary of Handel's death, the "Messiah" was performed at the Crystal Palace with an orchestra of ____ and a chorus numbering ____.
10. Handel testified to his belief in the ___ of Christ.
11. Handel considered Psalm 2 a ___ psalm.
12. What was Beethoven's estimate of Handel? ____
13. The length of the "Messiah" demands about ___ hours of listening time.
14. For Jennans and Handel the center of the Bible was ____.
15. They believed in ___ prophecy.
16. Isaiah 7:14 was understood as ____.
17. Handel could never have produced the Messiah if he had received his theological instruction from ____.
18. Luther emphasized the ____ of the Bible.

Reflections and Observations on Isaiah's "Servant Songs" for Lent and Holy Week

Christian News, March 7, 1983

The second section of Isaiah (chs. 40-66) contains a number of passages or pericopes which are known in scholarly works as "the Servant of the Lord" (Hebrew: Ebed Yahweh) passages.[1] usually there are said to be four: 42:1-9, 49:1-13, 50:4-11 and 52:13-53:12, although Edward Young would also call Isaiah 61:1-3 a "Servant passage," even though the word "Servant" does not occur in these verses.[2] However, in the latter passage the same ideas are enunciated as in the earlier ones and in the synagogue of Nazareth Jesus read this unique pericope and stated that it had been fulfilled in Him. Thus, it would not be improper to speak of five "Ebed Yahweh" passages. A specialized literature has grown up on the meaning of these five pericopes, although most scholars only allude to the passages that are found in chapters 42, 49, 50 and 52:13-53:12.

In the old Lutheran church year calendar, Isaiah 52:13-53:12 is the appointed epistle reading for Karfreitag, the German name for Holy Friday or Good Friday. The Inter-Lutheran Commission (ILC) on Worship has appointed the four passages having the expression "Servant of the Lord" as readings for the different days of Holy Week.[3] The ILC has also designated Isaiah 52:13-53:12 as a scripture for Good Friday.

The Uniqueness of the "Servant of Yahweh," Passages" in Isaiah

In Isaiah 40-53 the word servant (Hebrew: ebed) is a keyword. Yahweh calls Israel His Servant. In fact, between 42:1 and 53:12 the phrase "Ebed Yahweh" occurs over twenty times. Sampey claimed that evidently the word servant in the singular throughout these chapters refers to Israel in some sense. But who and what is Israel? Is it always a collective referring to a body of people? Or may it also refer to a single individual identified with Israel as its head?[4]

That in certain passages the nation of Israel is mentioned and meant becomes clear from the context. Thus Leupold wrote:

> And though it is true enough that in a certain sense Israel herself may be thought of as the servant of the Lord, as in the case in the second half of our chapter (i.e. 42), nevertheless there are many references of the New Testament that support our view of his identity with the Messiah. Yet we would note at the very outset that a certain "duality" runs through the Old Testament already, so that on the one hand the servant's work is done by a human agent; but on the other hand it is viewed as the work of God himself.[5]

Three of the "Servant Passages" are quoted in the New Testament and are applied to Christ; in fact, the only possible interpretation of these New Testament assertions can be the one, that the prophet Isaiah in the "Ebed Yahweh" periscopes was predicting various aspects of the prophetic and priestly offices of Christ, and in the Fourth, by implication and deduction also truths about the kingly office of Jesus Christ. Erroneous Theories about the identity of the "Servant of the Lord."

That Jewish and Hebrew scholars, except those who have accepted Christ as the promised Messiah of the Old Testament, should refuse to identify the Servant with Jesus Christ is not surprising. In Jewish literature one finds that the view that the "Servant of Yahweh" is either the nation of Israel or a remnant within the nation.[6] This remnant is considered to be righteous in comparison with those who are not in the nation of Israel. However, Leupold argued that already in 42:6, the first Servant Song, the servant is thought of very clearly distinct from the nation of Israel, for in verse 6 he stands over against the nation as the mediator of the covenant and its light.[7] Furthermore, in the Second Servant Song, where the servant speaks and declares in verse 5: "And now the Lord says, who formed me from the womb to be his servant, to bring Jacob back to him," the clear implication is that the servant of Yahweh is an individual, not a nation or group within Israel, and has the mission direct to the nation (called Jacob and Israel), and again in verse 6 Yahweh says: "It is too light a thing that you should be my servant to raise up the tribes of Jacob, and to restore the preserved of Israel, I will give you a light to the nations, that my salvation may reach the end of the earth."

Professor North has pointed out another difficulty with the collective theory, when he wrote:

> The fact that the Servant does not, like Israel, suffer for his own sins, but for the sins of others, and that this patience under suffering is in marked contrast to the querulousness of Israel in the main prophecy, was an obvious difficulty for the 'full collective theory.' The difficulty, it was thought could be obviated, or at any rate minimized, by identifying the Servant with a pious remnant of faithful Israelites, or with the order of the prophets.[8]

The theory that the pious remnant in Israel was the Suffering Servant of Isaiah 50 and 52:13-53:12 goes directly counter to various Old Testament passages that teach the universality and culpability of all men, including the Jews of the Old Testament. Solomon declared: "There is not a just man upon earth that doeth good and sinneth not."[8] David confessed: "Yes I was born guilty, and when my mother conceived me I was in sin (Psalm 51:5)."[9] David confessed: "They have all turned away together and become corrupt. Not one does right, not a single one" (Psalm 14:3).[10] Isaiah exclaimed:

> "We've all become like an unclean person, and all our righteousness are like rags dirtied by menstrual flow." (64:6)."[11] David declared in Psalm 143:2: "Don't bring your servant into court because no one living is righteous before thee."[12] Korah's descendants confessed: "No one can buy anyone's freedom or pay God a ransom for him" (Psalm 49:7)."[13]

The Identification of the Servant of Yahweh with Some Israelite Personality

The attempts by a number of scholars to identify the Servant of Yahweh with some historical individual mentioned on the pages of the Old Testament, must be labelled as not adequate and correct. Among historical personages suggested for this role have been the following: Hezekiah, Uzziah, Isaiah, Zerubbabel, Meshullam, the son of Zerubbabel, Jehoiachin, Moses and even Cyrus. North has pointed out correctly:

> The servant not only suffered as a consequence of his mission; suffering was the means whereby he was to bring his mission to a successful issue. It is sufficient to say that these theories fixing as they do upon individuals so diverse in character and calling cancel one another out, and that none of them has any serious backing today.[15]

Extreme Views about the Identity of the Servant

Some scholars have advocated some far out views about the identity of the Servant of the Lord. A few savants have proposed what has been denominated the "historico-Messianic theory." According to this interpretation the suffering servant was a contemporary of the prophet and that the latter considered the former destined to be the Messiah. After discovering the Suffering Servant he encouraged him to undertake the political restoration of Judah in exile. This allegedly brought the Suffering Servant into conflict with the Babylonian authorities who subjected him to a violent death. Thus the Prophet was responsible for bringing about the death of the Suffering Servant. However, correctly North says, that the Servant's mission was spiritual and not political.[16]

One of the strangest views, at least from a sound Biblical perspective, proposed by Old Testament Scholarship was the pagan view that the figure of the Suffering Servant was related to the Near Eastern myth of the dying and rising of the god Tammuz. North wrote about its unacceptability as follows:

> The obvious objection to this is that Tammuz was a nature God pure and simple and that the death had no atoning significance. That there are occasional features of Tammuz in the portrait of the Serpent (notably in 53.2, 22ff) is not improbable... To say that the Servant is Tammuz or any other cultic figure is quite another matter, and no one has the hardihood to maintain it.[16a]

The Messianic Interpretation of Isaiah 53

Professor North, a critical scholar, admitted: From the very beginning Christians interpreted Isa. 53 as a prophecy of Christ. There is abundant evidence for this in the New Testament (e.g. Acts 8.27-39; I Pet. 2:22-25), and there seems no doubt that Jesus read the passage as pointing to himself (e.g. Mark 1:11 and 10:45).[17]

Until the eighteenth century there was hardly a dissenting view found in Christendom relative to the truth that the Suffering Servant of the Lord was Jesus Christ. However, with the coming and introduction of the historico-critical method, the repudiation of the unity of Isaiah, the rejection of the concept of predictive prophecy, there can be no doubt that there then developed also theories previously enumerated which rejected the New Testament's testimony and interpretation of the meaning of the

Servant Passages that speak of a unique individual.

The Uniqueness of the Servant of the Lord Songs

Fitch, in *The New Bible Commentary* correctly has claimed that in Isaiah 42:1-9; 49:1-9; 50:4-9 and 52:13-53:12 the reader of the Old Testament comes to one of the most remarkable sections of all divine revelation.[18] Not only are these four pericopes unique in character, but as has been truly said, they are allied with all that is greatest in the scheme of the divine revelation. In thought and teaching they are connected more closely with the New Testament than any other Old Testament Scripture.

The second major section of Isaiah has been divided by Franz Delitzsch into three segments: 40-48,49-57, 58-66.[19] The first segment of the second section or half of Isaiah, 40-66, i.e. 40-48 deals with the salvation and deliverance of the Jews from the Babylonian Captivity; the second segment, chapters 49-57 announces the spiritual deliverance of Israel, and the third segment, chapter 58-66 predicts the deliverance of the true Israel of God from sin and damnation. The first Servant Song is found in 40-48, while the other three are interwoven with the thoughts in chapters 49-57, which emphasize especially the salvation which Yahweh's Servant, the Messiah, will effect by his suffering, death and resurrection.

With chapter 42 the reader of Isaiah reaches a distinctive stage in the thought of the prophet Isaiah. After having discussed the great themes of the majesty and sovereignty of God and after having dealt with his own people and the nations of the earth, Isaiah now proceeds under inspiration of the Holy Spirit to make known to his readers the means Yahweh will utilize to bring about an effectuation of His will. Israel is informed as to what mighty purposes God has in store for her to fulfill; the nations of the world must know the truth which Yahweh was going to disclose to them. "With the sure touch of inevitability the prophet therefore continues to speak of those things and to refer in particular to the Servant or Minister by whom the blessed will and purpose of heaven is to be completed."[20]

Beginning with the New Testament, Christian believers who hold that the Triune God is the God of the Holy Scriptures, have accepted the truth that Christ is the center both of the Old and New Testaments. Jesus claimed that the Old Testament Scriptures spoke of Him. Christ was the red thread running through the Old Testament, beginning with Genesis 3:15 and ending with Malachi 4 in the canon of the Old Testament as found in our European Bibles.

The history of Messianic prediction in the Old Testament may be studied according to the following time periods:

1. The ages before the Flood, Genesis, Chapters 1-8.

2. The Patriarchal age, from the Flood to Israel's arrival at Sinai, where patriarchal government yielded to national organization. Genesis 9-Exodus 19.

3. The age of the Judges, of whom Moses was the first, and Samuel the last. Exodus 19 to I Samuel 12.

4. The period of the Kings, including the United Kingdom, the Division of the Kingdom of the Twelve Tribes, and Judah after the Fall of Israel. 1 Samuel 13-11 Kings 25, together with many of the prophetic books and Psalms.

5. The Babylonian Exile, Ezekiel, Daniel and some Psalms.

6. The time of reconstruction after the Exile. Books dealing with this period would be Haggai, Zechariah, Ezra, Nehemiah and Malachi.[21]

The Book of Psalms and the Prophecy of Isaiah contain many predictions about the coming Messiah, with whom Christ identified Himself; this was also the identification made by a number of New Testament writers.[22] A significant fact of Yahweh's revelation as contained in the Old Testament is that during the long prophetic career of Isaiah, Yahweh vouchsafed a number of new insights about the conception, birth (7:14), person, work, ministry and kingdom of the Messiah, God's Servant. The Four Servant Songs make a special contribution to the some sixty odd Messianic prophecies, the high water mark of the Old Testament Scriptures. The threefold offices of Christ are set forth uniquely in these Servant Passages, delivered in the course of the eighth century before Christ.

Features Held in Common by the Four Servant Songs

The distinctive impression a reading of the Four Servant Passages gives is that a remarkable individual is spoken of, whose preparation, attitude work under no circumstances would be applicable to a nation, or to a normal mortal, except it be the Jesus, the God-man.

When studying and interpreting the Four Servant Songs, it is necessary to distinguish the different speakers who utter the teachings found in them. In the 29 verse that comprise the Four Songs, in most cases, it is Yahweh who is either speaking about His Servant or addressing the Servant directly. In other verses it is the Servant Himself who speaks, while in chapter 53:1, it is the believing portion of the nation of Israel that declares: "Who hath believed our report?"[23]

The different efforts which the Lord's Servant will perform are not merely meant for Israel, but for the nations. The Lord says to His Servant: "I formed you and have appointed you to be a Covenant, a Light for the nations (42:6), the same is also stated in 49:6. Some critical scholars of the past have argued that the Servant Songs were not an integral part of Isaiah 40-55,[24] denominated by them as the Second or Deutero-Isaiah. In this connection it may be noted that the expression "the Holy One" or "the Holy One of Israel," a designation for Yahweh (Lord) is found 26 times in Isaiah and only 30 times in the Old Testament.[25] This title, the Holy One of Israel, is found in the Second Servant Song, and in 49:7 which reads: "The Lord, who redeems Israel and his Holy One, says to Him whom the people despise and national abhor." The use of Holy One is one of the characteristics of the Book of Isaiah and supports the concept of the unity of the Book of Isaiah and also is supportive of the view that the Servant Songs cannot be removed from the fabric of chapters 40-55.[26]

The Mission of Yahweh's Servant

The purpose of the Messiah's mission is set forth in a number of the Servant Songs. The Lord's servant had a mission for his own people, many of whom, as Isaiah predicted in 6:9-10, would suffer from hardening of the heart. Therefore when Jesus began His ministry He called upon His Jewish hearers to repent. He told the Syro-Phoenecian woman that He was sent to the lost sheep of the house cf Israel. In chapter 49:6 (Second Servant Song) Yahweh states: "It is not enough that you are My Servant to raise the tribes of Jacob to bring back those in Israel who have been preserved-I have made You a Light for the nations that My salvation might reach to most distant part of the world."[27] The Messiah was to be a Savior for all people. Jesus undoubtedly had this passage in mind as fulfilled in Him when He asserted about Himself: "I am the Light of the world" (John 8:12). According to Mathew 28:18 Jesus commanded His followers to make disciples of all nations, thereby also claiming that all nations needed His message of redemption and salvation.

The Relationship of Yahweh to the Servant

The relationship between Yahweh and His anointed is emphasized in a number of the Servant Songs. The first of these remarkable songs begins: "Here is My Servant whom I support; I have chosen Him, and I delight in Him I put My Spirit on Him," and in 42:8 the Lord says: "I the Lord have called You for My righteous purposes and have taken hold of Your hand, I formed You and have appointed You to be a Covenant of the people, a Light for the nations." In 49:1 the Servant declares: "The Lord called Me from the womb, from the body cf My Mother he named my name." In 49:51 there is repeated the unique description of the Messiah's origin: "And now the Lord says, who formed me from the womb to be his servant — for I am honored in the eyes of the Lord, and my God has become my strength." In the third Servant Song, 50:4-9 the Lord God is depicted as giving the Servant the ability to instruct those to whom He is sent (v. 4). The same God opens his ear (v. 5), helps His Servant (v. 7); it was the will of the Lord to bruise His Servant (53:10), it was Yahweh who puts His Servant to grief (v. 10).

In this song the Servant's office is particularly described. Under the inspiration of the Holy Spirit, the Servant of the Lord will truly fulfill the glorious purpose for which He was called. Beck translated verse 1: "Here is My Servant whom I support, I have chosen Him, and I delight in Him, I put my spirit on Him. He will bring righteousness to the nations."[28] The particular task assigned to the Servant is described by Leupold as follows: "It is almost impossible to find an adequate equivalent for the word that we, with many others, have translated as 'truth,' as a 'norm of judgment,' or even as the true religion. None of these is quite satisfactory. The term implies all that the nations need for their salvation, the blotting out their spiritual ignorance."[29]

The Servant will accomplish this work without demonstrations of human powers which others so blatantly display (v. 2). The name of Yahweh will be spread throughout the nations by the Servant and men will know the Lord's glory. As the Servant fulfills His ministry and office. He will experience the blessings of the gracious God of all the earth.

Yahweh who has chosen and sent the Servant is the Creator of heaven and earth; He is the Giver of life to all creatures, and He is the God who will not share His glory with any of the heathen gods, whether they be the Babylonian gods of Isaiah's time or of our times. As the omniscient Lord He also predicts what will happen in the future, and such predictions the heathen deities will not make because they have no basis in reality. The tragedy is that the Babylonians and Assyrians created these gods but they were non-existent and "nothings" (Hebrew: elilim).

In chapter 40:1-3 the forerunner of the Messiah, who as the New Testament states, was none other than John the Baptist.[30] Now in chapter 42 the Messiah is mentioned. Isaiah 42:3 is a passage which is definitely applied to Jesus Christ in Matthew 12:17-21: "He shall not break a bruised reed, nor quench the smoking flax." The record of Christ's life shows that He evinced a spirit of meakness, of gentleness and undaunted perseverance. The Messiah would be sustained by divine power and would be a light to the Gentiles, to open the blind, to bring out the prisoners from prison, and to bring them that sit in darkness out of the prison house (vv. 5-6). In such a ministry all the followers of Christ may have a share, but they must show His spirit of sympathy and gentleness. His matchless courage and His dependence on the sustaining power of God (Acts 26:17-18).

The type of deliverance which the Servant of Yahweh is to effect does not refer to the kind of "liberation theology", now preached in Mexico, Central America, Africa and other countries where Biblical teaching is employed to undergird Marxist thinking and to justify the use of force to change the political order.[30] Various verses in the Servant Songs, including chapter 61:1-3 are interpreted to mean that Christ really came to bring about the freedom of economically impoverished and politically oppressed peoples. That such is not the case is shown by the manner in which Christ conducted His missionary activities in connection with His Galilean, Perean and Judean ministries, during which He never preached or incited revolt against Rome but taught: "Render unto Ceasar the things that are Ceasar's and unto God the things that are God's" (Matt. 22:21). Those in prison house in need of being freed from their bonds were all men and women and children under Satan's power, held in the bonds of sin.[31] Christ came to defeat the Devil and release men from the bondage of sin and transplant them out of the kingdom of darkness into the kingdom of light, and not primarily to bring deliverance from economic and political oppression by the use of force. Christ's kingdom is not established by the sword; it is a spiritual kingdom and its citizens are no longer in the grip of sin and under Satan's control. The church was given the sword of the spirit and not an iron sword with which to fight its battles against the forces of evil.

The Second Servant Song (49:1-13)
The mention of the Servant as an individual in 42:1-9 and thereafter

the Servant as a collective concept has led George Robinson, one-time professor at McCormick Theological Seminary to write:

> It is somewhat confusing, after the lofty picture of the ideal and apparently individual Servant described in 42:1-9, that the prophet should refer to all Israel, as Jehovah's Servant, as in 42:18-22; 43:10; 44:1-5, 21-28; 45:4; 48:20-22; for it is quite obvious that in all these passages he is alluding to the masses of people, reproving, consoling, admonishing and reassuring them.[32]

However, in 49:1-13 Isaiah makes a distinct advance over 42:1-9 relative to his depiction of the Servant's mission and experience. In 49 the Servant is an individual, a Person, a Prophet whose mission is worldwide. No less than twice it is stated by the Servant that the Lord called Him when He was in the womb, before His mother gave birth to Him, and pronounced the Servant's name. Here it is not impossible that there is a prediction of the Virgin's conception or to the annunciation of the angel Gabriel to Mary of her forthcoming Virgin conception and Birth (Luke 1:31-33).

The Second Song is the natural sequel to the First Song of 42:1-9. The new features of the Second Song are: 1. The Servant's consciousness of His mission (49:1-3); 2. His confession of failure in the past (49:4), and 3. His quickened faith in the revelation that Yahweh has raised him up for a still greater purpose, namely, as an organ of salvation to the ends of the earth (49:5-6). Moreover, before the Lord can accomplish His mission for all of mankind, there is a preliminary work which must be done for Israel.

The Second Servant Song announces that the Messiah will meet with discouragement, for the Servant has a mission to Israel and Jacob and this fact therefore does not agree with the view of those who claim that it is Israel who is the Servant spoken of in the Servant Songs. No, it will be God's Son who first of all was sent to the lost sheep of the house of Israel and then later His message would be for all nations. But as the Servant was carrying His mission to Israel, to the tribes of Jacob, He would meet with disappointment.

The Servant of Yahweh claims that He has a divine call for His prophetic mission or task; His words were like a sharp sword would pierce the consciences of sinners and administer judgment as well (Rev. 19:15). Although the Servant's service seems fruitless at first, and He fails to bring His people into fellowship with God, He is divinely encouraged by the assurance of the future return of some of Israel and of His mission's success to the world. His humiliation would be followed by the state of exaltation; after the resurrection victory the Servant would see the Gentiles as well as a remnant of the Jewish nation saved.

The Third Servant Song (50:4-11)

In this song the Messiah is introduced as Himself speaking. "The Lord Jehovah hath given men the tongue of them that are taught, that I may know how to sustain with words him that is weary." (v. 4). It was already stated in the previous song (49:1-6) that the Servant was conscious of the fact that

His ministry would involve suffering and pain. In this song, as Orelli has stated: "He possesses the two fundamental qualifications of an ideal prophet: willingness to listen as often as God's speaks, and willingness always to utter without demur whatever God commands."[33]

In the Third Song this consciousness is deepened and some forms of the suffering are begun to be spelt out. However, it will be in the Fourth Song that the full intensity of the Servant's suffering will be clearly delineated. It is in the Third Song that for the first time is heard the bitter scorn and contumely through which the Servant is forced to go (50:6-9). The patient manner in which, in the discharge of his task. He endured the abuse and insult to which He was subjected, is stressed. The Servant knew well what men usually mete out to prophets who proclaim God's will; they are scorned and are scourged, they are sawn in half as probably Isaiah was according to Jewish tradition, or are burned, beheaded or stoned to death.[34]

In this song the Servant of the Lord is addressing neither the nation nor His own people. His utterance is in the form of a soliloquy. The Servant realized the dignity and importance of His prophetic office, but also its peril. Especially emphasized in this Song are His obedience and trust. Daily the Messiah listens for the Lord's message and thereby is enabled to give courage to those who have faith:

The Lord hath given men the tongue of the learned, that I should know how to speak a word in season to him that is weary:

He waketh morning by morning, he waketh mine ear, and I was not rebellious, neither turned away my back.

The believer who reads this Servant Song will here find a wonderful example of trust in adversity. For the Servant declares:

For the Lord will help me;
Therefore I shall not be confounded;
therefore I have set my face as flint,
and I know that I shall
not be ashamed (v. 7).

This song also mentions for the first time, only to be intensified in the Fourth Song, that he would endure as priest for Israel and the nations, sufferings and torture.

I gave my back to the smiters and my cheek to them that plucked off the hair; I hid not my face from shame and spitting.

What was predicted as going to happen to the Messiah was fulfilled according to the Passion Account in the Gospels.[36]

On the other hand, the prophet Isaiah announced that only retribution and sorrow await those individuals who refuse to listen to the Lord's Servant and who oppose Him (50:10-11). Correctly Robinson has noted about the Third Servant Song, that like in the First Song, the Servant is free from all national limitations.[37] He asserts that the concept of the Servant is not bound to Israel either in the latter's totality, or as a spiritual church. Rather the Servant is portrayed as an individual, as a prophet, sinless, and obedient to the divine will; submissively patient, because of the Lord's unfailing support. In short, the Servant is described as an ideal prophet made perfect through sufferings.

The Fourth Servant of the Lord Song (52:13-53:12).

With the fourth of the Servant Songs in which the distinctive phrase, or designation, **Ebed Yahweh** (Servant of Jehovah or Lord) is employed, the Biblical student comes to the climax of the prophet's symphony.[38] Here the Old Testament reader will find the acme of Hebrew prophecy. In this Song all the leading ideas of the previous three Songs are gathered up and are presented in a manner which gives a complete and coherent picture of the life, service, suffering, death, burial and resurrection of God's Servant.

Chapter 52:13-53:12, one of the best known chapters of the Old Testament, is the middle chapter of the second major segment of the second half of Isaiah. Its position is no accident, because the theological truths enunciated in this Song belong to the very heart of the Gospel of Jesus Christ.

Many scholars and people, including orthodox and liberal Jews, deny that this Fourth Song refers to the Lord Jesus Christ,[39] but the proofs of the Messianic character are varied and many. While as has already been shown Israel as a nation is called Yahweh's servant, in this pericope (52:13-53:12) only an individual can be meant. The history of the Old Testament clearly reveals that in Biblical times, whether this be in the Old Testament or in the New, Israel proved to be a disobedient and perverse nation, a nation who was constantly being punished for its sins. The two great Pre-Christian deportations, the Assyrian captivity in 721 B.C. and the Babylonian captivity (597, 587 B.C.), were the just punishments visited upon a people who periodically violated the first restriction of the Mosaic Covenant, namely, to worship no other gods besides Yahweh. Beginning with the wilderness stay right to 587 B.C. both Israel, the Northern Kingdom and Judah, the Southern Kingdom, were guilty not only of being unfaithful to Yahweh, but also violated and ignored many of the laws which God had given them through Moses. Therefore, when they were punished, it was not that they were innocent, but that they were receiving the just reward for their failures and deliberate sins. Thus the innocent suffering of the Lord's Servant cannot be applied to Israel as a nation, or for that matter to a pious remnant among the people.

That modern Jewish commentators reject the individual view about the identity of the suffering Servant is not surprising.[40] The so called collective theory about who the Suffering Servant is adhered to both by Jewish scholars and Christian scholars.[41] Thus the Jewish scholar Slotki, in commenting of Isaiah 53, wrote:

The servant is the ideal Israel or the faithful remnant. That he is not an individual is the opinion of all Jewish commentators.[42]

Thus Whitehouse (a Christian Hebraist) also asserted:

Whatever causes may have tended to stimulate the advocacy of this form of interpretation (viz. the Christological), it is important for Christian exegetes to recognize that this path of Jewish exposits is in the main right, and that the path of Christian interpreters down to the time of Rosenmuller (i.e. 1820) has been in the main wrong.[43]

The Luther scholar Quanbeck (now deceased) in an essay delivered before the Lutheran Professors' conference took the position that it was perfectly legitimate for Jewish scholars to find in the suffering servant of Isaiah the people of Israel and also hold that in the Old Testament that man was saved by performing good works (a Jewish view), while Christians might find Christological meanings in the Old Testament and in Isaiah 53 a picture of Christ's suffering.[44] One is forced to ask, how it is possible for the same scriptures to have two different meaning at the same time, dependent upon whose interpreting the passage or chapter! This surely violates basic laws of interpretation and does not agree with the meaning of the whole Fourth Servant passage as understood by a number of different New Testament writers.

The person who reads Isaiah 52:13-53:12 and then compares it with the suffering and death of Christ described by the four Gospel writers will see how Isaiah has predicted these crucial events that represent the climatic happenings in the life of Christ. Martin has pointed out that there are eighty references to Isaiah in the New Testament (indirect and direct) and many of these references relate to this one chapter of Isaiah (the 53rd).[45] An unbiased reader of Acts 8 would realize that Philip told the Ethiopian eunuch, who happened to be reading Isaiah 53 on his return trip to his home land, and did not understand precisely what he was reading, was told by Philip the evangelist, that he had been reading about Christ (Acts 8:35).[46] Philip baptized the Ethiopian who accepted Christ as the lamb who was taken to the slaughter and through whose death he and many others were declared righteous. Martin has pointed out that there are at least six direct quotations from Isaiah 52:13-53:12. They are the following:

     52:15 is quoted in Romans 15:21
     53:1 is cited in John 12:38 and in Romans 10:16
     53:4 is quoted in Matthew 8:17
     53:5,6 cited in I Peter 2:22-25
     53:7,8. is quoted in Acts 8:32, 33
     53:12 is cited in Mark 15:28 and Luke 22:37.[47]

In addition to these references from Isaiah, there are also brief allusions to terms and phrases found in Isaiah 53. It would be profitable to study and compare:

     Romans 4:25 with 53:5
     I Peter 1:19 with 53:7
     Revelation 5:6 with 53:7
     Revelation 7:14 with 53:7
     John 1:29, 36 with 53:7 and 11
     I John 3:5 with 53:9, 11
     I Corinthians 15:3, 4 with 53:8-11

II Corinthians 5:21 with 53:8-11.[48]

It was Franz Delitzsch's contention that "all the references in the New Testament to the Lamb of God (with which the corresponding allusions to the Passover are interwoven) spring from this passage in the book of Isaiah, i.e. the dumb type of the Passover now finds a tongue."[49]

Isaiah 52:13-53:12 has been called the "holy of holies of the Old Testament." Polycarp described the Fourth Servant Song as "the golden passion of the Old Testament." This Isaianic chapter may be said to be the link between Psalm 22, the Great Passion Psalm and Psalm 110, the psalm's description of Christ's royal priesthood.

Hebrew scholars are aware of the fact that there are textual problems in the present Massoretic text. Some have found no less than 26 words which only occur in this pericope and which Bible translators know as **hapax legomena**, present interpretative difficulties as to the exact meaning of these words in the verses in which they occur.[50] Despite this fact, Leupold correctly argued: "Yet for all the difficulties that the chapter offers it is and will remain one of the grandest and most beloved passages of Sacred Writ. Faith grasps these verities, gratitude feeds on them, hope is nourished by them."

Concerning the Fourth Servant Song it may properly be claimed that in it the Old Testament has reached the high water mark of its revelation, for Archor has so aptly stated it: "Nowhere in all the Hebrew Scripture is there to be found a more profound treatment of the person and work of our Redeemer, and indeed even the New Testament can show no fuller discussion of the meaning of the cross."[51]

The Fourth Servant Song properly begins with the last paragraph of Chapter 52, that is, verses 13-15. The present division between chapters 52 and 53 is not the most felicitous. The last of the Four great Servant Songs may be divided into five strophes of three lines each.

The following is an outline of Isaiah 52:13-53:12:
    The Servant Exalted (52:13-15)
    The Servant Despised (53:1-3)
    The Servant Wounded (53:4-6)
    The Servant Cut Off (53:7-9)
    The Servant Satisfied (53:10-12)[52]

H. J. Stolee has called Isaiah 52:13-53:12 "A Preview of Calvary." In his helpful study of the Book of Isaiah, entitled, *Isaiah Saw the Lord* he has summarized, or outlined the Fourth Servant Song in this way:[53]

A Preview of Calvary
I. The Prophet Sketched Calvary (52:13-15)
1. Many are astonished at a suffering Messiah
2. Yet He shall prosper and be exalted
II. Man's attitude to Christ and to the Gospel (53:13-15)
1. Man despises the Gospel
2. Man despises the Christ

III. The Vicarious Atonement described (53:4-9)
1. Christ offered in our stead
2. He was obedient unto death
IV. Christ is not a victim but a Victor (53:10-12)
1. He dies according to God's plan
2. He shares His righteousness and victory with His people

One would think that Isaiah had stood on Calvary's hill and witnessed the crucifixion of Jesus; the details which are set down in this climactic poem are as clear and as clear as if the author was present at Christ's crucifixion in the first century B.C. and yet this remarkable passages was written about 700 years before its historical occurrence. The Fourth Servant Song is a remarkable Messianic prophecy; in fact there is nothing in the Old Testament more clear and complete relative to the very essentials of Christology (the doctrine of the person and work of Christ), both as to the humiliation and exaltation of the Lamb of God, who takes away the sins of the world. It parallels the great Christological passage of Paul in Philippians 2:5-11.

General Observations about the Fourth Servant Song

Besides containing the profoundest thought of the Old Testament revelation, this poem is a vindication of the Servant, "so clear and so true, and wrought out with such pathos and potency, that it holds first place in Messianic prophecy. As far as fact and accuracy of description are concerned, it might well have been composed after the tragedy of Calvary. It was for this reason, as already stated, Polycarp called it "the golden passion of the Old Testament."[54]

While the prophetic office is mentioned in 53:1, like the previous Song (50:4-11) the priestly office is again referred to, but more prominently than even in the Third Song. In the Fourth Song the Bible reader will find the Messiah described also as a priest vicariously suffering for the sins of others, to whom the stroke was due (53:8). Jesus is both depicted prophetically as priestly offer and propitiatory sacrifice. He would be both the Lamb and the Priest offering the Lamb.

No clearer passage is found in all Scripture, Old or New Testaments, which teaches the vicarious and substitutionary nature of the death of Christ.[55] The striking part of the picture in Isaiah 53 is the Servant's unparalleled suffering. In the Fourth Song inspired Isaiah has given Jew and Gentile a graphic pan-portrait of the Suffering Savior and tell them of the glorious work He was to undertake in order that the sin question might be settled forever to the perfect satisfaction of God, the infinitely Holy One.

This Song also proclaims the extension of the Servant's life after he has been put to death and buried. The resurrection of the Servant is thus taught, just as Psalm 16:10 announced the resurrection: "Thou wilt not let thine Holy One see corruption." The Lutheran Confessions quote Isaiah seven different times as proofs for its doctrinal stance on a number of doctrines.[56]

Footnotes

1. J .D. Yoder, "Servant of the Lord," *Wycliffe Bible Encyclopedia*, Charles F. Pfeiffer, Howard Vos and John Rea, editors (Chicago: Moody Press, 2, 1554).
2. Edward J. Young, *An Introduction to the Old Testament* (Grand Rapids: Wm. B. Eerdmans Publishing Company, Severn printing, 1975), p. 225.
3. *The Lessons*, The appointed First Lesson, Second Lesson, and Gospel for the Series C of the three-year lectionary prepared by the Inter-Lutheran Commission on Worship (Minneapolis: Augsburg Publishing House, no date), pp. 36, 37, 38, 40.
   The Lessons, Series B (Minneapolis: Augsburg Publishing Company, no date), pp. 35, 36, 37, 39.
   The Lessons, Series A (Minneapolis: Augsburg Publishing House, no date) pp. 39, 40, 41, 44.
4. John H. Sampey, *A Syllabus for Old Testament Study* (New York: George H. Doran Company, 1922), pp. 210, 28-282.
5. H.C. Leupold, *Exposition of Isaiah* (Grand Rapids: Baker Book House, 1968), II, p. 60.
6. Joseph Klausner, *The Messianic Idea in Israel*. Translated from the Third Hebrew Edition (New York: The Macmillan and Company, 1958), p. 162.
7. Leupold, **op. cit.**, p. 60.
8. C.R. North, *Isaiah 40-55* (London; SCM Press LTD, 1952), p. 30.
9. William F. Beck, *The Holy Bible, An American Translation* (New Haven: Leader Publishing Company, 1976), p. 658 (Old Testament).
10. **Ibid.**, p. 629 (Old Testament).
11. **Ibid.**, p. 863 (Old Testament).
12. **Ibid.**, p. 727 (Old Testament).
13. **Ibid.**, p. 657 (Old Testament).
14. North, **op. cit.**, pp. 31-32.
15. **Ibid.**, p. 32.
16. **Ibid.**, p. 32.
17. **Ibid.**, p. 33.
18. W. Fitch, "Isaiah," *The New Bible Commentary,* Professor F. Davidson, Editor, assisted by A.M. Stibbes and E. F. Kevan (Grand Rapids: Wm. B. Eerdmans Publishing Company, 1953), p. 591.
19. Franz Delitzsch, "Isaiah," *Fairbairns Imperial Standard Bible Encyclopedia*, edited by Patrick Fairbairn (Grand Rapids: Zondervan Publishing House, 1957), reprint of 1897 edition. III, 167.
20. Fitch, **op. cit.**, p. 591.
21. Edward Mack, *Christ in the Old Testament* (Richmond: Presbyterian Committee of Publication, 1926), p. 39.
22. **Ibid.**, pp. 18-31.
23. M. Reu, Thomasius, *Old Testament Selections* (Columbus The Wartburg Press, 1959), p. 287.
24. C.R. North, "Servant of the Lord", *Interpreter's Dictionary of the Bible*, George Arthur Buttrick, editor (New York: Abingdon Press), IV, 2923.
25. Cf. William Wilson, *Old Testament Word Studies* (Grand Rapids: Kregels Publications, 1978), p. 221.
26. Gleason Archer, *A Survey of Old Testament Introduction* (Chicago: Moody Press, 1964), p. 332.
27. Beck, **op. cit.**, (Old Testament), p. 845.
28. **Ibid.**, **op. cit.**, (Old Testament), p. 835.
29. Leupold, **op. cit.**, p. 61.
30. Paul E. Kretzmann, *Popular Commentary Old Testament* (St. Louis: Concordia Publishing House, 1924), II, p. 351.
31. Cf. William F. LeRoy, "Liberation Theology." *Christian News Encyclopedia* (Washington, Missouri: Missourian Publishing Co., 1982), II, 1133.
32. G.L. Robinson, *The Book of Isaiah* (Grand Rapids: Baker Book House, 1954), p.

143.

33. As quoted by Robinson, p. 149.
34. Cf. Raymond F. Surburg, *Introduction to the Intertestamental Period* (St. Louis: Concordia Publishing House, 1975), p. 133.
35. Robinson, p. 144.
36. Matthew 2:27-30.
37. Robinson, **op. cit.**, p. 145.
38. Horace D. Hummel, *The Word Becoming Flesh* (St. Louis: Concordia Publishing House, 1979), p. 221.
30. Frederick Alfred Aston, *The Challenge of the Ages* (Scarsdale, NY: Research Press, 1972), pp. 18-19.
40. I.W. Slotki, *Isaiah, Soncino Books of the Bible* (London: The Soncino Press, 1949), p. 260.
41. Peter Ackroyd, "The Book of Isaiah," *The Interpreter's One Volume Commentary on the Bible* (New York and Nashville: Abingdon Press).
42. Slotki, **op. cit.**, p. 260.
43. O.C. Whitehouse, *Isaiah, Century Bible*, as cited by Slotki, p. 260.
44. Quanbeck, "The Bible," in Robert Bertram, *Theology in the Life of the Church* (Philadelphia: Fortress Press, 1963).
45. Alfred Martin, Isaiah, "The Salvation of Jehova." (Chicago: Moody Press, 1956), p. 90.
46. F. F. Bruce, *The Acts of the Apostles – The Greek Text with Introduction and Commentary* (Grand Rapids: Wm. B. Eerdmans Publishing Company, reprinted 1949), II. 306.
47. Martin, **op. cit.**, p. 91.
48. **Ibid.**, p. 91.
49. Franz Delitzsch, *Commentary on Isaiah* (Grand Rapids: Wm. B. Eerdmans Publishing Company, reprinted 1949), II, p. 306.
50. North, **op. cit.**, p. 131.
50a. Leupold, **op. cit.**, pp. 22-223.
51. Gleason Archer, "Isaiah," Carl F. Henry, Editor, *The Biblical Expositor* (Philadelphia: A. J. Holman Company, 1960), II, p. 152. Leupold, II, p. 223.
52. Taken from Martin, **op. cit.**, p. 92.
53. H. J. Stolee, *Isaiah Saw the Lord* (Minneapolis: Bible Banner Press, 1955), pp. 161-165.
54. Robinson, pp. 145-46.
55. The official exposition of Luther's *Small Catechism* called *A Short Explanation of Dr. Martin Luther's Small Catechism – A Handbook of Christian Doctrine* (St. Louis: Concordia Publishing House, 1943), p. 115 quotes Is. 53:4,5 to teach the vicarious atonement. *Doctor Martin Luther's Small Catechism – Explained for Children and Adults*. Originally edited by C. Gausewitz (Milwaukee: Northwestern Publishing House, 1954) also cited is. 53:5-6 in behalf of the doctrine of the vicarious atonement.
56. Cf. the Biblical References, Index Theodore G. Tappert, *The Book of Concord* (Philadelphia: Fortress Press, 1959), p. 640.

Questions

1. What are the "Servant of the Lord" passages? ____
2. Isaiah in the "Ebed Yahweh" periscopes was predicting ____.
3. In Jewish literature one finds the view that the "Servant of Yahweh" is ____.
4. Was the pious remnant in Israel the suffering servant? ____
5. What came with the introduction of the historical-critical method? ____
____ is at the center of both the Old and New Testaments?

7. Psalms and Isaiah contain many ____.
8. The Servant will bring ____ to the nations.
9. The gods of the Babylonians and Assyrians are ____.
10. The forerunner of the Messiah was none other than ____.
11. What is "liberation theology?" ____
12. Christ never incited revolt against ____.
13. Christ's kingdom is not established by the ____.
14. Chapter 52:13-53:12 is one of the ____ of the Old Testament.
15. The innocent suffering of the Lord's Servant cannot be applied to ____.
16. How many references to Isaiah are there in the New Testament? ____
17. H. J. Stolee has called Isaiah 52:13-53:12 ____.
18. Isaiah 53 parallels the great Christological passage of Paul in ____.
119. Psalm 16:10 announced the ____.

The Contribution of Lutheran Handel to Ecclesiastical Music

(In commemoration of Handel's 300th birthday)

Christian News, May 20, 1985

During the year 1985 musicologists, historians of musical history and laymen especially interested in the influence of religion and theology upon music, are noting the 400th anniversary of the birth of Heinrich Schuetz, and the 300th anniversary of the births of Frederic Handel, Johann Sebastian Bach and Domenico Scarlatti, son of the more famous Alessandro Scarlatti. The first three of these were Lutherans, who made significant contributions to the field of church music. This year a great deal of attention has been and is and will be given to Johann Sebastian Bach, so that the birthday and contributions of Handel are being neglected, although this past Easter a number of churches have recalled Handel's 300th birthday by using his music from the "Messiah" for the Lenten and Easter season. Bach was born on March 21, 1685 and Handel on February 23, 1685.[1] Both Bach and Handel were contemporaries who hailed from the same Saxon Thuringian geographical area, made famous some two hundred and fifty years before Bach's and Handel's time by Luther. Both of these musicians and composers were the products of the musical culture of the Saxon-Thuringian region.[2]

A Brief Comparison of the Outward Lives of Bach and Handel

Although Bach and Handel[3] hailed from the same geographical region and were contemporaries, they never personally met, though at one time they held positions within a hundred miles of each other. Of the two, Handel did much more extensive travelling, Bach never visited Italy or England, which was not the case relative to Handel. In fact, Handel became a citizen of England and is usually classified with English composers rather than with those of Germany.[4] In his lifetime Handel achieved greater fame than did Bach. After Handel's death his fame was not dimmed as was that of Bach's.[5]

Handel never married and consequently left no heirs, while Bach married twice and sired twenty children, of whom a number died while young. But Bach left four sons who achieved considerable fame, in fact, one of his sons was in Bach's lifetime considered greater than his father. Handel appears to have been more ecumenical-minded than was Bach. Thus Handel wrote music for the Lutherans, for Roman Catholics (while living in Italy) and hymns and anthems for the Episcopalians in England.[7] Both men applied for the position of organist at Luebeck, where Buxtehude was organist, and would have been the successor of Buxtehude had they been willing to marry the latter's daughter. To the latter condition Bach and Handel refused to accede and therefore failed to secure the organist's position.[8]

Both Bach and Handel are considered the greatest representatives of the baroque period of European musical history; in fact they are also said to conclude it.[9] Toward the end of their lives both became blind.[10] Both of these Lutherans believed in a life after death and were conscious of their coming ends. A few days before his death, Handel expressed the hope that he might die on Good Friday, a wish God granted him, for Handel breathed his last on Good Friday, April 14, 1759, in the hope of meeting his good God and sweet Lord and Savior on the day of the resurrection.[11] Bach composed the following in anticipation of his coming death: "When in the Hour of Utmost Need," but then he found his spiritual balance and directed that the composition be renamed: "Before Thy Throne, My God I Stand."[12] After Bach's debts were paid practically nothing was left for his widow who within two years found herself in an almshouse, unable to support herself. Handel had accumulated considerable wealth so that he was able to leave money to relatives in Germany.[13] Bach's funeral was a very inauspicious affair, while Handel was buried in Westminster Abbey with pomp and circumstance.[14]

For seventy-five years Bach was nearly forgotten, with the exception of a few people who realized what a great musician and composer Bach had been. Handel's fame and music were not forgotten but he continued to be honored and his music performed.[15]

Weinstock made his comparison of these two contemporaries: "Handel remains one of the most attractive figures in the history of music as both man and composer. An extrovert, the familiar of the famous noble, and royal, he was a citizen of the world, the exact opposite in temperament and circumstance of his contemporary Bach."[16]

A number of years after their respective deaths, organizations were founded in Europe and in America, as The Hayden and Handel Society and the Bachgesellschaft, who were dedicated to the publication, singing and perpetuation of Handel's and Bach's musical works.

The Life and Activities of Handel (1685-1759)

The author of the article in *The Encyclopedia Britannica, Makropedia*, begins his discussion of the life and musical accomplishments of the German-born Handel in this way:

"One of the greatest composers of the late Baroque era, George Frederic Handel, German by birth, and English by adoption, mastered the techniques of German, French, and Italian musical style and adapted them to a new environment to create works of such power that he became a familiar institution in Britain and a key figure in the national traditions of Germany. Ultimately, his work became an essential factor in the popularization of European music throughout the world."[17]

George Frederic Handel, the son of a sixty-three year old barber-surgeon, with his mother the daughter of a Lutheran pastor, was born on February 23, 1685. His father was a surgeon at the court of the duke of Weissenfels. Like many another composer, Handel revealed musical talent at an early age. At the court where his father served, Handel had opportunity to hear good secular as well as church music. After his father's death Handel was able to concentrate on music. The Duke of Weissenfels recognized Handel's ability and recommended to his father before he died that young Handel's musical abilities should be developed and later supported Handel's efforts to become a composer and a musician. At nine years already he was writing spiritual cantatas; at ten he wrote a set of cantatas; at twelve he was in Berlin to continue his musical education. After his father's death he began the study of law, but music had such an appeal for him that he returned to it for the rest of his life.[18]

In Hamburg he continued his musical studies and became second violinist in the orchestra; at eighteen he was appointed organist of the Cathedral at Moritzburg, However, after a year he left that position for a stay at Hamburg.[19]

In the opening years of the eighteenth century Handel spent a number of years in Italy writing operas. Handel also demonstrated proficiency in the playing of the harpsichord. At nineteen years of age he composed "The Passion of St. John," a major work.[20] At twenty he wrote the opera "Amira." In 1710 Handel visited London where he acquired fame because of his operas. Beginning with 1712 and continuing to the year of his death (1759), England became the permanent home of the German Handel, who never succeeded in mastering the English language. For a number of years Handel majored in writing operas, of which he eventually wrote forty. However, a time came when the English public tired of them and Handel went bankrupt producing them. In eight years he lost $51,000 on Italian opera. Slanders of various kinds were circulated about him and his works and his productions were than no longer well received. In the midst of this adversity sickness overtook him and he suffered a partial stroke.[21]

Handel then went to Italy and after some time, he returned to England. Again he tried writing more operas but after more operatic failures he turned to the writing of oratorios. It was by means of them that Handel made his name famous forever.[22]

Handel and the Writing and Production of Oratorios

Handel is reputed once to have said: "Sacred music is best suited to a man descending into the valley of tears." Handel's first oratorio "Esther," was in reality a mask, while "Semele," "Alexander Balus," and "Susanna" are veritable chorus operas. "Hercules," called "a musical drama" by Handel himself, should, according to Lang, be considered the highest peak of the baroque music drama.[23] The subject matter for Handel's Biblical oratorios was taken mostly from the Old Testament, from events connected with the intertestamental period and from the New Testament (parts of the Messiah).

"Saul" and the colossal "Israel in Egypt," written in 1740, head the list of wonderful oratorios. In 1742 "the Messiah" was produced. This was followed by "Samson," "Joseph," "Semele," "Belshazzar," and "Hercules," which were also successful.[24] But even during these successes his enemies continued their conspiracies against the German composer and in 1744 he was once more bankrupt. For a year his pen remained idle. In 1746 the "Occasional Oratorio" and "Judas Maccabaeus" appeared, and these were speedily followed by "Joshua," "Solomon," "Susanna," "Theodra," and "Jephtha." It happened that while he was working on "Jephtha" that he suffered an attack of his last illness. Handel died on April 14, 1759 and was buried at Westminster Abbey.

Handel and English Music

H. Lang, one time professor of musicology at Columbia University, claimed the following about Handel's relationship to English music:

It is a singular fact that the composer who has left the deepest impression on English music should have been a German who came to England as an upholder of a purely Italian art.[25]

The same scholar further characterized Handel's art in this manner:

Handel's art embraces scintillating forms, colors, and figures of a gigantic imagination, the chief characteristics of which are a wholesome power of form, monumental dramatic conception, and a flowing poetic inspiration, abandoning itself in the contemplation of nature and its creatures.[26]

In the oratorio Handel gave England a national substitute for the opera. Observed Lang in his volume, *Music in Western Civilization*:

This oratorio was not humble church music, but entertainment of musico-dramatic kind, though on a higher moral plane, closer to and befitting English taste. Handel glorified the rise of the free people of England in his oratorios. The people of Israel became the prototype of the English nation, the chosen people of God reincarnated in Christendom, and magnificent Psalms of thanksgiving and marches of victory in imperial baroque splendor proclaimed the grandiose consciousness of England's world-conquering power.[27]

It is Lang's contention that the Handelian oratorios were entirely the product of England's social and spiritual environment, a circumstance instantly obvious, if we place any of them beside the master's German compositions especially the Passion music.[28] Handel has a pietistic touch, totally missing in the heroic English style, and this is understandably present in the German works, and there is also present the searching introspective spirit of the north German Lutheran, entirely different from the self-assuredness of the Anglican. Therefore the road to Handel's oratorios leads through English history.

Altogether Handel composed thirty-two compositions written in oratorio form. In what now follows a few of his more important ones will be discussed relative to their characteristics and contents. They are "Israel in Egypt," "Saul," "Solomon," "Messiah," and "Judas Maccabaeus."

The Oratorio "Israel in Egypt"

"Israel in Egypt" was the fifth of the nineteen oratorios which Handel composed in England and was written in 1738.[29] The Exodus, which is the second part, was written between the first and fifteenth of October, and had the superscription "Moses' Song, Exodus, chap. xv," and was begun on October 15th. At first this part was a cantata, but later Handel decided that the plagues of Egypt should not only be a good subject, but would prove a logical historical introduction to the second part. Four days later he began what now is the first part, and finished it on the 11th of November. This colossal work was written in 27 days. "Israel in Egypt" was performed on April 4, 1739, at the Kings Theatre.[30] The second performance took place on April 11, 1739 with alterations and additions; the latter were made to admit songs. The third performance, given on April 17, upon which occasion there was given "the Funeral Anthem," which Handel had written for Queen Caroline and was entitled "Lamentation for the Israelites for the Death of Joseph." During Handel's life time this oratorio was performed only nine times, despite its great excellence and so it was a failure from the viewpoint of the box office.

Years after it was presented in a mutilated form, but in 1849 the Sacred Harmonic Society of London gave it as it was originally written and as it is known now, without any of the songs of the "Funeral Anthem."[31]

The words for "Israel in Egypt" were written by Handel himself, although the words are taken literally from the Biblical text. Upton has given the following synopsis of this oratorio: The first part opens with the wail of the Israelites over the burdens imposed upon them by their Egyptian taskmasters, and then in rapid succession follow the plagues, the water of the Nile turned into blood, the reptiles swarming even unto the kings chambers, the pestilence scouring man and beast, the insect-cloud heralding the locusts, the pelting hail and the fire running along the ground, the thick darkness, and the smiting of the first-born. Then came the passage through the Red Sea and the escape from bondage, closing the first part.

The second part opens with a triumphant song of Moses and the Children of Israel rejoicing over the destruction of Pharaoh's host, and closes with the exultant strain of Miriam the prophetess, "Sing ye to the Lord, for he hath triumphed gloriously; the Horse and His Rider both he has thrown into the Sea."[32]

Actually, "Israel in Egypt" is essentially a choral oratorio, having no less than twenty-eight massive double choruses which are linked together by a few bars of recitative, with five arias and three duets interspersed among them.

The Oratorio "Saul"

"Saul" occupies an important place on the oratorio repertory. It was written before "Israel in Egypt," and according to Upton was composed between July 23, 1738 and August 28, 1738, and was thus produced within the period of two months and four days.[33] It was presented at the King's Theatre in Haymarket. Handel hired the latter theatre with the idea of presenting two oratorios a week. "Saul" was the first oratorio in this planned series of productions. "Saul" was announced as having within it "several new concertos for organ," an instrument which plays an important part in the oratorio itself, not only in amplifying, but also in solo work.

In 1740 "Saul" was performed by the Academy of Ancient Music in London and in 1742 in Dublin. Selections from it were also given in the great Handel Commemoration at Westminster in 1784 and in 1840 it was revived by the Sacred Harmonic Society of London, since which time it has occupied an important place in the oratorio repertory.[34]

"Saul" follows the Biblical narrative of the relations between David and Saul. The libretto has been attributed both to Jennens and Marell, but Upton believes that the balance of evidence favors Jennens, a poet, who lived at Gopsall. The overture, called "Symphoniae" is the longest of all of Handel's introductions in his oratorios. According to Upton "is an exceedingly graceful and delicate prelude and makes a fitting introduction to the dramatic story which follows. The characters introduced are Saul, the king of Israel, Jonathan, his son, Abner, captain of the host, David, the apparition of Samuel, Doeg, a messenger, an Amelekite, Abiathar, Merab and Michal, daughters of Saul, the witch of Endor and the Israelites. Avers Upton: "The very dramatic character of the narrative admirably adapts it to its division into acts and scenes."[35]

The Oratorio "Samson"

This oratorio was written in 1741 and was begun immediately after the completion of the Messiah and finished September 14, 1741.[36] The text of "Samson" was compiled by Newburgh Hamilton from "Samson Agonists," and from a "Hymn of the Nativity" and "Lines in a Solemn Musick."[37] "Samson" was first sung at Covent Garden, February 18, 1743. The principal parts were assigned as follows: Samson, to Mr. Beard, Manoah to Mr. Savage; Micah to Mr. Cibbes, Delilah to Mrs. Clive. The aria "Let the bright Seraphim" was sung by Signora Avolio, for whom it was written, and the triumphal obbligato was played by Valentine Snow, a virtuoso of that period. The presentation of "Samson" was greeted with extraordinary enthusiasm and it became very popular, so that many would-be hearers were turned away.[38]

The characters who appeared in "Samson" are: Samson, Micah, his friend, Manoah, Samson's father, Delilah, his wife, Harapha, a giant of Gath, an Israelite woman, priests of Dagan, Israelitish virgins and Philistines. After a brilliant overture, closing like that of "Saul," with a minute movement, the scene opens before the prison of Gaza, with Samson blind and in chains.[39] "Samson" is an oratorio in three acts, which contains a number of beautiful choruses. Upton in his volume: The Standard Oratorios has given an analysis and summary of this oratorio on pages 132-140.

The Oratorio the "Messiah"

When many people hear the name of Handel, they at once think of Christmas time and the Messiah."

Paul Lang wrote about the Messiah as follows:

The Messiah has become the epitome of the modern oratorio. This is understandable, for it unites choruses, arias, and recitatives into a great hymn and conjured up without denominational coloring. But we

may misjudge the essence of the Handelian style if we confuse our acquaintance to the one lyric among his thirty-two compositions in that
form.[40]

Another musicologist made this statement about the Messiah:

> Handel's Messiah is the most representative of its class. Not in
> opera, not in any form of music, does one composition stand out head
> and shoulders above its fellows as does this. It is not asserted that
> it is the first from the viewpoint of the musician, but no other ora-
> torio has enjoyed such enduring popularity – such positive adora-
> tion. Many generations have approved of it, and as different as the
> tastes of Eighteenth Centuries in most particulars, by this work
> they both have been melted to tears and aroused to higher aspira-
> tions.[41]

The Oratorio "Judas Maccabaeus"

"Judas Maccabaeus" was begun when Handel was sixty years old.
Most of his oratorios had been composed by this time, such as "Israel in
Egypt," "Messiah," "Samson," and "Saul."[58] On April 16, 1746, at Culloden
Muir, near Inverness, Charles Edward Casimir was defeated by the Duke
of Cumberland, who was William's brother, George II's younger brother.
This defeat ended the Stuart's attempt to regain control of the English
throne. In 1746 Handel had given the "Occasional Oratorio" at Covent
Garden on April 14, preceded in that same year by "Judas Maccabaeus."[59]

The Origin of Judas Maccabeus

Frederick, Prince of Wales, the Duke Cumberland's elder brother, suggested to Handel that he prepare an oratorio for the Duke's forthcoming
triumphal return to London. Weinstock gave the historical occasion as
follows: "It was to praise Cumberland under the thin disguise of Judas
Maccabaeus, the great solider who had battled (166-161 B.C.) against the
attempt of the Seleucid king Antiochus IV Epiphanes to turn Judaea into
a Hellenistic colony and to replace Judaism with a return to Greek paganism. Handel accepted the Prince of Wales' suggestion."[60] The Rev-
erend Thomas Moreall was asked to supply a text for the oratorio. Handel
began to compose "Judas Maceabaeus" on either Monday, July 8, or Tuesday, July 9, 1748 and had it completed in less than five weeks, by Sunday, August 11. However two famous musical pieces were added later,
namely, "See the conquering Hero comes," which was transferred from
the oratorio "Joshua" in 1748, and the chorus "Sion now her head shall
raise," was dictated when Handel was nearly blind to his assistant in
1757, just before his death.[61]

"Judas Maccabaeus" was rendered in April 1, 1748 at the Theatre
Royal in Covent Garden. It was sung six times during the first season, a
total of about fifty-five performances, of which thirty-three were conducted by Handel himself. It turned out to be a very popular oratorio and
was well received by Jewish Londoners. Weinstock claims that "it was
one of the first important stage presentations in England of a Jewish national hero in an entirely favorable light".[62] Because of the popularity of

"Judas Maccabaeus" Handel at once set about to deal with one of the heroes of the Maccabean era, namely, Juda's successor, Jonathan and this became the Oratorio "Alexander Balus." Weinstock contends that "Judas Maccabaeus" and "Alexander Bales" were the reason for the fact and the longest of Handel's rises to financial success and a great fame, an ascent that time was to lead to his apotheosis as a British national institution.[63]

The Oratorio "Solomon"

"Solomon" was written during the May and June of 1748 and heard for the first time in Covent Garden Theatre. At this time Handel's genius was at its height, having written "Messiah," "Judas Maccabaeus," "Samson" and "Joshua." Although there is considerable difference in character and style between each of these masterpieces, as yet, there remains to be found so much variety of mood in "Solomon."[64]

This is said to be due in part to the fact that there are more than a dozen numbers of a purely secular nature, and the religious side plays a rather modest part. What remains of it is devoted mainly to praise of the Great Temple left unfinished at the death of David, and now, finally completed.[65]

Handel's "Solomon," like many other of Handel's oratorios, is seldom given in its entirety. Some of the main characters used by Handel are: Solomon, the priests, Zadok, the high-priest, the queen, Pharaoh's daughter, a peasant girl, Nicaule, the Queen of Sheba.[66] "Solomon" ends with a double chorus, in which the first chorus sings:

Praise the Lord with harp and tongue
Praise Him, all ye old and young.
He's in mercy ever strong.

The second chorus sings:
Let the loud Hosannas rise
Widely spreading through the skies
God alone is just and wise.[67]

The "Chandos Anthems"

James Lord Brydges, first Duke of Chandon, was one of the most remarkable personalities of the early eighteenth century English society. He was Paymaster General under the reign of Queen Anne; he had gathered a fortune as well as a reputation on which Swift and Pope have recorded caustic comments.[68] On the edge of London he had built a residence known as the Palace of Cannons, said to be an architectural monument of finesse and extravagance.[69]

The Duke of Chandon maintained an excellent musical establishment.[70] Its director was Christopher Pepusch, a distinguished composer and founder of the Academy of Ancient Music.[71] Interesting details are preserved in the Family Register, letters, and Inventories of Cannons, now in Huntington Library at San Marino, California.

For two years (1717-1719) Handel may have lived at Chandos, where he composed six anthems, now referred to as "The Chandos Anthems, I-

VI." They are all based on various psalms and psalm verses. Psalms 66, 42, 51, 11, 145 and 100 were utilized by Handel.[72]

The "Chandos Anthems" according to Alfred Mann are described thus:

They have an unusual scoring in common: three part chorus supported by a three-part string orchestra - avoiding alto and viola sections, but using the vocal and instrumental parts and the wind and string compliments of the orchestra in such a manner that often the six-part or seven-part sound results. Oboe, violins, and the three bass instruments move independently or reinforce the vocal and instrumental lines so that the wonderfully string melodic contours arise which distinguish Handel's writing.[73]

It has been suggested by Mann that the limitations of the "Chandos Anthems", occasioned by the Duke's prejudice against the alto register and Pepusch's hostile attitude toward Handel, may be the reasons for the employment of the three part chorus and orchestra in the first six Chandos. Still, Mann believes that the trio sonata and the favored tessitura of the English Chapel singers served as points of departure for a scoring with which Handel wished to experiment.

From the earliest periods of his musical work, the trio sonata interested Handel and it was used in the music of the Chandos overtures. Yet he departed from the original trio setting, he ventured into new textures of orchestra writing, and the oboe assumes a binding function in the sound of the classical orchestra.[74]

In the "Chandos Anthems" the voice, however, predominates over the instruments, as it does in Handel's writing. The chorus becomes established as the main protagonist. A wealth of choral movements, ranging from arioso and recitative to the extended motet are absorbed in the choral movements.[75]

Handel and Sacred Music

While Handel wrote for the concert hall primarily, for that is the way he made a living, there are also found in the large number of musical productions of Handel compositions created for the church and for religious occasions. For Holy Week of 1704 he composed a Passion work, entitled "Johannes passion" or "Das Leiden und Sterben Jesu Christi," which was based on the Gospel of John with words of an aria by Christian Heinrich Postel. This was written and given in Hamburg. The other known Passion, written and given in 1716, possibly also in Hamburg, was entitled: "Der fur die Suenden der Welt gemartete und sterbende Jesus," whose words were composed by Barthold Heinrich Brocken.[76]

W. Dean in his article in *The New Catholic Encyclopedia* stated this about Handel's contribution to church music:

He was brought up a Lutheran, but composed for the rites of each country in which he lived, for Lutheran Germany, two settings of the Passion story, for Catholic Italy a group of Latin psalms and motets (it has been suggested by J .S. Hall that they formed a set of Vespers for the Carmelite church at Santa Maria di Monte Santo in Rome), for the Anglican Church 25 anthems with English words. Many of these

1175

were for special occasions, such as the treaty of Utrecht (1713) and the coronation of George II (1727). One of tile four coronation anthems has been sung at every British coronation since.[77]

The "Dettingen Te Deum"

Among Handel's religious compositions are at least four Te Deums. The most famous of them, is the Dettingen Te Deum, which was written to commemorate the British victory at Dettingen. It has been claimed that the British victory should go to the king's horse, which took fright and bolted off in the direction of the French forces, thus initiating a rather spontaneous charge on the enemy. So it is claimed that Handel's Te Deum was taken from another Te Deum by an Italian composer named Urio. Thus the musical commentator for Nonesuch Records of Handel's "The Dettigen Te Deum" wrote: "Therefore neither the king's attack nor Handel's 'Dettingen Te Deum' can be certified as authentic. We can say, however, that either Handel's refurbishing of the Urio work is the sole factor which makes it one of the supreme masterworks of the eighteenth century, or else that fellow Urio must be the most undeservedly neglected composer in history."[78] Handel also composed the Dettingen Anthem, "The King Shall rejoice," (1743) for the same English victory over the French.[79]

Handel's Hymn Tunes With Words by Charles Wesley

Handel's Church Music compositions range from the year 1696 to 1750, with "Laudate pueri, F ma," written about 1702 until Hallelujahs for soprano (1735-45). Three hymns were written for the Anglicans, namely, "O Love divine, how sweet thou art," "Rejoice the Lord is King "and" Sinners, obey the Gospel Word," for which Charles Wesley wrote the words dating 1726 and edited by Samuel Wesley, about 1826.[80]

Handel's Operas and Cantatas

Handel composed many Italian operas; there exist no less than thirty-eight that bear Italian titles, testifying to Handel's stay in four different Italian cities, including Rome. These are all secular. However, in 1719 he composed a religious cantata, entitled "Lobe den Herrn meine Seele," written for four voices, instruments and continuum. Concerning it one musicologist has stated that it is possibly a copy of an earlier work, or wrongly attributed to Handel. From the year 1696 there is supposed to be a church cantata "Ach Herr, mich armen Suender."[81] Weinstock claims that Handel composed a number of church cantatas around 1696.

Handel and the Organ

Handel appears to have had a flare for the organ and became an accomplished organist. As a boy of eight he showed an astonishing precocity in music, playing the organ at the ducal court at Weissenfels at the age of eight. At nine he began to study several instruments and the rudiments of composition with Friedrich Wilhelm Zachau, an organist at Halle. While a law student at Halle University, he was appointed organist of the local Calvinist Domkirche, though himself was an Evangelical Lutheran.[82] In1703 Handel and Mattheson travelled to Luebeck to apply for the position of organist held by Buxtehude, which Handel could have had, provided he would marry Buxtehude's daughter which he refused to do. Bach in 1705 also applied and failed to obtain this position, because he also did not wish to marry Buxtehude's daughter. Handel wrote 21 organ concertos.[83] On occasion he used the organ in his oratorios.

Bach and Handel's Place in Musical History Evaluated

In his comprehensive, Music in Western Civilization, Lang has made a final evaluation of Bach and Handel on pages 526-528. The former Columbia professor of music history wrote:

> With his conception of Christianity and antiquity as expressed in the music dramas, both Biblical and classical, Handel ventured deep into the era of the Enlightenment and renewed humanism. Bach represents a thoroughly German art, centered around the Lutheran Church and the organist's bench. Handel's workshop was opened wide to all forces and influences — without, however jeopardizing a particle of his individuality. Bach was a German with roots deeply imbedded in his native soil, Handel a citizen of the world who finally settled down in Britain.[84]

That Handel did not remain true to his German heritage has been held against him to the unstinted glorification of Bach and to the detriment of Handel. Lang believed that such a comparison is unfair and that the two men complement each other, a national person being complemented by an international personality. Although Handel was an internationalist yet in the final analysis he must be considered an English composer, the perfect counterpart of his German colleague.[85]

According to Lang, "Bach approached every new style, every new form with caution, sampling and selecting then carrying with him the newly acquired goods for a trial period. Handel gladly accepted everything, instantly assimilating it is a most personal style. Polyphony was for Bach a source of mystic struggle, in spite of his boundless versatility and apparent ease in the most complicated contrapuntal constructions. But it always drove him deeper and deeper, as if in quest of the final secrets of music."

"Barriers dissatisfied him and he broke them, trespassing boundaries, changing dimensions, and forcing the caesurae to conform to his own points of quintessence."[86]

By contrast according to Lang: "Handel did not wrestle with his creations; his polyphony had an almost Latin clarity and balance; its chief aim was not mysticism but a powerful architectonic of the very elements."[87] In turn Bach's "thematic material is heavy with forebodings: we feel that untold vistas will be opened if we follow him." Handel, on the other hand, his thematic invention is of a plasticity without equal; often a few introductory measures to an aria tell a whole story in the most pregnant and categorical manner.[88]

Both Bach and Handel close the long period of the baroque. Bach

1177

looked back; while Handel looked forward. Handel who outshone Bach in his day in public perception is mainly today honored for his "Messiah," while Bach today is respected for a plethora of outstanding secular and religious compositions.

Footnotes

1. Walter A. Buszin, "Bach, Johann Sebastian," Julius Bodensieck, ed. *The Encyclopedia of the Lutheran Church* (Minneapolis: Augsburg Publishing House, 1965), I, p. 172.
2. Paul Henry Lang, *Music in Western Civilization* (New York: W.W. Norton & Company, 194-1), p. 213.
3. Dean Arnold, *The New Oxford Companion to Music* (New York; The Oxford University Press, 1983; Ellen T. Harris, *Handel and the Pastoral Tradition* (New York: Oxford University Press, 1980). John Tobin, *Handel at Work* (New York: St. Martin's Press, 1964; P.H. Lang, *George Frederic Handel* (New York; E.P. Dutton, 1966: William C. Smith, "Handel, George Frederic," in *Grove's Dictionary of Music and Musicians.* Fifth edition by Eric Blohm (New York: St. Martin's Press, 1964), IV (H-K), pp. 36-60; David Ewen, *The Complete Book of Classical Music* (Englewood Cliffs, New Jersey, 1969), pp. 126-150.
4. P. M. Young, "Handel, George Frederic," *The Encyclopedia Britannica*, Maktropedia, 8, p. 603.
5. **Ibid.**
6. Buszin, "Bach, Johann Sebastian," **op. cit.**, p. 173.
7. W. Dean, "Handel, George Frederic," *New Catholic Encyclopedia*, 6, p. 912.
8. Young, **op. cit.**, p. 603.
9. Lang, **op. cit.**, p. 512; p. 489; p. 471.
10. *Grove's Dictionary of Music and Musicians*, **op. cit.**, p. 437.
11. Lang, **op. cit.**, p. 527.
12. **Ibid.**, p. 527.
13. Young, **op. cit.**, 8, pp. 139-141.
14. Lang, **op. cit.**
15. Young, **op. cit.**, p. 604.
16. Herber Weinstock, "Handel, George Frederic," *The Encyclopedia Americana,* 7, p. 672.
17. Young, **op. cit.**, p. 602.
18. **Ibid.**, pp. 602-603; Dennis Arnold, *The New Oxford Companion to Music* (New York: Oxford University Press, 1983.
19. Weinstock, **op. cit.**, pp. 672-673; Wolfgang, Schmieder, "Handel, George Frederic, Die Musik in Geschichte und Gegenwart (Kassel und Basel: Baerenreiter Verlag, 1956), Band 5, p. 1235.
20. Ingetraut Ludophy, "Handel, George Frederic," *The Encyclopedia of the Lutheran Church*, **op. cit.**, II, p. 978,
21. George P. Upton, *The Standard Oratories* (Chicago: A.C. McClurg Company, 1899), p. 166.
22. **Ibid.**
23. Lang, **op. cit.**, pp. 524-525.
24. **Ibid.**
25. **Ibid.**, p. 519.
26. **Ibid.**, 520.
27. **Ibid.**, p. 527.
28. **Ibid.**, p. 524.
29. Upton, **op. cit.**, p. 118; Cf. Westminster Records, WGSO-8200, "Handel, Israel in Egypt." Ewen, **op. cit.**, p. 139.
30. **Ibid.**
31. **Ibid.**

32. **Ibid.** p. 121.
33. **Ibid.**, p. 125.
34. **Ibid.**, p. 126.
·35, **Ibid.**, p. 127.
36. Edward Applebaum, in "Samson," booklet with EVEREST 3125, three-set record.
37. Upton, **op. cit.**, 132-135.
38. **Ibid.**, p. 134.
39. **Ibid.**, p. 135.
40. Lang, *Music in Western Civilization*, **op. cit.**, p. 526.
41. Josephine Thrall, *Oratorios and Masses* (New York and Chicago: Irving Square. 1908), p. 93.
42. Sir Thomas Beechem, Music Booklet accompanying RCA Record "The Messiah," (no date), p. 8.
43. Upton, **op. cit.**, p. 140.
44. Beechem, **op. cit.**, p. 4.
45. Sir Thomas Beechem, *The Mingled Chime*, quoted in the Booklet referred to in note 42, p. 4.
46. Joseph McCabe, *Handel's Messiah: A Devotional Commentary* (Philadelphia: The Westminster Press, 1978).
47. Upton, **op. cit.**, p. 140.
48. Cf. Raymond F. Surburg, "The Text, Music and Employment of the Bible in Handel's Messiah," *Christian News Encyclopedia* (Washington, Missouri: Missourian Publishing Company, 1982), II, p. 1378.
49. Anthony Mibler, "Handel's Messiah (Completer Version) London ffrr-Record, LLA-19.
50. **Ibid.**
51. **Ibid.**
52. **Ibid.**
53. Young, **op. cit.**, 605.
54. Surburg, **op. cit.**, p. 1378.
55. **Ibid.**
56. Upton, **op. cit.**, p. 144.
57. Surburg, **op. cit.**, p. 1380.
58. Lang, **op. cit.**, pp. 524-525.
59. Herbert Weinstock, "Judas Maccabaeus," booklet for Westminster Records, WGS0-201-203, Handel's "Judas Maccabaeus."
60. **Ibid.**, p. 3.
61. **Ibid.**
62. **Ibid.**, p. 5.
63. **Ibid.**
64. Sir Thomas Beechem, Handel's Solomon, back of Seraphim Record Set SB-6039.
65. Upton, **op. cit.**, p. 135.
66. Beechem, **op. cit.**, Back of Record Set, referred to in footnote 64.
67. Young, **op. cit.**, p. 604.
68. W. Dean. "Handel, George," *New Catholic Encyclopedia*, **op. cit.**, 6, p. 604.
69. Musical information on the back in the jacket for Nonesuch Records, "The Dettingen Te Deum," by George Frederic Handel.
70. **Ibid.**
71. Alfred Mann, Musical Notes on back of the jacket of Vanguard Records, "The Chandos Anthems, I-VI."
72. **Ibid.**
73. **Ibid.**
74. **Ibid.**
75. **Ibid.**
76. W.C.S. William, "Handel, George Frederic," in *Grove's Dictionary of Music and Musicians*, **op. cit.**, IV, p. 53.

77. Dean, **op. cit.**, p. 912.
78. Musical information on back of jacket of Nonesuch Records, M-71003," Handel, "The Dettingen Te Deum."
79. Williams, **op. cit.**, p. 54.
80. **Ibid.**, p. SA.
81. Williams, **op. cit.**, p. SA.
82. **Ibid.**, p. 38.
83. **Ibid.**
84. Lang, **op. cit.**, p. 526.
85. **Ibid.**, p. 528.
86. **Ibid.**, p. 527.
87. **Ibid.**, p. 528.
88. **Ibid.**, p. 528.

Questions

1. Schuetz, Handel, and Bach were ____.
2. Did Bach and Handel ever meet? ____
3. Handel became a citizen of ____.
4. Handel never ___ and left no ____.
5. Bach had ___ children.
6. Bach and Handel are considered representatives of the ____ period.
7. What happened to both toward the end of their lives? ____
8. Bach's funeral was an ___ affair and Handel was buried in ____.
9. Handel wrote ____ operas.
10. In the ___ Handel gave England a substitute for ____.
11. "Israel in Egypt" is essentially ____.
12. What has become the epitome of modern oratorio? ____
13. The first performance of the Messiah was given in ____.
14. King George II ____ when he heard the words ____.
15. Handel became a powerful proclaimer cf ____.
16. Handel refused to marry ____ daughter.
17. Bach today is respected for ____.

Mendelssohn - A Jewish Christian

The Contribution of the Lutheran Felix Mendelssohn to Church Music With Special Reference to His 'Reformation Symphony'

Christian News, November 9, 1987

November 4, 1987 marked the 140th anniversary of the death of Felix Mendelssohn, a Jew who was a Christian affiliated with the Lutheran Church.[1] Lutherans especially associate with Mendelssohn the fact that he wrote a symphony designed to be played on the 300th anniversary of The Augsburg Confession's presentation before the Emperor Charles V.[2] Another great contribution was Mendelssohn's rediscovery of the musical writings of Johann Sebastian Bach (1685-1750), whose music was forgotten for about seventy-five years after his death. With Mendelssohn there began a great revival of the musical compositions of one of the greatest musicians of all times.[3] For that alone Lutherans would be grateful. But as a Jewish Christian Mendelssohn used his pen in contributing to some great church music which has edified hundreds of thousands of people in the world. During the Luther's days (October 31 to November 10th and 11th), it certainly would be appropriate to recall Mendelssohn's life and contributions to the field of church music.

A Brief Life of Mendelssohn

Felix Mendelssohn Bartholdy (1809-1847) was the grandson of the great Jewish philosopher Moses Mendelssohn and the son of a wealthy banker and of a mother of exceptional culture and refinement.[4] He was born on February 3, 1809 in Hamburg and had the good fortune to enjoy every advantage which wealth could provide. Felix belonged to a rich and cultivated family, many of whose forebears had adopted Christianity in the generation before the emancipation of German Jews in 1812.[5] Yet his father was a deist who had not truly embraced Christianity. Burkley contends that "Felix, however, along with his brother Paul and devoted sisters Fanny and Rebecca became thoroughly, if somewhat ambivalently, assimilated into German Protestant culture of the romantic era."[6]

Professor Lang has characterized the family into which Mendelssohn was born as follows:

> The Mendelssohn home presented a family of character and integrity, equally devoted to each other and to the noble and artistic in life. As far as sheer talent was concerned, Mendelssohn belongs to the class of Pergolesi, Mozart and Schubert but is the child of an era that regarded intellectual culture as integral part of the composer's trade. These natural gifts were equally manifest in other fields.[7]

In 1811 during the French occupation of Hamburg, the family moved to Berlin where Felix studied piano with Ludwig Berger and composition with K. F. Zelter, who was a composer and teacher. The latter exerted an enormous influence on Mendelssohn's development. Besides his mother, Lea Solomon gave him his first piano lessons. His teachers also included Marie Bigot, Berger, and Moschelles.[8] His parents' home in Berlin was frequented by the leading artists of the day. From an early age Felix was given the opportunity of conducting his own works, played by small orchestras at family music parties.[9] At the age of nine he appeared in public as a pianist in Berlin and afterwards in Paris. Since his parents were interested in various phases of the arts, young Mendelssohn received instructions in the fine arts and became proficient in languages, literature, painting and music. However, his main interest was in music.

As a seventeen-year old adolescent Felix created works of maturity and genius, among them the bewitching overture to Shakespeare's Midsummer Night's Dream.[10] Up to that time Mendelssohn, although baptized as a Lutheran Christian, was floundering around as to the real meaning and purpose for his life. As a result of reading the words of the St. Matthew Passion he was so touched that he truly was converted and became a believing Christian and a true Lutheran.[11] In 1829, Mendelssohn was instrumental in having the great St. Matthew Passion produced and that event marked the beginning of the revival of the great music of Johann Sebastian Bach,[12] one of the greatest musicians and proclaimers of the Gospel of Jesus Christ to appear in the history of Lutheranism. In the 1830's and 1840's Mendelssohn became an authority on Bach and was frequently consulted for advice in matters pertaining to his music.

Mendelssohn's 1829 concert in London carried his fame all over the world. In 1839, he traveled to Italy, France and then to England and back to Germany but his father insisted that Felix settle down and in obedience to his father's wish, he found a permanent position in Duesseldorf.[13] Two years later, 1835, he became conductor of the famous Gewandhaus orchestra and its concerts. In that city he also became one of the founders and leading members of the conservatory of music. However, it was Leipzig which became the focal point of his musical activity until the time of his death in 1847. His stay in Leipzig was interrupted from time to time by many great performances.[14]

Mendelssohn was a prolific composer of many musical works. He wrote numerous compositions during his boyhood period, among them five operas, 11 symphonies for string orchestra, concerti, sonatas and fugues, most of which were preserved in Preussische Staatsbibliothek, Berlin, where they were lost during World War II.[15]

The famous pianist was also a contemporary of Chopin (1810-49). Robert Schumann (1810-1856) was a great admirer of Mendelssohn. In 1837 Felix married the daughter of a minister of the Reformed Church in Frankfort, a woman reputed to have been very beautiful.[16] This marriage was blessed with five children. Felix formed a warm friendship with Goethe and Schumann, besides being a great admirer of Bach as well of the works of Beethoven.[17]

Mendelssohn made ten trips to England where he presented his own musical compositions. The English liked him nearly as much as they did Handel, who had become an English citizen. For one year Mendelssohn served as chapel master being appointed to this position by the King of

Prussia. Felix also helped found the Berling Academy of Arts. The University of Leipzig conferred upon him the honorary degree of Doctor of Philosophy. He had a gifted sister Fanny who preceded him in death in 1845. Her death greatly affected his health and may have contributed to his own early death on November 4, 1847 in the City of Leipzig where he spent the last years of his life.[18]

Mendelssohn as a Musical Artist

Mendelssohn left a large and rich collection of musical works which became famous the world over. He was a composer, pianist, organist and conductor. Three great oratorios were given to the world by this musical genius. In addition to these oratorios, his exquisite music to "Midsummer Night's Dream" which was familiar the world over. He has left the musical world his stately and dramatic "Antigone" besides bequeathing five symphonies of which the "Scotch," "The Italian" and "The Reformation" are the best known. In addition to these are the best known overtures, "Rau Blas," "Com Sea," "Prosperous Journey," "Hebrides," and "Melusina" and the very dramatic "The Walpurgis Night." Mendelssohn authored a long list of beautiful trios and other specimens of chamber music, and the lovely "Song Without Words."[19] Felix also wrote a grand opera. He obtained from Geibel a libretto for the opera "Lorelei" of which he had finished the finale of the first act when death occurred on November 4, 1847 at the age of 39. At that time he was the idol of the musical world. Moyer claimed that "from the time of his first tour when he was twenty years until his last trip shortly before his death, he was crowned with the highest glory and honor that men and nations can give. An artist and a genius, a remarkable versatile composer, his compositions were light and easily understood. His works were noted for their grace, delicacy, and sweet melody. "[20]

Upton made the following assessment of Mendelssohn's works:

> Mendelssohn was a man of remarkable beauty and his character corresponding to his charms as a person ... Possessed of these graces of mind and person, and having all the advantages that wealth could bestow, he lacked those incentives which in other composers have brought out the deepest, highest, and most majestic forms of musical expression. His music is a reflex of his life: grace, eloquence, culture and finish are its characteristics.[21]

Mendelssohn's Contributions to Church Music

Mendelssohn used different musical art forms in giving the church and the public religious music. The first to be described in this presentation is the oratorio of which Felix wrote three.

The "St. Paul" Oratorio

This was the first of three produced by Mendelssohn and it was begun in Düsseldorf and finished in Leipzig in the winter of 1831. The libretto as it now stands was the joint effort of Fuerst and Schubring. The oratorio has three main themes: namely, the martyrdom of Stephen, the conversion of Saint Paul and Paul's career after his conversion. The Biblical text is found in Acts: chapters 7:9ff, 13-18.[22]

"St. Paul" was written upon a commission by the Cecilian Verein of Frankfort in 1831 where it was first performed. The next performance was on May 22, 1831 on the occasion of the Lower Rhine Festival of Duesseldorf. On October 3, 1836 "St. Paul" was presented at Liverpool. Between the two performances Mendelssohn revised it and dropped fourteen numbers. Lampadius, a contemporary of Felix has this general impression of the oratorio:

> The main thought which runs throughout the whole work is too high and broad to be linked by the tie of a personal interest to any single man. It is the glorification of Christianity, its joy in living and dying for the Lord, in contrast with the blind self-righteousness of Judaism and the mere sensuous morality of the last two with the former, and the victory of the light and love of the gospels, the thought eternal, the love divine. This thought is reincarnate in the persons of Stephen, Paul and Barnabas, and it is concentrated at that point which is really the central point of interest to the oratorio - the conversion of Saint Paul.[23]

"St. Paul" has two sections: the first is essentially dramatic; the second lyrical and contemplative.[24] The overture opens with the Lutheran chorale "Wachet auf," in clarinets, bassoons, and lower strings. Then comes "Saul, Saul Why Persecuted Thou Me?" in anticipation of Paul's conversion. Ewen states: "The main part of the overture has for its main subject a fugal episode depicting the struggle of the convert's soul. The chorale is repeated in the winds and serves as a second theme. A loud restatement of the chorale which points up the victory of faith ends the overture."[25]

St. Paul" opens with an elaborate chorus, "Lord! Thou Alone Art God."[26] Then follows the martyrdom of Stephen in detail in which Stephen eloquently utters: "My, Brethren and Fathers." The chorus then shouts: "Take Him Away," the soprano warns the city of Jerusalem in the aria: "Jerusalem Thou that Killeth the Prophets ..." A poignant tenor recitative relates the stoning of St. Stephen, the first adult Christian martyr, followed by Stephen's lament: "Happy and Blessed Are They ..." Then Saul appears on the scene exclaiming in a fiery aria: "Consume Them All." This is followed by the beautiful alto arioso: "But the Lord is Mindful of His Own." This is followed by the conversion of Saul, who then prays: "O God Have Mercy Upon Us" which in turn is preceded by a Jubilant chorus "Oh, Great Is the Depth of the Riches and Wisdom," which ends this portion of the oratorio.

A five-part fugal chorus: "The Nations Are Now the Lord's" opens the second part of the "St. Paul" oratorio. A number of choruses follow, among them the lovely "How Lovely are the Messengers," and the passionate "Is This Who in Jerusalem." Then comes the chorale: "Oh Thou, the True and Only Light,' a tenor recitative informs the hearers of the departure of Paul and Barnabas. The scene of the sacrifice at Lystra gives the occasion for two powerful choruses: "The Gods Themselves Are Mortals" and "Oh, Be Gracious You Mortals." The opposition to Paul by the Jews is expressed in "This is Jehovah's Temple." Paul then takes pathetic leave of his Christian brethren in " Be Thou Faithful Onto Death." . . . Two mighty choruses conclude the oratorio "What Love Hath the Father" and "Now Only Unto Him."

Annie Pattison in her book *The Story of the Oratorio* claimed: "that an examination of the work discloses musicianship and beauty of conception and construction decidedly Mendelssohnian. There is all the symmetry and design, the delicious yet ever enervating melody, and the clear and smooth harmonization of the tone-painter of the concert overtures."[27] It is her further contention that Johann Sebastian Bach influenced Mendelssohn's style. She averred: "In 'St. Paul' especially in the treatment of the Chorales, we see the triumph of modern constructive skill in the weaving together of solid, mainly diatonic harmony. In his four-part unaccompanied writing no one has so nearly approached the great model as Mendelssohn."[28] Pattison believed that Mendelssohn must ever remind his listeners of Bach as he might have been under the irresistible charm of Mozart's melody. "If anyone possesses the skill of beautifying counterpoint, it was Mendelssohn ..."[29] We are powerfully struck with this in the interludes and accompaniments of his Chorales. As example, she cited "O Thou, the True and Only Light" ("St. Paul") and the masterly setting of "nun danket alle Gott" (from the "bobgesang").[30]

The Hymn of Praise ("Der Lobgesang")

Another oratorio from the pen of Mendelssohn was "Der Lobgesang" or "Hymn of Praise." This oratorio was written in 1840, the occasion being the fourth centennial of the art of printing.[31] The musical features for this festival were entrusted to Mendelssohn, and the ceremonies celebrating Gutenberg's great accomplishment; the ceremonies occupied two days, June 24th and 25th. On the morning of June 24th there was a service in the church followed by the unveiling of the statue of Gutenberg in the public square, and an open air performance of Mendelssohn' s *Der Festgesang* for two choirs, with trombone accompaniment. David conducted one choir and Mendelssohn the other one. In the afternoon of the 25th "The Hymn of Praise" was given for the first time in the St. Thomas Church, preceded by Weber's "Jubilee Overture" and Handel's "Dettingen Te Deum." Mendelssohn himself conducted the "Hymn of Praise" on September 23, 1840 at Birmingham, England. After that performance the composer changed his work by also adding the whole scene of the watchman.[32]

The text of the "Hymn of Praise" is not in narrative form, nor has it any particular dramatic significance. Lampadius claimed "that the composer undertook to show the triumph at the creation of light over darkness. With his pious and believing heart he could easily enter into that theme and show with matchless power and skill the closing-in of those ancient foes, and the victory of light when darkness covered the ignobly shrank away."[32a]

Upton believed:

The expression of delight over the victory is very well brought out, not only in the music, but also in the arrangement of the Scriptural texts, which begin with exhortations of praise, and appeals with those who have been in distress and in affliction to trust the Lord. The tenor, who may be regarded as the Narrator, calls upon the Watchman, "What of the Night?" The response comes that the night is passing. In exaltation over the victory, once more the text ascribes praise to the Lord ... All that has life and breath sing to the Lord.[33]

Some musical critics have pronounced "The Hymn of Praise" Mendelssohn's greatest work. Averred Upton: "In its combination of Symphony and the voice parts, the one growing out of the other and both so intimately connected, it stands almost alone."[34]

The Oratorio "Elijah"

The oratorio "Elijah" is the most admired of all of Mendelssohn's compositions. It was finished in 1846, although the plan for it was already considered in 1837.[35] In 1840 Mendelssohn began to put his ideas into shape. The work when finished pleased him as may be seen by his words written to a friend: "I am jumping about my room for joy. If it only turns out half as good as I fancy, how pleased I shall be!" The "Elijah" oratorio was performed on August 18, 1846 in London. Although the composer was delighted, he was not satisfied with the oratorio as a whole. He made numerous changes and rewrote portions of it. The first performance of the revised "Elijah" occurred on April 16, 1847 when it was given by the Sacred Humanistic Society. Queen Victoria and Prince Albert were in attendance and the latter sent the composer his score with an appreciative paragraph.[36]

The text of "Elijah" was written by Mr. Bartholomew and based upon the First Book of Kings. According to Hiller the oratorio was suggested by the words in I Kings 19: "Behold, the Lord passed by." The prominent scenes treated in "Elijah" are: the prophecy of the coming drought, the raising of the widow's son, the rival sacrifices, the appearance of rain in answer to Elijah' s appeal, Jezebel's persecution of Elijah, the sojourn in the desert, his return, Elijah' s disappearance in the fiery chariot and the finale, which reflects upon the meaning of the sacred narrative.[37]

The scenes of "Elijah" are very dramatic and in this respect Mendelssohn may also be said to have created a new school of oratorio construction. It has been said that "Elijah" could be placed upon the stage with scenery, costumes, and the properties as a sacred opera and make a powerful impression upon those viewing and hearing the oratorio.

Straatton in his book "Mendelssohn" asserted:

"Marked by an interval of ten years Elijah shows a great advantage upon "St. Paul," not in scholarship, but in the development of the composer's individuality. The formers are more free; the chorale virtually disappears, the spirit of the composition is modern, dramatic, and frugal writing is nowhere obtrusive, though the counterpoint is rich and varied."[38]

"Elijah" has two parts. The first describes how the prophet brings on a drought on Israel and concludes with the contest of Elijah with the priests of Baal and the dooming of the false prophets and their destruction. The second part Elijah is hounded by Jezebel, but under the protection of Yahweh he triumphs over all enemies and in the end is carried alive on a fiery chariot to heaven.[39]

The dramatic element which Mendelssohn wished to stress throughout the whole oratorio is found already in the opening. Elijah announces in a stern recitative that the drought will be inflicted on the people. Then only, comes the overture which is written in a dirge-like mood, reflecting the people's anguish. The overture concluded, the people express their terror in the first dramatic chorus, "Help, Lord! Wilt Thou Destroy Us?" Then there follow stirring duets, choruses and recitatives which carry the drama on with telling theatrical effects. With the raising of the widow's son from death a climatic point is reached in the chorus: "Blessed are the Men that are Free" and in Elijah's pronouncement of doom for the priests of Baal; following by the recitative, "Oh Thou Who Makest Thine Angeles Spirits" followed by "Is Not His Word like Fire?"

Although the dramatic plays such an important role in this oratorio, lyricism is not sacrificed completely. It is found in such arias as that of Obadiah, "If with all your Hearts;" also in the prayer of Elijah: "Lord God of Abraham," which is immediately followed by the poignant chorale "Cast Thy Burden Upon the Lord." The first part of "Elijah" concludes with the peoples' hymn of praise and joy: "Thanks be to God!" Part II of the oratorio opens with a brilliant soprano aria: "Hear, Ye Israel" and soars to heights with Elijah's plea for death, "Is is Enough." Other beautiful musical compositions are: "Oh, Rest in the Lord," the tenor aria: "Then Shall the Righteous Shine Forth as the Sun," and the exultant chorus, "Oh! Come, Every One that Thirsteth." "Elijah" concludes with the mighty chorus, "And then shall your light Break Forth."

The Unfinished Oratorio "Christos"

Mendelssohn was working on a third oratorio which together with "St. Paul" and "Elijah" would have constituted an outstanding trilogy of important Old and New Testament personalities.[40] The words were written by Chevalier Bunsen and given to the musical composer in 1844. Before "Elijah" was begun by Mendelssohn. It was only after 1847, after "Elijah" was finished that he touched the music of "Christus." At this time he was in delicate health and had not recovered from the sudden death of his sister Fanny which deeply affected him. He spent time in working on "Christus" and "Lorelei," neither of which he finished, because he died on November 4, 1847, in his thirty-ninth year, caused by two serious attacks of apoplexy.[41]

There is not much information available in Mendelssohn's own letters or in those of his biographer on "Christus." Lampadius, a contemporary of Mendelssohn, wrote of the unfinished oratorio: "The oratorio was laid out upon a grand scale. It was in three parts, the career on earth, the descent into hell, and the ascent into heaven."[42] This plan must have been later altered by the composer because in the fragments of the oratorio that have survived are only two parts, and they pertain entirely to Christ's earthly career. There are in all eight complete numbers: three from the first part, and five from the second. The first part ended with the German chorale "Wie schoen leuchtet der Morgenstern." Fragments of the second part are in the form of passion music, including five tenor recitatives. Part II closes with a beautiful chorale: He leaves his heavenly portals endures grief of mortals to raise our fallen race.

O Love beyond expressing
He gains for us a blessing
He saves us by redeeming grace
When thou O sun are shrouded
By night or tempest clouded,
Thy rays no longer dark,
Though earth be dark and dreary
If, Jesus art near to me,
'Tis cloudless day within my heart.[44]

The Cantatas of Mendelssohn
Mendelssohn in his short life wrote music for six cantatas: namely, "The Walpurgis Night," "Antigone," "Oedipus," "Colonos," "As the Heart Panteth," "The Gutenberg Fest Cantata" and the "Lauda Sion."[45]

"As the Heart Panteth" Cantata
The music for the Forty-Second Psalm, familiarly known by the opening words of this psalm, begins Book II of the Psalter. This musical work was first performed at the tenth subscription of the Gewandhaus Concert in Leipzig in 1838, Clara Novello taking the soprano part when it was rendered.

Upton claimed that "though not composed on a large scale as the "Hymn of Praise" or even as the "Walpurgis Night," it is a work which is thoroughly artistic and just as complete and symmetrical in its way. It contains seven numbers.[46] After a low and well sustained introduction, the work begins with a chorus: "As the Hart panteth after the water brooks, so panteth my soul for Thee, O God." which is a veritable prayer in its tenderness and expression of passionate longing. After the chorus a delicate and refined solo, "For my soul thirsteth for God" continues the sentiment first given out in an oboe solo and then uttered by the voice in a beautiful melodious adagio. The third number is a soprano recitative, "My Tears have been my meat," leading to a chorus in march time by the soprano and altos, "For I had gone with the Multitudes: I went with them to the House of God." Then follows a full chorus of male voices in unison, "Why, my Soul art thou cast down?" answered by the female voices, "Trust thou in God." Again the soprano voice is heard in a pathetic recitative "O my God! my soul is cast down within me; all Thy waves and Thy billows are gone over me." A beautiful quartet replies with string accompaniment: "The Lord will command His loving kindness in the Day- time;

and in the Night His Song shall be with me, and my Prayer unto God of my Life." The response is full of hope and consolation but through it all runs the mournful strain of the soprano (forming a quintet at the end) coming to a close only when the full chorus joins in a repetition of the fourth number, "Trust Thou in God," this time elaborated with still greater effect, and a closing with a stately ascription to the God of Israel."

"The Lauda Sion" Cantata

This is the shortest of all the cantatas composed by Mendelssohn.[47] He was somewhat ecumenically minded because, although a Lutheran who must have known the fundamental doctrinal difference between Roman Catholicism, which also involved the difference on the Lord's Supper or the Holy Eucharist; he was agreeable to write a cantata for the Feast of Corpus Christi.[48] Some claim that this cantata' 'The Launda Sion" was one of his most beautiful cantatas. The work was composed for the celebration of this Festival by the church at St. Martin Liege and was first performed in that church June 11, 1846.[49]

This composition is written in seven numbers; the voices give out the theme: "Lauda, Sion" followed by a chorus "Lauda Thema" full of devotional spirit. The solo then enunciates in "Sit Laus Plena" phrases repeatedly by the chorus, followed by a beautifully accompanied quartet "In hac Mensa."

The fifth number is a solemn chorale in unison, leading to a soprano solo in the arioso style, "Car cibus," which is exquisitely beautiful. The work concludes with a very dramatic solo and chorus, "Sumit unus," set to the words "Bone pastor" and the closing verses of the hymn itself. Short as the cantata is observes Upton, "It is one of the most felicitous of all Mendelssohn's settings of the ritual."[50]

Church Music in General

Between November 15, 1830 and October 28, 1846 Mendelssohn composed different kinds of church music according to the listing given in Grove's *Dictionary of Music and Musicians*.[51] The catalogue of compositions classified as church music in Grove's volume gives fourteen different works. On November 15, 1830 he published Three Pieces for Church Music: 1. "Aus Tiefer Not;" 2. "Ave Maria" and 3. "Mitten wir." These were for solo voice, chorus and organ. At the same time he also authored Psalm 115, for solo voice and orchestra. On December 30, 1830 he published three motets for female voices and organ. They were: "Hear my Prayer, O Lord." 2. "O Praise the Lord;" and 3. "O Lord, Thou Hast Searched Me Out." On February 20, 1831 he issued "Verleih uns Frieden" for chorus and orchestra. On March 24, 1833 he made available Psalm 42 for solo voice, voices, chorus and orchestra. During that same year he published "Lord Have Mercy on Us" for the Anglican Evening Service for unaccompanied chorus. On February 1839 he issued for mixed voices the hymn tune "Defend me, Lord from shame."

On August 11, 1839 Mendelssohn published Psalm 95 for tenor, chorus and orchestra. April 11, 1839 he issued Psalm 114 for eight parts and orchestra. The same year on August 8th he published three English church pieces: 1. The Nunc Dimittis; 2. Jubilate and 3. Magnificat. On June 17th, 1844 there came from his facile pen Psalms 2, 43, and 22 for solo voices and orchestra. January 25, 1844 and hymn "Hear My Prayer" for soprano, orchestra and organ was produced. The next year December 25, 1845 he wrote six anthems: 1. "Rejoice O Ye People (Christmas)," "Thou Lord Our Refuge Has Been" (New Year's Day); "Above All Praise" (Ascension); 4, "Lord, on Our Offenses" (Passion Week); 5. "Let Our Hearts Be Joyful" (Advent), and 6. "For Our Offenses" (Good Friday). December 27, 1845 witnessed the publication of Psalm 98 for 8-part orchestra and chorus. December 14, 1840 (Opus 91) was a hymn with three choruses added, written for Alto, chorus and orchestra. Opus 111 is entitled "Tu Petrus" for chorus and orchestra, written in November 1827. On October 28, 1846 Mendelssohn produced "Kyrie Eleison" for the German Liturgy, written for double chorus. Opus 121 contains a Responsorium et Hymnus (for sale voices, cello and organ), also three Sacred Pieces: 1. "Ehre sei Gott" (for double chorus). 2. "Heilig" (for double chorus) and 3. "Psalm 100" (for mixed voices) also the "Te Deum" in ma for the Anglican Service (for mixed voices).

The Reformation Symphony No. 5 in D Minor, Op. 107

Mendelssohn wrote a number of symphonies especially during the earlier times of his musical career but the ones that are still being played today are the Italian, the Scotch and the Reformation.[52] They are the product of that period when he traveled rather extensively between 1830 and 1831. John Burk asserted about this period: "Mendelssohn's coming of age was doubly a peak in his life. He then traveled about Europe extensively for the first time, and, stimulated by the experience, composed his greatest orchestra works - his last three symphonies."[53] After his twentieth birthday Mendelssohn's father decided Felix needed broadening by travel so he spent most of 1829 in England with an excursion to Scotland. After his return to Berlin he also "did" Italy covering it from Milan in the north to Sorrento in the south in the season of 1830-31. It was during this time that Mendelssohn began and in some instances completed his three great symphonies.[54] Between the traveling for pleasure he composed his Reformation Symphony, began his "Scottish" Symphony, and worked on his "Italian Symphony.[55]

The "Reformation" Symphony was begun on September 1829 and completed in Berlin during the winter of 1829, when the composer was only twenty-one. He planned to conduct it during a German Tercentenary Festival commemorating the writing and presentation to Emperor Charles of the Augsburg Confession the one Confession recognized by all Lutheran Churches.[56] The author of The Augsburg Confession was Philip Melanchthon. The presentation of The Reformation Symphony was delayed for a number of reasons, including political and religious disturbances which followed the July Revolution in Paris. The work was not performed until September 15, 1832 with the composer at the podium of the Berliner Singakadamie.[57]

Joseph Singmaster claimed that "at first Mendelssohn Entertained high hopes for the symphony but later his enthusiasm waned." On one occasion he called it "a complete misfit."[58] His misgivings were founded upon the first movement — in his own exasperated words "a fat bristly animal." He later reworked the score but it was not published until 1868, twenty years after his death.

The first reception given the symphony was cool and a number of musical critics underrated it. Even in the first part of the present century it was not appreciated but later it was more favorably accepted, especially since it is "The Symphony of the Reformation." Singmaster claimed "that the Symphony No. 5 is stamped with Mendelssohn's great gift for melody, his lucid orchestration and generally felicitous style."[59] Although some mark the work in five movements, it is actually played in four. The powerful first movement symbolizes the struggle between the old faith and the new. The **Andante** opening states and briefly develops an important motive to which the strings respond softly with the "Dresden Amen," otherwise known as the cadence of the Eucharistic motif in Wagner's **Parsifal**.[60] The main body of the movement is dominated by the theme of religious conflict (Allegro con fuoco) but after a climax the "Amen" is heard again.

The second movement **Allegro vivace** is actually a Scherzo and Trio, distinguished by Mendelssohn's grace and lightness of touch whenever he approached the dance form.[61] The serious mood returns in the third movement **Andante**, which is a tender main subject and fervent second theme. In the Finale, which follows without pause, the liturgical theme is the dominant one. The solo flute starts **Andante con moto**, the melody of Martin Luther's "Ein Feste Burg ist unser Gott," heralding a new faith.[62] As the pace of the movement quickness the hymn serves as background for some brilliant counterpoint and is majestically proclaimed at the close of the full orchestra. The arrangement of the old chorale melody which Mendelssohn resurrected differs slightly from the form familiar to us in Bach's arrangement of the chorale and his cantata based upon it.[63]

Thus the "Reformation symphony" had an introduction as a concert piece two years after its intended presentation. Burk states that "The sturdy and noble chorale subject, and the beautiful 'Amen' cadence, with all their churchly association, are developed in unchurchly symphonic fashion. The music bespeaks his personal style, fervid in melody, lucid in orchestration, felicitous in every bar."[64]

Mendelssohn and the Bach Revival

One of the greatest accomplishments of Mendelssohn's short career was his own discovery of the works of a great Lutheran musician, namely, J. S. Bach, whose works were forgotten for seventy-five years. Lang called the presentation of the St. Matthew Passion in 1829 one of the great events in musical history.[65] This supposedly gave the movement in music an impetus for discovering the German past in literature and music. The result was that oratorios, a cappela choruses, and fugues began to be composed in great numbers in the first half of the nineteenth century. Had Mendelssohn only rediscovered Bach and became an advocate and publisher of his music, that alone would be sufficient for Lutherans ever gratefully to remember Mendelssohn, a Jew by physical birth and a Christian by the spiritual new birth.

Footnotes

1. For the Life of Felix Mendelssohn Bartholdi consult Percy A. Scholes *The Oxford Companion to Music* (Oxford: At the University Press, 1970), the 10th edition, pp. 627a-628a; *The Concise Encyclopedia* of *Music and Musicians* (New York : Hawthorn Books, 1958), p. 309.
2. John H. Burk, Musical Notes on the Back of RCA VICTOR Record LM-2221 Mendelssohn's Italian and Reformation Symphonies.
3. Paul Henry Lang, Music in *The History of Western Civilization* (New York: Norton and Company, 1941).
4. Herbert Weinstock, "Mendelssohn, Felix," *Encyclopedia Americana*, 18, p. 688 (1987 edition).
5. F. J. Burkley, "Mendelssohn, Felix," *The New Catholic Encyclopedia*, 9, p. 647.
6. **Ibid.**
7. Lang, **op. cit.**, p. 809.
8. Edward Lockspeiser, "Mendelssohn, Felix," *Encyclopedia Britannica*, Makropedia, 9, p. 901.
9. Lockspeiser, **op. cit.**, p. 901.
10. Weinstock, **op. cit.**, p. 689.
11. Cf. a sermon on cassette of James Kennedy, delivered at Fort Lauterdale, Florida, Spring of 1987.
12. Stephen F. Stratton, Mendelssohn. *The Muter Musicians Series* (New York: E. P. Dutton and Co., 1901), p. 40.
13. Lockspeiser, **op. cit.**, p. 901.
14. **Ibid.**, p. 902.
15. Cf. the listing of his compositions and the titles in *The New Grove Dictionary of Music and Musicians*, edited by Stanley Sadie (New York: St. Martin's Press, 1980), pp. 153ff.
16. Burkley, **op. cit.**, p. 647.
17. **Ibid.**, p. 647.
18. Elgin S. Moyer, *Who Was Who in Church History* (Chicago: Moody Press, 1962), p. 281.
19. As enumerated by George P. Upton, *The Standard Oratorios* (Chicago: A.C. McClurg and Company, 1899), pp. 207-208.
20. Moyer, **op. cit.**, p. 281.
21. Upton, **op. cit.**, p. 208.
22. "Felix Mendelssohn," David Ewen, *The Complete Book of Classical Music* (New Jersey: Englewood Cliffs, 1965), p. 460.
23. As cited by Upton, **op. cit.**, p. 209.
24. **Ibid.**
25. **Ibid.**, p. 460.
26. Cf. the analysis of the music in Upton, **op. cit.**, pp. 210-213.
27. Annie W. Pattison, *The Story of the Oratorio* (New York: Charles Scribner's Sons, 1915), pp. 19ff.
28. **Ibid.**, p. 133.
29. **Ibid.**
30. **Ibid.**, pp. 133-134.
31. Stratton, **op. cit.**, p. 90.
32. Upton, **op. cit.**, p. 213.

32a. **Ibid.**

33. Upton, p. 215.

34. **Ibid.**, p. 218.

35. Pattison, *The Story of the Oratorio*, **op. cit.**, pp. 136·137.

36. Upton, **op. cit.**, p. 221.

37. "Felix Mendelssohn," Ewen, **op. cit.**, p. 446.

38. Stratton, **op. cit.**, p. 157-158.

39. For an analysis as well as the words of the entire "Elijah" oratorio, cf. the booklet accompanying VOX 208 Mono, SVBX 5208bStereo, 3" 12 Records, Mendelssohn "Elijah;" or Upton, **op. cit.**, pp. 223-229.

40. Stratton, **op. cit.**, p. 160.

41. Upton, **op. cit.**, p. 208.

42. As cited from Lampadius, Upton, **op. cit.**, p. 232.

43. **Ibid.**, p. 232.

44. **Ibid.**, p. 233.

45. George Upton, *The Standard Cantatas* (Chicago: A.C. McClurg and Company, 1887), pp. 246-2267.

46. Upton, *The Standard Cantatas*, **op. cit.**, p. 202.

47. Cf. analysis of this cantata in Upton, *Standard Cantatas*, **op. cit.**, pp. 262-263.

48. Burkley, **op. cit.**, p. 647.

49. Stratton, **op. cit.**, p. 116.

50. Upton, *The Standard Cantatas*, **op. cit.**, p. 267.

51. Grove's *Dictionary of Music and Musicians* (New York: St. Martin's Press, 1954), V, p. 700.

52. Burkley, **op. cit.**, p. 647a.

53. Musical Notes on back of RCA VICTOR LM-221" Italian and Reformation Symphonies, Charles Munch Boston Symphony Orchestra.

54. **Ibid.**

55. **Ibid.**

56. Joseph Singmaster, Musical Notes on back of jacket for DECCA DL710 710144, Mendelssohn: Symphony No. 5 (Reformation) and Berwald: Symphony in C Major (Simgliere).

57. **Ibid.**

58. **Ibid.**

59. **Ibid.**

60. **Ibid.**

61. Ewen, **op. cit.** pp. 456-457.

62. Singmaster, **op. cit.**

63. Cf. Bach "Ein Feste Burg," Cantata BWV. 80, SERAPHIM, Record S-60248.

64. Burk, **op. cit.**

65. Paul Henry Lang, *Music in the History of the Western Civilization* (New York: Norton and Company, 1941), p. 804.

Questions

1. Mendelsohn wrote a symphony designed to be played at the ____.

2. Mendelsohn began a rediscovery of ____.

3. What did the words of St. Matthew passion do to Mendelsohn? ____

4. Mendelsohn became an authority on ____.

5. ____ became the focal point of his career.

6. His marriage was blessed with ____.

7. ____ became familiar all over the world.

8. Mendelsohn died at the age of ____.

9. "St. Paus is the glorification of ____ in contrast to the blind self-righteousness of ____.

10. "Der Lobgesang" celebrated ____.
11. The "Hymn of Praise" shows the triumph of ____.
12. The most admired of all of Mendelsohn's compositions is ____.
13. The author of the Augsburg Confession was ____.
14. One of Mendelsohn's greatest accomplishments was ____.

The Contribution of J.S. Bach to Lutheran Orthodoxy

Christian News, March 15, 1993

Johann Sebastian Bach died on July 28, 1750.[1] In general, Bach was not appreciated by his contemporaries. He was buried in an oak coffin, at that time considered an extravaganza.[2]

In the meeting that picked his successor there was not one word of appreciation or regret expressed at his passing. Publications of that day contained a brief notice of his death. Field wrote concerning Bach's passing: "there was also a sort of perfunctory praise, mostly for the Bach the acrobat at the organ. A few friends who understood Bach, praised him warmly, sorrowfully, knowing that a prophet had been among them. But their voices were largely unnoticed."[3] Bach had died practically a poor man. Two years later, Magdalena, his second wife, was a pauper, forced to live in a public almshouse, where she died on February 27, 1760.

J.S. Bach was dead for 52 years before finally a biography was written about one of the great musical geniuses in the history of music. It was published by Johann Nicholas Forkel in 1802.[4] The great master had been dead for 75 years before there was a revival of his music. He had been in the grave for a hundred years before any systematic or comprehensive efforts were made to make his works available to the world. The Bach Gesellschaft began to publish his works, and it took fifty years for that task to be accomplished.[5] The 250th anniversary celebration of his birth made a tremendous effort to give Bach the rightful appreciation and standing in musical history that he deserved.

March 21, 1985 will be the three hundredth anniversary of his birth. This year hundreds of thousands will celebrate the tercentenary with a great deal of fanfare and in a magnificent manner. This year Bachanalian events are planned in America, Europe and even in Japan for Bach's birthday celebration.

Frederick M. Winship, United Press International writer, recently wrote:

The 300 anniversary of the birth of Johann Sebastian Bach will begin officially in March, but the crescendo of the commemorative festivals, concerts, lectures, symposiums, recordings, and publications already has reached a high pitch wherever the great German composer is revered.[6]

Birmingham, Alabama, is planning to celebrate Bach basically all year long; in Flint, Michigan, they are remembering Bach from February 12 to June 1; the Oregon Bach festival in Eugene, Oregon, will be held from June 25 to July 8; in Toronto, Canada, Bach will be heard from March 8 to 24; and the Tribach Festival in Edmonton, Canada, is scheduled to be observed from March 21 to April 6.

Festivals are planned in Minneapolis (which will sponsor 120 concerts), Philadelphia, Carmel, California; Boulder, Colorado; Winter Park, Florida; Dearborn, Michigan; Raleigh, North Carolina; Dayton, Ohio;

Louisville, Kentucky; and Spokane, Washington are cities that will remember Bach's music achievements. Fort Wayne, Indiana, is paying Bach tribute with everything from many organ concerts at area churches to instrumental and choral performances. Concordia Theological Seminary has set in motion a series of musical offerings in honor of Bach. On March 21, *The St. Matthew Passion* will be given by the Fort Wayne Philharmonic at St. Paul's Lutheran Church. The San Francisco Symphony has scheduled a massive Bach Festival to be held from October 15 to November 17th.

Europe is also getting into the celebration act this year also will be the 300th birthday of Frederick Handel and Domenico Scarlatti. The Parliament of Europe is promoting the renaissance of baroque music in 1985. The Parliament of Europe is observing 1985 as "The European Music Year" (EMY). Bach, Handel, and Scarlatti are to be honored by the presentation of various types of their musical works. The EMY activities are scheduled to take place all year. This 1985th year is called MUSICA 85, and it started on January 1st with a program of carillon concerts all over the Netherlands. The Annual Vienna Festival will be sponsored from May 15 to June 16th and is dedicated to Bach.

Naturally West Germany and East Germany (Leipzig is in the East zone) are planning Bach celebrations, being proud of one of their greatest sons.

The city of Paris, France, is sponsoring a celebration from July 15 to September 18 in dozens of its churches. All Bach's organ works will be heard in Amsterdam's Nieuwe Kirk from April through August.

Newsweek already devoted one of its winter issues to Bach.[7] *The Lutheran Annual* has Bach's picture on its cover; the Aid Association for Lutherans in its magazine has an informative article by Kleinhans on the German master.[8] *Christian News* has called attention to the coming Bach anniversary a number of times.[9]

If Bach could arise from the dead right now he would not only be surprised but flabbergasted by the amount of attention given him and his works worldwide. What a contrast between 1750 and 1985! *Newsweek* has completely reevaluated Bach and his contribution. It has reversed the 18th century judgment about Bach and bestowed on him ecomiums his own age did not give him!

In the past, Bach's non-religious works have received more attention and praise but that he was a thoroughly religious person and that this even affected his secular music has not been emphasized.[9a] Will this happen again in connection with the observance of Bach's tercentennial?

In this essay the religious nature of his person and life will especially be stressed and many of his religious musical works will be specifically discussed. It will be the major concern of this commemorative essay to show that Bach made a significant contribution to Lutheran ecclesiastical music and also to orthodox Lutheran theology.

The Life of J. S. Bach (1685-1750)

Johann Sebastian Bach was born in Eisenach, Germany, (now Eastern

Zone), youngest son of a family of noted musical ancestry. He is said to have brought the baroque epoch in musical history to a close. The three strains of the Bach family had at least 120 descendants who were organists in cathedrals and churches over a period of two hundred years.[10] J. S. Bach is universally acknowledged as one of the most important composers of all time and he was also the foremost member of a family musical dynasty that scanned two centuries of Thuringian history.[11]

J.S. Bach was the youngest child of Johann Ambrosius Bach and Elisabeth Laemmerhirt.[12] Ambrosius was a string player employed by the town council and the ducal court at Eisenach. Johann Sebastian began school in 1692 or 1693 and did well despite frequent absences. Little is known about his musical training at this time, although he may have learnt the rudiments of string playing from his father, and no doubt attended the Georgenkirche, where Johann Christian Bach was organist until 1703. By the time he was ten years old, both of his parents were dead, in 1695 his older brother took him into his home; his brother's name was Johann Christoph (1671-1721), organist ar Ohrdruf. Johann Christoph had been a pupil of the keyboard composer Johann Pachelbel, and he apparently gave him his first formal keyboard lessons.

Sebastian Bach's years at Ohrdruf were quiet years, yet they were important years in his character development. This was also true of his spiritual development. Field wrote about this period: "For it was at Ohrdruf where the deep piety and interest in theology and the church that so characterized his whole life, were born. Sebastian Bach was the product of an intensely religious but stern and anti-pietistic training. Nevertheless, his simple faith and hearty devotion mark him as pious in the world's best and finest meaning. The roots of that tremendously spiritual earnestness that makes us love him so were laid, as is to be expected, during the confirmation days."[13]

After his confirmation Bach's voice secured him a place in a select choir of poor boys in the school of the Michaelskirche in Luenenberg (now in West Germany). This was in 1700. Even though his voice broke soon, his knowledge of a number of musical instruments allowed him to remain at that school. He probably studied in the school library, which had a large and up-to-date collection of church music.[14] At this time he also heard Georg Boehm, organist of the Johanniskirche, and he also visited Hamburg to hear the renowned organist Johann Adam Reinken at the Katharinakirche.

A few months in 1703 were spent in the employ of the Duke of Weimar, Johann Ernst, before becoming organist of the St. Boniface Church in Arnstadt, where he remained for four years.[15] In 1703 he was appointed as organist at Arnstadt, at the age of eighteen. There he remained till 1707, and he devoted himself to keyboard music, to the organ in particular. While playing at Luenenberg, he had the opportunity to become acquainted with the flamboyant playing and compositions of Dietrich Buxtehude, the most significant representative of the North German school of organ music. In October 1705 he walked 200 miles to Luebeck to hear Buxtehude. From his trip he only returned in the middle of January, 1706.[16]

In 1708 Bach was organist at the St. Blasius Church in Muelhausen. He moved there soon after he had married his cousin Maria Barbara Bach at Dornheim on October 17.[17] For a time things seem to have gone quite well. He produced several church cantatas; all of them were in a very conservative mold, based on biblical and chorale texts and did not display any of "the modern operatic" style of the Italians which was to appear in later cantatas. The famous *Toccata and Fugue in D Minor* (BWV 565) and the *Prelude and Fugue in D Major* (BWV 532) and the *Pasacaglia in C Minor* (BWV 582) come from this time in Bach's life. Cantata No. 71 *Gott ist mein Koenig* was also a product of the Muelhausen period.

At Muelhausen Bach was confronted with a rector who belonged to a pietistic movement, which was an offshoot of Lutheranism, but led away from the objectivity of the Scriptures as the sole foundation for faith and religion to a subjectivity of feelings as reflecting true faith and relationship with God.[18] Before long Bach seized the opportunity to move to Weimar. At the latter place Bach shifted his interest to instrumental-vocal ensemble into which he then poured his creative impulse. At orthodox Weimar, Bach was at the outset court organist and a member of the orchestra. At the encouragement of Wilhelm Ernst, Bach concentrated upon the organ during the first few years of his tenure. On March 2, 1714 he became concertmaster, with the duty of composing a cantata every month.

During the years 1708-14 his style is said to have changed. Between 1714-16 his style is alleged to have been decisively influenced by new styles and forms of the contemporary Italian opera and by the innovations of such Italian composers as Antonio Vivaldi. The J.S. Bach article in the *Encyclopedia Britannica* stated that the results of his influence may be seen in such cantatas as numbers 182, 199, and 61 in 1714; 31 and 161 in 1715; and 70 and 147 in 1716.[19] The same Britannica article explained: "His favorite forms appropriated from the Italians were those based on refrain (**tritornello**) or **da capo** schemes in which wholesale repetition — literal or with modifications — of entire sections of a piece permitted him to create coherent musical forms with much larger dimensions than had hitherto been possible. Those newly acquired techniques henceforth governed a host of Bach's arias and concerto movements, as well as many of his larger fugues (especially the mature ones for organ) and profoundly affected his treatment of chorales."[20]

At Weimar Bach composed most of the *Orgelbuechlein* (*The Little Organ Book*) and all but the last of the 18 "Great" chorale preludes; the earlier organ trios; and most of the organ preludes and fugues. *The Great Prelude and Fugue in G Major* for organ (BWV 541) was finally revised about 1715 and the *Toccata and Fugue in F Major* (BWV) may have been played at Weissenfels.[21]

When Bach was passed over for the position of musical director at Weimar, which became vacant on December 1, 1716, he requested a transfer to Koethen (or Coethen), where he became musical director and assumed the task of supervising the chamber and orchestral music. Although some of these works were composed earlier, they were revised at this time. It was at Koethen that the sonatas, for violin and clavier, viola da gamba were put into something like their present form. By March 24, 1721 Bach had completed his *Brandenberg Concertos*.[22]

In his position at Koethen Bach had very little, if any, contact with the sphere of organ music. In 1723 he returned to the field of church music and continued in it to his death on July 28, 1750.

Maria Barbara Bach died unexpectedly and was buried on July 7, 1720.[23] About November, Bach visited Hamburg; his wife's death may have unsettled him and led him to inquire about the vacant post at the Jacobikirche. But at the Katharinenkirche he played in the presence of Reinken. Unable to donate four thousand marks, he failed to get the appointment. On December 3, 1721, Bach married Anna Magdalena Wilcke, daughter of a trumpeteer at Weissenfels. Apart from his wife's death the four years at Koethen are said to have been the happiest of his life.

Bach's Years at Leipzig

Bach was the third choice for the Director of Music for the city of Leipzig. Telemann and Graupner had been offered the position of Kappelmeister but both turned it down. Bach had given a trial performance playing Cantata No. 22, "Jesu Nahm zu sich die Zwoelfe," (Jesus called unto him the Twelve) February 7, 1723. In being given the Leipzig position he was obligated to furnish performers for four churches. At the Peterskirche the choir merely led the hymns. At the Neukirchen, Nikolaikirche, and the Thomaskirche part singing was required, but Bach conducted his own church music, which was performed at the last two churches. Bach's first public performance occurred on May 30, 1723, with the presentation of Cantata 75, "Die Elenden sollen essen." This was on the first Sunday after Trinity. During this year many new cantatas were written and performed as was also the first version of *The Magnificat*. The year 1724 saw the production of the *St. John Passion*, later on revised. During 1724 he produced 62 church cantatas, of which 39 were new works. On June 11, 1724 Bach began a new cycle with the first Sunday after Trinity. Within the year he composed 52 of the so-called chorale cantatas. The Sanctus of the *Mass in B-Minor* was also a product of 1724. For the next three years Bach produced an average of one cantata per week.

Bach's Family and Offspring

Bach's first wife Maria Barbara Bach bore him seven children and his second wife Anna Magdalena Bach became the mother of thirteen children. To the second wife Bach dedicated many pieces. Many children died early in life. The most celebrated son was Carl Phillipp Emanuel, born in 1714, known as the "Berliner Bach." Johann Christian Friedrich, born 1732, became known as the "Buecheburger Bach," and Johann Christian, born in 1735, became famous as "the London Bach," who became an English citizen and a Roman Catholic Convert, the only Bach not to be a

Lutheran.[24] At one time the Bachs were a large family but the last descendant died a spinster in 1908.

Bach died on July 28, 1750 and was buried in a church cemetery in Leipzig, his grave was unmarked.[25] His last composition, written in his last illness was: "Wenn wir in goessten Noeten sind," (When My Last Hour Is At Hand). Johann Sebastian was an incessant and laborious writer from necessity and his earnings hardly sufficed to maintain his large family.[26] Much of his music was prepared for the service of the church.

Bach's Contribution to Religious Music

Bach acquired fame as a virtuoso organist and contrapuntist, a learned but old-fashioned player.[27] His music never enjoyed in his lifetime the success which Handel's had because the latter was addressing audiences of the opera house and choral concert halls.[28] He had to please them in order to be popular and earn a living. While by contrast, Bach always remained a payed employee of either a prince or town council and thus was not altogether dependent for his livelihood on public approval. Milner claimed that "whereas Handel's music looks outward, ever designed to make an immediate impression on the audience, Bach's is introspective, full of detail that is perceived only through careful listening and sympathetic understanding."[29]

Although Bach wrote much instrumental music, he designed the bulk of his work for use in the Lutheran church. In writing to his student Niedt, Bach asserted: "The aim and reason for all music should be none else but the glory of God and the recreation of the mind. Where this is not observed, there will be no music but only a described hubub."[30]

During six years of his Leipzig cantorate, Bach wrote 295 church cantatas (5 yearly cycles of 59 each) of which 200 are extant. About them Milner wrote: "To study them profitably it is important to remember their intimate connection with the liturgy of the Lutheran Sunday morning or festal services; their texts frequently contain quotations from, or references to, the Epistles and Gospels of the day, and the concluding chorale is always that of the particular Sunday or feast day."[31] In describing the nature of the Bach cantata Milner further observed:

> The music is full of symbolism, allusion, and word painting that becomes clear only when the works are viewed in their liturgical context. Most of the cantatas commence with a large-scale movement, frequently blended with the Italian concerto style; but where Handel would have a largely homophonic texture, Bach develops the chorus in elaborate counter point, e.g. the Ascension Cantata No. 11.[32]

William H. Scheidt, Director of the Bach Aria Group, described the standard Bach cantata as opening with a chorus, followed by perhaps four solo numbers, usually recitatives and arias, and closes with a simple chorale. The most important exception was the solo cantata, which dispenses with the opening chorus. A few other cantatas begin with an aria with chorus following. Some cantatas have contemporary texts but most of those composed in 1723-1724 are set to Bible verses. Many cantatas use hymn stanzas with the chorale tune confined to the choruses. Such verses, however, were ill-adapted for recitative of de capo aria settings. Thus, for his second series of cantatas, composed about 1735-1740, and all based on chorales, Bach had the texts for the middle movements paraphrased (or paraphrased them himself). Thus Scheidt opined:

> The roughly three years of extant cantatas, plus the organ chorales in the *Clavierübung* (published 1739) are Bach's **reaffirmation of orthodox Lutheranism** as opposed to the rationalistic tendencies of the day.[33] (Bold face supplied.)

Lang in his evaluation of Bach's cantatas asserted:

> The center of Lutheran religion is the inner struggle of the individual. This traditional subjective religion was transmitted in the Bach family for generations and accepted with the deepest convictions. Ardor, humility, fear, and soaring hope are embodied in Bach's cantatas with an intensity and effect which made these works the highest expression of Lutheran religiousness.[34]

According to Lang, the variety of the cantatas was great. Thus there are religious pastorals, oratorio-like dramatic scenes, pictorial Biblical episodes, lyrico-epic poems, and, finally, transfigurations steeped in pious contemplation, avoiding dramatic, pictorial, and characterizing effects, but filled with mystic symbolism.[35]

The same musicologist gave this impression of the cantatas:

> Bach's cantatas give the uninitiated the impression that here speaks one, who rising above earthly confusion, is entirely immersed in the worship of the celestial. But when we become more intimately acquainted with them we are struck by the earthiness of this man and realize that from day to day and from hour to hour he longed for salvation. From hundreds of arias and choruses ring the cry "and deliver me from my sins."[36]

The Oratorio Works of Bach
The Christmas Oratorio

There are a number of musical compositions that Bach labelled as "oratorium." The most famous was the "Christmas Oratorio," written by Bach in 1754, based on texts taken from Luke, chapters 1-2 and Matthew 1-2. Upton has informed us that "it is not, as its name suggests a work to be performed at a single hearing, but a composition divided into six parts of divine service, arranged for three days of Christmas, New Year's Sunday and Epiphany, each part being a complete cantata for each day, all linked together by chorales which give a unity of subject and design."[37] The oratorio was completed in installments, each part separate and complete in itself and yet combining to illustrate a given subject in its entirety. In the modern meaning of the term, Bach's "Christmas Oratorio" is not an oratorio, but it is so called because Bach's own title for his work was "Oratorium Tempore Navitatis Christi."[38]

The entire score embraces no less than sixty-four numbers. The oratorio has six parts, whose complete rendition would take a number of hours. Upton has summarized the contents of its six parts as follows:

In the first three parts the connecting narratives, recited by the evangelist, are assigned to tenor and bass, and declare the events associated with the birth of our Lord — the journey to Bethlehem, the birth in the manger, the joy of Mary, and the thanksgiving over the advent of the Lord — the choral parts being sung by the shepherds. The fourth part, that for New Year's Day, relates the naming of Jesus, and follows his career in a grand expression of faith and hope. The fifth part illustrates the visit of the three kings, the anxiety of Herod when he hears of the advent of the Lord, and the assurances given him to alloy his fears. In the sixth section the visitors depart to frustrate Herod's designs and choruses of rejoicing over the final triumph of the Lord close the work.[39]

The *Christmas Oratorio* concludes with "Glory to God in the highest," which is an exultant song of the heavenly host.[40]

The Magnificat in D

This is known as the "Great Magnificat," to distinguish it from the smaller one. It was composed on Christmas Day 1723. Spitta considered it one example of the genius of Bach. On Christmas Day 1723 in the evening the same cantata, which had been sung in the Nicolas church, was repeated in the evening at the Thomaskirche. But after the sermon the *Hymn of the Virgin* was sung, set in its Latin form and in an elaborate style. For the occasion of the Festival of Jesus' birth Bach expanded it into four vocal numbers. Upton has given an analysis of the Magnificat as now presented on pages 48-50 of his book, *The Standard Oratorios*. *The Great Magnificat* ends with a triumphant "Gloria," a chorus of extraordinary power and majesty.[41]

The Passions of Bach

Bach wrote five passions — the "St. John," probably about 1723 and first performed in the following year; another, which is lost, in 1725; the St. Matthew in 1731, and the St. Luke in 1734. Of these five only two are known, namely the "St. John" and the "St. Matthew," of which the St. Matthew is considered the greatest.[42]

Passion-music of Bach's time was the complement of the mysteries of the medieval times. The passion set forth the Lord's suffering and was performed at church festivals, in which the congregation participated in the singing of the chorales. They were the immediate predecessors of the modern oratorio.[43]

The idea for the form of the *St. Matthew Passion* was suggested to Bach by Solomon Deyling who filled an important position in Leipzig. The *St. Matthew Passion* was performed on Good Friday in an afternoon service, 1729, but was not heard again until young Mendelson revived it in Berlin, March 12, 1829.[44] After that it was frequently performed with great enthusiasm and still holds its place in the oratorio repertory.

The *St. Matthew Passion* is written in two parts, between which the sermon intervened in old times. Portions of chapters 26 and 27 according to St. Matthew are utilized; the remainder of the text being composed of hymns furnished to him by Christian Friedrich Henrici, who wrote under the name of "Picander," and was assisted in its compilation by Bach himself.[45] The dramatis personae are Jesus, Judas, Peter, Pilate, the Apostles, and the People or Turbae, and the narrative is interpreted by reflections addressed to our Lord. Two choruses "The Daughters of Zion" and "The Faithful," address the queries to Jesus. At times the questions addressed are by the Chorus, and at other times by single voices. Chorales were employed that were in common use in the Lutheran Church and were familiar to the congregation, who sang the melody, the harmony being sustained by the chorus and instruments. Upton described the nature of the *St. Matthew Passion* as follows:

The Gospel text is in recitative form throughout, the part of the evangelist, or narrator, being assigned to a tenor voice, while those of the persons incidentally introduced are given to the singers, in the dialogue, whenever the words of Jesus occur, the accompaniment is furnished by a string quartette, which serves to distinguish them from the others, and invests them with a peculiar gentleness and grace. There are 15 chorales in it, taken from the Lutheran service.[46]

St. John Passion of Bach

The *St. John Passion* dates from 1724. Both *Passions*, the *Matthew* and *John*, represent a compromise between the earlier "dramatic" and newer "opera" forms of the *Passion* composition. For the solo arias and accompanied recitatives of the St. John, Bach drew on a text by Heinrich Brocker. The St. John is more obviously dramatic by reason of the fewer lyrical interruptions to the narrative and the extended crowd sections.[47] St. Matthew, while it has dramatic moments, is more meditative and leisurely in its progress. Milner claimed that "Bach's treatment of the Gospel narrative is peculiarly his own; he abandoned every trace of the old chant intonations, substituting a vocal line ostensibly based on a secco recitative but with a lyrical turn of phrase not to found there, an effect that conformed entirely to the requirements of the German language and to the expressiveness required by the subject, in the Passions, **as in all his religious music, Bach's devotion and deep feeling for religion are manifest**"[48] (bold face supplied).

The Mass in B-Minor

The years 1730-1734 are said by Fields to have been the happiest of Bach's life. By this time his family was now sufficiently grown up to Provide musicals, his personal fame had spread abroad and many musicians came to Leipzig to see and hear Bach. About this time Augustus II, ruler of Saxony, died and was succeeded by Augustus III. He and his father had converted to Roman Catholicism. Bach decided to present a musical work to the new king and that turned out to be the "Mass B-Minor," which some musical critics have declared to be the most stupendous thing and placed it side by side with the *St. Matthew Passion* .[49] The *Mass in B-Minor* is not an exposition of the liturgical chants of the Roman Catholic Mass.[50] But the Mass or German Messe was the term used in

Germany and in the Scandinavian countries to designate the liturgical services of the Lutheran Church. Of course, the rubrics go back historically to the Roman Catholic Church. The *Mass in B-Minor* has six sections of the Mass — the Gratias, Qui Tollit, Patrem, Crucifixus, Osanna, Agnus Dei. Lang has observed that while this musical opus appears to be an entirely different work, when compared with the *Christmas Oratorio*, it is simply a gigantic collection of cantatas. It cannot be denied that the fact that the *B-Minor Mass* contains music that was originally the embodiment of a spirit diametrically opposed to the Latin text to which it is now fitted without radically alternations or noticeable effort and that together with its virtually prohibitive proportions and the great variety of forms and devices employed in the individual sections, makes the Mass somewhat different and heterogeneous.[51]

The Motets of Bach

Bach wrote 7 motets and 2 sanctus settings (3 others are based on works by other composers). The musical information on the back of *The Collectors Series*, Mace division of Scepter Records, stated: "the motets of Johann Sebastian Bach, unsurpassed as great church choral polyphonic compositions, dating from his Leipzig period, like most of his enduring works, owe their origin to official duty."[52] Musicologists tells us that originally the motet had its place at the beginning of the main service, in the vesper service, or on a special occasion during communion in the main service. By Bach's time there existed an extensive and highly useful compilations of music suitable for that purpose. Spitta has shown that Bach used the two-volume "Florilegium Portense" of Erhard Bodenschatz (1576-1636), a clergyman collector and publisher of sacred works consisting of 270 (?) motets which were published in 1618, respectively 1621.[53]

By Bach's time a new custom had developed, according to which, when a prominent citizen had died, or a group of people, they would be honored with an individual funeral service and sermon in place of the Sunday evening vespers. It appears that six authenticated motets were written by Thomas Santo on order for such service, in consideration for a fee. Thus it has been established that the five-part "Jesu meine Freude" (Jesus My Joy), a combination of choral and Bible text was composed for the funeral service of the wife of Postmaster Kaese on July 18, 1723. On October 16, 1729 the rector of the St. Thomas School and professor at Leipzig University, Johann Heinrich Ernesti, died. For this cultured friend of his, Bach composed the eight-part motet "Der Geist hilft unserer Schwachheit auf"[54] (The Holy Spirit Strengthens Our Weakness), the only motet with orchestral accompaniment. This was intended for the ceremonies to be held in St. Paul's Church of the University. The capella arrangement was to be rendered in the St. Thomas Church. The psalm-motet "Fuerchte dich nicht" (Do Not Fear) was composed for the burial ceremony of Mrs. Winkler, the wife of the town militia commandant, which took place on February 4, 1726. "Lobet den Herrn in allen Landen" (Praise the Lord in All the Lands) for four-part mixed choir appears to have been written for a happy occasion. Besides the use of basso continuo, it is characterized by a second peculiarity, the text of Psalm 117, has been freely set to music, without choral reference.[54]

Bach and the Organ

Bach was considered the top organist of his day. His mastery of the organ reached an unprecedented pinnacle.[55] In fact, as Schweitzer said: "He is not beginning but the end." Bach's real and most personal domain was instrumental music, especially the organ.[56] The musical symbol of the Christian congregation from the Middle Ages to the time of Bach had been the chorale and the polyphony based upon the chorale, the very expression of the blood and unity of the individual human being living under an eternal verity and law.[57]

Since Luther's reformation the specific character of Protestant Christianity shaped the baroque period in Germany and it was the congregation consciousness that speaks with convincing force in the Protestant chorales, which formed the basis of his art and in cantatas and oratorios which are the greatest treasure of Protestant church art.[58] The church became the sanctuary for central Germany. The solemn music they heard in their life gave them hope for his life as well as hope for eternity.[59] The organ was important for the members of Lutheran congregations; many an organ was built as a community project. The consecration of each organ was an occasion for great rejoicing for Lutherans loved the chorale which they enjoyed as good music but also as music rendered to the glory of God. For Bach the organ loft in a church was the place closest to his heart. [60]

When Bach appeared upon the scene, there were three different schools of organ playing and music in Germany. In central Germany, Thuringia and Saxony, there was a group of which belonged Johann Pachelbel of Erfurt and Nuremberg, Bach's Uncle Johann Christoph Bach of Eisenach, Johann Friedrich Sachau of Holle, who had adopted the Protestant chorale as the basis of their art. They mainly composed chorale preludes and organ chorales in a skillful polyphonic style. For Bach this organ tradition was of prime significance and remained throughout his life closely attached to it as the spiritual basis.[61]

In North Germany there was a school of organ music whose chief exponents were Nicholaus Bruhas of Hussum, Vincent Luebeck of Hamburg, and Dietrich Buxtehude of Luebeck. This school did not foster the chorale to any extent, but engaged in free fantasy and showed the influence of the Anglo-Dutch thought. However, it mastered all the possibilities of organ technique and discovered the richness of specific expressions. North Germany became the home of the most glorious organs. Hamburg and Luebeck had great instruments.[62]

In South Germany (a predominantly Roman Catholic area) there was an organ school, a third, represented by George Muffat at Passau, Johann Jacob Froberger in Vienna, and Johann Kaspar Kerll in Munich. They directly or indirectly were influenced by Girolamo Frescabaldi in Rome.[63] They favored the developed Italian form of the fugue and its subordinate species, the canzone and the ricercare. The organ music of Bach climaxed the German baroque; his organ music marks the complete synthesis and fusion of the Italian, French and German influence in his own personal style. About this fusion Fleischer wrote:

Through this synthesis and through the mighty broadening and deepening of the above mentioned styles, the organ works of Bach actually became a new and complete accomplishment. At the same time, they were also a final culmination beyond which further development would be impossible and incredible.[64]

Among Bach's organ compositions attention should be drawn to the organ preludes on the so-called Catechism hymns, a group of hymns arranged in the same order as the Six Chief Parte in Luther's Catechism. Part Three of Bach's *Klavieruebung* was composed "to illustrate the Lutheran Catechism by preludes treating the melodies of Luther's familiar hymns on the Commandments, Creed, Prayer, Baptism, Penitence, and Holy Communion." (Cs. Terry, Bach, London, 1940, p. 247). Since Luther had written a larger and a smaller catechism, "Bach gives us a larger and a smaller arrangement of each chorale." (Schweitzer, J. S. Bach, London, 1945, p. 289). Thus in going back to Christian truth not only for incentive, but also for subject matter to perform the work of his calling, Bach has given a striking illustration of the close connection between Christian doctrine and Christian practice.

Bach the Preacher of God's Word

Martin J. Naumann wrote a chapter "Bach the Preacher" for *The Little Bach Book*, in which the former Springfield Seminary professor, cogently argued: "The works of other great musicians speak to us, but the works of Bach preach to us."[65] "These sermons, his cantatas, and particularly his *St. Matthew Passion*, proclaim the glory of God in the Bible in a thousand voices in all places where men have learned to treasure the eloquence of the Thomaskantor."[66]

In his musical writings Bach preached Christ and Him Crucified. He extolled the Son of God as the Savior of the world. Bach preached powerfully through his music, in *The St. Matthew Passion* Bach brought the sufferings of Christ's, His crucifixion, and death to the public who attended it, but "presented the sacred story not only to his own, but all Christendom reverent confession to the Crucified. The music is charged with spiritual power and emotion."[67]

Bach's declared aim in life was to "advance music in the divine service to its very end and purpose, a regulated church music in honor of God." From 1723 to 1723 he was diverted from his goal, but with the acceptance of the St. Thomas position, he returned to his true element and for 27 years he was Kantor in Leipzig, where he showed his true form as a servant of the Word of God. Here he wrote most of his cantatas.[68] The latter were composed to fit into the Sunday worship service. They were rendered between the reading of the Epistle and the Gospel and the sermon. Usually a well-known chorale or hymn was employed at the beginning and the final stanza at the end with textual change, but the intermediate stanzas were altered to fit the movement. Bach believed that his compositions must serve the word of God and he treated the Epistle and Gospel pericopes not only according to the text of the chorale, but in accordance with his understanding and faith in the words read and preached. For today's worship services they are too long and should be shortened, averred Naumann, and he rendered in church rather than in the concert hall.[69]

Bach and Pietism

While Bach was musically active in Saxony, Pietism had become prominent and was opposing Lutheran orthodoxy. Pietism was characterized by subjectivity at the expense of the objectivity of Holy Scriptures. Already at Ohrdruf from 1695-1700, when still a child, Bach witnessed the conflict between the orthodox Lutheran and the pietistic element introduced by the opponents of orthodoxy. At Muelhausen Bach was faced by pietistic opposition where there were those who would even get rid of the organ.

Pietism had been generated and fostered by men like Spener and Francke and was spreading against dead orthodoxy and formalism; it led in certain people to emotionalism and radicalism.[70] The latter were found at Muelhausen and its community. This area had been a center for religious fanaticism ever since the days of the Anabaptists and the Zwickau prophets. At Bach's time one of Pietism's great advocates was Bach's pastor, Johann Adolph Frohne. At first Bach remained silent, but when there was talk of throwing out of the churches all altar paintings and statuary and the organ as well, Bach spoke out against Pietism. Bach became convinced that in such an atmosphere his musical art could not thrive or develop.[71]

In June 1708, hardly after a year, Bach handed in his resignation at Muelhausen, having accepted a position at Weimar. Bach's library contained a number of standard works of leading pietists; still he remained faithful to his Lutheran Confessions. Bach's whole attitude testifies to this. He was a confessionalist. When he applied for the Kantor position at the Thomas school he was obliged to be colloquized in Leipzig in May 1723 and found doctrinally sound.[72]

Pastor Erdmann Neumeister of Hamburg, author of about 600 hymns and pastor of the St. Jacobi church, wanted Bach as his Kantor, but the latter did not secure the position because he was unable to "donate" 4,000 marks to the church, if selected as Kantor. Neumeister wanted Bach, not only because he was a musical genius, but also because he was orthodox and so could help him in preaching the Word of God in a pure manner. Neumeister knew that Bach was opposed to Pietism, and that he was a staunch Lutheran and that Bach preached God's Word in a powerful way.[73]

Bach Opposition to Rationalism

Bach's problems at Leipzig were caused largely by those who turned away from orthodoxy and promoted a type of religion which was anti-

Scriptural and un-Lutheran. The University of Leipzig was the seat of this rationalistic religious teaching.[74] According to Walter Buszin, J.S. Bach and Martin Luther are the two most illustrious personages of Lutheranism. Bach had two sets of the writings of Luther in his library and was an avid follower of Luther. Wrote Buszin: "That Bach was a Lutheran by conviction may be seen from the theology of the sacred choral works and from the manner in which he interprets these texts."[75]

Buszin claimed that Bach's Lutheranism was altogether orthodox which may be seen from the following: (1) he left Muelhausen because of those who opposed Lutheran orthodoxy; (2) his favorite hymns were those of the golden age of the Lutheran chorale; (3) his problems in Leipzig were caused largely by those who turned away from orthodoxy to promulgate a type of belief which at times was even anti-Christian and unscriptural; (4) although Bach's texts at times betray a marked pietistic tinge and evince that he was also a child of his times, yet they never reveal anything that militates against the convictions of orthodox Lutheranism; (5) Bach employed forms in his music which were frowned upon by the pietists and approved by those who were orthodox.[76]

In many respects Bach was an exemplary Christian. Over his cantatas Bach wrote "in Jesus' name" and "to the glory of God." He believed that his whole life was to honor God. He accepted heartily Luther's dictum that all earthly service can be done to the Glory of God.

Columbia Broadcasting System's Evaluation of Bach

On Easter Sunday, 1948 and 1949, the Columbia Broadcasting System produced a special, hour long, religious program entitled, "The Son of Man." It consisted exclusively of readings from the four gospels, each impersonated by a separate reader, and of music by Bach.[77] The announcer explained that though Bach was not physically present at Jesus' death (and how many evangelists were?), that Bach through his music and his understanding of the record of the evangelists deserved to be ranked as "a fifth evangelist." William H. Scheide, in his Princeton University monograph, wrote: "Such a statement made over a nationwide radio network on Christianity's holiest day, surely deserves notice, is it truth or is it blasphemy — is it foolishness, a stumbling block, or the power of God?"[78]

Scheide in his study, *Johann Sebastian Bach as Biblical Interpreter* shows that Bach indeed could be called "a fifth evangelist" and has listed nearly one hundred passages from both the Old and New Testaments which were employed by Bach in his choral works.[79] Bach was a Biblical interpreter of the saving Gospel, as set forth in both the Old and New Testaments.

In 1950 Walter Buszin, a former Lutheran authority in liturgies and hymnology, wrote an excellent essay in which he showed how Orthodox Lutheran theology was clearly evident in the life and works of Bach.[80] It was written for the two hundredth anniversary of Bach's death (1950). By a number of quotations from the literature of that time, he showed that scholars of repute especially emphasized the profound Lutheran character of Bach's life and work. Thus he cited Gerhard Herz, musicologist of the University of Louisville, who had asserted:

Bach's personality and creations, which today move us chiefly, aesthetically and emotionally, are deeply rooted in the ethos of the Old Lutheran Church...The search for Bach's philosophy of life leads to the figure of Christ as understood by the orthodox Lutherans. Bach's art and his religion are but one and the same. Nobody in music perceived and interpreted the sacred and the miraculous more powerfully and more purely than Bach.[81]

In closing, we quote Huto Leichtentritt, who asserted:

In his cantatas, his Passion music, and his chorale preludes for the organ Bach interprets the meaning of the Holy Scriptures and the Christian Creed with a fervor, persuasiveness, penetration, and vast imaginative power never again exhibited by religious music. His religious music has, indeed, much similarity to a profound sermon of a great preacher.[82]

Footnotes

1. W. E. Bunin, "Bach, Johann Sebastian," Erwin L. Lueker, Editor, *Lutheran Cyclopedia* (St. Louis; Concordia Publishing House, 1975), p. 66.
2. Laurence Field, *Johann Sebastian Bach* (Minneapolis: Augsburg Publishing House, 1943), pp. 139-141.
3. **Ibid.**
4. **Ibid.**
5. "Bach, Johann Sebastian," *The Encyclopedia Britannica*, Macromedia Section, 2, p. 560.
6. "World Celebrates Bach's Birthday," *Ft. Wayne Sunday Journal Gazette*, February 10, 1965 (Cf. Travel Section).
7. *Newsweek*, December 1964.
8. AAL Correspondent, January-February, 1965.
9. *Christian News*, January 7, 1985.
9a. Field, **op. cit.**, p. vii; *Christian News*, January 7, 1985, p. 5.
10. "Bach, Johann Sebastian, Bach," *The Encyclopedia Britannica*, **op. cit.**, p. 556.
11. Paul Henry Lang, *Music in Western Civilization* (New York: W. W. Norton & Company, 1941), p. 489.
12. For the life of Bach, cf. the following books: L.C. Field, *Johann Sebastian Bach*, **op. cit.**, 166 pp.; J. A. Spitta, *The Life of Bach* (London: Novello & Co., 1899), 3 volumes; C.S. Terry, *Bach – A Biography* (London: Oxford University Press, 1962); C.S. Terry, *Bach – A Historical Approach* (London: Oxford University Press, 1930); Albert Schweitzer, *Bach* (8th edition, Liepzig: Bretkoph and Heartel, 1930), 2 volumes; A Pierro, *Johann Sebastian Bach*, tr. M. Savill (London, 1959); H.T. David and A . Mendels, eds., *A Bach Reader* (New York, 1954).
13. Field, **op. cit.**, p. 14.
14. "Bach, Johann Sebastian," *The Encyclopedia Britannica*, **op. cit.**, 2 p. 556.
15. Heinrich Fleisher, "Bach and the Organ," in Theo. Hoelty Nickel, *The Little Bach Book* (Valparaiso, Indiana: 1950), pp. 74-75.
16. **Ibid.**, p. 75.
17. Walter E. Buszin, "Bach, Johann Sebastian," in *The Encyclopedia of the Lutheran Church* (Minneapolis: Augsburg Publishing Company, 1965), I. p. 172.
18. Field, **op. cit.**, pp. 50-51.
19. "Bach, Johann Sebastian," *The Encyclopedia Britannica*, **op. cit.**, p. 557b.
20. **Ibid.**, pp. 557-558.
21. **Ibid.**, p. 558.

22. **Ibid.**
23. For his home and family life, cf. Field, **op. cit.**, pp. 72-76. Also cf. Buszin, *The Encyclopedia of the Lutheran Church*, **op. cit.**, I, pp. 172-173.
24. **Ibid.**, p. 173.
25. Field, **op. cit.**, pp. 139-141.
26. William H. Scheide, "Bach, Johann Sebastian," *The Encyclopedia Americana*, 1979 edition, 3, p. 16.
27. A. Milner, "Bach, Johann Sebastian," *New Catholic Encyclopedia*, 2, p. 6.
28. **Ibid.**
29. **Ibid.**
30. **Ibid.**, pp. 6-7.
31. **Ibid.**, p. 7.
32. **Ibid.**
33. Scheide, **op. cit.**, p. 18.
34. Lang, **op. cit.**, p. 498.
35. **Ibid.**
36. **Ibid.**, p. 497.
37. George Upton, *The Standard Oratorios – Their Stories, Their Music, and Their Composers* (Chicago: A. C. McClurg and Company, 1890), pp. 33-39.
38. **Ibid.**, p. 34.
39. **Ibid.**, pp. 34-35.
40. **Ibid.**, p. 35.
41. **Ibid.**, p. 50.
42. Milner, **op. cit.**, p. 7.
43. Upton, **op. cit.**, pp. 39-40.
44. *The Little Bach Book*, **op. cit.**, p. 1622; cf. Bach, *St. Matthew Passion* (Richmond Record, BA, 43001).
45. Upton, **op. cit.**, p. 41.
46. **Ibid.**, p. 41.
47. Lang, **op. cit.**, p. 509.
48. Milner, **op. cit.**, p. 6; Cf. also Joseph Braumstein, *Musical Notes for J. S. Bach, St. John's Passion*. BWV 245, Nonesuch Records, HC 73004 (Stereo).
49. Lang, **op. cit.** pp. 490-499.
50. **Ibid.**, p. 491. cf. Bach B Minor Mass RCA Victor. L86-6151.
51. **Ibid.**, pp. 498-499.
52. Bach of Folder for Mace Record M9016, put out by a Division of Scepter Records, Inc., New York, N.Y.
53. **Ibid.**
54. **Ibid.**
55. Milner, "Bach. Johann Sebastian," *New Catholic Encyclopedia,* 2, p. 6.
56. Fleischer, **op. cit.**, p. 74; Lang, **op. cit.**, pp. 504-505.
57. Fleischer, **op. cit.**, p. 69.
58. Lang, **op. cit.**, p. 392.
59. **Ibid.**
60. **Ibid.**
61. **Ibid.**, pp. 70-72.
62. **Ibid.**, p. 72.
63. **Ibid.**
64. **Ibid.**, p. 73.
65. Naumann, "Bach The Preacher", in *The Little Bach Book,* **op. cit.**, p. 14.
66. **Ibid.**
67. **Ibid.**, p. 17.
68. Cf. George Upton, *The Standard Cantatas, Their Stories, Their Music, and Their Composers* (Chicago: A. C. McClurg and Company, 1888), pp. 29-43.
69. Naumann, **op. cit.**, p. 18.
70. Field, **op. cit.**, pp. 50-51; Naumann, **op. cit.**, p. 19.

71. "Lutheran theology after 1580," *Lutheran Cyclopedia*, **op. cit.**, p. 506. Lang, **op. cit.**, pp. 471, 473, 475.
72. Naumann, **op. cit.**, p. 19.
73. **Ibid.**. p. 15.
74. Cf. Otto Heick, *A History of Christian Thought* (Philadelphia: Fortress, 1966), 11, pp. 13-15. Fleischer, **op. cit.**, p. 68; Robert Stephenson, *Anglican Theological Review*, Vol. xxxiii, October, 1951, No. 4, pp. 219-230; Cf. *Concordia Theological Monthly* , 23; 302-303, April, 1953, "Bach's quarrel with the Rector of the St. Thomas School."
75. Buszin, *The Encyclopedia of the Lutheran Church*, **op. cit.**, I, p. 172.
76. **Ibid.**
77. William H. Scheide, Princeton Pamphlets-8, *Johann Sebastian Bach as Biblical Interpreter* (Princeton Theological Seminary: Princeton, New Jersey Library, 1952), p. 5.
78. **Ibid.**
79. **Ibid.**, pp. 37-40.
80. Walter Buszin, "Lutheran Theology in Life and Works of Bach," *Concordia Theological Monthly*, 21: 896-913, December, 1950.
81. Gerhard Herz, "Bach's Religion," *Journal of Renaissance and Baroque Music*, Vol. 1, No. 2, June 1946, pp. 124-126.
82. Hugo Leichtentritt, *Music, History and Ideas* (Cambridge: Harvard University Press, 1938), p. 147.

Questions

1. Was Bach appreciated by his contemporaries? ____
2. Bach died practically a ____ man.
3. Bach had been dead almost ____ years before there was a revival of his music.
4. What happened at the 300th anniversary of Bach's birth? ____
5. Who called attention to the Bach anniversary several times____?
6. Bach made a major contribution to ___ music and orthodox ____.
7. Bach walked ____ miles to hear Buxtehude.
8. Bach was the father of ___ children.
9. Bach's grave was ____.
10. Bach asserted that the aim and purpose of all music should be ____.
11. Bach reaffirmed ____.
12. From hundreds of Bach's arias and choruses rings the cry ____.
13. Bach was considered the top ___ of his day.
14. Bach has given a striking illustration of the close connection between Christian ____ and Christian ____.
15. Martin J. Naumann argued that the works of other great musicians ___ to us but the works of Bach ___ to us.
16. In his musical writings Bach ____.
17. Bach's declared aim in life was ____.
18. Bach spoke out against ____.
19. According to Walter Buzin, ___ and ___ were the two most illustrious personages of the Reformation.
20. Over his cantatas, Bach wrote ___ and ____.
21. Bach could be called a ____ evangelist.

The Passion and Resurrection of Our Lord Jesus Christ as Reflected In Various Forms of Church Music

Christian News, June 14, 1993

The fine arts, such as sculpture, painting and music show a considerable influence by the Passion and Resurrection Narratives on church music. Some of the great Biblical choral works have been performed by outstanding conductors and great orchestras. Most of the great music of the church was created by the Roman Catholic Church and since the Reformation by Lutherans and Protestants.[1]

Various musical forms have been affected and used by different media to portray the main events and Passion and Resurrection of Christ.

This presentation will deal with the passion, death and resurrection of Christ as represented in different types of musical compositions. It will treat a number of outstanding music media, namely, the cantatas, the oratorios and choruses. A chronological sequence will generally characterize this presentation.

The Oratorio in General

An oratorio is said "to be an extension of a musical composition of solos and choruses with a more or less religious text, accompanied by full orchestra or organ, to be rendered without action, or scenery."[2] Its name was derived from the fact that it was sung in a large and public church of St. Maria in Valicelle, under the direction of St. Neri, the founder of the congregation of Oratorions.[3]

By contrast, the church cantata is a composition of less extent and less elevated than the oratorio set to religious words and primarily intended for church use, being sung without action, costume and scenery. Lorenz claims "there is really a very slight line of demarcation between a shorter oratorio and a lengthy cantata, hence they are treated concurrently in this study."[4]

German Oratorios

Ludwig Von Beethoven wrote an oratorio *Christ on the Mount of Olives*, Oratorio No. 80. It is believed that he was inspired by Hayden's *The Creation* in the early eighteen hundreds. Beethoven composed his Oratorio *Christus am Oelberg* in 1803 and performed it in Vienna.[5] It was composed to show the world that he owed nothing to his predecessors. This German Oratorio Op. 85 was written for three voices: Tenor, (Jesus), Soprano (the Seraphs), and Bass (Peter), with the accompanying of a modern choir (the disciples) and several voices (the warriors, the angels) plus brass and woodwind instruments.[6] Beethoven collaborated closely with Franz Savior Huber in setting the hastily written text of The Mt. of Olives oratorio. His **Oratorio, Op. 50**, is centered on Mt. Olives in Jerusalem. This musical piece is an expansion of Matthew 28:36, followed by Judas' betrayal of Jesus. Beethoven believed and subscribed to the New Testament account of Jesus' Passion. His faith is expressed thus: In recitative No. 4 where Beethoven asserts "Now tremble, nature for this is God's Son. Behold Him! on the earth He lies, of his Father quite forsaken, enduring unspeakable pain. The Holy One! He is prepared a bitter cruel death to suffer that so the sinner whom He loves may be delivered from death, and enter eternal life."[7]

Laudario 91 Di Cortone

Nonesuch has issued *Laudario 91 Di Cortone* in which the settings by Luciano Sgrizzi are for the soloists, and chorus of the rendition of The Societa Cameristica, under the direction of Edwin Loehrer. The *Laudario* is a laud collection; "laudarium, which is an old manuscript containing words and music for a group of lauds." Nonesuch's version may be found in the Etruscan Academy at Cortone, No. 91.[8]

What is a laud? The Lauds were popular religious songs, a sacred folk music, that originated in Northern Italy in the thirteenth century. "Their single line melodies were set to short-rhymed lines, part Italian dialect, part church Latin. They retell well-known stories and dogmas in simple dramatic style."[9] Their use begins with St. Francis of Assisi, who preached peacefully to the animals and to the tortured flagellants who went through the street, whipping their flesh to shreds to atone for men's sins. These dramatic contrasts are still found in the lauds.

Laudario 91 Di Cortone contains the *La Nativitta* (the Nativity and *the La Passion*). The latter begins with the kiss of Judas and ends with the resurrection and ascension of Christ. The kiss of Judas is followed by the flagellation of our Lord, then by the crucifixion, the lament of Man, and the lament of Mary.[10] The invocation by men and women followers. Part 7 gives the praise of the cross. The Passion ends with these words: "Let us praise the Resurrection and the wonderful Ascension of Jesus Christ, Son of God, who went to His Father and ascended into heaven."[11] St. Mark says in his Gospel, "the apostles then departed, and to all the world they preached eternal life and the precious Kingdom, God will give in recompense. Praise the Lord!"

The Transition from the Renaissance to the Baroque era was effected largely by the hands of the generation of Lutheran composers of which Michael Praetorius (1571-1621) is probably the most notable. Much of the Baroque period reflects the contemporary state of German music, the combination of tradition and innovation.

Christoph Demantius' Oratorio

One of the outstanding composers of the Baroque era was Christoph Demantius, who was born in Reichenberg (Bohemia) December 18, 1567. He studied at the University of Wittenberg but it is unknown how long he was a student there. Later he served as Kantor in Zittau and in Freibeurg (Saxony), where he died April 20, 1643 at the age of 76. The author of the notes on the Nonesuch records states: St. John Passion and Prophecy of the Suffering asserted about Demantius: "His native inventiveness and originality strongly grounded the formal resources of his own generation, were enhanced in his later years by exposure to the progressive musical ideas of younger composers, showing his music with a singular fusion of conservative and forward looking tendences."[12] A clear example of this aspect of his work is found in the *St. John Passion.*

The St. John Passion had its basis in Isaiah 52:13-53:12 where Isaiah portrays the vicarious atonement of Jesus. Demantius believed that Isaiah 53 was a prophecy of the suffering and death of Jesus.[13] How different is the faith of him when compared with modern Old Testament scholarship. Demantius and his contemporary Christians would be horrified and shocked if they attended the sessions of those scholars working at "the Jesus Seminar."[14]

Stainer's Crucifixion

The crucifixion has occupied an important place in religious art, poetry, sculpture, painting and religious music: vocal, instrumental and hymnody. In 1840 Stainer joined the choir at St. Paul's Cathedral, London. When he was 18 years old he was chosen by Sir Fredrich Gore as organist for the newly-formed St. Michael's College at Tenbury. After obtaining his B. Mus. at Christ College, Oxford, he was appointed organist at the University.[15] In 1872 leaving Oxford, he became the successor of his Master, Gore, as organist at St. Paul's Cathedral. He held this position till his vision failed him. In 1873 Stainer went to Oxford University as Professor of Music. He was busy with many appointments and he became a prolific composer. His death occurred in Italy in 1901.[16] For his D.Mus. degree he composed *GIDEON* written in 1865. *The Crucifixion* is Stainer's most important and popular of his four major works. It was given February 1887 in the parish church of Marylebone in London. *The Crucifixion* was originally described as a "Meditation on the Passion of the Holy Redeemer." The contents of this oratorio, according to Angel Record 35984 is as follows:

Side 1: Recitativ (tenor) and they came to a place named Gethsemane
The Agony (soloists and choir)
Processional to Calvary (choir and soloists)
Recitative (bass) And when they were come
The Mystery of the Divine Humiliation (choir and congregation)
Recitative (bass) He made Himself of no reputation
Side 2: Recitative (bass) And as Moses lifted up the serpent
Chorus: God so loved the world
Recitative (Tenor and choir) Jesus said. Father forgive them
Duet: So Thou lifted Thy divine petition
Recitative (bass and choir) And one of the malefactors
Recitative (Soloists and choir) When Jesus therefore saw His Mother
Recitative (bass) Is it nothing to you
The appeal of the Crucified (choir)
Recitative (Tenor and choir) After this Jesus, knowing
For the love of Jesus (choir and congregation)[16]

Stainer also authored the very popular melody: "Magdalene." He has been classified as belonging to a school of writers among whom were John Goss, Samuel Sebastian Westey, and later Barnby, West, Parry, Stanfort and others. Stainer also composed *"Gideon"* and *"The Daughter of Jairus."*

The Oratorio in Germany

In Germany, as in other European countries, the oratorio grew out of the miracle play, according to Lorenz. "The rage in Italy for the opera, however, had submerged the religious impulse of the oratorio. In the north the spirit of the Passion music and the traditional church melodies took possession of the miracle play and produced a composition of the miracle play of a profounder and more of a religious character. The modern oratorio is a child of the German oratorio."[17]

Heinrich Schuetz (1585-1672)

Some musicologists have acclaimed Schuetz as "the father of German music." It is certain that he was the "father of the German oratorio."[18] Lorenz claims that he links up with Italian church music by having spent three years of study under Giovani Gabrieli of Venice. Gabrieli, however, was an old man with more serious religious ideals of a century before. Schuetz had the benefit of the Venetian progressive attitude and the new broadening of musical resources in the monadic style, and in the emphasis of instrumentation, without the lightness and secularity which characterized the younger men of southern Italy.[19]

In 1623 Schuetz wrote a resurrection oratorio which was followed by the "Seven Words of the Cross," as well as four Passion Oratorios.

The musical notes on *Turnabout Record TU-534521* on the back of the jacket about Schuetz states: "With the Reformation a break came in the manifold but liturgically still unified Christian Church music and it was a double break: those Protestants who followed a Puritan outlook discarded polyphonic or no music at all."[20]

By contrast to the Puritanic, Luther, musician himself and a great admirer of Josquin de Pres, retained polyphonic music but Luther reformed it. One of the creations of German Lutheran music was the choral.[21]

Heinrich Schuetz (1672-1750) was forgotten in the seventeenth century, as were the musical computations of Gabrieli, but Carl von Westerfeld rediscovered Schuetz and the nineteenth century saw his works on programs. It was Philipp Spitta who collected Schuetz' music and issued a complete collection of his works. Spitta published *Psalms David, The Geistliche Konzerte, Die Music.* While the work is performed in a concert hall, it should be rendered in a church because they are part of the Lutheran liturgy. These works should be heard at Vespers or at Sunday services.[22]

The Seven Last Words are intended for Good Friday.

The seven final earthly sayings in the state of humiliation are:
1. "Father, forgive them for they know not what they do."

2. "Son, behold thy Mother."
3. "Mother, behold thy Son."
4. "My God, my God, why have you forsaken me?"
5. "I thirst."
6. "Father, into Thy hand I commit My Spirit."
7. "It is finished."

The musical commentary of Nonesuch TV-534521 claimed that *The Seven Words* from the Cross can really be termed an oratorio. The text, compiled from the four Gospels, is enlarged by additions to conform to the mysteriousness of Bach's Passion and *Beethoven's Missa Solemnis* are too long to be played in a church.

The Seven Last Words had its predecessor in the composition of Schuetz in the five part motets-cycle: *Was hast Du Verwirkt of the Continones sacrae*, 1625 and in turn this work had its predecessor in Senffs motet-cycle *Da Jesus an dem Krueze stand*.

Joseph Haydn's Oratorio

Information about the origin and presentation of Haydn's *Seven Words* is found in the writings by Baron Gottfieldv on Sweten, collaborator with Haydn in *The Creation* and *The Seasons*. In von Sweten's *Biographische Notizen uber Joseph Haydn* and also in Albert Christoph Dies' *Biographische Nachrichten on Joseph Haydn*; according to Diez, who visited Haydn thirty times between April 1805 and August 1808, Diez related that he had seen the Latin letter in which it was requested that on Good Friday Haydn should compose an oratorio as a part of the liturgy. The Good Friday liturgy was climaxed by commemorating the Crucifixion and in the unveiling and adoration of the Cross.[23]

D. Scarlotti's Oratorio

The year 1685 was a year uniquely auspicious for the tonal art. Within twelve months, the elder Bach and Guiseppe Scarlatti were born. The latter's father, Allessandrio was the maestero di capella in Naples and a composer of quite renown. His son, Domenico, however, outstripped his progenitor.[24] In his early twenties Domenico became a maestro di capella. He had written 550 keyboard sonatas between 1719. During the Roman period he wrote a notable number of vocal works, operas oratorios, chamber cantatas and church music. The greatest of these was the *Stabat Mater* which he conceived as a great multi-sectional motet for ten part chorus, compromising a pair of altos, tenors and basses, a capella except for contnuo.[25] The exact date of its composition is unknown. It is believed that *Stabat Mater* was composed during Scarlatti's five-year tenure at the Julian Chapel, which would be c.1719. It is a rhyming metrical text of twenty-three line stanzas, depicting the sorrowful Mary at the Cross. Horowitz quoted Ralph Kilpatrick's judgment: "It is a genuine masterpiece, perhaps the first really great work as we have seen from Domenico's hand. Large in scope, rich in imagination and of a lordly in the conduct of counterpoint, it does do justice in every way to the eloquence of the text."[26]

The words of *The Stabat Mater* are derived not only from the Gospels of St. Luke and St. John but also from other books of the New Testament. Who was the original author is a medieval mystery! It has been ascribed to Jacopone da Todi (died 1306) although Pope Benedict XIII gave his imprimatur to the Passion sequence as an official part of the Roman Missal, A.D. 1727.

Pergolesi's Stabat Mater

Giovanni Battista Pergolesi was born near Jesi, Ancona, Italy, January 4, 1710. He was originally interested in opera. In 1873 Pergolesi wrote *La Serva Padrona* which was to revolutionize the form of French opera until the works of Rossini were written.[27] Pergolesi was a prolific writer. His repertoire included four masses, two oratorios, eleven cantatas, twelve motets, five salve Reginas, several concertos for violin and flute, cello sonata, some harpsicord pieces and arias.

The Sabat Mater is Pergolei's most famous and finest work written at the monastery in Pozzjuoli during the last week of his life: he died on March 16, 1736.[28] It was originally written for two female voices, soprano and contralto, with strings and organ as accompaniment in its original form. After Pergolesi's death, Paisiello added wind instruments, and in the passage of time, it has finally been scored for full orchestra.

The massive dignity of the subject matter, the vocal treatment of great variety of effects and the extreme beauty of *The Stabat Mater* make it one of the salient works of all time.[29]

The Oratorios of Friedrich Handel

Although born in Germany, Handel was considered an Englishman. Lorenz claims that the English oratorio did not spring into being full orbed like Minerva from the head of Jupiter. There could be nothing in English music that could under any definition be constituted as an oratorio before the immigration of a German composer George Friedrich Handel into England in 1710. He wrote at least thirteen oratorios.[30]

In 1741 Handel wrote the oratorio "The Messiah," said to have been written in twenty-four days.[31] It was composed at the request of the Duke of Devonshire of Ireland. He wrote and produced it in Dublin, his greatest masterpiece. Many of Handel's oratorios are no longer reproduced and many of them lacked vitality but today "The Messiah" is very much alive.

The Oratorio "The Messiah"

Sir Thomas Beecham, who conducted "The Messiah" with the Royal Philharmonic Orchestra and chorus, wrote as follows: "The Messiah is unique among the twenty oratorios of Handel in being the only one which has any connection with the Christian faith. The others concern themselves with the exploits of a valiant people, ever seeking the fanciful security of a settlement home."[32]

The Messiah is usually divided into three parts: Part one deals with Christ's birth and ministry. Part two has the Lenten section. Part three contains the resurrection and the glorification of the Messiah.[33]

Part 2 is based on Isaiah 52:13-53:12, John 1:20, Matthew 11:28, Lamentations 1:12; Psalm 16:10; Psalm 24, Isaiah 40:11, Matthew 10:28-30.

Part 3 has the following: "Behold the Lamb of God," "He was despised and rejected." "All we have gone astray," "All they that see Him, laugh Him to scorn," "He trusted in God that He would deliver Him," "They rebuke Him broken in heart. Behold and see if there be any sorrow," "he was cut out of the land of the living," "But thou didst not leave His soul in hell," "Lift up your hearts, O ye gates," "How beautiful are the feet of them," "Why do the nations so furiously rage," "Let us break their bands asunder," "He that dwelleth in heaven. Thou shalt break them with a rod of iron." "Hallelujah!"

Part 3 also deals with Easter, Ascension and Christ's Second Coming. It is introduced by "I know that my Redeemer lives" followed by "Since by man came death," succeeded by "Behold I tell you a mystery," "the trumpet shall sound" concludes with "Worthy is the Lamb that was slain." Amen.

"The Messiah" is very much alive and is sung more often than Handel's other oratorios. Sir Thomas Beecham in the first volume of *A Mingled Chime* wrote: "Since his time mankind has heard no music written for voices which can feebly rival his for grandeur of build and tone, nobility and tenderness of melody. Scholastic skill and ingenuity and inexhaustible variety of effect."[34]

"The Hallelujah Chorus" made such an impression on its first rendition that when the majestic passage began, "For the Lord God Omnipotent reigneth," the audience, including the King who was present, rose to its feet and remained standing to the end of the chorus. Thus originated the present custom of standing while it is sung.[35]

The chief solo parts of the oratorio are: "I know that my Redeemer liveth," "He was despised," "Why do the heathen rage?" Whether musical minded or not, every minister should he familiar with the general features of this great oratorio.

Johann Sebastian Bach's Oratorios

Johann Sebastian Bach wrote four oratorios: *The St. Luke Passion*, *The St. John Passion*, *The St. Matthew Passion*, and *The Easter Oratorio* and *The Christmas Oratorio*.[35] *The St. Luke Passion*, Lorenz says is an early work and not as highly esteemed. Mendelsohn, the resurrector of Bach's music, declared it spurious after Bach had been dead for eighty years. The other oratorios, *St. Matthew's* and *St. John's* and *The Christmas Oratorio* are regarded as Bach's most splendid, monumental works in which German music for a century came to a climax.[36] Lang claimed that the *St. John's Passion*, the earlier of the two extent, is more youthful and impetuous than the latter *St. Matthew Passion*.[37] A great number of chorales are woven through its texture but with one exception the choral tunes are not expanded into choral paraphrases or fantasias. Lorenz says that the *St. John Passion*, considerably shorter than the second Passion, presents in a more summary, more vehement and more visually dramatic manner. It is especially in *St. John's Passion* that in the recitative, interrupted brusquely, the dramatic quality becomes more acute.[37a]

Content-wise, the Passion narratives in the New Testament have events and words by Jesus not found in the Gospel of St. Matthew. In *The Passion of St. John*, chapters 12-19 contain the account or the last days of Jesus' earthly life. Bach actually begins with chapter 18, Jesus going over the Brook of Kidrom. The St. John Passion may be divided into two parts. Part II includes the chorale: "See the Lord of Life and Savior meek and lowly," concluding with chapter 19:38-42. Lang categorically states that the recitatives in *The St. Matthew Passion* are entirely different from those in the *St. John Passion*.

Bach's St. Matthew Passion

Very early in the past the Church drove home its Christian lessons by dramatic dialogues.[38] From the ninth century various little scenes were staged in church with dialogue and music. Bach brought this form to its highest power in several settings of the Passion music libretto. In *The St. Matthew Passion*, Bach employed passages from the New Testament and partly from the poetry of C. H. Heinrich (1700-1761). He was Bach's friend who wrote under the pen name "Picander" with whom Bach collaborated his *St. Matthew Passion*. It was boldly laid out for two choruses, each with its orchestra for strings, flutes, oboes, harpsichords and two organs which St. Thomas Church had. About thirty people played a part in Bach's greater Passion.[39] The reeds were included besides ordinary oboes, the oboe de amore, which might be called a mezzo-soprano oboe and the oboe de caccia, representing the **cor anglais**, which is the alto oboe. The choruses should be much the same size as the orchestra, so that about sixty people took part on that Good Friday, April 15, 1729, when Bach conducted the first performance of his crowning achievement in his Church of St. Thomas in Leipzig.[40]

Solos and choruses follow the narrative. Interspersed are chorales, verses of hymn tunes as reflective commentary. The congregation joined in singing and sensed the feelings evoked by the drama. The choruses represented the people who took part in the momentous events describing the Crucifixion, both the believers and the opposition, the turba.[41]

Bach has the chief soloists as the Evangel (tenor) who relates the story, and Jesus (a bass Voice) was always accompanied by strings and continuo only. Peter (baritone) is also heard in a few sentences that fix him in memory. There are also in *St. Matthew Passion* brief recitations by Pilate's wife, two damsels, two false witnesses, the High Priest, Pilate and Judas.[42]

Soprano, alto, tenor and bass soloists comment on the story in arias. Variously accompanied by flutes, oboe or a solo violin. As one writer puts it: "These are often elaborate in their contrapuntal interplay." The *St. Matthew Passion* represents the peak of oratorio composition.[43]

Angel records has issued "Choruses and Chorales" from the *St. Matthew Passion* with Otto Klemperer, conductor. The Philharmonic Choir and Orchestra, giving twenty-eight choruses and chorales (Stereo S 36162).

Easter Oratorio by Bach

According to Lang, the Easter Oratorio is simply a string of cantatas while the Passions carry the cantatas with Protestant church music to its height. The musical notes accompanying Vanguard (SRV-156) asserted J.S. Bach's *Easter Oratorio* thus: "Yet, while undeniably recognized as a product of the master's maturest art, music lovers at large have been unable to make the acquaintance of the *Easter Oratorio* until the presentation of that recorded performance. At present not a single edition of the work is available. This is unpardonable, avers Van Guard music critic, Seymour Solomon."[45]

Philip Spitta, according to Seymour, states that of all of Bach's compositions, unlike his other two pieces so titled (*The Christmas* and *Ascension Oratorios*) which are merely enlarged cantatas, Bach's mysterious setting of Easter makes his *Easter Oratorio* a real oratorio. His style is Italianate and not Handelian.[46]

The Easter Oratorio is not in the somber style of Bach's "Christ lag in Totensbanden." Solomon said: "of *The Easter Oratorio* that it is fresh and verdant, spring-like in its innocence and reaffirmation of life."[47] *The Easter Oratorio* exists in three different versions: Vanguard SRV-156 is based on the text published by The Bach Gesellschaft, which is a compromise of three versions. The manuscript is probably dated back to about 1736.

In the oldest copy of *The Easter Oratorio*, solo parts are assigned to four people: Mary (Mother of James, Mary Magdalene, Peter and John). In later copies all four are omitted. Their omission, however, would make no sense and one must assume that Bach believed that the people would recognize them.[48]

The Easter Oratorio may be divided into three parts: Sinfonia, Adagio for oboe and strings, Duet and Chorus. This Oratorio must have been a favorite of Bach, judging by the time and effort he bestowed on making it perfect.[49]

Bach's Cantatas in General

A church cantata is a composition of less extent and less elevated style than the oratorio, set to religious words.[50] For Easter, Bach 1724, composed cantata No. 4 "Christ lag in Todesbande." Half of the work was primarily intended for church use, being sung without action, costume or scenery. Its text is that of a canticle by Luther, in seven numbers treated like so many variations on the theme of the chorale. The melody of this number is taken from the Gregorian hymn "Victimae Pascal" (Pascal sacrifices).[51]

The numbers are arranged in an absolutely symmetrical order. Numbers 1, 4 and 7 are entrusted to the chorus in four parts. No. 2, however, and No. 6 are duets, Nos. 3 and 5 are arias. In accordance, however, with the custom of choral numbers, in *The Easter Oratorio* the duets and arias, the vocal parts, are sung by the corresponding voices of the chorus.[52]

The orchestra is composed of two sections: violins, two violas, one trumpet, three trombones and continue.[53]

The Easter Oratorio is based on St. John 20:1-10. An opening Sinfonia, trumpets and drums, traditional heralds of pomp and circumstance, set the joyous tone of the Oratorio and usher in an extended instrumental piece which for sheer brilliance is unsurpassed in Bach's music. This orchestral introduction for strings only, expresses the theme of the chorale "Christus lag in Totenhanden."[54] The theme of this chorale is sustained notes sung by soprano in unison with three other choral sections, an accompanied by strings. The Hallelujah gives vent to a magnificent outburst of praise.

Lang wrote about Bach's beliefs as expressed in his cantatas as follows: "Its ardor, humility, fear and soaring hope embodied in Bach's cantatas with an intensity and effect which make the words the highest expression of Lutheran religiousness."[55]

Rimsky-Korsakov's Easter Music

One music historian claims that Rimsky-Korsakov (1844-1908) was without doubt the greatest orchestral soloist in the realm of Russian nationalistic art-music.[56] He was one of five: namely, Alexander Borodin, Mili Balakirev, Cesar Cui and Mousorski, to flourish in Russia in the 1880's and 1890's.[57] Rimsky-Korsakov decided to make himself proficient in every phase of musical technique so that he became the master of a whole generation of Russian musicians under Igor Stravinsky.[58] Rimsky-Korsakov was also the composer of the *Christmas Eve Suite*.[59]

Wagner's Good Friday Spell (Act 3)

Wagner's last music drama or "Consecration festival" stage drama, as he called it, occupied him off and on for more than thirty-seven years. It was in 1845 that he first read the trilogy of epic poems Titurei-Parsifal Loberangrin, written by the thirteenth century writer Wolfram Von Eschenhach. These poems were derived from a number of earlier sources, among them the account of the Knight Percefal in the poem *Li Contes del Graal*. It is possible that Christians were inspired by contemporary legends about the Knights of the Holy Grail.

The libretto for *Parcifal* was completed in 1872. Fragments of the incomplete poems *Jesus of Nazareth* and *The Victors*, based on a Buddhist theme were eventually incorporated by Wagner in *Parcifal*.[60]

Wagner based in the libretto Good Friday Spell, not first of all on the Bible, but on the story of the Holy Grail, not at all found in the New Testament. The stories about the Holy Grail embody certain Christian truths accepted by *Parsifal* that it was on Good Friday. Wagner declared, that the coming of inspiration for the verses that accompany the scene described in Act 3 came. For more information, consult Everest's *Parsifal* on the back jacket given by Herbert Glass, *Parliament* PLP-150.

In the category of different forms of music, one could also list the many hymns and chorales dealing with the Passion, Death, Burial, Resurrection and Ascension. That study will be developed in a future article.

Footnotes

1. Paul Lang, *Music in the History of the Western Civilization* (New York: N. W. Norton and Company, 1941), pp. 496-498.
2. Edmund S. Lorenz, *What a Minister Should Know About Church Music* (New York: Fleming H. Tevell Company, 1923), p. 368.
3. **Ibid.**, p. 365.
4. **Ibid.**, p. 365.
5. Musical Notations on the back jacket of phonograph Record VOX, ST 8766, Beethoven, *Christus am Oelberg*.
6. **Ibid.**, back side of jacket.
7. **Ibid.**
8. Cf. NONESUCH Record.
9. Lang, **op. cit.**, p. 113ff.
10a. Back of jacket VOX Record, *Laudario 91 Di Cortone*.
10b. **Ibid.**
11. **Ibid.**, columns 3 and 4.
12. Lang, **op. cit.**, p. 395.
13. NONESUCH Record, H 1138. On back side of record the text is given.
14. Robert H. Pfeiffer, *Introduction to the Old Testament* (New Harper and Brothers, Publishers, 1941), pp. 457-458; W. K. Lowth Clark *Concise Bible Commentary* (New York: The Macmillan Company, 1953), p. 542; Peter R. Ackroyd, in *The Interpreters One-Volume Commentary on the Bible* (Nashville; The Abingdon Press, 1871), p. 365.
15. Lang, **op. cit.**, pp. 378-379. Cf. also reverse side of phonographic Record, ANGEL 36980.
16. "Stainer John," E. Moyer, *Who Was Who in Church History* (Chicago: Moody Press, 1962), p. 385b.
17. Lang, **op. cit.**, p. 368.
17a. Moyer, **op. cit.**, p. 385.
18. Lang, **op. cit.**, p. 368; Lorenz, p. 358.
19. **Ibid.**, p. 369.
26. Cf. Turnabout Record, back jacket.
21. Chorale or choral, Edwin Lueker, *Lutheran Cyclopedia* (St. Louis: Concordia Publishing House, 1975), p. 158.
22. Lorenz, **op. cit.**, p. 368.
23. Cf. Joseph Haydn, *The Seven Last Words of Christ*, performed by The Little Orchestra of London as recorded on NONESUCH Record. H-71154.
24. Cf. E. Moyer, *Who Was Who in Church History*, **op. cit.**, p. 189a.
25. NONESUCH Record, **op. cit.**, back side of jacket.
26. Haydn, Joseph, *The Viking Desk Encyclopedia*, **op. cit.**, p. 574a.
27. As cited by James Lyons on the back of *DECCA Record, Scarlatti: Stabat Mater*, DC, 16114.
28. Lorenz, **op. cit.**, p. 358.
29. Cf. Pergolesi, *Stabat Mater*, MACE, M. 9614. Back side of jacket.
36. Lang, **op. cit.**, p. 368.
31. "George, Georg Frederick Handel," In Moyer, **op. cit.**, p. 186. "George F. Handel," *Lutheran Encyclopedia* 1954 edition.
32. Cf. The Booklet that accompanies the Multi-Record set of *The Messiah*.
33. Compare the Booklet that accompanies *The Messiah* of the Somerset Messiah Records, pp. 4ff.
34. Sir Thomas Beechem, in the *Manual Found in the Messiah* set of phonograph records.
35. Lorenz, **op. cit.**, p. 377. Lang, **op. cit.**, pp. 500-501.
36. *The Columbia Viking Encyclopedia*, **op. cit.**, Vol. I, p. 96.
35. Lang, **op. cit.**, pp. 499-501.
36. "Johann Sebastian Bach," *Concordia Cyclopedia*, p. 68.

37. Lang, **op. cit.**, p. 500.
37a. **Ibid.**
38. Lang, **op. cit.**, p. 566.
39. Lang, **op. cit.**, p. 561.
40. Cf. the booklet with Bach, *St. Matthew Passion* accompanying Richmond High Fidelity Recordings.
41. *The Great Choral Works of J. S. Bach*, produced and published by Murray Hill.
42. Lang, **op. cit.**, pp. 560-561.
43. Angel Stereo, *Choruses and Chorales of the St. Matthew Passion*, The Philharmonic Chorus and Orchestra conducted by Otto Klemperer.
44. Lang, **op. cit.**, p. 566.
45. Seymour Solomon, back side of *Vanguard Everyman Classics, Easter Ortorio*, SRV-156.
46. As cited by Solomon, **op. cit.**, back side of record of the *Easter Oratorio*.
47. **Ibid.**
48. Cf. libretto of *The Easter Oratorio*.
49. **Ibid.**
56. Lorenz, **op. cit.**, p. 365.
51. Solomon, **op. cit.**
52. Solomon, **op. cit.**, back jacket of *Easter Oratorio*.
53. **Ibid.**
54. **Ibid.**
55. Lang, **op. cit.**, p. 498.
56. Cf. Back side of Mercury Wing Stereo Record Kimskey-Korsakov *Russian Easter Overture*, Stereo S R W 18617.
57. "Rimsky-Korsakov," *The Columbia Viking Desk Encyclopedia*, II, p. 1138a.
58. Record Mercury Wing, SRV 18917, back side of jacket. Rimsky-Korsakov, *Russian Easter Overtures*.
59. *La Nuit De Noel* (Christmas Eve Suite). Cf. London Stereophonic Sound CS 6036.
60. Same reference given in footnote, No. 58.

Questions

1. Most of the great music of the church was created by ____.
2. What is an oratorio? ____
3. By contrast the church cantata is ____.
4. Beethoven believed and subscribed to ____.
5. What is a laud? ____
6. Who was Michael Praetorious? ____
7. The St. John Passion has as its basis ____.
8. What was Stainer's most important work? ____
9. Some musicologists have acclaimed ____ as "the father of German music."
10. One of the creation of German Lutheran music was ____.
11. Friedrich Handel was considered an ____ although born in ____.
12. The oratorio "The Messiah" is said to have been written in ____ days.
13. The chief solo parts of the oratorio are ____.
14. What oratorio's did Bach write? ____
15. Very early in the past the Church drove home its Christian lessons by ____.
16. About how many people took part when Bach conducted his first performance of ____ at ____.

www.ingramcontent.com/pod-product-compliance
Lightning Source LLC
Chambersburg PA
CBHW030633150426
42811CB00048B/92